Lecture Notes in Computer Science 16425

The series Lecture Notes in Computer Science (LNCS), including its subseries Lecture Notes in Artificial Intelligence (LNAI) and Lecture Notes in Bioinformatics (LNBI), has established itself as a medium for the publication of new developments in computer science and information technology research, teaching, and education.

LNCS enjoys close cooperation with the computer science R & D community, the series counts many renowned academics among its volume editors and paper authors, and collaborates with prestigious societies. Its mission is to serve this international community by providing an invaluable service, mainly focused on the publication of conference and workshop proceedings and postproceedings. LNCS commenced publication in 1973.

Baltasar Fernández-Manjón ·
António José Mendes · Marco Temperini ·
Zuzana Kubincová · Marc Spaniol ·
Guandong Xu · Elvira Popescu · Tianyong Hao ·
Xiangmeng Wang · Shuning He
Editors

Learning Technologies and Systems

24th International Conference on Web-based Learning, ICWL 2025
and 10th International Symposium on
Emerging Technologies for Education, SETE 2025
Hongkong, China, November 30 – December 3, 2025, Revised Selected Papers

Editors
Baltasar Fernández-Manjón
Universidad Complutense de Madrid
Madrid, Spain

Marco Temperini
Sapienza University of Rome
Rome, Italy

Marc Spaniol
Université Caen Normandie, ENSICAEN,
CNRS, Normandie University, GREYC
UMR 6072
Caen, France

Elvira Popescu
University of Craiova
Craiova, Romania

Xiangmeng Wang
The Hong Kong Polytechnic University
Hong Kong SAR, China

António José Mendes
University of Coimbra
Coimbra, Portugal

Zuzana Kubincová
Comenius University in Bratislava
Bratislava, Slovakia

Guandong Xu
The Education University of Hong Kong
Hong Kong SAR, China

Tianyong Hao
South China Normal University
Guangzhou, China

Shuning He
The Hong Kong Polytechnic University
Hong Kong SAR, China

ISSN 0302-9743 ISSN 1611-3349 (electronic)
Lecture Notes in Computer Science
ISBN 978-981-92-0041-2 ISBN 978-981-92-0042-9 (eBook)
https://doi.org/10.1007/978-981-92-0042-9

This Springer imprint is published by the registered company Springer Nature Singapore Pte Ltd.
The registered company address is: 152 Beach Road, #21-01/04 Gateway East, Singapore 189721, Singapore

Preface

This volume presents the proceedings of the Joint Conference of the 24th International Conference on Web-Based Learning (ICWL) and the 10th International Symposium on Emerging Technologies for Education (SETE), collectively referred to as ICWL-SETE 2025. The inaugural ICWL was held in Hong Kong in 2002, and since then, the conference has convened 23 more times across three continents, including Melbourne, Australia (2003); Beijing, China (2004); Hong Kong, China (2005, 2011); Penang, Malaysia (2006); Edinburgh, UK (2007); Jinhua, China (2008); Aachen, Germany (2009); Shanghai, China (2010); Sinaia, Romania (2012); Kenting, Taiwan (2013); Tallinn, Estonia (2014); Guangzhou, China (2015); Rome, Italy (2016); Cape Town, South Africa (2017); Chiang Mai, Thailand (2018); Magdeburg, Germany (2019); Ningbo, China (2020); Macao, China (2021); San Cristobal de La Laguna, Tenerife, Spain (2022); Sydney, Australia (2023); and Shanghai, China (2024). This year, ICWL 2025 was held from 30 November to 3 December in Hong Kong, China, organized by Hong Kong Polytechnic University.

Continuing the tradition initiated in ICWL 2016, the conference was held in conjunction with the 10th International Symposium on Emerging Technologies for Education (SETE). SETE collected the traditional workshop activities managed by ICWL in the past years. Workshops added new and hot topics on technology-enhanced learning, providing a better overall conference experience to the ICWL and SETE attendees.

In addition to the papers presented in the ICWL and SETE main tracks, this volume also includes contributions from six workshops: AIoT-MAPD, AIPL, LAAPL, LLMNE, OPEA, and UMLL, all held during the joint ICWL-SETE conference.

- AI and IoT-Enabled Technologies for Medical Education, Assessment, and Personalized Learning in the Digital Age (AIoT-MAPD 2025)
- The International Workshop on AI for Personalized Learning (AIPL 2025)
- The International Workshop on LLM and Agentic AI for Personalized Learning (LAAPL 2025)
- The International Workshop on Large Language Models for Next-generation Education (LLMNE 2025)
- The International Workshop on Optimizing Personalized Education with AI (OPEA 2025)
- The 9th International Symposium on User Modeling and Language Learning (UMLL 2025)

This year the theme of the initiative was "Advancing Educational Technology in the Age of AI". This research area is showing unprecedented developments and innovations, due to the continuing advancements in ICT, and developments of new methodologies allowed by artificial intelligence for education.

ICWL-SETE 2025 received 125 submissions, each reviewed by at least two experts appointed by the Program Chairs through a single-blind process. Following a rigorous review, 36 papers were accepted for presentation, resulting in an acceptance rate of

28.8%. These contributions span a wide range of topics, including AI Agent Applications in Education, Artificial Intelligence for Education, Assessment in Technology-Enhanced Learning, Big Data-Driven Education, Data-Driven Decision Making in Education, Education for Artificial Intelligence, Game-Based Learning, Generative AI in Education, and HTML5 Web-Based Learning.

We were honored to welcome Dragan Gašević and Jiannong Cao as distinguished keynote speakers at this year's conference. We sincerely thank all authors who submitted their work to ICWL-SETE 2025, as well as the Organizing Committee for their dedication and efforts in making the conference a success. Our appreciation also goes to the Program Committee members for their thorough evaluations, which made the selection of accepted papers possible. We are grateful to our sponsor, Springer, for their invaluable support, which enabled us to present the Best Paper Awards. We anticipate that the ideas and innovations emerging from ICWL-SETE 2025 will further benefit the scientific, industrial, and social communities. We hope that readers of this volume will find the contributions both relevant and inspiring.

December 2025

Baltasar Fernández-Manjón
António Josée Mendes
Marco Temperini
Zuzana Kubincová
Marc Spaniol
Guandong Xu
Elvira Popescu
Tianyong Hao
Xiangmeng Wang
Shuning He

Organization

General Conference Co-chairs for ICWL

Marc Spaniol	Université de Caen Normandie, ENSICAEN, CNRS, GREYC UMR6072, France
Guandong Xu	Education University of Hong Kong, China

General Conference Co-chairs for SETE

Elvira Popescu	University of Craiova, Romania
Tianyong Hao	South China Normal University, China

Program Committee Co-chairs for ICWL

Baltasar Fernández-Manjón	Universidad Complutense de Madrid, Spain
António José Mendes	University of Coimbra, Portugal

Program Committee Co-chairs for SETE

Marco Temperini	Sapienza University of Rome, Italy
Zuzana Kubincová	Comenius University in Bratislava, Slovak Republic

Workshop Chair

Xiangmeng Wang	Hong Kong Polytechnic University, China

Proceedings Publication Chair

Shuning He	Hong Kong Polytechnic University, China

Local Organization Chairs

Wenqi Fan	Hong Kong Polytechnic University, China
Yujuan Ding	Hong Kong Polytechnic University, China

Publicity Co-chairs

Ping Ji	City University of New York, USA
Feiran Zhang	Hong Kong Polytechnic University, China

Web Co-chairs

Shuning He	Hong Kong Polytechnic University, China
Da Ren	Hong Kong Polytechnic University, China

Steering Committee Representatives

Rynson W. H. Lau	City University of Hong Kong, China
Qing Li	Hong Kong Polytechnic University, China

Program Committee

Luca Addiucci	Sapienza University of Rome, Italy
Fernando Albuquerque Costa	University of Lisbon, Portugal
Jorge Luis Bacca Acosta	University of Girona, Spain
Lucia Budinská	Comenius University in Bratislava, Slovak Republic
Federica Caruso	University of L'Aquila, Italy
Fisnik Dalipi	Linnaeus University, Sweden
Tania Di Mascio	University of L'Aquila, Italy
Maya Dimitrova	Institute of Robotics, Bulgarian Academy of Sciences, Bulgaria
Jeffrey Gamble	National Chiayi University, Taiwan
Alicia García-Holgado	Universidad de Salamanca, Spain
Francisco José García-Peñalvo	Universidad de Salamanca, Spain
Carina Soledad	Universidad de La Laguna, Spain
Maria Jose Hernandez-Serrano	Universidad de Salamanca, Spain

Martin Homola	Comenius University in Bratislava, Slovak Republic
Min-Chai Hsieh	Tainan University of Technology, Taiwan
Juan Carlos Infante Moro	Universidad de Huelva, Spain
Theresa Kwong	Hong Kong Baptist University, China
Luigi Laura	UniNettuno University, Italy
Dennis Y. W. Liu	Hong Kong Polytechnic University, China
Victoria I. Marín	University of Lleida, Spain
Karolina Miková	Comenius University in Bratislava, Slovak Republic
Alexander Mikroyannidis	Open University, UK
Laurent Moccozet	University of Geneva, Switzerland
Ilaria Moschini	Università degli Studi di Firenze, Italy
Minoru Nakayama	Tokio Institute of Technology, Japan
Iosif Vasile Nemoianu	University Politehnica of Bucharest, Romania
Rainer Rubira-García	King Juan Carlos University, Spain
Filippo Sciarrone	Universitas Mercatorum, Italy
Sean Siqueira	Federal University of the State of Rio de Janeiro, Brazil
Andrea Sterbini	Sapienza University of Rome, Italy
Shu-Yuan Tao	Takming University of Science and Technology, Taiwan
Vladimir Trajkovik	Ss. Cyril and Methodius University, North Macedonia
Georgi Tuparov	New Bulgarian University, Bulgaria
Jesús Valverde-Berrocoso	Universidad de Extremadura, Spain
Pierpaolo Vittorini	University of L'Aquila, Italy
Shan Wang	University of Macau, China
Michal Winczer	Comenius University in Bratislava, Slovak Republic
Tak-Lam Wong	Douglas College, Canada
Wenxiu Xie	City University of Hong Kong, China
Wen Zhou	Anhui Normal University, China
Yingyi Zhuang	Chinese University of Hong Kong, Shenzhen, China

Contents

Workshop LAAPL

Workshop LLMNE

Workshop UMLL

Workshop OPEA

Intelligent Educational Tools and Personalized Learning

ChatGPT-Generated Comments Based on Scaffolding Theory for Online Learning Support

Jiaqi Wang[1] and Qun Jin[2(✉)]

[1] Graduate School of Human Sciences, Waseda University, Tokorozawa, Japan
jiaqi.wang.x@toki.waseda.jp

[2] Faculty of Human Sciences, Waseda University, Tokorozawa, Japan
jin@waseda.jp

Abstract. Online learning has significantly contributed to promoting educational equity, but learners often lack sufficient knowledge assistance and emotional support. While individualized comments (i-Comments) have proven effective in enhancing interaction, manual generation is labor-intensive and difficult to scale. This study proposes a framework for generating i-Comments using ChatGPT based on scaffolding theory and conducts a comprehensive assessment of content quality. Through systematic analysis of sentiment distribution, thematic relevance, and linguistic features, we evaluate the technical feasibility of the content of ChatGPT-generated i-Comments. Results demonstrate that ChatGPT-generated i-Comments achieve 97% positive or neutral emotional tone in emotional support comments and maintain thematic relevance with learning content. Word frequency usage patterns reveal that emotional support employs evaluative language to engage learners affectively; knowledge assistance utilizes technical terminology for precise information transmission, thereby offering insights for future optimization. This study assessed the features of i-Comments content generated by ChatGPT and experimentally validated the effectiveness of ChatGPT-generated i-Comments.

Keywords: Online learning support · artificial intelligence in education · ChatGPT · scaffolding theory

1 Introduction

Online learning has transformed educational accessibility by removing geographical and temporal barriers, enabling millions of learners worldwide to access high-quality educational resources [2]. However, this educational process also presents significant challenges, particularly the lack of interaction and support that characterizes traditional classroom environments. Learners frequently watch educational videos in isolation, without the immediate knowledge assistance and emotional support typically provided by instructors and peers [5].

B. Fernández-Manjón et al. (Eds.): SETE 2025/ICWL 2025, LNCS 16425, pp. 3–16, 2026.
https://doi.org/10.1007/978-981-92-0042-9_1

This isolation in online learning environments often leads to decreased motivation, increased dropout rates, and reduced learning satisfaction. The absence of timely feedback prevents learners from resolving confusion or deepening their understanding, making the learning process less engaging and effective [26]. Research has shown that interaction quality significantly impacts learning outcomes in online environments, particularly when supported by appropriate technological interventions [1].

To address these challenges, Wang et al. introduced individualized comments (i-Comments), which display contextually relevant scrolling text over educational videos to create a sense of companionship and provide real-time learning support [32]. While experimental validation demonstrated positive effects on learning satisfaction and engagement, it also showed a reduction in learners' loneliness. However, the manual generation process has significant limitations: high labor costs, subjective bias, and poor scalability for large-scale educational implementations.

Recent research in generative artificial intelligence, particularly large language models like ChatGPT, offer promising solutions for automated educational content generation. ChatGPT's ability to understand natural language input and generate coherent, contextually relevant responses makes it a potentially valuable tool for creating educational support materials [6]. However, the appropriateness and educational value of AI-generated content require systematic evaluation before widespread adoption in learning environments.

This study addresses the critical need for assessment of AI-generated educational content by developing and evaluating a ChatGPT-based framework for i-Comments generation. Grounded in scaffolding theory, which emphasizes providing appropriate support to bridge the gap between learners' current capabilities and their learning goals [31]. The study investigates three core questions: (1) Can ChatGPT generate knowledge assistance comments that maintain thematic correlation with educational video content? (2) Do ChatGPT-generated emotional support comments exhibit appropriate emotional characteristics for motivational purposes? (3) What characteristics emerge in the content of ChatGPT-generated instructional comments?

By conducting a systematic content analysis of the AI-generated comments, this study demonstrates the feasibility of automated learning support generation and contributes to the expanding field of AI applications in education. The findings provide essential groundwork for large-scale AI implementation in education while offering practical insights for optimizing AI-generated educational content.

The remainder of this paper is organized as follows. Section 2 provides an overview of ChatGPT use in education and scaffolding theory. Section 3 presents the technical framework for generating i-Comments using ChatGPT based on scaffolding theory. Section 4 describes experimental evaluation based on data analysis results using multiple linguistic and subjective metrics. Section 5 discusses the implications of these findings and directions for optimization, and

Sect. 6 concludes this study with major contributions and future research directions.

2 Related Work

2.1 ChatGPT in Education and Comment Generation

Generative Artificial Intelligence (GAI) is redefining the educational paradigm by influencing both instructional practices and the ways learners acquire knowledge [18]. Taking the representative ChatGPT as an example, research shows that it has many advantages in enhancing the educational experience. For example, one of the major advantages of ChatGPT is its ability to provide personalized real-time responses, providing instant feedback to help students correct misunderstandings and maintain learning progress [8]. Similarly, when applied to a flipped learning environment, ChatGPT can help students to participate more actively in pre-class activities and prepare for in-class interactive activities [12]. In educational environments such as debate training, ChatGPT has been shown to aid critical thinking by acting as a debate partner. The application helps students practice debating skills and receive feedback on their reasoning, thus improving their overall critical thinking skills [14]. ChatGPT is also an excellent tool for developing higher-order thinking skills by guiding students through tasks and challenges to help them solve problems in a structured learning environment [7].

In addition, ChatGPT has shown significant advantages in video comment generation, especially in real-time interactive environments. Researchers have developed automated comment generation systems such as 'LiveBot', which generates comments in real time based on the visual and textual content of the video. These comments are usually displayed on the screen while the video is playing, thus increasing viewer interactivity and engagement [17]. It has been proposed to use generative models to generate comments that are more in line with people's preferences by collecting user feedback (e.g., number of likes). This approach improves the quality of interactions by training reward models to make the generated comments more attractive [29]. Although ChatGPT shows many advantages in the field of real-time interaction and content generation, related research also faces some shortcomings and challenges. For example, generated comments sometimes lack precision or quality control, may be too generic or repetitive, and have limited enhancement of interaction depth and variety [29]. In addition, generated comments may not understand complex contexts well or accurately capture deeper meanings in the video or viewers' emotional feedback [17].

2.2 Scaffolding Theory in Educational Technology

Knowledge scaffolding is a fundamental strategy to enhance learners' knowledge acquisition and affective experience in online learning [16]. Knowledge scaffolding refers to the provision of support to help learners bridge the gap between their current level of understanding and their learning goals. This concept is usually based on various forms supported by Vygotsky's Zone of Proximal Development (ZPD) theory [27], including prompting, explanation, demonstration, and feedback [9].

Emotional scaffolding aims to enhance the learner's affective experience during the learning process. This includes addressing learners' emotional responses to the content, providing encouragement, and creating a supportive atmosphere [25]. This approach helps to reduce anxiety, increase enthusiasm, and foster a growth mindset. Emotional scaffolding is particularly important for overcoming learning challenges [11].

Some studies have confirmed that combining knowledge scaffolding and emotional scaffolding is more effective than using either method alone. For example, a conversational agent (CA) that combines both strategies can promote deeper learning and affective engagement [16]. Knowledge scaffolding can guide learners to explore concepts and construct knowledge through prompts and intriguing interactions. Emotional scaffolding can keep learners enthusiastic and engaged by responding to emotional changes and providing supportive feedback. Research has shown that students who use guided scaffolding perform better than those who do not have this type of support, indicating the effectiveness of scaffolding in online learning [11]. In addition, scaffolding can meet individual needs and provide the necessary assistance for different learning backgrounds to achieve learning goals. For example, knowledge scaffolding can target specific gaps in understanding, while emotional scaffolding can reduce anxiety and foster a growth mindset in learners by encouraging them to view challenges as opportunities for growth [25].

3 Method

3.1 Design of Technical Framework

We developed a comprehensive framework for generating i-Comments using ChatGPT, consisting of five integrated components: multimodal video analysis, individualized information setting, comment attribute setting, content generation, and customized display [34]. The proposed framework is illustrated in Fig. 1.

The multimodal video analysis component processes educational videos through two main channels. First, audio content is extracted and converted to timestamped text using an automatic speech recognition (ASR) method called Whisper [24]. It captures the instructor's explanations, key concepts, and temporal context. Second, keyframes containing important visual information, like concept definitions, diagrams, or summary slides, are identified and extracted to complement textual content understanding.

The individualized information setting component allows customization based on learner characteristics, including educational background, learning preferences, and proficiency levels. This enables the generation of differentiated content that suits different learner needs, such as more detailed explanations for beginners and in-depth discussions for advanced learners.

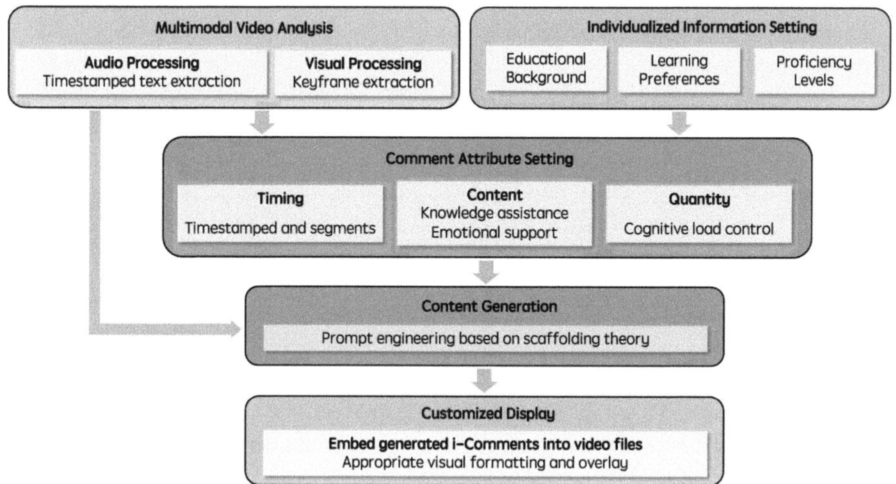

Fig. 1. The framework of individualized comments generation by ChatGPT

Comment attribute setting defines three critical parameters. Timing determines when comments appear, both at specific timestamps and during different video segments. The content is categorized into two distinct types: knowledge assistance, based on the principles of knowledge scaffolding, and emotional support, informed by the theoretical framework of emotional scaffolding. Quantity controls the number of comments per time segment to avoid cognitive overload while providing sufficient support. These attributes are informed by previous research on optimal i-Comments design [33].

The content generation component utilizes carefully designed prompts to instruct ChatGPT to create educational content aligned with scaffolding theory principles [34]. This is followed by a customized display component that embeds generated comments into video files with appropriate visual formatting.

3.2 I-Comments Content Generation Based on Scaffolding Theory

The generation of i-Comments content in this study is grounded in scaffolding theory, which posits that learners benefit from adaptive, temporary support that enables them to accomplish tasks beyond their independent capabilities within the Zone of Proximal Development (ZPD) [4,31]. In video-based learning, time-synchronized comments can be designed as scaffolding support, serving a dynamic assisting function by directing attention, providing explanations, and sustaining learning motivation [21]. Building on the notion of distributed scaffolding, which emphasizes the provision of multiple complementary supports across contexts [22], we translated theoretical principles into content generation rules that systematically integrate cognitive and emotional assistance.

Knowledge scaffolding was implemented through the following aspects: providing explanatory clarifications for challenging concepts, offering supplementary information, designing inquiry-based questions that prompt reflection, emphasizing key points requiring focus, and contextualizing abstract knowledge within concrete scenarios through personal insights. These strategies are intended to reduce intrinsic and extraneous cognitive load while fostering germane cognitive processing [30], thereby facilitating deeper comprehension and schema construction. Meanwhile, emotional scaffolding was incorporated to address the affective dimension of learning, which is critical for sustaining engagement and persistence [20]. Social presence and learning motivation are enhanced by generating comments that include encouraging affirmations, empathetic acknowledgment of challenges, recognition of learner effort, and sharing of personal experiences. This design aligns with research findings that emotional identification enhances persistence among online learners [28].

To maintain readability and prevent cognitive overload during learning, each comment is constrained to a maximum of 20 words, ensuring a balance between information density and fluency. Furthermore, based on prior research that instructional support is most effective when integrated into optimal moments of processing [35], we determined the optimal timing through video entropy analysis, preferentially inserting comments during lower entropy segments where cognitive resources are available. In this way, scaffolding theory is systematically operationalized into concrete content generation rules [13], enabling individualized and pedagogically informed i-Comments that support both cognitive and emotional dimensions of learning in video-based contexts [10].

4 Experimental Evaluation

4.1 Experiment Overview

Evaluating the quality of generated i-Comments is crucial, as it directly impacts learners' online learning experiences and performance. To address this evaluation challenge, we designed a comprehensive experimental framework that analyzed multiple dimensions of i-Comment quality and real-world application effectiveness.

We generated two different categories of i-Comments, knowledge assistance and emotional support using ChatGPT across six rounds, with each round producing 20 comments of each type for the same video content. The content used in the experiment was taken from NHK's learning video "High School Lecture Japanese History" website. The selected video focused on social and cultural developments from the Jomon to the Yayoi period in Japan. We obtained 120 emotional support comments and 120 knowledge assistance comments. We then conducted systematic analyses examining several key aspects: the sentiment distribution of ChatGPT-generated i-Comments, their relevance to the learning video content, and word frequency patterns to understand linguistic characteristics.

To validate our method in real-world scenarios, we created an enhanced learning video incorporating ChatGPT-generated i-Comments based on our proposed framework. Subjects evaluated these i-Comments using four established criteria:

naturalness, consistency, timing, and helpfulness. This enabled a direct comparison between human-generated and ChatGPT-generated i-Comments in real learning environments, providing insights into the practical effectiveness of AI-generated interactive comments for educational purposes.

4.2 Sentiment Analysis

We conducted an experiment to analyze the sentiments expressed in i-Comments generated by ChatGPT. i-Comments with positive sentiments can provide emotional support to learners. However, not all comments need to convey positive emotions. Some neutral or relatively serious emotions can be related to the learning content.

We analyzed two types of i-Comments content using the VADER sentiment analyzer, which is a dictionary and rule-based sentiment analysis tool specifically designed for analyzing sentiments in social media text and short text. The output of VADER sentiment analysis typically includes three aspects: positive, negative, and neutral sentiments.

Table 1. The results of sentiment analysis

	Emotional Support	Knowledge Assistance
Positive	93	68
Neutral	23	44
Negative	4	8

We then applied a pre-trained VADER sentiment analysis model to calculate the compound sentiment scores for these comments. Comments with a compound score greater than or equal to 0.05 were classified as positive sentiment, while those with a compound score less than or equal to -0.05 were classified as negative sentiment. The remaining comments were classified as neutral sentiments. The results are presented in Table 1.

We summarized the sentiment distribution proportions of each i-Comment type in Fig. 2. The results indicate that, in the emotional support category, the proportion of positive and neutral sentiment comments reached 97%, suggesting that the emotional support comments provided positive feedback to encourage and motivate learners. On the other hand, the proportion of negative sentiment comments increased in the knowledge assistance comments, which may be related to the nature of the learning content. For instance, a comment such as "Food was really scarce in ancient times" was identified as expressing negative sentiment.

4.3 Correlation Analysis

We analyzed the correlation between the two types of i-Comments and the original video content. It is crucial to ensure that the i-Comments are relevant to

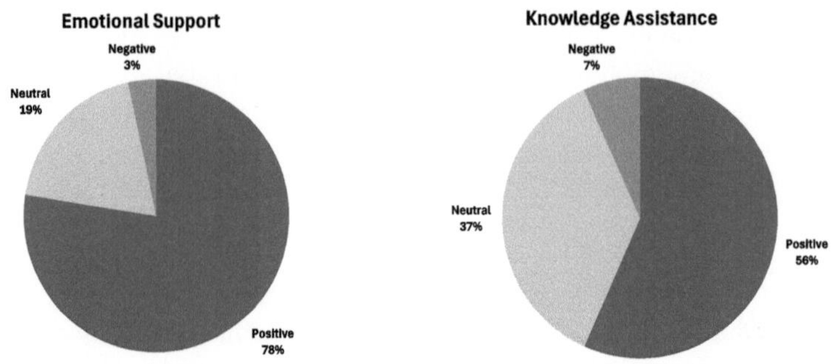

Fig. 2. Overall sentiment distribution proportions by i-Comment type

the original video content to avoid distracting the learner with irrelevant information.

First, we perform text preprocessing on each document, including translation, removal of stop words, and punctuation, to facilitate subsequent analysis [19]. Next, we extract keywords from the text. Then, we employ a text vectorization method to convert the text into numerical representations, allowing for the calculation of similarity between different pairs of texts. Specifically, we utilize the TF-IDF (Term Frequency-Inverse Document Frequency) method, which measures the importance of each word by calculating its frequency in the document (TF) and its rarity across the entire document set (IDF) [23].

We use three main metrics to evaluate the correlation between the content. Cosine similarity reflects the thematic consistency between comments and learning video content, with higher values indicating that comments remain aligned with the core subject matter and thereby help learners maintain focus and deepen comprehension. Jaccard index, by capturing the degree of lexical overlap, highlights whether comments reinforce key domain-specific terminology or introduce complementary concepts, this balance between repetition and extension supports both consolidation of essential knowledge and expansion of learners' cognitive frameworks [15]. Euclidean distance measures the absolute divergence between comment content and video text, providing evidence of functional differentiation between knowledge and emotional scaffolding. Smaller distances in knowledge comments suggest tight coupling with learning content, reinforcing comprehension, whereas larger distances in emotional comments demonstrate the provision of motivational and affective support distinct from factual narratives [3]. These indicators clarify how i-Comments simultaneously serve cognitive alignment, knowledge reinforcement, and emotional engagement, highlighting their multidimensional role in online learning support. The results are shown in Table 2.

The analysis results indicate that knowledge documents exhibited moderate correlation with learning content (Cosine = 0.2234, Jaccard = 19.10%), while emotional documents showed extremely low correlation with learning content (Cosine = 0.0083, Jaccard = 11.52%). The Euclidean distance analysis

Table 2. Correlation Metrics

	Cosine Similarity	Jaccard Index	Euclidean Distance
Knowledge-Learning content	0.2234	19.10%	0.0442
Emotional-Learning content	0.0083	11.52%	0.0634

further confirmed this finding, with the distance between emotional documents and learning content (0.0634) being 43% greater than that between knowledge documents and learning content (0.0442). The consistency across all three metrics validates the reliability of the analysis and confirms the functional differentiation of the three document types: learning content provides educational narratives, knowledge documents successfully extract key concepts (maintaining relevance while avoiding duplication), and emotional documents focus on the expression of subjective experiences, maintaining functional independence from factual content.

4.4 Word Frequency Analysis

We conduct a word frequency analysis of emotional support i-Comments and knowledge assistance i-Comments to compare the linguistic features, and the primary nouns used in the two sets of comments. Initially, the data was cleaned, including the removal of words without substantial meaning, followed by tokenization to segment the texts into individual nouns. The word frequency statistics for the processed words are shown in Fig. 3

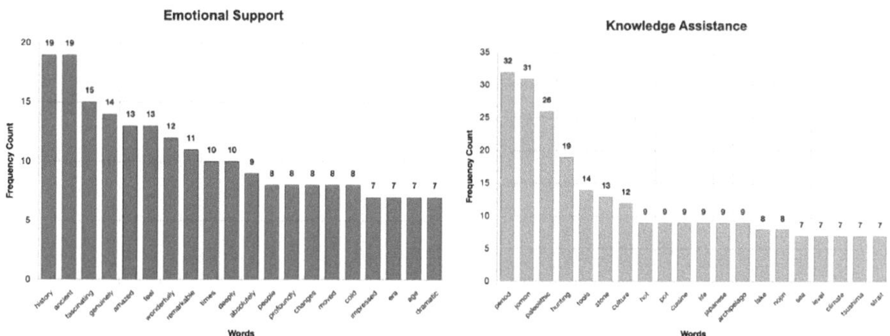

Fig. 3. Top 20 frequency words in two types of GPT-Generated i-Comments

The word frequency analysis revealed distinct linguistic patterns across the two types:

Emotional support was characterized by high-frequency affective vocabulary, with "history" and "ancient" (both n=19) as the most prominent terms.

The lexical profile demonstrated a strong presence of emotional adjectives and adverbs, including "fascinating" (n=15), "genuinely" (n=14), "amazed" (n=13), and "wonderfully" (n=12). The frequent occurrence of terms such as "feel" (n=13), "deeply" (n=10), "profoundly" (n=8), and "moved" (n=8) indicates a discourse focused on personal emotional responses and subjective reflections regarding historical content.

Knowledge assistance exhibited a predominance of domain-specific terminology related to archaeology and prehistory. The most frequent terms were "period" (n=32), "Jomon" (n=31), and "Paleolithic" (n=26), reflecting a focus on temporal frameworks. Additional high-frequency words included specialized vocabulary such as "hunting" (n=19), "tools" (n=14), "stone" (n=13), and geographical references like "Lake Nojiri" (n=8 combined) and "Tsushima Strait" (n=7 combined). The term cluster "hot pot cuisine" (n=9 each) appeared consistently, indicating a thematic history and food-related content.

In summary, the emotional support demonstrates a preference for evaluative and affective language, strategically employing emotional adjectives and adverbs to engage learners and foster subjective connections with historical content. In contrast, the knowledge assistance is characterized by domain-specific technical terminology and archaeological vocabulary, optimized the accuracy of information transmission and academic reliability.

4.5 Subjective Evaluation

We recruited ten graduate students from Japanese universities as subjects to evaluate the generated comments. Subjects were required to watch a learning video with i-Comments generated by ChatGPT and another video with human-generated i-Comments, then complete a questionnaire to evaluate the quality of the generated comments.

The subjects assessed the comments on the following four criteria: naturalness, consistency, timing, and helpfulness, and each item is answered on a 5-point Likert scale ranging from one (strongly disagree) to five (strongly agree). This experiment aims to conduct a comparative analysis of the effectiveness of ChatGPT in generating i-Comments.

We conducted a t-test analysis on the evaluations of human-generated i-Comments and ChatGPT-generated i-Comments. The results in Table 3 indicate that, except for Helpful, where the p-value is 0.02 (< 0.05), implying that the difference in this indicator is significant. The remaining three attributes: naturalness, consistency, and timing are all greater than 0.05, indicating no statistically significant differences. By comparing the means, we can see that the mean score of Human-Generated i-Comments on helpful (4.7) is significantly higher than that of ChatGPT-Generated i-Comments (4.0). This could be attributed to GPT often generating relatively broad content that lacks specificity and consideration of the context. As a result, learners may find ChatGPT-generated comments less helpful, leading to lower scores for the helpful attribute.

Table 3. t-test results between the two groups

	Group Condition			
	Human-Generated i-Comments (n=10)	GPT-Generated i-Comments (n=10)	t	p
Naturalness	4.40±0.69	3.90±1.10	1.21	0.24
Consistency	4.80±0.42	4.70±0.48	0.49	0.63
Timing	4.30±0.82	3.80±0.92	1.28	0.22
Helpful	4.70±0.48	4.00±0.67	2.69	0.02*

5 Discussion

5.1 Assessment of ChatGPT Basic Capabilities in Generating I-Comments Based on Scaffolding Theory

Based on our systematic content feature analysis, ChatGPT demonstrates fundamental capabilities necessary for implementing both knowledge and emotional scaffolding functions in educational contexts. The thematic correlation (Euclidean distance 0.0442) indicates that ChatGPT can maintain cognitive coherence essential for effective knowledge scaffolding, while the appropriate emotional distribution (97% positive/neutral in support comments) suggests capability for providing basic emotional scaffolding.

However, an important distinction must be made between demonstrating basic technical capabilities and achieving effective educational support. Our analysis reveals that ChatGPT meets fundamental requirements for scaffolding implementation, such as content relevance, emotional appropriateness, and systematic delivery, but the gap in perceived helpfulness indicates that additional factors contribute to educational effectiveness beyond these basic features.

While our results demonstrate that ChatGPT can generate content with appropriate characteristics for scaffolding functions, translating appropriate characteristics into effective learning support likely depends on factors such as depth of individualization, contextual relevance, and alignment with learning preferences that require further investigation.

5.2 Optimization Directions Guided by Scaffolding Theory

Our findings reveal specific optimization opportunities for enhancing AI-generated educational content effectiveness. For knowledge scaffolding improvement, the comparison with human content suggests that incorporating more helpful information could enhance the educational value of AI-generated cognitive support.

Emotional scaffolding optimization should focus on increasing individualization and situational awareness in supportive messaging. While AI successfully generates appropriate emotional tone, developing greater sensitivity to individual learner contexts, progress patterns, and specific challenges could improve the perceived relevance and effectiveness of emotional support.

The integrated optimization approach should consider how knowledge and emotional scaffolding functions can be coordinated more effectively. Human instructors naturally blend cognitive and affective support based on real-time assessment of learner needs, suggesting that AI systems could adjust the balance between informational and motivational content based on learner responses and progress indicators.

6 Conclusion and Future Work

In this study, we proposed a scaffolding theory-based technical framework utilizing ChatGPT to generate individualized comments (i-Comments), enhancing cognitive and emotional support in video-based learning, and assessing the technical feasibility of using ChatGPT to generate learning support content. The research validates that ChatGPT possesses capabilities for generating educationally appropriate content, as evidenced by thematic correlation with learning contents and appropriate emotional characteristics for support functions. However, we also identify important distinctions between technical competence and perceived educational value, particularly regarding the specificity and helpfulness that contribute to effective learning support.

In our future work, we will compare the proposed method with other existing methods in more depth, for example, with the manual generation of i-Comments, in order to evaluate its validity. In addition, more research subjects should be recruited, especially learners from different backgrounds. More learning content should be included, and more patterns should be generated by adjusting the parameters of ChatGPT to conduct experiments. By increasing the diversity of subjects, the breadth and credibility of the experimental results will be enhanced. Moreover, the evaluation in this study mainly relied on subjective assessment. The lack of objective evaluation methods may limit the comprehensiveness of the results. In future work, more objective evaluation indicators will be added to provide a more comprehensive evaluation of the effectiveness of the proposed method.

References

1. Abrami, P.C., Bernard, R.M., Bures, E.M., Borokhovski, E., Tamim, R.M.: Interaction in distance education and online learning: using evidence and theory to improve practice. J. Comput. High. Educ. **23**(2), 82–103 (2011)
2. Altinay, F., Ossiannilsson, E., Altinay, Z., Dagli, G.: Accessible services for smart societies in learning. Int. J. Inf. Learn. Technol. **38**(1), 75–89 (2020)
3. Bakker, J.D.: Common distance measures. Appl. Multivariate Stat. R (2024)
4. Belland, B.R., Kim, C., Hannafin, M.J.: A framework for designing scaffolds that improve motivation and cognition. Educ. Psychol. **48**(4), 243–270 (2013)

5. Bradley, T., Lomicka, L.: A case study of learner interaction in technology-enhanced language learning environments. J. Educ. Comput. Res. **22**(3), 347–368 (2000)
6. Chang, C.Y., Chen, I.H., Tang, K.Y.: Roles and research trends of ChatGPT-based learning. Educ. Technol. Soc. **27**(4), 471–486 (2024)
7. Chen, Y., Zhang, X., Hu, L.: A progressive prompt-based image-generative AI approach to promoting students' achievement and perceptions in learning ancient Chinese poetry. Educ. Technol. Soc. **27**(2), 284–305 (2024)
8. Chen, Y., et al.: HOTVCOM: generating buzzworthy comments for videos. arXiv preprint arXiv:2409.15196 (2024)
9. Cong-Lem, N.: Emotion and its relation to cognition from Vygotsky's perspective. Eur. J. Psychol. Educ. **38**(2), 865–880 (2023)
10. Grévisse, C., Rothkugel, S., Reuter, R.A.: Scaffolding support through integration of learning material. Smart Learn. Environ. **6**(1), 28 (2019)
11. Huang, W.L., Li, L.Y., Liang, J.C.: Exploring learners' learning performance, knowledge construction, and behavioral patterns in online asynchronous discussion using guidance scaffolding in visual imagery education. Educ. Technol. Soc. **27**(1), 1–17 (2024)
12. Jeon, J., Lee, S.: The impact of a chatbot-assisted flipped approach on EFL learner interaction. Educ. Technol. Soc. **27**(4), 218–234 (2024)
13. Kim, N.J., Belland, B.R., Axelrod, D.: Scaffolding for optimal challenge in k-12 problem-based learning. Interdisc. J. Prob. Based Learn. **13**(1), 3 (2019)
14. Lee, U., et al.: Can ChatGPT be a debate partner? Developing ChatGPT-based application "DEBO" for debate education, findings and limitations. Educ. Technol. Soc. **27**(2), 321–346 (2024)
15. Levy, A., Shalom, B.R., Chalamish, M.: A guide to similarity measures and their data science applications. J. Big Data **12**(1), 188 (2025)
16. Liu, Z., Duan, H., Liu, S., Mu, R., Liu, S., Yang, Z.: Improving knowledge gain and emotional experience in online learning with knowledge and emotional scaffolding-based conversational agent. Educ. Technol. Soc. **27**(2), 197–219 (2024)
17. Ma, S., Cui, L., Dai, D., Wei, F., Sun, X.: LiveBot: generating live video comments based on visual and textual contexts. In: Proceedings of the AAAI Conference on Artificial Intelligence, vol. 33, pp. 6810–6817 (2019)
18. O'Dea, X.: Generative AI: is it a paradigm shift for higher education? Stud. High. Educ. **49**(5), 811–816 (2024)
19. Papageorgiou, G., Economou, P., Bersimis, S.: A method for optimizing text preprocessing and text classification using multiple cycles of learning with an application on shipbrokers emails. J. Appl. Stat. **51**(13), 2592–2626 (2024)
20. Park, M.H.: Emotional scaffolding as a strategy to support children's engagement in instruction. Univ. J. Educ. Res. **4**(10), 2353–2358 (2016)
21. Van de Pol, J., Elbers, E.: Scaffolding student learning: a micro-analysis of teacher-student interaction. Learn. Cult. Soc. Interact. **2**(1), 32–41 (2013)
22. Puntambekar, S.: Distributed Scaffolding: scaffolding students in classroom environments. Educ. Psychol. Rev. **34**(1), 451–472 (2022)
23. Qaiser, S., Ali, R.: Text Mining: use of TF-IDF to examine the relevance of words to documents. Int. J. Comput. Appl. **181**(1), 25–29 (2018)
24. Radford, A., Kim, J.W., Xu, T., Brockman, G., McLeavey, C., Sutskever, I.: Robust speech recognition via large-scale weak supervision. In: International Conference on Machine Learning, pp. 28492–28518. PMLR (2023)

25. Rosiek, J., Beghetto, R.A.: Emotional Scaffolding: the emotional and imaginative dimensions of teaching and learning. In: Advances in Teacher Emotion Research: The Impact on Teachers' Lives, pp. 175–194 (2009)
26. Salta, K., Paschalidou, K., Tsetseri, M., Koulougliotis, D.: Shift from a traditional to a distance learning environment during the COVID-19 pandemic: university students' engagement and interactions. Sci. Educ. **31**(1), 93–122 (2022)
27. Shabani, K., Khatib, M., Ebadi, S.: Vygotsky's zone of proximal development: instructional implications and teachers' professional development. Engl. Lang. Teach. **3**(4), 237–248 (2010)
28. Shahidzade, F., Fazilatfar, A.M., Razmi, M.H.: The correspondence between students' and teachers' views on teachers' emotional scaffolding strategies in English classes in Iran. Front. Psychol. **13**, 874747 (2022)
29. Su, J., Yang, W.: Unlocking the Power of ChatGPT: a framework for applying generative ai in education. ECNU Rev. Educ. **6**(3), 355–366 (2023)
30. Sweller, J., Van Merriënboer, J.J., Paas, F.: Cognitive architecture and instructional design: 20 years later. Educ. Psychol. Rev. **31**(2), 261–292 (2019)
31. Vygotsky, L.S., Cole, M.: Mind in Society: Development of Higher Psychological Processes. Harvard University Press, Cambridge (1978)
32. Wang, J., Chen, J., Jin, Q.: i-comments: on-screen individualized comments for online learning support. In: 2022 IEEE International Conference on Dependable, Autonomic and Secure Computing, International Conference on Pervasive Intelligence and Computing, International Conference on Cloud and Big Data Computing, International Conference on Cyber Science and Technology Congress (DASC/PiCom/CBDCom/CyberSciTech), pp. 1–5. IEEE (2022)
33. Wang, J., Chen, J., Jin, Q.: Experimental design and validation of i-comments for online learning support. In: International Conference on Human-Computer Interaction, pp. 201–213. Springer (2023)
34. Wang, J., Chen, J., Jin, Q.: Assessing ChatGPT-generated comments for video content viewing in online learning. In: 2024 IEEE Cyber Science and Technology Congress (CyberSciTech), pp. 230–237. IEEE (2024)
35. Wang, X., Lin, L., Han, M., Spector, J.M.: Impacts of cues on learning: using eye-tracking technologies to examine the functions and designs of added cues in short instructional videos. Comput. Hum. Behav. **107**, 106279 (2020)

BugC: A Conversational GenAI Tutor for Learning to Code

María Ferrándiz-Díaz[1], Andrea E. Cotino-Arbelo[1,2], Jezabel Molina-Gil[1,2], and Carina S. González-González[1,2](✉)

[1] University of La Laguna, La Laguna 38202, Spain
{alu0101475899,acotinoa,jmmolina,cjgonza}@ull.edu.es
[2] Women's Research Studies Institute, La Laguna 38202, Spain
http://www.ull.es

Abstract. Learning to program in C remains a significant challenge for first-year students in engineering degrees, often due to abstract concepts and limited personalized support. While generative Artficial Intelligence (GenAI) offers new opportunities for educational tools, most existing solutions focus on languages like Python, leaving C underexplored despite its foundational role in computer science curricula. This study presents the design, development, and comparative analysis of two GenAI-based solutions aimed at supporting C programming learning: a chatbot prototype built on Botpress AI and a custom web platform named BugC. Developed through an iterative process, the first solution enabled rapid prototyping and conversational flow experimentation, while the second offered a fully integrated environment combining theoretical content, interactive exercises, and contextual AI support. A comparative analysis highlights key differences in scalability, customization, maintenance, and pedagogical integration. Results show that while no-code platforms facilitate initial development, they present limitations in cost, flexibility, and long-term sustainability. In contrast, the custom web architecture of BugC offers greater control, adaptability, and alignment with educational needs.

Keywords: Human-Computer Interaction · Generative Artificial Intelligence · Conversational Agents · Programming Learning · Chatbot

1 Introduction

Learning to program remains one of the most formidable challenges for first-year students in technical degrees [1] [2]. The difficulty in grasping abstract concepts, combined with the lack of constant support outside the classroom, often generate anxiety and frustration among students beginning their university education [1]. These challenges frequently translate into poor academic performance, increased demotivation, and in some cases, the decision to drop out of the program [3]. Furthermore, research suggests that these difficulties may disproportionally affect female students, who often face additional barriers such as stereotype threat, lack

B. Fernández-Manjón et al. (Eds.): SETE 2025/ICWL 2025, LNCS 16425, pp. 17–29, 2026.
https://doi.org/10.1007/978-981-92-0042-9_2

of female role models in computing, and impostor syndrome, which can further hinder their programming learning experience [4]. While various digital educational resources currently exist to support programming learning [5–7], they typically offer static or non-personalized approaches, limiting their effectiveness for students with different knowledge levels and learning rhythms. Nonetheless, the emergence of Generative Artificial Intelligence (GenAI onwards) opens new possibilities for transforming the teaching-learning process within higher education institutions [8,9]. Conversational Agents (CAs onwards), capable of interacting with users through natural language and generating responses adapted to their level and specific queries, emerge as an innovative solution to bridge this gap [10]. Their ability to provide immediate support, contextualized feedback, and continuous guidance positions these systems are key allies in reinforcing autonomous and meaningful learning [11]. Research has demonstrated that CAs have been well-received by the university community, as their intuitive and accessible design can reduce anxiety associated with learning complex subjects [12–14]. And higher education institutions must embrace intelligent technologies to enhance teaching-learning processes, particularly in technical fields that require progressive and active mastery, such as programming [15,16]. This educational transformation responds not only to technological evolution but also to new pedagogical demands: flexibility, personalization, and accessibility in student support [17].

Building on this need, this study presents the design, development, and comparative evaluation of two GenAI-powered solutions aimed at supporting C programming learning: a CA prototype built on Botpress AI and a fully integrated web-based learning platform named BugC. What distinguishes this work is its specific focus on the C programming language. Numerous studies have explored AI-driven tools for learning more modern or beginner-friendly languages such as Python [18]. Nonetheless, there remains a significant gap in solutions tailored to the syntactic and conceptual challenges of C, particularly in contexts requiring low-level understanding, memory management, and hardware interaction [19]. Accordingly, the present study adopts a design-based research approach centered on the iterative design, development, and formative evaluation of both tools. Rather than focusing on learning outcomes, the goal of this phase is to explore the technical, pedagogical, and practical implications of two distinct implementation strategies. The study is therefore exploratory in nature, emphasizing design feasibility and refinement based on informal user feedback. The article is structured as follows: Sect. 2 presents the methodology. Section 3 describes the development process and key results, including the two technological solutions and their comparative analysis. Sections 4 and 5 discuss the main findings, limitations, implications for future work, and conclusions.

2 Method

2.1 Research Design

This study follows a design-based research approach, with an emphasis on iterative development and comparative analysis of two technological solutions for supporting C programming learning. The development process was structured around four phases: (1) research and concept, (2) scoping and design, (3) creation and development, and (4) evaluation. Each phase informed the next through continuous reflection and revision, allowing the research team to adapt the design decisions to emerging technical and pedagogical insights. Importantly, the primary goal of this work was not to assess learning outcomes, but to examine the technical, pedagogical, and practical implications of two distinct implementation approaches: a no-code chatbot platform (Botpress AI) and a custom-built web environment (BugC). In line with the exploratory and formative nature of this phase, the evaluation focused on identifying usability challenges, integration constraints, and opportunities for pedagogical enhancement rather than measuring participants performance. To inform refinements, preliminary feedback was gathered through informal debriefings with a small group of volunteer users (educators and students) who interacted with the prototype in short, guided sessions. No systematic data collection or statistical analysis was performed at this stage. Instead, the interactions were used to surface design insights and guide iterative improvements. As such, this implementation should be understood as a formative pilot study, a preparatory step for future empirical validation of the tools.

2.2 Aim

The aim of this research is to design, develop, and compare two technological approaches for integrating a GenAI-based CA into C programming education. Rather than assessing pedagogical impact, this study focuses on the technical and pedagogical trade-offs between using a rapid-development platform (Botpress AI) and a custom-built web solution (BugC). The central research questions are: (1) how can a GenAI-based CA be designed to enhance the learning of C programming learning among first-year technical university students, and (2) what are the implications of choosing one technological approach over another?

2.3 Procedure

The creation and development phase began with the implementation of the first functional prototype using Botpress AI, a conversational AI platform that combines Natural Language Processing (NLP onwards), flow-based dialogue management, and seamless integration with advanced language models such as OpenAI's GPT [20–22]. This setup enabled the development of a responsive and context-aware chatbot capable of understanding user queries and generating human-like, pedagogically appropriate responses. In parallel, the BugC platform was developed through an iterative, user-centered methodology emphasizing the needs, preferences, and experiences of the target users. Building on insights from preliminary research, the process was organized into the four phases described in the design framework (see Sect. 2.1). The research and concept phase focused on a comprehensive analysis of existing tools for programming education, including both GenAI-based systems and non-AI chatbots used as educational companions. A systematic review of current AI applications in educational settings was conducted, with attention to their pedagogical strategies, technical architectures, and interaction models. Based on this analysis, a set of functional and non-functional requirements was defined (summarized in Table 1), tailored to the needs of university-level programming courses. This phase also established the theoretical and pedagogical foundations of the study, identifying how the proposed tool could help mitigate common learning challenges. The scoping and design phase involved the conceptualization and visual structuring of the tool. This included the design of the user interface and the conversational flow, aiming to ensure intuitive and pedagogically coherent interaction. The design process was informed by principles of accessibility, clarity, usability, and inclusivity [23], with particular emphasis on supporting diverse learning styles. Special care was taken to construct dialogue structures that promote progressive learning, deliver contextual feedback, and encourage active engagement through a natural and supportive conversational tone. During the creation and development phase, the initial prototype was refined into a fully integrated system that combines an interactive web interface with theoretical content, practical exercises, and the GenAI-powered chatbot. The development process prioritized modularity, scalability, and maintainability to facilitate future improvements. Finally, the evaluation phase was designed to validate the functionality and pedagogical relevance of the prototypes through informal, formative testing. Early versions of both tools were reviewed by a small group of students and educators during guided pilot sessions. These sessions focused on usability, technical performance, and pedagogical alignment, rather than quantitative assessment. Feedback was gathered through informal debriefings and observational notes, allowing the research team to identify interface issues, conversational breakdowns, and opportunities for refinement. This feedback was systematically integrated into successive iterations, ensuring that the tools evolved in alignment with real educational needs. During the requirements analysis stage, a use case diagram was developed to formally capture the functional interactions between the main actors: students, instructors, and the system. This diagram, shown in Fig. 1, served as a blueprint for the subsequent design and implementation phases, providing a high-level specification of the intended functionalities, such as accessing theoretical content, solving exercises, interacting with the CA, and managing educational resources. The model functioned as a methodological artifact guiding system development. In later stages, the implementation of these use cases diverged according to the selected technological approach: Botpress AI realized only a subset of conversational flows, whereas the BugC platform operationalized the complete set of functionalities through its modular architecture. Overall, this procedure emphasized iterative design, continuous improvement, and formative evaluation, consistent with the exploratory purpose of the study and the broader principles of design-based research.

Table 1. Key functional features and specifications of BugC.

Functional requirements	Description
Display of theoretical content	The system must allow structured access to the C programming language syllabus, organized by topics and subtopics.
Interactive exercises linked to each topic	Each theoretical block must include a set of practical exercises with response validation, hints, and solutions, aimed at promoting active understanding.
Context-aware conversational support	A chatbot must be integrated and accessible from any section, capable of answering content-related questions, adapting to the user's knowledge level, and retrieving relevant information from the loaded knowledge base. Additionally, it must be able to log interactions into an existing external tool.
Real-time progress feedback	The system must provide immediate feedback on exercise outcomes (correct/incorrect) to inform users about their learning progress.
Dynamic interaction without page reload	Content loading must be dynamic, allowing the displayed material to update automatically when a topic is selected from the sidebar menu, without requiring a page reload.

3 Results

The research led to the development of two distinct technological solutions designed to support C language programming learners through conversational AI. These tools emerged iteratively from the design-based research process, representing two complementary approaches to integrating GenAI intro programming education. Rather than focusing on quantitative evaluation, this section presents the outcomes of the design and development phases, highlighting how the iterative methodology informed the technical, pedagogical, and structured characteristics of each prototype.

3.1 Educational Chatbot Using Botpress AI

From a technical and pedagogical perspective, Botpress AI offered several advantages. Its visual interface for designing conversational flows enabled the creation of complex dialogue structures without requiring advanced programming skills (see Fig. 2), making it accessible to educators without a technical background. This feature supports future adaptability, allowing instructors to modify conversation nodes, integrate custom knowledge bases, and adjust responses autonomously. Additionally, the platform supports conditional logic, external data integration, and NLP, enabling the chatbot to retrieve topic-specific content (e.g.: theory and exercises in C) and implement intent-based transitions that provide immediate feedback and real-time support during self-paced learning.

Fig. 1. Use case diagram of the proposed system.

However, several technical, usability, and economic limitations emerged during development and testing, ultimately indicating that this solution, while functional, was not sustainable as a final product. First, the monthly subscription cost of €89 for the required plan posed a significant barrier to scalability, especially in educational contexts with limited budgets. Second, the platform exhibited stability issues during advanced editing. Frequent bugs occurred when rearranging nodes, such as broken, duplicated, or misaligned connections, which often required manual correction or even partial reconstruction of the flow. This significantly hindered project maintenance, particularly in later stages with a high number of interconnected nodes. Furthermore, the chatbot struggled with ambiguous or misspelled inputs, revealing weaknesses in intent recognition and conversational recovery mechanisms. Advanced features such as dynamic node reuse and complex cross-flow conditionals were either limited or non-intuitive, restricting the system's ability to deliver highly personalized interactions.

3.2 The BugC Educational Web Platform

The BugC web platform could serve as an effective solution for supporting C programming learning, distinguished by its accessibility, modularity, and user-centered pedagogical design. As illustrated in Fig. 3, the platform provides a clean and intuitive interface. Among its main advantages is the integration of theoretical content, interactive exercises, and conversational assistance within a single environment, combined with a clear and adaptable interface that responds to the user's level of interaction. BugC offers a seamless and structured learning experience by organizing the curriculum into well-defined topics, each containing concise theoretical explanations followed by hands-on exercises. These exercises

Fig. 2. Visual interface of Botpress AI for creating conversational flows.

include immediate feedback, hints, and sample solutions, fostering active learning and self-assessment. The evaluation of the practical component is based on comparing the student's output against a regular expression to determine correctness. Additionally, the system can provide hints and display the correct solution when necessary, helping to guide learning without discouraging students. The integrated chatbot, powered by GenAI via the OpenAI API, provides contextual support at any point in the learning journey, answering questions in a way that aligns with the current topic and avoids introducing out-of-scope concepts. This tight integration of resources reduces the need to switch between tools, minimizing cognitive load and helping learners stay focused and engaged. Technically, the platform was built using standard web technologies—HTML, CSS, JavaScript, and Node.js—ensuring broad compatibility and ease of deployment. Content is managed dynamically through structured JSON and TXT files, allowing for straightforward updates and adaptation to different teaching contexts without requiring deep technical expertise. This modular architecture enhances the platform's flexibility and scalability, making it a practical option for educators looking to implement AI-supported learning tools in programming courses.

Despite these strengths, several limitations were identified during the pilot phase. The most critical is the reliance on a stable internet connection and continuous access to the OpenAI API, which means the chatbot cannot function offline and may be affected by latency, service interruptions, or usage costs. Additionally, the current exercise validation system is rule-based and relatively basic, primarily checking for exact output matches or syntax correctness, which limits its ability to recognize semantically correct but structurally different solutions. Expanding this system to support more sophisticated code analysis would greatly improve its educational value. Another key limitation is the lack of user progress tracking. At present, BugC does not store data on completed activities, performance trends, or individual learning paths. As a result, it cannot provide personalized feedback or adaptive content recommendations, nor does it offer instructors insights into student engagement or common difficulties. Imple-

Fig. 3. User interface of the BugC web platform, integrating theoretical content, exercises, and chatbot support.

menting user authentication and a backend data layer would enable formative assessment features and support more individualized learning experiences.

3.3 Comparative Insights

While both tools aim to support C programming learning through conversational AI, they represent distinct approaches with complementary strengths and limitations (illustrated in Table 2). The Botpress AI chatbot was primarily designed as a conversational assistant, focusing on delivering contextual answers to student queries. In contrast, the BugC web platform was conceived as a comprehensive learning environment, integrating theory, practice, and AI support into a single, cohesive experience. This fundamental difference in scope is reflected in their respective architectures: Botpress relies on a proprietary conversational engine with a visual flow editor, whereas BugC is built on open web standards combined with direct integration of the OpenAI API, allowing for greater technical control and customization. In terms of accessibility and UX, BugC offers a more structured and navigable interface. Its responsive web design enables seamless access across devices and allows users to browse content by modules, while the Botpress solution depends on the platform's native interface or basic integrations, limiting design and navigation options. Similarly, visual design control is constrained in Botpress, where modifications are bound to the platform's editor, while BugC enables full customization ensuring alignment with pedagogical functional and non-functional requirements.

One shared feature is level-based adaptation, implemented in both systems to tailor content to the learner's proficiency. However, BugC enhances this functionality by combining backend logic with a visible level selector in the interface, offering users more transparency and control. In contrast, the Botpress version relies solely on internal conversational flows, making the adaptation less explicit to the user. Regarding maintenance and scalability, BugC proves more sustainable in the long term. Content updates are managed through editable TXT and

Table 2. Comparative analysis of Botpress AI and BugC Platform.

Criteria	Botpress AI	BugC Platform (personalized web)
Aim	Conversational assistance on C programming	Complete ecosystem: theory, exercises, and chatbot
Main technology	Botpress AI with proprietary interface	Web development technologies
Accessibility	Botpress interface or basic integration	Responsive web access, modular navigation
Design and UX	Limited to Botpress editor	Fully customizable
Adaptation	Pre-programmed conversational flows	Dynamic adaptation by level and interface selector
Customization	Low–medium (restricted to Botpress environment)	High (full control over code, logic, and style)
Generative AI	Flow rules + response modules	Full integration with OpenAI via dynamic prompts

JSON files on the server, enabling quick revisions without touching the core code. In Botpress, although the visual flow editor simplifies initial development, complex edits often lead to interface instability, as previously noted. Moreover, future expansion is more straightforward in BugC. New topics can be added as independent HTML/JS modules, while Botpress requires creating and linking new conversational flows, which becomes cumbersome as complexity grows. Finally, integration with GenAI differs significantly. In Botpress, AI responses are mediated though predefined rules and response modules, limiting dynamic adaptability. BugC, on the other hand, enables full integration with OpenAI via dynamically generated prompts, allowing for richer, context-aware interactions that can evolve with the user's input and learning path.

4 Discussions

The comparative analysis between Botpress AI and BugC suggest that effective support for programming learning requires more than simply integrating conversational AI capabilities. Our analysis shows that while no-code platforms like Botpress offer rapid prototyping capabilities, they present inherent limitations in customization flexibility and long-term sustainability. In contrast, custom-built solutions like BugC provide greater control and adaptability, through requiring more initial development effort.

Three key design principles emerged from this work. First, curricular alignment and contextual awareness are essential. The CA must not only answer questions but do so in a way that respects the scope and progression of the course. Both systems implemented content filtering based on syllabus coverage and user level, preventing cognitive overload and maintaining pedagogical coherence. Second, integration matters more than isolation. Placing the CA within a broader learning ecosystem, where students access theory and practice in the same place, reduces cognitive load and supports self-regulated learning. Third, flexibility and maintainability are critical for sustainability. While no-code platforms offer accessibility, they often limit control and increase dependency on external services. A custom web architecture, though requiring more initial effort, allows for greater adaptability, easier content updates, and better alignment with institutional needs.

These findings align with and extend previous research by [1,2], who identified anxiety and lack of support as primary barriers in programming education. Our work builds upon existing chatbot implementations such as the Python tutoring systems reviewed by [5,7], but addresses the specific challenges of C programming through structured content integration and level-based adaptation. Unlike static educational platforms, our approach incorporates dynamic GenAI support within a comprehensive learning environment.

Nevertheless, it is essential to situate our work within the landscape of GenAI chatbot implementation in programming education, where significant concerns have been identified. In a recent study on AI chatbots in programming education [24], instructors reported concerns about inaccurate responses, need for sufficient prior knowledge for effective use, and concerns about negative impact on education, particularly on students' development of transversal skills for future professional practice. Notably, this study observed that when students used ChatGPT for their programming learning, pair programming practices were negatively affected, with students only acting as the driver while deploying ChatGPT as the navigator. According to instructors, this approach compromised students' development of essential collaboration skills. It is important to recognize that ChatGPT was not specifically designed for educational purposes, particularly not for structured programming instruction. This fundamental mismatch between general-purpose GenAI tools and specific educational needs underscores the necessity of purpose-built solutions like our BugC platform, which integrates pedagogical principles and curriculum alignment from the ground up.

However, positive outcomes have also been reported in more controlled educational contexts. A study on the impact of educational chatbots on student learning experience demonstrated that chatbots can greatly enhance student learning experiences by allowing them to study at their own speed with less stress, saving them time, and keeping them motivated [25]. Furthermore, integrating these AI systems into educational environments can create supportive conditions that encourage positive interactions and improve academic outcomes. It should be noted, however, that this latter study was conducted in secondary school contexts, highlighting the need for different approaches when implementing chatbots in university-level technical education where learning objectives and study autonomy differ significantly.

Despite these contributions, this study has limitations. First, the evaluation was conducted as a pilot with a small and non-representative sample, which limits the generalizability of the findings. Second, the lack of longitudinal data prevents conclusions about the long-term impact of the chatbot on learning outcomes such as retention, confidence, or programming skill development. Third, while the system adapts to user level, it does not currently track individual progress or learning trajectories, missing opportunities for personalized feedback and adaptive content delivery. Additionally, the reliance on the OpenAI API introduces external dependencies, including potential costs, latency, data privacy concerns, and lack of full control over model behavior, particularly in detecting or avoiding biased or inappropriate language.

Looking ahead, several directions for future work emerge. First, incorporating user analytics and a progress-tracking system would enable the platform to offer adaptive recommendations and support formative assessment. Second, expanding the exercise validation engine to include semantic code analysis, beyond syntax or output matching, would allow the system to better assess alternative correct solutions and provide more meaningful feedback. Third, exploring local or open-source language models (e.g.: Llama, Mistral, among others) could reduce dependency on commercial APIs and improve data sovereignty, especially in academic contexts. Finally, extending the platform to other programming languages or courses would test its scalability and adaptability across different technical domains.

Moreover, future iterations could integrate emotional awareness into the conversational agent, enabling it to detect the learner's emotional state at the beginning of the interaction, such as frustration, confusion, or motivation, through language cues or explicit input. This would allow the chatbot to adjust its tone, pacing, and type of support accordingly, fostering a more empathetic and responsive learning experience. Additionally, enhancing the backend data collection, such as through Airtable or a custom database, to include demographic variables like gender, age, and country of origin could enable intersectional analysis of user interactions. Identifying potential patterns in how students from different backgrounds engage with the tool can inform more inclusive design decisions and help uncover hidden biases in usage or perception.

5 Conclusions

This proposal explored how a GenAI-based CA can be conceptually designed and technically implemented to support C programming learning among first-year university students. Through an iterative, user-centered process framed within a design-based research approach, two technological solutions were conceived and developed: a chatbot prototype built on Botpress AI and a custom web platform named BugC. The outcomes of this formative phase highlight that the effective integration of GenAI in programming education goes beyond conversational functionality. It requires a holistic design perspective that combines pedagogical structuring, curricular alignment, and technical sustainability. The comparison between both tools revealed that while no-code platforms such as Botpress AI enable rapid prototyping and early experimentation, they entail trade-offs in customization, maintenance, and long-term scalability. In contrast, the BugC platform demonstrated greater flexibility and integration potential, unifying theoretical content, interactive exercises, and AI-driven support within a modular architecture. From a design standpoint, key lessons include the importance of contextual and pedagogical awareness, the value of embedding AI within broader learning ecosystems, and the need for maintainable, educator-friendly infrastructures that can evolve alongside curricular and technological changes. Although this phase did not involve formal data collection, the insights derived from the development and formative testing process provide a practical foundation for future empirical studies and large-scale implementation. In sum, this research demonstrates that GenAI holds substantial promise for programming education when thoughtfully embedded within coherent, user-centered designs. The future of AI in learning lies not in isolated chatbots, but in integrated intelligent environments that empower both students and educators through meaningful, adaptive, and sustainable technological innovation.

Acknowledgments. This study is part of the research project "Playful Experiences with Interactive Social Agents and Robots: Social and Communication Aspects (PLEISAR-SOCIAL)", reference PID2022-136779OB-C33, led by principal investigators Francisco Gutiérrez Vela (University of Granada) and Carina González González (University of La Laguna). The project is funded by the Spanish Ministry of Science and Innovation through the "Knowledge Generation Projects – Coordinated Oriented Research" call. The authors also acknowledge the support provided by the Canary Islands Agency for Research, Innovation and the Information Society (ACIISI) under the Ministry of Economy, Knowledge and Employment, as well as the European Social Fund (ESF) through the 2021–2027 Integrated Operational Programme of the Canary Islands (RIS3 Extended), and the project 2024POB40 Aulas Hospitalarias y Brecha Digital: Implementación de Herramientas de IA y Robótica Social para la Inclusión, funded by CajaCanarias Foundation.

References

1. Atiq, Z., Loui, M.C.: A qualitative study of emotions experienced by first-year engineering students during programming tasks. ACM Trans. Comput. Educ. (TOCE) **22**(3), 1–26 (2022). https://doi.org/10.1145/3507696
2. Yusoff, K.M., Ashaari, N.S., Wook, T.S.M.T., Ali, N.M.: Analysis on the requirements of computational thinking skills to overcome the difficulties in learning programming. Int. J. Adv. Comput. Sci. Appl. **11**(3), 244–253 (2020)
3. Saavedra, E.J.D., Martínez, M.F.B.C., Escorza, Y.H.: Aprendizaje invertido como estrategia didáctica para incentivar la motivación y disminuir la deserción de los estudiantes en el curso Fundamentos de Lenguajes de Programación de la Universidad del Valle (sede Tuluá) (2021)
4. Silva, U.F., Ferreira, D.J., Ambrósio, A.P.L., Oliveira, J.L.D.S.: Problems faced by female computer science undergraduates: a systematic review. Educação e Pesquisa, vol. 48 (2022)
5. Kaggle, "Kaggle" (2010). https://www.kaggle.com/
6. BitDegree, "BitDegree" (2017). https://es.bitdegree.org/
7. Code.org, "Code.org" (2013). https://code.org/es

8. Katsamakas, E., Pavlov, O.V., Saklad, R.: Artificial intelligence and the transformation of higher education institutions: a systems approach. Sustainability **16**(14), 6118 (2024). https://doi.org/10.3390/su16146118
9. García-Peñalvo, F.J.: Generative Artificial Intelligence. Open challenges, opportunities, and risks in higher education. In: Proceedings 14th International Conference on eLearning, vol. 3696, pp. 4–15 (2023)
10. Wölfel, M., Shirzad, M.B., Reich, A., Anderer, K.: Knowledge-based and generative-AI-driven pedagogical conversational agents: a comparative study of Grice's cooperative principles and trust. Big Data Cogn. Comput. **8**(1), 2 (2023). https://doi.org/10.3390/bdcc8010002
11. Tan, S.C., Chen, W., Chua, B.L.: Leveraging generative artificial intelligence based on large language models for collaborative learning. Learning: Res. Pract. **9**(2), 125–134 (2023). https://doi.org/10.1080/23735082.2023.2258895
12. Wang, H., Tang, S., Lei, C.U.: AI conversational agent design for supporting learning and well-being of university students (2024)
13. Akpan, I.J., Kobara, Y.M., Owolabi, J., Akpan, A.A., Offodile, O.F.: Conversational and generative artificial intelligence and human-chatbot interaction in education and research. Int. Trans. Oper. Res. **32**(3), 1251–1281 (2025). https://doi.org/10.1111/itor.13522
14. Hsu, T.C., Huang, H.L., Hwang, G.J., Chen, M.S.: Effects of incorporating an expert decision-making mechanism into chatbots on students' achievement, enjoyment, and anxiety. Educ. Technol. Soc. **26**(1), 218–231 (2023)
15. Leoste, J., et al.: Integration of artificial intelligence in higher education programming courses: insights from student perspectives and practices. In: International Conference on Interactive Collaborative Learning, pp. 417–427 (2024). https://doi.org/10.1007/978-3-031-85652-5_42
16. Chen, L., Chen, P., Lin, Z.: Artificial intelligence in education: a review. IEEE Access **8**, 75264–75278 (2020). https://doi.org/10.1109/ACCESS.2020.2988510
17. Rane, N., Choudhary, S., Rane, J.: Education 4.0 and 5.0: integrating artificial intelligence (AI) for personalized and adaptive learning (2023)
18. Martínez, J.H.H.: Diseño e implementación de un Chatbot de IA para la Enseñanza Personalizada de Python en estudiantes de Décimo Grado del Colegio Internacional Camino a la Cima: Evaluación de un Recurso Educativo Digital para el área STEAM," Doctoral dissertation, Universidad de Cartagena (2024)
19. Subero, A.: The C programming language. In: Programming PIC Microcontrollers with XC8 (2024). https://doi.org/10.1007/979-8-8688-0467-0_2
20. Botpress, "Botpress" (2017). https://botpress.com/
21. OpenAI, "GPT-4.1-nano" https://platform.openai.com/docs/models/gpt-4.1-nano
22. Reddy, V.S., et al.: Quantum enhanced tour and travel recommendation AI chatbot utilizing bot press. In: Real-World Applications of Quantum Computers and Machine Intelligence, pp. 249–262 (2025)
23. Emma, L.: User-centered design to enhance accessibility and usability in digital systems (2024)
24. Groothuijsen, S., et al.: AI chatbots in programming education: students' use in a scientific computing course and consequences for learning. In: Computers and Education: Artificial Intelligence, pp. 1–9 (2024). https://doi.org/10.1016/j.caeai.2024.100290
25. Baha, T.A., et al.: The impact of educational chatbot on student learning experience. In: Education and Information Technologies, pp. 10153–10176 (2024). https://doi.org/10.1007/s10639-023-12166-w

First Experiences with a Tool for Collaborative Creation of Quiz Questions by Students

Zuzana Kubincová(✉) and Katarína Krupková

Faculty of Mathematics, Physics and Informatics, Comenius University, Mlynská Dolina, Bratislava, Slovakia
kubincova@fmph.uniba.sk, krupkova6@uniba.sk

Abstract. Quizzes are an effective learning tool that promotes active and self-regulated learning. As research shows, quizzes are motivating, stimulate critical thinking and their regular use helps students identify gaps in their understanding of the subject matter and better retain newly acquired knowledge for a longer period of time. The benefits of quizzes are even more pronounced when the quizzes are created directly by students. In our paper, we present the Quiz module, which was developed for collaborative creation of quiz questions by students. However, after its deployment in teaching, students were not very involved in activities with this tool. To find out the reasons, we conducted qualitative research through interviews. In this paper, we present students' opinions on this type of activity, the reasons for their low participation, and their suggestions on how to increase student engagement and how to integrate AI into this tool.

Keywords: Quiz · Testing · Quiz Questions · Collaborative Question Creation · Educational Activity · Qualitative Research · Interview

1 Introduction

Tests and quizzes are often used as formative assessment tools at various levels of education and in various educational fields [1–3]. As Kwan showed in his comparative study [4], quizzes are more effective in formative assessment than some other commonly used tools.

Regular use of quizzes in teaching can help students better understand the subject matter and improve their academic performance [5]. Cohen [1] demonstrated a positive relationship between students' attitudes toward learning and their scores on online quizzes. After completing a series of quizzes, students showed significant improvements in the time they spent taking online quizzes, and their results also improved. Similarly, the results of other studies also indicate a strong correlation or causal relationship between completing formative quizzes and improved performance on final exams [2, 6]. A study conducted among first-year students at a Dutch university [2] showed that students who completed all modules of the formative quiz had significantly higher scores on the final exam. This was true for students who had previously achieved good results, but an even

B. Fernández-Manjón et al. (Eds.): SETE 2025/ICWL 2025, LNCS 16425, pp. 30–40, 2026.
https://doi.org/10.1007/978-981-92-0042-9_3

more significant improvement was seen in students who had previously achieved only poor results.

Zhang [7] even claims that formative quizzes can not only improve students' performance on exams, but also predict their academic results. Kibble came to similar conclusions in his study on self-testing as formative assessment [8], pointing out that students' performance on their first attempt at online quizzes was predictive of their performance on final exams.

The results of ongoing quizzes can also be included in the final assessment, but even in this case, they usually only make up a fraction of the overall assessment, so students tend to perceive them as an engaging or even fun activity that helps them focus better on the material being covered [9, 10]. Several studies show that students highly value the use of online quizzes as part of lessons and consider them a useful educational tool [10, 11]. Quizzes as a tool for online formative assessment can increase student motivation and engagement in educational activities [3, 5], which is even more evident in the case of adaptive quizzes that adjust the difficulty based on students' previous performance [9].

However, the aforementioned improvement in student performance thanks to quizzes may also be related to the fact that continuous assessment of their knowledge motivates them to learn actively and organize their education better, which ultimately helps improve their results [12–15].

In his literature review [9], Surip also mentions research showing that if quizzes are only an optional part of the course and do not contribute to the overall assessment, students do not use them, but when a reward in the form of even a minimal number of points is offered, students use the quizzes and ultimately benefit from them in the final exam.

Another study [6] concluded that most students tend to take self-testing quizzes just before the final exam, which, in our opinion, reduces their effectiveness as an educational tool. If quizzes are administered regularly, students are forced to keep up with the teaching and gradually learn the material covered throughout the course [11, 12, 15], which contributes to better and longer-term retention [13, 14, 16].

The use of quizzes has many advantages not only for students but also for teachers. Quizzes used for formative assessment provide teachers with information about students' results and attitudes [1]. They are among the key methods for quickly and effectively identifying students' strengths and weaknesses and assessing their ongoing progress, which is information that can help improve teaching and achieve the goals and objectives of the study program [17].

Research investigating the benefits of student-created quizzes in educational settings takes a slightly different direction. Studies have shown that this approach can lead to greater student engagement, help them gain a deeper understanding of the subject matter, and improve their academic performance [18, 19]. Creating quizzes for classmates is a form of active learning that promotes students' understanding of the course objectives, self-reflection, and increases their ability to self-regulate their learning [19]. The authors of several studies also present digital platforms that allow students to create, take, and discuss quizzes [18–21] and report positive student responses as well as objective findings, such as statistically significant improvements in students' performance on tasks.

In an effort to motivate and engage our students, we have decided to incorporate activities into our teaching in which students will collaboratively create quiz questions for a given course. In this paper, we present the first version of the Quiz module, which was developed for this purpose as part of our educational environment courses.matfyz.sk. The first testing of the module with students helped to fine-tune some of its shortcomings and add the required features, but it also showed their interest in activities of this type. Despite the positive results of testing the tool, after its implementation in teaching, it was found that students did not engage much in activities with it. Therefore, we conducted qualitative research through interviews to identify the reasons for the low use of the tool and possible solutions to this problem. The paper also includes a presentation of the research results: students' opinions on the tool and activities with it; the reasons they reported for their low participation; their ideas on how to improve students' motivation and interest in these collaborative activities; and their opinions on integrating artificial intelligence into this tool.

2 Quiz Module

2.1 Functionality and Implementation

The Quiz module, as part of the Courses virtual learning environment, is developed as a web application using the React library based on JavaScript. The Redux library and its Redux Toolkit extension are used for global management of the application state and for communication with the backend.

The home page of the tool shows a list of all questions added by course participants (Fig. 1). It is possible to view question details, generate a quiz, or add a new question.

Any member of the course can add a quiz question (Fig. 2). The module currently supports questions with predefined answer options. It is necessary to create at least two answer options, and at least one must be marked as correct. Images can also be added to the question and to the answer options.

Course members can also see a detailed view of submitted questions with the question text and answer options which are marked correct or incorrect. As this view is intended for discussion and feedback on the question, there is a comment section below where any course member can submit a comment. The question's author, or the teacher, can edit the question (Fig. 3a). If there is a previous version of the question, it is also accessible from here. Unlike the student view, the teacher view also offers the option to approve questions that they consider to be of sufficient quality. Editing an existing question uses the same view as adding the question. The editor can make any changes, but the edited question must also pass validation.

If the teacher approves a sufficient number of questions, it is possible to generate a quiz (Fig. 3b) from them: 10 items are randomly selected and displayed from the bank of approved questions. Users can fill out the answers and check them afterwards.

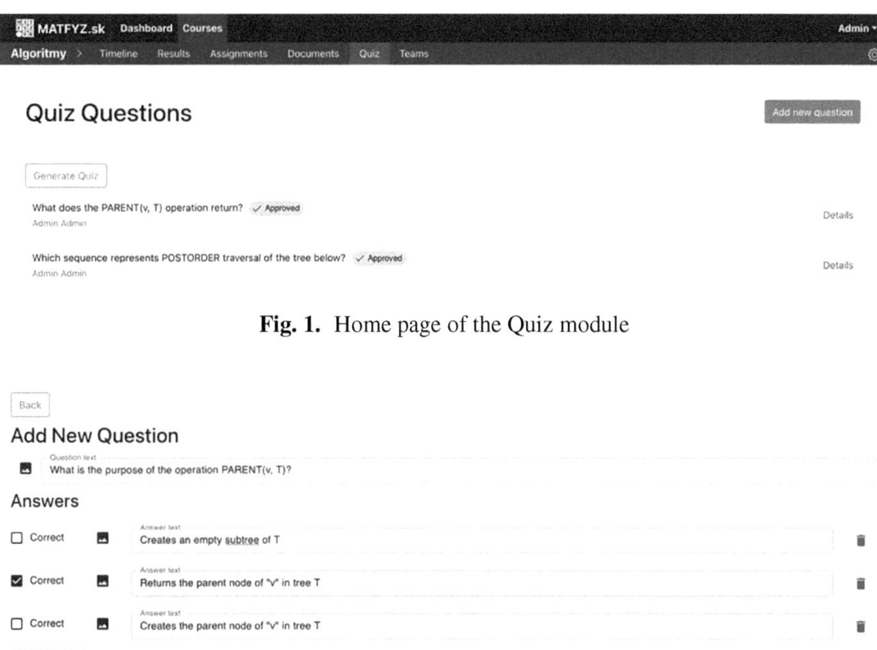

Fig. 1. Home page of the Quiz module

Fig. 2. Adding a question

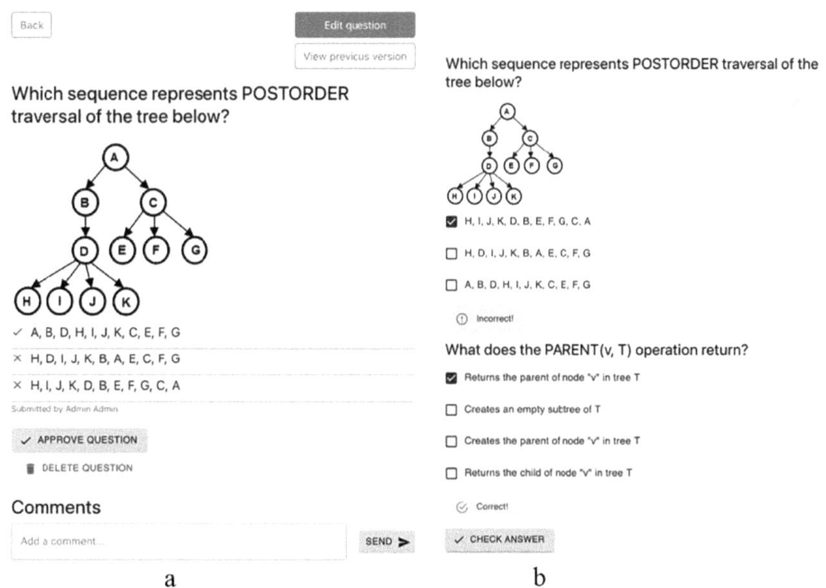

Fig. 3. a. Question detail – teacher view. b. Generated quiz with checked answers

2.2 Module Testing

The Quiz module was tested in three rounds. In each round, participants received instructions on how to work with the test version of the module, completed the tasks, and filled out a questionnaire. The questionnaire questions covered their experience working in the module, any errors they encountered, or recommendations for possible improvements. In the first two rounds, the participants were student teachers. For these groups we included questions about potential use in their teaching practice.

The pilot testing was conducted with a small group of student teachers. No serious errors were found, and all participants were successful in working with the module. We received positive feedback regarding the potential use of the tool in teaching, although several participants noted the time-consuming nature of coming up with questions.

The second round of testing was conducted with a group of 10 student teachers as part of an Algorithms and Data Structures course. The participants of this round again found the environment intuitive and useful for teaching. The aspects of collaboration and active learning were noted as main advantages, while the lack of functionality for adding images was mentioned as a shortcoming.

The third round of testing involved a group of 116 secondary vocational school students specializing in programming. This group was instructed to search for errors and vulnerabilities in the system, and to propose improvements. Most participants found the module useful saying they would use such an activity in their own education. Several students reported using a similar method. About a quarter of participants considered the module unsuitable to their learning style, or lacking functionality, and they noted the inefficiency of coming up with questions and distractors. This round led to several technical improvements and prepared the module for deployment in teaching.

3 Deploying the Tool in the Course Teaching

3.1 Assignment Settings

After improving the Quiz module based on some comments from testing, we deployed it in the Algorithms and Data Structures course in the bachelor study program for student teachers of informatics. There were 13 students (9 female and 4 male) enrolled in the course.

In one of the lectures, the module was introduced to students who were instructed to try it out during the lesson. Afterward, a whole-semester assignment of collaboratively creating and commenting on questions that could be used in the final test was announced. The assignment was set as optional.

3.2 Activity Progress

In the introductory lesson, students tried out and created questions, with some of them also commenting on the questions of the others. Although the students seemed to enjoy this activity, for most of them it was their only interaction with the Quiz module. The teacher reminded students of the long-term assignment several times during the semester, but only a few students contributed questions. Only at the end of the semester, when the final test was approaching, several new questions appeared in the system.

Students posted as few as 14 questions related to the course topics altogether. The questions were authored by only six students, with four students posting one question each, one student posting two questions, and another one posting eight questions. Two of the questions created by the latter student were not fully completed, as the suggested distractors were only sketched out. None of the students posted any comments.

In the teacher's opinion, all the questions composed by the students were too simple to be used in the final test. The students did not take advantage of the opportunity to collaboratively improve their newly created questions, as no one commented on the questions of the others. Thus, none of the questions proposed by the students were used in the final test.

After the final test, the teacher inquired among the students about the reasons why they had not engaged in the activity. According to their responses, the primary reason was a lack of time due to many responsibilities during the semester.

4 Why were Students Not Using the Tool?

4.1 Research Setting

To better understand students' attitudes towards the activity, we conducted further investigation after the end of the exam period. We used qualitative research design and carried out a semi-structured interview with two male students who performed particularly well on the course. Each contributed one question as part of the assignment.

The interview focused on students' opinions on the Quiz tool in general, their experiences with the tool and creating questions, the reasons why course participants did not post questions, how to increase their involvement, etc. The interview was recorded, and after transcription it was analyzed using open and axial coding method.

4.2 Interview Results

Students' Opinions on the Tool. The tool was generally perceived positively by students ("It's a very good idea") as a valuable aid that can help them learn, review material, and prepare for tests ("a way for students to repeat it themselves, to use it as a method to prepare for the test on their own"). They also saw its potential in creating a database of questions that could serve as study material for future students ("...maybe not us or those after us, but later [students] can use it as study material. To test themselves."). They consider creating questions to be a great way to learn and organize their knowledge. Similarly, students appreciate the ability to generate quizzes that they can use to identify gaps in their knowledge ("when real quizzes are generated from it, it's probably the best way to find out what they know and what they don't know"). However, they also expressed some reservations, particularly regarding the use of the tool for generating graded tests or for grading question creation.

The students were also asked to evaluate the tool from the perspective of their future careers as teachers. They confirmed that they would like to use this tool in their future teaching practice because it is useful for students ("very good way to give students some assistance"). In their opinion, it is suitable for use from lower secondary school to university level. They also pointed out that questions created by students could help them, as teachers, to reveal how students understand the individual areas taught ("what students find easy and what they find difficult").

Reasons for Low Participation in Question Creation. The students identified several key factors as to why the course participants did not use the tool. They stated that the main reason was that they were not used to this type of collaboration in learning and content creation ("...creating questions is simply not something that students are used to."). They were also not used to providing feedback ("For example, until I came here [to university], we never gave verbal feedback on anything. So, when you're not used to it, it takes a while.").

The tool and the activity were new and unfamiliar to them. Although the tool was introduced to them and they had no major problems working with it, they did not quite know what questions to create.

Another reason was a lack of motivation to engage in the task. Since the activity was set up as optional, they did not consider it important enough to participate in. As the interviewed students stated, motivation such as "it's for you, it will help you learn" only works for a certain type of student, not for the majority. The opinion emerged in the interview that if the task is not mandatory, most students simply will not do it ("[the teacher] will not make anyone do anything like this unless it is compulsory ...").

The students also saw a problem in creating questions, because it is not easy to come up with a good question that is neither too easy nor too difficult ("They were reluctant to write anything because they weren't sure what style [of questions] to use... in terms of scope, length, difficulty... And how should they even start?"). In addition, a common problem was that a student would formulate a question and only when they wanted to enter it into the system would they discover that someone else had already posted the same or at least a very similar question before them. The students were then frustrated because their efforts had been wasted.

Perhaps an even bigger problem than creating questions was coming up with suitable wrong answers to the questions ("So, the hardest part is probably to find something that can be asked in such a way that you can also come up with some answers that are not completely obvious, that you look at them and immediately see [which answer is correct and which is incorrect].").

Another factor that emerged in relation to the topic of commenting on questions created by classmates was a kind of social uncertainty or concerns related to group dynamics. Students did not comment on others' questions because they were afraid of how their classmates would react to critical comments ("it's one thing what the teacher will think about it, but it's another thing what the other classmates will think about it"). They explicitly stated that this was related to relationships in the classroom.

The interviews also revealed that students prefer individual learning, especially in programming and informatics courses. This was a surprising finding for us, and we perceived it as one of the obstacles to student participation in this activity, which was intended to promote collaborative learning.

Proposals for Increasing Student Engagement. In terms of increasing their involvement in the collaborative creation of quiz questions, students came up with several specific suggestions that can be classified into several categories.

Motivation. To increase motivation, students suggested making this activity a mandatory homework assignment. Later they agreed that it did not have to be completely mandatory but rather should be evaluated by bonus points ("This is quite a good motivation and it is not completely mandatory"). In any case, students need to be encouraged to use this tool more and the benefits of using it need to be better explained to them. Students should be required not only to create questions, but also to comment on their classmates' questions, and the whole task should be presented to them as a normal part of teaching ("...we will do it this way ... you will not get a mark for it, so you do not need to worry about it, but we will simply use it in class").

Educational Level of Users. Students recommended the use of this type of educational activity across all years of study, even starting in lower secondary school ("...lower secondary – so from then on, even up to university. In my opinion, as far as years of study are concerned, it's not entirely limited in this respect.", "...the younger the students are, the easier it is to teach them a new system when they are not used to anything else").

Question Examples. The problems with the difficulty of creating questions due to the fact that students do not know how to start and do not know what questions are expected of them could be solved by preparing a larger number of sample questions ("... Show students from the very beginning, when they are introduced to it: this style of questions - example, or this style of questions - example,...").

Assignment Timing. A situation where a student does not upload their question to the system because someone else has already uploaded a similar or identical question can be resolved by better timing of the activity: setting deadlines for creating questions. All created questions would be displayed to students at once after the deadline, i.e., not continuously. This way, several students could create similar questions, but each of them could receive a bonus for the posted question and, in addition, they could subsequently collaborate on creating of the final question. After the first deadline, students would be randomly assigned 1–3 questions, followed by a second deadline in which they would have to write meaningful feedback on them. Such timing of the activity would also help solve the problem that the interviewees reported as "not wanting to be the first to post a question or comment."

Anonymity. The students agreed that anonymity in creating questions and especially in providing feedback would greatly help to alleviate concerns about embarrassment, peer judgement, and uncertainty when commenting ("...if it were anonymous, yes, I can imagine that in a sense it would probably help"). It would also encourage more honest criticism and creativity.

Use of AI in the Quiz Tool and in Education. One of the areas we discussed in the interview was the potential use of artificial intelligence (AI) in connection with the Quiz module. According to their own statements, students already have experience with using AI in their learning. They most often use it to explain the subject matter, especially when it comes to complex concepts, and to test themselves by generating questions and assignments from the topic they are currently studying. However, they also appreciate the assistance of AI in searching for sources and grammatical correction of their texts.

The students' first proposal for incorporating AI into activities with the Quiz module was to automatically generate quiz questions. However, this approach is not in line with the original intention of using the tool for collaborative question creation by students to help them better understand the subject matter. After highlighting this issue, interviewees suggested utilizing AI to generate sample questions that could be used when assigning tasks, so that it would be clear what was expected of students.

Their other suggestions in this area were directed towards assessment and feedback. For example, they suggested that, after further modification the module, AI could automatically evaluate answers to open-ended quiz questions, which would save the teacher's time. From the students' point of view, it would be useful to use AI to generate dynamic feedback, where incorrect answers would be followed by an explanation of why they are incorrect and links to specific parts of lectures or videos where the topic is explained would also be provided.

During the interview, we also discussed the risks and concerns associated with the use of AI. As soon as we objected to the respondents' original proposal to use artificial intelligence in the Quiz module to automatically generate questions, arguing that this approach would reduce the original educational value of this activity, they themselves pointed out the first risk: artificial intelligence could easily be misused by students to automatically generate questions or tasks for them.

Their other concern was related to their experience that general AI models are unable to correctly solve specialized tasks. They cited graph drawing in mathematics as an example. However, we believe that the rapid development of AI will soon solve this problem. For the time being, however, it would probably be necessary to incorporate specialized AI models for certain courses.

4.3 Discussion and Research Limitations

Since the LMS environment was still under development when the tool was introduced into teaching, students occasionally encountered technical problems that made it difficult for them to work with the tool. Although these problems were not related to the module itself, they could have affected students' willingness to use the tool.

Another limitation of the research is the relatively small number of students in the group in which the tool was used and the short period of time it was used. Therefore, in the future, we would like to use this tool after its improvement in other courses with the same as well as other students to obtain more data on its use.

Despite the many problems they mentioned, the students confirmed that they would like to use this tool in other courses in their studies and also, as future teachers, with their future students, especially if the tool was further improved, e.g., with additional types of questions, the possibility of anonymous student participation, or if it was integrated with AI. They agreed that they would use it not only to create questions but also to comment on them. They would use the tool as a learning aid for students and also as a way to get feedback from them on the difficulty of the learning material. They see great potential in integration with artificial intelligence, especially for automatic assessment or providing personalized feedback.

Although their initial proposal to use AI together with the Quiz module to automatically generate questions is not in line with the original assignment, as it undermines the original goal of learning through collaborative question creation, it should be reconsidered whether or not it would be appropriate to adapt the assignment. For example, questions could be generated by AI, and students could focus on evaluating and commenting on them instead of creating them.

5 Conclusions

In this paper, we presented a module for collaborative creation of quiz questions. The aim of educational activities with this tool is to help students organize their knowledge, discover their strengths and weaknesses in a particular area, and motivate them to adopt a new approach to collaborative learning.

The module has been tested in teaching, but student engagement in activities with this tool has been very low. In our research, we therefore sought to identify the cause of this phenomenon and possible remedies. We used a qualitative approach and conducted in-depth semi-structured interviews. The analysis showed that students perceive the collaborative question-creation tool as an innovative and useful idea that supports active learning. They attribute its low initial usage to a lack of motivation, unfamiliarity with this method of learning, uncertainty in creating questions, and fear of criticism in a non-anonymous environment, which, in the context of not very good relationships within the group, prevented them from posting questions and especially comments.

They offered several ideas for overcoming these obstacles, which we would like to draw inspiration from in our future work. In our further research, we plan to focus on improvements to the tool that would enhance its quality and usability, as well as on modifying the methodology of its use in our courses.

Acknowledgments. This work was supported by grants VEGA - 1/0621/22 and APVV-20-0353.

Disclosure of Interests. The authors have no competing interests to declare that are relevant to the content of this article.

References

1. Cohen, D., Sasson, I.: Online quizzes in a virtual learning environment as a tool for formative assessment. JOTSE **6**(3), 188–208 (2016)
2. Zijlstra, S.-J.J., et al.: Formative quizzing and learning performance in Dutch first-year higher education students. In: Computer Assisted Assessment. Research into E-Assessment: 18th International Conference, CAA 2015, Zeist, The Netherlands, Proceedings 18. Springer International Publishing (2015). https://doi.org/10.1007/978-3-319-27704-2_15
3. Gikandi, J.W., Morrow, D., Davis, N.E.: Online formative assessment in higher education: a review of the literature. Comput. Educ. **57**(4), 2333–2351 (2011)
4. Kwan, F.: Formative assessment: the one-minute paper vs. the daily quiz. J. Instr. Pedagogies **5** (2011)
5. Yang, C., Luo, L., Vadillo, M., Yu, R., Shanks, D.: Testing (quizzing) boosts classroom learning: a systematic and meta-analytic review. Psychol. Bull. **147**(3) (2021)

6. Aravinthan, V., Aravinthan, T.: Effectiveness of self-assessment quizzes as a learning tool. In: Proceedings of Engineering Education Conference (EE 2010) (2010)
7. Zhang, N., Henderson, C.N.R.: Can formative quizzes predict or improve summative exam performance? J. Chiropr. Educ. **29**(1), 16–21 (2015)
8. Kibble, J.: Use of unsupervised online quizzes as formative assessment in a medical physiology course: effects of incentives on student participation and performance. Adv. Physiol. Educ. **31**(3), 253–260 (2007)
9. Surip, N., Som, Z., Palanisamy, M., Mohamad, M.: Ideas for designing better quizzes: a literature review and suggestion. Int. J. Acad. Res. Progressive Educ. Dev. **10**(8) (2021)
10. Sandi, S., Dangin, D.: Benefits and barriers on quizizz application as formative assessment tool in vocabulary teaching: students side. EDULIA: English education. Linguist. Art J. **4**(2), 166–177 (2024)
11. Salas-Morera, L., Arauzo-Azofra, A., García-Hernández, L.: Analysis of online quizzes as a teaching and assessment tool. J. Technol. Sci. Educ. **2**(1), 39–45 (2012)
12. McDaniel, M., Agarwal, P., Heusler, B., McDermott, K., Roediger, H.: Test-enhanced learning in a middle school science classroom: the effects of quiz frequency and placement. J. Educ. Psychol. **103**, 399–414 (2011)
13. Roediger, H.L., III., Karpicke, J.D.: The power of testing memory: basic research and implications for educational practice. Perspect. Psychol. Sci. **1**(3), 181–210 (2006)
14. Karpicke, J.D., Roediger, H.L., III.: Repeated retrieval during learning is the key to long-term retention. J. Mem. Lang. **57**(2), 151–162 (2007)
15. Roediger III, H.L., Putnam, A.L., Smith, M.A.: Chapter one - ten benefits of testing and their applications to educational practice. Psychol. Learn. Motiv. **55**, 1–36 (2011)
16. Roediger, H.L., III., Karpicke, J.D.: Test-enhanced learning: taking memory tests improves long-term retention. Psychol. Sci. **17**(3), 249–255 (2006)
17. Stufflebeam, D.L.: The CIPP Model for Program Evaluation. Nijhoff Publishing, Boston, Kluwer (2003)
18. Stelovsky, J., Ogawa, M.B., Ogata, B., Stelovska, U.: Constructive learning by teaching: flip-flop, peer evaluation, and agile tooltip: making and taking peer quizzes synchronized with lecture screencasts. In: Designing for the User Experience in Learning Systems, pp. 177–200 (2018)
19. Posselt, C., Flyger, C., Kjaersgaard, N.: Strengthening students' learning outcomes through students working with quizzes. In: Towards a new future in engineering education, new scenarios that European alliances of tech universities open up, pp. 1454–1461. Universitat Politècnica de Catalunya (2022)
20. Di Pierro, M., Hastings, P.: Social quizzes with scuiz. Recent Adv. Inf. Syst. Technol. **2**(5), pp. 975–982. Springer International Publishing (2017). https://doi.org/10.1007/978-3-319-56538-5_97
21. Thurzo, A., Makovník, M., Lysý, J., Valkovič, L., Javorka, V.: Medical e-learning and testing system powered by crowdsourcing and based on social networks designs. Mefanet Report **03**, 126 (2010)

PockeTA: Virtual Teaching Assistant Platform with Course Context

Zackary P. T. Sin[1(✉)], Miffy H. T. Cheung[1], Ye Jia[1], XiangZhi Eric Wang[1], Matthew W. H. Lai[1], Chen Li[1,2], Xiao Huang[1], Peter H. F. Ng[1], George Baciu[1], and Qing Li[1]

[1] Department of Computing, The Hong Kong Polytechnic University, Hong Kong, China
{zackary-p-t.sin,miffy-ho-ting.cheung,aimmeng-ye.jia,richard-chen.li, xiao.huang,peter.nhf,csgeorge,qing-prof.li}@polyu.edu.hk, {xiangzhi.wang,22056774d}@connect.polyu.hk

[2] Department of Applied Social Sciences, The Hong Kong Polytechnic University, Hong Kong, China

Abstract. PockeTA is a pedagogical agent using AI, accessible on and off campus. It can be used in a variety of situations, such as on PCs for studying and on mobile devices during field trips. The pedagogical agent, supported by a multi-agent system, is deeply integrated with a graph-based knowledge base, K-Cube, which is managed by teachers. The system collects student questions, organizes them into learning-analytics metrics, and visualizes them for instructors to help them monitor students' progress and learning experiences. In this paper, we outline the framework of our system and share some promising early results. Positive feedback from early adopters suggests PockeTA may help address TA scalability; rigorous controlled studies are required to evaluate effects on learning outcomes and TA workload. These challenges are particularly evident in many regions worldwide, where universities often struggle to improve the TA-to-student ratio due to resource constraints and growing student populations.

Keywords: virtual teaching assistant · e-learning · large-language models

1 Introduction

Teaching assistants (TAs) play a pivotal role in the landscape of university education, serving as a critical bridge between faculty and students. TAs not only facilitate the dissemination of knowledge but also contribute to the overall academic development of students by providing supplementary instruction, personalized feedback, and mentorship. Their involvement is particularly significant in large classes, where individualized attention from the primary instructor is often limited. Through leading discussion sections, conducting laboratory sessions, and offering office hours, TAs enhance the learning experience and foster a more interactive and supportive educational environment.

B. Fernández-Manjón et al. (Eds.): SETE 2025/ICWL 2025, LNCS 16425, pp. 41–55, 2026.
https://doi.org/10.1007/978-981-92-0042-9_4

Despite their importance, several challenges undermine the effectiveness of TAs in universities, particularly in the context of scalability and resource allocation. One of the most pressing issues is the insufficient ratio of TAs to students, which is a concern in many higher education systems worldwide. These challenges are often exacerbated by the increasing scale of higher education institutions and the growing demand for quality education. As a result, students in many regions may not receive timely feedback or sufficient guidance, which can negatively impact their academic performance and overall university experience. Rapidly rising student enrollments, coupled with constrained institutional resources, have created scenarios where a single TA may be responsible for supporting dozens, or even hundreds, of students. This imbalance significantly hampers the ability of TAs to provide meaningful, individualized support, thereby diminishing the quality of education on a global scale.

Fortunately, the advent of large language models (LLMs) and the progress on multi-agent architectures provide us with various paradigm-shifting tools to address this issue. Utilizing LLMs for e-learning is a current hot topic in education and Human-Computer Interaction (HCI) research. They mostly focus on specific tasks, such as writing assistance, code teaching [8,16,28,32], language learning [6,18], physical activity coaching [17] and integration with current pedagogy [27]. As LLMs can display human-like intelligence, it is a natural next step to consider them as the thinking module for virtual TAs as well. The underlying idea is not new. However, there seems to be a lack of effort in actually realizing it. Further, recent works seem to focus on text-based communication. On the other hand, previous studies have demonstrated that an avatar can help establish social presence with users, thereby enhancing Human-AI trust and learning engagement, which in turn leads to improved learning outcomes [15,31]. There is a lack of virtual TA work that considers this point as well.

To this end, PockeTA has been developed as an ubiquitously accessible virtual teaching assistant, accessible across a university campus. The system is designed to be available across multiple platforms, including personal computers and mobile devices (Fig. 1). The user interface draws inspiration from remote meeting software (e.g., Zoom). Specifically, the PC and mobile interfaces emulate conventional remote meeting environments, wherein students can visually interact with the virtual TA avatar and engage in real-time dialogue. As the interface is similar to how students interact with a human TA remotely, it is easy to learn and intuitive to use. The platform supports document sharing, enabling PockeTA to review and provide commentary. This innovative approach fosters a sense of presence and interactivity, allowing students to engage with the virtual agent in a manner analogous to interactions with human instructors.

At the core of PockeTA's functionality is its integration with a graph-based knowledge base named K-Cube [21,29], which systematically connects course content and instructional materials. This architecture empowers the virtual assistant to deliver contextually relevant support and actively engage students in alignment with their curricular requirements. Furthermore, data generated from student interactions with PockeTA are systematically uploaded and visualized

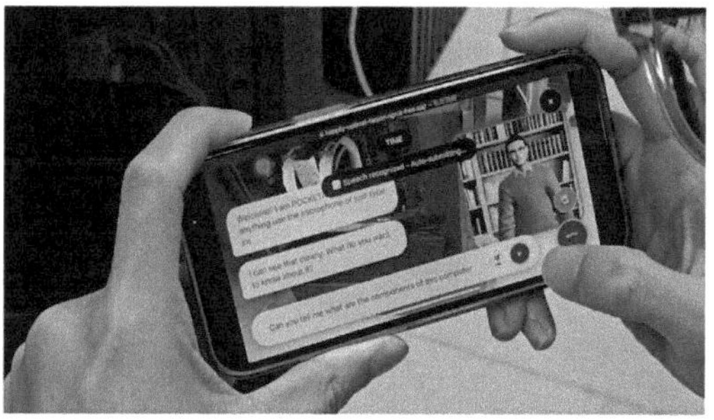 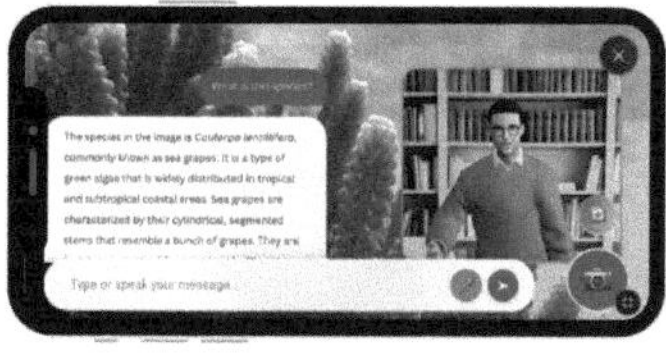

Fig. 1. Students can access PockeTA via mobile devices anytime, anywhere.

for instructors, providing a novel mechanism for educators to monitor, analyze, and respond to students' learning experiences. This dual focus on student support and instructional feedback positions PockeTA as a transformative tool in the landscape of university education.

2 Related Work

There are discussions on the application and benefit of virtual teaching assistants (vTAs). Early vTAs, such as Jill Watson, developed at Georgia Institute of Technology [11,30], demonstrated the feasibility of using AI-driven agents to answer student queries in online forums with high accuracy, thereby addressing scalability challenges in Massive Open Online Courses (MOOCs). Subsequent developments have focused on increasing personalization, as seen in architectures that incorporate student modeling and context-aware responses, enabling vTAs to recommend tailored learning materials and cluster students based on interaction patterns [7]. A vTA on WhatsApp, called KNUSTbot [9], has been shown, via empirical studies, that such a form of vTA can significantly improve academic performance and student engagement, particularly by providing immediate feedback and support outside regular office hours. There was a survey focusing on China, which presents a discussion that further highlights vTAs' potential to reduce teacher burden and improve access to educational resources, aside from underscoring the importance of cultural adaptation and ethical considerations [4]. More recent research has explored the integration of text-based generative AI models, specifically ChatGPT, which offer enhanced content creation and information retrieval capabilities, but also raise concerns regarding bias, privacy, and the depth of interaction. Despite these challenges, the literature consistently identifies vTAs as valuable tools for personalization, scalability, and accessibility in education, while calling for further research into their long-term impact, cross-cultural applicability, and ethical deployment [1]. However, previous works have yet to present a discussion on the system, interface, and presentation of the vTA in such platforms. We believe that our work is one of the pioneering efforts toward this endeavor.

The integration of LLMs into e-learning platforms marks a significant technological leap, fundamentally reshaping pedagogical strategies by creating more personalized, interactive, and efficient learning environments with the goal of approximating a 1:1 teacher-to-student ratio [24]. A primary application is the development of sophisticated virtual tutors that offer on-demand, individualized assistance; for instance, AI tools in Harvard's CS50 course were designed to guide students toward solutions, making them feel as if they had a "personal tutor", while the Iris chatbot uses subtle hints to foster independent problem-solving [5]. Empirical studies, such as a semester-long trial with the "CodeTutor" assistant, have validated this approach by showing significant improvements in student scores, although they also highlight student concerns that such tools may not sufficiently develop critical thinking skills [22]. This transformative potential is particularly evident in computer science education, where LLMs assist with code generation, debugging, and algorithmic explanation, with platforms for "prompt programming" and AI-assisted pair programming demonstrating enhanced student performance [3,23,25]. However, this is counterbalanced by the significant risk of over-reliance, where students can become trapped in a "vicious cycle" of submitting incorrect AI-generated code without developing a fundamental understanding, necessitating a pedagogical shift towards teaching verification and security for AI-generated artifacts [10,19,26]. Beyond direct student support, LLMs also empower educators by automating the creation of learning materials, such as generating initial drafts of worked examples in Java or drafting responses for TAs in class forums, thereby freeing up instructor time for more complex pedagogical tasks [12,13,20]. This highlights a critical gap that this paper addresses: the lack of a holistic, personified vTA that is deeply integrated with specific course contexts. Many existing systems face challenges with academic integrity, the potential for social erosion, and a growing digital divide [2,14]. PockeTA is designed to fill this gap by moving beyond simple Q&A to offer a comprehensive platform that combines a personified agent with K-Cube for true course-awareness, multi-modal interaction, and integrated learning analytics for instructors, thereby addressing the need for a more robust and contextually-grounded vTA as called for by the research community.

3 Features of PockeTA

In this section, we present the features of PockeTA, and highlight the difference between PockeTA and typical LLM-based e-learning systems.

Q&A Assistant: Naturally, one of the most common uses of PockeTA is to use it as a Q&A assistant to learn from (Fig. 2). It serves as an advanced query resolution system capable of delivering immediate responses to academic inquiries. Users submit questions via text input, and the AI leverages a connected knowledge base, course-specific materials, and general academic resources to generate explanations. The system supports conversational follow-up, enabling iterative clarification and deeper conceptual discussion. Questions asked by students will also be recorded for learning analytics.

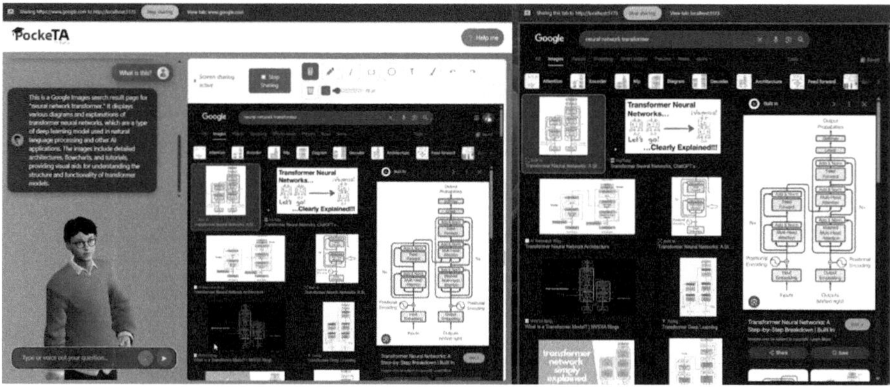

Fig. 2. PockeTA can answer academic questions in lieu of human TAs.

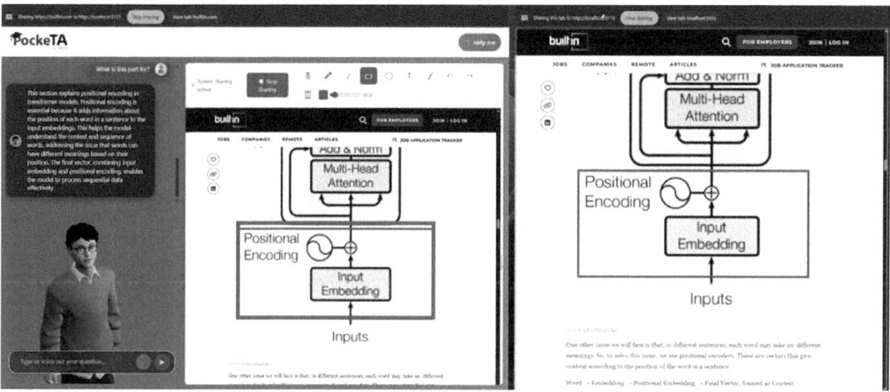

Fig. 3. Students can use the interactive drawing tools to express a question or bring PockeTA's attention to the annotated part(s).

Interactive Drawing: PockeTA incorporates a visual collaboration tool that enables users to sketch ideas on a digital canvas, thereby facilitating non-textual input and interaction. The canvas offers intuitive drawing tools, including freehand sketching, circling and annotation. Upon submission, the AI interprets the drawing—utilizing image recognition to provide relevant explanations. This feature is particularly advantageous for annotating non-textual content (Fig. 3).

Course Integration: To ensure contextual relevance, PockeTA is embedded within academic curricula through direct integration with course-specific resources. Upon configuration—typically via the upload or linkage of syllabi, lecture slides, textbooks, or learning management systems—the AI retrieves these contents or information (via retrieval-augmented generation (RAG)) in interactive time during user interactions. This alignment with curricular materials aims

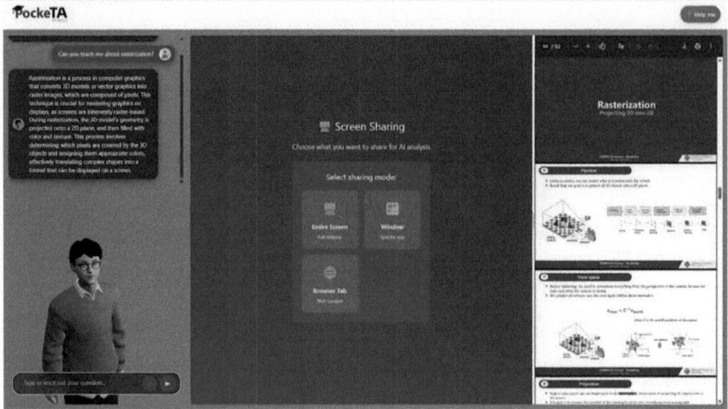

Fig. 4. PockeTA is course-aware. If relevant teaching materials (e.g., lecture slides) are available, PockeTA can present them to the student.

to minimize misinformation and enhance the applicability of responses. The system accommodates various file formats, which can support the management of multiple courses. It also includes usage tracking, which can later be used to understand the popularity of a particular teaching material (Fig. 4).

Academic Advising: PockeTA offers a personalized academic advising module, providing tailored recommendations to guide students' educational trajectories. By analyzing user-provided data—such as academic goals, performance metrics, and assessment results. The AI can work with the student to design individualized study plans, provide course selection advice, and offer skill development suggestions.

Learning in the Field: PockeTA has a mobile version that supports off-campus, on-the-go learning that can benefit field-based learning (Fig. 5). The platform offers offline functionality with data synchronization upon reconnection and incorporates location-aware features, such as contextualizing queries based on the physical environment of the user. This capability is particularly valuable for disciplines that involve fieldwork, such as environmental or construction.

Visualizing Learning Experience: It is important for the teachers to understand the learning experience of their students. By connecting to K-Cube, PockeTA can provide learning analytics and enable visualization on students' learning trajectories through data-driven insights. The system aggregates interaction data—such as question frequency and employs expressive analytics to generate visual representations (e.g., charts, heatmaps, timelines) of knowledge gaps, strengths, and progress trends.

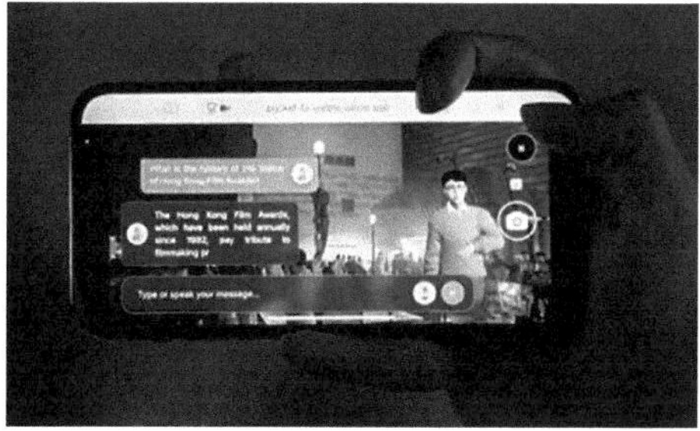

Fig. 5. The mobile version of PockeTA can be used to support field-based learning.

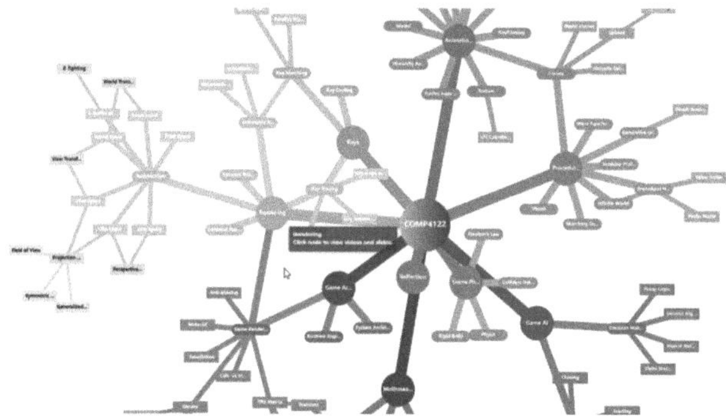

Fig. 6. PockeTA is linked with K-Cube, a graph-based knowledge base for context.

K-Cube Connected Knowledge Base: Underlying PockeTA's functionalities is K-Cube, a graph-based knowledge base (Fig. 6) that describes the content of a course and interconnects it with teaching material. Teachers will be editing the graph to change the content of their course; this will, in turn, change the course context of PockeTA and change how it delivers content and interacts with the students.

Comparisons with Other LLM-Based E-Learning Solutions: Of course, it is possible to use a typical LLM-based (e.g. ChatGPT) interface or systems to engage in Q&A activities or text-based mini-lecture. However, we believe this would ignore several deficiencies in directly applying LLMs to an e-learning system. In Table 1, we highlight the benefits and differences of PockeTA compared to other LLM-based systems.

4 System Design

PockeTA's system is fundamentally driven by a sophisticated multi-agent framework responsible for orchestrating the system's intelligence, adaptability, and

Table 1. Comparison of capabilities between PockeTA and general LLM-based systems for educational support tasks. Notes: ✓ = Supported; × = Not Supported; * Partially supported but requires technical prompt manipulation by the teacher; † Supported via knowledge graph defining the teaching context.

Capability	LLMs (e.g., ChatGPT)	PockeTA
Answer to General Knowledge Questions	✓	✓
Answer to Course-specific/aware Questions	×	✓
Avatar for Engagement	×	✓
Invocation of Trust and Learning Confidence	×	✓
Academic Advising	×	✓
Course Content Linkage	×	✓
Learning Analytics Visualization	×	✓
Teacher Controllability	✓*	✓†

interactive behaviors (Fig. 7). At the heart of PockeTA lies a graph-based knowledge base, which serves as the central repository for course content, instructional materials, and domain-specific information. This graph database is structured to model the hierarchical and relational organization of each course, enabling not only efficient retrieval of relevant educational resources but also facilitating advanced learning analytics. For instance, the system can track and analyze student engagement by monitoring the frequency and distribution of questions posed on particular topics, thereby providing valuable insights into learning patterns and areas requiring further instructional support.

The multi-agent architecture comprises a collection of specialized agents, each designed to handle distinct aspects of student interaction, such as question answering, academic advising, and the delivery of ad hoc mini-lectures. These agents operate in concert, leveraging their individual expertise to deliver a seamless and contextually appropriate learning experience across various PockeTA frontends, including desktop, mobile, and immersive environments. When a student initiates a query—whether seeking clarification on a complex concept, requesting personalized academic guidance, or engaging in interactive mini-lectures—the system employs RAG to dynamically fetch the most pertinent context, content, and information from the underlying databases. RAG acts as an intelligent intermediary, synthesizing data from the graph-based knowledge base, course material database, and study information repositories to ensure that responses are both accurate and tailored to the student's immediate needs.

This architecture is further enhanced by an interaction database, which continuously updates with new data generated from student-agent exchanges. These interactions are visualized and made accessible through K-Cube, a dedicated interface for instructors and administrators. The portal empowers educators to exert granular control over PockeTA's behavior, edit and curate course contexts, and access a suite of learning analytics tools. Through these analytics, teachers can identify commonly asked questions, monitor student progress, and adapt instructional strategies to better address emerging learning challenges.

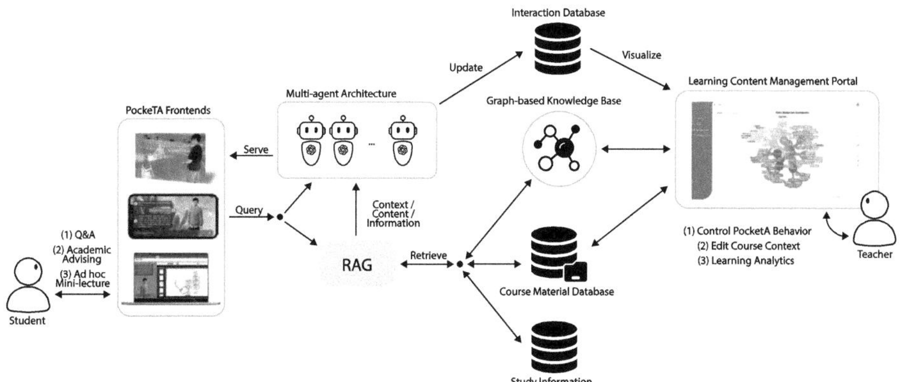

Fig. 7. PockeTA system architecture

5 Use Case Narrative

To illustrate the practical applications and potential impact of PockeTA, two representative use case scenarios are presented: the student perspective and the teacher perspective.

Student Perspective: Consider the case of a university student who engages in self-directed study during late-night hours. In such circumstances, access to human teaching assistants (TAs) is typically constrained due to limited availability outside of standard working hours. PockeTA, as an AI-powered vTA, addresses this gap by providing on-demand academic support. While it does not fully replicate the nuanced expertise of human instructors, PockeTA is designed to facilitate natural, dialogic interactions that emulate the back-and-forth communication recognized as effective in constructivist learning paradigms. Furthermore, the virtual agent possesses the capacity for unlimited patience, enabling extended learning sessions tailored to the student's pace and needs. This persistent availability and adaptability can foster a more supportive and responsive learning environment, particularly for students who require additional time or repeated explanations to master complex concepts.

Teacher Perspective: From the instructor's standpoint, PockeTA offers valuable insights into student learning behaviors and areas of difficulty. Following each student interaction, the system generates a session report that is transmitted to a backend analytics platform. This report includes metadata such as the topics discussed and the specific questions posed by students. The aggregated data are visualized atop a knowledge graph, allowing instructors to identify frequently asked questions and common areas of confusion. Such data-driven feedback enables educators to make informed adjustments to their teaching strategies, curricular content, or supplementary materials, thereby enhancing the overall effectiveness of instruction. By integrating PockeTA into the teaching workflow, universities can leverage real-time learning analytics to support continuous pedagogical improvement.

6 User Study

Our system has been released for beta testing. To understand how learners interact with PockeTA, we recruited 16 volunteer users for system testing and conducted online structured interviews. To analyze the data, we conducted thematic analysis with coding to extract qualitative insights. The thematic analysis of the structured interview data revealed a range of user perspectives, expectations, and concerns regarding the development and deployment of PockeTA. The analysis identified six major themes: (1) Personalized and Contextual Learning Assistance, (2) Emotional and Social Dimensions, (3) Technical Reliability and Safety Concern, (4) Requested Features and (5) Requested Use Cases. Each theme is illustrated below with representative participant quotes.

6.1 Personalized and Contextual Learning Assistance

Analysis of student feedback reveals that PockeTA's most valued attribute is its ability to deliver highly personalized, context-aware support that is closely integrated with course materials and responsive to individual learning needs. Participants consistently described the system as both innovative and practical, with one student noting: *"My first thought on PockeTA is that it's a very useful and forward-thinking idea. Having a personal vTA that's connected to my course material could really improve how I learn, ask questions, and get help whenever I need it."*

The platform design was seen as encouraging active engagement and curiosity. As one user shared: *"It looks very interesting, and the digital teacher encourages me to ask some interesting questions."*

The availability and personalization of support were also highlighted as key strengths. One participant remarked: *"I think developing a personalised, 24/7 TA is a great idea," while another praised the immediacy of the system's responses: "Its ability to read from the screen in real time is great."*

Several students expressed that PockeTA exceeded their expectations, with one stating: *"That's amazing and beyond my expectations. I truly anticipate its further development and deployment."*

The convenience and creativity of the platform design were also frequently mentioned. As one respondent put it: *"It is a very convenient and creative design. If the effect is significant, it will be very helpful for students to learn."*

Importantly, students appreciated PockeTA's ability to provide course-specific explanations and practical examples. One user explained: *"It can retrieve the slides on the subject of the course I enrolled in, explaining the idea in a way that includes analogical real-life examples and application examples, allowing me to grasp the concept quickly, then start digging down step by step."*

Finally, the system's capacity to deliver immediate, tailored academic support was emphasized by another participant: *"PockeTA can help me study by giving quick, accurate answers when I'm stuck, explaining difficult concepts in a way that matches my course material, helping me review with summaries or practice questions, and making it easier to stay organized and focused throughout the semester."*

Collectively, these responses illustrate that students perceive PockeTA as a transformative tool that not only provides timely academic assistance but also can adapt to their unique learning contexts, thereby having strong potential to enhance both engagement and learning outcomes.

6.2 Emotional and Social Dimensions

While most feedback focused on functional aspects, several participants highlighted the emotional and social support that PockeTA could provide. The sense of having a companion or support system during study was valued by some users.

One participant described the assistant as a supportive presence: *"I like the idea that a man is standing aside. It feels like someone is accompanying the study."*

Another suggested that the assistant could offer more than just academic help: *"I suggest that the TA offer more emotional support."*

The ability to escalate questions to a real teaching assistant was also seen as a way to provide reassurance and human connection: *"Provide the option to escalate questions to a real TA when needed."*

6.3 Technical Reliability and Safety Concern

Participants raised several technical concerns, particularly regarding bugs, interface issues, and privacy. These concerns underscore the importance of robust, user-friendly, and secure design.

Interface usability was also a concern: *"I think the selection box cannot effectively select the content I want, especially since it cannot adapt to different screens, which will cause relatively serious deviations. I hope it can be improved."*

Privacy and control over the assistant's actions were highlighted: *"I don't feel safe when it asks me to share the screen."* *"I can't really control the TA speaks out the answer or not. Sometimes I typed the question wrongly, the TA speaks the answers out, but I cannot stop him, which I still need to wait for him to finish his sentence and then I can finally get my true answer...."*

6.4 Requested Features

Beyond Q&A, participants envisioned a suite of advanced features to support their learning. Summarization, quiz generation, and multimedia explanations were among the most frequently requested enhancements.

For example, one participant described the value of content summarization and practice questions: *"Summarizing lecture slides or notes to help me revise faster before exams and generating practice questions or mini-quizzes based on recent topics I've studied."*

The potential for multimedia support was also highlighted: *"If it can create some images or animations to match with the answers, it will help me to understand the answers better."*

Participants also wanted the assistant to help them monitor their learning journey: *"Perhaps it can help to summarize the questions that I asked? And show my learning progress?"*

The desire for features that facilitate active learning and self-assessment was echoed by another respondent: *"It can give me a short quiz to verify my knowledge."*

Participants also mentioned the importance of being able to input information in various ways, such as through voice or audio: *"I think it would be beneficial to add functions like audio recognition and analysis. If I have any doubts about a certain statement taught in class, I can obtain the knowledge imparted by the professor by inputting and analyzing this audio."*

Participants also expressed interest in the assistant adapting to their learning progress and needs: *"In the future, I'd like PockeTA to offer context-aware answers based on the course I'm studying, track my learning progress to highlight weak areas, generate practice quizzes or flashcards automatically, help me plan my study time with reminders, provide the option to escalate questions to a real TA when needed, and support multimedia content like diagrams or videos to explain complex topics more clearly."*

6.5 Requested Use Cases

Finally, participants envisioned a wide range of potential use cases for PockeTA, extending beyond individual study to classroom integration, research, teaching, and even programming support.

For classroom use, one participant suggested: *"I think this app can be extended for use in the classroom. When students share the teacher's live broadcast on this app, they can quickly solve the problems they encounter in class."*

Some tutors saw value in research and teaching: *"Give me some ideas on the concepts, helping me to do my research or perhaps helping me teaching."*

The potential for programming and debugging support was also noted: *"Not just a simple chatting, and help to understanding some concepts. But also help me in other learning process, like debugging, programming, and creating ..."*

6.6 Discussion

Students consistently describe PockeTA as a "forward-thinking idea" and a "very convenient and creative design," emphasizing its value as a personalized, always-available assistant integrated with their academic materials. Users particularly appreciate features such as real-time screen reading, intuitive navigation, and the ability to retrieve and explain course slides, provide analogies, and deliver quick clarifications or summaries. This feedback highlights strong usability and user satisfaction, suggesting that PockeTA supports engagement and streamlines access to academic content. While students frequently characterize their experience with PockeTA as highly beneficial to their learning, such appraisals primarily reflect perceived support and motivation rather than empirically demonstrated learning gains. The motivational aspect—such as having a digital assistant that encourages inquiry and reinforces active engagement—may contribute to more sustained academic habits. However, distinguishing between perceived utility and actual instructional impact remains essential. The assistant's versatility in handling diverse content and learning scenarios further enhances its appeal, suggesting broad potential for integration into different educational contexts. In summary, the expanded feedback confirms and deepens the initial thematic analysis: students value PockeTA for its personalized, context-aware support, ease of use, and motivational presence. These qualities position PockeTA as a promising tool for improving learning outcomes and fostering a more engaging, supportive educational environment.

7 Conclusion

This paper demonstrates that an AI-powered virtual teaching assistant like PockeTA has strong potential to address scalability and limited personalization in higher education. By integrating course-specific knowledge, real-time analytics, and interactive features, PockeTA offers students immediate, tailored support and provides educators with insights into learning experiences. User feedback highlights its role in enhancing engagement, organization, and confidence, which suggests high potential for improving learning efficacy and supporting a more responsive, student-centered educational environment.

References

1. Agarwal, K.: AI in education-evaluating ChatGPT as a virtual teaching assistant. Int. J. Multi. Res. (IJFMR) **5**(4) (2023)
2. Ali, A., Collier, A.H., Dewan, U., McDonald, N., Johri, A.: Analysis of generative AI policies in computing course syllabi. In: Proceedings of the 56th ACM Technical Symposium on Computer Science Education, vol. 1, pp. 18–24 (2025). https://doi.org/10.1145/3641554.3701823
3. Alpizar-Chacon, I., Keuning, H.: Student's use of generative ai as a support tool in an advanced web development course. In: Proceedings of the 30th ACM Conference on Innovation and Technology in Computer Science Education, vol. 1, pp. 312–318 (2025). https://doi.org/10.1145/3724363.3729106

4. Audras, D., Zhao, A., Isgar, C., Tang, Y.: Virtual teaching assistants: a survey of a novel teaching technology. Int. J. Chin. Educ. **11**(2), 2212585X221121674 (2022)
5. Bassner, P., Frankford, E., Krusche, S.: Iris: an AI-driven virtual tutor for computer science education. In: Proceedings of the 2024 on Innovation and Technology in Computer Science Education, vol. 1, pp. 394–400 (2024). https://doi.org/10.1145/3649217.3653543
6. Bendarkawi, J., et al.: Conversar: exploring embodied LLM-powered group conversations in augmented reality for second language learners. In: Proceedings of the Extended Abstracts of the CHI Conference on Human Factors in Computing Systems, pp. 1–11 (2025)
7. Benedetto, L., Cremonesi, P., Parenti, M.: A virtual teaching assistant for personalized learning. arXiv preprint arXiv:1902.09289 (2019)
8. Chen, J., et al.: Learning agent-based modeling with LLM companions: Experiences of novices and experts using ChatGPT & netlogo chat. In: Proceedings of the 2024 CHI Conference on Human Factors in Computing Systems, pp. 1–18 (2024)
9. Essel, H.B., Vlachopoulos, D., Tachie-Menson, A., Johnson, E.E., Baah, P.K.: The impact of a virtual teaching assistant (chatbot) on students' learning in Ghanaian higher education. Int. J. Educ. Technol. High. Educ. **19**(1), 57 (2022)
10. Fernandez, A.S., Cornell, K.A.: Cs1 with a side of AI: teaching software verification for secure code in the era of generative AI. In: Proceedings of the 55th ACM Technical Symposium on Computer Science Education, vol. 1, pp. 345–351 (2024). https://doi.org/10.1145/3626252.3630817
11. Goel, A.K., Polepeddi, L.: Jill Watson: a virtual teaching assistant for online education. In: Learning engineering for online education, pp. 120–143. Routledge (2018)
12. Hassany, M., Ke, J., Brusilovsky, P., Lekshmi Narayanan, A.B., Akhuseyinoglu, K.: Authoring worked examples for java programming with human AI collaboration. In: Proceedings of the 39th ACM/SIGAPP Symposium on Applied Computing, pp. 101–103 (2024). https://doi.org/10.1145/3605098.3636160
13. He, K., Liu, X., Xu, Y., Bustamante, A.S., Warschauer, M.: "Carlitos the curious caterpillar": exploring teacher-AI co-creation of culturally responsive educational materials for young learners, pp. 236–254 (2025). https://doi.org/10.1145/3713043.3727056
14. Hou, I., Man, O., Hamilton, K., Muthusekaran, S., Johnykutty, J., Zadeh, L., MacNeil, S.: 'All roads lead to ChatGPT': how generative AI is eroding social interactions and student learning communities. In: Proceedings of the 30th ACM Conference on Innovation and Technology in Computer Science Education, vol. 1, pp. 79–85 (2025). https://doi.org/10.1145/3724363.3729024
15. Jia, Y., et al.: Nivta: towards a naturally interactable edu-metaverse teaching assistant for cave. In: 2024 IEEE International Conference on Metaverse Computing, Networking, and Applications (MetaCom), pp. 57–64. IEEE (2024)
16. Jin, H., Lee, S., Shin, H., Kim, J.: Teach AI how to code: using large language models as teachable agents for programming education. In: Proceedings of the 2024 CHI Conference on Human Factors in Computing Systems, pp. 1–28 (2024)
17. Jörke, M., et al.: GPTCoach: towards LLM-based physical activity coaching. In: Proceedings of the 2025 CHI Conference on Human Factors in Computing Systems, pp. 1–46 (2025)
18. Kim, M., Nallbani, A.L., Stovall, A.R.: Exploring LLM-based chatbot for language learning and cultivation of growth mindset. In: Extended Abstracts of the CHI Conference on Human Factors in Computing Systems, pp. 1–5 (2024)

19. Kirova, V.D., Ku, C.S., Laracy, J.R., Marlowe, T.J.: Software engineering education must adapt and evolve for an LLM environment. In: Proceedings of the 55th ACM Technical Symposium on Computer Science Education, vol. 1, pp. 666–672 (2024). https://doi.org/10.1145/3626252.3630927
20. Laney, M., Dewan, P.: Human-AI collaboration in a student discussion forum. In: Companion Proceedings of the 29th International Conference on Intelligent User Interfaces, pp. 74–77 (2024). https://doi.org/10.1145/3640544.3645215
21. Li, Q., et al.: KCUBE: a knowledge graph university curriculum framework for student advising and career planning. In: International Conference on Blended Learning, pp. 358–369. Springer (2022). https://doi.org/10.1007/978-3-031-08939-8_31
22. Lyu, W., Wang, Y., Chung, T.R., Sun, Y., Zhang, Y.: Evaluating the effectiveness of LLMs in introductory computer science education: a semester-long field study. In: Proceedings of the Eleventh ACM Conference on Learning @ Scale, pp. 63–74 (2024). https://doi.org/10.1145/3657604.3662036
23. Lyu, W., Wang, Y., Sun, Y., Zhang, Y.: Will your next pair programming partner be human? An empirical evaluation of generative AI as a collaborative teammate in a semester-long classroom setting. In: Proceedings of the Twelfth ACM Conference on Learning @ Scale, pp. 83–94 (2025). https://doi.org/10.1145/3698205.3729544
24. Mahon, J., Mac Namee, B., Becker, B.A.: Guidelines for the evolving role of generative AI in introductory programming based on emerging practice. In: Proceedings of the 2024 on Innovation and Technology in Computer Science Education, vol. 1, pp. 10–16 (2024). https://doi.org/10.1145/3649217.3653602
25. Pădurean, V.A., Denny, P., Gotovos, A., Singla, A.: Prompt programming: a platform for dialogue-based computational problem solving with generative AI models. In: Proceedings of the 30th ACM Conference on Innovation and Technology in Computer Science Education, vol. 1, pp. 458–464 (2025). https://doi.org/10.1145/3724363.3729094
26. Rahe, C., Maalej, W.: How do programming students use generative AI? Proc. ACM Softw. Eng. (2025). https://doi.org/10.1145/3715762
27. Ravi, P., et al., Abelson, H.: Co-designing large language model tools for project-based learning with k12 educators. In: Proceedings of the 2025 CHI Conference on Human Factors in Computing Systems, pp. 1–25 (2025)
28. Shochcho, M.I., et al.: Improving user engagement and learning outcomes in LLM-based python tutor: a study of pace. In: Proceedings of the Extended Abstracts of the CHI Conference on Human Factors in Computing Systems, pp. 1–12 (2025)
29. Sin, Z.P., et al.: Toward an edu-metaverse of knowledge: immersive exploration of university courses. IEEE Trans. Learn. Technol. **16**(6), 1096–1110 (2023)
30. Taneja, K., Maiti, P., Kakar, S., Guruprasad, P., Rao, S., Goel, A.K.: Jill Watson: a virtual teaching assistant powered by ChatGPT. In: International Conference on Artificial Intelligence in Education, pp. 324–337. Springer (2024). https://doi.org/10.1007/978-3-031-64302-6_23
31. Jia, Y., et al.: Towards ai-assisted immersive learning: factor analysis of learning effect in k-cube edu-metaverse. In: IEEE International Conference on Metaverse 2025 (2025)
32. Zhu, Y., Ye, Z., Yuan, Y., Tang, W., Yu, C., Shi, Y.: AutoPBL: an LLM-powered platform to guide and support individual learners through self project-based learning. In: Proceedings of the 2025 CHI Conference on Human Factors in Computing Systems, pp. 1–26 (2025)

Empowering Educators as AI Co-designers: Developing Advanced Digital Competencies with a Customized LLMeducakit for Large Language Model Personalization

Roberto Feltrero[1(✉)] and Luis-F. López-López[2]

[1] Universidad de Salamanca, Salamanca, Spain
rfeltrero@usal.es
[2] University of Eastern Finland, Joensuu, Finland
luislop@uef.fi

Abstract. The integration of Large Language Models (LLMs) in education requires educators to develop advanced digital competencies that encompass technical, pedagogical, and ethical dimensions. This study presents an analysis of a comprehensive training initiative involving the design and implementation of a specialized course on LLM personalization for academic instructors, vocational trainers, corporate learning and development managers, as well as designers of educational and training materials. This experience includes the development of a software tool, the ProyectoHeliox LLMeducakit, an open-source platform based on OpenWebUI and tailored for educators to ease the LLM personalization process and management. We propose a systematic analysis of student projects of this course to assess advanced digital competences development. Results reveal six principal categories of advanced LLM personalization options in educational contexts, each fostering skills such as computational thinking, ethical AI use, data management, and pedagogical innovation. The features of LLMeducakit, including accessible, privacy-preserving, and customizable AI workflows, were instrumental in supporting these advancements. The findings demonstrate that a combination of targeted professional development and dedicated technological tools enables trainers to move from passive AI users to active co-designers of AI-driven educational solutions, aligning with international frameworks and highlighting the importance of ethical, inclusive, and reflective AI integration in education.

Keywords: Large Language Models · Advanced Digital Competencies · AI in Education · Retrieval-Augmented Generation · Personalized Learning · ProyectoHeliox · LLMeducakit

1 Introduction

Considering the widespread use of Generative Artificial Intelligence (henceforth Gen AI) in schools, the development of advanced digital competencies (henceforth ADCs)—which extend beyond digital competence to include ethical, pedagogical, and reflective

B. Fernández-Manjón et al. (Eds.): SETE 2025/ICWL 2025, LNCS 16425, pp. 56–66, 2026.
https://doi.org/10.1007/978-981-92-0042-9_5

capacities—has become a critical priority for twenty-first-century education [1, 2]. International frameworks such as UNESCO's AI Competency Framework for Teachers and the European DigCompEdu stress that educators must move from basic digital literacy toward the capacity to critically evaluate, adapt, and create AI-driven educational solutions [3]. These frameworks propose a progressive structure guiding teachers from initial awareness and adoption of AI tools to the integration and critical assessment of AI-based innovations [4].

Responding to these challenges, this project was organized in three interrelated phases. The first involved the design and implementation of a specialized training program enabling educators to personalize LLMs for educational use through theoretical sessions, hands-on workshops, and collaborative projects fostering both technical mastery and critical reflection. The second focused on developing LLMeducakit—accessible at https://llmeducakit.proyectoheliox.org— a set of tools designed to adapt generative artificial intelligence (GAI) for educational purposes. The first of these tools is a platform for personalizing large language models (LLMs) based on the open-source software OpenWebUI and adapted for educational use, incorporating advanced support systems and workflows that reduce technical barriers for users across different educational levels. The third phase comprised a systematic review of participants' projects, identifying and classifying the ADCs developed.

To interpret these outcomes, a conceptual framework for ADCs in AI was developed, drawing on recent research and policy documents emphasizing computational thinking, ethical and critical evaluation, data management, pedagogical innovation, and continuous professional development. By integrating targeted training, a dedicated technological platform, and rigorous outcome analysis, this project contributes to understanding how educators can acquire the competencies and mindsets needed to lead AI-driven educational transformation, informing both policy and practice toward more inclusive, ethical, and innovative educational ecosystems.

2 Conceptual Framework: Advanced Digital Competencies for AI and LLM Personalization in Education

This section provides an analysis of advanced digital competencies identified in the scientific literature, selecting dimensions relevant for developing tools and educational strategies through the personalization of large language models (LLMs), focusing on dimensions 1 to 4 of the DigCompEdu [4] framework, which delve into the technical and pedagogical skills of educators. The concept of Advanced Digital Competences applied to artificial intelligence in education refers to a set of high-level skills, knowledge, and practices that enable individuals or organizations to create, understand, evaluate, and apply AI technologies effectively in educational settings. These go far beyond basic digital literacy or mere familiarity with ICTs, and encompass areas such as information literacy, digital content creation, secure and responsible technology use, and problem solving with digital tools, with both technical and critical implications. The relevance of AI due to its multiple uses in educational settings requires teacher trainers and educators to develop a set of ADCs. These competencies are multidimensional, and imply a wide range of technical, pedagogical, ethical, and reflective skills. They are increasingly recognized in international frameworks such as DigCompEdu, UNESCO's AI Competency Framework for Teachers, and recent research on AI literacy and competency [5]. The following were identified:

ADC 1. AI Literacy and Computational Thinking. Educators must master the fundamental, technical principles of AI, which imply how LLMs process data, generate language, and can be adapted to different educational requirements through techniques such as RAG and fine-tuning. It requires the development of computational thinking skills, which include the ability to decompose problems, recognize patterns, abstract concepts, and even design algorithmic solutions—which is foundational for critically engaging with AI tools and customizing them for educational needs. Amongst others, skills under this area would include: ADC 1.1 Proficiency in designing, implementing, and evaluating machine learning and deep learning based educational strategies; ADC 1.2 Knowledge about the basics of supervised, unsupervised, and reinforcement learning; ADC 1.3 Continuous learning and keeping up with AI Advancements; ADC 1.4 Engaging in ongoing learning to follow new developments in AI algorithms, tools, and ethical best practices.

ADC 2. Data Literacy and Responsible Data Management. Data literacy must necessarily be one of the competences required to effectively apply AI in educational settings. It comprises the capacity to select, prepare, and manage relevant datasets for training or augmenting models, while ensuring data quality, diversity, privacy and compliance. Educators must also understand the implications of data-driven AI, including potential biases and the importance of equitable representation [2, 4, 6]. Amongst others, this competence would imply skills such as: ADC 2.1 Ability to collect, clean, manage, and analyze large and complex datasets; includes finding patterns, reading charts and graphics, collecting, analyzing, and drawing insights from data; ADC 2.2 Understanding data preprocessing for AI training, including data normalization, feature engineering, and bias detection; ADC 2.3 Knowledge base management, refers to the practice of creating, organizing, maintaining, and optimizing a centralized repository of information using AI technologies; ADC 2.4 Communicating arguments and decisions based on data, and using reasoning to inform decisions to improve learning, identifying trends, and supporting equitable outcomes.

ADC 3. Ethical, Human-Centered, and Critical AI Use. Personalization tools of LLMs enable educators to modify, adapt, and assess the risks, bias and efficacy of LLMs. Thus, the development of advanced competence in terms of critical and ethical evaluation of AI tools is a must for educators. They should always promote transparency and ensure the responsible and human-centered use of AI in teaching and learning process. This includes fostering inclusivity, safe-guarding privacy, and supporting students' digital agency [5]. Amongst the possible skills, we could highlight: ADC 3.1 Designing user interfaces that facilitate effective human-AI collaboration; ADC 3.2 Understanding usability and cognitive principles for explaining AI decisions to end-users; ADC 3.3 Show awareness of ethical issues such as bias, transparency, accountability, and privacy, enabling for explanations of AI systems; ADC 3.4 Implementation and popularization of fair practices related to AI.

ADC 4. Design and Innovation with AI. This ADC involves the AI-assisted design, customization, and adaptation, of materials as well as innovative and pedagogically appropriate use of AI-powered tools. Thus, advanced competences in the design and innovative use of AI for educational purposes cover dimensions 2 and 3 of the DigCompEdu framework, since they do not only imply the technical ability to design, but also the necessary pedagogical skills to effectively assess and evaluate the learning process. Educators must be able to adapt LLMs to specific curricular goals, learning contexts, and student needs—such as creating accessible content, simulating real-world scenarios, or supporting multilingual and inclusive education [6]. This advance competence requires skills such as: ADC 4.1 AI-assisted creation of educational materials: ability to design, create, and adapt digital educational resources in specific contexts using AI (text/image/video production, adaptive learning content, and algorithmic resource curation); ADC 4.2 Proficiency in prompt engineering, since it is necessary for educators to develop and master prompting in order to obtain the best outcomes from LLM; ADC 4.3 Customizing AI resources: skills to fine-tune, integrate, or even develop AI-powered tools or educational resources (e.g., customizing chatbots, creating AI-based interactive content, or developing small instructional algorithms); ADC 4.4 Intellectual property and attribution for AI content: understanding of proper licensing, copyright, and attribution practices for AI-generated created digital materials.

ADC 5. Assessment and Reflective Practice. This ADC is related to dimensions 3 and 4 of the DigCompEdu. The teaching and learning process would not be complete if educators are not able to assess the impact of AI-enhanced learning environments, using multimodal and formative assessment strategies, and reflect on their own practice to continuously improve AI integration through critically assessing the reliability, bias and quality of AI-generated digital content for educational purposes. IT would consequently lead to adapting instructional approaches, and, ultimately, sharing best practices with peers [6]. Some possible signs of the acquisition of this competence would be reflected by the ability to: ADC 5.1 Collecting and analyzing evidence of student learning in AI- enhanced learning environments; ADC 5.2 Interpret, question, and validate AI-generated results and identify potential errors or limitations in AI-driven recommendations; ADC 5.3 Understand the societal impact and legal or regulatory requirements involving AI technologies and development of an iterative evaluation model, repeatedly testing, assessing, and refining AI models—such as grading systems or intelligent tutoring tools—to improve their accuracy, fairness, and educational impact.

Throughout this section, the main dimensions for advanced competences applied to AI in education identified in the literature have been shown and succinctly explored.

3 Methodology

This section outlines the methodological framework for designing and implementing a course on advanced digital competencies (ADCs) oriented toward the personalization of Large Language Models (LLMs). Integrating theoretical, practical, and ethical dimensions, the process combines curriculum design with the development of an open-source toolkit to enable educators to adapt LLMs for effective, responsible, and context-sensitive innovation in education [7, 8].

3.1 Course Design and Implementation

Developed by a multidisciplinary team in educational innovation and technology, the course aimed to enhance educators' advanced digital competencies, particularly in applying Retrieval-Augmented Generation (RAG) techniques. Offered through a university continuing education programme, it promoted openness, flexibility, and inclusivity across educational sectors.

Grounded in active learning, the module combined lectures, debates, and project-based workshops to accommodate varied professional and technical backgrounds. Learning activities progressed from theory to practice and reflection, introducing core concepts in LLMs, AI, and digital pedagogy alongside ethical considerations such as bias, privacy, and human oversight [9].

The LLMeducakit—an open-source toolkit for prompt engineering, dataset design, and RAG experimentation [10] was used in workshop sessions. Continuous assessment was applied through exercises, collaborative projects, and a final integrative task which was designed to consolidate conceptual, practical, and ethical skills, illustrating best practices in advanced digital competence [11].

3.2 LLMeducakit: Design, Adaptation, and Customization

The LLMeducakit is an open-source, user-centred toolkit enabling educators to personalize LLMs in privacy-compliant, locally managed environments. Built on OpenWebUI and the Ollama framework, it supports local or API-based models to ensure data sovereignty and mitigation of cloud-related risks. At the same time, it fosters adoption within education, where technical expertise can be highly variable. Furthermore, robust, open-source communities supporting these projects are also available, providing not only ongoing software updates but also extensive documentation and peer collaboration, which are essential for the sustainability and continuous improvement of the toolkit. Such active ecosystems enable educators and developers to troubleshoot, customize, and expand the toolkit effectively over time, ensuring it remains responsive to evolving educational needs.

The toolkit offers multi-model support, configurable parameters (temperature, top-p, token limits), and RAG integration for contextually accurate, evidence-based outputs [12, 13]. Its modular design allows integration of datasets, tools, and automations for tasks such as grading or resource retrieval, with forthcoming features like role-based access control [14].

A participatory approach was adopted in the adaptation process. The tool evolved through iterative prototyping and user feedback collection after being piloted in educational settings. It ensured that the toolkit responded to real-world challenges faced by educators, such as the necessity for seamless integration with existing educational resources, multilingual content support, and reliable mechanisms to assess the pedagogical effectiveness of customized models [15, 16]. This cycle of feedback and refinement is central to aligning technological capabilities with the practical demands of educational environments, thereby bridging the gap between technology-based innovation and classroom applicability.

Consequently, the LLMeducakit can be adapted to the specific requirements of diverse educational contexts. It supports multilingual content, model evaluation, and academic document formats such as Markdown and LaTeX. Extensible through APIs, the framework integrates seamlessly with institutional databases and digital tools, empowering educators with autonomy without necessitating advanced technical expertise. These features position LLMeducakit as a sustainable and pedagogically grounded framework that advances responsible AI innovation while reinforcing institutional sovereignty [7].

4 Results: Advanced Competencies Developed Through RAG-Based Educational Projects

The analysis of student submissions from the advanced digital competencies course reveals six main categories of applied projects, all leveraging RAG as the core technique to achieve to optimize the LLM tool and achieve the pedagogical objectives. The categorization reflects the development of specific advanced competencies required by educators and highlight mastery of certain technical features within LLMeducakit, as well as key objectives from the educational model. Throughout the following paragraphs, the categories will be developed, including a conceptual description, together with the description of the ADCs involved in the different submissions and the technical skills required to produce them, in accordance with the intended pedagogical objectives sought after by the participants.

LLM as a Customized Textbook Aligned to Curricular Stages. Through RAG, participants designed and adapted LLMs that function as adaptive textbooks, tailored to the requirements and curricula of a variety of areas for different educational stages. These models were able to retrieve and generate content aligned with official learning objectives, thus enabling dynamic, contextualized explanations and resources for a myriad of topics. The inception of LLMs which would perform as adaptative textbooks, imply, from our point of view, the application of digital advanced competences such as computational thinking and AI literacy, which implies decomposition of curricular content into modular knowledge bases and engineering of prompts for targeted retrieval; and pedagogical innovation, as demonstrated by the ability to redesign learning materials for personalization and adaptability [7]. To translate these competencies into practice, students demonstrated technical mastery of LLMeducakit, particularly in creating and managing domain-specific knowledge bases and designing retrieval parameters and general prompt templates for curriculum alignment. The educational objectives pursued in these initiatives included enhancing student engagement through tailored content, as well as empowering educators to curate and adapt digital resources at scale.

LLM for Accessible Educational Information for Special Needs. Projects focused on adapting LLMs to deliver educational content in accessible formats, including real-time translation, simplified language, and multimodal outputs for students with special needs. The creation of accessible content implies the application of advanced competencies such as user experience design and accessibility, thanks to which students learned to configure LLMs for inclusive communication and equitable access; and ethical data management, as shown by the management of privacy and sensitivity when dealing with student profiles [15, 17]. Implementation of these ideas involved integrating multilingual embeddings, translation plugins, and accessibility settings within the LLMeducakit. The main educational objectives emphasized the importance of universal design in AI-driven education and raised awareness of ethical and regulatory considerations in personalized learning.

LLM for Perspective-Specific Discussion. LLMs were adapted to simulate discussions from defined philosophical, cultural, or disciplinary perspectives, supporting critical thinking and argumentation skills. The inception of LLMs which would perform in specific educational situations to provide further discussion and interact with students imply the application of digital advanced competences on the teachers' part such as critical evaluation and bias awareness, since students configured models to represent diverse viewpoints and analyzed potential biases in generated content; and prompt engineering, since mastery in designing prompts that guide the model to adopt specific stances is shown [18]. Technically, students mastered tools such as advanced prompt templates, scenario-based retrieval, and role-based moderation. The educational objectives centered on cultivating digital literacy, improving debate skills, and recognizing the close link between model configuration and discourse quality.

LLM for Generating Metaphors, Analogies, and Conceptual Tools. The design of projects involved configuring LLMs to generate metaphors, analogies, and advanced conceptual elements for the analysis of literary or scientific texts. Regarding the ADCs implied in the design of LLMs suitable for the analysis of different textual taxonomies, we can highlight creative computational thinking, since students explored the generative capabilities of LLMs for abstract reasoning and interdisciplinary innovation as seen through the Application of AI to bridge humanities and STEM education [19]. These projects required technical skills such as adjusting creativity parameters (temperature, top-p) and selecting embeddings to achieve semantic richness. The resulting educational aims included expanding analytical and interpretive skills through AI and fostering cross-disciplinary approaches to digital education.

LLM as Virtual Debate Avatars. Students designed LLMs to act as virtual avatars, facilitating and participating in educational debates, either as moderators or as representatives of specific viewpoints. The advanced digital competences developed to design the projects which enacted avatars able to produce debates and interact with learners on specific topics assuming certain roles are simulation and role-play design as shown in the mastery in configuring LLMs for interactive, scenario-based learning, and collaboration and communication as detected in the Development of systems for multi-user engagement. In technical terms, students employed multi-agent workflows, real-time interaction plugins, and scenario scripting with dynamic knowledge base switching. Educationally, these projects highlighted the potential of AI to foster collaborative learning, as well as the importance of adaptability in real-time educational environments.

LLM as Simulation Environments for Practice. LLMs were used to simulate real-world scenarios, such as acting as a virtual patient, student, or client, enabling experiential learning and practice in safe, controlled environments. These types of projects required the most advanced development of technological competencies. In fact, the student responsible for this initiative decided to incorporate proprietary tools in the design of the virtual patient, thereby strengthening and expanding their digital skill set. Specifically, the scenario generation module was used to construct a dialogue environment in which the virtual patient and the trainee doctor could engage in structured dialogue. Persona embedding allowed the system to simulate diverse disease profiles, each with characteristic symptom patterns that the virtual patient could reproduce in response to the trainee's inquiries. Finally, interaction logging was implemented to capture the exchanges between the student and the simulated patient, providing a data layer for subsequent learning analytics. As a result, the project provided a clear demonstration of competencies such as problem-solving and adaptive reasoning as Students created complex, context-aware simulations; and Data management and privacy, as seen when handling sensitive data securely. Such projects reinforced the educational value of AI-enabled experiential learning while stressing the critical importance of robust data governance in simulation-based education (Table 1).

Table 1. Categories of RAG-Based Student Projects and Associated Advanced Competencies mapped onto them

P. Categ.	ADC developed	Project Application	LLMeducakit Features Master
1	ADC 1.2 ADC 2.3 ADC 4.1 & 4.2	Creation of an adapted textbook; textual environments	Custom knowledge base creation; general prompt; tailored content delivery
2	ADC 4.1 ADC 3.1	Adapting information; interface for easy reading	Multilingual embeddings; output customization
3	ADC 3.1 ADC 4.2 ADC 5.1	Adaptation for students; perspective-specific discussion	Advanced prompt design for targeted responses, content moderation and filtering tools
4	ADC 4.3 ADC 5.3	Metaphor/analogy generation; AI tools to foster creativity	Creativity control; embedding selection to enhance semantic richness
5	ADC 1.2 ADC 4.1 ADC 3.3	Debate avatars; customized textbook	Multi-agent conversation workflows; scenario scripting
6	ADC 1.1 ADC 2.3	All categories	Persona embedding; integration for realistic simulations; interaction logging

These results illustrate that the educational model, centered on hands-on RAG-based projects and the flexible use of the LLMeducakit, fosters not only technical proficiency but also ethical, creative, and critical digital competencies. Students in our module were able to develop a range of advanced digital competences to achieve their educational objectives. As can be seen from the table above, the design of educational materials with LLMeducakit through RAG techniques is, on the one hand, suitable for a wide array of educational purposes, and on the other hand, subsume a series of complex and advanced competences which ultimately lead to the development of Key advanced competences in AI applied to education. The analysis shows how LLMeducakit can be used for a variety of educational purposes, and when applied with clear educational objectives in mind, it becomes a valuable tool for educators. However, it is necessary to develop a series of competences. For example, the creation of adapted textbooks is carried out through the customization of the knowledge base, training the machine for a specific form of content delivery through managing prompting. The realization of these technical skills to meet the educational objectives clearly indicate the development and mastery of dimensions 1 and 2 in our framework, related to technical knowledge of AI and data literacy, since the educator must be aware of how LLMs work and process data, as well as competences belonging to dimension 4, related to the design and creation through AI. The creation of materials suitable for students with educational needs, as in the category analyzed here, also implied development of competences related to dimension 3, since educators were able to critically analyze the possibilities of the tool to deliver an accessible, student-centered educational product.

5 Conclusions

This study demonstrates that integrating open-source LLM personalization tools—particularly RAG within privacy-preserving, locally controlled environments—enables educators to develop advanced digital competencies. Grounded in active, practical, and ethical pedagogy, the course design fostered not only technical mastery but also critical, creative, and reflective capacities essential for feasible AI-enhanced education. The development of LLMeducakit bridges cutting-edge AI technologies with educational practice. Built on OpenWebUI and adapted for educators the platform offers specialized features, advanced help systems, and dedicated interaction environments to facilitate LLM personalization across educational levels. By enabling control over data privacy, model configuration, and workflow extensibility, LLMeducakit supports responsible and innovative educational practice.

Analysis of participant projects revealed six main application types—from adaptive textbooks to simulation environments—requiring competencies in computational thinking, AI literacy, data management, ethics, creativity, and professional growth. These outcomes reflect a progression beyond basic digital skills toward integrated advanced competences aligned with frameworks such as DigCompEdu and UNESCO's AI Competency Framework for Teachers [20]. The findings highlight that technical proficiency must be accompanied by ethical awareness, inclusivity, and lifelong learning. The project-based, participatory approach proved effective in enabling educators to shape and lead responsible AI integration within their institutions.

Overall, this experience shows that with the right methodological and technological framework—embodied in LLMeducakit—educators can evolve from passive users to active co-designers of AI-driven educational innovation. This transition is essential to ensure AI adoption that is pedagogically meaningful, ethically grounded, and socially equitable. Future research should explore scalable training models, long-term educational impacts, and the evolving dimensions of AI literacy.

Acknowledgments. This research was partially funded by the Ramón y Cajal programme (MICIU/AEI/10.13039/501100011033 and ESF) grant number RYC2024-049375. The article has also benefited from the activities within the scope of the project EDARCLUSION, PID2021-127124OB-I00 (financed by MCIN/AEI/https://doi.org/10.13039/501100011033) and by "FEDER Una manera de hacer Europa").

Disclosure of Interests. The authors have no competing interests to declare that are relevant to the content of this article.

References

1. European Commission. Joint Research Centre: DigComp 2.1: the digital competence framework for citizens with eight proficiency levels and examples of use. Publications Office, LU (2017)
2. AI competency framework for teachers. UNESCO (2024). https://doi.org/10.54675/ZJTE2084
3. Cruz-Meléndez, C., López García, A.C.: Competencias digitales para el uso de la inteligencia artificial en la formación de administradores públicos. IESED - Rev. Int. Estud. Sobre Sist. Educ. **3**, 653–673 (2024)
4. INTEF: Marco Común de Competencia Digital Docente (2017). http://educalab.es/documents/10180/12809/Marco+competencia+digital+docente+2017/afb07987-1ad6-4b2d-bdc8-58e9faeeccea
5. UNESCO Intelligence I.R.C. on AI: Challenging systematic prejudices: an investigation into bias against women and girls in large language models. UNESCO and IRCAI, Paris, Francia (2024)
6. Perini, M., Wubbels, C., Sartori, R., Tommasi, F.: AI-pioneers toolkit resources for choosing and using AI tools in education (2024). https://aipioneers.org/wp-content/uploads/2024/09/D.4.2-ENG.pdf
7. García Peñalvo, F.: Towards augmented pedagogy: the role of AI in personalized learning (2024)
8. Carmona-Mesa, J., Quiroz-Vallejo, M.: Innovations in AI personalization for educational contexts. J. Educ. Technol. **12**, 45–62 (2024)
9. Floridi, L., Chiriatti, M.: GPT-3: its nature, scope, limits, and consequences. Minds Mach. **30**, 681–694 (2020). https://doi.org/10.1007/s11023-020-09548-1
10. Kasneci, E., et al.: ChatGPT for good? On opportunities and challenges of large language models for education. Learn. Individ. Differ. **103**, 102274 (2023). https://doi.org/10.1016/j.lindif.2023.102274
11. Redecker, C.: European framework for the digital competence of educators: DigCompEdu. https://publications.jrc.ec.europa.eu/repository/handle/JRC107466. Accessed 22 May 2025. https://doi.org/10.2760/178382
12. Agarwal, S., et al.: LitLLM: a toolkit for scientific literature review. arXiv:2402.01788 (2024)
13. Scherbakov, D., Hubig, N., Jansari, V., Bakumenko, A., Lenert, L.A.: The emergence of large language models as tools in literature reviews: a large language model-assisted systematic review. J. Am. Med. Inform. Assoc. **32**, 1071–1086 (2025). https://doi.org/10.1093/jamia/ocaf063
14. Open University: Use of LLM tools within higher education: Report 1. The Open University (2024)
15. Binns, R.: Fairness in machine learning: lessons from political philosophy. arXiv:1712.03586 (2017)

16. Birhane, A., et al.: Power to the people? Opportunities and challenges for participatory AI. Equity Access Algorithms Mech. Optim. 1–8 (2022)
17. Mittelstadt, B.: Principles alone cannot guarantee ethical AI. Nat. Mach. Intell. **1**, 501–507 (2019). https://doi.org/10.1038/s42256-019-0114-4
18. Bender, E.M., Friedman, B.: Data statements for natural language processing: toward mitigating system bias and enabling better science. Trans. Assoc. Comput. Linguist. **6**, 587–604 (2018). https://doi.org/10.1162/tacl_a_00041
19. Guettala, M., Bourekkache, S., Kazar, O., Harous, S.: Generative artificial intelligence in education: advancing adaptive and personalized learning. Acta Inform. Pragensia. **13**, 460–489 (2024). https://doi.org/10.18267/j.aip.235
20. Dilek, M., Baran, E., Aleman, E.: AI literacy in teacher education: empowering educators through critical co-discovery. J. Teach. Educ. **76**, 294–311 (2025). https://doi.org/10.1177/00224871251325083

DyslexIA: Empowering Dyslexic Students with Accessible Learning Through AI

Stefano D'Urso(✉) and Filippo Sciarrone

Faculty of Technological Sciences and Innovation Piazza Mattei, Universitas Mercatorum, Rome 10 00186, Italy
stefano.durso@studenti.unimercatorum.it,
filippo.sciarrone@unimercatorum.it

Abstract. Students with dyslexia face persistent challenges in accessing and processing written content, which can compromise learning opportunities and motivation. While recent advances in generative AI have shown promise in education, few systems explicitly address the needs of dyslexic learners. This paper presents *DyslexIA*, an AI-powered learning assistant that combines text adaptation, readability-aware fine-tuning, and structured scaffolding techniques to support inclusive learning. The system introduces several innovations: customizable interaction modes, fine-tuned models optimized for readability and active voice, and contextual as well as cumulative concept and mind maps. Moreover, DyslexIA embeds reflective scaffolding inspired by the *ICAP framework* and *Improved Vee Questions*, guiding learners beyond comprehension toward constructive engagement. Widely used accessibility features such as text-to-speech, speech-to-text, and customizable fonts are also integrated in a unified environment. Preliminary evaluation with about 25 students and educators shows measurable improvements in readability metrics and highlights the usefulness of summarization, concept mapping, and reflective prompts. These findings, although exploratory, suggest that DyslexIA can serve as a communication bridge between students and teachers and as a step toward empowering dyslexic learners through AI-enabled accessible and reflective learning.

Keywords: Artificial Intelligence in Education · Dyslexia · Accessible Learning · Readability Metrics · Summarization · Concept Maps · Inclusive Education

1 Introduction

Dyslexia is one of the most widespread Specific Learning Disorders (SLD), with an estimated prevalence of 5–15% worldwide [12,21]. It is characterized by persistent difficulties in decoding and processing written content, which often result in slower study processes, limited comprehension, and increased cognitive load. These challenges can compromise not only academic performance but also motivation and self-confidence. Worldwide, dyslexia is the most common of all SLDs;

B. Fernández-Manjón et al. (Eds.): SETE 2025/ICWL 2025, LNCS 16425, pp. 67–82, 2026.
https://doi.org/10.1007/978-981-92-0042-9_6

the EDA describes it thus: *No matter which country – No matter which language – Dyslexia is everywhere.* To mitigate these effects, Technology-Enhanced Learning (TEL) has progressively introduced compensatory solutions such as text-to-speech systems [29], speech recognition [3], spell-checkers [15], and adaptive multimedia content. While effective in improving accessibility, these tools typically focus on isolated tasks (e.g., reading aloud or correcting spelling) and rarely support higher-level processes such as comprehension, reflection, and knowledge organization.

Artificial Intelligence (AI) has recently emerged as a transformative force in education, ranging from Intelligent Tutoring Systems (ITS) to conversational agents based on Large Language Models (LLMs). These systems can provide summaries, explanations, and personalized dialogue. However, despite the growing availability of generative AI in mainstream education [17,30], its application to dyslexic learners remains limited. Existing systems largely address detection or low-level assistance, leaving unexplored the potential of AI to scaffold inclusive and reflective learning

Building on this, we developed *AI4LA*, a generative AI-based prototype capable of producing contextual concept maps and personalized support, with encouraging results in terms of usability and engagement [11]. These studies confirmed the opportunity to design systems that go beyond compensatory support and actively scaffold learning.

In this paper we present *DyslexIA*, an AI-powered learning assistant that integrates text adaptation, readability-aware fine-tuning, and structured scaffolding techniques. The system introduces several innovations: (i) **customizable interaction modes** (full, standard, smart+, smart), offering different levels of guidance; (ii) **readability-aware fine-tuning**, trained on dialogues optimized for high readability indexes (Gulpease [20], Flesch [10], LIX [4]) and Active Voice usage; (iii) **contextual and cumulative concept maps** and **expressive mental maps**, supporting both session-level comprehension and long-term knowledge integration; and (iv) **multi-level summarization**, which adapts from lightweight previews to full map-reduce synthesis of complex texts. Furthermore, DyslexIA includes a *tutor mode*, designed to ensure coverage of key concepts before activating reflective Improved Vee questions [1,24], and a *reflective mode*, which begins directly from comprehension prompts. In addition, DyslexIA unifies widely adopted accessibility features for dyslexic learners, including text-to-speech, speech-to-text, and customizable fonts with adjustable size and spacing, thereby consolidating compensatory tools within a single inclusive environment.

The contribution of this work is guided by the following Research Questions (RQs):

- **RQ1:** How can different chatbot interaction modes adapt to the heterogeneous needs of dyslexic learners?
- **RQ2:** To what extent does readability-aware fine-tuning improve the clarity and accessibility of generated texts, as measured by established readability metrics?

- **RQ3:** What is the educational potential of combining readability-driven text adaptation with scaffolding tools such as concept maps and reflective prompts?

By addressing these questions, this paper explores how generative AI can evolve from a tool for accessibility to a structured assistant for inclusive and reflective learning. Preliminary results show measurable improvements in readability metrics (higher Gulpease, Flesch, and Active Voice ratios) and positive qualitative feedback from early adoption in study centers. These findings, though exploratory, highlight the potential of DyslexIA as a step toward empowering dyslexic students through AI-enabled learning support.

2 Background and Related Work

Numerous research efforts have investigated the use of technology to assist learners in overcoming reading and writing challenges, particularly in comprehension and short-term memorization. Traditional assistive technologies include speech recognition systems, which enable students to vocalize rather than write sentences [3], and text-to-speech solutions, particularly beneficial for dyslexic learners [29]. Other tools such as smart pens [25], spell-checkers [15], and multimedia resources are also widely adopted, often incorporating gamification to sustain engagement [28]. While valuable in mitigating surface-level difficulties, these approaches primarily focus on accessibility and compensation rather than fostering deeper comprehension, reflection, or structured knowledge construction.

The rise of Deep Learning and Large Language Models (LLMs) has expanded possibilities for educational support. Conversational agents can generate explanations, answer questions, and validate knowledge across sources. However, most are designed for general learners, without explicit adaptation to dyslexic students or other Specific Learning Disorders (SLDs) [17,30]. In large-scale contexts where teacher support is limited, this gap highlights the need for AI-powered tools that integrate cognitive and pedagogical scaffolding.

Against this background, we consider several strands of research that inform the design of *DyslexIA*: (i) assistive technologies for dyslexia; (ii) readability metrics for text adaptation; (iii) cognitive principles of chunking and engagement; (iv) structured visualizations through concept and mind maps; and (v) the trajectory from our earlier AI4LA prototype to the present DyslexIA system.

2.1 Readability Metrics and Text Adaptation

Readability assessment is critical to ensuring accessible texts, particularly for learners with dyslexia. Over the years, several indices have been developed to quantify textual difficulty on the basis of sentence length, word complexity, and other surface-level linguistic features.

For Italian, the Gulpease Index [20] is the most widely adopted. Unlike English-centric formulas, it relies on letters, words, and sentences, producing a score between 0 and 100, where higher values correspond to easier texts. Values above 60 indicate material accessible to middle school students, while values below 40 denote challenging academic texts. This index has been shown to be particularly suitable for Romance languages, where syllable-based measures are less reliable.

For English, the Flesch Reading Ease score [10] remains a standard. It combines average sentence length and average syllables per word, with scores ranging from 0 (very difficult, legal/technical texts) to 100 (very easy, children's books). Texts scoring between 60–70 are typically considered accessible to a general adult audience. The Flesch score is widely applied in education and publishing to align materials with intended audiences.

The LIX (Läsbarhetsindex), developed by Björnsson [4], provides a language-independent measure of readability. Its formula is based on the ratio of words to sentences and the percentage of long words (over six letters). Typical values range from 25–30 (very easy, children's books) to over 50 (very difficult, legal or technical texts). A simplified variant, RIX, focuses only on the density of long words, and has been shown to strongly correlate with LIX [2]. Recent applications confirm its usefulness in cross-linguistic readability assessment [5,27].

Across these indices, empirical evidence highlights that higher readability (shorter sentences, fewer long words, and a preference for active voice) reduces cognitive load and improves comprehension for students with dyslexia. DyslexIA incorporates these metrics both in the fine-tuning of its language models and in the evaluation pipeline, ensuring that generated outputs are not only correct but also linguistically accessible.

2.2 Concept Maps, Mind Maps, and Structured Visualizations

Visual representations have long supported learners with dyslexia by externalizing complex relations. Concept maps, introduced by Novak and Gowin [24], foster meaningful learning through semantic networks of nodes and labeled links, while mind maps, popularized by Buzan [6], emphasize expressive and mnemonic synthesis [13]. Meta-analyses confirm their effectiveness in improving comprehension and retention [13,23]. Our earlier AI4LA prototype already introduced contextual concept maps [11]. DyslexIA extends this with cumulative concept maps that persist across sessions and expressive mind maps for personal synthesis, creating a dual layer of structured and associative representations.

2.3 Cognitive Principles: Chunking and Engagement

According to Cognitive Load Theory (CLT), working memory has a limited capacity, and instructional design must therefore segment complex information into manageable units to avoid overload [22,26]. Miller's seminal work established the "magical number seven, plus or minus two" as a limit for short-term memory elements, a result later refined by Sweller and colleagues to highlight the importance of reducing extraneous load and fostering germane processing.

In practice, research suggests that breaking texts into coherent chunks of approximately 2–4 pages or 3,000–4,000 words facilitates schema acquisition and comprehension while keeping cognitive demands within sustainable levels [26,31]. Each chunk thus represents a self-contained learning unit that can be processed deeply and connected sequentially to construct larger knowledge structures.

In parallel, the ICAP framework (Interactive, Constructive, Active, Passive) provides a model for categorizing the quality of learner engagement [7]. The framework predicts a hierarchy of outcomes: Interactive activities (e.g., dialogic co-construction) promote deeper understanding than Constructive ones (e.g., self-explaining or mapping), which in turn outperform Active (e.g., highlighting) and Passive modes (e.g., listening or reading without response). Applied to AI-driven environments, ICAP emphasizes the need for systems that not only deliver content but also prompt learners toward constructive and interactive exchanges.

DyslexIA operationalizes these principles by automatically chunking large documents into cognitively manageable segments and by scaffolding reflective interactions that align with the higher levels of ICAP. This design ensures that learners are not merely consuming adapted texts but are actively engaging in comprehension, reflection, and knowledge construction.

2.4 The Vee Heuristic and Reflective Learning

Beyond readability and structural visualization, an important strand of research concerns the role of metacognitive scaffolds in learning. The Vee heuristic, first proposed by Gowin [24] and later refined by Åhlberg as the Improved Vee [1], is designed to make the process of knowledge construction explicit. It distinguishes between the conceptual domain (theories, principles, value basis) and the methodological domain (data, operations, observations), connected through a focus question that guides inquiry.

Empirical studies show that activating reflection around a clear epistemic question helps learners connect new information to prior knowledge and to critically examine how knowledge is generated [32]. The Improved Vee incorporates iterative cycles such as Plan–Do–Check–Act (PDCA), encouraging learners to refine their understanding through successive reflection and application.

In the context of dyslexia, such structured reflection is rarely embedded in assistive technologies, which tend to emphasize surface accessibility rather than metacognition. DyslexIA adopts the Improved Vee as an invisible but integral scaffold: learners are periodically prompted with reflective questions derived from the focus question, ensuring that comprehension goes beyond decoding to include conceptual integration and critical awareness.

2.5 Summarization and Concept Extraction

Recent progress in LLM-based summarization enables the automatic reduction of long documents while preserving coherence. Techniques such as MapReduce-style summarization [9], clustering-based chunk selection [18], and structure-preserving or hierarchical approaches [33] have proven effective in handling oversized inputs. DyslexIA leverages these methods to generate both lightweight previews and comprehensive summaries, as well as to extract ranked concept lists with salience scores. These features allow learners to track what has been covered and to identify underexplored concepts, thereby fostering semantic completeness.

2.6 From AI4LA to DyslexIA

Our previous system, AI4LA, pioneered the use of generative AI for dyslexic learners by combining contextual conversations with automatic concept map generation [11]. An initial evaluation with high school students showed encouraging feedback on usability and engagement [11]. However, AI4LA remained limited in scope, primarily offering compensatory support. DyslexIA represents the next stage: it integrates readability-aware fine-tuning, multi-level summarization, customizable interaction modes, cumulative concept and mind maps, and reflective scaffolding grounded in the ICAP framework. This transition moves beyond compensation toward a model of inclusive and reflective learning assistance, aligned with recent calls for leveraging generative AI in education for dyslexic students [8].

3 System Design and Features of DyslexIA

DyslexIA is an AI-powered learning assistant that integrates accessibility, readability optimization, and structured scaffolding into a unified architecture. The system is designed to support dyslexic learners not only in accessing texts but also in constructing and reflecting on knowledge. It operates bilingually (Italian and English), ensuring inclusivity across different educational contexts. This section describes the main components and features of the system.

At the technological core, DyslexIA relies on two large language models: **GPT-4.1** and **GPT-4.1-mini**. The former is used for complex tasks such as reflective scaffolding, concept map generation, or long-document summarization, while the latter supports lightweight interactions and fast responses.

Importantly, DyslexIA can operate in two complementary modes:

- **Pure Chat Mode**, where the assistant interacts directly with the learner using its pretrained and fine-tuned capabilities.
- **Retrieval-Augmented Generation (RAG) Mode**, where the assistant leverages a personal knowledge library built by the learner. Users can upload diverse sources—textual documents (PDF, TXT, DOCX), images processed via OCR, or YouTube videos—which are transformed into vector embeddings and stored in a Qdrant vector database. These resources become retrievable context for subsequent tasks such as summarization, Q&A, or concept map generation. When documents are below a threshold of about 5000 tokens ($\approx$ 3–4 pages), the system can also activate a dedicated *Tutor Mode*, providing step-by-step coverage and reflective prompts.

This architecture reflects current advances in RAG [19], which combine the generative power of large language models with targeted retrieval from a dynamic vector store, thereby enhancing factuality and personalization. In DyslexIA, RAG is crucial not only to ground answers in user-provided content, but also to build cumulative knowledge artifacts over multiple study sessions.

Equally central is the use of **prompt engineering**. Each interaction level (Full, Standard, Smart+, Smart) is governed by a dedicated system role, carefully designed to regulate verbosity, readability, scaffolding, and reflective engagement. This ensures that DyslexIA adapts its conversational strategies to the learner's needs, providing clear, accessible, and pedagogically consistent support.

3.1 Readability-Aware Fine-Tuning

To ensure that generated outputs are clear and accessible, DyslexIA employs fine-tuning strategies grounded in readability metrics. A specific fine-tuning was performed on GPT-4.1-mini, using about 150 bilingual (Italian and English) conversations across diverse topics. Each assistant response in the dataset was explicitly constrained to:

- adopt **active voice**, reducing syntactic complexity;
- maintain **Gulpease and Flesch readability scores above 80**, whenever possible.

In cases where domain-specific or disciplinary terms could not be simplified without loss of meaning, these were flagged as *non-reducible words*. Readability indices were then recalculated excluding these terms, allowing optimization of all other parts of the text while preserving conceptual precision. This strategy ensured a balanced compromise between accessibility and fidelity of the content.

3.2 Customizable Chatbot Modes

A distinctive feature of DyslexIA is the availability of four interaction modes, which adapt the level of guidance to the learner's needs:

- **Full mode**: comprehensive guidance with detailed explanations, broad concept coverage, maps, and reflective prompts at each step.
- **Standard mode**: balanced support with summaries, clarifications, and optional scaffolding, with an intermediate breadth of concepts.
- **Smart+ mode**: concise answers enriched with simplified rephrasing and readability-optimized output. Conceptual coverage is reduced to the essential set, relying on the fine-tuned model.
- **Smart mode**: minimal guidance, focused on quick and accessible responses. It also leverages the fine-tuned model, and proactively provides contextual suggestions to help the learner continue the conversation.

These modes are not the result of simple stylistic variation: they are the outcome of targeted prompt engineering, which defines system roles that regulate verbosity, conceptual breadth, scaffolding strategies, and reflective prompts. The spectrum thus ranges from broad conceptual exploration (Full mode) to minimal yet guided support (Smart mode).

3.3 Summarisation Pipeline

An essential component of DyslexIA is its ability to transform complex documents into accessible summaries that serve both as orientation tools and as study aids. The system adopts a two-stage summarisation strategy, aligned with cognitive load principles and scalable to different input sizes:

- **Initial Summary:** generated from the first segments of an uploaded text, it provides a lightweight overview of the main themes. This anticipatory guide acts as an *advance organizer*, activating prior knowledge and helping the learner frame expectations before engaging with the full material.
- **Full Summary:** produced through a map-reduce pipeline, where each chunk of the text is first summarized independently and then combined into a coherent global narrative. When documents exceed token limits, clustering-based chunk selection ensures thematic diversity and semantic coverage.

Summaries are presented in a consistent format (headings, bullet points, math in LaTeX, code blocks with syntax highlighting) and are dynamically adapted to the learner's language preference (Italian or English). Importantly, summaries are not static outputs: they form the basis for subsequent stages of interaction, including concept extraction, coverage tracking, and reflective prompts.

3.4 Concept Maps and Knowledge Integration

DyslexIA supports the generation of contextual concept maps, which represent the main ideas and their relationships within a text or a dialogue. Map generation is personalized according to the **interaction level** chosen by the learner:

- **Full or Standard mode:** maps contain a larger set of concepts and links, providing comprehensive coverage.
- **Smart+ or Smart mode:** maps are generated with fewer nodes, highlighting only the most salient elements.

From the initial representation, learners can **drill down** to expand or collapse parts of the map, visualizing more or fewer concepts and links according to their preference. This flexibility allows them to adjust the cognitive load of the visualization, moving seamlessly between an overview and a detailed exploration. Beyond single sessions, the system can also **merge concept maps across multiple interactions**, helping learners track progress, identify recurring or missing concepts, and gradually build a personalized knowledge graph.

3.5 Guided and Reflective Learning Modes

When documents stored in the library are within the threshold of 5000 tokens, DyslexIA can activate advanced study modes:

- **Tutor Mode:** the system extracts and ranks the key concepts from the uploaded text, presents an initial summary enriched with hints, and guides the learner through a dialogue aimed at covering all concepts. Coverage is tracked dynamically via the vector store. Once sufficient coverage is reached, the assistant introduces an **Improved Vee Question**, an open-ended reflective prompt that stimulates deeper reasoning by inviting learners to compare, apply, or reframe the material. This ensures that reflection is scaffolded upon comprehension.
- **Reflective Mode:** learners can bypass the coverage phase and start directly from an Improved Vee Question. This mode is particularly useful in exploratory learning or revision, where the goal is to activate metacognition from the outset. By beginning with a reflective prompt, the assistant positions itself as a partner in epistemic dialogue rather than a content provider.

3.6 Simplified Text Generation

In addition to summarisation, DyslexIA offers a dedicated *simplified version* of the learner's material. Starting from the original content *as-is*, the assistant rewrites the text according to three complementary constraints:

- **Maximisation of readability indices:** the system optimises the output to achieve high values of the Gulpease index (for Italian texts) or the Flesch Reading Ease score (for English texts). This is obtained through shorter sentences, reduced lexical complexity, and overall improved accessibility.
- **Active voice transformation:** whenever possible, passive constructions are reformulated in active voice. Active phrasing enhances clarity, reduces syntactic load, and supports sequential processing of information.
- **Concept highlighting:** automatically extracted key concepts are emphasised in **bold**. This visual cue directs attention to the most relevant terms, facilitates scanning and re-reading, and provides learners with clear anchors for note-taking, memorisation, and concept mapping activities.

These constraints work in synergy: readability optimisation reduces surface complexity, active voice restructuring improves the flow of ideas, and concept highlighting ensures that the semantic backbone of the text remains immediately visible. Importantly, the **meaning of the original content is never altered**: technical terminology and domain-specific expressions are preserved, while surrounding elements are adapted to minimise cognitive effort.

By combining linguistic simplification with visual structuring, DyslexIA enables dyslexic learners to engage directly with study materials in a form that is easier to process, while retaining conceptual precision. The simplified version thus reduces barriers to comprehension and recall, and also serves as a scaffold for subsequent learning activities such as summarisation, concept map generation, or guided reflection.

4 Preliminary Results

To assess the potential of DyslexIA, we conducted an initial evaluation focusing on two complementary perspectives: (i) quantitative readability analysis of generated texts, and (ii) qualitative observations collected during early adoption in study centers and pilot activities with teachers and students. While preliminary, these findings provide encouraging evidence of DyslexIA's effectiveness and usability.

4.1 Quantitative Analysis Readability Gains

We conducted two main types of quantitative tests: (i) **simplification of textbook chapters**, to evaluate DyslexIA's ability to make study materials more accessible; and (ii) **readability of chatbot responses**, comparing DyslexIA's modes with a standard ChatGPT 5 configuration.

Textbook Chapters (Simplification). Chapters were acquired either from PDF files (including *OCR* when needed) and converted into a learner-friendly *Markdown* version. The simplified output preserves technical terminology, maximizes readability indices (Gulpease for Italian, Flesch for English), transforms passive into active voice where possible, and additionally **highlights key concepts in bold** to facilitate scanning and recall. Table 1 reports aggregate improvements over 10 chapters.

Table 1. Readability indicators for original vs. simplified textbook chapters (averages over 10 chapters).

Metric	Original	DyslexIA Simplify
Gulpease	50.5	60.4
Gulpease (filtered)	53.0	65.5
Active Voice Ratio	0.44	0.83
Information Density	0.35	0.43

The simplified versions consistently show higher readability, a marked increase in active voice usage (44% $\rightarrow$ 83%), and higher information density, indicating clearer yet content-preserving texts.

Chatbot Responses (By Interaction Level). We then compared the readability of answers produced by DyslexIA (in its four interaction levels: *Full*, *Standard*, *Smart+*, *Smart*) against ChatGPT 5. The evaluation covered 50 questions in Italian, including: "What is a quantum computer?", "Tell me about Ancient Rome", "Explain the concept of derivative", and "What is the Big Bang?". Table 2 reports the averages.

Table 2. Readability indicators for chatbot responses (averages over 50 questions).

Metric	ChatGPT 5	Full	Standard	Smart+	Smart
Gulpease	45.9	50.0	53.7	62.3	67.9
Active Voice Ratio	0.92	0.88	1.00	1.00	1.00
Information Density	0.62	0.54	0.52	0.57	0.70
Extracted Key Concepts	177	129	100	30	19

Findings. DyslexIA improves readability across all modes (Gulpease rises from 45.9 in ChatGPT 5 to 67.9 in Smart), while guaranteeing almost perfect active voice usage. The *Full* mode maintains information density comparable to the baseline, with fewer concepts extracted (177 $\rightarrow$ 129). More concise modes (*Smart+*, *Smart*) progressively reduce the number of concepts (down to 19 in Smart) while preserving or even increasing information density (0.70). This indicates an adaptive trade-off: from broad coverage and scaffolding (*Full*) to concise, high-accessibility outputs (*Smart*), enabling both teachers and learners to select the desired balance between completeness and readability.

4.2 Qualitative Observations Student and Teacher Feedback

DyslexIA was piloted in two study centers supporting middle and high school students with dyslexia (approximately 25 learners in total). In addition, non-continuative activities were conducted with high school students and special education teachers or educational tutors. Although feedback was collected in an informal and anecdotal way, it has provided valuable insights for system refinement and evolution.

Several key observations emerged:

- **A communication bridge:** both students and teachers emphasized how DyslexIA often served as a "bridge" in the learning process. In some cases, teachers reported not being fully confident in the subject domain (e.g., technical or scientific topics). DyslexIA's explanations and summaries provided crucial support, enabling more effective mediation between teacher and student.
- **Most used features:** the functions most frequently employed were summarization, concept map generation, and simplified mode. These were perceived as directly useful for clarifying and reorganizing complex content.

- **Tutor mode as teaching aid:** interestingly, the tutor function was more often used by teachers than by students themselves. Teachers exploited DyslexIA's reflective prompts and guided questioning as scaffolds to stimulate student reasoning during support sessions.
- **Stimulus for improvement:** the feedback received has been directly used as input for new developments, such as adaptive control of concept map density and fine-tuning of simplification strategies.

Overall, the qualitative feedback highlights that DyslexIA is not only a tool for learners but also a resource for educators, helping to create a shared space of interaction and reflection.

5 Discussion and Limitations

The preliminary results provide an initial indication of how DyslexIA can support inclusive learning for students with dyslexia. The findings can be interpreted in light of the research questions (RQ1–RQ3) introduced in Sect. 1 and, more broadly, in relation to ongoing debates about the responsible integration of generative AI in education.

RQ1. Adaptivity of Interaction Modes. The availability of multiple chatbot modes emerged as a key factor in addressing the heterogeneous needs of learners. Some students valued the structured guidance of *tutor mode*, while others preferred the brevity of *smart+ mode*. This confirms that no single interaction strategy is universally optimal, and that adaptivity should remain central to the system's design. More generally, the data suggest that flexibility in scaffolding depth is particularly relevant in inclusive contexts, where learning profiles vary widely. A promising avenue for future work will be to explore dynamic switching between modes, possibly informed by learner profiles or real-time engagement analytics, so that the assistant can seamlessly adapt its role as facilitator, tutor, or summarizer.

RQ2. Readability-Aware Fine-Tuning. Improvements in Gulpease, Flesch, LIX, and RIX scores confirm that readability-driven adaptation enhances clarity. Importantly, students and teachers also perceived texts as easier to understand, suggesting that quantitative gains corresponded to real improvements in accessibility. These findings reinforce the value of integrating readability metrics into generative models as an explicit optimization goal, rather than treating accessibility as a by-product of general text generation. Still, further validation with larger corpora and across diverse subject domains will be needed. It will also be important to investigate the trade-off between simplification and precision: while disciplinary terminology must be preserved, surrounding context can be simplified without altering meaning. Understanding where this boundary lies will be key to scaling the approach.

RQ3. Adaptation and Scaffolding. The combination of adapted texts with concept maps and reflective prompts appeared promising. Learners were able to visualize and recall content more effectively, while reflective prompts encouraged deeper engagement and reasoning. These results resonate with research that links scaffolding to metacognitive development and long-term retention. At the same time, some maps were perceived as overly complex, highlighting the need for adaptive depth management to ensure that visual scaffolds remain supportive rather than overwhelming. In practical terms, this calls for adjustable levels of detail, so that learners and teachers can decide whether to prioritize overview, detail, or synthesis.

Beyond these specific findings, recent research has highlighted the role of learners' *GenAI literacy*, i.e., their ability to critically interpret AI outputs. Studies show that learners with higher GenAI literacy are better able to benefit from conventional chatbots, whereas scaffolding-oriented chatbots can reduce reliance on such literacy by providing structured prompts and guidance [16]. DyslexIA's design—embedding Improved Vee Questions and ICAP-based reflective scaffolds—can thus be interpreted as a strategy to mitigate disparities in GenAI literacy, ensuring that even less experienced users can interact productively with the system. At the same time, by encouraging students to interrogate and reflect upon AI-generated responses, DyslexIA may also foster the gradual development of GenAI literacy as a secondary outcome.

A related concern is the risk of *metacognitive laziness*, i.e., the tendency of learners to over-rely on AI outputs without engaging in deeper reflection. Recent work has warned that high performance with AI support may create an illusion of mastery, while in fact reducing metacognitive engagement [14]. DyslexIA explicitly addresses this risk by requiring coverage of key concepts before reflective prompts are triggered, thereby ensuring that reflection builds on prior comprehension. In this sense, the system exemplifies how design strategies can counterbalance the efficiency of generative AI with structured opportunities for critical thinking. Taken together, these results suggest that DyslexIA moves beyond compensatory support to foster a participatory and reflective model of inclusive learning, aligning with calls to design AI systems that engage learners in higher-order cognitive processes rather than delivering static content.

5.1 Limitations

The exploratory nature of this evaluation must be emphasized. The sample size was limited (about 25 students in study centers and a small number of teachers), and the activities were not conducted under controlled laboratory conditions but in real support contexts. Feedback was collected informally, without standardized instruments. Moreover, the quantitative analyses were based on a restricted set of chapters and prompts, which may not capture variability across disciplines or educational levels. Controlled studies with larger and more diverse populations are required to validate the system's impact on learning outcomes, motivation, and long-term knowledge retention.

6 Conclusion and Future Work

This paper introduced *DyslexIA*, an AI-powered learning assistant that combines readability-aware fine-tuning, customizable interaction modes, and structured scaffolding tools. The preliminary evaluation suggests that the system can improve text accessibility and foster more active engagement for dyslexic learners, moving beyond compensatory support toward a reflective model of inclusive learning.

At the same time, the study remains exploratory, limited in scale and scope. Future work will focus on larger controlled experiments, systematic comparisons with existing tools, and the integration of adaptive orchestration strategies for interaction modes and scaffolding depth. We also plan to extend DyslexIA to additional learning disorders and multilingual contexts, consolidating its role as a flexible and inclusive learning assistant.

In summary, DyslexIA contributes to the ongoing debate on how generative AI can be responsibly leveraged in education to support inclusivity. By embedding readability-aware adaptation and metacognitive scaffolding, the system illustrates a pathway toward AI tools that not only compensate for specific learning difficulties but actively foster deeper cognitive engagement. We hope that future iterations of DyslexIA can serve as a model for inclusive AI design, bridging accessibility and pedagogy in ways that benefit diverse learners.

References

1. Åhlberg, M., Ahoranta, V.: Two improved educational theory based tools to monitor and promote quality of geographical education and learning. Int. Res. Geogr. Environ. Educ. **11**(2), 119–137 (2002)
2. Anderson, J.: Lix and Rix: variations on a little-known readability index. J. Read. **26**(6), 490–496 (1983)
3. AAthanaselis, T., Bakamidis, S., Dologlou, I., Argyriou, E.N., Symvonis, A.: Making assistive reading tools user friendly: a new platform for Greek dyslexic students empowered by automatic speech recognition. Multimedia Tools Appl. **68**, 681–699 (2014)
4. Björnsson, C.H.: Readability of newspapers in 11 languages. Read. Res. Q. 480–497 (1983)
5. Brosens, D., De Donder, L., Smetcoren, A.S., Dury, S.: Exploring educational opportunities for foreign national prisoners in Europe. Scand. J. Educ. Res. **64**(3), 389–407 (2020)
6. Buzan, T., Buzan, B.: The Mind Map Book. Pearson Education (2006)
7. Chi, M.T., Wylie, R.: The ICAP framework: linking cognitive engagement to active learning outcomes. Educ. Psychol. **49**(4), 219–243 (2014)
8. Dabaghi, K., D'Urso, S., Sciarrone, F.: Artificial intelligence and learning of students with dyslexia: a brief review. In: International Symposium on Emerging Technologies for Education, pp. 155–169. Springer (2023). https://doi.org/10.1007/978-981-97-4243-1_13
9. Dean, J., Ghemawat, S.: Mapreduce: simplified data processing on large clusters. Commun. ACM **51**(1), 107–113 (2008)

10. Dobbs Ferry, N.: A new readability yardstick. J. Appl. Psychol. **32**(3), 221–233 (1948)
11. D'Urso, S., Sciarrone, F.: AI4LA: an intelligent chatbot for supporting students with dyslexia, based on generative AI. In: International Conference on Intelligent Tutoring Systems, pp. 369–377. Springer (2024). https://doi.org/10.1007/978-3-031-63028-6_31
12. Edition, F.: Diagnostic and Statistical Manual of Mental Disorders, pp. 205–224. American Psychiatric Association, Washington, DC (1980)
13. Eppler, M.J.: A comparison between concept maps, mind maps, conceptual diagrams, and visual metaphors as complementary tools for knowledge construction and sharing. Inf. Vis. **5**(3), 202–210 (2006)
14. Fan, Y., et al.: Beware of metacognitive laziness: effects of generative artificial intelligence on learning motivation, processes, and performance. Br. J. Edu. Technol. **56**(2), 489–530 (2025)
15. Gotesman, E., Goldfus, C.: The impact of assistive technologies on the reading outcomes of college students with disabilities. In: Proceedings of the Chais Conference on Instructional Technologies Research (2009)
16. Jin, Y., et al.: Chatting with a learning analytics dashboard: the role of generative ai literacy on learner interaction with conventional and scaffolding chatbots. In: Proceedings of the 15th International Learning Analytics and Knowledge Conference, pp. 579–590 (2025)
17. Shankar, K., Perumal, E., Elhoseny, M., Nguyen, P.: An IoT-cloud based intelligent computer-aided diagnosis of diabetic retinopathy stage classification using deep learning approach. Comput. Mater. Continua **66**(2), 1665–1680 (2021)
18. Khan, R., Qian, Y., Naeem, S.: Extractive based text summarization using k-means and tf-idf. Int. J. Inf. Eng. Electron. Bus. **13**(3), 33 (2019)
19. Lewis, P., et al.: Retrieval-augmented generation for knowledge-intensive NLP tasks. In: Advances in Neural Information Processing Systems, vol. 33, pp. 9459–9474 (2020)
20. Lucisano, P., Piemontese, M.E., et al.: Gulpease: una formula per la predizione della leggibilita di testi in lingua Italiana. Scuola e città 110–124 (1988)
21. Mazefsky, C., McPartland, J., Gastgeb, H., Minshew, N.: Brief report: comparability of DSM-IV and DSM-5 ASD research samples. J. Autism Dev. Disord. **43**(5), 1236–1242 (2013)
22. Miller, G.A.: The magical number seven, plus or minus two: some limits on our capacity for processing information. Psychol. Rev. **63**(2), 81 (1956)
23. Nesbit, J.C., Adesope, O.O.: Learning with concept and knowledge maps: a meta-analysis. Rev. Educ. Res. **76**(3), 413–448 (2006)
24. Novak, J.D., Gowin, D.B.: Learning How to Learn. Cambridge University Press (1984)
25. Olabisi, S.B., David, A.A.: Digital smart pen: a portable media with endless benefits. Int. J. Comput. Appl. **74**(14), 28–30 (2013)
26. Paas, F., Renkl, A., Sweller, J.: Cognitive load theory and instructional design: recent developments. Educ. Psychol. **38**(1), 1–4 (2003)
27. Papanikolaou, K.A., Mabbott, A., Bull, S., Grigoriadou, M.: Designing learner-controlled educational interactions based on learning/cognitive style and learner behaviour. Interact. Comput. **18**(3), 356–384 (2006)
28. Sella, F., Tressoldi, P., Lucangeli, D., Zorzi, M.: Training numerical skills with the adaptive videogame "the number race": a randomized controlled trial on preschoolers. Trends Neurosci. Educ. **5**(1), 20–29 (2016)

29. Taylor, P.: Text-to-Speech Synthesis. Cambridge University Press (2009)
30. Tiron, K., Ghergut, A.: The predictors of dyslexia in a regular orthography. Ann. AII Cuza Univ. Psychol. Ser. **28**, 67–90 (2019)
31. Van Merrienboer, J.J., Sweller, J.: Cognitive load theory and complex learning: recent developments and future directions. Educ. Psychol. Rev. **17**(2), 147–177 (2005)
32. Wheeldon, J., Ahlberg, M.K.: Visualizing Social Science Research: Maps, Methods, & Meaning. Sage (2011)
33. Zhang, X., Wei, F., Zhou, M.: HIBERT: document level pre-training of hierarchical bidirectional transformers for document summarization. arXiv preprint arXiv:1905.06566 (2019)

Criterium: Assisting Teachers in Fair and Consistent Grading of Open-Ended Questions

Stefano D'Urso(✉) and Filippo Sciarrone

Faculty of Technological Sciences and Innovation Piazza Mattei, Universitas Mercatorum, 10 00186 Rome, Italy
stefano.durso@studenti.unimercatorum.it,
filippo.sciarrone@unimercatorum.it

Abstract. Open-ended questions offer deep insights into students' reasoning, but present persistent challenges in terms of grading consistency and bias. In this paper, we introduce Criterium, a teacher-assistant system designed to support fair, explainable, and scalable evaluation of open-ended student responses, particularly in the humanities. Unlike traditional automated grading solutions, Criterium places the teacher at the center of the evaluation loop, offering structured rubrics, prompt-based LLM scoring, and optional content retrieval to anchor judgments in curricular material. We present the system architecture, the underlying scoring model – which distinguishes minimum from advanced criteria – and results from a real-world pilot involving multiple classes and assignments. Criterium aims not to replace teacher judgment, but to enhance its objectivity and traceability in both formative and summative contexts.

Keywords: Large Language Models · Automated Assessment · Open-ended Questions · Human-in-the-Loop · Educational Technology · Scoring Rubrics · Explainable AI

1 Introduction

Evaluating open-ended responses is among the most valuable yet complex tasks in education. Particularly in disciplines such as history and literature, these tasks enable students to express critical thinking, contextual reasoning, and personal interpretation [11]. However, their richness comes at a cost: open-ended assessments are time-consuming to grade, prone to inconsistency and bias [16], and difficult to scale in large or online learning environments [5].

To address these challenges, we present *Criterium*, a system designed not to automate grading, but to *support* teachers through transparent, structured evaluation of student-written responses. Criterium adopts a **dual-criteria scoring model**, distinguishing between *minimum* and *advanced* criteria. This distinction reflects well-established pedagogical practice: minimum criteria capture the essential elements required for a response to be considered correct,

B. Fernández-Manjón et al. (Eds.): SETE 2025/ICWL 2025, LNCS 16425, pp. 83–95, 2026.
https://doi.org/10.1007/978-981-92-0042-9_7

while advanced criteria reward deeper understanding and extended reasoning. As noted by Brookhart [3], effective rubrics should separate core requirements from additional merit indicators to guide both fair evaluation and instructional improvement. Similarly, Wiggins and McTighe [15] emphasize the importance of identifying essential evidence versus desirable extensions when designing assessment tasks. Evaluations are performed via large language models (LLMs), guided by structured prompts that incorporate rubrics, model answers, and optional curriculum-aligned content [4,14].

Criterium explicitly preserves teacher agency. Educators define the evaluation rubrics, review system outputs, and may customize key parameters—such as the contribution of linguistic form, or the balance between basic and advanced content—according to pedagogical intent or student needs. This makes the system adaptable to a wide range of classroom settings, including those requiring accommodations.

We validate our approach through a classroom-based pilot study, involving a sample of over 60 students and 2 teachers, showing that Criterium can produce fair, interpretable evaluations while aligning closely with teacher expectations. Our findings complement existing work on rubric-based LLM grading [8,12], and contribute to a growing body of research that seeks to harness the capabilities of LLMs in educational assessment without removing human oversight. Specifically, we address the following Research Question (RQ):

> **RQ:** *Can a rubric-aligned, prompt-based LLM evaluation framework reliably support teachers in grading open-ended student responses while preserving transparency, fairness, and pedagogical validity?*

2 Related Works

Open-ended questions have long been recognized as a valuable tool for assessing comprehension, opinion, and reasoning beyond the constraints of fixed-response formats [6,7]. Their strength lies in their ability to capture nuanced, self-generated responses, which can reflect not only content knowledge but also critical thinking and personal interpretation [11]. However, open-ended formats present notable challenges for evaluation: they are time-consuming to grade, prone to subjective bias, and difficult to scale, especially in large educational or survey contexts [16].

Despite these difficulties, researchers have continued to emphasize the cognitive and diagnostic value of open-ended questions [7,16]. Their inclusion in assessments is essential when the goal is to measure the depth and salience of understanding, rather than the mere recognition of facts. Recent work has further demonstrated that open-ended and multiple-choice questions tap into different cognitive processes, highlighting the complementary role of each in educational evaluation [11].

The emergence of automatic grading systems has aimed to address these limitations. In particular, short-answer and essay scoring tools have gained prominence in online learning environments, where scalability and consistency are key.

Del Gobbo et al. [5] provide a systematic mapping of recent work in the field, identifying a growing but still immature research landscape characterized by diverse methodologies, from rule-based systems to machine learning classifiers.

In this evolving context, Large Language Models (LLMs) offer a promising new paradigm. Unlike earlier systems based on surface features or handcrafted rules, LLMs exhibit the ability to understand, summarize, and evaluate open-ended content using context-rich prompts. Pioneering work by Caines et al. [4] and Tan et al. [14] has explored the use of generative models like GPT-3 and GPT-4 in educational settings, demonstrating potential applications in content generation, feedback delivery, and automated assessment—particularly when guided by well-defined rubrics.

Several studies have focused on the specific task of evaluating student responses. Mendonça et al. [8] compared LLMs with human grading in a programming education setting, showing close alignment when detailed rubrics were used. Pinto et al. [12] extended this evaluation to workplace training, finding that ChatGPT could identify semantic nuances typically missed by simpler metrics, and that expert raters generally agreed with its feedback.

A more targeted line of research examines LLMs as tools to simulate student behavior. Benedetto et al. [1] showed that LLMs can be prompted to generate plausible responses at different skill levels across multiple domains, which may serve both as a benchmarking tool and a means to train or test evaluators.

Beyond general-purpose models, Bernard et al. [2] introduced EQUATOR, a deterministic framework that leverages vector-based retrieval and structured scoring to assess reasoning quality and factual accuracy in open-ended questions—offering an alternative to the fluency bias often seen in generative outputs.

Lastly, in the context of open-ended question design, Raz et al. [13] demonstrated how LLMs can be used to score the complexity of questions themselves using Bloom's taxonomy. This work complements answer evaluation by enabling automated quality control over the questions that students are asked.

Our work builds on these contributions through the design of *Criterium*, a system for rubric-aligned evaluation of open-ended student responses. Distinct from fully generative or classifier-based approaches, Criterium employs prompt-based evaluation via LLMs to match responses against structured criteria, while also providing linguistic form analysis and configurable weighting.

Unlike prior work focused on fully automated scoring or benchmark datasets, our system is explicitly designed to operate *in real classroom settings*, addressing the practical gap between experimental LLM applications and their pedagogical integration. The goal is not only to support fair and transparent grading, but also to preserve teacher agency through human-in-the-loop interaction. We present this as an *exploratory study*, aimed at evaluating the feasibility and alignment of rubric-driven LLM evaluation in authentic school contexts.

3 System Overview

This section outlines the architecture and functioning of our automatic evaluation system for open-ended student responses. The system is structured around two main components: a formal scoring model based on pedagogical criteria, and an implementation layer powered by LLMs using a prompt-based evaluation.

3.1 Evaluation Model

The evaluation model is designed to quantify two complementary dimensions of student responses: *structural correctness* and *formal quality*.

Structural correctness refers to the content-level alignment with the expected answer, based on a two-level rubric:

- *Minimum criteria* capture essential elements that must be present for the response to be considered valid.
- *Advanced criteria* reward elaboration, contextualization, and higher-order understanding beyond the essentials.

Formal quality, by contrast, refers to linguistic and expressive aspects of the response—such as lexical variety, grammatical accuracy, orthographic correctness, and clarity of exposition. This dimension is assessed independently and can be weighted via a personalization parameter.

Together, these two components define a hybrid scoring model that ensures both the *substantive accuracy* and the *communicative effectiveness* of a student's answer are taken into account.

Let n and m be the number of satisfied minimum and advanced criteria respectively, and N and M their total counts for a given question. The normalized structural score $s(n, m) \in [0, 1]$ is defined as:

$$s(n,m) = \alpha \cdot \left(\frac{n}{N}\right) + (1-\alpha) \cdot \left(\frac{n}{N} \cdot \frac{m}{M}\right)$$

This function ensures that advanced criteria contribute to the score only if at least some minimum criteria are satisfied. The parameter $\alpha \in [0, 1]$ governs the global weight of minimum criteria versus advanced ones.

The parameter $\alpha \in [0, 1]$ controls the balance between correctness and elaboration in the scoring function. Its effect can be better understood by analyzing the structure of the formula:

- The first term, $\alpha \cdot \frac{n}{N}$, measures the degree to which the minimum (essential) criteria are satisfied.
- The second term, $(1 - \alpha) \cdot (\frac{n}{N} \cdot \frac{m}{M})$, captures the contribution of advanced criteria, but only proportionally to the number of minimum criteria met.

This formulation ensures that:

- When α is high (e.g., 0.8), the final score is mainly driven by basic correctness. The system prioritizes essential requirements.

- When α is low (e.g., 0.3), more weight is given to elaboration and depth—as long as the answer satisfies at least part of the minimum expectations (due to the multiplicative condition $\frac{n}{N}$).

To illustrate this behavior, Table 1 shows some numerical examples with varying values of n, m, and α.

Table 1. Numerical examples showing how the normalized score $s(n, m)$ varies with different values of α.

n	m	N	M	$s(n,m) \mid \alpha = 0.8$	$s(n,m) \mid \alpha = 0.3$
2	0	2	2	$0.8 \cdot 1 + 0.2 \cdot 0 = \mathbf{0.8}$	$0.3 \cdot 1 + 0.7 \cdot 0 = \mathbf{0.3}$
2	2	2	2	$0.8 \cdot 1 + 0.2 \cdot 1 = \mathbf{1.0}$	$0.3 \cdot 1 + 0.7 \cdot 1 = \mathbf{1.0}$
1	2	2	2	$0.8 \cdot 0.5 + 0.2 \cdot 0.5 = \mathbf{0.5}$	$0.3 \cdot 0.5 + 0.7 \cdot 0.25 = \mathbf{0.425}$

Each question is assigned a maximum weight W_i, and its score is computed as $S_i = W_i \cdot s(n_i, m_i)$. The total structural score is:

$$S_{tot} = \sum_{i=1}^{k} S_i$$

In addition to structural correctness, the model accounts for language form (e.g., lexical richness, spelling, clarity of exposition) through a separate formal score $L \in [0, L_{\text{max}}]$, which is modulated by a factor $\gamma \in [0, 1]$. This defines how much linguistic form contributes to the overall result:

$$T = S_{tot} + \gamma \cdot L$$

The parameter γ is defined per student, allowing adaptive evaluation. For instance, $\gamma = 0$ fully excludes the formal score—useful in case of learning accommodations such as dyslexia—while $\gamma = 1$ applies full weight. Intermediate values reflect a partial contribution.

Finally, the total score can be normalized to a fixed scale (e.g., 30 points) as follows:

$$T_{\text{norm}} = \frac{T}{W_{\text{tot}} + \gamma \cdot L_{\text{max}}} \cdot 30$$

where $W_{\text{tot}} = \sum_i W_i$. Qualitative thresholds (e.g., *insufficient*, *correct*, *excellent*) may be associated with ranges of T_{norm} to support pedagogical interpretation and reporting.

3.2 LLM-Based Scoring Implementation

The scoring process is implemented via prompt-based evaluation using large language models (LLMs). In our implementation, we use **GPT-4o-mini** [9], a lightweight variant of GPT-4 optimized for fast inference. The model is accessed via the OpenAI API and operates in a deterministic configuration (temperature = 0) to ensure reproducibility and stability across evaluations. For each question, a structured prompt is generated, including:

- the text of the question;
- a list of minimum and advanced evaluation criteria;
- a model answer;
- the student's answer;
- the question weight.

The LLM is asked to return a JSON object specifying:

1. the number of minimum and advanced criteria met;
2. a short qualitative comment (max 3 lines).

A separate prompt is used to assess the formal quality of the response, with scoring on a 0–5 scale. This component outputs a second JSON with the form score and a brief justification. To ensure factual accuracy, the system optionally uses retrieval-augmented generation (RAG) [10] to inject reference materials into the prompt. This improves alignment with curriculum content and evaluation expectations. Structured prompts and standardized JSON outputs ensure the responses are machine-readable and consistent with the scoring function. This promotes reproducibility, transparency, and human-in-the-loop supervision.

4 Experimental Setup

To evaluate the effectiveness and realism of the proposed scoring model, we conducted a pilot study involving real student assignments in the context of secondary education. The study included six different open-ended assessments drawn from standard school curricula: two history tasks and four on Italian literature. All prompts were taken from widely adopted textbooks and delivered within the normal teaching schedule.

A total of 62 students participated:

- **History**: 25 students from a second-year class of a Liceo Scientifico (Applied Sciences track) completed two history assignments.
- **Italian Literature**: 20 students from a fourth-year class and 17 students from a fifth-year class worked on four literature tasks.

All assignments were administered and evaluated by the subject teacher as part of the normal coursework. For each assignment, the teacher:

- created an original rubric including a set of *minimum* and *advanced* criteria for each open-ended question;
- corrected each student response manually, assigning a numerical grade and annotating comments directly on the paper.

In parallel, our tool processed the same assignments as follows:

- the system generated a structured *reference* answer for each question, based on the textbook content and didactic materials shared by the teacher;
- all student responses were digitized and anonymized before evaluation;
- automated scoring was applied using the model described in Sect. 3.

The teacher-provided materials—including the question, model answer, evaluation criteria, and maximum score—were transformed into structured JSON format to be used in the system prompt. An example of this transformation is shown in Appendix A.

This setup allows for a direct comparison between traditional teacher-based evaluation and the system-generated scoring, enabling both quantitative and qualitative analysis of agreement and discrepancies.

5 Results and Evaluation

The proposed evaluation model was applied to six open-ended assessments in history and Italian literature, involving 62 students across three classes. For each assignment, the automated system computed:

- a score per question based on the number of satisfied minimum and advanced criteria;
- a qualitative explanation justifying the score;
- a lexical quality score (clarity, grammar, and spelling), modulated via the γ parameter.

Per-question Evaluation

For each student response, the system computed the normalized score s for each question as described in Sect. 3, using the rubric provided by the teacher. An example output includes:

- **Criteria satisfied:** 2/2 minimum, 3/5 advanced;
- **Score:** $s = 0.3 \cdot 1.0 + 0.7 \cdot (1.0 \cdot 0.6) = \mathbf{0.72}$;
- **Qualitative explanation:** "The student covers all core ideas but omits one of the higher-level insights discussed in class."

Lexical Score and Personalization

The system assigns an additional score L to formal aspects of the text (e.g., lexical variety, orthographic accuracy). The overall impact of L is scaled by γ, which can be customized per student:

- $\gamma = 1$ for full inclusion (standard evaluation),
- $\gamma = 0$ for DSA accommodations (form excluded),
- $0 < \gamma < 1$ for partial weight (teacher-tuned).

Summary Table and Parameter Sensitivity

A summary table aggregates the total scores across all questions and students. Teachers can interactively adjust:

- the weights of individual questions;
- the α parameter (impact of advanced criteria);
- the γ coefficient (impact of form).

This enables them to explore how different pedagogical priorities (e.g., content focus vs expression) affect the overall distribution of scores. Table 2 shows an excerpt.

Table 2. Example of final scores with $\gamma = 0.3$ and $\alpha = 0.3$.

Student	Structural Score	Form Score ($\gamma \cdot L$)	Total
User 1	21.2	1.5	22.7
User 3	18.4	2.3	20.7
User 5	24.0	0.0	24.0

Qualitative Feedback

Each student received a per-question diagnostic explaining:

- which criteria were met or missed,
- suggestions for improvement,
- linguistic issues detected (where applicable).

This feature was especially appreciated by teachers, who confirmed that the system-generated feedback closely aligned with their manual annotations, and provided pedagogical value even in cases of partial correctness.

6 Discussion

The criteria-based evaluation model implemented in Criterium enables interpretable scoring and consistent feedback generation, grounded in pedagogical intent. A key strength of the system lies in its ability to produce structured outputs—both numerical and qualitative—aligned with teacher-defined rubrics.

Importantly, Criterium operates independently from teacher grades: during the initial evaluation phase, the system does not have access to teacher-assigned scores. This blind scoring approach was essential to ensure that system outputs remained unbiased and fully driven by the criteria. Teachers later entered their own grades for comparison, enabling a posteriori analysis of scoring alignment and discrepancies.

To explore this alignment, we carried out a systematic review phase where teacher scores were compared against those automatically generated by Criterium. Across all evaluated tasks, we observed a clear pattern: **increasing α consistently reduces the average discrepancy between Criterium and teacher scores.** That is, placing more weight on minimum criteria aligns better with human evaluations. The trend is visualized in Fig. 1.

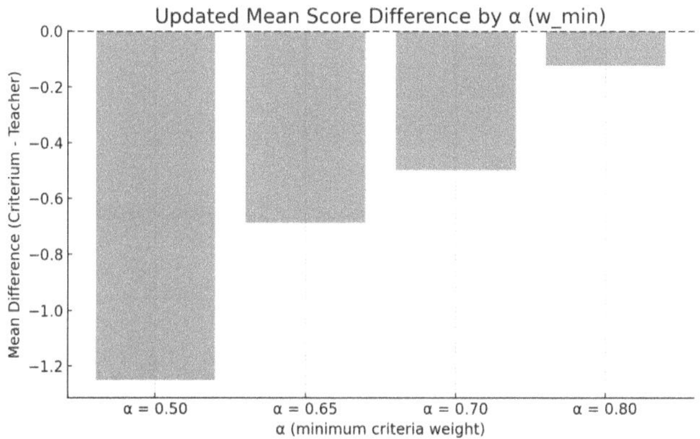

Fig. 1. Mean differences (Criterium - Teacher) for a representative test task, plotted against increasing values of α. Higher α values reduce the discrepancy.

Although the magnitude of the discrepancy varies across tasks and evaluators, the directional trend remains consistent. In more demanding tasks or weaker student groups, the system tends to diverge more. Notably, **Criterium is consistently more severe than human evaluators**, particularly at lower α values.

The explanation lies in the different logic applied by teachers versus the algorithm:

- Teachers tend to base evaluation primarily on *correctness*, i.e., satisfaction of minimum criteria.
- Achieving a passing or good grade typically depends on meeting essential requirements.
- Advanced criteria are only partially and variably considered, often in a subjective or compensatory way.
- When α is low (e.g., 0.5), the system penalizes answers that lack depth or advanced features, *even if structurally correct.* This results in lower scores and a perception of higher severity.
- As α increases, the scoring logic becomes more *teacher-centric*, rewarding correctness and tolerating the absence of sophistication.

6.1 Analysis of Score Dispersion

We also analyzed the **standard deviation** of the score differences (Criterium - Teacher) across α values. As shown in Fig. 2, this metric remained relatively stable across α configurations.

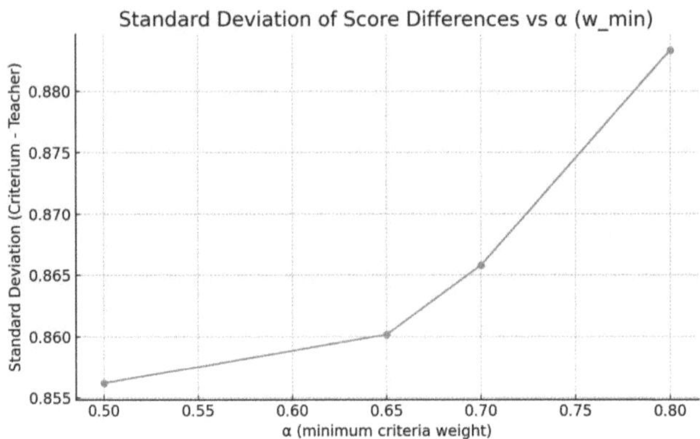

Fig. 2. Standard deviation of score differences at increasing α values. Overall dispersion is stable, but varies by student group.

However, when grouping students by performance level (based on teacher scores), different behaviors emerge:

- **High-performing students** (teacher score > 6) show *lower variability* at low α values. The system aligns more consistently when advanced criteria are emphasized.
- As α increases, dispersion in the high group grows slightly.
- **Low-performing students** (teacher score ≤ 6) show *consistently high variability* across all α values. They are more affected by system penalties when failing to meet minimum or advanced criteria.

This suggests that low-performing students are more sensitive to strict rubric enforcement, while high-performing students benefit from a balanced integration of minimum and advanced components.

The qualitative feedback generated by the system was consistently judged as relevant and pedagogically aligned. The lexical scoring component also proved valuable, particularly when γ was adjusted to neutralize its impact for students with learning accommodations (e.g., dyslexia).

While the system shows strong potential, it currently depends on manual rubric input and calibration. Future work should explore how LLMs could assist in deriving criteria from model answers or curricular content, and in providing natural-language explanations for scoring decisions.

7 Conclusion and Future Work

This paper presented Criterium, a teacher-assistant system for the fair and consistent evaluation of open-ended student responses. Grounded in pedagogical principles and implemented via prompt-based LLMs, Criterium offers a structured yet adaptable framework that preserves teacher agency while improving assessment objectivity and transparency.

Initial results from real classroom deployments suggest that Criterium can replicate teacher judgments with high fidelity while providing structured feedback to students. However, broader validation is needed.

As future work, we aim to expand the testing to include a wider range of subjects (e.g., philosophy, civic education, scientific reasoning) and a more diverse pool of teachers, including those from different school levels and educational systems. Furthermore, we plan to explore the integration of Criterium into university-level settings and massive online courses (MOOCs). In these contexts, the scalability of assessment is a major challenge: open-ended questions are pedagogically valuable but often avoided due to the high cost of manual grading. Criterium can help bridge this gap by offering a reliable, semi-automated evaluation layer that enables instructors to maintain high-quality assessment practices without compromising on scale or fairness.

A Example of Input Data Transformation

The following example illustrates how teacher-provided materials are structured into JSON format for automatic evaluation by the Criterium system.

Original Material (Teacher-Provided)

Question: Chi erano gli optimates ed i populares?

Answer Material: A detailed explanation including definitions of both groups, historical context, and examples of key political figures, as found in standard history textbooks.

Minimum Criteria:

- Definition of optimates (e.g., aristocrats, pro-Senate, conservative)
- Definition of populares (e.g., reformers, support from the people, use of plebeian tribunes or assemblies)

Advanced Criteria:

- Mention of the conflict between the two groups as a cause of instability
- Examples of optimates (e.g., Sulla, Cato, Cicero)
- Examples of populares (e.g., Caesar, the Gracchi, Marius)
- Mention of political instruments (e.g., Senate vs. Tribunes/Comitia)
- Reference to the lack of formal party structure

Question Weight: 5

Transformed JSON Input


```
{
  "id": 1,
  "domanda": "Chi erano gli optimates ed i populares?",
  "risposta_modello": "Gli optimates e i populares erano due gruppi
    politici informali...",
  "criteri_minimi": [
    "Definizione di optimates (es: aristocratici, pro-Senato, conservatori)",
    "Definizione di populares (es: riformatori, appoggio del popolo,
     uso del tribunato o dei comizi)"
  ],
  "criteri_avanzati": [
    "Conflitto tra optimates e populares come causa di instabilit\'{a}
     della Repubblica",
    "Esempi di personaggi optimates (es: Silla, Catone, Cicerone)",
    "Esempi di personaggi populares (es: Cesare, Mario, i Gracchi)",
    "Strumenti politici utilizzati (es: Senato vs tribunato/comizi)",
    "Riferimento all'assenza di partiti formali (non erano partiti moderni,
     ma schieramenti ideologici)"
  ],
  "peso": 5
}
```


References

1. Benedetto, L., Aradelli, G., Donvito, A., Lucchetti, A., Cappelli, A., Buttery, P.: Using LLMs to simulate students' responses to exam questions. In: Findings of the Association for Computational Linguistics: EMNLP 2024, pp. 11351–11368 (2024)
2. Bernard, R., Raza, S., Das, S., Murugan, R.: Equator: a deterministic framework for evaluating LLM reasoning with open-ended questions.# v1.0.0-beta. arXiv preprint arXiv:2501.00257 (2024)
3. Brookhart, S.M.: How to Create and Use Rubrics for Formative Assessment and Grading. ASCD (2013)
4. Caines, A., et al.: On the application of large language models for language teaching and assessment technology. arXiv preprint arXiv:2307.08393 (2023)
5. Del Gobbo, E., Guarino, A., Cafarelli, B., Grilli, L., Limone, P.: Automatic evaluation of open-ended questions for online learning. A systematic mapping. Stud. Educ. Eval. **77**, 101258 (2023)
6. Geer, J.G.: What do open-ended questions measure? Public Opin. Q. **52**(3), 365–367 (1988)
7. Geer, J.G.: Do open-ended questions measure "salient" issues? Public Opin. Q. **55**(3), 360–370 (1991)
8. Mendonça, P.C., Quintal, F., Mendonça, F.: Evaluating LLMs for automated scoring in formative assessments. Appl. Sci. **15**(5), 2787 (2025)
9. OpenAI: Gpt-4o technical report (2024). https://platform.openai.com/docs/models/gpt-4o. Accessed 24 Apr 2025
10. OpenAI: Retrieval-augmented generation with OpenAI models (2024). https://platform.openai.com/docs/guides/retrieval. Accessed 24 Apr 2025
11. Ozuru, Y., Briner, S., Kurby, C.A., McNamara, D.S.: Comparing comprehension measured by multiple-choice and open-ended questions. Can. J. Exp. Psychol. **67**(3), 215 (2013)

12. Pinto, G., Cardoso-Pereira, I., Monteiro, D., Lucena, D., Souza, A., Gama, K.: Large language models for education: grading open-ended questions using ChatGPT. In: Proceedings of the XXXVII Brazilian Symposium on Software Engineering, pp. 293–302 (2023)
13. Raz, T., Luchini, S., Beaty, R., Kenett, Y.: Automated scoring of open-ended question complexity: a large language model approach (2024)
14. Tan, K., Yao, J., pang, t., Fan, C., Song, Y.: Elf: educational LLM framework of improving and evaluating ai generated content for classroom teaching. ACM J. Data Inf. Q. (2025)
15. Wiggins, G.: Understanding by Design. Association for Supervision and Curriculum Development (2005)
16. Züll, C.: Open-ended questions (version 2.0) (2016)

Educational Practice, Culture, and Student Development

The Lion Dance VR Revival: Gamified Cultural Preservation Through a Tri-Modal Design Framework

Tip Ying Li(✉) and Anthony Kong(✉)

School of Design, The Hong Kong Polytechnic University, Hung Hom, Hong Kong SAR, China
tipying.li@connect.polyu.hk, anthony-pui-keung.kong@polyu.edu.hk

Abstract. Intangible Cultural Heritage (ICH), exemplified by the lion dance, faces pressing challenges in the digital era, particularly regarding the transmission of complex, embodied skills that are indispensable for sustaining cultural competency. Prevailing digital media platforms privilege passive observation, offering limited avenues for the acquisition and reproduction of embodied practices central to ICH. This study introduces the Lion Dance VR Revival – an immersive learning platform designed through the proposed Tri-Modal Design Framework. This integrative framework synthesizes cognitive load theory, scaffolding theory, and self-determination theory to address cognitive, pedagogical, and motivational dimensions while embedding cultural context within embodied learning. The structured learning trajectory comprises three modules: (1) Meaning, (2) Motion, and (3) Mastery. It guides learners from cultural orientation to progressive skill acquisition. A mixed-methods evaluation was conducted with 37 novice participants. Quantitative findings demonstrated significant increases in learning motivation (M = 4.51/5) and engagement (M = 4.31/5). Complementary qualitative analyses further corroborated these outcomes, underscoring the framework's efficacy in fostering cultural authenticity, leveraging gamification, and utilizing real-time feedback from the "Digital Sifu" to support learning. Collectively, these results substantiate the pedagogical validity of the Tri-Modal Design Framework and provide a theoretically grounded model for developing immersive technologies aimed at the preservation and transmission of practice-based ICH.

Keywords: Virtual Reality · Intangible Cultural Heritage · Gamification · Embodied Learning · Skill Acquisition

1 Introduction

Lion dance, one of the most iconic intangible cultural heritages (ICH) in Hong Kong, is a tradition passed down through generations via a rigorous master-apprentice system [1]. However, digital media has brought great challenges to traditional skills such as lion dance, which takes a long time to practice and has a high threshold [2–8]. The demanding training [9], limited access to specialized equipment [10, 11] and practice venues [12, 13], raise the entry barrier, confining public engagement to festival-time

B. Fernández-Manjón et al. (Eds.): SETE 2025/ICWL 2025, LNCS 16425, pp. 99–114, 2026.
https://doi.org/10.1007/978-981-92-0042-9_8

spectatorship rather than sustained practice. This reflects a broader waning of participation in traditional cultural practices [8, 14] and exemplifies the global struggles faced by ICH.UNESCO emphasizes that the value of ICH is in the knowledge and know-how transferred from generation to generation [15]. Preserving these practices is vital, since it requires preserving not only the performance, but also the rich network of knowledge and skill and cultural meaning contained in that performance [20, 21]. Therefore, the conservation of lion dance is important for the retention of a distinctive traditional cultural heritage of Hong Kong [22, 23] and for preventing the loss of its wisdom for posterity [24]. More effective entry points are needed and training mechanisms—especially for youth and first-time learners [15–17]—to convert observation into practice and ensure the continuity of this intangible cultural heritage [18, 19]. In this light, we introduce an accessible, safe, and motivating virtual reality (VR) platform called the "Lion Dance VR Revival" for training and practice. Through a dynamic transition from passive viewing to active participation, this project aims to contribute directly to the continuation of the lion dance tradition. To elaborate on this work, this paper first reviews the related literature in Sect. 2, then presents our 'Tri-Modal Design Framework' in Sect. 3 and system implementation in Sect. 4. We then report on the platform's user evaluation in Sect. 5 and conclude with a discussion of the findings in Sect. 6.

2 Literature Review

This literature review provides a framework for the 'Lion Dance VR Revival' project, explore gaps in current research. We examine the established efficacy of VR in skill acquisition, the motivational role of gamification, key pedagogical principles for complex skill learning, and the current landscape of VR applications in cultural heritage.

2.1 VR for Traditional Skill Transmission

VR stands out among other technologies for learning complex motor tasks thanks to its characteristics. First, VR offers safety and repeatability that allows a learner to practice high-risk moves, such as pole-jumping in lion dance, without fear of injury. Such a controlled environment enables uniform exposure to be provided, which has been shown to improve performance in "high-stakes" learning environments such as surgical training and occupational safety training [51–54]. Second, VR supports embodied interaction, meaning that the users' physical activities are reflected in virtual events. This will make tasks more comprehensible, and learning will benefit from embodied, interactive tasks with avatars and objects [26]. Third, VR can provide real-time feedback, knowledge of results (KR) and/or knowledge of performance (KP) at crucial stages, facilitating immediate error correction and skill practice [27]. Together, these features involve learners in activity beyond passive observation, practice-oriented skill making oriented to the principles of deliberate practice [50].

2.2 Gamification for Enhanced Motivation in Education

Apart from the medium, the motivation for learning needs to be sustained. Gamification, the use of game mechanics in non-game environments, is a successful way to increase user engagement and motivation [36]. To support engagement that supports immanent learning, we draw heavily from Self-Determination Theory (SDT). SDT claims that intrinsic motivation is maximized if learning experiences satisfy three basic psychological needs: the need for autonomy (offering meaningful choices, enabling self-paced learning), the need for competence (setting clear goals and giving immediate feedback through knowledge of results or knowledge of performance), and the need for relatedness(promoting interpersonal relations and giving a mentor-like support) [35].

2.3 Key Pedagogical Principles for Complex Skill Learning

To address the complex, culturally situated nature of the skill involved, we combine two well-documented pedagogical frameworks. The first is based on the context-practice decoupling principle that we derive from cognitive load theory. This theory explains the limits of working memory through the intrinsic, extraneous, and germane cognitive load. This principal advocates for a strict separation of learning stages. Initially, learners internalize meanings and rules in an environment designed to minimize extraneous cognitive load. Subsequently, they engage in focused embodied practice, aided by timely KR and KP feedback. This structured approach optimizes germane load while managing intrinsic load, thereby enabling more efficient learning in both the cognitive and psychomotor domains. [55, 55]. Second, we recast scaffolding theory to emphasize the value of mentorship/apprenticeship to learning. Best learning happens when support structures like digital models or coaching are progressively faded away as the student's skills improve. This scaffolding approach is well rooted in cognitive apprenticeship principles and guides our approach to mentoring and the pursuit of objective advancement [55].

2.4 VR in Cultural Heritage: The Need for an Integrated Design Framework

Applications in cultural heritage range from virtual museums to interactive storytelling [42–44, 48, 49] but also include mixed-mode experiences with informational and interactive components. But these actions enable knowledge to be transmitted and contextualized, and a profound gap remains. Existing models, including those which interactive technology, often generate limited cultural insights and lack the pedagogical support required for skill development, especially for embodied cultural practices.. This gap highlights a disconnection: although the enhancement of motor skill learning has been proven using VR, the motivational results of gamification are well documented, and the significance of pedagogical strategies, such as scaffolding, is recognized; these components were not systematically integrated in VR applications for cultural heritage. As a result, there is a pressing need for an organized, pedagogically grounded approach to the transmission of such complex, embodied intangible cultural heritage skills. This research aims to fill this critical gap by introducing and testing such a framework, more precisely in relation to lion dance.

3 Research Gap and Conceptual Framework

Inspired by the broad research gap of complex ICH motor skill transmission, this section outlines the conceptual framework guiding the "Lion Dance VR Revival" project. We start by formulating the research questions to which this framework is directed.

RQ1: How can VR learning environments be designed to support the effective integration of cultural context with embodied skill practice, while ensuring pedagogical principles of safety, motivation and authenticity are maintained?
RQ2: What is the effectiveness of a platform built on such a framework in enhancing novice users' learning motivation and engagement with ICH?
RQ3: What is the initial effect of such a platform on novice users' acquisition and learning confidence of complex ICH motor skills?

3.1 The Tri-Modal Design Framework: A Holistic Approach

To answer RQ1, we propose a novel "Tri-Modal Design Framework". Rather than proposing new theories, the framework systematically synthesizes established pedagogical and psychological theories (i.e., cognitive load theory, self-determination theory and scaffolding theory) to meet the challenge of embodying ICH skills into practical use. This framework is based on a clear hierarchy of principles, structure, and mechanisms.

3.1.1 Core Design Principles (Guiding Philosophy)

We propose three guiding principles that ensure technology serves the mission of cultural preservation and education. First, we prioritize safety and repeatability, using VR to provide risk-free environments for practicing complex ICH motor tasks [51–54]. This approach facilitates the practice of intricate movements without the danger of injury or real-world expense, enhancing learner readiness for real-life scenarios. Second, in terms of sustaining engagement, the focus of our framework is on promoting motivation through gamification. Based on SDT, our design incorporates carefully chosen game mechanics to fulfil participants' basic psychological needs for autonomy, competence and relatedness, thereby enabling deeper and more sustainable interaction with the learning material [34–40]. Finally, the general principle of authenticity in preservation asserts that any design intervention must serve genuine cultural heritage preservation goals. This necessitates inputs and collaborations with community experts and practitioners to achieve the nuances, customs, and spirit of the lion dance [41–49]. The media needs to reflect not just the technical capabilities required, but also deep cultural importance of this cultural art.

3.1.2 Framework Structure: Meaning, Motion, Mastery

The design principles are encapsulated in our "Tri-Modal Design Framework" that guides the learning support and is based on three interrelated dimensions. The first dimension, meaning (cultural understanding), provides the grounding structure by providing various cultural and historical background information on the lion dance, which in turn leads to an appreciation and value placed on the dance. Secondly, the second dimension, motion (skill practice), based on the first one, literally involves learners in their bodies by making them practice lion dance movements with interactive, real-time feedback in an embodied environment. The third dimension, mastery (expert demonstration), is the pinnacle of the framework, and it provides learners with opportunities to observe and analyze expert performances, inspiring advanced skill acquisition and cultural immersion.

3.1.3 Key Pedagogical Mechanisms

Two pedagogical mechanisms are used to direct the shape and purpose of the framework. The first segment is Context-Practice Decoupling, a technique (informed by Cognitive Load Theory) that separates the contextual learning from hands-on analogue skill practice [55, 55]. This division prevents participants from being overloaded with concurrent requirements and allows them the chance to focus on cultural subtleties before performance-based skills and blurring the lines conversely. This staged approach is expected to support better schema building by reducing unnecessary cognitive load. The second mechanism is the "Digital Sifu," [55] - a new scaffolding approach for promoting gradual skills mastering. Based upon Scaffolding Theory and cognitive apprenticeship principles of modelling, coaching, and fading, the Digital Sifu offers contingent support that falls off as the learner progresses. This provides good insight for beginners and breaks complex skills down. However, we recognize the inherent tension in the concept of a technologically mediated "Digital Sifu" and cultural authenticity. In the traditional context, a "Sifu" is a holistic mentor who imparts discipline, ethics, and a cultural worldview—a role far exceeding that of a technical instructor. A purely algorithmic agent may reduce this intimate relationship to a mere learning app process, lacking in human connection. To mitigate this problem, our design integrates narrative and symbiotic layers in our architecture in the feedback loop. Besides, the Digital Sifu's instruction is enhanced by integrating audio recordings of traditional master sayings and providing responsive feedback that addresses not only motor accuracy but also cultural and behavioral norms. This design ensures the Digital Sifu acts as a bridge to deeper cultural understanding, rather than merely a technical scaffold (Fig. 1).

3.2 Prototyping: Lion Dance VR Revival

This conceptual framework underpins the design process and development of our prototype platform, known as the "Lion Dance VR Revival". The "Tri-Modal Framework" is translated into the three key modules in our system: The "Meaning" dimension matches the "Meaning" Module (VR Cultural Storytelling Exhibition), the "Motion" dimension is symbolized by "Motion" Module (VR Lion Dance Learning Platform), and the "Mastery" dimension is the equivalence of "Mastery" Module (VR 180° Immersion Video). This transition between abstract models and a more concrete and vivid user experience demonstrates the effectiveness of our approach inside a real VR learning environment.

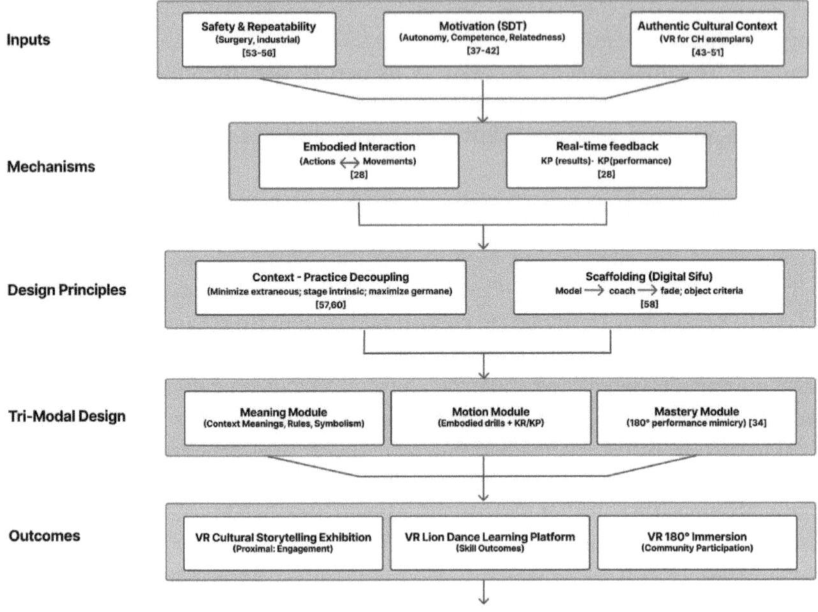

Fig. 1. Conceptual Framework of "Lion Dance VR Revival"

4 Method

4.1 System Overview and Architecture

The "Lion Dance VR Revival" platform consists of three main modules: the "Meaning" Module, the "Motion" Module, and the "Mastery" Module. This modularity allows the user to progress from cultural appreciation through embodied practice towards the pursuit of mastery.

4.2 Implementation Choices and Technical Architecture

To achieve this, the present study uses virtual reality (VR) technology as the basis of implementation, which is chosen for its unique capability of promoting first-person embodied interaction, an essential factor contributing to its potential to demonstrate physical techniques like the lion dance. To realize the Tri-Modal Framework, decisions with respect to hardware, software, and development pipelines were strategically made to facilitate accessibility, performance, and cultural authenticity. The Meta Quest 2 was chosen as the main development platform, and its standalone feature greatly decreases the hardware threshold for potential users, which makes the research more accessible and recruits a more diverse user base. We used Unity 3D (2022.3 LTS) for software: for the cross-platform compatibility and the extended reality (XR) interaction toolkit, which was crucial for rapidly prototyping the complex feedback system. The system features a modular architecture (Meaning, Motion, Mastery) with a host system managing user progression. A host system controls the user's progress and movement among the modules. The development pipeline was greatly enriched by continuous communication with professional lion dance practitioners. This partnership was crucial to bringing native 3D content into Blender and Maya, in turn animating realistic movement for the "Digital Sifu." It was also crucial to cover 180° videos for the "Mastery" Module with high-end VR cameras for true visual realism.

4.3 Module Implementations

4.3.1 The "Meaning" Module: VR Cultural Storytelling Exhibition

This module is designed to realize the "Context" component of the "Context-Practice Decoupling" principle articulated in Sect. 3, managing cognitive load by separating cultural learning from skill practice. It features an interactive museum in a virtual Chinese Temple where users explore the lion dance's legend, history, and cultural meaning. The user experience emerges as a sequence of scenes in a movie, guiding users from a "Misty Entrance" to a History Hall, a Symbolism Chamber, and finally an Incense Ritual. We have included interactive features such as ceremonial drum playing and lion's head touching, which are integrated into the program flow to build emotional ties to the culture. Besides, an AI-driven narration system adjusts generated responses as per the interaction characteristics of users, providing tailored depth and detail, while a special navigation unit provides help for users to navigate the exhibits (Fig. 2).

Fig. 2. Scenes from the 'Meaning' Module: The VR Cultural Storytelling Exhibition"

4.3.2 The "Motion" Module: VR Lion Dance Learning

This module materializes the "practice" part of the "Context-Practice Decoupling" principle, plugged in with the "Digital Sifu" scaffolding mechanism and SDT-compatible gamification aspects, reviewed in detail in Sect. 3. It helps to obtain lion dance motor skills with a step-by-step curriculum, multi-modal feedback, and game mechanics. The learning progression deconstructs complex movements into foundational lessons: Basic Stance and Arm & Head Movement; Arm & Blink Eye Action Coordination; and Rhythm & Full-Body Flow. Authentic demonstrations by an expert instructor are used as a reference for the "Digital Sifu" animations. A fully evaluated motion tracking and feedback system compares a user's movements with reference data, providing instant visual feedback - in the form of "Perfect" or "Bad" messages and glowing targets - and audio feedback, such as drum beats and crowd noise. Motivation and progression are encouraged through the addition of gamification elements, including a star rating system, achievement badges, unlockable lion heads and performance scoring (Fig. 3).

Fig. 3. Feedback Mechanisms in the 'Motion' Module.

4.3.3 The "Mastery" Module: VR 180° Immersion Video

This module represents the "Expert Demonstration" component of the framework, supported by the pedagogical argument for it—the safe observation of high-risk skills — being discussed in the "Safety and Repeatability" principle of Sect. 3. It has panoramic 180° VR videos which allow users to experience first-person on-stage professional lion dance performances without any danger. Spanning up-to-the-minute footage of high-jumping pole attempting, filmed from every possible angle to a detailed lesson on lion head rituals and how to handle the same. Produced in a project partnership with a professional lion dance troupe, using leading 180° VR video technology, this module aims to motivate and guide learners, and to supplement traditional technical analysis with the ability to appreciate the cultural engine that runs in the lion dance, showing the artistic aspect of lion dance (Fig. 4).

Fig. 4. First-person and Multi-angle Views in the 'Mastery' Module's High-Stakes Pole Challenge

5 Platform Evaluation and Findings

This section reports the findings of a mixed-methods user study, on the "Lion Dance VR Revival" system, focusing on the nuanced user experience, that are studied by examining the four key constructs (Learning Motivation, Engagement, Cultural Identification, and Self-Perceived Skill Acquisition). The questionnaire items for these constructs were self-designed, not adapted from validated instruments, to align with the study's theoretical frameworks, such as Self-Determination Theory (SDT). We recruited 37 novice users (N = 37) to participate in the study. The group consisted of 21 females and 16 males, with ages 12–35 years (n = 3 for 12–18, n = 23 for 19–25, n = 11 for 26–35). Most participants (28/37) had prior VR experience, but all were lion dance novices (36 with no experience; one, P5, with 1.5 years non-professional practice). Informed consent was obtained from all subjects. High values for every construct were observed from the quantitative results. Motivation to learn was particularly high (M = 4.51, SD = 0.65); the overall engagement was also highly encouraging (M = 4.31, SD = 0.83). Cultural identity was also significantly improved (M = 4.03, SD = 0.83) and high self-reported sense of skill acquisition (M = 3.89, SD = 1.01), as detailed in Table 1.

Table 1. Descriptive Statistics for Measured Constructs from User Questionnaire

Construct	Questionnaire Item	Mean (M)	Standard Deviation (SD)
Learning Motivation	"This VR experience made me want to learn more about lion dance."	4.62	0.59
	"Gamified elements (scores, unlocks) motivated me to practice repeatedly."	4.40	0.71
Engagement	"I felt completely immersed in the virtual environment."	4.54	0.61
	"While using the platform, I lost track of time."	4.08	1.05
Cultural Identification	"The platform enhanced my sense of identification with lion dance culture."	4.11	0.75
	"The 'Meaning' module gave me a deeper understanding of the cultural background of lion dance."	3.95	0.91
Self-Perceived Skill Acquisition	"I felt I had mastered the basic lion dance steps."	3.92	0.98
	"The 'Digital Sifu's' feedback was very helpful for my learning."	3.86	1.04

5.1 Qualitative Insights

These quantitative trends were confirmed and expanded upon by rich qualitative feedback, revealing a deep sense of the user experience. To provide context for the qualitative feedback, specific participants are quoted using an anonymous identifier (e.g., P1, P2).

The demographic information for the participants quoted in Sects. 5.1 and 5.2 is summarized in Table 2. Participants consistently highlighted how gamified elements played a motivating role, with P21 stating: "The points system and getting new lion heads was the motivation I needed to do better. It was all fun and game like, but it was fun learning something so totally awesome simply. And it didn't seem to me like I was working." The highly engaging nature of the platform further led to high levels of engagement with P12 remarking on the strong sense of presence, "When I put it on (that VR) it just made sense, and you just feel like you were there". Also, "Meaning" enhanced cultural identification significantly as P5 mentioned: "The temple environment is nice, and to hear about the history about all these lion dances, it makes them more meaningful. It was more than just exercise; it was a cultural experience." The "Digital Sifu" was also widely complimented for how it helped you learn the ropes, with players often praising it for its real-time corrective feedback and visual cues. P7 added, "The green lines that tell me where to put my hands were super helpful. It let me sort of sense right then and there whether I was doing any of that correctly or not, and then I could make all sorts of adjustments from there. You would be coaching yourself in real time." Together, these findings highlight the platform's success in designing a culturally appropriate, engaging and efficient learning environment.

Table 2. Demographic information of all study participants (N = 37)

Participant ID	Age Group	Gender	VR Experience	Lion Dance Experience	Participant ID	Age Group	Gender	VR Experience	Lion Dance Experience
P1	19–25	Female	Yes	No	P20	26–35	Female	Yes	No
P2	19–25	Male	Yes	No	P21	19–25	Female	Yes	No
P3	26–35	Female	Yes	No	P22	19–25	Male	Yes	No
P4	19–25	Male	No	No	P23	12–18	Female	No	No
P5	19–25	Female	Yes	1.5 years	P24	19–25	Male	No	No
P6	26–35	Female	Yes	No	P25	26–35	Female	Yes	No
P7	19–25	Male	Yes	No	P26	19–25	Female	Yes	No
P8	19–25	Female	Yes	No	P27	19–25	Male	Yes	No
P9	26–35	Female	Yes	No	P28	26–35	Male	No	No
P10	19–25	Male	Yes	No	P29	19–25	Female	Yes	No
P11	19–25	Female	No	No	P30	19–25	Male	Yes	No
P12	19–25	Female	No	No	P31	12–18	Female	Yes	No
P13	26–35	Male	Yes	No	P32	26–35	Female	No	No
P14	19–25	Female	Yes	No	P33	19–25	Male	Yes	No
P15	12–18	Male	Yes	No	P34	19–25	Female	Yes	No
P16	19–25	Male	Yes	No	P35	26–35	Male	Yes	No
P17	19–25	Female	Yes	No	P36	19–25	Female	No	No
P18	26–35	Male	Yes	No	P37	26–35	Female	Yes	No
P19	19–25	Female	No	No					

5.2 User Feedback and Directions for Improvement

The overall feedback was positive with some good suggestions for improvements. First, participants universally requested content expansion, suggesting advanced levels (a "Higher Training Crate") and a wider variety of lion dance styles. Second, there was strong demand for social interaction, with P15 expressing a desire to "play with others in VR." Third, users recognized the framework's broader applicability. P9, for instance, noted that "The opportunity is massive" for porting the educational model to other forms of ICH. Collectively, this feedback highlights a desire for deeper content, social connectivity, and broader application, providing a clear roadmap for the future development of the Tri-Modal Design Framework.

6 Discussion and Conclusions

This section integrates the results of the study, relating the empirics to the research questions and theory developed in the beginning. We discuss the implications of our findings and acknowledge its limitations and present potential directions for future research before concluding with a comprehensive conclusion.

6.1 Positioning the Tri-Modal Design Framework

Prior studies on virtual reality (VR) have successfully demonstrated its utility for immersive viewing [56], gamifying knowledge transfer [57], and evaluating user acceptance in cultural learning [58]. Nevertheless, these models are limited in that they mainly address the cognitive and affective domains, enabling users to learn about culture. By contrast, our work tackles the more complex challenge of transmitting the embodied knowledge and skills inherent to ICH. Our "Lion Dance VR Revival" platform, built based on the Tri-Modal framework, proposes a psychomotor-centric approach to educate users about performing physically challenging routines. This achievement lays bare how powerfully this system addresses the Tri-Modal Design Framework designed for motor learning and distinguishes our work from prior research. Two aspects are especially important in our approach. The first is the principle of Context-Practice Decoupling, grounded in Cognitive Load Theory, which consciously isolates culture learning from physical practice to facilitate more focused development of skills. Second, is our approach to "Digital Sifu" influenced by Scaffolding Theory (ST) which provides guided, immediate and progressively fading feedback for motor learning. Ultimately, the key of success is an intentional combination of learning theories and the affordances of modern consumer VR leading to a embodied learning experience.

6.2 Discussion of Findings in Relation to Research Questions

Building on the context established above, the results confirm the usability of the "Tri-Modal Design Framework." Regarding RQ1 (how cultural context is integrated with embodied practice) the framework design was particularly well-targeted. For instance, qualitative feedback from one participant P5 showed the practice became more meaningful after interacting with the temple context in "Meaning" module: reflecting the

"Context-Practice Decoupling" design principle. Also, the "Digital Sifu" was identified as an effective scaffolding tool; participant P7 referred to it as a "personal coach", confirming that Scaffolding Theory can be applied successfully to a virtual environment. With respect to RQ2, i.e. helping to motivate and engage users, both the quantitative (Motivation M = 4.51; Engagement M = 4.31) and the qualitative feedback show strong success. These findings align with the broader potential of VR for cultural heritage engagement. The high motivation and engagement observed are consistent with the user acceptance finding of Ch'ng et al. [58], and our use of SDT-based gamification echoes the approach of Zhang et al. [57]. This is vividly captures by P21, who noted "I think I'm having fun learning something really awesome." Furthermore, the strong sense of presence reported by users, such as P12 feeling they were 'actually there', illustrates the potential for virtual reality (VR) to create an immersive learning environment. For RQ3, concerning the initial effect on skill acquisition by the platform, we find promising results, as underpin the self-reported learning score (M = 3.89). As established in our comparative analysis, our study extends beyond simply validating engagement to address the more complex challenge of transmitting embodied practice. Unlike earlier applications focused on virtual reconstruction [56] or knowledge dissemination [57], our platform yielded high self-perceived skill acquisition. We attribute this learning outcome directly to the pedagogical mechanisms of our framework. This is supported by qualitative insights: P18's mention of the importance of both "direct, clear guidance" and "real time corrections for mistakes" delivered by the Digital Sifu supports that an embodied, interactive system which offers immediate, multi-modal feedback does effectively teach novices the basic steps of complex ICH motor skills.

6.3 Implications of the Study

This study has important theoretical and practical implications. Theoretically, as presented in our comparative analysis (Sect. 6.1), this pedagogical situation goes beyond a digitize and display approach, representing an important shift from static archiving to the dynamic transmission of practice-based ICH. It also provides some actionable design principles. The notion of Context-Practice Decoupling acknowledges the significance of culture before skill-based training to manage cognitive load. To promote users' internal motivation, we adopt the SDT- based gamification to design game mechanics that meet players' autonomy, competence and relatedness needs. The Digital Sifu's success is due to its focus on Scaffolded Feedback, where adaptive support gives real-time, multi-modal feedback that gradually reduces as learners master concepts. Finally, all design decisions must be rooted in Authenticity and Embodiment, which means working closely with heritage specialists to ensure authentic cultural representation.

6.4 Limitations and Future Research

Although the present results are encouraging, there are several limitations to our study that will guide future research. First, a primary limitation, shared with the broader field of research [56–58], is the reliance on subjective measures for skill acquisition; future work should therefore integrate objective motion-tracking analysis. Additionally, the lack of a non-VR control group prevents a definitive statement about the relative efficacy of the platform. Future studies will need to include comparative control groups and objective measures of performance to confirm the subjective experience of skill development. Furthermore, the relatively small test group (N = 37) and the single context setting lead to restrictions as to the generalizability of the results, and future studies to explore bigger and more diverse groups of participants would be desirable. Finally, users feedback suggests critical future directions include implementing multiplayer features to stimulate social learning and exploring the transferability of the "Tri-Modal Design Framework" to other forms of intangible cultural heritage.

6.5 Conclusion

At a time when all the digital distractions threaten the survival of old school ways, such research shines some light on a potential way forward. Inspired by the "Tri-Modal Design Framework", the "Lion Dance VR Revival" has presented a validated transference solution for maintaining and transmitting complex embodied ICH. By fusing immersive technology together with pedagogically sound principles and authentic cultural representation, this innovative work not only serves as an educational resource but also establishes a new paradigm, grounded in the framework, for how technology can bridge the gap between a past rich in tradition and a future rich in potential.

References

1. Intangible Cultural Heritage Office (LCSD): ICH Inventory of Hong Kong, sec. 2.1. Lion Dance, pp. 4–5. (2024)
2. Census and Statistics Department (HKSAR): Thematic Household Survey Report No. 80: Internet and smartphone penetration (2023). https://www.info.gov.hk/gia/general/202406/27/P2024062700313.htm. Accessed 26 Aug 2025
3. Serrano-Sanchez, J.A., et al.: Associations between screen time and physical activity in adolescents. J. Phys. Act. Health **8**(5), 657–665 (2011)
4. Lennox, R.D., et al.: Physical activity, screen time and subjective well-being in adolescents from a disadvantaged area. Int. J. Environ. Res. Public Health **17**(12), 4280 (2020)
5. Robinson, J.P.: Arts and leisure participation among IT users: further evidence of time enhancement over time displacement. Soc. Sci. Comput. Rev. **29**(4), 470–480 (2011)
6. Meier, E.H., Reinecke, L.: Media use, sports participation, and well-being in adolescence. Media Psychol. **17**(4), 393–414 (2014)
7. Twenge, J.R., et al.: Screen time and mental health: a prospective analysis. BMC Public Health **24**, 2102 (2024)
8. Heung, S.: Why lion dance is 'dying' in Singapore and Hong Kong. South China morning post (2019). https://www.scmp.com/week-asia/lifestyle-culture/article/2185286/going-going-gong-why-lion-dance-dying-singapore-a. Accessed 26 Aug 2025
9. South China Morning Post (Young Post): It takes a lion's share of discipline and training to lion dance (2015). https://www.scmp.com/yp/discover/lifestyle/features/article/3067982/it-takes-lions-share-discipline-and-training-lion. Accessed 26 Aug 2025
10. Jonie Uniforms: Hong Kong style lion dance head/tail (Style SL-12AG). https://www.jonieuniforms.com/. Accessed 26 Aug 2025
11. Kungfu Direct: Lion & dragon - drums. https://www.kungfudirect.com/catalog/lion-and-dragon. Accessed 26 Aug 2025

12. Leisure & Cultural Services Dept. (LCSD): Hire charges of leisure facilities (urban area) (2023). https://www.lcsd.gov.hk/en/leisure-link/ls_booking_charges_urban.html. Accessed 26 Aug 2025
13. Leisure & Cultural Services Dept. (LCSD): Guide to the booking procedure for use of fee-charging recreation & sports facilities (individuals) (2024)
14. HKSAR Government: LCQ6: Regulation of lion, dragon and unicorn dances (2022). https://www.info.gov.hk/gia/general/202211/16/P2022111600484.htm. Accessed 26 Aug 2025
15. UNESCO: What is intangible cultural heritage? https://ich.unesco.org/en/what-is-intangible-heritage-00003. Accessed 26 Aug 2025
16. Intangible Cultural Heritage Office (LCSD): ICH funding scheme purpose and objectives (2025). https://www.icho.hk/en/web/icho/ich_funding_scheme_introduction.html. Accessed 26 Aug 2025
17. HKSAR Government (LegCo): Safeguarding and promoting intangible cultural heritage, panel paper CB (2)973/2024(4) (2024)
18. UNESCO: Text of the 2003 convention for the safeguarding of the intangible cultural heritage. https://ich.unesco.org/en/convention. Accessed 26 Aug 2025
19. HKSAR Government: LCQ1: Intangible cultural heritage (2023). https://www.info.gov.hk/gia/general/202305/31/P2023053100293.htm. Accessed 26 Aug 2025
20. UNESCO: Text of the convention for the safeguarding of the intangible cultural heritage, Art. 1 & Art. 2 (Definitions). https://ich.unesco.org/en/convention. Accessed 26 Aug 2025
21. UNESCO: Operational directives for the implementation of the convention for the safeguarding of the intangible cultural heritage (2022)
22. Intangible Cultural Heritage Office (LCSD): Representative list of the intangible cultural heritage of Hong Kong. https://www.icho.hk/en/web/icho/representative_list.html. Accessed 26 Aug 2025
23. Intangible Cultural Heritage Office (LCSD): ICH inventory of Hong Kong-general criteria (2024)
24. HKSAR Government, leisure and cultural services department: safeguarding and promoting intangible cultural heritage, paper CB (2)973/2024(4) (2024)
25. Radianti, J., Majchrzak, T.A., Fromm, J., Wohlgenannt, I.: A systematic review of immersive virtual reality applications for higher education: design elements, lessons learned, and research agenda. Comput. Educ. **147**, 103778 (2020)
26. Dourish, P.: Where the Action Is: The Foundations of Embodied Interaction. MIT Press, Cambridge (2001)
27. Salmoni, A.W., Schmidt, R.A., Walter, C.B.: Knowledge of results and motor learning: a review and critical reappraisal. Psychol. Bull. **95**(3), 355–386 (1984)
28. Gallagher, A.G., Satava, R.M.: Virtual reality as a training and assessment tool in surgery. World J. Surg. **36**(4), 775–782 (2012)
29. Faure, C., Bideau, B.: Virtual reality for sports training: a review. J. Sports Sci. **37**(1), 1–10 (2019)
30. Parncutt, R., McPherson, G.E. (eds.): The Science and Psychology of Music Performance: Creative Strategies for Teaching and Learning. Oxford University Press, New York (2002)
31. Virtual Reality Stereoscopic 180-degree video-based immersive environments: applications for training surgeons and other medical professionals. ResearchGate (n.d.)
32. Impacts of Immersive 3D videos on students' surgical learning. PMC (n.d.). https://pmc.ncbi.nlm.nih.gov/articles/PMC11634195/. Accessed 26 Aug 2025
33. Yazdi, M.: Augmented reality (AR) and virtual reality (VR) in maintenance training. In: Advances in Computational Mathematics for Industrial Applications, pp. 165–174. Springer (2024). https://doi.org/10.1007/978-3-031-53514-7_10

34. Deterding, S., Sicart, M., Nacke, L., O'Hara, K., Dixon, D.: From game design elements to gamefulness: defining gamification. In: CHI 2011 Extended Abstracts on Human Factors in Computing Systems, pp. 9–12 (2011)
35. Ryan, R.M., Deci, E.L.: Self-determination theory and the facilitation of intrinsic motivation, social development, and well-being. Am. Psychol. **55**(1), 68–78 (2000)
36. Hamari, J., Koivisto, J., Sarsa, H.: Does gamification work?—A literature review of empirical studies on gamification. In: Proceedings of the 47th Hawaii International Conference on System Sciences, pp. 3025–3034. IEEE (2014)
37. Kapp, K.M.: The Gamification of Learning and Instruction: Game-Based Methods and Strategies for Training and Education. John Wiley & Sons (2012)
38. Dicheva, D., Dichev, C., Agre, G., Angelova, G.: Gamification in education: a systematic mapping study. J. Educ. Technol. Soc. **18**(3), 75–88 (2015)
39. Subhash, S., Cudney, E.A.: Gamified learning in higher education: a systematic review of the literature. Comput. Hum. Behav. **87**, 192–206 (2018)
40. Landers, R.N.: An uncomfortable truth about gamification and motivation. Ind. Organ. Psychol. **7**(2), 199–203 (2014)
41. Styliani, M., Kounavis, M., Vrailas, N.: Virtual reality in cultural heritage: a review of applications. In: Proceedings of the 2009 International Conference on Virtual Reality and Visualization, pp. 1–8. IEEE (2009)
42. Bruno, F., Bruno, S., De Sarno, L., Muzzupappa, M.: Virtual Museum: an immersive experience for cultural heritage. J. Cult. Herit. **11**(4), 438–445 (2010)
43. Tsiouris, M., Koutsabasis, P.: Virtual reality in museums: a systematic review. J. Cult. Herit. **38**, 1–10 (2019)
44. Forte, M.: Cyber-archaeology: towards a new paradigm for archaeological research. Digit. Appl. Archaeol. Cult. Heritage **1**(1), 2–10 (2014)
45. Champion, E.: Playing with the Past: Digital Games and the Simulation of History. Springer (2011). https://doi.org/10.1007/978-1-84996-501-9
46. Garau, C.: Virtual reality for cultural heritage: a review of recent applications. J. Cult. Herit. **33**, 1–10 (2018)
47. Jung, T., Han, D.: Augmented reality (AR) and virtual reality (VR) in cultural heritage tourism. In: Information and Communication Technologies in Tourism 2014, pp. 521–532. Springer (2014).
48. Bruno, F., Bruno, S., De Sensi, G., Luchi, M.L., Mancuso, A., Muzzupappa, M.: From 3D reconstruction to virtual reality: a complete methodology for digital archaeological exhibition. J. Cult. Herit. **11**(1), 42–49 (2010)
49. Rizvic, S., Boskovic, D., Okanovic, V., Sljivo, S., Zukic, M.: Interactive digital storytelling: bringing cultural heritage in a classroom. J. Comput. Educ. **6**(1), 143–166 (2019)
50. Ericsson, K.A., Krampe, R.T., Tesch-Römer, C.: The role of deliberate practice in the acquisition of expert performance. Psychol. Rev. **100**(3), 363–406 (1993)
51. Satava, R.M.: Virtual reality and surgical simulation. World J. Surg. **25**(11), 1485–1489 (2001)
52. Seymour, N.E., Gallagher, A.G., Roman, S.A., O'Brien, M.K., Andersen, D.K., Satava, R.M.: Virtual reality training improves operating room performance: results of a randomised, controlled trial. Ann. Surg. **236**(4), 458–464 (2002)
53. Aggarwal, P.R., Singh, A.K., Singh, S.K.: Immersive virtual reality as a surgical training tool: a cohort study. J. Surg. Educ. **81**(6), 723–730 (2024)
54. Feng, Z., Lovreglio, R., Yiu, T.W., Acosta, D.M.: Immersive virtual reality training for excavation safety and hazard identification. Smart Sustain. Built Environ. (2024)
55. Sweller, J.: Cognitive load theory. Psychol. Learn. Motiv. **55**, 37–76 (2011)
56. Wood, D., Bruner, J.S., Ross, G.: The role of tutoring in problem solving. J. Child Psychol. Psychiatry **17**(2), 89–100 (1976)

57. Braun, V., Clarke, V.: Using thematic analysis in psychology. Qual. Res. Psychol. **3**(2), 77–101 (2006)
58. Sweller, J.: Cognitive load during problem solving: effects on learning. Cogn. Sci. **12**(2), 257–285 (1988)
59. Gaitatzes, A., Christopoulos, D., Roussou, M.: Reviving the past: cultural heritage meets virtual reality. In: Proceedings of the 2001 Conference on Virtual Reality, Archeology, and Cultural Heritage (VAST 2001). Association for Computing Machinery, New York, NY, USA, pp. 103–110 (2001). https://doi.org/10.1145/584993.585011
60. Zhang, L., Qi, W., Zhao, K., Wang, L., Tan, J., Jiao, L.: VR games and the dissemination of cultural heritage. In: Streitz, N., Konomi, S. (eds.) Distributed, Ambient and Pervasive Interactions: Understanding Humans. DAPI 2018. Lecture Notes in Computer Science, vol. 10921. Springer, Cham (2018). https://doi.org/10.1007/978-3-319-91125-0_35
61. Ch'ng, E., Li, Y., Cai, S., Leow, F.T.: The effects of VR environments on the acceptance, experience, and expectations of cultural heritage learning. J. Comput. Cult. Herit. **13**(1), 21 (2020). https://doi.org/10.1145/3352933

Graph Tasks Worksheets to Develop Computational Thinking Skills in Middle School: A Case Study

Lucia Budinská(✉), Karolína Miková, and Zuzana Kubincová

Comenius University in Bratislava, Mlynská dolina, Bratislava 842 48, Slovakia
{lucia.budinska,mikova,kubincova}@fmph.uniba.sk

Abstract. The topic of graphs is a commonly used informatics concept that contributes to the development of computational thinking skills. As research shows, it can be used effectively, for example, in STEM education at various school levels. However, the form of incorporating this topic into teaching is still the subject of research.

Tasks related to this topic commonly appear in the International Bebras Challenge task database. The contestants' results in these tasks show that well-formulated tasks can be reasonably demanding for middle school students. Therefore, our research focused on investigating possible implementations of graph tasks in lessons. Three tasks from the Bebras challenge were selected, and a worksheet was created for each of them. The worksheets were then verified with a smaller group of students in class. These worksheets consisted of so-called microworlds, each focusing on a different graph representation. Our research problem was to determine how to appropriately grade the difficulty of the tasks in the worksheets so that the topics are motivating for the students and the tasks are not overly cognitively demanding. To address this, qualitative methods of data collection and analysis were used, working with over 100 students aged 10–14 at three different schools. The main goal was to better understand the cognitive demands of graph tasks for middle school students and to formulate specific recommendations for practice. One of our results indicates that the connection of motivation with real-life experiences has a significant impact on students' results and understanding.

Keywords: Bebras · Graph · Microworlds · Worksheets · Unplugged activities · Computational thinking · STEM · Qualitative research

1 Introduction

1.1 STEM and Computational Thinking Skills

STEM education, which combines four areas – science, technology, engineering, and mathematics – is often implemented through project-based learning. In projects, students usually have to solve practical challenges, engage in analysis,

B. Fernández-Manjón et al. (Eds.): SETE 2025/ICWL 2025, LNCS 16425, pp. 115–130, 2026.
https://doi.org/10.1007/978-981-92-0042-9_9

experimentation, modeling, testing, etc. When confronted with real-life problems, they are forced to identify what is relevant, how to divide the problem, how to plan a solution, how to implement it, and also how to evaluate it. These problem-solving steps directly correspond to the individual components of computational thinking (CT), such as abstraction, decomposition, algorithmic thinking, etc. CT thus provides a methodological framework for tackling problems solved in STEM projects, e.g., tasks in physics, biology, or mathematics.

The connection between CT and STEM education is currently the subject of several research projects and pedagogical innovations.

In their study [1], Cantlon et al. presented an interesting interdisciplinary STEM project in which elementary school students wrote a computer program to test the intelligence of primates and used it directly in a zoo with real monkeys. This unique project, which tapped into kids' natural curiosity, showed that well-designed STEM education can also develop CT skills.

Sen et al. conducted research [2] with gifted students, working with them for several weeks on STEM activities based on the engineering design process. The results of the study showed that STEM activities helped to develop students' creativity, collaboration, critical thinking, and also improved their CT skills.

In a study [3] carried out in elementary schools in China and Macau, Peng et al. used a STEM approach in a computer programming course that included incorporating interdisciplinary knowledge acquisition into the task process and providing practical rules to guide each stage of the task. The results show that after completing the course, students' computational thinking skills, especially their ability to decompose complex tasks improved.

Bedar and Al-Shboul conducted an experiment in which they used the STEAM approach (STEM areas plus arts) in geography subject in high school [4]. The results showed significant development of computational thinking, particularly algorithmic thinking and abstraction in students from the experimental group.

When developing CT in students, it is necessary to introduce them also to the concept of data structures, which are important for effective problem-solving. One such structure is the graph, which is used to solve a number of practical problems in STEM: in chemistry, graphs are used to model molecules; in geography and engineering, to plan routes and infrastructure networks; in computer science, to represent social networks or internet connectivity; in mathematics, for modeling relationships between entities, etc.

As shown by the results of several studies, graph tasks implemented in the STEM environment lead to improved CT skills across all age groups and contexts. For example, a study [5] using network graphs in a STEM intervention in solving transportation and logistics optimization problems reported an average 23% improvement in CT indicators, particularly in problem decomposition, pattern recognition, and abstraction.

Junior et al. [6] employed an educational board game based on graph grammars to K-12 teaching. Their results show the development of computational thinking skills in most of their students.

In their research [7], Barana et al. examined the computational thinking processes associated with the creation of animated graphs. Their analysis showed that the creation of animated graphs activates all the processes behind the mental strategies of CT that are useful in problem solving.

To find the best way to develop CT in students at lower levels of education, we have explored various approaches. One of them is involving students in informatics competitions or using interesting tasks from competitions in teaching.

1.2 Computational Thinking in Bebras Challenge

The Bebras is an international challenge on informatics and computational thinking, and its main goals include: "Show the variety of informatics topics and concepts. Showing that solving informatics problems is interesting and challenging" [8]. This is done by a set of small tasks in three different difficulty levels, that students should be able to solve within 3 min each. This fact makes it not trivial to create a good Bebras task that shows some informatics concepts and, at the same time, enhances CT. Many tasks are therefore connected to algorithmic thinking, as decomposition and evaluation (as higher levels of CT) are not so easy to be introduced and performed in this short time [9]. Therefore, researchers from the Bebras community use modifications of Bebras tasks in many different ways in educational content. They often use these tasks as unplugged activities [10–12], or introduction to programming and CT in different levels of education (primary [13], secondary [14,15]).

There are a lot of different unplugged activities, outside of the Bebras, that acquaint students with different informatics concepts. For example, Rodriguez and his colleagues [16] used unplugged projects in the middle school classroom. They suggest letting students get their own hands-on experiences with the topic, using a relevant real-world connection, and try to have short and precise instructions and be consistent. They also claim that a naive way of problem-solving (or trial and error) can be useful in getting students' attention. The trial and error method is often used in learning as a first step, but it could be more challenging to use in Bebras tasks. If we want students to create a strategy, Datzko [17] suggests having a lot of possible answers to minimize the use of this method. But sometimes trial and error can help. For example, Vaníček [18] tried to enhance it in interactive tasks, where students can find rules on their own, and therefore there is no need to explain everything in the task body. But it is crucial to find an appropriate task in a challenge that can be solved like this as it is in lower levels of computational thinking skills and also cognitive skills, and the contest aims for higher levels.

Can we somehow use naive ways of problem-solving, while also supporting students to create some clever strategies? How can we support it in schools and let students use different methods to understand some concepts? One answer to this can be a word *microworld* by Papert [19]. Papert's idea was to let students explore and, as a result, understand abstract ideas. Microworld is an "incubator", a world of its own where students can learn a specific thing in one area. Students should learn the concepts by working with this world and testing their hypotheses. This could also help to enhance an abstraction, as part of computational thinking. Abstraction could be used to represent data as models or simulations [20]. The national curriculum in Slovakia, where our research was conducted, states [21] that students in middle schools (10 to 14 years old) should learn to work with data structures (as tables, sequences, and graphs), they should be able to understand them, to organize information in them, and interpret them. In this paper, we try to use ideas from Papert's microworlds and from the Bebras challenge to show how unplugged worksheets (microworlds) based on Bebras tasks can help students acquire informatics concepts of graph data structures and enhance their abstraction skills.

2 Research Methodology

The main goal of our research was to find out how to use graph tasks worksheets in middle schools (for 10–14 years old students). The focus was on the cognitive demand of tasks, their motivation, and their appropriateness for this age group. Two research questions were set. **Question 1:** *How can worksheets created from Bebras graph tasks be used in middle schools so that they are suitable for various types of students?* **Question 2:** *What influences students' preferences and their understanding of graph tasks?*.

The qualitative analysis was conducted in two phases. In the first phase, we observed the gradation of tasks, their cognitive demand, and how the students solved them. In the second phase, we observed the implementation of the worksheets in school lessons. In both phases, the main data collection resources were artifacts (worksheets completed by students), interviews (semi-structured with students or teachers), field notes, and records of students' commented solving. Data were analysed using coding (both selective and axial), categorization, and constant comparison [23], as well as narrative analysis [24]. To minimise researcher bias, the triangulation of all collected data was performed. The interviews were transcribed and coded by one researcher. Field notes were discussed between two researchers, and assumptions, if any, were confirmed by artifacts or interviews. Parents of students agreed to their children's participation in the research and their recording. All students were also asked for their own consent to participation and recording. Students used their first names in worksheets, but these were visible only to main researcher.

First Phase: In the first phase of research, two different schools were included. School A was a secondary grammar school, where the research was conducted on 12 sixth-grade students (11–12 years old, 4 boys and 8 girls) and 9 seventh-grade students (12–13 years old, 6 boys and 3 girls). School B was a middle school, where the research sample was 7 fifth-grade students (10–11 years old, 2 boys and 5 girls). In this phase, students solved the worksheets (one per lesson) individually. At the beginning of the lesson, their teachers gave them a few instructions and introduced the topic. The students then solved the tasks on the worksheets. Three students were recorded during the lessons, while solving worksheets and they were asked to comment on what they had been doing (this was not done for the first worksheet). Participating researchers took notes during the whole lesson. After the lesson, semi-structured interviews with randomly selected students were recorded, and students were asked their opinions on tasks and they described how they understood the tasks.

Second Phase: In the second phase of research, a school C was included in the research. This was a middle school with a research sample of 6 groups of fifth-grade students (10–11 years old), comprising a total of 62 students (34 girls and 28 boys). At the beginning of the lesson, the teacher introduced the topic, gave instruction, and then she let students work in pairs or groups of three (exceptionally alone). In many groups, students verbalized what they were doing, correcting each other, or arguing about their solutions. At the end of the lesson, the teacher led the discussion about tasks, students talked about their solutions, and they tried to find out the correct answers. The teacher was walking among the groups, and when she saw that some students were stuck or were arguing for a long time, she asked them guiding questions. The researcher took notes of both whole-class discussions and discussions in pairs or groups during the lesson. After the lesson, a semi-structured interview with the teacher was recorded. She was asked to talk about her view of the lesson and her opinion on worksheets.

The number of students who solved the worksheets in each phase are shown in Table 1. In the first phase, students from School A solved all three worksheets; in the second phase, each worksheet was solved by a different group of students.

Table 1. The number of participants in each phase

	First phase			Second phase
	School A		*School B*	*School C*
	6th grade	*7th grade*	*5th grade*	*5th grade*
Family relationships	11 (7 girls)	7 (3 girls)	-	18 (10 girls) in 9 groups
Tram lines	12 (8 girls)	9 (3 girls)	-	22 (12 girls) in 10 groups
Bracelet machine	12 (8 girls)	9 (3 girls)	7 (5 girls)	22 (12 girls) in 11 groups

3 Bebras Tasks and Worksheets

As we have mentioned before, it is essential for us to investigate various options for implementing graph tasks in informatics lessons. We chose three tasks from Bebras challenge with graphs. Tasks without algorithms, optimization, or more advanced structures were intentionally selected to focus on abstraction. The first worksheet, called Family Relationships, uses graphs to show relationships in a family. This is not a commonly used family tree, as there are oriented edges in both directions. The second worksheet, Tram Lines, shows a map of tram and bus lines in a city. This is a common type of graph we see in real life, and this could show students how they could use their CT outside the school. In the third worksheet, the finite state automaton is used as a machine that creates bracelets. This shows an informatics concept in a form that can be understood even by students in this age group. All worksheets were created with the Bloom taxonomy of cognitive domain [25] in mind. We tried to create at least one task for each category and arrange it in the worksheet so that the order according to the level of cognitive difficulty was respected. One of the most important things was to differentiate tasks in one worksheet, so that they have different motivations and/or different types of answers, so that (1) every student can find some task they can solve, and (2) they help students to look at the problem from different sides. The whole process and reasons why we chose these tasks is described in more detail in the previous paper [22]. In this paper, our main focus was on the students and their perception of these tasks. Worksheets were used as an instrument that helped us better understand the students' reasoning and find out how differently they can grasp the concept of graphs. This also served as validation that our worksheets help them understand these concepts. In many studies, the main goal is to obtain students' results, but sometimes the answers we perceive as incorrect can be explained by students as stemming from a misunderstanding or a real-life connection. As CT is mostly about the process of thinking about problems, we find it crucial to observe this process.

In the next parts, we will describe the results from both phases of our research for each worksheet individually.

3.1 Family Relationships

The first worksheet was based on task 2013-CZ-04a[1] about relationships in one family. The worksheet consisted of 11 tasks. (1) finding relations from graph, (2) finding relations that are not directly drawn in graph, but can be deducted, (3) filling in sentences: "X is *name of relation* of Y" and "X has *name of relation* Y", (4) adding information (an edge or a node) to the graph, (5) choosing which of the four graphs represents relations in text, (6) drawing graph based on instructions, (7) answering questions from graphical information, (8) answering questions from textual information, (9) choosing which task from the previous two was easier, and find pros and cons for each representation, (10) drawing own family graph, (11-bonus) define own representation of family relations.

Tasks (1) to (4) used one graph, see Fig. 1, so that students could first understand how it works. The graph used in tasks (7) and (8) was the same (different than in previous tasks) but with different names of people to compare cognitive demand and difficulty of graphical and textual representation.

Results: First phase: The most cognitively demanding tasks, where errors were made, were tasks (or subtasks) where the language and orientation of arrows did not match. Arrows in the graph were oriented so that they used "is" orientation ("X is [relation written on arrow] of Y"), but in the text, there

[1] This means that the task was used in the school year 2013/14 and it was created by the Czech team.

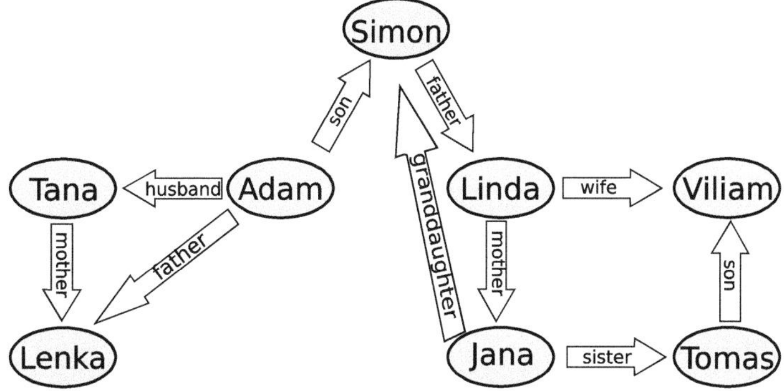

Fig. 1. Graph from Family relationships worksheet. Translated to English.

were often sentences with "has" ("X has [relation] Y"). These were often solved incorrectly. Other mistakes resulted from reading without comprehension when parsing longer sentences or not reading the instructions. For example, the sentence: *"Kristof's mother is called Patricia"*. was drawn incorrectly by 6 students, 4 of them were in sixth grade. And from the sentence: *"Lujza is a mother of Dano and a daughter of Emilia."* 6 students deduced that Lujza is Emilia's mother.

In task (9), where students were choosing either graphical or textual representation, most of the students chose graphs, as it was "easier" and they did not need to "construct it in their head". Students in sixth grade could not find situations where it's better to use textual representation, but students in seventh grade found some (e.g. if they should create a family tree, it is easier to write down than to draw, or it can require less space). The task (10) gave students a chance to draw their own family graph. In this task, the differences between boys' and girls' answers were the most visible. Girls mostly drew bigger and more difficult graphs, including even distant relations in their families (e.g. stepfamily, cousins twice-removed, godparents, etc.). Boys drew graphs with the minimum required number of people and relations. This could show that girls liked the idea behind the worksheet more than boys and were motivated enough to put on more work. Many students did not solve the last bonus task (to create their own representation of family relations), because they did not like the theme or, as they said, they were "not so creative". Some students, mostly those who liked the worksheet, came up with different ideas – e.g. using well-known family trees, or more complicated schemes for different relations.

Second Phase: When introducing this worksheet, the teacher made sure that students knew the names of relations it used, so it would not alter the results. In this group, there was a problem with arrows' orientation too. In some groups, students resolved it, but some students were confused throughout the work with the worksheet. Many groups finished their work early, so that they had a lot of time to work on tasks (10) and (11). They created graphs that were thought through and very detailed (they even dealt with divorces, same-sex marriages, and so on). Approximately half of the groups created their own representations of family relations, and the teacher let them present them to their peers at the end of the lesson. The teacher highlighted these tasks as a good opportunity for skilled and talented students to work on challenging tasks, while also believing that every student can solve this task at their own level. The second phase showed that this worksheet can be used for group or pair work, and it could be helpful in understanding the graph. But it is not true for everyone, as for some students, the orientation of arrows was still challenging.

3.2 Tram Lines

The second worksheet was created from task 2015-HU-04, and it is connected to the map of public transportation. The decision not to create a separate map for each task or group of tasks (as it is used in the other two worksheets) was made as this allowed us to use one bigger map (see Fig. 2), which is more similar to real maps of public transportation. The map was on a separate sheet to allow students to work with it during the whole lesson. On the first page of the worksheet, there was a paragraph with some basic information (what is on a map and what is represented by some objects). The worksheet consisted of 7 tasks. (1) answering questions about information from the first paragraph describing the graph, (2) finding lines from/to named stop, (3) choosing between lines based on certain criteria, (4) completing short stories with name of a stop or numbers, (5) finding combination of lines based on certain criteria, (6) completing short stories with name of a stop or numbers, with transitions, (7) drawing own line based on stated criteria and writing how to get to specified places.

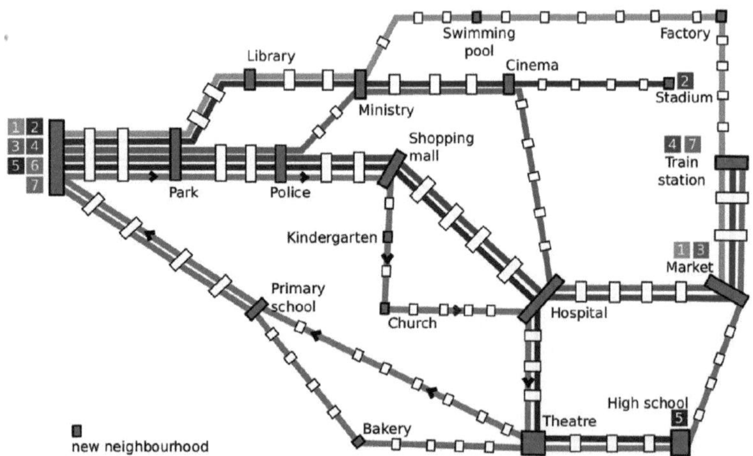

Fig. 2. Graph from Tram lines worksheet. Places translated into English.

Results: First phase: This worksheet was the most difficult, and it took longer for students to solve all the tasks, than the other two worksheets. Based on the students' answers, it was obvious that they did not carefully read the introduction and later only guessed what was represented by different things in the map. Most of them realized their mistakes later on (mostly in tasks (4) and (6)). Seventh graders connected their real-life experiences to tasks. For example, they knew that the bus or tram was empty at the first stop, "so passengers could sit down". That is why they chose this stop when planning their route, which had several options for where to transfer. Or they took into account that if there is a large stop where many lines pass, there is a greater chance that there will be many people there, so "it is not a good choice for a teacher with kindergarten children". Their connection to their own experiences affected their solution – if they do not like to transfer, they usually try to find a line without transferring, even if it is longer. In the sixth grade, more students from our research sample do not use public transport very often, and therefore, some tasks were difficult for them, for example, they used to forget to write the name of the stop where to transfer. And they also had problems with orientation in the map, even though we added some elements to the original map (from Bebras task) to make it easier (line numbers on the first and the last stop, names of bigger stops...). Another problem we saw in sixth grade students was that some tasks had more than one correct answer. These students were not used to this and therefore they were rechecking their answers multiple times.

Some of the students liked tasks where they were "helping people" (task (5)), others liked "logic puzzles" (tasks (4) and (6)). Considering students' work with the structure, older students navigated it more easily; they were dismissing lines that could not be suitable, pre-counting the number of stops to help them in the next tasks, and so on. Younger students had more difficulties with orientation in the map, and were more likely to get lost in it.

Second phase: This worksheet proved to be too difficult for younger students when it was introduced to fifth-graders in the second phase. Even though they worked in pairs or groups, they did not finish all the tasks in the worksheet. In this round of testing, more misconceptions emerged, many of them directly connected to the graphical representation of maps (e.g. they considered rectangles to be buildings, not stops). At the end of the lesson, the teacher went through the tasks and explained how they should have been solved, because many students were demotivated when they got stuck on some tasks. She showed real public transportation maps from around the world, and they discussed their importance. The discussion showed that many students in this group are not using public transportation on their own or often. And this could have added more cognitive demand to tasks – as they were not only trying to understand the structure, but also the rules of how to use public transportation.

3.3 Bracelet Machine

The third worksheet, called the Bracelet machine, is based on task 2013-AT-05. It introduces finite state automata in an easier and graphically suitable version.

The graph in the story represents rules for a machine that creates bracelets (see Fig. 3). In the introduction, it is written where the machine starts creating a bracelet and where it ends. This worksheet consists of 8 tasks. (1) drawing a path to the automaton picture of how the bracelet was made, (2) filling in missing pieces from bracelets, (3) choosing which bracelets were made by the given automaton, (4) choosing which of two automata could make the given bracelets, (5) drawing bracelets made by automaton, (6) identifying rules for automaton in previous tasks, (7) adding missing elements to a pre-defined automaton based on three already made bracelets, (8) creating own automaton and its products.

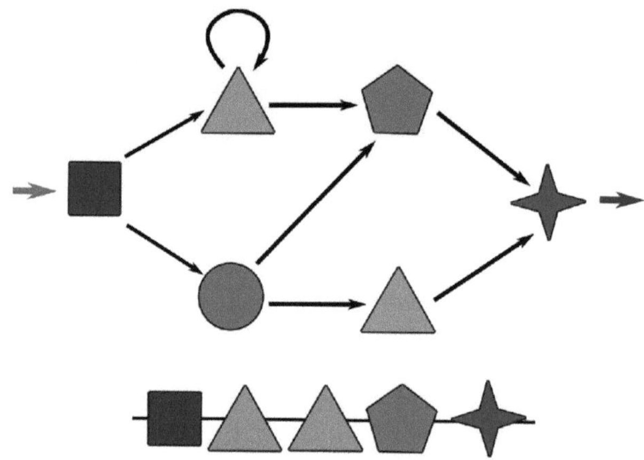

Fig. 3. Graph from Bracelet machine worksheet, bracelet made by automaton is shown below.

Results: First phase: The most cognitively demanding part was the concept of loop. As this was not explained on purpose, to make students construct their own idea while working with tasks, we were aware that this could happen. For many students, later tasks were helpful in understanding how the loop works, but getting stuck on tasks in the first part of the worksheet was demotivating for many of them. Therefore, changes were made to the worksheet, and this new version was tested in School B. Some changes concerned task (1), where bracelets with 0, 1, and 2 uses of the loop were used. And, most importantly, the order of tasks (2) and (3) was interchanged. This resulted in a lower mistakes rate in the subtask that had previously been the most difficult for students at School A.

While working with a loop, many problems stemmed from real-life connections, as in interviews, many students argued that the loop cannot be used many times, because "the bracelet would be long", "we don't have enough pieces" and so on. In task (8), there were differences between automata made by girls and those made by boys. On one hand, boys used original motivation from the worksheet (bracelets) and their automata were easier and used less number of pieces, but were still effective. On the other hand, girls created more complicated rules and with different motivations than the bracelets (Santa's bag, necklaces, school marks...). In school B, all of the fifth-graders used bracelets, even with the same pieces as in previous tasks.

Second phase: The students worked on this worksheet only for about 35 min, which was the shortest time of all three worksheets. In this phase, students still had most issues with the concept of the loop. Many pairs and groups were stuck on the third task (originally (2)), many discussions were led, some with real-life connections, some with using their mathematical mindset to better describe the situation, e.g. "that is like x", "the longest bracelet will be $\infty + 4$, as this bead could be repeated infinity times and you need another four", "based on examples in other tasks [the loop] shouldn't be used more than 3 times"). Still, this worksheet was perceived as easy for a big majority of students, with the exception of a few groups who were not sure how to solve these tasks. The teacher liked that the concept of the loop was interesting to skilled students because it made them think, and it was not trivial, while other students could still solve most of the tasks with only a naive understanding of the concept, but without misconceptions.

4 Results

Two research questions were proposed. **Question 1:** *How can worksheets created from Bebras graph tasks be used in middle schools so that they are suitable for various types of students?*

Based on our results, several factors were identified that can help create better tasks for middle school students and to integrate this topic into the education process. One factor is to create different types of tasks that work with the same graph structure, ensuring they suit different learning styles and students' preferences. This allows students to work at their own cognitive level and, moreover, at their level of abstraction. In the final tasks of all worksheets, students created their own graphs or structures, and while everyone could solve these tasks, different levels of abstraction between students were evident. These tasks, therefore, offer a low floor and a high ceiling and do not limit more skilled students.

Another factor is the clarity and precision of instructions. If students skipped them or did not understand them, they often struggled with solving tasks because they made up their own rules. Providing different ways of working with the graph can help students fix their mistakes or initial misconceptions, as they need to rethink what they are doing and adopt a skeptical mindset. We observed that girls tended to go back and correct their previous mistakes, while boys switched their approach to working with the structure in the middle of the worksheet, but did not correct their earlier mistakes. However, both groups still corrected their misconceptions during the process, which is what matters.

The way the worksheet is used in the lesson creates another factor. In the first phase, students worked alone. In the second phase, students worked in pairs or groups, and this led to more fruitful discussions that often helped resolve misunderstandings and misconceptions. Discussing tasks, trying to understand different viewpoints, and arguing and reasoning their perspectives could lead to better results. Teacher-led discussion with all students could also be helpful, providing a teacher with an opportunity to connect the information students learned with other informatics concepts or real-life scenarios.

Question 2: *What influences students' preferences and their understanding of graph tasks?*

It is possible to examine the tasks that were solved without problems by the majority of students, but these are not necessarily preferred by them. To verify our results by triangulating the data, we included a short reflection at the end of each worksheet. Almost every student could name at least one task they liked. For some students, it was the most difficult task; for others, it was the easiest. Some students' preferences were based on the type of tasks.

In the first phase, students worked on all the worksheets, which allowed them to identify their favourite worksheets. Most boys preferred the second worksheet, Tram lines, because they found it "challenging". Most girls favoured the last worksheet, Bracelet machine, because it was "colourful". The girls in our research sample enjoyed tasks involving family, helping others, and colourful pictures, while the boys preferred logic puzzles and more challenging tasks. This is consistent with research from Germany, where Hubwieser [26] found that girls performed better in Bebras tasks involving real-life situations and colourful pictures, and tasks which are less difficult. In contrast, boys in Hubwieser's study were more successful in tasks with abstract structures; they did not require a real-life connection and often used the trial-and-error method.

For older students (seventh grade), the Tram lines worksheet was easy, while younger students found it difficult. This trend was also observed in the second phase. This worksheet involves real-life skills that not all students possess, making it more cognitively demanding as both the structure and the operations required to use are new to them. The concept of loops in finite state automata posed a similar problem due to its higher cognitive demand. It was demonstrated that the order of tasks is crucial for understanding the structure and rules, as changing the order of tasks helped students to better grasp this concept.

5 Discussion

During the testing of our worksheets, we identified some problems that may limit their use in classrooms. The first issue was found in the Family Relationships worksheet. The type of graph used in this worksheet is not very intuitive and may not be suitable for representing family relationships, leading to some mistakes. Although using different graphical and verbal descriptions ("X is/has *name of relation* Y") can be confusing. In real life, language often does not match its visual representation. It is important for students to discover this to understand the significance of consistency in the rules used to create graphs. Nevertheless, for introducing family relationships to younger students, a more appropriate graph type could be chosen. Additionally, the family theme can be problematic in group work, as the names used in the graphs can coincide with the names of students in the classroom, potentially leading to teasing. To avoid this, names from history or other subjects, such as monarchs, could be used. However, this may result in some students relying on their knowledge from other classes rather than focusing on understanding the graph itself.

Concept in the second worksheet, Tram lines, proved too difficult for younger students and for those without prior experience with public transportation. It is important for teachers to assess whether this theme is appropriate for their students. For students with no prior experience, it may be helpful if teachers provide more guidance and explain the concept in greater detail. These instructions should be discussed rather than written down, as we have observed that students tend to skip longer texts and often struggle with reading comprehension, which then affects their ability to complete the tasks.

Some students found it challenging to work with questions that had more than one correct answer. In our examined groups, this was mostly true for girls, who tended to second-guess their answers. However, we believe that this should not discourage the inclusion of such tasks. Students need to practice solving more tasks of this type to build self-confidence. Both this issue and difficulties with reading comprehension are common problems in education across various subjects, so we assume they are not entirely specific to our worksheets.

6 Conclusion

We consider it important for the development of computational thinking that students grasp the concept of a graph as a data structure at a level that allows them to interpret the data stored in it and use it to solve relevant problems. For this reason, we find it appropriate to introduce this structure to students at lower levels of education. We have therefore prepared three worksheets based on three graph tasks from the Bebras Challenge and tested them with middle school students. Each worksheet featured one graph data structure, and the goal was for students to retrieve information from it, navigate within it, and understand how it functions. These objectives align with the goals of our national informatics curriculum for the early years of middle school.

During our research, we discovered several interesting findings. Some differences between different age groups and between boys and girls were identified. These groups used different strategies to solve the tasks, or assessed the task difficulty differently. The results also underlined the importance of personal prior experience with the context of the task. If a task models a real-life situation, it can be more challenging for students who lack experience in that area. Therefore, it is important to consider whether certain experiences are standard for the age group, and this can limit the applicability of the story and setting used in the task.

We also identified several issues that provided insights into how to improve these worksheets. Despite these challenges, we believe that unplugged worksheets represent a valuable way to adapt Bebras tasks for use in schools. They offer an opportunity to introduce students to informatics concepts in a more detailed manner, enabling them to construct their understanding in a meaningful way.

We consider it most important that working in a microworlds with graded tasks offers students different perspectives on a given concept. This improves their understanding and stimulates motivation, as each student can find a task that interests them. Linking tasks to the microworld reduces the cognitive demand on students, as they encounter a structure created according to the same rules in all the tasks. In these tasks, the graph is used as a data structure, so students use natural language to describe the data or processes represented in the graph. It is precisely the ambiguity of natural language that leads to errors in data representation. Group discussion has proven to be a suitable solution here, which we consider to be an essential part of the development of CT skills. And, as the results of the second phase of the research showed, it is exactly the discussion that helps students grasp the concept of graphs at different levels. We aimed to provide students with a space with a low floor and a high ceiling so that no group would be demotivated. It turned out that when the worksheets were assigned to the appropriate grade, this aspect was respected, and all participating students had the opportunity to develop their computational thinking.

Acknowledgments. This work was supported by grants VEGA-1/0621/22 and VEGA-1/0407/25.

References

1. Cantlon, J.F., Becker, K.T., DeLong, C.M.: Computational thinking during a short, authentic, interdisciplinary STEM experience for elementary students. J. STEM Educ. Res. **7**(3), 425–443. Springer (2024)
2. Sen, C., Ay, Z. S., and Kiray, S. A.: Computational thinking skills of gifted and talented students in integrated STEM activities based on the engineering design process: the case of robotics and 3D robot modeling. Thinking Skills Creativity **42**, 100931. Elsevier (2024)
3. Peng, J., Hao, M., Chen, B., Wang, M.: Cultivating computational thinking in a STEM course through the ICDCO instructional model. Educ. Inf. Technol., 1–39. Springer (2025)
4. Bedar, R. A.-H., Al-Shboul, M.: The effect of using STEAM approach on developing computational thinking skills among high school students in Jordan. Int. Assoc. Online Eng. (2020)
5. Marsidi, M.: The integration of the RBL-STEM learning model and graph theory in solving transportation and logistics optimization problems to enhance students' computational thinking skills. Jurnal Ilmiah Soulmath: Jurnal Edukasi Pendidikan Matematika, **13**(1) (2025). https://doi.org/10.25139/smj.v13i1.10025
6. da Silva Junior, B.A., da Costa Cavalheiro, S.A., Foss, L.: "The Last Tree", exercising the Computational Thinking through a Graph Grammar based educational game. J. Comput. Thinking (JCThink) **2**(1), 3–3 (2018)

7. Barana, A., Conte, A., Fissore, C., Floris, F., Marchisio, M., Sacchet, M.: The creation of animated graphs to develop computational thinking and support STEM education. In: Maple Conference, pp. 189–204. Springer (2019)
8. Dagiene, V., Futschek, G.: Introducing informatics concepts through a contest. In: IFIP Working Conference: New Developments in ICT and Education. Universite de Picardie Jules Verne, Amiens (2010)
9. Dagiene, V., Sentance, S.: It's Computational Thinking! Bebras Tasks in the Curriculum. In: 9th International Conference on Informatics in Schools: Situation. Evolution, and Perspectives, ISSEP 2016, pp. 28–39. Münster, Germany (2016)
10. Dagiene, V., Futschek, G., Stupuriene, G.: Creativity in solving short tasks for learning computational thinking. Constructivist Found. **14**(3) (2019)
11. Bellettini, C., Lonati, V., Monga, M., Morpurgo, A., Palazzolo, M.: Situated learning with Bebras Tasklets. In: Pozdniakov, S.N., Dagienė, V. (eds.) ISSEP 2019. LNCS, vol. 11913, pp. 225–239. Springer, Cham (2019). https://doi.org/10.1007/978-3-030-33759-9_18
12. Kim, J.A.: Flipped learning and unplugged activities for data structure and algorithm class. In: Software Engineering in IoT, Big Data, Cloud and Mobile Computing. Stud. Comput. Intell., **930**. Springer, Cham (2021)
13. Vinikienė, L., Dagienė, V., Stupurienė, G.: Introducing programming concepts through the Bebras tasks in the primary education. In: Keane, T., Fluck, A.E. (eds) Teaching Coding in K-12 Schools: Research and Application, pp. 145–156, Springer, Cham (2023). https://doi.org/10.1007/978-3-031-21970-2_10
14. Keane, T.: Introduction: the need for programming and computational thinking from early childhood education through to secondary schooling. In: Keane, T., Fluck, A.E. (eds) Teaching Coding in K-12 Schools: Research and Application, pp. 1–9. Springer, Cham (2023). https://doi.org/10.1007/978-3-031-21970-2_1
15. Jasutė, E.: Computational thinking unplugged in CS middle class lessons in Lithuania. In: Proceedings of International Teacher Forum on International Conference on Computational Thinking Education 2020. Hong Kong, pp. 11–12 (2020)
16. Rodriguez, B., Rader, C., Camp, T.: Using student performance to assess CS Unplugged activities in a classroom environment. In: Proceedings of the 2016 ACM Conference on Innovation and Technology in Computer Science Education. ACM, pp. 95–100 (2016)
17. Datzko, C.: Openness and creativity in solving short tasks for learning computational thinking. Constructivist Found. **14**(3) (2019)
18. Vaníček, J.: Bebras informatics contest: criteria for good tasks revised. In: International Conference on Informatics in Schools: Situation, Evolution, and Perspectives, pp. 17–28. Springer (2014)
19. Papert, S.: Mindstorms: Children, Computers, and Powerful Ideas. Basic Books, Inc., New York, NY, USA (1980)
20. CSTA and ISTE: Operational Definition of Computational Thinking for K-12 Education. https://cdn.iste.org/www-root/Computational_Thinking_Operational_Definition_ISTE.pdf (2011)
21. ŠPÚ: Štátny vzdelávací program. Informatika - nižšie stredné vzelávania. https://www.statpedu.sk/files/articles/dokumenty/inovovany-statny-vzdelavaci-program/informatika_nsv_2014.pdf (2014)
22. Budinská, L., Mayerová, K.: From Bebras tasks to lesson plans–graph data structures. In: International Conference on Informatics in Schools: Situation, Evolution, and Perspectives, pp. 256–267 (2019)
23. Lichtman, M.: Qualitative Research in Education, 3rd edn. SAGE, USA (2013)

24. Creswell, J.W.: Educational Research: Planning, Conducting, and Evaluating Quantitative and Qualitative Research. Inc., Pearson Education (2015)
25. Bloom, B., et al.: Taxonomy of Educational Objectives the Cognitive Domain, vol. 1, pp. 20–24. McKay, New York (1956)
26. Hubwieser, P., Hubwieser, E., Graswald D.: How to attract the girls: gender-specific performance and motivation in the Bebras challenge. In: International Conference on Informatics in Schools: Situation, Evolution, and Perspectives, pp. 40–52. Springer, Cham (2016). https://doi.org/10.1007/978-3-319-46747-4_4

Technology for Emotions: A Review of Tools for Enabling Children to Self-report Their Emotions in Learning

Andrea Fladmark[1], Marie Holmeide[1], Feiran Zhang[2(✉)], Boban Vesin[1,3], Isabella Possaghi[1], and Sofia Papavlasopoulou[1]

[1] Department of Computer and Information Science, Norwegian University of Science and Technology, Trondheim, Norway
{andrea.fladmark,marie.holmeide,boban.vesin,isabella.possaghi, sofia.papavlasopoulou}@ntnu.no

[2] School of Design, The Hong Kong Polytechnic University, Hong Kong SAR, China
feiran.zhang@polyu.edu.hk

[3] Department of Business, History and Social Sciences, USN School of Business, Vestfold, Norway
boban.vesin@usn.no

Abstract. Understanding and supporting children's emotions has become increasingly recognized as a critical factor in effective learning, with growing research exploring methods for capturing emotional states in educational contexts. This literature review examines the role of technology in enabling children to self-report their emotions during educational activities. Drawing on 23 studies, we analyze various tools for capturing children's emotions to identify the state of the art in the types of tools used and their impacts. Our findings reveal that the prevalence of both paper-pencil-based and technology-based self-reporting tools features graphical user interfaces (GUIs), while tangible user interfaces (TUIs) remain underrepresented in educational settings despite their potential for less intrusive and real-time reporting. Accordingly, we discuss future research directions and advocate for integrating subjective self-report data with objective physiological data from sensors, such as wristbands or AI-driven facial recognition systems, to achieve a more comprehensive understanding of children's emotional states.

Keywords: Affective Computing · Children · Emotions · Self-Reporting · Learning

1 Introduction

Emotions significantly influence children's learning processes, engagement, and collaboration. Understanding and adapting to children's emotional states is therefore essential to foster effective learning environments. To optimize learning, educators may need to understand children's emotional states and adjust teaching strategies to promote positive emotions in children [1]. Consequently, there is

B. Fernández-Manjón et al. (Eds.): SETE 2025/ICWL 2025, LNCS 16425, pp. 131–144, 2026.
https://doi.org/10.1007/978-981-92-0042-9_10

an urgent need for tools that enhance our understanding of children's emotional experience throughout their learning process [2]. However, emotions encompass expressive, physiological, behavioral, and subjective components, necessitating practical tools for the timely identification of students' emotional states. Self-report tools, whether used in-the-moment or retrospectively by children, are widely used and offer educators and researchers insights to support learning and encourage reflection. Unlike other techniques for capturing the emotional experience of children, self-reports allow the evaluation of a wide range of psychological processes and can provide a more nuanced understanding of human thought than most other methods [3]. Nevertheless, there is limited knowledge about how self-report tools facilitate the capture of children's emotions in learning contexts [3].

With the growing integration of technology, such as mobile devices, in educational contexts, incorporating in-the-moment self-reporting becomes more feasible without disrupting the learning process. Technology offers the potential for effective, user-friendly solutions and for enhancing smooth communication between students and teachers. However, a knowledge gap persists regarding how technology enables self-reports for children in learning contexts [4]. Therefore, this paper aims to investigate how technology can empower children to self-report their emotions during learning activities. To achieve this goal, we conducted a systematic review of the literature to identify research gaps and identify future opportunities.

2 Related Works

Current reviews primarily focused on technologies for detecting students' emotions using alternative sensing techniques such as artificial intelligence (AI) and wearable devices, rather than self-reporting. For instance, Ba and Hu [5] investigated the use of wearable devices to measure emotions in education. Their findings from 50 reviewed papers showed that, while most studies focused on university students in controlled settings, recent advances in wearable devices now enable the measurement of emotions in younger students within more natural settings. Rather than inquiring into educational contexts, Saganowski et al. [6] narrowed the investigation to the use of wearable devices for emotion recognition in everyday life, considering 34 relevant papers. They concluded that while most studies were conducted in laboratory settings, using wearables for emotional recognition in real-life scenarios is feasible, provided additional considerations, such as device comfort and new self-assessment procedures tailored to an authentic setting. Through a review of 41 selected papers, Vistorte et al. [2] examined how AI can improve emotional assessment in educational settings. Their results indicated that machine learning and facial recognition are the most widely used AI techniques for emotion assessment.

In particular, one related review by Fuentes et al. (2015) [7] focused on the features of user interfaces for self-reporting emotions across varying contexts, including workplace and healthcare, based on 13 included papers. They found a predominance of graphical user interfaces (GUIs) over tangible user interfaces (TUIs) and emphasized the importance of validating self-reported emotions with physiological signals. They called for more research in real-world contexts and suggested new interaction styles for groups like children and older adults. In their later review (2017) [8], they expanded their review to 40 papers, identifying the emotional information captured for self-reports and types of technologies employed. However, both reviews focused on broader contexts rather than educational settings and did not address children as the primary users.

In summary, previous reviews have investigated different technologies for self-reporting or wearable devices to capture emotions. However, the research primarily addressed users across various age groups, rather than focusing on a more defined target, such as children. To address this gap, we conducted a literature review to uncover the role of technology in enabling children to self-report their emotions during learning activities. More specifically, this review aims to identify: *(1)* the types of tools utilized, and *(2)* the impacts of these tools in enabling children to self-report emotions. This review contributes to a deeper understanding of how technology can empower children to self-report their emotions and identifies research directions for this underexplored topic.

3 Methods

3.1 Research Strategy

The keywords selected for our review include *"Self-report"*, *"Technology"*, *"Emotion"*, *"Children"*, and *"Learning"*. We compiled different strings and combinations for each keyword using the Boolean "OR" operator and constructed the collection of keywords using the Boolean "AND" operator, as shown in Table 1. We conducted the initial search in October 2024 across multiple databases and digital libraries, yielding 1270 records. These returned records are from ACM Digital Library (N = 7), IEEE Xplore Digital Library (N = 17), Scopus (N = 804), ERIC (N = 45), Taylor & Francis (N = 2), and Web of Science (N = 396). In early 2025, we extended the search again to include relevant studies published by December 2024 and identified additional studies (N = 11) using the snowballing technique.

3.2 Selection Procedure

We included articles presenting tools designed for or used by children to self-report their emotions in educational settings. To guide our selection process, we apply the following exclusion criteria: *(a)* the article is written in languages other than English; *(b)* the article is a literature review or does not pass the quality assessment (e.g., the information about the tool presented is too minimal to articulate its underlying technique); and *(c)* the article presents a study only involved users over 18 years old. Given that this is an underexplored field, we opted to include all relevant papers that met our inclusion criteria, regardless of publication year, to ensure a comprehensive review of the existing literature.

Table 1. Keywords and search strategy.

Keywords	The strings and combinations of keywords
Self-report	("self report*" OR "self evaluat*" OR "self access*" OR "self reflect" OR "self track*" OR "self record*" OR "quantified self")
Technology	("technology" OR "tech" OR "AI" OR "digital tool" OR "software" OR "application" OR "smart device" OR "system" OR "platform")
Emotion	("emotion*" OR "feeling*" OR "sentiment*" OR "affective state*" OR "mood" OR "emotional state*" OR "mental state*")
Children	("child*" OR "student*" OR "pupil*" OR "youth" OR "teenager*" OR "pre-teen*" OR "adolescent")
Learning	("learning" OR "learner" OR "K-12")

This approach allowed us to capture the full scope of available research without imposing temporal restrictions.

Before screening the returned records, we removed duplicates, including papers that presented the same tool to the same user group. Our paper selection followed the systematic approach proposed by Kitchenham [9]. Namely, we started by scraping based on titles, then reviewing the abstracts of the remaining records, and screening the full texts of the remaining papers. After the exclusion process, we eventually considered 23 studies that fully met the inclusion criteria.

4 Results

The 23 reviewed articles were published from 2006 to 2024, with five [10–14] published in the last five years. As shown in Table 2, the research reviewed was conducted across five continents (i.e., Europe, Asia, South America, Australia, and North America), with most of the research conducted in the United Kingdom (UK). While two studies [12,15] did not specify the setting, another two studies [16,17] took place in two different countries.

To varying degrees, all reviewed studies aimed to enable children to self-report their emotions, but most did not explicitly refer to existing emotion theories or models. Among those that did, the selection of emotions was justified based on the achievement emotion theory proposed by Pekrun [18] (e.g., [14,17,19,20]), basic emotions [21], and Desmet and Hekkert's model of product emotions [22], while only a few combined multiple references to come up with their unique set of emotions [13,15,23].

These tools have been used in diverse educational settings of varying formality. These educational contexts include small cognitive tasks (e.g., reading texts [23], matching and naming [19]), playful learning activities through educational games [16,22,24] and Audino-based tasks [13], emotional education [11,15,25] for children with special needs, and classes as part of the formal education such as language [20,26,27], design [14,28,29], science [30,31], and mathematics [17,32] course.

Table 2. Overview of the 23 reviewed studies. Countries abbreviations: UK (United Kingdom), USA (United States), DE (Germany), TR (Turkey), CH (Switzerland), IE (Ireland), NL (Netherlands), AU (Australia), IN (India), CL (Chile).

Source	Year	Age	n	Place	Learning Domain	Self-report Tool
[20]	2009	9–12	20	UK	German language	Subtle Stone
[26]	2018	14–15	12	TR	English language	Melisa
[27]	2010	12–13	15	UK	German language	Subtle Stone
[33]	2015	~18*	3	CL	n.a.	EmoBall
[10]	2021	15–17	23	AU	n.a.	Ecological Momentary Assessment
[22]	2009	8–11	25	UK	Serious game	Sorémo
[16]	2016	9–11	130	UK, DE	Serious game	Five Degrees of Happiness; Smiley Face Likert scale
[23]	2019	15–18	103	CH	Reading texts from psychology class	Self-Assessment-Manikin
[25]	2015	15–17	43	IE	Social-emotional learning	CopeSmart
[15]	2013	7+	n.a.	n.a.	Social-emotional learning	CaptureMyEmotion
[17]	2012	7–12	1189	USA, DE	Mathematics learning	AEQ-ES
[12]	2023	4–7	20	n.a.	n.a.	Child EMA app
[13]	2024	12–14	36	TR	Arduino-based learning tasks	Geneva Emotion Wheel
[19]	2014	7–11	60	IN	Matching and naming tasks	Graduated Achievement Emotions Set
[24]	2006	7–13	73	UK	Online games	Fun Toolkit – Smileyometer
[30]	2016	13–14	220	AU	Science learning	Emotion diary
[11]	2021	5–10	n.a.	USA	Social-emotional learning	Dot's World
[21]	2010	7–12	38	USA	n.a.	Electronic Diaries
[31]	2016	13–14	n.a.	AU	Science learning	Emotion diary
[32]	2014	12–16	295	USA	Mathematics learning	Wayang Outpost
[14]	2022	14–15	17	NL	Design-based learning	Fireflies
[28]	2018	12–13	9	NL	Design-based learning	Emotion card; Geneva Emotion Wheel
[29]	2019	13–14	30	NL	Design-based learning	EmoForm

4.1 Types of Tools for Self-Reporting Children's Emotions

Overall, 11 reviewed studies [10,13,16,17,19,23,24,28–31] used paper-and-pencil-based surveys to support children in self-reporting their emotions in learning. In comparison, 12 reviewed studies employed either tangible [14,20,27,33] or digital [11,12,15,21,22,25,26,32] technology-based tools. Interestingly, a few used both sensors and self-reporting for comparative purposes [10,15,23].

Paper-And-Pencil Based Tools: In our review, we define paper-and-pencil-based tools as those that can be administered as written tests, either on paper or via touchpads. Table 3 presents the appearance of tools reported in the reviewed studies. These tools offer broad accessibility to people with limited digital access and serve as a cost-effective, low-tech alternative for allowing children to self-report their emotions. For example, some studies [17,30] used this type of tool to achieve a higher number of children's engagement, while another enabled repeated self-reports through *EmoForm* [29]. Furthermore, we observed that another motivation for using these tools is the low barriers to rapid adaptation of existing or valid survey instruments or techniques. As an illustration, two reviewed studies adapted their instruments from the Achievement Emotions Questionnaire (AEQ) proposed by Pekrun et al. [34], such as the Graduated Achievement Emotions Set (GR-AES) [19], and the Achievement Emotions

Questionnaire-Elementary School (AEQ-ES) [17] by modifying AEQ to fit elementary school students' cognitive and language ability levels. While the Fun Tool Kit [24] comprises the four evaluation methods for children, the Smileyometer, Fun-o-meter, Again-Again Table, and the Fun Sorter, Five Degrees of Happiness [16] was designed based on the Smileyometer [24].

In contrast, Hirt et al. [23] compared AI-based facial emotion recognition (using FaceReader) with secondary school students' self-reports. Gao et al. [10] investigated the reliability of self-report data by examining participants' confidence in self-report responses and comparing perceived and physiological measures of student engagement using the *Empatica E4* wristband. Children wore wristbands during school hours and were reminded to complete online questionnaires about their mood three times a day at specific times. This study found that perceived self-report engagement is not always consistent with physiologically measured engagement, suggesting the potential risk of relying solely on subjective annotations as ground truth.

Additionally, these tools are often administered after a specific task or event. For example, in two studies [30,31], children were asked to fill out the emotion diary at the end of each lesson. Slightly differently, in another study, children reported their emotions during their learning processes using a self-reporting tool such as the Emotion Card [29], which was adapted from the Five Degrees of Happiness Smiley Face Likert [16]. Özture Yavuz et al. [13] was the only study to develop a predictive model of gifted students' engagement levels using self-report and behavioral data. Self-reports from multiple sources, including Geneva Emotion Wheel [35], were collected before, during (while students watched video instructions), and retrospectively regarding the task.

Digital Interactive Tools: As shown in Table 4, only 6 of 8 reviewed studies explicitly presented the interfaces of the digital web-based tools or mobile apps. We found that web-based self-reporting tools were often used to generate adaptive feedback during learning. For example, Aslan et al. [26] studied how emotion-aware interventions affect children's behavior and emotional states through the learning companion, *Melisa* [26], which collected the students' emotional self-labels and suggested various real-time interventions based on them. Self-reporting was carried out intrusively, where children were randomly asked to submit mandatory self-reports during the activity. Children could also report their emotions voluntarily at any time during the activity. *Wayang Outpost* [32] is used as part of an intelligent tutoring system (ITS). While children used the ITS to solve individual mathematics problems and self-report their emotions approximately every five minutes, the ITS includes a learning companion, which adapts its behavior based on students' self-reports and effort. While *Sorémo* [22] is an affective educational software for children self-reporting emotions. However, it is unclear whether this was implemented as part of an ITS.

Furthermore, mobile apps enabled flexibility in connecting children to other actors, such as parents, and in use scenarios beyond the classroom. For example, Electronic diaries [21] were used by children to self-report independently at home

Table 3. Paper-and-pencil based tools.

Self-Report Tool	Year	Tool Appearance	Time Point	Source
Ecological Momentary Assessment	2021	n.a.	In-the-moment	[10]
Five Degrees of Happiness Smiley Face Likert Scale	2016		Retrospective	[16]
Modified Self-Assessment-Manikin	2019	n.a.	Retrospective	[23]
Achievement Emotions Questionnaire–Elementary School (AEQ-ES)	2012	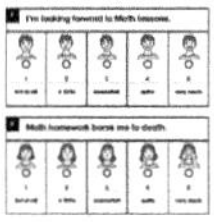	Retrospective	[17]
Geneva Emotion Wheel [35]	2024	n.a.	Retrospective	[13]
Graduated Achievement Emotions Set	2014	n.a.	Retrospective	[19]
The Fun Toolkit – Smileyometer	2006		Retrospective	[24]
Emotion Diary	2016	n.a.	Retrospective	[30]
Emotion Diary	2016	n.a.	Retrospective	[31]
Emotion Card & Modified Geneva Emotion Wheel [35]	2018	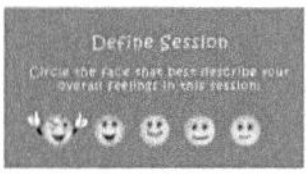	In-the-moment & Retrospective	[28]
EmoForm	2019	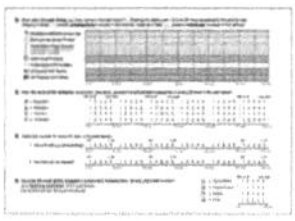	Retrospective	[29]

for one week. The electronic diary prompted the children four times a day, asking them how they were feeling. Similarly, a Child Ecological Momentary Assessment (EMA) smartphone app was used in [12] for children to complete surveys about their mood and behavior twice daily for 14 days. Parents also completed surveys twice a day to allow parent-child comparisons of responses. A chatbot-based app called *Dot's World* [11] was designed to foster emotional education exercises in children. *Dot's World* encourages children to self-report an emoticon that represents how they feel and why they choose it. A related app designed for parents allows them to become actively involved in their children's emotional development and identify needs for early intervention.

Three other digital tools, in the form of mobile apps, were developed for children's social-emotional learning. For example, *CaptureMyEmotion* [15] is designed for autistic children to take photos, videos, and sounds, report their emotions, and simultaneously sense their arousal level using a wireless sensor. *CopeSmart* [25] is introduced to help children engage in emotional self-monitoring and learn positive coping strategies.

Table 4. Digital interactive tools.

Self-Report Tool	Year	Tool Appearance	Time Point	Source
Melisa	2018		In-the-moment	[26]
Sorémo	2009		In-the-moment	[22]
CopeSmart	2015		In-the-moment	[25]
CaptureMyEmotion	2013		In-the-moment	[15]
Child EMA app	2023	n.a.	In-the-moment	[12]
Dot's World	2021	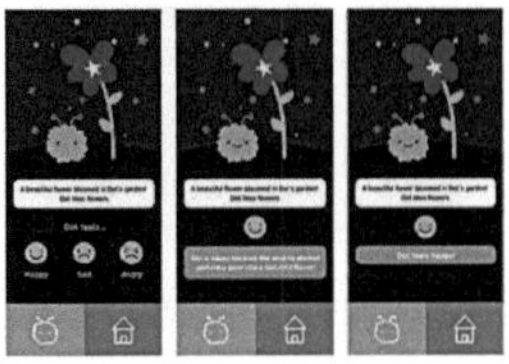	In-the-moment	[11]
Electronic Diaries	2010	n.a.	In-the-moment	[21]
Wayang Outpost	2014	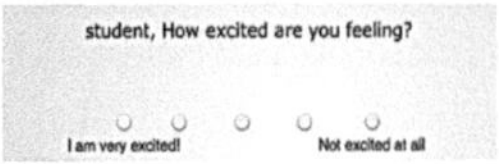	In-the-moment	[32]

Tangible Interactive Tools: We found a total of four studies featuring three tools that used tangible user interfaces (TUIs) for self-reporting (Table 5). For example, *Subtle Stone* [20,27] is a squeezable handheld tool that communicates emotions through different colors, which children decode themselves, functioning as a secret language. Children were asked to use their Subtle Stones whenever they wanted to communicate an emotion to their teacher during lessons. Similarly, *EmoBall* [33] includes the ball TUI and a base with a touch screen. Users can self-report their emotions on the touch screen, and the ball vibrates

Table 5. Tangible interactive tools.

Self-Report Tool	Year	Tool Appearance	Time Point	Source
Subtle Stone	2009		In-the-moment	[20]
Subtle Stone	2010		In-the-moment	[27]
EmoBall	2015	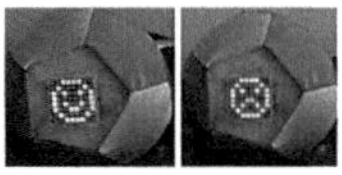	In-the-moment	[33]
Fireflies	2022	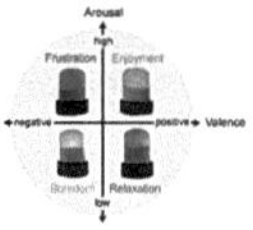	In-the-moment	[14]

once an emotion is selected. In a more contextualized setting, *FireFlies* [14] is a tangible interactive lamp that children can use to change its color to visualize and communicate their emotions to the whole class. A set of task cards was used, combined with *FireFlies*, to provide additional contextual insights into the tasks involved when a child is experiencing an emotion.

Diaries as Self-Reporting Tool: Three reviewed studies used diaries as their primary self-reporting tool. In the emotion diary, participants are encouraged to share their emotions and detail the events that led to them. Tomas et al. [31] stated that self-reporting through the emotion diary helped teachers better understand children's emotions, consistent with the finding in Ritchie et al. [30]. However, Ritchie et al. [30] also reported that the children found it annoying to complete emotion diaries at the end of each lesson. Conversely, Suveg et al. [21] proposed an electronic diary. Compared to the other two diaries, this diary did not require further explanation of an emotion, as it was designed to be more suitable for school-aged youths. Despite this adaptation, the results showed that only 60% of the electronic diary prompts were answered successfully.

4.2 Impacts of self-reporting tools

Self-Reporting Tool Integrated to Intelligent Tutoring System (ITS) and Mobile Technology: The self-reporting offered on the *Wayangng Outpost* [32] ITS appeared to have a positive effect on the students' emotional valence. Still, it remains unclear whether this is due to the empathy shown or to their ability to vent their negative emotions to the system. Aslan et al. [26] investigated the effect of emotion-aware interventions using a learning companion named Melisa. This preliminary study showed that emotion-aware interventions positively impacted the students' emotional states. Milojevich et al. [12] tested a child EMA smartphone app for reporting young children's emotions, which achieved good results, with a high response rate across child surveys and high agreement between parents and children. However, Milojevich et al. [12] raised concerns about providing young children with mobile phones or tablets, as they could be used for non-study purposes. Leijdekkers et al. [15], on the other hand, argue that mobile technology offers several advantages and emphasize the importance of leveraging its full potential.

Self-Reporting Tool Adapted from Validated Scales Using Pictorial Likert Scale: Milojevich et al. [12] adapted their mobile application for children by having a star cartoon character that read out questions and offered thumbs-up/thumbs-down or pictorial Likert scales as response options. Their results indicated a high response rate across child surveys with high agreement between parents and children. AEQ-ES [17] and *EmoForm* [29] were adapted and modified by incorporating pictorial 5-point Likert scales. AEQ-ES was shown to measure achievement emotions successfully, and the data collected from *EmoForm* was shown to be reliable.

Tangible User Interface (TUI) as Self-Reporting Tool: Our review revealed promising potential of employing TUIs to yield emotional communication and sharing beyond simply self-reporting. These tools, such as *Subtle Stone* [20,27] and *FireFlies* [14], have similar functionality, allowing children to signal their emotions by choosing a color to display on the tool. In particular, *FireFlies* enable social sharing of emotions during learning in a less disruptive yet effective way, thereby strengthening team cooperation and providing emotional relief. *Subtle Stone* allowed high school students to self-report their emotional experiences of the moment to their teacher without disrupting the lesson. Some students from the study stated that having to think about what emotion to report to their teacher helped them become more aware of how they were feeling throughout their lessons. It is worth noting that the students had different privacy needs. Since *Subtle Stone* lacks the ability to control who sees your content dynamically, some students wanted absolute privacy, while others saw benefits in sharing emotional information with others.

5 Discussion

These self-report tools, implemented in 23 reviewed studies, have been used in diverse educational settings of varying formalities, highlighting the acute need for mechanisms that allow children to account for their emotions. However, it remains unclear how AI-powered techniques, such as automated emotion recognition, can enhance children's self-reports of their emotions. For example, a study reviewed [23] showed a low agreement between automated emotion recognition and children's self-reports of interest and boredom, suggesting the risks of over-reliance on solely established emotion recognition software in intelligent tutoring and adaptive learning systems without accounting for the relevance of specific contexts. Although self-report annotations are often regarded as the ground truth for predicting emotions, another reviewed study [10] called for a better way to infer emotions rather than using subjective self-reports alone, based on their findings of some inconsistencies between perceived engagement in self-reports and physiologically measured engagement. In the age of hybrid human-AI intelligence, a research direction could be to complement self-reports with other objective measures, such as AI-powered emotion processing and recognition using algorithms and sensors [36], to reduce bias [3]. We argue that more research is needed to understand how emerging technologies, such as AI, can be leveraged to support children's emotional self-reporting across different learning tasks. For example, future research could examine how children and AI can collaborate and complement each other's strengths in recognizing emotions promptly and contextualizing events to the feelings they elicit.

Two studies [30,31] examined the use of emotion diaries as a paper-pencil-based self-reporting tool in a learning context involving high school students as participants. The concrete developmental discrepancies in children of different ages, such as language, reading, and motor skills, consequently affect their ability to provide detailed answers to questions [24]. Considering this, a potential research direction could investigate how emotion diaries can be adapted to the different ages and developmental levels of children in long-term intervention, incorporating gamified design and other considerations to motivate regular use.

A common challenge across the reviewed studies is developing an in-the-moment self-reporting tool that does not interfere with learning activities. Retrospective self-reporting has its benefits, as it avoids interrupting lectures and repetitive measures during lessons [29]. Reporting emotions in-the-moment makes it easier to connect emotions to their causes [21]. TUIs such as Subtle Stone and *FireFlies* offer in-the-moment self-reporting without interfering with learning. However, TUIs are less represented than graphic user interfaces (GUIs) for children in the reviewed studies, which aligns with findings from [7]. This indicates a potential research direction for exploring new methods of employing TUIs as self-reporting tools in learning contexts.

Social sharing of emotions through *FireFlies* has shown promising results [14], and Balaam et al. addressed privacy concerns in student-teacher emotion sharing by inventing secret color languages in *Subtle Stone* [27]. Their results showed that children tend to express different emotions depending on who they know is listening. Despite the secret language in *Subtle Stone*, it has limitations: children cannot select audiences on an ad hoc basis. Therefore, a potential research direction could involve exploring ways for children to express their emotions and control dynamically shared audiences.

We acknowledge that this work is subject to a few limitations. First, there might be some commercial tools designed for children to track their emotions that were not included in this review. Future work can expand the pool to include available commercial tools and gray literature from research reports to identify further the design patterns and qualities that enable children to self-report emotions during learning activities. Second, the choice of keywords for the search string and the focus on English-language articles may have affected the scope and coverage of the review. Future studies are encouraged to include additional languages and to explore alternative keywords to provide a more comprehensive review of the field.

6 Conclusion

This represents the first review of tools designed to enable children's emotional self-reporting in learning environments. Based on 23 reviewed papers, we present three types of tools: paper-and-pencil-based, digital interactive, and tangible interactive. Our results revealed that self-reporting tools adapted from validated scales using a pictorial Likert scale appeared to be an easy starting point, while tools integrated into intelligent tutoring systems or presented in a tangible modality offer features such as affective feedback and social sharing of emotions, providing added value to self-reporting emotions. Despite self-reporting being a widely adopted approach for capturing emotions, tools designed for children in learning contexts remain limited. We call for future research to explore ways to use tangible interfaces, complement self-reporting with other subjective measures such as sensors, and integrate AI augmentations, e.g., facial analysis, to enhance personalized emotional support.

Acknowledgments. We want to thank the support from the UTFORSK project of the Norwegian Directorate for Higher Education and Skills (HK-dir) under project number: UTF-2021/10186; Start-up Fund from The Hong Kong Polytechnic University under project number: P0058157; and Exten.D.T.2 - Extending Design Thinking with Emerging Digital Technologies, which has received funding from the European Union's Horizon Europe Framework Programme for Research and Innovation under Grant Agreement No. 101060231. Views and opinions expressed are, however, those of the authors only and do not necessarily reflect those of the European Union. Neither the European Union nor the granting authority can be held responsible for them.

Disclosure of Interests. The authors have no competing interests to declare that are relevant to the content of this article.

References

1. Domitrovich, C.E., Durlak, J.A., Staley, K.C., Weissberg, R.P.: Social-emotional competence: an essential factor for promoting positive adjustment and reducing risk in school children. Child Dev. **88**(2), 408–416 (2017)
2. Vistorte, A.O.R., Deroncele-Acosta, A., Ayala, J.L.M., Barrasa, A., López-Granero, C., Martí-González, M.: Integrating artificial intelligence to assess emotions in learning environments: a systematic literature review. Front. Psychol. **15**, 1387089 (2024)
3. Pekrun, R.: Self-report is indispensable to assess students' learning. Frontline Learn. Res. **8**(3), 185–193 (2020)
4. Salloum, S.A., Alomari, K.M., Alfaisal, A.M., Aljanada, R.A., Basiouni, A.: Emotion recognition for enhanced learning: using ai to detect students' emotions and adjust teaching methods. Smart Learn. Environ. **12**(1), 21 (2025)

5. Ba, S., Xiao, H.: Measuring emotions in education using wearable devices: a systematic review. Comput. Educ. **200**, 104797 (2023)
6. Saganowski, S., Perz, B., Polak, A.G., Kazienko, P.: Emotion recognition for everyday life using physiological signals from wearables: a systematic literature review. IEEE Trans. Affect. Comput. **14**(3), 1876–1897 (2022)
7. Fuentes, C., Gerea, C., Herskovic, V., Marques, M., Rodríguez, I., Rossel, P.O.: User interfaces for self-reporting emotions: a systematic literature review. In: Garcia-Chamizo, J., Fortino, G., Ochoa, S. (eds) International Conference on Ubiquitous Computing and Ambient Intelligence, pp. 321–333. Springer (2015). https://doi.org/10.1007/978-3-319-26401-1_30
8. Fuentes, C., Herskovic, V., Rodríguez, I., Gerea, C., Marques, M., Rossel, P.O.: A systematic literature review about technologies for self-reporting emotional information. J. Ambient Intell. Hum. Comput. **8**(4), 593–606 (2017)
9. Kitchenham, B., et al.: Procedures for Performing Systematic Reviews, vol. 33, pp. 1–26. Keele University, Keele, UK (2004)
10. Gao, N., Rahaman, M.S., Shao, W., Salim, F.D.: Investigating the reliability of self-report data in the wild: the quest for ground truth. In: Adjunct Proceedings of the 2021 ACM International Joint Conference on Pervasive and Ubiquitous Computing and Proceedings of the 2021 ACM International Symposium on Wearable Computers, pp. 237–242 (2021)
11. Ryu, S.J., Tan, J.M., Wohn, D.Y.: Dot's World: an emotional development support platform for children. In: Proceedings of the 20th Annual ACM Interaction Design and Children Conference, pp. 568–572 (2021)
12. Milojevich, H.M., et al.: Building an ecological momentary assessment smartphone app for 4-to 10-year-old children: a pilot study. Plos ONE **18**(8), e0290148 (2023)
13. Yavuz, G.Ö., Akçapınar, G., Sarıca, H.Ç., Usluel, Y.K.: Investigating features that play a role in predicting gifted student engagement using machine learning: video log and self-report data. Educ. Inf. Technol. **29**(13), 16317–16343 (2024)
14. Zhang, F., Markopoulos, P., An, P., Schüll, M.: Social sharing of task-related emotions in design-based learning: challenges and opportunities. Int. J. Child-Comput. Interact. **31**, 100378 (2022)
15. Leijdekkers, P., Gay, V., Wong, F.: CaptureMyEmotion: a mobile app to improve emotion learning for autistic children using sensors. In: Proceedings of the 26th IEEE International Symposium on Computer-Based Medical Systems, pp. 381–384. IEEE (2013)
16. Hall, L., Hume, C., Tazzyman, S.: Five degrees of happiness: Effective smiley face likert scales for evaluating with children. In: Proceedings of the the 15th International Conference on Interaction Design and Children, pp. 311–321 (2016)
17. Lichtenfeld, S., Pekrun, R., Stupnisky, R.H., Reiss, K., Murayamam, K.: Measuring students' emotions in the early years: the achievement emotions questionnaire-elementary school (AEQ-ES). Learn. Individ. Differ. **22**(2), 190–201 (2012)
18. Pekrun, R., Stephens, E.J.: Achievement emotions: a control-value approach. Soc. Pers. Psychol. Compass **4**(4), 238–255 (2010)
19. Raccanello, D., Brondino, M., Pasini, M., et al.: Achievement emotions in technology enhanced learning: development and validation of self-report instruments in the Italian context. IxD&A **23**, 68–81 (2014)
20. Alsmeyer, M., Luckin, R., Good, J., Harris, E.: Supporting affective communication in the classroom with the subtle stone. Int. J. Learn. Technol. **4**(3–4), 188–215 (2009)

21. Suveg, C., Payne, M., Thomassin, K., Jacob, M.L.: Electronic diaries: a feasible method of assessing emotional experiences in youth? J. Psychopathol. Behav. Assess. **32**(1), 57–67 (2010)
22. Girard, S., Johnson, H.: Developing affective educational software products: Sorémo, a new method for capturing emotional states. J. Eng. Des. **20**(5), 493–510 (2009)
23. Hirt, F., Werlen, E., Moser, I., Bergamin, P.: Measuring emotions during learning: lack of coherence between automated facial emotion recognition and emotional experience. Open Comput. Sci. **9**(1), 308–317 (2019)
24. Read, J.C., MacFarlane, S.: Using the fun toolkit and other survey methods to gather opinions in child computer interaction. In: Proceedings of the 2006 Conference on Interaction Design and Children, pp. 81–88 (2006)
25. Kenny, R., Dooley, B., Fitzgerald, A.: Feasibility of "copesmart": a telemental health app for adolescents. JMIR Mental Health **2**(3), e4370 (2015)
26. Aslan, S., Alyuz, N., Okur, E., Mete, S.E., Oktay, E., Esme, A.A.: Effect of emotion-aware interventions on students' behavioral and emotional states. Educ. Technol. Res. Dev. **66**(6), 1399–1413 (2018)
27. Balaam, M., Fitzpatrick, G., Good, J., Luckin, R.: Exploring affective technologies for the classroom with the subtle stone. In: Proceedings of the SIGCHI Conference on Human Factors in Computing Systems, pp. 1623–1632 (2010)
28. Zhang, F., Markopoulos, P., Bekker, T.: The role of children's emotions during design-based learning activity. In: Proceedings of the 10th International Conference on Computer Supported Education (CSEDU 2018), Funchal, Portugal, pp. 15–17 (2018)
29. Zhang, F., Markopoulos, P., Bekker, T., Schüll, M., Paule-Ruíz, M.: EmoForm: capturing children's emotions during design based learning. Proc. FabLearn **2019**, 18–25 (2019)
30. Ritchie, S.M., Hudson, P., Bellocchi, A., Henderson, S., King, D., Tobin, K.: Evolution of self-reporting methods for identifying discrete emotions in science classrooms. Cult. Stud. Sci. Educ. **11**(3), 577–593 (2016)
31. Tomas, L., Rigano, D., Ritchie, S.M.: Students' regulation of their emotions in a science classroom. J. Res. Sci. Teach. **53**(2), 234–260 (2016)
32. Wixon, M., Arroyo, I.: When the question is part of the answer: examining the impact of emotion self-reports on student emotion. In: Dimitrova, V., Kuflik, T., Chin, D., Ricci, F., Dolog, P., Houben, GJ. (eds) International Conference on User Modeling, Adaptation, and Personalization, pp. 471–477. Springer, Cham (2014). https://doi.org/10.1007/978-3-319-08786-3_42
33. Fuentes, C., Rodríguez, I., Herskovic, V.: EmoBall: a study on a tangible interface to self-report emotional information considering digital competences. In: Bravo, J., Hervas, R., Villarreal, V. (eds) Ambient Intelligence for Health, pp. 189–200. Springer, Cham (2015). https://doi.org/10.1007/978-3-319-26508-7_19
34. Pekrun, R., Goetz, T., Frenzel, A.C., Barchfeld, P., Perry, R.P.: Measuring emotions in students' learning and performance: the achievement emotions questionnaire (AEQ). Contemp. Educ. Psychol. **36**(1), 36–48 (2011)
35. Scherer, K.R., Shuman, V., Fontaine, J.R.J., Soriano, C.: The GRID meets the Wheel Assessing emotional feeling via self-report. In: Components of Emotional Meaning: A Sourcebook, vol. 53, pp. 1689–1699 (2013)
36. Possaghi, I., et al.: Integrating multi-modal learning analytics dashboard in K-12 education: insights for enhancing orchestration and teacher decision-making. Smart Learn. Environ. **12**(1), 1–34 (2025)

Responsible Video Game Development for Gaming Disorder Prevention: From Review Insights to the GameDev MentorHub Proposal

Federica Caruso[1(✉)], Sara Peretti[2], Valentino Giona[1], and Tania Di Mascio[1]

[1] Department of Information Engineering, Computer Science and Mathematics, University of L'Aquila, L'Aquila 67100, Italy
{federica.caruso1,tania.dimascio}@univaq.it, valentino.giona@student.univaq.it

[2] Center of Excellence DEWS, University of L'Aquila, L'Aquila 67100, Italy
sara.peretti@univaq.it

Abstract. Gaming Disorder (GD) has been recognized by the World Health Organization as a behavioral addiction with severe consequences, especially among adolescents. Current prevention approaches are mainly downstream, implemented after video games are released and placing responsibility on players rather than on upstream development choices. To investigate how GD prevention is currently supported upstream, this paper first presents an integrative review of tools and education and training programs in video game development, as these two resources reflect how developers are concretely equipped in their practice. The review highlights a double gap: existing tools improve efficiency, collaboration, and engagement but lack approaches to address GD risks, while education and training provide technical and creative skills but rarely include GD prevention as a learning outcome. Then, to respond to this double gap, this paper presents GameDev MentorHub, an "on-the-job" Technology-Enhanced Learning tool that aims to embed GD prevention directly into the video game development process, providing development support, real-time GD risk evaluation, and context-aware learning grounded in psychological science. By aligning GD prevention with everyday development practice and fostering ongoing knowledge development, the proposed tool seeks to complement existing downstream approaches and advance upstream approaches to prevent GD.

Keywords: Responsible Video Game Development · Gaming Disorder Prevention · Technology-Enhanced Learning · "on-the-job" Learning · Developers Education

1 Introduction

Video games are one of the most pervasive forms of digital entertainment, particularly among adolescents, who represent a substantial proportion of the global

B. Fernández-Manjón et al. (Eds.): SETE 2025/ICWL 2025, LNCS 16425, pp. 145–159, 2026.
https://doi.org/10.1007/978-981-92-0042-9_11

player population [54]. A growing body of research has highlighted the positive impact of playing video games on cognitive skills, creativity, and social interaction [39,70]. At the same time, however, a ever-increasing number of players experience problematic gaming behavior that, in severe cases, may escalate into Gaming Disorder (GD), classified by the World Health Organization (WHO) in the 11th revision of the International Classification of Diseases (ICD-11) as a behavioral addiction that causes severe impairment in personal, social, or educational functioning [67]. Although GD can occur at any age, adolescents are consistently reported as the most susceptible group, being disproportionately represented in prevalence data [16,30]. This susceptibility makes the potential consequences of GD particularly critical, since difficulties such as sleep disruption, reduced academic performance, mental health problems, and social isolation directly interfere with developmental milestones and overall well-being during this life stage [40,42,56]. As a result, GD has increasingly been recognized as a *public health concern* involving multiple stakeholders, including caregivers and educators, health authorities and policymakers, as well as the video gaming industry and video game developers, although debates often focus on assigning *responsibility* to these actors rather than promoting more effective prevention approaches [19,30,34,56].

This emphasis on responsibility is reflected in current GD prevention approaches, which remain largely *downstream*, meaning that they are applied *after* video games have already been developed. In particular, these approaches are mostly reactive and rely on self-regulation, thereby placing the burden of responsibility on players, particularly adolescents who are the most susceptible group, to manage problematic gaming behavior [17,40]. For example, among current GD prevention approaches, Digital Self-Control Tools (DSCTs), such as screen timers and app blockers, are the most widespread adopted and exemplify its downstream nature, since they require players to assume ongoing responsibility for self-regulation after being exposed to video games designed to maximize engagement, thereby reinforcing an approach that overlooks the upstream design choices contributing to problematic gaming behavior [1,52]. Beyond DSCTs, other current GD prevention approaches include parental control [45], public awareness campaigns promoted by health authorities [41], and, in some countries, regulatory measures such as playtime restrictions or bans on loot boxes [4,13,14,61]. In parallel, psychological research has identified several video game features associated with GD risk (e.g., [26,29,31,36,42,51,53,55]) and has proposed scales and checklists to assess them [10,50]. However, these findings are typically applied post hoc, after a video game has already been developed, and remain largely disconnected from actual video game development practice [12,26,58,61].

Thus, the purely downstream nature of current GD prevention approaches, together with the persistent disconnection between research findings and development practice, underlines the need for complementary *upstream* prevention approaches that promote responsible video game development grounded in research findings on GD risks. At the core of such upstream prevention approaches are video game developers, broadly understood to include programmers, designers, artists, and other professionals directly involved in the video game development process [58]. As central actors in shaping video game features, developers are frequently identified, along with the video gaming industry more broadly, in academic and policy debates as partly responsible for exacerbating GD risks [9,61], which raises the question of *what tools and knowledge they can draw upon in practice to prevent such risks during video game development?*. To address this research question, an integrative review was conducted of both the tools widely employed in the video game development process and the education and training programs through which knowledge is acquired. The results of this review, presented in Sect. 2, highlight a double gap affecting upstream GD prevention in current video game development practice: *(i)* tools that support video game development focus on efficiency, collaboration, and sustaining engagement, but offer no explicit support to identify or mitigate GD risk; *(ii)* education and training programs provide video game developers with solid technical and creative skills, but they rarely incorporate knowledge about responsible video game development or GD prevention as explicit learning outcomes.

To address this double gap, this paper introduces GameDev MentorHub [11], an "on-the-job" Technology-Enhanced Learning (TEL) tool designed to serve as an upstream prevention approach by making GD prevention a seamlessly integrated part of the video game development practice (as detailed in Sect. 3). Indeed, the proposed tool, built on the Multiperspective Framework [12], pursues a double goal: *(i)* serving as a development support *tool* in which GD prevention is an explicit and integral dimension of the video game development process while *(ii)* fostering *knowledge* acquisition on GD risks through experiential learning supported by evidence-based resources, thereby knowledge acquisition occurs *on-the-job*, through the tool adopted in the video game development process, aligning learning directly with practice.

2 Review of Tools and Knowledge in Video Game Development Practice

This section presents an integrative review [66] of the existing tools currently used in the video game development process, as well as the education and training programs through which developers acquire knowledge. The review combines academic literature (e.g., [2,6,15,18,23,43,46–48,63,65]) with practice-oriented sources, including developer communities (e.g. Reddit [49], Discord [21]) and industry reports from professional associations (e.g., [28,35]), in order to provide a comprehensive perspective that integrates scholarly knowledge and real-world practice and assesses the tools and knowledge developers are equipped with, particularly in relation to GD prevention.

2.1 Tools in the Video Game Development Process

Video game developers require a heterogeneous set of tools due to the interdisciplinary and iterative nature of the development process, which combines artistic, technical, and design disciplines and must adapt to evolving requirements [2,6,23]. These tools comprise both video game-specific ones, such as video game engines and content authoring tools for constructing game worlds [57,65], and general-purpose ones, such as version control systems and project management software [47,48], which are widely used across other application domains. These two categories are employed in different ways across the main stages of the video development process, commonly identified as (1) *pre-production*, which covers conceptual design, planning, and documentation; (2) *production*, which entails the implementation of the video game and the integration of graphics, audio, and gameplay features; and (3) *post-production*, which focuses on quality assurance, refinement, and release support [2,43,46]. The tools commonly associated with each stage of the video game development process are outlined below, with attention to those most widely adopted in practice:

1. **Pre-production** is the stage in which the conceptual foundations of a video game are established and the overall project is planned. Tools in this stage mainly serve four functions: project management and coordination, conceptual design and documentation, narrative design, and prototyping [35,43,63,65]. Project management software is central to coordination, with video game developers relying on either domain-specific solutions (e.g., *HacknPlan, Favro*) or widely adopted general-purpose tools such as *Jira* or *Trello*, the latter being especially popular among small teams and independent developers, as reported both in industry surveys and community discussions [28,49,63]. Instead, conceptual design and documentation are often supported through flexible platforms like *Miro*, *Mural*, or *Notion*, which enable collaborative brainstorming and visualization [49,60,62]. A central outcome of these activities is the Game Design Document (GDD) [15,18], traditionally compiled in static formats but today more frequently maintained through collaborative platforms (e.g., *Google Docs*, *Confluence*) or supported by project management software such as *HacknPlan*, which integrate documentation into coordination functions [21,49]. Rather, narrative design benefits from dedicated authoring tools such as *Articy:draft* and *Twine* that facilitate the structuring of branching dialogues. Finally, prototyping activities, ranging from low-fidelity sketches to advanced gameplay simulations, utilize a broad range of tools. Lightweight solutions such as *Balsamiq* and *Figma* are frequently highlighted in practice-oriented sources as entry points for small teams and independent developers [21,49], while more advanced tools such as *World Machine* and *Machinations.io* support specialized prototyping of terrains, objects, and gameplay mechanics [21,49]. Recently, AI-based tools have also begun to support pre-production activities [3,5,28,68,69]. Generative AI-based tools such as *Scenario* or *Ludo.ai* are used to generate concept art and video game ideas, while large language models like GPT are increasingly employed to assist in drafting design documents and prototyping narrative elements. In parallel, image generation tools such as *Stable Diffusion* or *MidJourney* are adopted to rapidly produce concept art and mood boards that support the early stages of ideation [69].

2. **Production** is the stage in which the video game is implemented and its audiovisual components (commonly referred to as *assets* in video game development practice) are created and integrated into a playable form. Tools in this stage mainly serve three core functions: software development, audiovisual component creation, and component integration supported by version control systems [23,63,65]. Game engines are central to software development, with *Unity* and *Unreal Engine* dominating video game industry use, and *Godot* gaining increasing adoption among independent developers thanks to its open-source nature [28,35,49]. These engines are commonly used in combination with general-purpose Integrated Development Environments (IDEs) such as *Visual Studio* or *Rider*, which support coding and debugging. Then, the audiovisual component creation function relies on specialized tools for 2D and 3D graphics, animation, and audio, including *Adobe Photoshop* and *Illustrator* for 2D, *ZBrush*,*Adobe Substance 3D*, *Blender* and *Maya* for 3D modeling and animation, and *Audacity* or *FMOD Studio* for audio design [57,65]. Finally, component integration and collaborative development functions are supported by version control systems such as *Git*, *GitHub*, *GitLab*, or *Perforce*, which are essential for managing both source code and large audiovisual files in team-based projects [23,48]. During production, AI-based tools are being increasingly applied to accelerate software development and the creation of audiovisual components. Examples include *Promethean AI* and *Meshy*, which generate 3D environments and models, as well as GPT-based systems that provide assistance with coding tasks and implementing gameplay mechanics. In practice, code completion assistants such as *GitHub Copilot* are also increasingly used to support scripting and debugging in production pipelines [28,69].
3. **Post-production** is the stage in which the video game is refined, tested, and prepared for release. Tools in this stage mainly serve three core functions: quality assurance and testing, performance optimization, and release and player monitoring [22,23,43,63]. Quality assurance and testing rely on bug tracking and test management tools such as *Bugzilla* or *TestRail*, which support the systematic reporting and resolution of issues. Automated testing frameworks and continuous integration systems (e.g., *Jenkins*, *TeamCity*) are also adopted to streamline build validation and detect regressions early in the pipeline [48,65]. Then, performance optimization is supported by profiling and debugging tools integrated in game engines (e.g., *Unity Profiler*, *Unreal Insights*) or provided as standalone solutions (e.g., *RenderDoc*), which allow developers to identify bottlenecks in graphics rendering, memory management, or CPU/GPU usage [23,57]. Finally, release and player monitoring rely on analytics platforms [22], such as *Unity Analytics*, *GameAnalytics*, or *Steamworks*, which enable developers to track player behavior and engagement metrics after video game launch. In fact, given the commercial dependence of the video game industry on long-term engagement and monetization, behavioral analytics has become a standard component of the video game development process, shaping decisions on balancing and content updates. These tools are frequently complemented by crash reporting tools

like *Backtrace* or *Sentry*, which provide real-time data on software stability in the wild [23,59]. At this stage, too, AI-based tools are emerging. Recent studies have explored the use of GPT models for detecting glitches and bugs, analyzing player feedback, and synthesizing behavioral data to inform balancing decisions and content updates. AI has also been applied to sentiment analysis of player reviews and community discussions, providing additional insights to guide post-release refinements [69].

Taken together, these reviewed tools constitute the technological backbone of the contemporary video game development process and are widely adopted across both large studios and independent teams [2,6,23,49,63]. Although indispensable in the pre-production, production, and post-production stages, their primary focus is on efficiency, collaboration, creativity, and sustaining player engagement and retention [6,23,63], rather than on addressing risks linked to GD. This tendency is reinforced by the fact that the set of tools is heterogeneous and fragmented, as each tool is designed for a specific function, and their interoperability relies on external integrations or manual workflows rather than on a *unified hub* [15,24,44]. This fragmentation complicates the development of a consistent and integrated view of GD-related risks across the entire video game development process [24,44,48]. At the same time, the growing adoption of AI-based tools accelerates the video game development process but does not provide preventive functionalities, as these applications concentrate on coding assistance, assets creation, or playtesting rather than on identifying or mitigating video game features associated with GD [3,5,68,69]. Consequently, the preventive role of the tools currently used in the video game development process remains largely indirect, as their contribution to GD prevention depends entirely on how they are used in practice. As a result, GD prevention becomes contingent on video game developers' knowledge and practices, revealing a structural gap in current video game development tools in terms of explicit support for GD prevention.

2.2 Education and Training on Video Game Development

Education and training play a crucial role in shaping the knowledge and practices of both current and future video game developers. Academic curricula, professional courses, and industry-led initiatives provide the primary channels through which video game developers acquire technical expertise, creative skills, and business-oriented competencies [32,35,64]. Over the last two decades, these education and training programs have expanded significantly, reflecting both the economic growth of the video game industry and the recognition of video game development as a distinct academic and professional field [23,33]. The scope and limitations of current education and training in relation to GD prevention are examined across three complementary dimensions: (1) the structure and orientation of academic curricula and professional courses, (2) video game developers' perspectives as expressed in community surveys, and (3) emerging initiatives that aim to integrate responsibility and awareness of design risks into learning practices. Each dimension is discussed in turn below:

1. **Academic curricula and Professional Courses.** Research and institutional reviews indicate that video game development academic curricula are predominantly structured around four knowledge pillars: creativity and design, technical programming and engineering, audiovisual production, and business and marketing strategies [23,24,33,64]. These knowledge pillars reflect the interdisciplinary nature of the field and align closely with video game industry priorities such as innovation, production efficiency, and sustaining player engagement and retention [23,32,33,64]. A comparative perspective highlights that this orientation is consistent across geographical contexts. In Europe, Tunnel and Norbisrath [64] show that bachelor's curricula in game development overwhelmingly emphasize technical, creative, and business competencies, while offering little systematic integration of responsible design or GD prevention. A similar picture emerges from North America and Canada, where the HEVGA 2025 report documents that university programs remain centered on technical, artistic, and business aspects, with limited attention to ethical, psychological, or public health dimensions [32]. Taken together, these studies indicate that while curricula provide video developers with strong technical and creative knowledge, they rarely address the potential health risks associated with specific development practices, leaving GD prevention outside the scope of formal education.
2. **Video Game Developers' Perspectives.** Surveys conducted within the video game development community corroborate this academic evidence by providing the viewpoint of video game developers themselves. The IGDA Developer Satisfaction Survey (2023), which gathered responses from more than 3,000 developers worldwide, reports that while developers acknowledge the importance of ethical and player well-being issues, such concerns are not consistently addressed in education or professional development pathways [35]. Similar results emerge from the 2025 State of the Game Industry Report conducted by the Game Developers Conference, based on a comparable sample of developers, which highlights that professional development and training remain primarily focused on production skills and sustaining engagement rather than on responsible practices or GD prevention [28].
3. **Emerging initiatives**. In recent years, some learning-oriented initiatives have been dedicated to integrating responsibility into education and training on video game development. Frommel et al. [27] highlight initiatives that explicitly incorporate critical reflection on harms and benefits of video game design into curricula, fostering students' ability to balance engagement goals with responsible practices. Aagaard et al. [1] propose design frameworks that enable developers to recognize and avoid dark patterns while still achieving high levels of engagement. In parallel, ongoing discussions around ethical guidelines and responsible game design (e.g., the Ethical Games Initiative [25], Birk et al. [7]) illustrate a growing awareness in the field, although the systematic translation into mainstream education and training programs remains limited.

Therefore, the review of current education and training programs in video game development suggests that they are primarily aligned with the video game industry's priorities, providing video game developers with robust technical and creative knowledge [23,32,33,64]. However, they do not systematically integrate knowledge related to GD prevention, leaving awareness dependent on the individual sensitivity of developers rather than being an expected learning outcome. As a consequence, developers are well prepared to sustain player engagement and retention, but insufficiently equipped to identify and mitigate video game features empirically associated with GD [26,29,51,55].
Therefore, as mentioned in Sect. 1, this integrative review evidences the existence of a double gap in current video game development practice:

(i) As highlighted in Sect. 2.1, current tools are primarily oriented toward efficiency and sustaining engagement without explicit support for GD prevention;
(ii) as highlighted in Sect. 2.2, education and training provide strong technical and creative knowledge but do not systematically integrate knowledge on GD prevention.

Taken together, these findings demonstrate that developers lack both technological and educational upstream support for translating evidence on GD risks into responsible video game development practices. This double gap can suggest why GD prevention has remained largely downstream, outlining the need for complementary upstream approaches. It also provides the rationale for introducing GameDev MentorHub, presented in the next section, as an upstream approach integrated into the video game development process.

3 GameDev MentorHub

GameDev MentorHub is designed as an "on-the-job" TEL tool that embeds situated, experiential learning on GD prevention directly into the video game development process [11]. Unlike traditional approaches, in which education and training are separated from video game development practice, GameDev MentorHub aims to integrate knowledge acquisition with everyday video game development activities, enabling developers to learn about preventing GD while working with tools on real projects. In this way, it addresses the double gap identified in Sect. 2, by providing developers with a tool that explicitly supports GD prevention and by embedding knowledge acquisition into video game development workflows rather than leaving it dependent on developer sensitivity.

Theoretical foundation

The conceptual foundation of GameDev MentorHub builds on the *Multiperspective Framework* [12], conceived as a *knowledge base* that bridges real-world video game development practice (e.g., [2,43,46,58]) with evidence-based findings from psychology science on GD (e.g., [51,55]). Specifically, this framework structures the video game development process into four interconnected levels spanning the three main stages of pre-production, production and post-production [2,43,46]: (1) the *Target Audience Level*, focusing on demographic and cognitive profiles of intended users (e.g., age, vulnerabilities); (2) the *Abstract Level*, which considers both Gaming Aspects (e.g., rules, mechanics, progression systems) and Serious Aspects (e.g., psychological wellbeing, supervision); (3) the *Concrete Level*, covering presentation and technology choices (e.g., interface, input/output devices, interaction models); and (4) the *Actual Level*, where prototypes and final implementations are created and evaluated, including usability and GD risk assessment. Moreover, the development pathway defined by the framework aims to minimize GD risks by prioritizing the game elements most influential in shaping adolescents' problematic gaming behaviors. Indeed, it maps the functional, temporal, and GD-related relationships among these elements and embeds targeted, evidence-based recommendations within each level, thereby providing a structured pathway for developers to identify how specific video game features may contribute to or mitigate GD risks. A detailed description of the Multiperspective Framework is provided in [12].

The Proposed Tool

The GameDev MentorHub tool [11] operationalizes the Multiperspective Framework by providing an interactive environment that represents the video game development process as a graph. In this representation, *nodes* correspond to framework elements, while *edges* encode functional, temporal, and GD-related relationships. The disclosure of nodes is progressive, first at the framework level and then by GD-related priority, guiding developers to work through video game elements in a structured and risk-aware sequence. At each node, developers can define design choices, reflect on their implications, and attach relevant resources while receiving targeted micro-learning content, reflective prompts, and evidence-based recommendations. In this way, the tool embeds situated learning directly into the workflow, supporting developers in making informed design choices regarding the prevention of GD.

Unlike current fragmented tools, GameDev MentorHub is conceived as a centralized *hub* that connects functionalities usually distributed across different tools employed in the various stages of the video game development process. By integrating project management, design documentation, collaboration features, and evidence-based recommendations within a single graph-based environment, and by supporting future interoperability with widely adopted tools such as Unity, Blender, GitHub, or Figma [11], it aims to transform a dispersed set of tools into a unified workflow explicitly oriented toward GD-aware video game development. A further innovation under development is the AI-based component, designed to act as a *mentor* by analyzing video game developers' input in real time, identifying potentially GD-prone patterns, and suggesting mitigation strategies or additional resources. While a first set of core functionalities (e.g., project management, documentation, role management, and collaboration features) has already been implemented, advanced AI-driven GD risk assessment and full interoperability with external tools remain at the prototypical stage and will require further validation in real-world settings [11]. A detailed description of the GameDev MentorHub tool and its functionalities is provided in [11].

Therefore, GameDev MentorHub aims to directly address the double gap identified in Sect. 2. On the side of *tools*, it introduces preventive functionalities absent from current video game development tools, such as real-time GD risk assessment and embedded evidence-based guidance, transforming tools from neutral productivity enhancers into active supports for responsible video game development. On the side of *knowledge*, it integrates micro-learning and critical reflection directly into the workflow, ensuring that GD prevention becomes an explicit outcome of the video game development process rather than an optional, sensitivity-driven practice. This integration is grounded in established perspectives in TEL that emphasize the effectiveness of situated and experiential approaches. It reflects the principles of *cognitive apprenticeship*, which situates learning in authentic contexts through modeling, coaching, and reflection-in-action [8], resonates with Kolb's *experiential learning* cycle of experience, reflection, conceptualization, and experimentation [37], and is consistent with previous TEL initiatives designed to support experiential and reflective learning (e.g., [20]). In line with the notion of *situated learning*, which emphasizes that knowledge is best acquired through participation in communities of practice [38], GameDev MentorHub integrates GD prevention into everyday video game development workflows. By doing so, it provides not only a technological support system but also a pedagogical foundation that increases the likelihood that GD prevention knowledge is applied consistently in real-world video game development practice.

Practical implications

The practical implications of GameDev MentorHub can be articulated along the two dimensions of the double gap, namely *tools* and *knowledge*. On the side of *tools*, for video game developers, the prototype suggests that upstream GD prevention approaches could be embedded into everyday video game development practice, reducing dependence on individual sensitivity and minimizing the need for additional external training. At the team and industry level, it points to the possibility of standardizing responsible video game development practices, thereby mitigating reputational risks and anticipating potential regulatory demands. On the side of *knowledge*, GameDev MentorHub could complement existing education and training programs by turning GD prevention into a situated and continuous learning process within development practice, rather than leaving it as an optional or extra-curricular activity. Finally, for research purposes, by unifying documentation, reflection, and evidence-based guidance within a single hub, the tool offers the prospect of generating real-time data on development decisions, thereby supporting the study of upstream prevention approaches in authentic video game development practice.

While these implications remain prospective, given that GameDev MentorHub is still at a prototypical stage, they illustrate how embedding preventive functions into tools and situated learning into knowledge pathways may contribute to addressing the double gap identified through an integrative review detailed in Sect. 2.

4 Conclusions and Future Directions

This paper examined how tools and education shape video game development practice in relation to GD prevention. The integrative review identified a double gap: *(i)* while existing development tools are effective in supporting efficiency, collaboration, and engagement, they do not provide explicit mechanisms for upstream GD prevention; likewise, *(ii)* current education and training programs equip developers with strong technical and creative knowledge but rarely integrate knowledge on GD prevention as a structured learning outcome.

Therefore, in this paper, GameDev MentorHub is introduced as a prototype designed to address this double gap by combining GD preventive functions with situated, experiential learning directly embedded in the video game development process. Although still in its early stages of implementation, it illustrates a possible pathway for transforming GD prevention from an optional, individually driven practice into an integrated component of the video game development process.

Future work will focus on empirical evaluation in both educational and professional settings, carried out in collaboration with video game industry partners. Within this context, a central question will be whether upstream GD prevention can be effectively integrated into video game development practice, demonstrating that these will not reduce player engagement and retention, and possibly even contribute to them. Addressing this question will be critical to understand whether GD prevention can become not only ethically desirable but also practically viable within the video game industry.

Acknowledgments. This work has been funded by the European Union - NextGenerationEU under the Italian Ministry of University and Research (MUR) National Innovation Ecosystem grant ECS00000041 - VITALITY - CUP E13C22001060006.

Disclosure of Interests. The authors have no competing interests to declare that are relevant to the content of this article.

References

1. Aagaard, J., Knudsen, M.E.C., Bækgaard, P., Doherty, K.: A game of dark patterns: designing healthy, highly-engaging mobile games. In: CHI Conference on Human Factors in Computing Systems Extended Abstracts (2022)
2. Aleem, S., Capretz, L.F., Ahmed, F.: Game development software engineering process life cycle: a systematic review. J. Software Eng. Res. Dev. **4**(1), 6 (2016)
3. Alharthi, S.A.: Generative ai in game design: enhancing creativity or constraining innovation? J. Intell. **13**(6), 60 (2025)

4. BBC News: Video game loot boxes declared illegal under Belgium gambling laws (2018). https://www.bbc.com/news/technology-43906306. Accessed 13 Jan 2025
5. Begemann, A.: Do you know where your games come from? Artificial intelligence and game development. Int. J. Emerging Disruptive Innov. Educ. VISIONARIUM **2**(1), 8 (2024)
6. Berg Marklund, B., Engström, H., Hellkvist, M., Backlund, P.: What empirically based research tells us about game development. Comput. Games J. **8**, 179–198 (2019)
7. Birk, M.V., Van Der Hof, S., Hodent, C., Gerling, K., Van Rooij, A.J.: Behavioural design in video games: Ethical, legal, and health impact on players. In: Extended Abstracts of the 2023 CHI Conference on Human Factors in Computing Systems. New York, NY, USA (2023). https://doi.org/10.1145/3544549.3573801
8. Brown, J.S., Collins, A., Duguid, P.: Situated cognition and the culture of learning. Educ. Res. **18**(1), 32–42 (1989)
9. Caffarone, A.: Virtual gaming, actual damage: video game design that intentionally and successfully addicts users constitutes civil battery. Duke Law & Technology Review, Forthcoming (2023)
10. Carmona, A., Carbonell, X., Bonilla, I., Ivern, J., Chamarro, A.: Video game structural features are related to internet gaming disorder and motivations of play: design and validation of the video game structure scale (VGSS). Int. J. Mental Health Add., 1–19 (2025)
11. Caruso, F., Peretti, S., Pino, M., Di Mascio, T.: GameDev MentorHub: an "on-the-job" TEL environment for video game developers. In: Methodologies and Intelligent Systems for Technology Enhanced Learning, 15th International Conference. MIS4TEL 2025. Lecture Notes in Networks and Systems, vol. 1619 (2025). https://doi.org/10.1007/978-3-032-05070-0_14
12. Caruso, F., Peretti, S., Pino, M., Di Mascio, T.: Risk of gaming disorders in adolescents: a multiperspective framework for video games development. In: Proceedings of the 17th International Conference on Computer Supported Education (CSEDU), vol. 2, pp. 838–845 (2025). https://doi.org/10.5220/0013467600003932
13. Chambers, Partners: Gaming law 2024: South Korea. https://practiceguides.chambers.com/practice-guides/gaming-law-2024/south-korea (2024). Accessed 13 Jan 2025
14. China Legal Experts: China gaming laws. https://www.chinalegalexperts.com/news/china-gaming-laws (2025). Accessed 13 Jan 2025
15. Chueca, J., Verón, J., Font, J., Pérez, F., Cetina, C.: The consolidation of game software engineering: a systematic literature review of software engineering for industry-scale computer games. Inf. Softw. Technol. **165**, 107330 (2024)
16. Colasante, E., Pivetta, E., Canale, N., Vieno, A., Marino, C., Lenzi, M., et al.: Problematic gaming risk among European adolescents: a cross-national evaluation of individual and socio-economic factors. Addiction **117**(8), 2273–2282 (2022). https://doi.org/10.1111/add.15843
17. Colder Carras, M., Aljuboori, D., Shi, J., Date, M., Karkoub, F., García Ortiz, K., et al.: Prevention and health promotion interventions for young people in the context of digital well-being: rapid systematic review. J. Med. Internet Res. **26**, e59968 (2024)
18. Cormio, L., Giaconi, C., Mengoni, M., Santilli, T.: Exploring game design approaches through conversations with designers. Des. Stud. **91**, 101253 (2024). https://doi.org/10.1016/j.destud.2024.101253

19. Council of Europe International Cooperation Group on Drugs and Addictions: risks and harms associated with online gaming and gambling (2024). https://rm.coe.int/p-pg-it-2024-2-report-risks-and-harms-online-gaming-and-gambling-final/1680b07d35
20. Di Mascio, T., Gennari, R., Melonio, A., Tarantino, L.: Engaging "new users" into design activities: the terence experience with children. In: Caporarello, L., Di Martino, B., Martinez, M. (eds) Smart Organizations and Smart Artifacts: Fostering Interaction between People, Technologies and Processes, Lecture Notes in Information Systems and Organisation, vol. 7, pp. 241–250. Springer, Cham (2014). https://doi.org/10.1007/978-3-319-07040-7_23
21. Discord channel "GameDev Community": user posts on public discussion on essential tools for development. https://discord.com/invite/gamedev (2025). Accessed 27 Aug 2025
22. El-Nasr, M.S., Drachen, A., Canossa, A.: Game analytics. Springer (2016)
23. Engström, H.: Game development research. University of Skövde (2020)
24. Engström, H., Marklund, B.B., Backlund, P., Toftedahl, M.: Game development from a software and creative product perspective: a quantitative literature review approach. Entertainment Comput. **27**, 10–22 (2018)
25. Ethical Games Initiative: Ethical games: a code of ethics for the game industry (2024). https://ethicalgames.org
26. Flayelle, M., Andronicos, M., King, D.L., Billieux, J.: Understanding the interplay between video game design features and dysregulated gaming patterns: a call to anchor future research directions in interactionist frameworks. Addictive Behaviors Reports, p. 100609 (2025)
27. Frommel, J., Freeman, G., Gerling, K., Johnson, D., Mandryk, R.L.: Building creative strategies and solutions to promote benefits while mitigating harms of video games. In: CHI PLAY 2024, pp. 462–465 (2024). https://doi.org/10.1145/3665463.3678860
28. Game Developers Conference, Omdia: 2025 state of the game industry report. https://reg.gdconf.com/state-of-game-industry-2025 (2025)
29. Griffiths, M.D., Nuyens, F.: An overview of structural characteristics in problematic video game playing. Curr. Addict. Rep. **4**, 272–283 (2017)
30. Griffiths, M.D., Stavropoulos, V., Pontes, H.M., Carbonell, X., King, D.L., Lin, C.Y., et al.: Gaming Disorder Among Children and Adolescents, pp. 187–194. Springer Nature Switzerland, Cham (2025). https://doi.org/10.1007/978-3-031-69362-5_26
31. Guan, J., Chen, T.: Exploring addiction mechanism of different game types. J. Educ. Humanit. Soc. Sci. **8**, 1490–1496 (2023)
32. Higher Education Video Game Alliance: HEVGA 2025 Report on University Games Programs in USA and Canada. https://hevga.org/wp-content/uploads/2025/03/HEVGA-2025-Report-on-University-Games-Programs.pdf (2025)
33. Hou, H.T.: Diverse development and future challenges of game-based learning and gamified teaching research. Educ. Sci. **13**(4), 337 (2023). https://doi.org/10.3390/educsci13040337
34. Imataka, G., Izumi, S., Miyamoto, Y., Maehashi, A.: Gaming disorders: Navigating the fine line between entertainment and addiction–gaming history, health risks, social consequences, and pathways to prevention. J. Clin. Med. **13**(17), 5122 (2024)
35. International Game Developers Association (IGDA) and Western University: 2023 developer satisfaction survey summary report. https://igda-website.s3.us-east-2.amazonaws.com/wp-content/uploads/2024/05/01161842/2023-04-14_IGSA-DSS-2023_SummaryReport.pdf (2024)

36. Karhulahti, V.M.: Vitality structures in 'addictive' game design. Open Res. Europe **4** (2024)
37. Kolb, D.A.: Experiential learning: Experience as the Source of Learning and Development. Prentice Hall, Englewood Cliffs, NJ (1984)
38. Lave, J., Wenger, E.: Situated Learning: Legitimate Peripheral Participation. Cambridge University Press, Cambridge (1991)
39. Li, Y., Wang, C., Liu, J.: A systematic review of literature on user behavior in video game live streaming. Int. J. Environ. Res. Public Health **17**(9), 3328 (2020). https://doi.org/10.3390/ijerph17093328
40. Limone, P., Ragni, B., Toto, G.A.: The epidemiology and effects of video game addiction: a systematic review and meta-analysis. Acta Physiol. (Oxf) **241**, 104047 (2023)
41. Long, J., et al.: Public health approaches and policy changes after the inclusion of gaming disorder in ICD-11: global needs. BJPsych Int. **19**(3), 63–66 (2022). https://doi.org/10.1192/bji.2021.57
42. Lopez, D.A., Foxe, J.J., van Wijngaarden, E., Thompson, W.K., Freedman, E.G.: The longitudinal association between reward processing and symptoms of video game addiction in the adolescent brain cognitive development study. J. Behav. Addict. **13**(4) (2024)
43. Murphy-Hill, E., Zimmermann, T., Nagappan, N.: Cowboys, ankle sprains, and keepers of quality: How is video game development different from software development? In: Proceedings of the 36th International Conference on Software Engineering, pp. 1–11 (2014)
44. Musil, J., Schweda, A., Winkler, D., Biffl, S.: A survey on a state of the practice in video game development (report number: Ifs-qse 10/04). Technische Universität Wien, Tech. Rep. (2010)
45. Nursalam, N., Iswanti, D.I., Agustiningsih, N., Rohmi, F., Permana, B., Erwansyah, R.A.: Factors contributing to online game addiction in adolescents: a systematic review. Int. J. Public Health Sci. (IJPHS) **12**(4), 1763 (2023)
46. O'Hagan, A.O., O'Connor, R.V.: Towards an understanding of game software development processes: a case study. In: O'Connor, R., Umay Akkaya, M., Kemaneci, K., Yilmaz, M., Poth, A., Messnarz, R. (eds) European Conference on Software Process Improvement, pp. 3–16. Springer, Cham (2015). https://doi.org/10.1007/978-3-319-24647-5_1
47. Pieva, L., Pillat, R., Mossmann, J.B., Bernardino, M.: What are the project management practices in the digital games industry? A survey study. J. Interact. Syst. **16**(1), 427–440 (2025)
48. Politowski, C., Petrillo, F., Montandon, J.E., Valente, M.T., Guéhéneuc, Y.G.: Are game engines software frameworks? A three-perspective study. J. Syst. Softw. **171**, 110846 (2021)
49. Reddit Community "GameDev": Community discussion threads. https://www.reddit.com/r/gamedev/ (2025). Accessed 27 Aug 2025
50. Rehbein, F., Gentile, D.A., Lemmens, J., Rumpf, H.J.: Structural game characteristics and problematic gaming: introduction of the risk characteristics checklist for games (RCCG). Sucht (2024). https://doi.org/10.1024/0939-5911/a000859
51. Rehbein, F., King, D.L., Staudt, A., Hayer, T., Rumpf, H.J.: Contribution of game genre and structural game characteristics to the risk of problem gaming and gaming disorder: a systematic review. Curr. Addict. Rep. **8**(2), 263–281 (2021)
52. Roffarello, A.M., De Russis, L.: Achieving digital wellbeing through digital self-control tools: a systematic review and meta-analysis. ACM Trans. Comput.-Hum. Interact. **30**(4) (2023). https://doi.org/10.1145/3571810

53. Sachu, B., Kadeswaran, S., Jayseelan, R.: Investigating online game addiction: an in-depth analysis of design elements through the player engagement model. ShodhKosh: J. Vis. Performing Arts **5**(3), 91–100 (2024). https://doi.org/10.29121/shodhkosh.v5.i3.2024.1222
54. Sage, D.: How Many Gamers Are There? (2025 Worldwide Statistics). https://www.demandsage.com/gamers-statistics/ (2025). Accessed 05 Nov 2025
55. Saini, N., Hodgins, D.C.: Investigating gaming structural features associated with gaming disorder and proposing a revised taxonomical model: a scoping review. J. Behav. Addict. **12**(2), 352–374 (2023). https://doi.org/10.1556/2006.2023.00019
56. Satapathy, P., et al.: Burden of gaming disorder among adolescents: a systemic review and meta-analysis. Public Health Pract. **9**, 100565 (2025)
57. Shaker, N., Togelius, J., Nelson, M.J.: Procedural Content Generation in Games. Springer, Cham (2016). https://doi.org/10.1007/978-3-319-42716-4
58. Shrestha, A., Zuo, F., Qian, G., Rhee, J.: A survey and insights on modern game development processes for software engineering education. In: Feng, W., Rahimi, N., Margapuri, V. (eds) Software and Data Engineering, pp. 65–84. Springer, Cham (2025). https://doi.org/10.1007/978-3-031-75201-8_6
59. Sobota, B., Pietriková, E.: The role of game engines in game development and teaching, chap. 5. IntechOpen (2023). https://doi.org/10.5772/intechopen.1002257
60. Staniewska, A., Konopacki, J.: Minecraft games and public participation in landscape design-current teaching experience. World Trans. Eng. Technol. Educ. **19**(2), 238–243 (2021)
61. Stevens, M.W., Delfabbro, P.H., King, D.L.: Prevention approaches to problem gaming: a large-scale qualitative investigation. Comput. Hum. Behav. **115**, 106611 (2021)
62. Tech Leader Advance: Miro: a visual collaboration hub for game and software teams. https://www.techleaderadvance.com/blog/miro-a-visual-collaboration-hub-for-game-and-software-teams (2025). Accessed 27 Aug 2025
63. Toftedahl, M., Engström, H.: A taxonomy of game engines and the tools that drive the industry. In: Proceedings of DiGRA 2019 Conference: Game, Play and the Emerging Ludo-Mix (2019)
64. Tunnel, R.H., Norbisrath, U.: Classification of video games bachelor's curricula. J. Educ. Learn. **12**(2), 39–51 (2023). https://doi.org/10.5539/jel.v12n2p39
65. Ullmann, G.C., Politowski, C., Guéhéneuc, Y.G., Petrillo, F.: Game engine comparative anatomy. In: Gobl, B., van der Spek, E., Baalsrud Hauge, J., McCall, R. (eds) International Conference on Entertainment Computing, pp. 103–111. Springer, Cham (2022). https://doi.org/10.1007/978-3-031-20212-4_8
66. Whittemore, R., Knafl, K.: The integrative review: updated methodology. J. Adv. Nurs. **52**(5), 546–553 (2005)
67. WHO: International Classification of Diseases, 11th revision (ICD-11). https://icd.who.int/en (2019). Accessed 05 Nov 2025
68. Wu, Z., Chen, Z., Zhu, D., Mousas, C., Kao, D.: A systematic review of generative ai on game character creation: applications, challenges, and future trends. IEEE Trans. Games (2025)
69. Yang, D., Kleinman, E., Harteveld, C.: GPT for games: an updated scoping review (2020–2024). IEEE Trans. Games (2025)
70. Zhang, L., Han, J., Liu, M., Yang, C., Liao, Y.: The prevalence and possible risk factors of gaming disorder among adolescents in China. BMC Psychiatry **24**(1), 381 (2024). https://doi.org/10.1186/s12888-024-05826-9

A Dialogue-Centered Framework for Reducing Transactional Distance in Online Photography Education: Design-Based Research in the Vietnamese Context

Bin Youn(✉) and Surendheran Kaliyaperumal

Digital Media, RMIT University, Ho Chi Minh City, Vietnam
bin.youn@rmit.edu.vn

Abstract. This paper presents the DILA (Dialogue-Interaction-Learning-Autonomy) framework developed through design-based research in an online undergraduate photography course at RMIT University Vietnam. Addressing the challenge of replicating studio-based pedagogy in digital environments with dialogue-centered approaches using accessible tools, we implemented four integrated dialogue channels across 131 students over a 12-week semester. The framework combines synchronous consultations (39 sessions, 54% participation), asynchronous discussions, strategic support workshops using Miro boards for persistent visual reference, and sustained email correspondence with visual collaboration tools. Observable outcomes include a 45% reduction in procedural questions following High-Distinction exemplary showcases and documented progression from technical dependency to creative autonomy. Unlike technology-intensive approaches, the framework leverages structured dialogue as primary pedagogical technology. The study contributes a theoretically-grounded, empirically tested model for online creative arts education, particularly relevant as AI-generated imagery challenges traditional photography pedagogy, shifting focus from technical execution to critical thinking and aesthetic judgment. Limitations include single-context implementation and absence of control comparison.

Keywords: online learning · photography education · transactional distance theory · dialogue framework · creative arts pedagogy · design-based research

1 Introduction

The migration of practice-based creative courses to online environments has exposed fundamental pedagogical challenges that transcend simple content delivery. Photography education, traditionally anchored in studio critique and hands-on experimentation, exemplifies these challenges. Recent studies indicate that 67% of creative arts programs struggled with online transition compared to 42% in other disciplines [1], with the core challenge lying not in content delivery but in replicating the dialogic nature of studio pedagogy—what Barab & Squire identify [2] as iterative cycles of creation, critique, and feedback that define "critique culture" in authentic learning environments.

B. Fernández-Manjón et al. (Eds.): SETE 2025/ICWL 2025, LNCS 16425, pp. 160–169, 2026.
https://doi.org/10.1007/978-981-92-0042-9_12

Photography education traditionally relies on iterative cycles of creation, presentation, and feedback that develop both technical skill and aesthetic judgment. When migrated online, this pedagogical model encounters multiple barriers: students' reluctance to share work-in-progress due to vulnerability in digital spaces, absence of informal peer learning that occurs naturally in physical studios, difficulty providing nuanced visual feedback through standard LMS platforms, and cultural factors affecting participation styles, particularly in Asian educational contexts.

This paper addresses these challenges through the DILA framework, developed and tested in Photography 101 at RMIT University Vietnam across two semesters. The initial semester revealed critical issues: students frequently misread assignment requirements despite detailed written instructions, struggled with technical-aesthetic integration, and demonstrated reluctance to engage in peer critique. These observations informed systematic interventions in Semester 2 (July-September 2025), where we reconceptualized dialogue as pedagogical technology rather than mere communication tool.

Our contribution extends Moore's [3] Transactional Distance Theory through practical implementation in a creative arts context, integrating Kaliyaperumal's [4] multi-dimensional interaction model to create a transferable framework for resource-constrained institutions. By demonstrating how systematic dialogue design can reduce transactional distance and foster creative autonomy without AR/VR infrastructure, we offer an alternative path for online photography education in the AI era.

2 Theoretical Foundation

2.1 Transactional Distance in Creative Arts Education

Moore's [3] Transactional Distance Theory identifies three variables affecting online learning effectiveness: Structure (S), Dialogue (D), and Learner Autonomy (LA). The relationship $TD = S/D$ suggests that increased dialogue reduces perceived distance. However, this linear model oversimplifies creative arts education where multiple interaction types occur simultaneously and recursively.

In this study, we operationalize Structure (S) as the degree of rigidity in course design, measured by the ratio of fixed to flexible learning activities. Dialogue (D) represents the frequency and depth of meaningful interactions, calculated as (synchronous hours $\times$ participation rate) + (asynchronous posts $\times$ engagement depth). While this linear formulation simplifies complex relationships, it provides a practical heuristic intervention design.

Photography education presents unique challenges for transactional distance management. Unlike procedural disciplines where structured content can compensate for limited dialogue, photography requires constant negotiation between technical execution and aesthetic interpretation. The absence of physical studio spaces eliminates what Stein et al. [5] call "ambient learning"—the informal knowledge transfer that occurs through observation and proximity. This loss is particularly acute in photography, where seeing others work, handling physical prints, and engaging in spontaneous critiques constitute essential pedagogical elements.

To address these complexities, we integrate Kaliyaperumal's [4] extension of Moore's theory, which identifies four critical interaction dimensions:

- **Learner-Content (LC)**: In photography, this encompasses both theoretical understanding (composition rules, lighting principles) and aesthetic judgment (visual narrative, emotional impact)
- **Learner-Instructor (LI)**: Requires personalized feedback on creative choices, technical problem-solving, and conceptual development guidance
- **Learner-Learner (LL)**: Enables peer critique essential for developing visual literacy and understanding diverse aesthetic perspectives
- **Learner-Interface (LInt)**: Encompasses both learning platforms (LMS, discussion boards) and creative tools (editing software, sharing platforms)

2.2 Dialogue as Pedagogical Technology

While literature emphasizes AR/VR solutions for practice-based online learning [6, 7], with studies showing increased engagement through simulated studio environments, we propose an alternative approach: reconceptualizing dialogue itself as technology—a designed system for achieving pedagogical outcomes. Hrastinski's [8] distinction between synchronous and asynchronous e-learning suggests that carefully orchestrated dialogue can create "cognitive presence" equivalent to physical proximity.

The emergence of AI-generated imagery adds urgency to this dialogue-centered approach. Recent automated critique systems for generative image tools (e.g., Midjourney's rating system, DALL-E's iterative refinement, Stable Diffusion's aesthetic scoring) primarily emphasize technical execution—fidelity to prompts, rendering quality, compositional coherence. However, critique of deeper conceptual or aesthetic levels remains less developed in these systems. Our dialogue-centered approach complements these AI tools by fostering capabilities that algorithms cannot replicate: contextual interpretation within cultural frameworks, ethical judgment about representation and authenticity, and development of personal artistic voice grounded in human experience.

The DILA framework thus positions structured dialogue not as a temporary pandemic solution but as essential pedagogy for developing irreplaceable human creative capabilities—particularly critical as AI democratizes technical image production while leaving conceptual development and critical thinking as uniquely human domains.

3 The DILA Framework Development

3.1 Research Context and Methodology

Following design-based research methodology [2], we developed the DILA framework through iterative cycles of design, implementation, and refinement. The context was *Photography 101*, a foundation course delivered fully online to 131 students across Hanoi and Ho Chi Minh City campuses at RMIT University Vietnam.

Semester 1. Observations (Baseline Data)

- Widespread misinterpretation of assignment requirements despite detailed written instructions

- Limited peer interaction in discussion forums
- Technical competence without aesthetic development
- High dependency on instructor validation

Semester 2. Interventions (July–September 2025)

- Redesigned visual instructions with annotated examples
- Implemented structured dialogue interventions at strategic points
- Introduced visual collaboration platforms for feedback
- Created persistent reference materials using Miro boards

Course structure included three progressive assignments: technical mastery (A1), genre exploration (A2), conceptual development (A3). Data collection involved systematic observation, participation metrics, and pedagogical documentation. Aggregated data available upon request, subject to privacy constraints.

3.2 Framework Architecture

The DILA (Dialogue-Interaction-Learning-Autonomy) framework integrates four dialogue channels, each targeting specific aspects of transactional distance (Fig. 1):

Synchronous Consultations (Small-Group Format)

- Design: Voluntary 30-min sessions with flexible 1:1 to 1:4 ratio
- Implementation: 39 sessions conducted (19.5 h) across 17 unique days
- Participation: 54% of eligible students (39/72) attended at least once
- Pedagogical Function: Personalized guidance with peer learning benefits
- Key Innovation: Group format enabled students to learn from others' critiques

Asynchronous Discussion Boards (Canvas Integration)

- Design: Structured threads for procedural and conceptual discussions
- Implementation: Evolved from 20 procedural to 11 interpretive threads
- Participation: All students engaged at varying levels
- Pedagogical Function: Persistent community dialogue and peer support
- Observable Pattern: 45% reduction in questions post-HD showcase

Strategic Support Workshops (Miro Board Delivery)

- Design: 90-min sessions with persistent visual materials
- Implementation: Two sessions strategically timed before assignment deadlines
    - o Session 1 (Week 6): HD exemplar showcase with 33 attendees

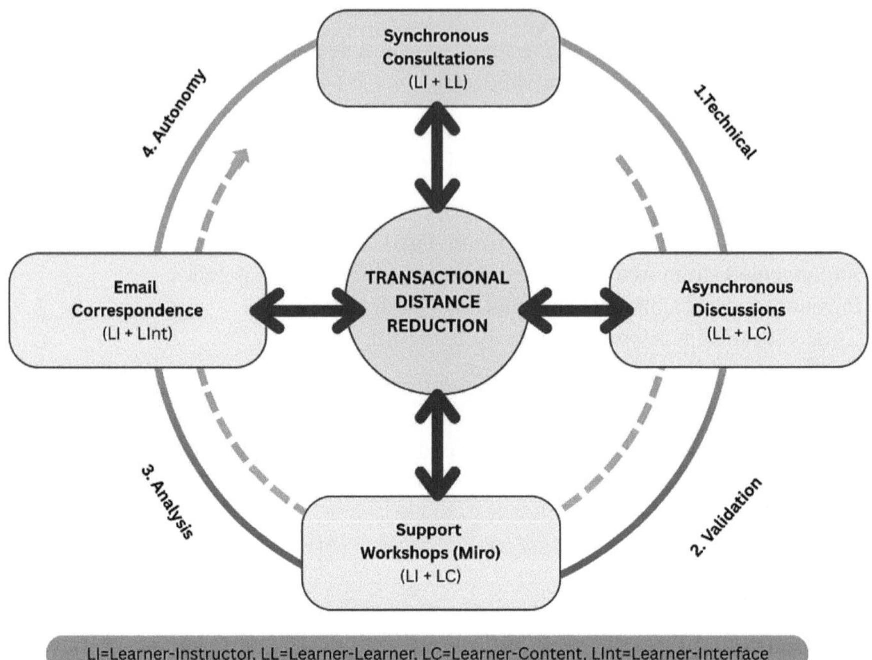

Fig. 1. The DILA Framework for Online Photography Education. Four dialogue channels (*solid arrows*) are mapped to interaction types with feedback loops (*dashed arrows*). Numbers 1–4 indicate progression phases from Technical Dependency to Creative Autonomy

  - o Session 2 (Week 8): Genre exploration with 27 artist references, 22 attendees

- Platform Innovation: Miro boards provided persistent visual reference for asynchronous access
- Pedagogical Function: Making excellence transparent and connecting theory to practice

Sustained Email Correspondence (Visual Platform Integration)

- Design: Iterative exchanges with visual feedback capabilities
- Implementation: 35+ exchanges with 10 highly engaged students
- Platform Integration: Miro, Canva, Figma for visual annotation
- Pedagogical Function: Extending personalized support beyond scheduled sessions
- Key Evolution: Students progressed from folder-dumping to curated presentation

4 Implementation and Empirical Findings

4.1 Deployment Timeline and Participation Metrics

The timeline and participation metrics are given in Table 1 as follows:

Table 1. Dialogue intervention metrics across semester weeks

Week	Intervention Type	Participation	Focus Area	Observable Outcome
1–3	Initial Consultations	12 sessions	Technical basics	Equipment/software clarification
4–5	Discussion Threads	20 procedural posts	Assignment 1 prep	Format/submission queries
6	Support Workshop 1	33 students (25%)	HD Showcase	Transparency of excellence
7–8	Intensive Consultations	18 sessions	Assignment 2 development	Shift to aesthetic questions
8	Support Workshop 2	22 students (17%)	Genre/Artist study	Theory-practice connection
9–10	Email Intensification	10 students, 35 + msgs	Project refinement	Folder sharing → curated selection
11–12	Final Consultations	9 sessions	Conceptual development	Autonomous decision-making

While this study focused on behavioral indicators and participation metrics as proxies for learning engagement, we acknowledge the absence of direct learning outcome assessments. The 45% reduction in basic queries and progression to autonomous decision-making suggest improved comprehension, though future iterations should incorporate rubric-scored assignments for validation.

4.2 Student Progression Phases

Through systematic observation, we identified a consistent progression in student dialogue patterns.

Phase 1. Technical Dependency (Weeks 1–3). Students' initial engagement focused entirely on procedural and technical concerns. Discussion board posts averaged 2–3 sentences requesting clarification on file formats, export settings, and equipment access. Consultation sessions were dominated by "how-to" questions, with students seeking step-by-step instructions. Email exchanges were brief and transactional. One representative query: "What DPI should I use for submission?" This phase reflected high structure dependence and minimal autonomous exploration.

Phase 2. Validation Seeking (Weeks 4–6). As technical confidence grew, dialogue shifted toward quality validation. Students began sharing work but primarily sought binary approval ("Is this good enough?"). Consultation requests increased, with students bringing multiple options and asking instructors to choose. The HD showcase intervention at Week 6 marked a turning point—seeing peer excellence made quality criteria tangible. Post-showcase, questions became more specific: "How can I achieve the lighting quality in the HD example?".

Phase 3. Comparative Analysis (Weeks 7–9). Following the HD showcase, dialogue complexity increased markedly. Discussion threads evolved from procedural to interpretive, with students debating genre boundaries and aesthetic choices. The Support Workshop 2 introduction of 27 artist references catalyzed deeper engagement. Students began contextualizing their work within broader photographic traditions. Email exchanges lengthened, with students providing rationales for their choices rather than seeking approval.

Phase 4. Creative Autonomy (Weeks 10–12). Final weeks demonstrated genuine autonomous engagement. Consultation conversations became dialogues rather than Q&A sessions, with students articulating creative vision and seeking specific technical advice to achieve it. Peer-to-peer support emerged organically in discussion boards. Email exchanges showed sophisticated self-critique, with students identifying their own areas for improvement. One student's progression exemplified this evolution: from sending 50+ unedited photos seeking selection help to present 5–7 carefully chosen images with written artistic statements.

Table 2 summarizes the observable changes in student behavior following the framework implementation:

Table 2. Observable changes in student behavior after DILA framework interventions

Indicator	Before Intervention	After Intervention	Change
Question Type	20 procedurals	11 interpretive	-45% basic queries
Consultation Focus	"How to" technical	Creative rationale	Shift to autonomy
Email Pattern	Full folder sharing	5–7 curated images	Editorial judgment
Peer Interaction Engagement	Minimal (1.2 posts)	Active dialogue	Increased Engagement

These quantifiable changes validate the framework in reducing transactional distance and developing learner autonomy through structured dialogue interventions.

4.3 Platform Innovation: Miro Boards for Persistent Visual Dialogue

The integration of Miro boards for support workshops addressed a critical challenge in online photography education: the ephemeral nature of synchronous visual presentations. Traditional screen-sharing in live sessions meant students who missed the session or wanted to review materials had no visual reference.

The Miro implementation provided:

- Persistent Visual Reference: Students could access and review HD exemplars asynchronously
- Layered Annotation: Instructor comments directly on images explaining quality indicators

- Comparative Layout: Side-by-side arrangement enabling pattern recognition
- Student Interaction: Comments and questions added asynchronously by 47 additional students post-session

This approach transformed the support workshop from a one-time event to an ongoing resource, with board access statistics showing continued engagement throughout the semester (average 3.2 visits per student).

4.4 Cultural Considerations in Vietnamese Educational Context

The Vietnamese educational context presented specific challenges requiring framework adaptation:

Communication Preferences. Students demonstrate a strong preference for text-based verbal communication. In live sessions, despite encouragement, only 1–2 students used voice, while 20–30 actively engaged via chat. We leveraged text dialogue as legitimate participation, developing chat facilitation strategies, and creating structured text-based critique protocols.

Face-Saving Culture. Direct peer critique proved culturally challenging. Students hesitated to comment critically on peers' work, potentially causing loss of face. We addressed this through structured critique frameworks emphasizing constructive language, anonymous peer review options, and instructor modeling of respectful critical dialogue.

Instructor Dependency. Vietnamese educational traditions emphasize instructor authority, creating initial resistance to peer learning. Group consultations shifted traditional authority dynamics as students observed peer feedback value.

5 Discussion and Implications

5.1 Theoretical Contributions

Our contribution operationalizes Moore's theory through practical dialogue-channel mapping to interaction dimensions. The framework extends theory in three ways:

Dialogue as Primary Technology. Demonstrates structured dialogue using accessible tools to replicate studio pedagogy. The 45% support reduction suggests that well-designed dialogue surpasses technological simulation.

Multi-dimensional Distance Reduction. Mapping reveals transactional distance comprises multiple distances requiring targeted interventions—synchronous consultations address LI/LL dimensions while Miro workshops strengthen LC connections.

Progressive Autonomy Development. Documented progression validates dialogue's role developing critical judgment through recursive cycles rather than linear skill acquisition or content mastery.

5.2 Resource Efficiency and Transferability

Framework implementation demonstrates cost-effectiveness: 19.5 consultation hours reached 54% of students using free/institutional tools (Canvas, Miro free tier, Figma education). Group consultations and persistent boards serve multiple students simultaneously with 45% efficiency gains.

Principles transfer broadly: music (virtual masterclasses with score annotations), design (iterative collaborative critique), creative writing (workshop models with layered text feedback), architecture (virtual studio with 3D model reviews).

5.3 Implications for AI-Era Photography Education

As AI tools democratize technical image creation, the DILA framework's emphasis on dialogue-developed competencies becomes increasingly vital. The framework cultivates capabilities AI cannot replicate:

- Critical Evaluation: Assessing aesthetic merit beyond technical execution
- Cultural Interpretation: Understanding images within social contexts
- Ethical Judgment: Navigating representation and authenticity
- Creative Vision: Developing unique artistic voice

The progression from technical dependency to creative autonomy mirrors the shift photography education must make—from teaching tools to developing critical creative thinkers.

6 Limitations and Future Research

6.1 Study Limitations

This research acknowledges several constraints:

- Single Context: Implementation in one institution limits generalizability
- Control Group: Absence of control comparison limits causal inference
- Learning Measures: Lack of standardized outcome assessments
- Temporal Scope: Single semester without longitudinal tracking
- Platform Specificity: Canvas/Miro implementation may affect transferability
- Selection Bias: Voluntary participation favored motivated students
- Cultural Context: Vietnamese setting may not translate directly
- Ethical Constraints: Individual performance tracking was not permitted

6.2 Future Research Directions

Building on this foundation, future research should explore:

1. Cross-Cultural Validation: Implementing DILA across diverse contexts
2. Longitudinal Impact: Tracking autonomy development across courses
3. AI Integration: Exploring AI-assisted dialogue facilitation at scale
4. Comparative Studies: Controlled experiments comparing DILA with traditional approaches
5. Discipline Adaptation: Customizing framework for specific disciplines
6. Scale Testing: Implementation in MOOC environments with 500+ students

7 Conclusion

This paper presents the DILA framework as a theoretically grounded, empirically tested approach to online photography education. Through systematic implementation across 131 students, we demonstrate that structured dialogue interventions can effectively reduce transactional distance using widely accessible digital tools.

The framework's key innovations include reconceptualizing dialogue as pedagogical technology, mapping specific interventions to multi-dimensional interaction types, and using persistent visual platforms (Miro boards) for asynchronous reference. Observable outcomes—including 45% reduction in support needs, documented progression from dependency to autonomy, and successful integration of theoretical knowledge with practical application—validate the approach's effectiveness.

As AI transforms creative industries, photography education faces an existential challenge: what value does human instruction provide when machines can generate technically perfect images? The DILA framework offers a clear answer: human dialogue develops critical thinking, aesthetic judgment, and creative vision—competencies that remain fundamentally human. Through structured dialogue across multiple channels, online photography courses can maintain studio pedagogy's essence while adapting to digital delivery constraints.

The study contributes not merely to a successful case study but a transferable framework for resource-constrained institutions seeking to deliver quality online creative education. By demonstrating that dialogue design can substitute for expensive infrastructure, we democratize access to effective online photography education. In an era where content is commoditized and AI-generated imagery proliferates, dialogue emerges as the irreplaceable core of creative education.

References

1. Sun, A., Chen, X.: Online education and its effective practice: a research review. J. Inf. Technol. Educ. Res. **15**, 157–190 (2016)
2. Barab, S., Squire, K.: Design-based research: putting a stake in the ground. J. Learn. Sci. **13**(1), 1–14 (2004)
3. Moore, M.G.: Theory of transactional distance. In: Keegan, D. (ed.) Theoretical Principles of Distance Education, pp. 22–38. Routledge, London (1993)
4. Kaliyaperumal, S.: Development and validation of an evaluation framework for assessing quality of massive open online courses. Doctoral dissertation, Karunya University (2021). https://shodhganga.inflibnet.ac.in/handle/10603/407600
5. Stein, D.S., Wanstreet, C.E., Calvin, J., Overtoom, C., Wheaton, J.E.: Bridging the transactional distance gap in online learning environments. Am. J. Distance Educ. **19**(2), 105–118 (2005)
6. Garzón, J., Acevedo, J.: Meta-analysis of the impact of augmented reality on students' learning gains. Educ. Res. Rev. **27**, 244–260 (2019)
7. Khan, T., Johnston, K., Ophoff, J.: The impact of an augmented reality application on learning motivation of students. Adv. Hum.-Comput. Interact. **2019**, 1–14 (2019)
8. Hrastinski, S.: Asynchronous and synchronous e-learning. Educause Q. **31**(4), 51–55 (2008)

Benefits and Challenges of Implementing Retro Arcade in Informatics: A Case Study in Secondary Education

Karolína Miková(✉), Jakub Krcho, and Pavla Blažeková

Comenius University in Bratislava, Mlynská Dolina, 84248 Bratislava, Slovakia
{mikova,krcho}@fmph.uniba.sk, nunukova1@uniba.sk

Abstract. This paper explores the integration of the Retro Arcade game console as a follow-up extension module to the Micro:bit in secondary school informatics education. The objective of the study was to assess the educational potential of combining hardware (Retro Arcade) with a visual programming environment (MakeCode Arcade), and to identify both the strengths and limitations of this approach. The research design was a case study, based on qualitative methods and involved active student participation in creating original games. The project focused on the development of programming skills, analysis of informatics-related content, and the enhancement of digital literacy, computational thinking, and social competencies. Data were collected through classroom observations, semi-structured interviews, and analysis of students' final products. The results indicate a high level of student motivation and engagement, with notable educational benefits in terms of programming practice, teamwork, and interdisciplinary learning. Despite encountering certain technical and methodological challenges, these did not prevent the effective use of the console in the classroom setting. The Retro Arcade platform proved to be a valuable educational tool for reinforcing and expanding students' programming knowledge, encouraging creativity, and supporting critical thinking within the context of modern informatics education. The study suggests that integrating playful, game-based development tools into formal curricula can enhance learning outcomes and foster deeper student involvement in informatics.

Keywords: STEM Education · Retro Arcade Game Console · Programming · Social Skills · Case Study

1 Introduction

Incorporating educational robotics into the teaching process is an engaging way to show students the practical applications of programming. Today, students across all levels of education may already encounter robots, which allows them to learn to create simple programs and become acquainted with modern technologies such as sensors [1, 2]. As well as programming skills, they learn to decompose a problem into smaller, more manageable sub-tasks [3] and to cooperate with classmates, thereby practicing soft skills,

B. Fernández-Manjón et al. (Eds.): SETE 2025/ICWL 2025, LNCS 16425, pp. 170–180, 2026.
https://doi.org/10.1007/978-981-92-0042-9_13

particularly communication [4]. In this paper, we conduct a case study at one experimental school, in which high school students engage with Micro:bits [5] and LEGO Education sets [6]. During lessons with these robots at experimental school, students were solving basic tasks, creating their own assignments, and exploring the limits of both the robots and their own skills. For quite some time, we have been interested in how to build upon these knowledge and skills. After a careful analysis, we decided to employ a Micro:bit extension—the Retro Arcade game console [7]. In Slovakia [8, 9] as well as in the Czech Republic [10] there were already some experiences with its online simulator from COVID period in primary and secondary schools, mostly on informatics lessons [9, 11]. Most existing research studies use only software environments, without hardware. In our study, we will focus precisely on the potential of combining both hardware and software of Retro Arcade in educational process.

2 The Retro Arcade Game Console

In combination with the MakeCode Arcade platform, this console allows students to create their own games in a simple and fun way. It has the potential to introduce students to the creative process of game design [12]. This can be applied to both graphical design and programming. Students can explore different types of game for this console through tutorials [13]. Students can choose tutorials thematically or by type to align with their vision for a new game [14]. Using the console allows students to create playful electronic artefacts more easily than programming games in typical children's software environments [15, 16].

2.1 Hardware

Retro Arcade with the Micro:bit (Fig. 1) is an extension for the Micro:bit version V2. It has a TFT colour display of 160 × 128, four directional buttons, two buttons labelled A/B, and a reset button. This "gamepad with a colour screen" can be used for online game programming and offline play. Its current price is about €35 in Europe, and it is still available for purchase online. We consider this information to be important because many different robots, robotic toys, and games eventually become unavailable.

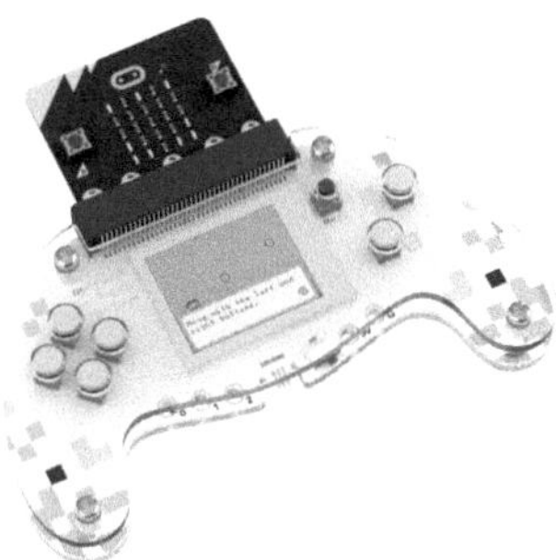

Fig. 1. The Retro Arcade console with Micro:bit. (Image source: https://wiki.elecfreaks.com/en/microbit/expansion-board/microbit-retro-arcade/.)

2.2 Software

The programming environment for the console is called MakeCode Arcade (Fig. 2). It is not yet localized into Slovak, so at least a basic knowledge of English commands is required. However, we do not consider this a serious obstacle for use in secondary and high school. Like the MakeCode environment [17], it is divided into multiple sections: online simulator (marked 1), command panel (marked 2) - additional commands can be added via connected extensions and canvas for program (marked 3). Code can be built either by dragging blocks or by writing source code in JavaScript or Python.

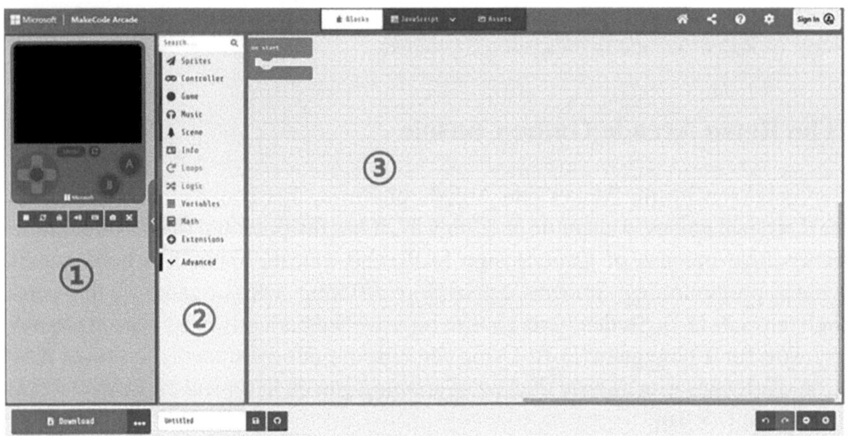

Fig. 2. The MakeCode Arcade software environment.

3 Methodology

The primary research problem addressed in this study was the lack of understanding of how students would engage with the Retro Arcade console in an educational setting. Specifically, it was unclear whether this tool would support the acquisition of new programming concepts, whether the time available in regular lessons would be sufficient for the development of a final product, and whether the activity itself would serve as a motivating factor for students.

To investigate these questions, we adopted a qualitative design research approach, specifically a case study [18]. This approach allowed us to explore the integration of the console within the educational process and to observe its influence across multiple domains of learning, including programming skills, motivation, and project-based collaboration.

For the purposes of the case study, we designed and tested a structured set of learning tasks to help students transition smoothly between different programming interfaces. Students were subsequently guided to design and implement their own games, resulting in fully playable first levels of arcade games.

The overarching **goal of our research** was to explore the potential of using the Retro Arcade game console at a secondary school with general education. We therefore formulated the following **three research questions**:

1. Which areas or topics of computer science might be taught using the Retro Arcade game console?
2. What are the benefits of incorporating activities with the Retro Arcade Console into education classes?
3. In order to incorporate Retro Arcade into teaching, what restrictions and limitations must be taken into account?

3.1 Participants

In order to explore the potential of the console for educational purposes, we required a suitable group of students. Based on our research questions, we decided that they should already have been taught Python programming so that we could focus on the application rather than teaching basics of programming. Therefore, we selected students in the higher years of secondary school (during the evaluation phase, we also extended the study to younger students based on the results). As well as age grouping, we needed to select a specific class. In the first iteration, the console was evaluated with a class of 28 students in the fourth year of a bilingual gymnasium in capital city of middle Europe, with an extended mathematics curriculum. There were 22 girls and 6 boys aged from 17 to 19 years old. The second iteration involved 15 students in the second year of the same gymnasium, specializing in mathematics. There were 4 girls and 11 boys aged from 15 – 17 years old. Both iterations took place in the 2023/24 academic year. The two groups were very different, which contributed to the richness of the data collected.

3.2 Data Collection and Analysis

In view of the qualitative nature of the research, qualitative data was also collected [19]. All observations made during the work with the console were meticulously recorded as field notes. In addition, we conducted interviews with the students and took photographs of their final products. All actions were undertaken in accordance with the GDPR, which was resolved within the school's responsibility at the beginning of the school year. All participants were informed. The data collected in this manner was then processed through qualitative methods of open and selective coding [20].

4 Implementation

When selecting and designing learning activities, we focused on two basic game concepts: (1) the player moving in a static environment and (2) the player moving in a dynamic environment. We created time frames so that each concept could be covered in a single lesson. Due to the already saturated informatics curriculum, we divided the students' work into four lessons: two for introductory content and tutorials, and two for independent student work. As game creation also involves graphics, we added an additional two lessons. These two lessons were taken from a subject called '*Art, Culture and Literature*', during which the students presented their work. In the following chapters, we present the content of these six lessons in more detail. Students had the option to choose whether they would work in groups or independently. Most worked in pairs.

4.1 First and Second Lessons

The first lesson began with a discussion about games in general. We discuss topics like: (1) Who plays what games?, (2) What types of gaming environments are they familiar with?, (3) How much time do they spend playing games? and so on.

After a short discussion, we asked students what they thought about programming their own game. Initially, this seemed unrealistic to them, but we managed to ignite interest. We then introduced them the MakeCode Arcade environment, since students were familiar only with MakeCode as they worked with Micro:bit. There are several tutorials available in the MakeCode environment, from which we have selected one that is quite simple and familiar to them. For this first lesson we choose "Chase the Pizza" tutorial [21] to familiarize them with the environment. Students completed the tutorial and then were tasked with modifying it by selecting commands and adding extensions to create their own variant of the game. The active part focused on working with sprites:

- creation (drawing or selecting from a database),
- placing a sprite in the game,
- assigning "good" and "bad" roles,
- and adding effects.

During the second lesson, students completed the "Basketball" tutorial [22]. No major issues were encountered. They continued with tutorials of their own choosing, then formed teams to begin brainstorming their own final game concepts. Interestingly, they automatically divided into pairs, where one was a good programmer and the other was a more creatively minded student. In other words, they were good at designing the theme of the game and creating graphics.

4.2 Third and Fourth Lessons

These lessons were focused on students developing their own game. They could consult the prepared tutorials when they ran into difficulties and collaborate with each other, particularly those who were less experienced programmers. The teacher's role was primarily to guide rather than actively design, and students also had access to them. The teacher would suggest where to find commands or offer hints about possible solutions but would avoid altering the students' design decisions. By the end of the lessons, the students had produced simple arcade games (i.e. the first levels) based on standard arcade principles.

If time allowed, students could continue developing additional levels or adding more gameplay elements individually outside of class, but the time allocated during lessons was insufficient for this.

4.3 Fifth and Sixth Lessons

These lessons were dedicated to student presentations of their projects. All games were uploaded to Micro:bits and connected to the console (see Fig. 3), enabling students to present their game ideas and implementations and allow others to play them. Significant time was allocated to this stage because obtaining feedback was very important. Students compared different projects, discussed ways to improve them, and had time to play multiple games.

Fig. 3. Backgrounds of students' final games

5 Results

The results are organised according to the three research questions. The first question was about which informatics content could be taught using the Retro Arcade console. Our analyses therefore focused on programming skills, digital literacy, and computational thinking. The second question explored the potential for additional educational benefits, including the development of social skills, opportunities for interdisciplinary learning, and the use of modern instructional strategies. The third question examined the constraints of the console's hardware and software, as well as limitations arising from students' prior programming knowledge.

5.1 Informatics Content

Upon thorough examination of the tutorials designed to facilitate orientation with the environment, it was determined that a more advanced level of programming expertise is requisite. In order to successfully program a complex game, it is essential that students must master at least the following programming constructs:

Basic Constructs:

- creation of objects with properties (appearance, name, etc.)
- placement of objects in space and modification of their x, y coordinates
- object movement (using arrow keys or following another object)

Advanced Constructs:

- detection of other objects' positions
- communication and interaction among objects
- repetition of command sets

- usage of variables in different contexts (e.g. object creation)

In the context of working with tutorials, students naturally discovered commands associated with their selected game. These commands have been either incorporated into prior games or have been self-taught when necessary to achieve the desired game vision. Retro Arcade, as an extension, benefits students in the field of programming by these specific commands, which rarely occur when solving common programming tasks—based on our experience in education with Micro:bits.

Specific Constructs Related Particularly to Game Creation:

- adding/subtracting points or lives
- using a timer
- interval display of objects
- setting up multiplayer options
- repeating or otherwise dynamic scene animation
- music (in the background of the game; sounds during object interactions)
- updating – objects, environment, etc.
- resetting the game/early termination

Since the students created different games, it was necessary for them to explain during the presentation of their game which new commands they had learned and how they could be used not only in the game but also in solving other programming tasks.

In terms of digital literacy [23], students were forced to confront the idea that their arcade game was a synthesis of arcade game creation principles that had already been used in the past. It was not our goal for the game they designed to have a completely new principle or plot. Our goal was for students to find suitable game forms and learn to apply the skills and knowledge they had acquired in their previous studies to simple games with familiar principles.

In terms of computational thinking, we identified skill development as the main benefit. Students learned how to divide the entire project into smaller tasks that would be solvable for them (i.e., problem decomposition). Sometimes, it was possible for them to work on sub-tasks in parallel within the group. Often, however, they had to collaborate on a single task, without which progress on the project would have been difficult. Analysing the task and synthesising the solution was essential for successfully programming the Retro Arcade project.

5.2 Educational Benefits

Given the interdisciplinary nature of the project, contributions in the fields of computer science and art, culture, and literature were to be expected. It proved crucial to get to know the students in the class, as their programming skills and personalities were important parameters in designing the scope of the individual parts of the project and also the skills we wanted to focus on primarily.

Social Skills: The work of students who worked on the same goal, even though each created a different game, resulted in the strengthening of social relationships within the group. Almost everyone needed to communicate with other members of their group, but also interact with students from other groups when necessary. Especially for students skilled in programming, it was relatively new and interesting to collaborate on a single project with more creatively minded classmates who did not have programming skills but had a vision of what the game should look like. The programmers then had to either incorporate the design as envisioned or, more complicatedly, explain to their more creatively minded classmates that the vision was unfeasible for some reason. The creatively minded students, in turn, faced challenges in clearly expressing their visions to the programmers.

The group of programmers found many discussions about different solutions to specific situations and the analysis of their individual proposals interesting. They often had different mechanisms for achieving their vision, but sometimes it was not possible to program them because their programming skills were not yet at the required level. In such cases, they had to come up with alternative solutions, often with compromises compared to the desired version. It was also very interesting for the teacher to observe these discussions (see Fig. 4). It was often challenging not to intervene in the problem-solving process and let the students find their own approaches.

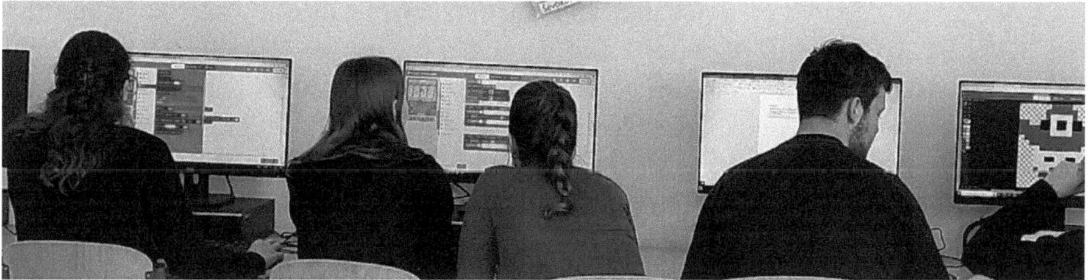

Fig. 4. Discussions during problem solving.

5.3 Constraints and Limitations

When you open the MakeCode Arcade environment after creating an account, it only offers a basic range of commands. If the user needs additional types of commands or other game attribute settings, they must extend the command panel individually. This extension is not entirely intuitive at first, but given previous experience with the MakeCode environment, it is manageable. This is not an extreme limitation, but rather suggests that it is more suitable for older students or those with more experience.

Other limitations we identified concerned the form and possibilities of working with music. For example, it was not possible to insert pre-prepared audio tracks in various formats into the environment. The user must set up all music in the musical staff available within the environment, which requires sufficient musical education and time.

As this is a retro version (see Fig. 5), the range of possible colours is also significantly limited. The resulting graphics do not meet the requirements of today's teenagers, who are used to high resolutions. This is also related to the size of the screen, which was another limitation for the students. 160 x 128 pixels is really small, and although the characters in the story are recognizable, they are really tiny and blurry.

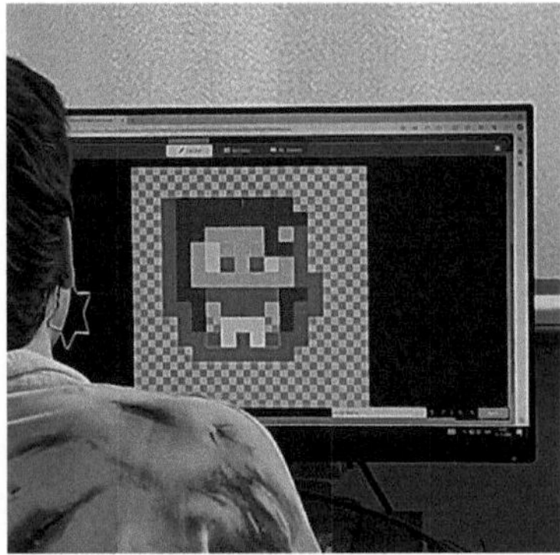

Fig. 5. Student working in the limited "retro" graphics mode

6 Conclusion

Students appear to learn best when they feel that they are playing, or when they know that their work has real significance (for example, when it is linked to authentic problems). In this case study, gamification [24] was employed as a motivational element. The main objective was to identify and explore Micro:bit extensions that could serve students after completing introductory work with Micro:bit in lower grades, enabling them to engage in more complex, interdisciplinary problem-solving tasks. After evaluating several potential add-on modules, the Retro Arcade game console was selected. The study therefore aimed to determine whether the console (hardware and software) is suitable for a school environment and whether its capabilities make it a viable instructional extension.

Regarding the **first question**, "Which areas or topics of computer science might be taught using the Retro Arcade game console?" we found that basic operations like: variables, object creation, and movement programming are essential.

Students can also learn specialized game-oriented commands like: interval display of objects, timers, scene animation, multiplayer options, etc.

In exploring the **second question**, "What are the benefits of incorporating activities with the Retro Arcade Console into education classes?", several benefits were observed. In addition to improvements in programming and computational thinking, there were also notable gains in interpersonal skills, communication, project planning, time management, and presentation abilities.

In response to the **third question**, which requested an identification of restrictions and limitations that must be taken into account when incorporating Retro Arcade into teaching, several limitations were identified. However, none of these were deemed to be so critical as to prevent its incorporation into teaching. Constraints such as a limited colour range and a small game area are rooted in the game's retro nature and are regarded as minor in the current context of high-fidelity graphics. From a software perspective, the current environment is adequate for secondary school students to program a relatively simple arcade game.

It should be noted, however, that these findings are based on qualitative data obtained from two smaller groups of students. As such, they should be interpreted as indicative rather than conclusive. Nevertheless, the results provide valuable insight into the educational potential of the Retro Arcade console and serve as a basis for subsequent quantitative research aimed at validating and extending these findings on a larger sample of participants.

In consideration of the limited time within the informatics curriculum, engagement with Retro Arcade appears adequate for introducing students to the process of game development. The complexity and diversity of the components supported understanding of essential programming concepts. Students were often confronted with the gap between their game-idea expectations and their actual programming skills, which promoted decomposition, analysis, and synthesis of partial solutions. In conclusion, all students successfully developed the first level of their game within the allocated time, allowing for peer testing and feedback. Overall, the integration of the Retro Arcade extension into instruction appears highly beneficial—both in terms of informatics education and the development of social and presentation skills.

Acknowledgments. We would like to thank referees for their comments on this paper. We would like to thank to projects VEGA 1/0621/22 and VEGA 1/0407/25 for the provided funding and have our results published.

Disclosure of Interests. The authors have no competing interests to declare that are relevant to the content of this article.

References

1. Coufal, P.: Project-based STEM learning using educational robotics as the development of student problem-solving competence. Mathematics **10**(23), 4618 (2022). https://doi.org/10.3390/math10234618
2. Veselovská, M., Mayerová, K.: Programming with motion sensor using LEGO WeDo at lower secondary school. Int. J. Inf. Commun. Technol. Educ. **4**(3), 40–52 (2015)
3. Informatické myšlení. Jihočeská univerzita v Českých Budějovicích. https://imysleni.cz/index/co-je-informaticke-mysleni. Accessed 07 Feb 2025
4. Rubinacci, F., et al.: Robotics for soft skills training. Res. Educ. Media **9**(2), 20–25 (2017)
5. SPy: Učíme s hardvérom. https://ucimeshardverom.sk. Accessed 20 Oct 2024
6. LEGO: Robotika EV3. www.eduxe.sk/les/robotika-ev3. Accessed 19 Oct 2024
7. Elecfreaks: Retro Console for micro:bit. https://wiki.elecfreaks.com/en/microbit/expansion-board/microbit-retro-arcade/. Accessed 08 Feb 2025
8. Voštinár, P.: MakeCode arcade: interesting environment for programming 2D games. In: IEEE World Conference on Engineering Education (EDUNINE), pp. 1–6 (2021)
9. Voštinár, P.: MakeCode arcade platform for game-based learning. Comput. Sci. Inf. Syst. **21**(3), 971–988 (2024)
10. Horáčková, H.: MakeCode arcade aneb vytvořte si vlastní arkádovou hru. https://bastlirna.hwkitchen.cz/makecode-arcade-vlastni-arkadova-hra-1/. Accessed 05 Aug 2021
11. Siever, B., Rogers, M.P.: Game on! Inspired CS education with MakeCode arcade. In: Proceedings of the 52nd ACM Technical Symposium on Computer Science Education, p. 1355 (2021)

12. Seyed, T. et al.: MakerArcade: using gaming and physical computing for playful making, learning, and creativity. In: Extended Abstracts of the 2019 CHI Conference on Human Factors in Computing Systems, pp. 1–6 (2019)
13. MakeCode Tutorials. https://arcade.makecode.com/tutorials. Accessed 07 Feb 2025
14. Spieler, B., et al.: Evaluation of game templates to support programming activities in schools. arXiv preprint arXiv:1805.04517 (2018)
15. Espejo, B., Dávila, J., Cordero, M., de León, J.: Game on! Inspired CS education with Make-Code arcade. In: Proceedings of the 52nd ACM Technical Symposium on Computer Science Education, p. 1345 (2021). https://doi.org/10.1145/3408877.3432494
16. Kafai, Y.B., Burke, Q.: Connected Code: Why Children Need to Learn Programming. MIT Press, Cambridge (2014)
17. MakeCode. https://www.microsoft.com/en-us/makecode/about?oneroute=true. Accessed 25 Dec 2024
18. Creswell, J.W.: Educational Research: Planning, Conducting, and Evaluating Quantitative and Qualitative Research. Pearson, New Jersey (2008)
19. Billups, F.D.: Qualitative Data Collection Tools: Design, Development, and Applications, 1st edn. SAGE Publications, Thousand Oaks (2020)
20. Saldaña, J.: The Coding Manual for Qualitative Researchers, 5th edn. SAGE Publications, London (2025)
21. "Chase the Pizza" tutorial. https://arcade.makecode.com/tutorials/chase-the-pizza. Accessed 07 Feb 2025
22. "Basketball" tutorial. https://arcade.makecode.com/tutorials/dunk. Accessed 07 Feb 2025
23. Gilster, P.: Digital Literacy, 1st edn. Wiley, New York (1997)
24. Smiderle, R., Rigo, S.J., Marques, L.B., Coelho, J.A.P.M., Jaques, P.A.: The impact of gamification on students' learning, engagement and behavior based on their personality traits. Smart Learn. Environ. **7**, 3 (2020). https://doi.org/10.1186/s40561-019-0098-x

Revised Findings on Students' Preconceptions of Robot Control

Barbora Stenová and Karolína Miková(✉)

Comenius University in Bratislava, Mlynská dolina, 84248 Bratislava, Slovakia
{barbora.stenova,karolina.mikova}@fmph.uniba.sk

Abstract. As technologies develop rapidly, the experiences that students gain outside of school are also changing rapidly. In order to develop a modern, student-centered education system that effectively shapes students' knowledge, it is important to understand the experiences that students bring with them and the foundations on which teachers can build when delivering lessons. This study explores the preconceptions that 10–15-year-old students have about robot control. To obtain relevant data, we designed an electronic questionnaire divided into three sections. We collected responses from over 200 students at three different schools. Our analysis focused on three key open-ended questions from the first section of the questionnaire. The responses were evaluated using qualitative methods and the ESRA model, which considers the relationships between the environment, sensors, the program and actuators. Twelve different models of student thinking were identified, with six occurring most frequently, which we are mentioning in this paper. Many students described robots as devices that perform isolated actions, without referencing control mechanisms. Others attributed decision-making to sensors rather than the program, or viewed robot behavior as a fixed sequence of tasks. Only a minority demonstrated a partial understanding of the interaction between system components, although even these explanations were typically incomplete. The findings reveal that there is a tendency towards fragmented or incorrect conceptions, which highlights the need to address intuitive but inaccurate ideas in robotics education.

Keywords: revised findings · educational robotics · pre-concepts · programming · computer science · secondary education · prior knowledge

1 Introduction

In this paper, we present new results that follow up on a pilot study [1] in which we identified students' basic preconceptions about the functioning and control of robots. The results showed that although most students knew that a robot must be programmed to perform a specific task, their explanations remained mostly at the level of specific examples. Only a few students were able to describe the control process in more detail and explain the relationships between the robot's

B. Fernández-Manjón et al. (Eds.): SETE 2025/ICWL 2025, LNCS 16425, pp. 181–191, 2026.
https://doi.org/10.1007/978-981-92-0042-9_14

environment, sensor activity, robot program, and the actual execution of the task.

These results helped us in the subsequent stage of the research to better set up the [2] coding rubric for an expanded sample of participants, which covers the entire second level of elementary school (ages 10–15) and is also four times larger. The main research objective of this research is to identify the preconceptions of students (aged 10 to 15) regarding the control of robots. In order to fulfill the research objectives, two research questions were formulated as follows:

RQ1: What preconceptions about robot control do students aged 10–15 have?

RQ2: What implications might these preconceptions have for teaching educational robotics in practice?

2 Related Work

Our research is conducted in Slovakia, where we have been systematically integrating programming and robotics from primary education for about 10 years [3]. Educational robotics, as a modern and interesting didactic intervention, allows for the simultaneous teaching of various educational content and the development of many skills [4,5]. In Slovakia is often taught in computer science classes. The analysis and identification of preconceptions in educational robotics is therefore for us one from many essential steps in developing effective and student-centered teaching methods.

2.1 Preconceptions

In this article, the term 'preconceptions' is employed to denote the initial ideas that students form prior to their exposure to formal education in a given field [6]. This knowledge is based on their everyday personal experiences with objects, events, and phenomena they encounter in real life, the media, and films. From birth, children learn intuitively through informal observation of the world around them, manipulation of objects, and experimentation [7]. To map these preconceptions, let us select appropriate methodological materials, forms and teaching methods that can help students identify their incorrect preconceptions more quickly and effectively [8] and build deeper and more structured knowledge.

2.2 Conceptual Change

Building correct knowledge, conceptual change is crucial. We understood it as the restructuring of existing knowledge, represents a key area of research in science education, where students often enter the learning process with incorrect or naïve conceptions [9]. These misconceptions are shaped by intuitive reasoning, everyday experiences, media influence, and shortcomings in traditional instruction [10]. A significant contribution to understanding this process is diSessa's epistemological model Knowledge in Pieces (KiP) [11], originally developed for physics education, but later applied across various domains, including mathematics, chemistry, ecology, computer science, and issues related to race and racism [12].

In recent years, there has been a growing interest in applying conceptual change theories to computer science education, particularly in programming. Burkhardt et al. [13] identified differences in mental representations of object-oriented programming between novices and experts, closely linked to learners' prior knowledge. Aonar and Soloway [14] highlight how novice programmers often fill knowledge gaps with intuitive but incorrect conceptions, which can result in persistent misconceptions. While much of the research has focused on students' preconceptions, increasing attention is being paid to teachers' preconceptions as well, for instance in the context of artificial intelligence [15]. Misconceptions among younger learners have also been studied, particularly regarding their understanding of the Internet at the K–8 level [16,17], with further elaboration by Brom et al. [18,19]. We have not yet found any research on preconceptions about how robots work.

2.3 Interactivity of Robotics Model

Interactivity constitutes an essential aspect of robotics, as it enables robots to dynamically engage with their environment [20]. Through the use of sensors, robots are able to replicate basic human senses such as hearing, sight, and touch, allowing them to perceive external stimuli and make decisions based on this input. This feature significantly distinguishes robotics programming from traditional programming approaches found in widely used educational programming languages for children [21]. The principle that underpins this type of robotic interactivity is known as Sense–Reason–Act (SRA) programming, which enables robots to respond dynamically to changing conditions in their environment [22]. This approach is based on a recurring cycle of three core processes: sense—perceiving the environment; reason—processing information and making decisions; and act—executing an action. For the purposes of our research, we have included one more state in this model, namely "environment," so the model we use is ESRA (see Fig. 1). The robot first senses (relation 1) information from its environment (E) using sensors (S), then sends it (relationship 2) to the program (R), where it is processed according to predefined rules and conditions, and finally the decision is sent (relationship 3) to the actuator (A), which performs a specific action.

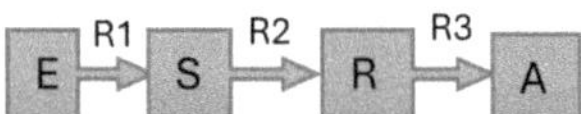

Fig. 1. Graphical representation of the ESRA model with 7 components: E, R1, S, R2, R, R3, A.

3 Methodology

The main goal of this research is to gain a deeper understanding of the students' initial knowledge, which they acquired before the start of formal robotics education, about how robots work, how they perform various activities, how they make decisions, and more. We want not only identify in detail students' preconceptions about robot control, but also to contribute practical recommendations for teaching robotics based on the identified preconceptions of students.

3.1 Participants

Compared to the pilot study, we expanded the research sample to include two additional types of schools and a wider age range (to cover entire second level of elementary school). We have responses from 204 students aged 10 to 15 (85 girls and 119 boys) from three different schools in a capital city. Forty-eight first-year students (aged 11–13) with general intellectual giftedness and higher mathematical and logical thinking were selected from an eight-year grammar school (school A). From a local primary school with a larger number of students (school B), 58 children from grades 6 and 8 (aged 11–14) participated in the research. The largest group was made up of students from School C, a smaller elementary school, where 98 students from grades 5, 6, 7, and 9 (aged 10–15) participated in the research.

3.2 Data Collection

Given the nature of our research, we chose a questionnaire method with open-ended questions [23], which allowed students to express their ideas in their own words, providing us with additional data that gave us a more detailed insight into their thinking. Based on the results of the pilot study, the questionnaire was modified and currently consists of 17 questions. The students completed the questionnaire electronically, which simplified its distribution, administration, and subsequent processing of the data obtained. We evaluated the tool through pilot testing, which was observed by a researcher. Data collection was carried out according to the GDPR, with particular emphasis placed on adherence to ethical principles. Prior to participation, students were informed of the objectives and methodology of the research study. The responses provided by the students were anonymous, and their data was processed exclusively for research purposes.

The Structure of the Questionnaire was divided into three consecutive parts. The first part focused on the concept of a "robot," its functioning, and control options. The second part focused on sensors and actuators, i.e., the process of communication between robots and their surroundings, with questions based on descriptions of model situations. The third part concerned the concept of "sensor" itself, different types of sensors, and their functioning in the context of robotics.

The students' responses offer a comprehensive and varied set of data. In order to answer research questions, three specific questions were selected from the first part of the questionnaire. The focus of these questions corresponds to the main goal and offers more than enough valid data. An analysis of these questions was conducted by both authors. The following questions were selected from the questionnaire:

A: Choose two robots from the previous task and describe how they work (each separately).

B: How does a robot know that it has to perform a certain action? Try to describe it in general terms; if you don't know, use a specific example.

C: If a robot can perform multiple actions, how does it decide which action to perform?

4 Data Analysis

To process the collected data, we primarily used qualitative analysis methods [24], which allowed us to work in detail and distinguish even the slightest differences between students' preconceptions. We applied frequency analysis [25] to track how often different topics appeared in the students' answers. It provides us with the data to completed the overall picture of the quality of particular preconceptions and their prevalence among students. We analyzed each student response (to all three selected questions) in detail using the ESRA model (see chapter 2.3.).

Based on a pilot study, in which we coded students' answers according to five key IT concepts (programming, human–programmer, conditions, environmental dependencies, sensors), we paired individual key IT concepts with components of the ESRA model. Programming and human-programmer were included in component R (program) in our ESRA model, while the programmer could also be classified as component E (environment) in cases of direct human control of the robot. We also assigned conditions to component R (program). We included dependence on the environment in component E (environment) and sensors in component S. In addition, the ESRA model contains relationships between individual components, as it is precisely through these relationships that we can see the level of students' preconceptions, i.e., whether it is just a simple listing of terms or an understanding of these terms and their interconnection.

We coded all the students' answers and assigned them a score (from -1 to 2) for each component and relationship in the ESRA model separately. Since the students' preconceptions are not comprehensive and completely correct, only some parts of the ESRA model appeared in their models. Together, we identified 12 different models representing different student preconceptions about robot control. Using selective coding, we selected the six most common ones that best reflect their preconceptions about robot control.

The coding and scoring of individual student responses was carried out as follows:

0: If the component or relationship was not present in the response at all. For example: "The robot vacuums." Although the answer describes the activity, it does not contain any description of the ESRA model components, so we assigned a score of 0 to the student for each component and relationship.

1: If the component was described correctly, but only very superficially and without technical terminology, we assigned a value of 1. An example together with the assigned scores for individual components of the ESRA model is shown in Table 1.

Table 1. Example of assessment for a score of 1 in the ESRA model

"The robot vacuum cleaner moves because it has a sensor that sees and recognizes obstacles in its surroundings."

E	R1	S	R2	R	R3	A
1	1	1	0	0	0	1

-1: If a component was described but incorrectly interpreted, a value of -1 was assigned. For example, "The robot knows what to do because the sensor tells it." In this case, the student used the term sensor but incorrectly assigned it a decision-making function that belongs to the program, so we assigned a score of -1 for relationships 2 and 3, as the student has an incorrect preconception about them.

2: The component was explained correctly, in detail, and using technical terminology at a cognitively appropriate level. For example: "The robot vacuum cleaner uses a distance sensor that detects obstacles in its vicinity and then sends this information to a program that decides what the robot vacuum cleaner will do next." The scores assigned to the individual components of the ESRA model are shown in Table 2.

Table 2. Example of assessment for a score of 2 in the ESRA model

"The robot vacuum cleaner uses a distance sensor that detects obstacles in its surroundings and then sends this information to a program that decides what the robot vacuum cleaner will do next."

E	R1	S	R2	R	R3	A
2	1	2	1	2	1	1

When analyzing student responses according to the ESRA model, we also looked at the type of robot control the students described in their answers. We distinguished between direct and planned control. Direct control represented a situation where the robot acted on the basis of an immediate command from a human, for example via a mobile device or a button. Planned control is when the robot acts autonomously on the basis of a pre-prepared program and is able to respond to stimuli from sensors. This categorization allowed us to better identify whether students perceive robots only as human-controlled devices or whether they also recognize their autonomous behavior.

5 Results

Based on an analysis of student responses, we identified the most common preconceptions that appeared in all participating schools. These preconceptions about robot control range from completely naive and incorrect concepts to incomplete, non-complex but partially correct concepts. We list them in order from the simplest to the most complex. That is, from those that had only one or no components from the ESRA model to those that had more.

Students describe a robot as a device that performs one specific action without explaining the control process. Students are unaware of the principles of robot control and do not realize that its activity is controlled by inputs from sensors and a program. They perceive the robot as a machine that has a function and performs it mechanically, for example, "the robot vacuums" or "the robot walks."

Students identify the program as the only principle of robot operation and control. Students repeatedly mentioned the program as the basic principle of robot operation and control, e.g., that "the robot has a program inside it that determines its behavior." However, there is no acknowledgment of changes in behavior based on the state of the environment, sensors, actuators, and the relationships between them. They perceive the robot purely as a decision-making machine, without considering where the stimuli come from or how the program's decisions are translated into real action.

Students perceived robot control as performing tasks according to a specified priority of activities, regardless of stimuli from sensors in the robot's environment. The students believe that controlling the robot consists of having a pre-set order of activities according to which it performs tasks, i.e., the robot does not "decide" or, if it does, it decides which activity is more important and performs that one. "The robot vacuum cleaner first vacuums the house and then goes to recharge, because that is the order it has been programmed to follow."

Students attribute the task of controlling the robot only to sensors. They perceive sensors as devices that not only collect data from the environment, but also make decisions and directly determine the action of the actuator/robot. In their answers focused on robot control, the students described only the role of the sensor and the execution of the action. Other components of the ESRA model were not mentioned. They even have an incorrect preconception about sensors, as they attribute not only the function of sensing the environment to them, but also a decision-making function ("the sensor tells the robot what to do"). They do not realize that the decision-making function is performed by a program that, after processing the input information from the sensors, decides how the robot will behave.

Students describe that the robot's activity is controlled by a program and sensors. Students realize that the robot's sensor detects "something," then the program decides on the robot's next action and sends the result to the actuator. For example "The robot waiter can bring me my order because the sensor and program tell it to." In their minds, the robot responds to stimuli from the sensors and the program ensures that some action is taken. However, they still lack a conscious connection to the environment, i.e., where the sensors obtain this information and also that the data obtained from the sensor enters the program. This preconception is closest to the correct functioning and control of the robot, but it is still incomplete.

Students intuitively and implicitly distinguish between planning and direct control, but their understanding is mostly superficial and incomplete. The most common model in the students' answers was one in which the robot performs an activity independently "according to how it is programmed," i.e., they described planned control. Some students only mentioned direct control of the robot, where a person gave a command and the robot carried it out, without a deeper explanation of the process of input processing or the interconnection between individual system components, for example. "When someone gives it a command," "when we press a button," or "when we turn it on in the application." Students therefore lack knowledge about the second type of control or even the possible combination of both types of control.

Overall, it can be said that although students are able to describe how a robot works and how it is controlled, their understanding is superficial, often inaccurate, and sometimes even incorrect. The most common misconceptions simplify the control of a robot to simply entering commands, or perceive the principle of control through only one or two components of the ESRA model (program or sensor). Students therefore often lack awareness of the interconnection of all system components (sensors – program – actuators – environment) and their mutual relationships.

5.1 Recommendations

We consider it essential in these days that teachers systematically build on existing student preconceptions when teaching computer science and robotics and focus specifically on areas where students have incomplete, incorrect, or intuitively formed ideas. Incorrect preconceptions should not be eliminated, but gradually transformed into correct ones [26]. If the teacher creates activities that reveal these preconceptions, confront them, and gradually transform them into more accurate knowledge, students will be able to build a comprehensive and functional model of understanding the functioning and control of robots.

Teaching educational robotics should focus more on explaining the roles of individual components of the ESRA model (robot environment, sensors, program, actuators) and their interconnection. Of course, this should be age appropriate and linked to examples that students are familiar with from everyday life. It would be appropriate to use the ESRA model as a theoretical basis on which educators can create activities explaining the individual components of the ESRA model and their interrelationships. For example activities could focus on working with sensors, such as reacting to obstacles, changing light intensity, or distinguishing colors. After the activities, it is a good idea for students and teachers to work together to name or draw what role the sensor played, what the program did, and what the actuator did. In this way, students will gradually understand that the sensor only provides data from the environment, the program processes it, and the actuator performs the specific action. It is also beneficial to include tasks in which the robot behaves differently depending on the sensor's input. For example, it moves forward until it "detects" an obstacle, and only when it detects it does it turn around. Students will thus see that the robot can respond to changes in the environment.

6 Discussion

We are aware that our results must be interpreted with certain limitations in mind. The research sample included students from three different types of schools, but all were located in the capital city, which may affect the possibilities for generalization. For this reason, it would be appropriate to expand the research sample to include schools from other cities or villages in future research. In addition, it was a questionnaire survey, which provided rich data but did not allow for a more detailed observation of the students' thought processes. A further limitation of the research was the data analysis. The process of assigning scores to individual answers was challenging and time-consuming. It is considered a weakness of the research that the process was not always straightforward. Therefore, the authors conducted numerous discussions and used several tools to clarify and standardize the scoring procedures. They also established sample examples (see tables in Chap. 4) to assist in assigning scores to identical or similar student responses.

7 Conclusion

Nowadays, robotics, automation, and artificial intelligence are increasingly influencing our everyday lives, which is why we consider it important for students to understand at least the basic principles of how they work. With rapidly developing technologies, students' experiences are also developing rapidly. For this reason, we consider it important to know students' preconceptions about robot control even before formal teaching of educational robotics in schools. Such knowledge can guide the educational process in a way that helps students form correct ideas, eliminate misconceptions, and gradually develop the skills necessary for controlling and safely using robotic technologies.

We qualitatively analyzing student responses from 204 questionnaires and we identified 12 different models of student preconceptions. It was evident that students possessed an understanding of the necessity for programming in order to operate a robot; however, their explanations frequently remained at the level of specific examples, lacking a comprehensive grasp of the control principle.

This principle involves a multitude of components, including the environment, sensors, actuators, and the interrelationships between these components. Consequently, students frequently either reduce robot control to a single component (e.g., a program or sensor) or incorrectly attribute functions to components that do not belong to them.

Here are the six most common preconceptions among students aged 10–15:

- describe a robot as a device that performs one specific action without explaining the control process.
- identify the program as the only principle of robot operation and control.
- perceived robot control as performing tasks according to a specified priority of activities, regardless of stimuli from sensors in the robot's environment.
- attribute the task of controlling the robot only to sensors. They perceive sensors as devices that not only collect data from the environment, but also make decisions and directly determine the action of the actuator/robot.
- describe that the robot's activity is controlled by a program and sensors.
- intuitively and implicitly distinguish between planning and direct control, but their understanding is mostly superficial and incomplete.

We want to continue our research by processing the remaining two parts of the questionnaire and building a more comprehensive set of preconceptions about robotics. We believe that in the future we will also be able to develop recommendations that will lead to the creation of activities based on the identified preconceptions and systematically contribute to building students' knowledge.

Acknowledgments. This work was supported by national grants VEGA 1/0621/22 and VEGA 1/0407/25.

References

1. Stenová, B., Miková, K.: Students' Pre-concepts of Robot Control Before Their First Robotics Lesson: A Pilot Study. In: Learning Technologies and Systems (SETe), pp. 86–98. Springer, Singapore (2025)
2. Allen, D., Tanner, K.: Rubrics: Tools for making learning goals and evaluation criteria explicit for both teachers and learners. CBE—Life Sciences Education **5**(3), 197–203 (2006)
3. Kabátová, M., Kalaš, I., Tomcsányiová, M.: Programming in Slovak Primary Schools. Olympiads in Informatics **10**, 125–159 (2016)
4. Mikropoulos, T.A., et al.: Educational robotics as mindtools. Themes in Science and Technology Education **6**(1), 5–14 (2013)
5. Kandlhofer, M., Steinbauer, G.: Evaluating the impact of educational robotics on pupils' technical and social skills and science related attitudes. Robot. Auton. Syst. **75**, 679–685 (2016)
6. Henriques, L.: Children's Ideas About Weather: A Review of the Literature. Sch. Sci. Math. **102**(5), 202–215 (2002)
7. Paradise, R., Rogoff, B.: Side by Side: Learning by Observing and Pitching In. Ethos **37**(1), 102–138 (2009)

8. Otero, V.K.: Moving Beyond the "Get it or Don't" Conception of Formative Assessment. J. Teach. Educ. **57**(3), 247–255 (2006)
9. Sinatra, G.M.: The "warming trend" in conceptual change research: the legacy of Paul R. Pintrich. Educ. Psychol. **40**(2), 107–115 (2005)
10. Garrison, J.W., Bentley, M.L.: Science education, conceptual change and breaking with everyday experience. Stud. Philos. Educ. **10**(1), 19–35 (1990)
11. diSessa, A.A.: A friendly introduction to "knowledge in pieces": modeling types of knowledge and their roles in learning. In: Invited Lectures from the 13th International Congress on Mathematical Education, pp. 65–84. Springer, Cham (2018)
12. Philip, T.: A "knowledge in pieces" approach to studying ideological change in teachers' reasoning about race, racism and racial justice. Cogn. Instr. **29**(3), 297–329 (2011)
13. Burkhardt, J.M., Détienne, F., Wiedenbeck, S.: Mental representations constructed by experts and novices in object-oriented program comprehension. In: Human-Computer Interaction INTERACT'97: IFIP TC13 International Conference on Human-Computer Interaction, pp. 339–346. Springer, Boston (1997)
14. Bonar, J., Soloway, E.: Preprogramming knowledge: a major source of misconceptions in novice programmers. Hum.-Comput. Interact. **1**(2), 133–161 (1985)
15. Lindner, A., Berges, M.: Can you explain AI to me? Teachers' pre-concepts about Artificial Intelligence. In: IEEE Frontiers in Education Conference, pp. 1–9 (2020)
16. Pancratz, N., Diethelm, I.: Draw us how smartphones, video gaming consoles, and robotic vacuum cleaners look like from the inside: students' conceptions of computing system architecture. In: Proceedings of the 15th Workshop on Primary and Secondary Computing Education (WiPSCE '20). ACM, New York (2020)
17. Rücker, M.T., Pinkwart, N.: Review and discussion of children's conceptions of computers. J. Sci. Educ. Technol. **25**, 274–283 (2016)
18. Yaghobová, A., Drobná, A., Brom, C.: Are There gears and belts inside the computer?: preliminary results of research on preconceptions of 6–9-graders. In: Proceedings of the 2023 Conference on Innovation and Technology in Computer Science Education, vol. 2, pp. 659–659 (2023)
19. Brom, C., Yaghobová, A., Drobná, A., Urban, M.: 'The internet is in the satellites!': A systematic review of 3–15-year-olds' conceptions about the internet. Educ. Inf. Technol. **28**, 14639–14668 (2023)
20. Khatib, O.: Digital interactivity: human-centered robotics, haptics, and simulation. In: Liu, J., et al. (eds.) Active Media Technology. Lecture Notes in Computer Science, vol. 2252, pp. 4–4. Springer, Berlin, Heidelberg (2001)
21. Merkouris, A., Chorianopoulos, K.: Introducing computer programming to children through robotic and wearable devices. In: Proceedings of the Workshop in Primary and Secondary Computing Education, pp. 69–72. ACM, London (2015)
22. Slangen, L.A.M.P., Gravemeijer, K.P.E., Pepin, B.E.U., van Keulen, J.: Teaching Robotics in Primary School. Technische Universiteit Eindhoven, Eindhoven (2016)
23. Billups, F.D.: Qualitative Data Collection Tools: Design, Development, and Applications, 1st edn. SAGE Publications, Thousand Oaks (2020)
24. Creswell, J.W.: Educational Research: Planning, Conducting, and Evaluating Quantitative and Qualitative Research. Pearson, New Jersey (2008)
25. Creswell, J.W.: Concise Introduction to Mixed Methods Research, 2nd edn. SAGE Publications, Los Angeles (2021)
26. Posner, G.J., Strike, K.A., Hewson, P.W., Gertzog, W.A.: Accommodation of a scientific conception: toward a theory of conceptual change. Sci. Educ. **66**(2), 211–227 (1982)

AI and Learning Analytics Innovations

Simplifying Graph Neural Kernels: from Stacking Layers to Collapsed Structure

Lin Wang, Shijie Wang, Sirui Huang, and Qing Li(✉)

The Hong Kong Polytechnic University, Hong Kong SAR, China
{comp-lin.wang,shijie.wang,sirui.huang}@connect.polyu.hk,
csqli@comp.polyu.edu.hk

Abstract. Recent advances in Learning Analytics have shown the importance of modeling complex relationships among learners, learning resources, and interactions in online education environments. Graph-based representations naturally capture these multi-relational structures, enabling more accurate analysis of learning behaviors and personalized support. However, existing graph neural network models face challenges in terms of computational scalability and interpretability, which limit their applicability in large-scale e-learning platforms. To address these issues, this paper introduces two novel kernel-based methods for graph representation learning: the Simplified Graph Neural Tangent Kernel (SGTK) and the Simplified Graph Neural Kernel (SGNK). SGTK replaces the traditional multi-layer stacking mechanism with a continuous K-step aggregation procedure, reducing redundant computations while maintaining expressive power. SGNK further advances this approach by modeling infinitely wide graph neural networks as Gaussian Processes, allowing kernel values to be computed directly without explicit layer-wise operations. Applied to learning analytics tasks such as student performance prediction and resource recommendation, our methods demonstrate competitive accuracy compared to state-of-the-art graph neural models, while achieving superior computational efficiency. By integrating graph kernel methods with learning analytics, this work offers an efficient approach for analyzing complex learner-resource-interaction networks in e-learning environments. Extensive experiments on node classification task demonstrate that the proposed SGTK and SGNK achieve performance comparable to existing approaches while improving computational efficiency. Implementation details are available at https://github.com/WANGLin0126/SGNK.

Keywords: Gaussian Process Kernel · Graph Kernel · Neural Tangent Kernel · Graph Neural Tangent Kernel · Simple Graph Convolution

1 Introduction

In modern e-learning environments, massive amounts of heterogeneous data are generated from learners' interactions with digital platforms, including activi-

B. Fernández-Manjón et al. (Eds.): SETE 2025/ICWL 2025, LNCS 16425, pp. 195–209, 2026.
https://doi.org/10.1007/978-981-92-0042-9_15

ties such as course navigation, resource usage, assessments, and peer collaboration. Effectively analyzing these data is central to the field of Learning Analytics, which aims to understand learning behaviors, predict performance, and provide personalized feedback [17,21]. A common challenge in this context lies in modeling the complex relationships among learners, learning resources, and interaction events. Graph-structured representations naturally capture these multi-relational connections, making them a powerful tool for educational data mining and the development of intelligent tutoring and adaptive learning systems [2,9,11,27].

To process graph-structured data, existing research has mainly relied on Graph Neural Networks (GNNs) and Graph Kernels (GKs) [20,24,32,33]. GNNs learn node or graph representations through recursive message passing and feature transformations, enabling the extraction of higher-order relational patterns. In contrast, GKs embed graphs into high-dimensional feature spaces to measure similarity based on structural information and attributes. Both approaches are valuable for educational applications, such as modeling student-resource networks or identifying communities of learners with similar behavior [2,11]. However, they also exhibit critical limitations: GNNs are computationally intensive and require extensive training, while GKs, though training-free, often lack the expressive power to fully capture complex patterns in large-scale learning data [20,24].

To harness the advantages of both GNNs and GKs, [3] introduced the Graph Neural Tangent Kernel (GNTK), a novel kernel method that effectively bridges the gap between these two approaches. Specifically, the GNTK models the training dynamics of infinite-width GNNs, thereby integrating the powerful representational capabilities of GNNs with the computational efficiency of GKs. By capturing the strengths of both paradigms, the GNTK has demonstrated competitive—and, in some cases, superior—performance compared to GNNs across a variety of graph mining tasks [16,26].

In spite of its demonstrated effectiveness, the GNTK exhibits certain inherent limitations. Specifically, the GNTK employs a layer-stacking strategy to compute the kernel value, as illustrated in Fig. 1. In this strategy, each layer begins with an aggregation step, where information from neighboring nodes is collected, followed by a transformation step that applies non-linear operations to the aggregated data [7]. These steps are performed recursively across layers to iteratively update the kernel values. While this recursive stacking mechanism enhances the expressiveness of the kernel by incorporating information from multiple layers, it also leads to an increase in computational complexity, which grows linearly with the number of layers stacked.

Moreover, as the depth of the network increases, the transformations performed in the deeper layers contribute progressively less to the overall performance of the model [30]. This diminishing contribution limits the utility of excessively deep networks. As a result, while the GNTK is a powerful tool, its high computational cost and reduced benefits at greater depths may hinder its scalability and applicability in certain cases.

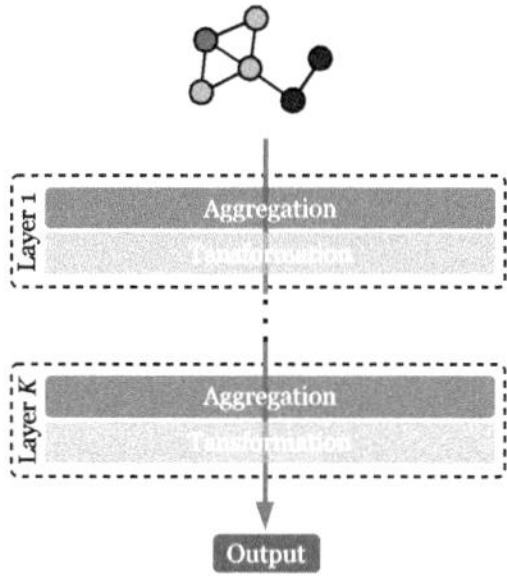

Fig. 1. The layer stacking structure.

In this paper, we investigate the structure of the GNTK method and identify computational redundancies. Specifically, as the number of stacked layers increases, the impact of the non-linear transformations in deeper layers diminishes. Thus, retaining only aggregations and a limited number of Neural Tangent Kernel [7] iterations within these layers suffices. This approach reduces computation time while maintaining the kernel function's effectiveness.

Building on this observation, we propose the **S**implified **G**raph Neural **T**angent **K**ernel (**SGTK**) method. This method involves performing K consecutive steps of aggregation operations, followed by a single update of the kernel function. SGTK reduces computational redundancy and enhances the efficiency of kernel function computation. Furthermore, we define an infinitely wide, simple graph neural model, deriving a Gaussian process (GP) [29] kernel function with reduced computational complexity, termed the **S**implified **G**raph **N**eural **K**ernel (**SGNK**). This method calculates the expectations of the post-activation output of the infinitely wide graph model to determine the kernel value. Compared to SGTK, SGNK further streamlines the process and reduces computational complexity while maintaining effectiveness in downstream tasks. Our main contributions are as follows:

- We propose SGTK, which replaces the stacking layers in GNTK with continuous K-step message passing to reduce computational redundancy.
- By interpreting the infinite-width simple graph neural model as a GP, we introduce SGNK, which further reduces computational complexity compared to SGTK.
- We conducted a theoretical analysis to demonstrate the low computational complexity of the proposed methods and validated their computational efficiency improvements through extensive experiments.
- We have experimentally validated the proposed methods in node classification task, demonstrating that our methods ensure excellent classification accuracy.

2 Related Works

Graph Neural Networks. GNNs have undergone significant advancements, addressing diverse aspects of graph learning through various models. For semi-supervised learning, GCNs [10] leverage spectral graph convolutions, while GATs [23] incorporate attention mechanisms to prioritize relevant neighbors. Extensions like R-GCNs [18] handle multi-relational data, and GraphSAGE [5] introduces sampling-based aggregation for scalable inductive learning. To enhance expressiveness, GINs [33] employ sum aggregation inspired by the Weisfeiler-Lehman test. Simplifying computations, SGC [30] removes non-linear activations and collapses weight matrices, while APPNP [4] integrates personalized PageRank with neural networks for improved performance.

Graph Neural Tangent Kernel. Neural tangent kernel (NTK) [7] fundamentally transforms our understanding of training dynamics in infinitely wide neural networks by equating them to kernel methods. CNTK [1] extends NTK to convolutional neural networks. GNTK [3] and GPGC [6] are introduced for graph neural networks, demonstrating their efficacy in graph-based tasks. Krishnagopal et al. [12] investigate the training dynamics of large-graph GNNs using GNTKs and graphons. GCNTK [35] shows that for wide GCNs, the output for semi-supervised problems can be described by a simple differential equation. A quantum graph learning model, GraphQNTK [22], leverages quantum parallelism to enhance computational efficiency; however, experiments reveal that its performance lags behind that of GNTK. Jiang et al. [8] employ sketching to accelerate GNTK, but they do not experimentally demonstrate efficiency improvements. Wang et al. [26] integrate structural information with the neural tangent kernel and propose the SNTK, a method designed to address graph condensation problems. Additionally, GCKM [31] employs stacked layers to compute graph kernels, but this approach involves redundant computations, which contribute to increased computational complexity.

3 Methodology

In this section, we begin with a brief review of the GNTK to establish the necessary background. Thereafter, we introduce the proposed SGTK and SGNK, as illustrated in Fig. 2. Subsequently, we present the implementation details of the proposed methods, outlining the key steps and considerations. Lastly, we provide a theoretical analysis of computational complexity, showing that the proposed kernel methods are more efficient than previous GNTK approaches.

3.1 Notations and Definitions

In general, a graph can be represented as $G = (\mathcal{V}, \mathcal{E})$, where $\mathcal{V} = \{v_1, v_2, \cdots, v_{|\mathcal{V}|}\}$ denotes the set of $|\mathcal{V}|$ nodes, and $\mathcal{E}$ represents the edge set. We use $X = [x_1, x_2, \cdots, x_{|\mathcal{V}|}]^\top \in \mathbb{R}^{|\mathcal{V}| \times d}$ to denote the node feature matrix, where d is the dimensional size of the node features. The structural information of the graph is captured by the adjacency matrix $A \in \{0,1\}^{|\mathcal{V}| \times |\mathcal{V}|}$, where $A_{ij} = 1$ indicates a connection between nodes v_i and v_j, and $A_{ij} = 0$ otherwise. In this study, we examine both graph-level and node-level downstream tasks. Given two graphs $G_1 = \{X_1, A_1\}$ and $G_2 = \{X_2, A_2\}$ with n and m nodes, respectively, the graph kernel is defined as $\mathcal{K}(G_1, G_2) : \mathbb{R}^{n\times d} \times \mathbb{R}^{m\times d} \to \mathbb{R}$. Conversely, the node-level kernel is defined as $\mathcal{K}(v_i, v_j) : \mathbb{R}^d \times \mathbb{R}^d \to \mathbb{R}$.

3.2 Brief Review of Graph Neural Tangent Kernel

The GNTK [3] is a kernel function derived from infinite-width graph neural networks. It serves as a tool for analyzing and understanding the training behavior of GNNs. Specifically, we consider a two-layer GCN [10], which is defined as:

$$f_{\text{GCN}}(X, A) = \text{softmax}\{\hat{A}\ \text{ReLU}\{\hat{A}XW^{(0)}\}W^{(1)}\}, \tag{1}$$

where $\hat{A} = \tilde{D}^{-\frac{1}{2}}\tilde{A}\tilde{D}^{-\frac{1}{2}}$, $\tilde{A} = A + I$, and $\tilde{D} = \text{diag}\left(\sum_j \hat{A}_{1j}, \sum_j \hat{A}_{2j}, \ldots, \sum_j \hat{A}_{nj}\right)$. The GNTK follows a structure similar to that of the GCN. It first uses adjacency information to aggregate the covariance matrix of the node features. This matrix is then input into the NTK iterations. Repeating these steps K times yields the kernel value for an infinite-width GCN with K layers, as illustrated on the left in Fig. 2. For two graphs G and G', the GNTK kernel matrix is computed as:

$$\boldsymbol{\Theta} = \text{NTK}\{\hat{A}_1\ \text{NTK}\{\hat{A}_1\boldsymbol{\Sigma}^{(0)}\hat{A}_2^\top\}\hat{A}_2^\top\}, \tag{2}$$

where $\Sigma_{ij}^{(0)} = c_i c_j x_i \cdot x_j$, and $c_i = (\|\sum_{p\in\mathcal{N}(i)\cup\{i\}} x_p\|_2)^{-1}$ serves as a scaling coefficient that facilitates subsequent NTK computations. $x_i \in G_1$ and $x_j \in G_2$. By conducting a readout operation on the kernel matrix in Equation (2), the similarity value between graphs G_1 and G_2 can be derived.

The performance and efficiency of GNTK greatly depend on its architecture, including the number of layers and NTK iterations. Although iterative stacking of layers enables GNTKs to match GCNs of arbitrary depths, minimally contributing NTK iterations in deeper layers introduce computational redundancy. This results in computational overhead, limiting their practical applicability [3,30].

3.3 Simplified Graph Neural Tangent Kernel

GNTK originates from the infinitely wide GCN. To simplify the redundant computations in GNTK, it is essential to first examine the computational complexity inherent in the infinitely wide GCN.

We propose streamlining the GCN structure by retaining K rounds of message passing to enhance the receptive field of node representations while reducing the nonlinear transformations to collapse the weight matrix. Specifically, considering the infinite-width graph neural network model with K-step message passing, we have:

$$\hat{X} = \hat{A}^K X, \tag{3}$$

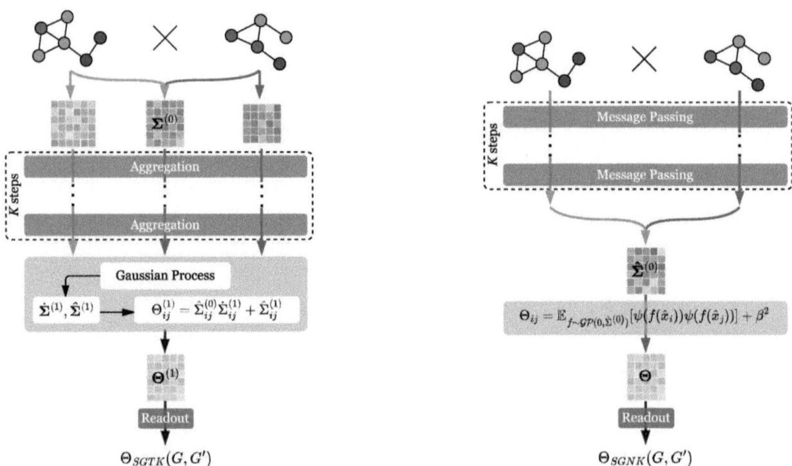

Fig. 2. This kernel structure includes SGTK and SGNK. The SGTK improves computational efficiency by using continuous K-step aggregation. Furthermore, the SGNK models the infinite-width simple graph neural network as a GP, requiring only the expectation of the infinite-width neural model's post-activation output to determine the kernel values. This approach further reduces computational complexity.

where $\hat{X} \in \mathbb{R}^{n\times d}$, with n representing the number of samples and d the input dimensionality.

To enhance the receptive field of the node's features, a two-layer neural network is employed, where the width of the hidden layer approaches infinity. Let the infinite-width neural network take $\hat{X}$ as its input. Each layer consists of a biased linear transformation $f^{(l)}: \mathbb{R}^{n\times d^{(l-1)}} \rightarrow \mathbb{R}^{n\times d^{(l)}}$, where $d^{(l)}$ is the width of the l-th layer. The parameters are initialized as $W^{(l)} \sim \mathcal{N}(0, \sigma_w^2)$ and $b^{(l)} \sim \mathcal{N}(0, \sigma_b^2)$. Let $\hat{X}^{(0)} = \hat{X}$. The output of the l-th layer of the network can be expressed as:

$$f^{(l)}(\hat{X}^{(l)}) = \sigma_w \hat{X}^{(l)} W^{(l)} + \beta b^{(l)}, \tag{4}$$

$$\hat{X}^{(l+1)} = \psi(f^{(l)}(\hat{X}^{(l)})), \tag{5}$$

where β is a hyperparameter adjusting the effect of the bias on training. Let $\sigma_b^2 = 1$. Under LeCun initialization [13], the variance of the weights $W^{(l)}$ is denoted as $\sigma_w^2 = \frac{1}{d^{(l)}}$. As the width of a neural network approaches infinity, its training dynamics can be represented by an explicit limiting kernel [7], which we term the Simplified Graph Neural Tangent Kernel (SGTK).

Specifically, for two graphs G_1 and G_2, with node features $X_1 = \{x_i\}_{i=1}^n$ and $X_2 = \{x_j\}_{j=1}^m$, respectively, the kernel preprocessing involves the covariance matrix of the enhanced node features:

$$\hat{\Sigma}_{ij}^{(0)} = \frac{1}{d}\hat{x}_i \hat{x}_j^\top + \beta^2. \tag{6}$$

Suppose the enhanced node features $\{\hat{x}_i\}_{i=1}^n$ and $\{\hat{x}_j\}_{j=1}^m$ are independently and identically distributed (i.i.d.). In the limit as the layer width tends to infinity, the node-level SGTK kernel value between node v_i of G_1 and node v_j of G_2 is defined by:

$$\Theta_{ij}^{(1)} = \hat{\boldsymbol{\Sigma}}_{ij}^{(0)} \dot{\boldsymbol{\Sigma}}_{ij}^{(1)} + \hat{\boldsymbol{\Sigma}}_{ij}^{(1)}, \tag{7}$$

where the intermediate calculation variables of the covariance matrix are:

$$\hat{\boldsymbol{\Sigma}}_{ij}^{(1)} = \mathbb{E}_{f^{(0)} \sim \mathcal{GP}(0, \hat{\boldsymbol{\Sigma}}^{(0)})}[\psi(f^{(0)}(\hat{x}_i))\psi(f^{(0)}(\hat{x}_j))] + \beta^2, \tag{8}$$

$$\dot{\boldsymbol{\Sigma}}_{ij}^{(1)} = \mathbb{E}_{f^{(0)} \sim \mathcal{GP}(0, \hat{\boldsymbol{\Sigma}}^{(0)})}[\dot{\psi}(f^{(0)}(\hat{x}_i))\dot{\psi}(f^{(0)}(\hat{x}_j))], \tag{9}$$

where $\dot{\psi}(\cdot)$ is the derivative of the activation function. As illustrated in Fig. 2, compared to GNTK, which requires iterative stacking of message passing and NTK iterations, the proposed SGTK enhances the receptive field of node features through K-step aggregation in a concentrated manner. This is followed by a single kernel update, effectively collapsing the layers to reduce computational redundancy.

3.4 Simplified Graph Neural Kernel

SGTK streamlines the computation process of GNTK by reducing redundant calculations. However, the computation of SGTK relies on the characteristics of infinite-width neural networks and the Gaussian process kernel. The computational efficiency of the kernel method is limited by its reliance on the Gaussian process kernel.

We further propose a kernel method with lower computational complexity than SGTK, termed the Simplified Graph Neural Kernel (SGNK). This approach directly models the defined infinite-width simple graph neural network as a Gaussian process, which is determined by the expectations of the post-activation outputs of the Gaussian process [14,15]. These expectations can be computed analytically without the need for iteration. Consequently, this direct kernel method further reduces computational complexity. For the node features x_i and x_j, the Gaussian process kernel is defined recursively by the following functions:

$$\Sigma^{(0)}(x_i, x_j) = \frac{1}{d} x_i x_j^\top + \beta^2, \tag{10}$$

$$\Sigma^{(l+1)}(x_i, x_j) = \mathbb{E}_{f^{(l)} \sim \mathcal{GP}(0, \boldsymbol{\Sigma}^{(l)})} \left[\psi(f^{(l)}(x_i))\psi(f^{(l)}(x_j))\right] + \beta^2. \tag{11}$$

For an infinitely wide simple graph neural network with K-step message passing, followed by a two-layer neural network, the node-level Simplified Graph Neural Kernel (SGNK) for the node features x_i and x_j is defined as follows:

$$\Theta_{ij} = \mathbb{E}_{f^{(0)} \sim \mathcal{GP}(0, \hat{\boldsymbol{\Sigma}}^{(0)})}[\psi(f^{(0)}(\hat{x}_i))\psi(f^{(0)}(\hat{x}_j))] + \beta^2. \tag{12}$$

Let the neural network adopt the Error Function as the activation function $\psi(x) = \frac{2}{\pi}\int_0^x e^{-t^2}dt$, then SGNK can be calculated analytically [28],

$$\Theta_{ij} = \frac{2}{\pi} sin^{-1} \frac{2\tilde{x}_i^\top \Sigma_w \tilde{x}_j}{\sqrt{(1 + 2\tilde{x}_i^\top \Sigma_w \tilde{x}_i)(1 + 2\tilde{x}_j^\top \Sigma_w \tilde{x}_j)}}, \tag{13}$$

where $\tilde{x} = (\hat{x}, 1)^\top$ is the augmented vector, and the variance matrix $\Sigma_w = \text{diag}(1, 1, \cdots, \sigma_b^2)$. In matrix form, the calculation process can be expressed as:

$$\boldsymbol{\Theta} = \frac{2}{\pi} sin^{-1} \frac{2\tilde{X}_1 \Sigma_w \tilde{X}_2^\top}{\sqrt{[\mathbf{1} + 2diag(\tilde{X}_1 \Sigma_w \tilde{X}_1^\top)]^\top [\mathbf{1} + 2diag(\tilde{X}_2 \Sigma_w \tilde{X}_2^\top)]}}. \tag{14}$$

Given that $\Sigma_w = diag(1, 1, \cdots, \sigma_b^2)$, we have,

$$\boldsymbol{\Theta} = \frac{2}{\pi} sin^{-1} \frac{2\tilde{X}_1 \tilde{X}_2^\top}{\sqrt{[\mathbf{1} + 2diag(\tilde{X}_1 \tilde{X}_1^\top)]^\top [\mathbf{1} + 2diag(\tilde{X}_2 \tilde{X}_2^\top)]}} \tag{15}$$

Finally, for the graph-level tasks, the readout operation yields the kernel value between G and G', which is:

$$\Theta(G, G') = \sum_{i \in G, j \in G'} \Theta_{ij}. \tag{16}$$

The detailed execution processes of our proposed SGTK and SGNK are shown in the Algorithm 1 and 2.

3.5 Computational Complexity Analysis

To demonstrate the reduced computational complexity of our proposed simplified methods compared to the GNTK, we present a comprehensive computational complexity analysis. The notations used are as follows: n and m represent the number of nodes in two different graphs, d stands for the node feature dimensionality, k indicates the average degree per node, and K represents the number of message-passing iterations.

In each layer, the computational complexity of GNTK comprises two parts: message passing and NTK iterations. The complexity of message passing is $O(nk^2)$, while the NTK iterations have a complexity of $O(n^2d + nmd + m^2d)$. Consequently, for the GNTK with K layers, the total computational complexity is $O(K(nk^2 + n^2d + m^2d + nmd))$.

In contrast, the proposed SGTK performs K steps of aggregation and eliminates multi-layer stacking, achieving an overall complexity of $O(Knk^2 + n^2d + m^2d + nmd)$. Furthermore, the SGNK reduces this complexity to $O(Knk^2 + nmd)$. This indicates that the complexity of our proposed kernels is lower than that of GNTK.

Algorithm 1. Simplified Graph Neural Tangent Kernel (SGTK)

1: **Input:** Graphs $G = \{X, A\}$, $G' = \{X', A'\}$.
2: **Output:** Node-level kernel matrix $\boldsymbol{\Theta}^{(1)}$ and graph-level kernel value $\Theta(G, G')$.
3: **Initialize:** $\boldsymbol{\Sigma}^{(0)} = X(X')^\top$, $\boldsymbol{\Sigma}_X^{(0)} = X(X)^\top$, $\boldsymbol{\Sigma}_{X'}^{(0)} = X'(X')^\top$, $\hat{A} = D^{-\frac{1}{2}}(A + I)D^{-\frac{1}{2}}$, $\hat{A}' = D^{-\frac{1}{2}}(A' + I)D^{-\frac{1}{2}}$, K.
4: K-step aggregation on covariance matrix.

$$\hat{\boldsymbol{\Sigma}}^{(0)} = \frac{1}{d}\hat{A}^K \boldsymbol{\Sigma}^{(0)}(\hat{A}'^K)^\top + \beta^2,$$

$$\hat{\boldsymbol{\Sigma}}_X^{(0)} = \frac{1}{d}\hat{A}^K \boldsymbol{\Sigma}_X^{(0)}(\hat{A}^K)^\top + \beta^2,$$

$$\hat{\boldsymbol{\Sigma}}_{X'}^{(0)} = \frac{1}{d}\hat{A}'^K \boldsymbol{\Sigma}_{X'}^{(0)}(\hat{A}'^K)^\top + \beta^2.$$

5: Update $\hat{\boldsymbol{\Sigma}}_X^{(1)}$ and $\hat{\boldsymbol{\Sigma}}_{X'}^{(1)}$ by Eq. (8).
6: Update $\hat{\boldsymbol{\Sigma}}^{(1)}$ and $\dot{\boldsymbol{\Sigma}}^{(1)}$ by Eq. (8), (9), $\hat{\boldsymbol{\Sigma}}^{(0)}$, $\hat{\boldsymbol{\Sigma}}_X^{(1)}$, and $\hat{\boldsymbol{\Sigma}}_{X'}^{(1)}$.
7: Calculate the nodel-level kernel value by Eq. (7),

$$\Theta_{ij}^{(1)} = \hat{\boldsymbol{\Sigma}}_{ij}^{(0)} \dot{\boldsymbol{\Sigma}}_{ij}^{(1)} + \hat{\boldsymbol{\Sigma}}_{ij}^{(1)}.$$

8: Readout, $\Theta(G, G') = \sum_{ij} \Theta_{ij}^{(1)}$.

4 Experiment

This section evaluates the effectiveness of the proposed kernel methods through extensive experiments on node classification tasks. We compare the performance and efficiency of our methods with neural network approaches and other graph kernel methods. Our experimental findings demonstrate the robust performance of our approach in classification tasks. Furthermore, they highlight computational efficiency improvements compared to neural networks and GNTK. The experiments were conducted on an Apple M1 Pro CPU with 16GB of RAM.

4.1 Experimental Settings

Datasets. Five widely-used node-level benchmark datasets are selected to evaluate the effectiveness of our methods: Cora, CiteSeer, PubMed [34], Photo, and Computers [19]. For node classifications, we utilize publicly available splits for the Cora, CiteSeer, and PubMed datasets. For the Computers dataset, the first 20 instances from each category are selected as the training set, while the last 100 instances of each class are chosen as the testing set (Table 1).
Baselines. To evaluate the effectiveness of the proposed SGTK and SGNK, we compare them against various graph neural networks and kernel methods. The baseline graph neural networks include GCN [10], GAT [23], SGC [30], GraphSAGE [5], APPNP [4], and GIN [33]. Additionally, we consider graph kernels such as the GNTK [3], SNTK [26], and GCKM [31].

Algorithm 2. Simplified Graph Neural Kernel (SGNK)

1: **Input:** Graphs $G = \{X, A\}$, $G' = \{X', A'\}$.
2: **Output:** Node-level kernel matrix $\boldsymbol{\Theta}$ and graph-level kernel value $\Theta(G, G')$.
3: **Initialize:** $\hat{A} = D^{-\frac{1}{2}}(A+I)D^{-\frac{1}{2}}$, $\hat{A}' = D^{-\frac{1}{2}}(A'+I)D^{-\frac{1}{2}}$, K.
4: K-step message passing on nodes features.

$$\hat{X} = \hat{A}^K X, \quad \hat{X}' = \hat{A}'^K X',$$

5: Calculate the node-level kernel matrix by Eq. (15),

$$\boldsymbol{\Theta} = \frac{2}{\pi} sin^{-1} \frac{2\tilde{X}_1 \tilde{X}_2^\top}{\sqrt{[\mathbf{1} + 2diag(\tilde{X}_1 \tilde{X}_1^\top)]^\top [\mathbf{1} + 2diag(\tilde{X}_2 \tilde{X}_2^\top)]}} \tag{17}$$

6: Readout, $\Theta(G, G') = \sum_{ij} \Theta_{ij}$.

Table 1. Node-level dataset details.

Dataset	# Nodes	# Edges	# Class	# Node feature
Cora	2,708	5,429	7	1,433
Citeseer	3,327	9,104	6	3,703
Pubmed	19,717	44,338	3	500
Photo	7,650	238,162	8	745
Computers	13,752	491,722	10	767

Parameter Settings. We tune the hyperparameter K over the range $\{1, 2, 3, 4, 5\}$ for GCKM, SNTK, GNTK, SGTK, and SGNK. For classification using SVM, its hyperparameter is optimized over the range $[10^{-2}, 10^4]$. Similarly, for KRR, the regularization parameter λ is tuned over the range $[10^{-2}, 10^2]$.

4.2 Node Classification Performance Comparison

This subsection explores the application of kernel functions to node classification tasks. Specifically, we apply the proposed kernel methods to node classification datasets, utilizing an SVM classifier to evaluate their performance. For GNN methods, we report the mean and standard deviation of the results from 10 runs and present the classification accuracy of the kernel methods using fixed training and testing set splits.

As shown in Table 2, the proposed methods, SGTK and SGNK, consistently demonstrate strong performance across all five node classification datasets. These methods achieve the highest classification accuracy in each dataset, outperforming both traditional kernel methods and GNNs. This consistent superiority underscores the effectiveness of the proposed kernel methods in capturing complex graph structures and node relationships.

The results obtained from the node classification datasets further emphasize the effectiveness of the proposed methods in addressing node classification tasks.

Table 2. Node classification accuracy (%). The top three performance methods are highlighted in varying shades of green, with darker shades representing superior performance.

Methods	Cora	Citeseer	Pubmed	Photo	Computers
GCN	81.1±0.5	71.7±0.1	77.1±0.3	91.4±0.8	84.2±0.3
GAT	79.5±1.0	68.8±0.2	75.7±0.9	90.1±0.6	83.3±0.7
SGC	79.0±0.3	67.4±0.2	76.9±0.1	91.0±0.5	84.1±0.2
APPNP	79.3±0.2	67.1±1.0	76.0±0.5	91.7±0.3	86.3±0.2
GraphSAGE	79.3±0.4	67.5±0.3	73.9±0.6	90.0±0.1	82.8±0.6
GIN	77.2±1.8	67.4±0.2	78.1±0.1	43.8±5.5	30.0±5.2
GCKM	82.4	72.3	79.8	91.30	84.20
SNTK	80.70	69.20	78.40	91.00	84.70
GNTK	80.50	69.20	77.20	91.00	84.70
SGTK(Our)	82.60	71.10	80.00	91.75	86.50
SGNK(Our)	82.80	72.60	79.90	90.88	85.50

Specifically, the capability of SGTK and SGNK to maintain high accuracy across diverse datasets highlights their robustness and generalizability. These findings suggest that the proposed methods are well-suited for graph-based learning tasks, contributing to advances in graph analysis techniques.

To comprehensively evaluate the classification performance of the proposed kernel methods, experiments were also conducted using Kernel Ridge Regression (KRR) [25], as detailed in Table 3. KRR, a widely used technique for regression tasks, ensures reliable performance and demonstrates the compatibility of the proposed methods with various classifiers. Given the set of training nodes $\mathcal{V}$ and their corresponding labels $\mathcal{Y}$, KRR models the optimal predictions for test nodes v_t by leveraging the kernel function to capture relationships between nodes. Furthermore, the proposed methods are compatible with Support Vector Machines (SVMs), showcasing their adaptability across different classification frameworks. The prediction for a test node v_t is computed as follows:

$$f(v_t) = \mathcal{K}(v_t, \mathcal{V})[\mathcal{K}(\mathcal{V}, \mathcal{V}) + \lambda I]^{-1}\mathcal{Y}, \tag{18}$$

where the kernel function $\mathcal{K}(v, v') : \mathbb{R}^d \times \mathbb{R}^d \to \mathbb{R}$ quantifies the similarity between nodes v and v', and $\lambda > 0$ is the regularization parameter that controls the trade-off between fitting the training data and maintaining model generalizability. By incorporating the kernel function $\mathcal{K}$, KRR effectively captures the complex relationships among nodes in the graph, making it a suitable choice for evaluating the proposed kernel methods.

The experimental results, summarizing the performance of the kernel methods under the KRR framework, are presented in Table 3. These results provide a comprehensive comparison and highlight the advantages of the proposed methods over existing approaches.

Table 3. Kernel method on kernel ridge regression results.

Methods	Cora	Citeseer	Pubmed	Photo	Computers
GCKM	82.50	71.70	79.90	93.25	86.80
SNTK	81.40	70.70	80.00	90.13	84.20
GNTK	81.30	71.10	78.60	89.63	83.80
SGTK(Our)	83.50	72.00	80.00	92.87	87.90
SGNK(Our)	82.60	72.40	80.00	92.12	86.50

4.3 Node Classification Efficiency

To validate the efficiency of the proposed methods in node classification tasks, we investigated the impact of the parameter K on the time consumption of GCKM, SNTK, GNTK, SGTK, and SGNK when calculating the kernel matrix. The experimental results, as shown in Fig. 4, indicate that GCKM, GNTK, and SNTK exhibit a linear increase in time consumption with an increase in K. In contrast, our methods remain largely unaffected by variations in the message-passing times, maintaining consistent efficiency in kernel matrix computations.

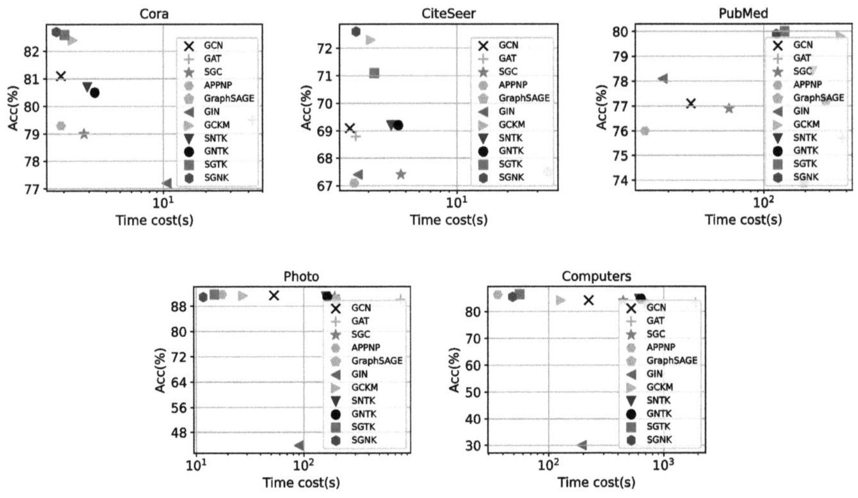

Fig. 3. Node classification time consumption and accuracy comparison.

Additionally, we present the time taken by each method to achieve the classification accuracy detailed in Table 2. This assessment allows us to evaluate the time efficiency of each method. The results of time consumption are presented in Fig. 3. SGNK demonstrates low time consumption across all five datasets, followed closely by SGTK. The proposed methods exhibit time efficiency at least three times faster than GNTK, with SGNK (0.015s) outperforming GNTK

(0.827s) by a factor of 53.7 on the Computers dataset. In contrast, GNN methods incur significantly higher time costs due to the need for iterative training over multiple epochs and the uncertainty of model convergence.

In conclusion, the proposed methods not only outperform the baselines in node classification performance but also exhibit consistent time efficiency. This consistency corroborates the theoretical analysis, providing strong evidence for the enhancement in time efficiency achieved by the proposed methods.

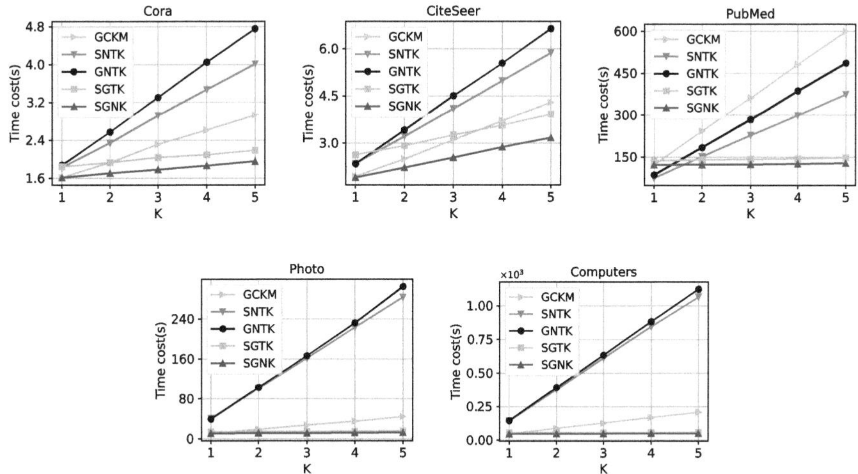

Fig. 4. The changes of node classification time consuming with respect to K.

5 Conclusion

In this paper, we propose the Simplified Graph Neural Tangent Kernel (SGTK) and its derivative, the Simplified Graph Neural Kernel (SGNK), to address the computational inefficiencies of graph kernels. By introducing continuous K-step aggregation and eliminating multi-block stacking, SGTK reduces redundancy in the Graph Neural Tangent Kernel (GNTK). SGNK further simplifies computations by interpreting an infinite-width simple graph neural network as a Gaussian process. Experimental results demonstrate that SGTK and SGNK achieve competitive classification accuracy while improving computational efficiency. These methods provide practical and scalable alternatives to traditional graph kernels and graph neural networks, particularly in resource-constrained scenarios.

Acknowledgments. This work was supported by the Hong Kong Research Grants Council under the General Research Fund (Grant No. 15200023).

References

1. Arora, S., Du, S.S., Hu, W., Li, Z., Salakhutdinov, R.R., Wang, R.: On exact computation with an infinitely wide neural net. Advances in neural information processing systems **32** (2019)
2. Brinton, C.G., Chiang, M.: Social learning networks: a graph-based analysis of student interaction patterns. IEEE Trans. Learn. Technol. **7**(3), 246–259 (2015)
3. Du, S.S., Hou, K., Salakhutdinov, R.R., Poczos, B., Wang, R., Xu, K.: Graph neural tangent kernel: Fusing graph neural networks with graph kernels. Advances in neural information processing systems **32** (2019)
4. Gasteiger, J., Bojchevski, A., Günnemann, S.: Predict then propagate: Graph neural networks meet personalized pagerank. arXiv preprint arXiv:1810.05997 (2018)
5. Hamilton, W., Ying, Z., Leskovec, J.: Inductive representation learning on large graphs. Advances in neural information processing systems **30** (2017)
6. Hu, J., Shen, J., Yang, B., Shao, L.: Infinitely wide graph convolutional networks: semi-supervised learning via gaussian processes. arXiv preprint arXiv:2002.12168 (2020)
7. Jacot, A., Gabriel, F., Hongler, C.: Neural tangent kernel: Convergence and generalization in neural networks. Advances in neural information processing systems **31** (2018)
8. Jiang, S., Man, Y., Song, Z., Yu, Z., Zhuo, D.: Fast graph neural tangent kernel via kronecker sketching. In: Proceedings of the AAAI Conference on Artificial Intelligence, vol. 36, pp. 7033–7041 (2022)
9. Joksimović, S., et al.: How do we model learning at scale? a systematic review of research on moocs. Rev. Educ. Res. **88**(1), 43–86 (2018)
10. Kipf, T.N., Welling, M.: Semi-supervised classification with graph convolutional networks. arXiv preprint arXiv:1609.02907 (2016)
11. Kizilcec, R.F., Piech, C., Schneider, E.: Deconstructing disengagement: Analyzing learner subpopulations in massive open online courses. In: Proceedings of the 3rd International Conference on Learning Analytics and Knowledge, pp. 170–179 (2013)
12. Krishnagopal, S., Ruiz, L.: Graph neural tangent kernel: Convergence on large graphs. In: International Conference on Machine Learning, pp. 17827–17841. PMLR (2023)
13. LeCun, Y., Bottou, L., Orr, G.B., Müller, K.R.: Efficient backprop. In: Neural networks: Tricks of the trade, pp. 9–50. Springer (2002)
14. Lee, J., Bahri, Y., Novak, R., Schoenholz, S.S., Pennington, J., Sohl-Dickstein, J.: Deep neural networks as gaussian processes. arXiv preprint arXiv:1711.00165 (2017)
15. Neal, R.M.: Bayesian learning for neural networks, vol. 118. Springer Science & Business Media (2012)
16. Nguyen, T., Chen, Z., Lee, J.: Dataset meta-learning from kernel ridge-regression. arXiv preprint arXiv:2011.00050 (2020)
17. Romero, C., Ventura, S.: Educational data mining: A review of the state of the art. IEEE Trans. Syst. Man Cybern. Part C (Appl. Rev.) **40**(6), 601–618 (2010)
18. Schlichtkrull, M., Kipf, T.N., Bloem, P., Van Den Berg, R., Titov, I., Welling, M.: Modeling relational data with graph convolutional networks. In: The semantic web: 15th international conference, ESWC 2018, Heraklion, Crete, Greece, June 3–7, 2018, Proceedings 15, pp. 593–607. Springer (2018)

19. Shchur, O., Mumme, M., Bojchevski, A., Günnemann, S.: Pitfalls of graph neural network evaluation. arXiv preprint arXiv:1811.05868 (2018)
20. Shervashidze, N., Schweitzer, P., Van Leeuwen, E.J., Mehlhorn, K., Borgwardt, K.M.: Weisfeiler-lehman graph kernels. J. Mach. Learn. Res. **12**(9) (2011)
21. Siemens, G.: Learning analytics: the emergence of a discipline. Am. Behav. Sci. **57**(10), 1380–1400 (2013)
22. Tang, Y., Yan, J.: Graphqntk: quantum neural tangent kernel for graph data. Adv. Neural. Inf. Process. Syst. **35**, 6104–6118 (2022)
23. Velickovic, P., Cucurull, G., Casanova, A., Romero, A., Lio, P., Bengio, Y., et al.: Graph attention networks. Stat. **1050**(20), 10–48550 (2017)
24. Vishwanathan, S.V.N., Schraudolph, N.N., Kondor, R., Borgwardt, K.M.: Graph kernels. J. Mach. Learn. Res. **11**, 1201–1242 (2010)
25. Vovk, V.: Kernel ridge regression. In: Empirical inference: Festschrift in honor of vladimir n. vapnik, pp. 105–116. Springer (2013)
26. Wang, L., Fan, W., Li, J., Ma, Y., Li, Q.: Fast graph condensation with structure-based neural tangent kernel. In: Proceedings of the ACM on Web Conference 2024, pp. 4439–4448 (2024)
27. Wen, M., Yang, D., Rose, C.P.: Linguistic reflections of student engagement in massive open online courses. In: Proceedings of the 8th International AAAI Conference on Weblogs and Social Media, pp. 525–534 (2014)
28. Williams, C.: Computing with infinite networks. Advances in neural information processing systems **9** (1996)
29. Williams, C.K., Rasmussen, C.E.: Gaussian processes for machine learning. MIT Press, Cambridge (2006)
30. Wu, F., Souza, A., Zhang, T., Fifty, C., Yu, T., Weinberger, K.: Simplifying graph convolutional networks. In: International Conference on Machine Learning, pp. 6861–6871. PMLR (2019)
31. Wu, Z., Zhang, Z., Fan, J.: Graph convolutional kernel machine versus graph convolutional networks. Advances in neural information processing systems **36** (2024)
32. Wu, Z., Pan, S., Chen, F., Long, G., Zhang, C., Philip, S.Y.: A comprehensive survey on graph neural networks. IEEE Trans. Neural Networks Learning Syst. **32**(1), 4–24 (2020)
33. Xu, K., Hu, W., Leskovec, J., Jegelka, S.: How powerful are graph neural networks? arXiv preprint arXiv:1810.00826 (2018)
34. Yang, Z., Cohen, W., Salakhudinov, R.: Revisiting semi-supervised learning with graph embeddings. In: International Conference on Machine Learning, pp. 40–48. PMLR (2016)
35. Zhou, X., Wang, H.: On the explainability of graph convolutional network with gcn tangent kernel. Neural Comput. **35**(1), 1–26 (2023)

Knowledge Pyramid Construction for Multi-level Retrieval-Augmented Generation

Rubing Chen, Xulu Zhang, Jiaxin Wu, Wenqi Fan, Xiao-Yong Wei(✉), and Qing Li

The Hong Kong Polytechnic University, Kowloon, Hong Kong SAR
cs007.wei@polyu.edu.hk

Abstract. This paper addresses the need for improved precision in existing knowledge-enhanced question-answering frameworks, specifically Retrieval-Augmented Generation (RAG) methods that primarily focus on enhancing recall. We propose a multi-layer knowledge pyramid approach within the RAG framework to achieve a better balance between precision and recall. The knowledge pyramid consists of three layers: Ontologies, Knowledge Graphs (KGs), and chunk-based raw text. We employ cross-layer augmentation techniques for comprehensive knowledge coverage and dynamic updates of the Ontology schema and instances. To ensure compactness, we utilize cross-layer filtering methods for knowledge condensation in KGs. Our approach, named PolyRAG, follows a waterfall model for retrieval, starting from the top of the pyramid and progressing down until a confident answer is obtained. We introduce two benchmarks for domain-specific knowledge retrieval, one in the academic domain and the other in the financial domain. The effectiveness of the methods has been validated through comprehensive experiments by outperforming 19 SOTA methods. An encouraging observation is that the proposed method has augmented the GPT-4, providing 395% F1 gain by improving its performance from 0.1636 to 0.8109. The source code and datasets can be accessed at https://github.com/Anya-RB-Chen/PolyRAG.

1 Introduction

Large Language Models (LLMs), such as GPT-4 and open-source variants like FLAN [35] and LLaMA [31], have achieved remarkable success in general knowledge tasks [26]. However, their generalist nature is ill-suited for professional domains requiring specialized knowledge, such as law [9,15] and finance [33,40]. While Supervised Fine-Tuning (SFT) can adapt LLMs to specific domains [23], as seen in models for medicine [41,42,44] and finance [6,37,40], this approach risks catastrophic forgetting of general knowledge [19] and is prone to model hallucination [14].

Retrieval-Augmented Generation (RAG) offers a compelling alternative by enhancing LLMs with domain-specific knowledge [16]. RAG frameworks retrieve

B. Fernández-Manjón et al. (Eds.): SETE 2025/ICWL 2025, LNCS 16425, pp. 210–224, 2026.
https://doi.org/10.1007/978-981-92-0042-9_16

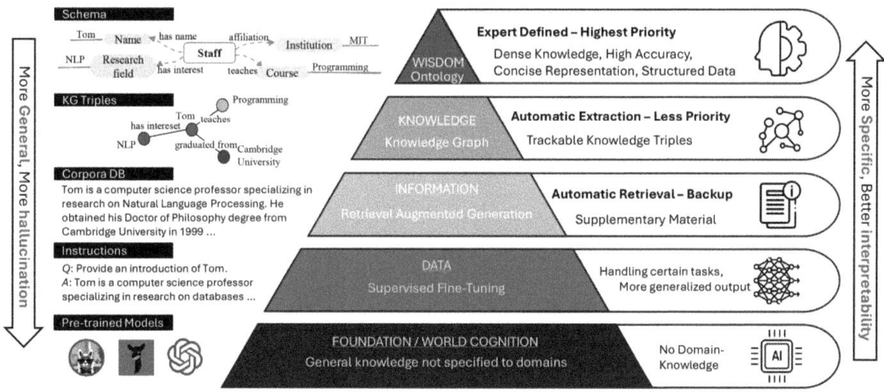

Fig. 1. PolyRAG Framework based on the concept of Knowledge Pyramid: different layers signify varying levels of specificity and richness. The layers are mutually complementary, working together for a balance between recall and precision.

relevant information from external sources to enrich the prompt's context, making the LLM's output more accurate and traceable [10]. However, early RAG methods often rely on unstructured text chunks, which lack organization [16,20]. To address this, Knowledge Graphs (KGs) have been integrated to provide structured knowledge [3]. While Ontologies offer even stricter, formally defined schemas ideal for domain-specific tasks [24], their use in RAG remains underexplored, largely due to the manual effort required for schema creation.

In educational contexts, where factual accuracy and verifiability are critical, the imprecision of existing methods poses a significant barrier. Answering a student's query with hallucinated information can undermine the learning process [36]. Therefore, developing a RAG framework that prioritizes precision is essential for building reliable educational technologies and intelligent tutoring systems.

Existing RAG methods primarily use KGs or Ontologies to improve information "recall" without a specific focus on "precision". As illustrated in Fig. 1, different knowledge representations offer a trade-off. Higher-level, structured sources like Ontologies are "precision"-friendly due to their formal definitions, while lower-level, richer sources like raw text are "recall"-friendly. Motivated by this observation, we propose a multi-layer knowledge pyramid and a corresponding querying strategy within the RAG framework to balance "precision" and "recall" by leveraging heterogeneous knowledge sources.

Our approach, named PolyRAG, organizes knowledge into a three-layer pyramid: a high-precision **Ontology** layer with a formal semantic framework; a balanced **Knowledge Graph (KG)** layer capturing entities and relations; and a high-recall **raw text** layer for comprehensive coverage. During construction, we employ cross-layer augmentation and filtering to dynamically update the Ontology and condense the KG, ensuring the knowledge base is both comprehensive and compact without extensive manual intervention. The retrieval

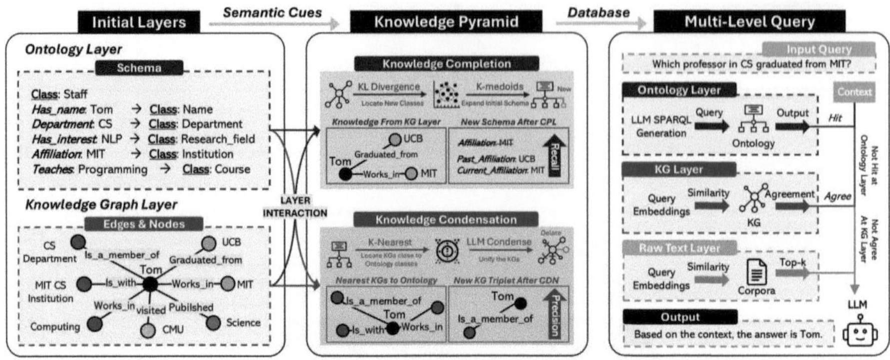

Fig. 2. The framework of PolyRAG includes: (1) Knowledge Pyramid Construction, starting from extracting knowledge from corpora data to form the initial layers, then performing the layer interactions, which are knowledge completion and condensation. (2) Given the refined Knowledge Pyramid, the LLM inference obtains the contexts through a multi-level query, which retrieves the knowledge from the higher layer down to the lower layer in a waterfall pattern.

process follows a waterfall model, querying from the top of the pyramid (Ontology) downwards to the raw text layer until a confident answer is found, as shown in Fig. 2. This multi-level strategy, particularly suited for educational applications, prioritizes precision while ensuring broad information access when needed.

To facilitate research in this area, we introduce two new benchmarks for domain-specific knowledge retrieval. The first is a comprehensive dataset for the academic domain, built by the authors to cover 1,319 staff members, 2,061 courses, and 31 departments at The Hong Kong Polytechnic University (PolyU). The second extends the public FiQA dataset [28] for the financial domain, restructured into our pyramid model. Both benchmarks will be made publicly available.

2 Related Works

2.1 Domain-Specific Large Language Models

Domain-specific LLMs are tailored for areas like law [9,15,43], medicine [42,44], or finance [33,40] to provide higher accuracy than general-purpose models [23]. A common adaptation method is instruction fine-tuning on domain-specific corpora [23]. However, this approach can degrade the model's general capabilities, a phenomenon known as catastrophic forgetting [19]. To mitigate these limitations without sacrificing specialization, prompting LLMs with external domain knowledge has become a widely adopted strategy.

2.2 Retrieval-Augmented Generation

Retrieval-Augmented Generation (RAG) enhances LLMs by incorporating retrieved knowledge for in-context learning, thereby reducing hallucinations and grounding responses in factual data [16]. The foundational NaiveRAG architecture segments a corpus, embeds the chunks, and retrieves the top-k most similar documents to augment the LLM prompt [20]. Advanced RAG methods improve upon this by adding components like rerankers to refine search results (e.g., Re2G [12], bge-reranker [39]) or prompt compression to reduce noise and context length (e.g., Selective Context [17], LLMLingua [1]).

Despite these advancements, RAG systems based on unstructured text still face a trade-off between knowledge detail and informational noise. They are less effective for complex queries that require synthesizing information from multiple sources or levels of abstraction. For instance, in an educational setting, answering a student's question might require integrating a formal definition from a glossary, a conceptual explanation from a textbook, and a practical example from a case study. This task challenges simple chunk-based retrieval. This highlights the need for more structured knowledge representations to build robust educational tools.

2.3 Knowledge-Augmented Language Models

To address the limitations of text-only retrieval, research has shifted towards knowledge-augmented models that integrate structured knowledge bases [18]. Beyond raw text, Knowledge Graphs (KGs) are a popular choice, with methods replacing text chunks with retrieved KG triplets [25]. KAPING [3] and RRA [38] are notable examples of this approach. Ontologies [24,32] are utilized less frequently, often serving as auxiliary tools to generate KGs [21,25] or to augment textual corpora [4,24]. However, effectively integrating and querying these heterogeneous forms of knowledge remains a significant challenge, which our work aims to address.

3 Knowledge Pyramid Construction

The knowledge pyramid serves as the foundation for PolyRAG. The construction process begins by creating three initial knowledge banks, each corresponding to a layer of the pyramid: an Ontology ($\mathcal{O}$), a Knowledge Graph ($\mathcal{K}$), and raw texts ($\mathcal{T}$). The core of our methodology lies in fostering interactions between these layers to enhance the overall comprehensiveness and compactness of the knowledge base.

3.1 Construction of Initial Layers

Ontology Layer: The Ontology layer $\mathcal{O} = \{\mathcal{O}_s, \mathcal{O}_i\}$ comprises a schema $\mathcal{O}_s$ and its instances $\mathcal{O}_i$. Since manually defining a comprehensive schema is resource-intensive, we simplify the process by extracting an initial sub-domain schema from general Ontologies like WordNet [22] or ConceptNet [29]. This schema is then refined using the semi-automatic knowledge completion method described later. Figure 3 illustrates an example Ontology for the academic domain.

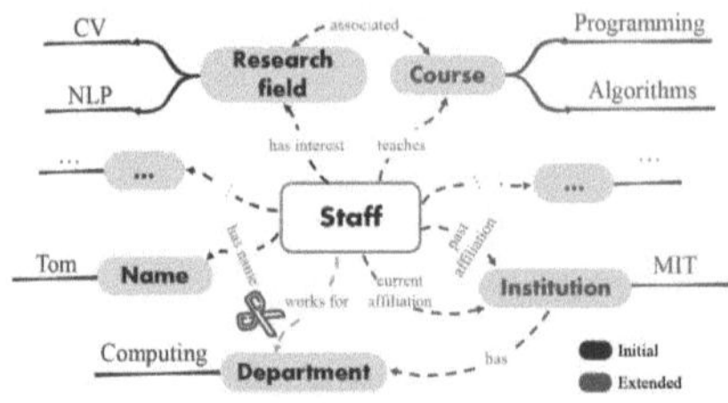

Fig. 3. Knowledge completion through cross-layer interactions. The comprehensiveness of the initial Ontology schema is improved with noteworthy concepts identified from the KG layer.

Algorithm 1 PolyRAG Querying

function POLYRAG(Q)
  result $\leftarrow$ Onto(Query$_{onto}$(Q, schema))
  if $result \neq \emptyset$ **then return** *result*
  end if
  triplets $\leftarrow$ EmbRetrieve$_{kg}$($Q, \mathcal{K}$)
  if Query$_{kg}$(Q, *triplets*) is "Yes" **then**
    return *triplets*
  end if
  return EmbRetrieve$_{rawtext}$($Q, \mathcal{T}$)
end function

With the schema $\mathcal{O}_s$ defined in Web Ontology Language (OWL) [2], we guide an LLM to extract instances from the raw text layer $\mathcal{T}$ for each class (e.g. *staff*) - property (e.g. *graduated_from*) pair $(c, a) \in \mathcal{O}_s$. This is achieved using a function:

> $f_{ins}(c, a; p)$: Given a paragraph $\{p\}$ from the $\{domain\}$ domain, please identify instances of the Ontology relationship where a class $\{c\}$ has the property of $\{a\}$. Note that the property may consist of multiple entities.

By applying f_{ins} across all paragraphs, the instance set $\mathcal{O}_i$ is constructed as:

$$\mathcal{O}_i = \{f_{ins}(c, a; p) \,|\, \forall (c, a) \in \mathcal{O}_s,\, \forall p \in \mathcal{T}\}. \tag{1}$$

The specific prompt implementation may vary, and in some cases, few-shot examples can improve extraction quality.

Knowledge Graph Layer: We employ Open Information Extraction (OpenIE) [11] to extract KG triplets from raw texts. To mitigate the noisy output of direct extraction, we adapt the multi-round prompting approach from LLM2KG [5], using four functions: $f_{par}(p)$ for paraphrasing, $f_{ent}()$ for entity extraction, $f_{rel}()$ for relation completion, and $f_{dis}()$ for disambiguation. These functions form a cascade for KG triplet extraction:

$$f_{kg}(p) = f_{dis}\big(f_{ent}(f_{par}(p)),\, f_{rel}(f_{par}(p))\big). \tag{2}$$

This process constructs the initial knowledge graph layer as:

$$\mathcal{K} = \{f_{kg}(p) \,|\, \forall p \in \mathcal{T}\}. \tag{3}$$

The detailed implementation of the four functions is as follows:

> $f_{par}(p)$: Determine the factual claims from a given paragraph $\{p\}$. Put these facts into short phrases with basic grammar. Remember that every statement should have a distinct meaning, and pronouns should be avoided.

$f_{ent}(f_{par}(p))$: Extract the noun entities in phrases from the given sentences $f_{par}(p)$. The entities should not contain any comma, and each entity should be unique during extraction.

$f_{rel}(f_{par}(p))$: Given the reference context $f_{par}(p)$ and relevant entities, complete the relations between two entities. Notice that a triple should only contain one entity as head, one verb or verb phrase as relation, and one entity as tail. Separate the head, relation, and tail with a comma.

$f_{dis}(f_{ent}(), f_{rel}())$: You are given several triples $f_{rel}()$ with their entities $f_{ent}()$. These triples consist of subject-predicate-object elements, separated with a comma, but may contain ambiguities or inaccuracies. Your task is to refine and disambiguate these triples to ensure that they accurately reflect the entities and relationships described in their source texts without duplication or omissions.

These Ontology, KG, and the raw-text backup, set the stage for the subsequent completion and condensation procedures required for the PolyRAG framework.

3.2 Knowledge Completion

As shown in Fig. 1, higher pyramid layers are more structured but often have limited coverage. A common issue is that expert-defined Ontologies may lack important classes or attributes. We address this in a data-driven manner by identifying noteworthy concepts and relations that exist in lower layers (KG, text) but are absent from the Ontology. For example, our analysis revealed that *past_affiliations* frequently appeared in the KG but was missing from the initial Ontology, which only included *current_department*. Incorporating both *past_affiliations* and *current_affiliations* enhances the Ontology's completeness, particularly for queries about alumni or former roles.

These missing concepts indicate where the Ontology and KG diverge in semantic coverage. To identify them, we map both layers into a common semantic space. We transform (c, a) pairs in the Ontology into subject+relation phrases matching the KG format and then encode all phrases using Instructor embedding [30]. We model the distribution of each layer as a multivariate Gaussian:

$$F(\mathbf{X}) = \frac{1}{(2\pi)^{\frac{n}{2}}|\mathbf{\Sigma}^{\frac{1}{2}}|} e^{-\frac{1}{2}(\mathbf{X}-\boldsymbol{\mu})^{\top}\mathbf{\Sigma}^{-1}(\mathbf{X}-\boldsymbol{\mu})}, \tag{4}$$

where $\mathbf{X}$ is a phrase embedding, and $\boldsymbol{\mu}$ and $\mathbf{\Sigma}$ are the mean and covariance matrix. The distributions are denoted as $\mathbf{X}_{\mathcal{O}} \sim \mathcal{N}(\boldsymbol{\mu}_{\mathcal{O}}, \mathbf{\Sigma}_{\mathcal{O}})$ and $\mathbf{X}_{\mathcal{K}} \sim \mathcal{N}(\boldsymbol{\mu}_{\mathcal{K}}, \mathbf{\Sigma}_{\mathcal{K}})$. We then measure the Kullback–Leibler (KL) divergence for each

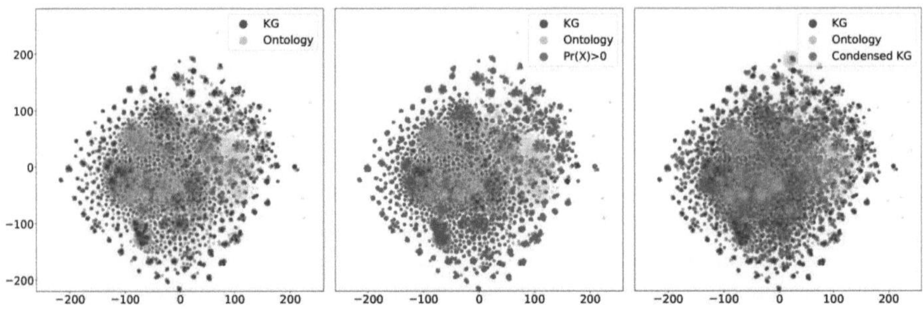

Fig. 4. The distribution of KG and Ontology: the original distributions (left), samples with a high priority for knowledge completion are highlighted in red (middle), and the condensed KG after knowledge condensation (right). (Color figure online)

X:

$$D_{\mathbf{X}}(\mathcal{O} \parallel \mathcal{K}) = -F_{\mathcal{O}}(\mathbf{X}) \log(F_{\mathcal{K}}(\mathbf{X})) \tag{5}$$

$$D_{\mathbf{X}}(\mathcal{K} \parallel \mathcal{O}) = -F_{\mathcal{K}}(\mathbf{X}) \log(F_{\mathcal{O}}(\mathbf{X})), \tag{6}$$

where $D_{\mathbf{X}}(\mathcal{O} \parallel \mathcal{K})$ measures divergence to $\mathcal{K}$, and vice versa for $D_{\mathbf{X}}(\mathcal{K} \parallel \mathcal{O})$.

We define a priority rating function to identify concepts for promotion from the KG to the Ontology:

$$Pr(\mathbf{X}) = D_{\mathbf{X}}(\mathcal{O} \parallel \mathcal{K}) - D_{\mathbf{X}}(\mathcal{K} \parallel \mathcal{O}). \tag{7}$$

As depicted in Fig. 4, this function effectively highlights areas where the KG is information-dense but the Ontology is sparse. We apply k-medoids clustering on KG triplets in these high-priority areas to identify new classes and attributes. These are then integrated into the Ontology schema and instances, progressively enhancing the pyramid's comprehensiveness. Figure 3 illustrates this process, where new connections between Staff and Research Interests were added, improving the system's ability to handle student queries for advisors.

3.3 Knowledge Condensation

While Knowledge Completion enriches the pyramid bottom-up to improve "recall", Knowledge Condensation refines it top-down to enhance "precision". The principle is to leverage the well-structured Ontology to eliminate redundancy in the lower KG layer. We implement this by using each Ontology class attribute as an anchor to explore its neighborhood and identify the k nearest KG triplets, $\mathbf{X_k}$. This top-down filtering prunes extraneous data and refines the knowledge base to include only the most pertinent information. An LLM is then instructed to summarize these triplets into a more compact form using the following prompt:

> $f_{con}(\{\mathbf{X_k}\})$: Please condense the set of knowledge graph triplets $\{\mathbf{X_k}\}$ obtained from the $\{domain\}$ domain by eliminating redundant triplets and summarizing the remaining ones in a more concise manner. Here are some examples for your reference: $\{examples\}$. The condensation process should follow the logic of $\{CoT\}$.

Repeating this process for all Ontology anchors systematically refines the entire KG, forming the condensed layer shown in Fig. 4. Redundant triplets with similar semantics, such as "Prof. A works in Z" and "Prof. A is with Z institute", are consolidated into a single, standardized relation like "*is_a_member_of*". This condensation not only reduces redundancy but also enhances the clarity of the KG, which is crucial for maintaining consistency and querying effectively.

4 Multi-level Querying

The knowledge pyramid enables a straightforward, top-down querying strategy for PolyRAG, following the sequence: Ontology → Knowledge Graph → Raw Texts. The process returns a result as soon as an answer is found, otherwise, it proceeds to the next layer. This flow is detailed in Algorithm 1. The framework requires two key components: a search method for each layer and a condition for proceeding to the next. The Raw Texts layer can be queried using a standard NaiveRAG approach, while the Ontology and KG layers utilize the specialized strategies described below.

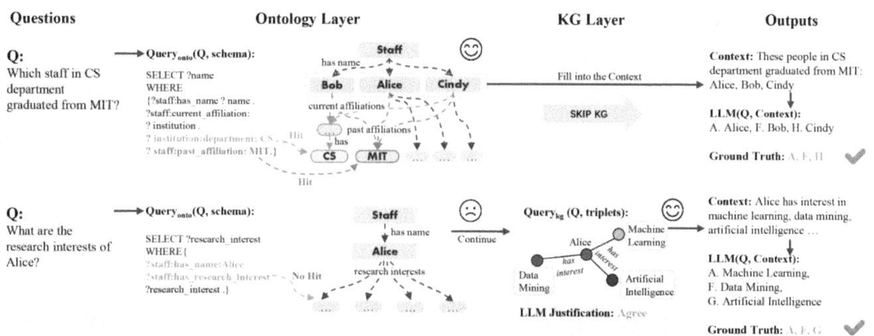

Fig. 5. Illustration of multi-level querying: the two queries are addressed at the Ontology and Knowledge Graph layers, respectively, bypassing the lower levels.

4.1 Search at Ontology Layer

At the Ontology Layer, we leverage SPARQL, a query language known for its precision with well-structured queries [32]. For instance, for the question "What are the research interests of Prof. James Wang?", the LLM would generate a SPARQL query to find a staff member matching that name and retrieve their "research_interest" attribute from $\mathcal{O}$. The result is either a list of interests or an empty set if the knowledge is absent. Figure 5 shows a query, "Which staff in CS department graduated from MIT?", being handled at this layer. The LLM uses the $Query_{onto}$ prompt to generate a SPARQL query with two constraints: "current_affiliation: CS" and "past_affiliation: MIT". If the Ontology contains this information, the query returns a precise and concise result, terminating the search. This direct retrieval of keywords reduces the contextual load on the LLM, making the approach efficient even for smaller models. We guide an LLM to generate the appropriate SPARQL query using the following prompt function:

> $Query_{onto}(Q, schema)$: Given a question $\{Q\}$ within the {domain} domain, please formulate a SPARQL query to retrieve the answer based on the provided Ontology schema. The namespace is $\{schema.base\}$, and the classes are $\{schema.class\}$. The object properties between classes are $\{schema.op\}$, and the classes may also have data properties such as $\{schema.dp\}$.

4.2 Search at Knowledge Graph Layer

At the knowledge graph layer, we use an embedding-based retrieval method similar to NaiveRAG, but applied to KG triplets instead of text chunks. Treating triplets as natural language has proven effective for KG-enhanced question-answering [3]. After retrieving relevant triplets, we use a prompt function to have the LLM assess if the information is sufficient to answer the question:

> $Query_{kg}(Q, triplets)$: Given a question $\{Q\}$ and the context information provided by the matched triplets from the knowledge graph $\{triplets\}$, please justify whether the provided information is sufficient to accurately answer the question. Respond with either "Yes" or "No" to provide your justification.

For example, given the query "Which CS staff has interest in cloud computing?", the LLM would respond "Yes" if the retrieved triplets contain facts like "Prof. A works in CS Department" and "Prof. A published on cloud computing journal". If not, the justification would be "No", and the search would proceed to the raw text layer. Figure 5 also illustrates a query, "What are the research interests of Alice?", that fails at the Ontology layer due to missing knowledge. The process then moves to the KG layer, where an embedding search retrieves the top-k semantically similar triplets. The LLM uses the $Query_{kg}$ prompt to confirm these triplets are sufficient. Upon receiving a "Yes", the retrieved triplets serve as the context, enabling the LLM to generate a correct answer.

Table 1. Dataset statistics of the two benchmarks.

Dataset	AcadChall	R-FLUE-FiQA
Domain	Academia	Finance
#Raw texts	5,019	17,072
Ontologies		
#Instances	25,481	225,085
#KG Triples	27,920	68,737
#QA pairs	512	1,705
QA type	MCQ&MAQ	Open-ended

5 Experiments

5.1 Experimental Setup

We evaluate our approach on two domain-specific benchmarks. The first, AcadChall, is a new benchmark we created for the academic domain, covering 31 departments, 1,319 faculty, and 2,061 courses from a university. It contains 512 challenging Multiple-Choice and Multiple-Answer Questions (MCQ/MAQ) with eight choices each, designed to rigorously test model precision. The second is R-FLUE-FiQA, a well-known finance benchmark derived from the FLUE benchmark [28], consisting of 1,705 open-ended questions. For both datasets, we constructed knowledge pyramids using the methods described in Sect. 3. Dataset statistics are shown in Table 1.

For retrieval, we use instructor-xl [30] for embeddings with cosine similarity. The number of retrieved items (k) was empirically set to 10 for the KG layer and 5 for the raw text layer.

5.2 Evaluation Metrics

We use Precision, Recall, and F1 for MCQ/MAQs, and BLEU and BERT similarity (based on MiniLM [34]) for open-ended questions. We also introduce HitRate (HR), a novel metric that measures the proportion of necessary domain-specific entities present in the generated response. This metric is designed to evaluate factual accuracy and relevance, complementing traditional metrics by focusing on the inclusion of key information.

5.3 Comparison to SOTA Methods

We compare PolyRAG against five groups of methods: 1) Frozen-LLMs (direct querying without external knowledge); 2) SFT (models fine-tuned on domain data, including LoRA [13] and models like Finance-Chat [7]); 3) NaiveRAG [16]; 4) Advanced RAG (ColBERTv2 [27], Bge-reranker [39]); and 5) KG-Augmented

Table 2. Performance comparison with SOTA methods on the AcadChall and R-FLUE-FiQA datasets.

Group	Method	Knowledge Base	Backend LLM	AcadChall			R-FLUE-FiQA			
				Precision	Recall	F1	BLEU-2	BLEU-4	BERT	HR(%)
Frozen-LLM	Direct Querying	Pretrained	LLaMA-7B	0.2892	0.5796	0.3470	0.4166	0.2612	0.4658	4.4914
	Direct Querying	Pretrained	LLaMA2-7B	0.2400	0.4039	0.2558	0.4106	0.2533	0.4540	4.8735
	Direct Querying	Pretrained	Vicuna-7B	0.3195	0.6622	0.3969	0.3552	0.2251	0.4509	4.7271
	Direct Querying	Pretrained	Vicuna-13B	0.3044	0.5423	0.3606	0.4098	0.2616	0.4933	5.6721
	Direct Querying	Pretrained	GPT-3.5	0.3716	0.4031	0.3677	0.2597	0.1525	0.5426	4.1965
	Direct Querying	Pretrained	GPT-4	0.1986	0.1453	0.1636	0.4109	0.2457	0.5415	7.6901
SFT	Finance-LLM	Raw Texts	LLaMA-7B	-	-	-	0.3990	0.2428	0.4265	3.8447
	Finance-Chat	Raw Texts	LLaMA2-7B	-	-	-	0.3669	0.2265	0.4531	5.0571
	LoRA	Raw Texts	Vicuna-13B	0.3234	0.6794	0.3914	0.3768	0.2382	0.4511	4.5854
Naive RAG	In-Context	Raw Texts	Vicuna-7B	0.3621	0.8386	0.4673	0.3159	0.2208	0.5858	7.5769
	In-Context	Raw Texts	Vicuna-13B	0.3665	**0.9043**	0.4923	0.2934	0.1866	0.5337	5.4326
	In-Context	Raw Texts	GPT-3.5	0.5105	0.5791	0.5315	0.3618	0.2147	0.5337	3.9153
	In-Context	Raw Texts	GPT-4	0.5032	0.5094	0.4651	0.3982	0.2404	0.5381	5.9918
Advance RAG	Colbertv2	Raw Texts	Vicuna-13B	0.3384	0.6693	0.3815	0.4229	0.2979	0.5918	7.1836
	Bge-reranker	Raw Texts	Vicuna-13B	0.3003	0.6400	0.3586	0.4400	0.3092	0.5965	7.4097
KG Augmentation	KAPING	KG	Vicuna-7B	0.4365	0.8581	0.5133	0.4079	0.2610	0.5389	5.5468
	KAPING	KG	Vicuna-13B	0.3446	0.8945	0.4742	0.3832	0.2403	0.5422	5.4149
	KAPING	KG	GPT-3.5	0.7326	0.6340	0.6433	0.2599	0.1742	0.5300	4.8785
	KAPING	KG	GPT-4	0.6327	0.7065	0.6238	0.3554	0.2319	0.5187	6.1383
Ours	PolyRAG	Pyramid	Vicuna-7B	0.5306	0.8337	0.5967	0.4485	**0.3235**	0.6008	8.6802
	PolyRAG	Pyramid	Vicuna-13B	0.4330	0.8148	0.5655	0.4444	0.3172	0.6089	8.6954
	PolyRAG	Pyramid	GPT-3.5	0.8667	0.7860	0.8039	**0.4459**	0.3204	**0.6114**	**8.7046**
	PolyRAG	Pyramid	GPT-4	**0.8711**	0.7992	**0.8109**	0.4002	0.2609	0.6012	7.7705

Table 3. Ablation results on the AcadChall shows the impact of: (1) Completion (CPL) and Condensation (CND); (2) knowledge layers, including various combinations of Ontology (Ont.), Knowledge Graph (KG), and Raw Text (Raw.).

Model	Metric	Knowledge CPL and CND					Influence of Knowledge Layers						
		Naive RAG	Baseline	+CPL	+CND	+CPL +CND	Ont.	KG	Raw.	Ont. +Raw.	KG +Raw.	Ont. +KG	PolyRAG
Vicuna-7b	Precision	0.3621	0.5306	**0.6888**	0.6557	0.5306	0.4383	0.4365	0.3621	0.4535	0.3673	0.5251	**0.5306**
	Recall	**0.8386**	0.8337	0.8325	0.7599	0.8337	0.6242	0.8581	0.8386	0.8393	**0.8758**	0.8266	0.8337
	F1	0.4673	0.5734	0.5874	0.5766	**0.5967**	0.4445	0.5133	0.4673	0.5368	0.4840	0.5608	**0.5967**
Vicuna-13b	Precision	0.3665	0.4230	0.4289	0.4236	**0.4330**	0.3363	0.3446	0.3665	0.4100	0.3747	0.4081	**0.4330**
	Recall	**0.9043**	0.8848	0.8045	0.8075	0.8148	0.5811	0.8945	**0.9043**	0.8908	0.9050	0.8814	0.8148
	F1	0.4923	0.5309	0.5595	0.5557	**0.5655**	0.3818	0.4742	0.4923	0.5187	0.4919	0.5166	**0.5655**
LLaMA2-70b	Precision	0.5673	0.7661	0.8633	0.8595	**0.8838**	0.5549	0.6666	0.5673	0.6198	0.7421	0.6833	**0.8838**
	Recall	0.3893	0.6479	**0.6836**	0.6445	0.6821	0.4501	0.6490	0.3893	0.5244	0.5083	0.5980	**0.6821**
	F1	0.4193	0.6678	0.7267	0.7166	**0.7380**	0.4501	0.6080	0.4193	0.5205	0.5505	0.5922	**0.7380**
Gemini-Pro	Precision	0.5152	0.7956	0.8217	0.8036	**0.8372**	0.3386	0.6388	0.5152	0.5905	0.6890	0.7755	**0.8372**
	Recall	0.3968	0.6513	0.8597	**0.8737**	0.8419	0.3089	0.4591	0.3968	0.4662	0.5428	0.6697	**0.8419**
	F1	0.4214	0.6899	0.7869	0.7439	**0.8107**	0.3157	0.5099	0.4214	0.5013	0.5821	0.6709	**0.8107**
GPT-3.5	Precision	0.5105	0.7855	0.8044	0.7985	**0.8667**	0.4107	0.7326	0.5105	0.6890	0.8339	0.8567	**0.8667**
	Recall	0.5791	0.7806	**0.8152**	0.8027	0.7860	0.3945	0.6340	0.5791	0.5818	0.6622	0.7710	**0.7860**
	F1	0.5315	0.7905	0.7939	0.7943	**0.8039**	0.3979	0.6433	0.5315	0.6020	0.7071	0.7939	**0.8039**
GPT-4	Precision	0.5032	0.7661	0.8063	0.8435	**0.8711**	0.3500	0.6327	0.5032	0.6464	0.8187	0.6083	**0.8711**
	Recall	0.5094	**0.8206**	0.7909	0.7853	0.7992	0.4369	0.7065	0.5094	0.6779	0.7729	**0.9032**	0.7992
	F1	0.4651	0.7639	0.7763	0.7873	**0.8109**	0.3677	0.6238	0.4651	0.6303	0.7636	0.6871	**0.8109**

LLMs [3]. We test across multiple LLM backbones, including LLaMA [31], Vicuna [8], GPT-3.5, and GPT-4, for a total of 23 comprehensive comparisons.

As shown in Table 2, PolyRAG outperforms other SOTA methods across all groups, backbones, and benchmarks, demonstrating a superior balance between precision and recall. Notably, with PolyRAG, GPT-4's F1 score on AcadChall surged from 0.1636 to 0.8109, a 395% increase over the frozen model and a 74% increase over NaiveRAG. This substantial improvement is attributable to the pyramid structure, with approximately 44% of questions on AcadChall being resolved at the high-precision Ontology layer and another 42% at the KG layer.

5.4 Ablation Studies

Knowledge Completion and Condensation. The left side of Table 3 shows the impact of Knowledge Completion (CPL) and Condensation (CND). Both modules individually improve performance, but their combination yields the largest gain (an average F1 improvement of 6.5% ± 6.4% over the baseline). CPL enriches the Ontology, allowing more queries to be resolved at this high-precision layer. CND consolidates the KG, reducing token load and helping smaller models better understand the context. For instance, with both modules, GPT-4's F1 score rises from 0.7639 to 0.8109, confirming their complementary benefits.

Influence of Knowledge Layers. The right side of Table 3 analyzes the contribution of each layer. The Ontology layer is crucial for precision, boosting it by an average of 25.8% when combined with raw text. The KG layer provides a balanced improvement in both precision and recall. These results empirically validate our hypothesis that the hierarchical structure of the knowledge pyramid effectively leverages the complementary strengths of each knowledge representation.

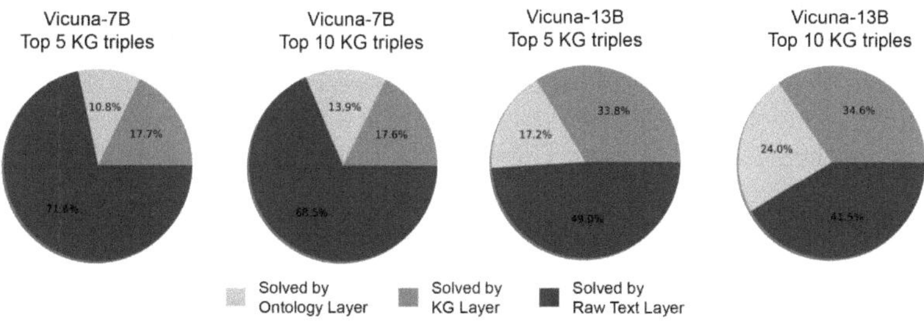

Fig. 6. Query proportion addressed by Ontology, KG, and Raw Text Layer.

5.5 Query Proportion Addressed by Each Knowledge Layer

Figure 6 shows the distribution of queries resolved by each layer. A significant portion of queries (over 28.5%) are answered by the structured Ontology and KG layers, highlighting their efficiency in the waterfall query process. This proportion increases with more powerful LLM backbones and when more KG triplets are provided as context, demonstrating the framework's ability to effectively utilize structured knowledge to improve accuracy and reduce reliance on less precise raw text retrieval.

6 Conclusion

This research outlines a preliminary investigation proposing a framework that integrates various knowledge representations to create a knowledge base and offers a multi-level query approach for applying the knowledge pyramid to domain-specific question answering. In this context, we addressed two significant challenges: the problem of prioritizing knowledge in a certain area and the presence of noise in retrieval situations. In order to overcome the limitations, we introduce Knowledge Pyramid multi-level retrieval framework as PolyRAG. PolyRAG utilizes a sequential retrieval approach and prioritizes knowledge extraction. This approach is designed to tackle the challenges posed by the high demand for dense knowledge in domain-specific scenarios and the distractions caused by noisy contexts. The accuracy of PolyRAG has been validated through extensive tests done in AcadChall and R-FLUE-FiQA, surpassing earlier approaches and generating state-of-the-art results.

Acknowledgments. This work was supported by National Natural Science Foundation of China (Grant No. 62372314). The experimental part of this work was supported by The Centre for Large AI Models (CLAIM) of The Hong Kong Polytechnic University.

References

1. Anderson, N., Wilson, C., Richardson, S.D.: Lingua: addressing scenarios for live interpretation and automatic dubbing. In: Proceedings of the 15th Biennial Conference of the Association for Machine Translation in the Americas (Volume 2: Users and Providers Track and Government Track), pp. 202–209 (2022)
2. Antoniou, G., van Harmelen, F.: Web Ontology Language: OWL, pp. 67–92. Springer, Heidelberg (2004). https://doi.org/10.1007/978-3-540-24750-0_4
3. Baek, J., Aji, A.F., Saffari, A.: Knowledge-augmented language model prompting for zero-shot knowledge graph question answering. In: Proceedings of the 1st Workshop on Natural Language Reasoning and Structured Explanations (NLRSE), pp. 78–106 (2023). arXiv preprint arXiv:2306.04136 (2023)
4. Baldazzi, T., Bellomarini, L., Ceri, S., Colombo, A., Gentili, A., Sallinger, E.: Fine-tuning large enterprise language models via ontological reasoning. In: International Joint Conference on Rules and Reasoning, pp. 86–94. Springer (2023)
5. Carta, S., Giuliani, A., Piano, L., Podda, A.S., Pompianu, L., Tiddia, S.G.: Iterative zero-shot llm prompting for knowledge graph construction. arXiv preprint arXiv:2307.01128 (2023)

6. Chen, W., et al.: Disc-finllm: a Chinese financial large language model based on multiple experts fine-tuning (2023)
7. Cheng, D., Huang, S., Wei, F.: Adapting large language models via reading comprehension. In: The Eleventh International Conference on Learning Representations (2024)
8. Chiang, W.L., et al.: Vicuna: an open-source chatbot impressing gpt-4 with 90%* chatgpt quality, March 2023. https://lmsys.org/blog/2023-03-30-vicuna/
9. Cui, J., Li, Z., Yan, Y., Chen, B., Yuan, L.: Chatlaw: open-source legal large language model with integrated external knowledge bases (2023)
10. Dong, Q., et al.: A survey on in-context learning (2023)
11. Etzioni, O., Banko, M., Soderland, S., Weld, D.S.: Open information extraction from the web. Commun. ACM **51**(12), 68–74 (2008)
12. Glass, M., Rossiello, G., Chowdhury, M.F.M., Naik, A.R., Cai, P., Gliozzo, A.: Re2g: Retrieve, rerank, generate (2022)
13. Hu, E.J., et al.: Lora: Low-rank adaptation of large language models (2022)
14. Huang, L., et al.: A survey on hallucination in large language models: principles, taxonomy, challenges, and open questions. arXiv preprint arXiv:2311.05232 (2023)
15. Huang, Q., et al.: Lawyer llama technical report (2023)
16. Lewis, P., et al.: Retrieval-augmented generation for knowledge-intensive nlp tasks. Adv. Neural. Inf. Process. Syst. **33**, 9459–9474 (2020)
17. Litman, R., Anschel, O., Tsiper, S., Litman, R., Mazor, S., Manmatha, R.: Scatter: selective context attentional scene text recognizer. In: Proceedings of the IEEE/CVF Conference on Computer Vision and Pattern Recognition, pp. 11962–11972 (2020)
18. Liu, A., Du, J., Stoyanov, V.: Knowledge-augmented language model and its application to unsupervised named-entity recognition. In: North American Chapter of the Association for Computational Linguistics (2019). https://api.semanticscholar.org/CorpusID:104292554
19. Luo, Y., Yang, Z., Meng, F., Li, Y., Zhou, J., Zhang, Y.: An empirical study of catastrophic forgetting in large language models during continual fine-tuning. arXiv preprint arXiv:2308.08747 (2023)
20. Ma, X., Gong, Y., He, P., hai zhao, Duan, N.: Query rewriting in retrieval-augmented large language models. In: The 2023 Conference on Empirical Methods in Natural Language Processing (2023)
21. Mihindukulasooriya, N., Tiwari, S., Enguix, C.F., Lata, K.: Text2kgbench: a benchmark for ontology-driven knowledge graph generation from text. In: International Semantic Web Conference, pp. 247–265. Springer (2023)
22. Miller, G.A.: Wordnet: a lexical database for English. Commun. ACM **38**(11), 39–41 (1995)
23. Ouyang, L., et al.: Training language models to follow instructions with human feedback. Adv. Neural. Inf. Process. Syst. **35**, 27730–27744 (2022)
24. Palagin, O., Kaverinskiy, V., Litvin, A., Malakhov, K.: Ontochatgpt information system: ontology-driven structured prompts for chatgpt meta-learning. arXiv preprint arXiv:2307.05082 (2023)
25. Pan, S., Luo, L., Wang, Y., Chen, C., Wang, J., Wu, X.: Unifying large language models and knowledge graphs: a roadmap. IEEE Trans. Knowl. Data Eng. (2024)
26. Radford, A., Narasimhan, K., Salimans, T., Sutskever, I., et al.: Improving language understanding by generative pre-training (2018)
27. Santhanam, K., Khattab, O., Potts, C., Zaharia, M.: Plaid: an efficient engine for late interaction retrieval (2022)

28. Shah, R.S., et al.: When flue meets flang: benchmarks and large pretrained language model for financial domain. In: Proceedings of the 2022 Conference on Empirical Methods in Natural Language Processing (EMNLP). Association for Computational Linguistics (2022)
29. Speer, R., Chin, J., Havasi, C.: Conceptnet 5.5: An open multilingual graph of general knowledge. In: Proceedings of the AAAI Conference on Artificial Intelligence, vol. 31 (2017)
30. Su, H., et al.: One embedder, any task: instruction-finetuned text embeddings (2022). https://arxiv.org/abs/2212.09741
31. Touvron, H., et al.: Llama: Open and efficient foundation language models. arXiv preprint arXiv:2302.13971 (2023)
32. Vamsi, K.K., Kommineni, V.K., Samuel, S.: From human experts to machines: an llm supported approach to ontology and knowledge graph construction (2024)
33. Wang, N., Yang, H., Wang, C.D.: Fingpt: instruction tuning benchmark for open-source large language models in financial datasets. In: NeurIPS Workshop on Instruction Tuning and Instruction Following (2023)
34. Wang, W., Wei, F., Dong, L., Bao, H., Yang, N., Zhou, M.: Minilm: deep self-attention distillation for task-agnostic compression of pre-trained transformers. In: Proceedings of the 34th International Conference on Neural Information Processing Systems (2020)
35. Wei, J., et al.: Finetuned language models are zero-shot learners. arXiv preprint arXiv:2109.01652 (2021)
36. Wei, X.Y., Yang, Z.Q.: Mining in-class social networks for large-scale pedagogical analysis. In: Proceedings of the 20th ACM International Conference on Multimedia, MM '12, pp. 639–648. Association for Computing Machinery, New York (2012). https://doi.org/10.1145/2393347.2393436
37. Wu, S., et al.: Bloomberggpt: a large language model for finance. arXiv preprint arXiv:2303.17564 (2023)
38. Wu, Y., et al.: Retrieve-rewrite-answer: a kg-to-text enhanced llms framework for knowledge graph question answering. ArXiv abs/2309.11206 (2023). https://api.semanticscholar.org/CorpusID:262054223
39. Xiao, S., Liu, Z., Zhang, P., Muennighoff, N.: C-pack: packaged resources to advance general Chinese embedding (2023)
40. Xie, Q., et al.: Pixiu: a large language model, instruction data and evaluation benchmark for finance (2023)
41. Yang, K., Zhang, T., Kuang, Z., Xie, Q., Huang, J., Ananiadou, S.: Mentallama: interpretable mental health analysis on social media with large language models, pp. 4489–4500 (2024)
42. Yang, S., et al.: Zhongjing: Enhancing the Chinese medical capabilities of large language model through expert feedback and real-world multi-turn dialogue (2024)
43. Yue, S., et al.: Disc-lawllm: fine-tuning large language models for intelligent legal services (2023)
44. Zhang, X., Tian, C., Yang, X., Chen, L., Li, Z., Petzold, L.R.: Alpacare: instruction-tuned large language models for medical application. arXiv preprint arXiv:2310.14558 (2023)

Learning Analytics by Design: Safeguarding Metadata for AI Services

Augmenting Open-Source Middleware with LRS Functionality

Truong-Sinh An[1(✉)], Alexander Streicher[2], Michael Wifling[3], Bach Do[1], Christopher Krauss[1], Daniela Altun[4], and The-Anh Nguyen[1]

[1] Fraunhofer FOKUS, Kaiserin-Augusta-Allee 31, 10589 Berlin, Germany
{truong-sinh.an,bach.do,christopher.krauss, the-anh.nguyen}@fokus.fraunhofer.de

[2] Fraunhofer IOSB, Fraunhoferstraße 1, 76131 Karlsruhe, Germany
alexander.streicher@iosb.fraunhofer.de

[3] Ausbildungskommando, Landsberger Str. 133, 04157 Leipzig, Germany
michael1wifling@bundeswehr.org

[4] Fraunhofer FKIE, Zanderstraße 5, 53177 Bonn-Bad Godesberg, Germany
daniela.altun@fkie.fraunhofer.de

Abstract. Modern learning platforms are modular ecosystems with decentralized storage of content, offerings, and metadata. LLM-based chatbots are increasingly integrated to support learners in their educational journey. This development highlights the importance of collecting and analyzing learning data to enable personalized and adaptive e-learning applications that improve outcomes across different offerings. Based on operational research [1] with the German Armed Forces (Bundeswehr, Bw), we identified the need for decentralized, middleware-based Learning Record Store (LRS) solutions that respect organizational policies for data governance, privacy, federated identities, and interoperability, using the Experience API (xAPI) as the standard for tracking learning experiences.

Current literature reveals a significant gap in the LRS landscape. Existing approaches often lack mechanisms for effective data flow control, interoperability, and strict data separation in decentralized environments. They also fail to maintain optimized metadata for AI services. To address these shortcomings, this research examines the organizational and technical requirements for a decentralized, middleware-based LRS. Our contribution is a novel concept designed to function as a network of data enclaves, enabling seamless queries and semantic control across the organization. A key feature is the data flow control mechanism, which complies with the xAPI specification and supports functions such as selective data merging to manage access and data flow, optimizing data processing with LLM agents.

Keywords: Learning Analytics · LRS · xAPI · Data Interoperability · Data Governance in Education · AI-optimized Metadata

B. Fernández-Manjón et al. (Eds.): SETE 2025/ICWL 2025, LNCS 16425, pp. 225–239, 2026.
https://doi.org/10.1007/978-981-92-0042-9_17

1 Introduction

Modern educational ecosystems must incorporate the effective collection and analysis of learning data which enables adaptivity, personalization, and the analysis of learning analytics to enhance learner engagement and improve educational outcomes following the conceptional tools introduced by [2]. Valid learner data is crucial for designing personalized learning paths and enhancing the quality of educational offerings [3]. Traditional approaches to learning data management are often insufficient to address the complexities of classic approaches like learning analytics [4,5] and modern learning contexts like educational AI-Assistants for the Metaverse [6]. In such landscapes, xAPI has emerged as a powerful tool for capturing learning activities, facilitating the seamless integration of data from multiple sources. However, despite the advantages offered by existing xAPI compliant LRS solutions (e.g., Learning Locker, Veracity), these platforms fall short in handling complex data flow control scenarios. Specifically, they face challenges with statement-forwarding and proxying based on semantic filtering mechanisms, which are essential for fully supporting the diverse organizational policies of various stakeholders.

Our concept, developed in alignment with the requirements of the German Armed Forces (Bundeswehr, Bw), is based on a requirements and performance specification that addresses their organizational policies and highlights the need for a more advanced approach to managing permissions, especially in environments where strict organizational boundaries and structured access hierarchies must be upheld (e.g., data security and data privacy constraints). Users act on the basis of their classification (e.g., non-military personnel or other classifications) with different identities and in different networks, which may be strictly encapsulated or only unilaterally accessible. These requirements make it difficult to support users across all identities and educational environments with learning analytics and AI functions during their learning process.

To address this critical gap, we present the concept of a middleware-based LRS which can be integrated as a microservice in other (open-source) middleware solutions which fully support interoperability standards and specifications. As part of the implementation of the German Armed Forces' virtual learning environment (VLBw) [7] for training and continuing education, the Common Learning Middleware (CLM) [8] is being used as an open-source solution which enforces the usage of interoperability standards. It enhances access and data flow control mechanisms through graph-based permission structures [27]. It facilitates the integration of external xAPI-compatible LRSs by allowing them to register as service providers with the middleware and routing xAPI statements to the appropriate LRS depending on permissions.

The basic functionality that allows organizations to grant applications and services access to and process these xAPI statements is expanded with our concept to address the organizational guidelines of the Bw. Across all identities and networks, applications and services should enable the aggregation and analysis of learning data from various sources – the special feature being the permissions for necessary or confidential contextual information as metadata.

A simple example is the reduction of redundant data when storing xAPI statements. A more concrete example is that xAPI statements are enriched with contextual information for further processing by specifically dereferencing educational and didactic metadata (e.g., from LOM) or by adding sensitive information to the response payload of aggregation queries. This is achieved, for example, by dereferencing, since the object ID in the xAPI statement corresponds to the activity and metadata for this activity is available in the middleware according to LOM and can be queried with the URI. Applications/services may not request this LOM, depending on their permissions. This is where the concept comes into play and checks whether the application/service is allowed or even required to process specific metadata from the LOM; this metadata is then added to the response payload. Another example is the fact that applications and services do not have the authorization to view specific metadata in the xAPI statements and to specifically remove it from the response payload of a query.

The verification of permissions to determine whether applications/services are allowed to request certain metadata via interfaces is already covered by the graph-based permission structures of the middleware. The concept must extend this approach, as the metadata in the xAPI statements must be controlled in a more granular manner. One of the main functions goes beyond the support of xAPI profiles (profiles). The concept does not provide an xAPI profile for all producers and consumers of xAPI statements, but rather each producer and consumer of xAPI statements can use an already approved profile or register their own. A profile is considered a usage right (policy) – the concept provides for the consistent use of profiles by assigning them to an API token and understands this process as a client usage right and the definition of statement templates as a promise to produce xAPI statements in this form or to require this amount of metadata for processing. Applications can define and register their own xAPI profile. The application defines statement templates as such, specifying the quality of metadata required for internal processing. The organization checks whether there is a justified and legitimate interest in metadata beyond the basic information for this application, and the API token for queries against the LRS is bound to this profile. For each query, the associated profile can be loaded via the API token, and its statement templates serve as a kind of template for the response payload, and information is removed or added accordingly, if available.

The concept is supplemented by a Data Preparation & Aggregation Service (DPAS) as an LRS companion. The aim of the concept is to make insights and patterns resulting from aggregation and analysis available to all applications and services in the Bw, thus providing an opportunity to standardize the interpretation of data. This would, for example, prevent multiple methods of calculating learning progress and avoid confusion among learners and teachers due to different values in different places. Server-side pre-aggregation in the database can be more efficient than regularly requesting xAPI statements as raw data and then calculating them. This makes it attractive for some services to shift this effort to the LRS. Services can request a list of all already registered aggregation functions, but only those that correspond to the associated profile are listed. If none of the aggregation functions are suitable, you can register your own. Conceptually, aggregation functions can be registered as remote procedure calls – context views – that merge metadata from the xAPI statements and store it in a way that is optimized for time series analysis. Applications such as LLM agents can decide, in accordance with the Resource-Oriented Architecture (ROA), whether they want to use the xAPI-compliant API for raw data or the DPAS-RPC API. The LRS comes with its own learning analytics dashboard based on Grafana. As part of this, aggregation functions are already registered with the DPAS by default.

2 Related Works

In recent years, the field of digital education and learning technologies has experienced significant growth [9]. A central focus is on effectively capturing and analyzing learning data to facilitate personalized learning [10]. xAPI, in its core related to the W3C Activity Streams specification, has emerged as a widely accepted data format that enables the tracking and documentation of learning activities across various platforms. Research indicates that xAPI enhances interoperability between different learning systems, providing valuable insights into learner behavior [11,12] and continues with Version 2 as IEEE specification.

Several LRS have been developed to manage xAPI data [13]. Commercial solutions like Watershed, Grassblade and Veracity provide strong analysis, and visualization features but easy adaptability and system integration are challenging. In contrast, open-source LRSs offer flexibility and cost advantages, but documented drawbacks include heavier self-support and customization needs and uneven documentation, which can make systems difficult to install, use, maintain, and troubleshoot [14]. Studies of learning-analytics (LA) deployments likewise report inadequate support and instructions, difficult user interfaces, and weak communication of use-cases and value to end-users [15]. More broadly, the LA literature identifies gaps in usability, access, and performance when projects scale [16], as well as mismatches between tool capabilities and user needs [17]. On the other hand, there are new solutions such as SQL LRS, which do not meet the requirements (see Chap. 3) of the Bw with their approaches.

Alongside xAPI [18,19], other standards like IMS Caliper address similar needs in educational technology [20]. Caliper offers a framework for collecting learning activity data and defines metrics to enhance interoperability between systems. While both standards aim to improve data exchange, xAPI is often preferred for its flexibility in capturing a wider range of learning experiences.

The integration of LRS functionalities into existing open-source middleware remains a relatively underexplored area. Some studies have highlighted the utility of middleware in educational settings, particularly in improving interoperability and data management [21,22]. Nevertheless, there is a clear need for further research specifically addressing the expansion of middleware to include LRS functionalities and the associated challenges and solutions in order to be a trusted source of metadata and learning analytics for advanced learning technologies in the age of AI.

3 Requirements Analysis

The design and implementation of the proposed LRS concept is based on a catalog of requirements that covers various use cases relevant to the organizational context of the German Armed Forces, specifically in relation to the upcoming introduction of the new training and continuing education platform—the German Armed Forces' virtual learning environment.

One notable scenario involves users navigating between different networks with different access policies within the military and its organizational guidelines, depending on their specific roles. Each network, along with its associated services and content, is considered a separate organization. Given the variability of corporate policies, these entities may be subject to different requirements regarding data management and control. In their most restrictive form, corporate policies may require that metadata remain within the boundaries of a single network, which is referred to as operating within a digital enclave. In addition, non-military personnel and other classifications may have different user identities in different networks.

In cases of unilaterally accessible networks, users who engage in learning activities within an enclave retain the ability to access learning objects stored in open networks. This multi-network scenario requires effective coordination of data flows, which was facilitated by the open-source middleware CLM, which was used as a demonstrator during the study. However, this scenario poses several challenges for both LRSs operating within enclaves and those operating on open networks. One of the biggest challenges is establishing organization-wide identities. This problem can be mitigated by implementing unique login credentials or introducing federated identity management systems that enable seamless user authentication across network or organizational boundaries.

A critical challenge is ensuring interoperability for clients consuming the LRS. Clients must interact with the LRS without altering the specification-compliant logic required for xAPI statement requests. Our concept enforces Learning Record providers and consumers to register their xAPI profiles as a promise between all stakeholders that their metadata will always comply with the specified templates in their profiles. Furthermore, semantic interoperability is a core requirement. Different clients across various sub-organizations shall utilize the same vocabulary to ensure that xAPI data and statements are semantically interoperable. In this context, semantic interoperability refers to the ability of different systems or applications to exchange (trace) data and interpret it meaningfully. In e-learning, this capability is important, as various platforms and tools may use different data formats and vocabularies. This poses a particular challenge when xAPI statements are only used in the form in which they are available when creating learning content, due to the authoring tools or standards and specifications used. Similarly, when using learning content from existing resources, a wide variety of xAPI profiles emerges over time, some of which can no longer be adapted.

An additional requirement arises from the need to store xAPI statements not only as raw data but also in a pre-aggregated format suitable for optimized processing by AI services, namely as safeguarded metadata that improves the efficiency of AI-driven analytics and insights while remaining aligned with the stored profiles. Clients applications and services have the ability to register pre-aggregation functions for SQL (materialized) views via a Remote Procedure Call (RPC) API in the Data Preparation & Aggregation Service. This functionality enables clients to create custom context views that meet their specific analytical requirements. A simple example is that a view can be registered that translates the xAPI statements produced by another service with a different vocabulary into its own vocabulary. A more complex example is the pre-calculation of learning progress in a user/learning object matrix. Additionally, clients can also view and use RPC views created by other clients, which promotes collaboration, increases the overall benefits of the LRS and makes insights and indicators accessible for all within the Bw.

Our concept, developed in alignment with the requirements of the Bw, is based on a requirements and performance specification that addresses these organizational policies and highlights the need for a more advanced approach to managing permissions, especially in environments where strict organizational boundaries and structured access hierarchies must be upheld (e.g., data security and data privacy constraints).

Furthermore, the requirements for optimized AI evaluation of metadata necessitate the outsourcing of data preparation tasks via customer-created and DPAS-registered (RPC) context views. By allowing customers to define and manage their own SQL (materialized) views, we enable them to better tailor data extraction and transformation processes to their analysis requirements. This delegation of responsibilities not only increases the efficiency of the overall system, but also enables customers to perform more effective and targeted analyses. This allows customers to leverage their specific expertise and requirements to optimize metadata for AI-driven insights, ultimately leading to improved performance and better results in their respective use cases (Table 1).

The requirements also included the use of SQL-based database management systems. The concept is database type agnostic and was adapted to SQL for the Bw. We opted for the DBMS PostgreSQL, but can abstract and exchange database communication via DAOs and DTOs.

Table 1. Comparison of LRS functions for AI services

Feature	Our Concept	Learning Locker	Commercial LRS
Real-time AI Integration	✓	Limited	✓
Privacy-preserving AI	✓	×	Partially
RPC / Custom Views	✓	×	Limited
Semantic AI Enrichment	✓	×	×

4 Concept

The middleware-based LRS concept is designed to meet the complex requirements of modern educational environments, typical for heterogeneous corporate or organizational system landscapes. Central is the integration of advanced data governance mechanisms that facilitate compliance with stringent regulatory standards. By safeguarding sensitive learning data, the LRS supports lifelong learning initiatives and effective skills-based training, which is essential for organizations operating under strict data protection regulations.

Deletion concepts as a requirement for data protection considerations of personal data with protection needs of non-military personnel and other classifications complicate the historical evaluation of learning experiences. Solutions were repeatedly questioned, and a conceptual solution was found. Our LRS concept stipulates that xAPI statements (statements) may only be generated for activities for which enrollment has been submitted. In addition, information requiring protection can be handled specially depending on the configuration. For example, all user-specific clear names and references such as name, username and group info as URL are being replaced by their Inverse Functional Identifier (IFI) (see chapter 2.4.2.3 in [18,19]), as a pseudonym. Furthermore, data of activities could be classified and has been replaced by the middleware's collision-free IRI. This approach ensures that classified information is not stored directly within the middleware or the LRS. Instead, sensitive information is retrieved and de-referenced from third-party sources such as LOM providers, LTI tool providers via Resource Search, or OIDC providers, and subsequently made accessible through the open-source middleware CLM.

A key innovation of our LRS concept is its modular architecture, allowing flexible deployment in diverse organizational contexts [24]. The implementation leverages a microservice infrastructure from the CLM, to foster scalability and flexibility in containerized environments (e.g., Kubernetes). To enhance scalability and analytics, we propose utilizing standard relational database management systems (RDBMS,) to store the data triples - we tested our approach with MariaDB, Azure Data Explorer and use PostgreSQL for the Bw. Unlike document-oriented databases like MongoDB (e.g., in Learning Locker), SQL-based databases are more widely adopted, easier to scale, and offer straightforward integration with analytics tools such as Grafana dashboards. For queries and analyses, the data is aggregated in advance, indexed using (materialized) views (see Fig. 1, point 3) and viewed as situational facts – the interpretation of the data is left to the dashboards and AI services, which interpret these facts as answers to questions based on the case studies in [25]. This choice is complemented by integrating a message queue and load balancing system, such as Apache Kafka, to manage ingest peaks in request loads and maintain system responsiveness.

To address identity management challenges, our LRS concept includes advanced access control mechanisms based on graph-based permission structures. This feature enables fine-grained control over data access, ensuring users interact with the system according to their roles and policies [27] and cannot generate learning experiences with activities they are not enrolled to. Federated identity management provides streamlined login experiences across different networks, enhancing user satisfaction.

When used in a school context with minors, our concept can specifically mark information that requires special protection [26]. Configuring the middleware as an ID broker is another option for generating pseudonymized identifiers for client applications via federated identities. These identifiers are generated for the authenticated user in their security context and the requesting service in accordance with the OpenID Connect specification as a subject identifier of the type "pairwise" in accordance with the Pairwise Identifier Algorithm of the OIDC specification as a Pairwise Pseudonymous Identifier (PPID) and correspond to the OIDC variant of an IFI [28]. With this approach, the results from multiple services, such as the activity overview and risk forecast, cannot be merged in order to avoid correlation, as the user IDs have been pseudonymized specifically for each service through the corresponding configuration in the dereferencing proxy.

Let us now follow the journey of a learning experience as an xAPI statement through the LRS, the LRS companion DPAS, and on to a client as a consumer:

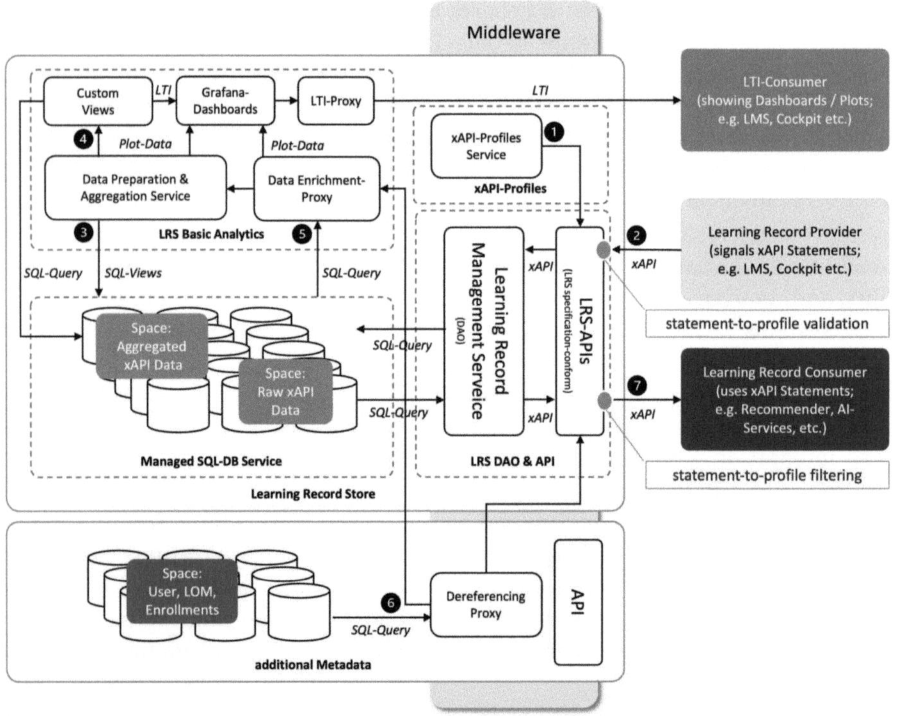

Fig. 1. Architecture of the middleware-based LRS concept with microservices and the LRS companion Data Preparation & Aggregation Service, a holistic view.

4.1 xAPI Profiles Service

The first point of contact with the LRS is the "xAPI Profiles Service" (Fig. 1, point 1). This service issues API tokens that enable applications and services to communicate with the LRS. Operators of a Learning Record Provider, such as a learning management system that can signal xAPI statements, register the service with their xAPI profile at the LRS in order to obtain an API token. In addition to the concepts (verbs, activities, and context extensions) as vocabulary, the xAPI profile also contains statement templates that define the semantic meaning and structure/schema of xAPI statements. Operators of LRS and learning record providers can agree on the mandatory fields. These profiles are transparently accessible to all applications and services within the virtual learning environment of the German Armed Forces.

4.2 Statement-to-Profile Validation

Signaled xAPI statements are communicated to xAPI-compliant interfaces. This is where "statement-to-profile validation" comes into play (Fig. 1, point 2). The xAPI statements are projected against the statement templates from the profile associated with the API token. Unknown attributes are removed in the interest of data minimization, and no provider can send more metadata in the xAPI statements than agreed upon. If promised attributes are missing, the LRS can be configured to either reject the statement or still store it as RAW data.

4.3 Data Preparation and Aggregation Service

The "Data Preparation & Aggregation Service" (DPAS, Fig. 1, point 3) allows client applications and services such as learning analytics or AI services to register aggregation functions as remote procedure calls (RPC), which contextually merge metadata (xAPI statements) and store them for further time series analysis into SQL (materialized) views. The registry provides an overview of all aggregation functions via its interfaces. According to the xAPI profile (1) associated with the API token, proprietary aggregation functions may not be able to take all metadata into account (2 & 7).

4.4 Custom Views

The aggregation functions registered in (3) are configured as SQL (materialized) views which can be seen as context views or "Custom Views" (Fig. 1, point 4) and allow SQL queries similar to raw data. The pre-aggregated metadata optimizes queries and processing times and allows clients such as LLM agents to use metadata whose context they understand. For learning analytics dashboards, a custom view can be created for each indicator, and for more complex metrics and representations, a resource-oriented architecture-compliant remote method invocation of a remote procedure call via custom views. A practical use case for AI services such as LLM-based chatbots is that a tool can be provided for MCP servers that lists the custom views with their descriptions so that LLMs can use them deliberately.

4.5 Data Enrichment-Proxy

In accordance with data protection and information security requirements, entities such as user or group information and sensitive information are stored exclusively as IFI in both raw data and (user-defined) custom views. The "Data Enrichment-Proxy" (Fig. 1, point 5) may add metadata to the result of a query against (4 & 7). For example, in the case of an aggregation query, where the result is extended with additional metadata that was not originally sent in the instructions before being returned. This is possible when a LOM provider is used in the ecosystem. This approach saves storage space in the LRS and reduces the amount of redundant data. The metadata can be extended according to the profile and instruction templates and, depending on the configuration, can also convert pseudonyms to plain text on the fly.

4.6 Dereferencing-Proxy

The "Dereferencing-Proxy" (Fig. 1, point 6) enables client applications such as learning analytics or AI services to receive the requested data already enriched with additional metadata. AI services such as recommender systems usually work internally with identifiers and only need the titles of the learning objects when displaying learning and recommendation for action. Some services, such as learning analytics dashboards or LLM chatbots, already require this information in the response payload of the aggregation or raw data query. When querying statements, the consumer's API token determines the extent to which the query response data is modified by a proxy. The service can return pseudonymized metadata as IRI, provided that the source systems are known. For example, some LRS also offer an aggregation interface where [22], in addition to the filter, a server-side data aggregation and transformation job is sent in the query (3 & 4). The result could be a HashMap over a list of competencies and skills with the aggregated performance levels. If the profile does not include the activity type Competence or Skill and the competencies and skills are included in the LOM metadata, these can be added to the xAPI context extensions by the proxy during processing and are then available for the data transformation step in the aggregation request. This Scenario might be helpful with Clients where it is challenging fetching the LOM metadata in parallel, e.g. Grafana.

4.7 Statement-to-Profile Filtering

Semantic interoperability is foundational to our LRS concept. Middleware solutions can act as intermediaries that translate and mediate communications between disparate e-learning systems. For example, a middleware application might convert data from an xAPI compatible tool into a format understandable by a SCORM-only compliant LMS. By implementing middleware that adheres to these standards, organizations can enhance semantic interoperability, enabling seamless data exchange and integration for a comprehensive view of learner progress and engagement. For this purpose, the concept proposes to implement "statement-to-profile filtering" (Fig. 1, point 7) in accordance to (2) for querying and aggregation - an approach that only allows statements to be queried via an API token that matches the corresponding profile (1). Clients cannot query more metadata than they are allowed according to their xAPI profile. Different profiles can carry the risk of different semantic interpretations of concepts. For this purpose, the middleware supports mapping if the registration of a custom "mapping" view is not an option. The verbs and activity types listed in a profile can come from different vocabularies and have the same semantic meaning; for this scenario, the specification allows the "relatedMatch" attribute [23]. This attribute lists a series of IRIs of concepts of the same type from another profile or version of the same profile that has a related meaning, e.g. the middleware will consider statements with the verbs initialized, launched and started, even the profile only has the concept of initialized as verb, but the verb is having relatedMatch listing launched and started.

4.8 Scenarios

Modern modular ecosystems can be enhanced with LLM-based chatbots that improve the learning experience through personalized assistance. A standard scenario involves a chatbot accessing an LRS via a Middleware Communication Platform (MCP) to retrieve xAPI statements.

Standard Approach with Processing Logic in Chatbot
In the standard method (Fig. 2), the chatbot sends a request to the API endpoint `/statements` to retrieve raw xAPI statements. This allows access to unprocessed data, which the chatbot aggregates and enriches with metadata. Upon receiving the raw data, the chatbot analyzes it to gain insights that enhance understanding of the learning context and improve user interactions. Strict data protection policies complicate this, as personal data is pseudonymized and sensitive metadata is removed.

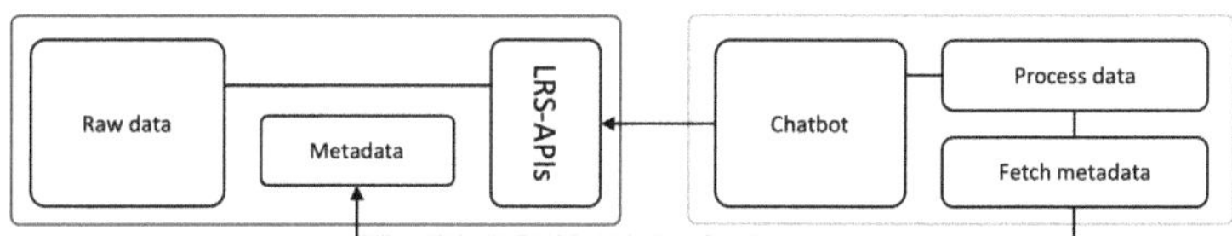

Fig. 2. Standard approach with processing logic in chatbot

For example, the API call may look like this:

```
GET /statements?agent={"mbox_sha1sum":"..."}&verb={"id"
    :".../completed"}&activity={"id":".../course"}
```

Approach with DPAS, Custom View and Dereferencing-Proxy
Our extended approach (Fig. 3) consists of the LLM chatbot querying a predefined SQL (materialized) view with aggregated data. Here, the chatbot receives a payload enriched with contextual information, allowing it to provide tailored responses quickly. This method streamlines data retrieval and ensures that the chatbot uses optimized metadata for personalized learning experiences.

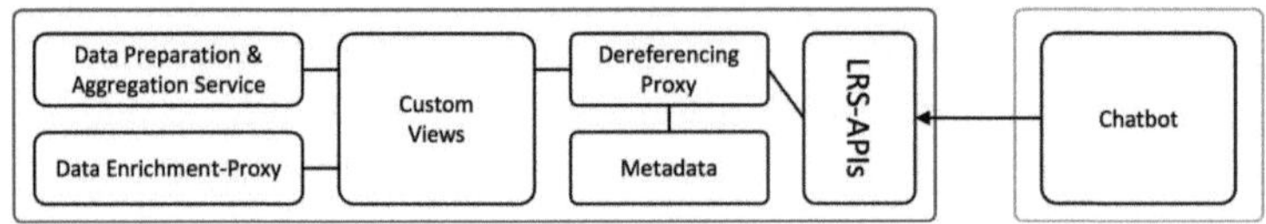

Fig. 3. Our concept with DPAS, custom View and Dereferencing-Proxy

An example API request for this scenario could look like this:

```
GET /custom_view?agent={"mbox_sha1sum":""}&context={"
    context_id":"activity"}
```

Approach with Custom Views in DPAS as MCP-Tool
One advantage of SQL (materialized) views is that they can be registered on an MCP server together with a description text using tools. This enables the LLM-based chatbot to decide independently which tools/views to use and, ideally, to have all the information needed to generate a response available with just one query (Fig. 4).
An example API request for via MCP could look like this:

```
POST https://mcp-server.example.com/api/data \
-H "Content-Type:␣application/json" \
-d '{
  "action": "retrieve_data",
  "view": "learning_progress",
  "parameters": {
    "user_id": "",
    "date_range": {
      "start": "2025-11-30",
      "end": "2025-12-03"
    }
  }
}'
```

Depending on the authorization level, the response payload of the interface could already be enriched with all the necessary metadata. This metadata includes both educational and didactic metadata from LOM and contextual metadata for classification in the learning setting. Unnecessary metadata is specifically removed from the response payload. We understand this as "safeguarding metadata for AI services."

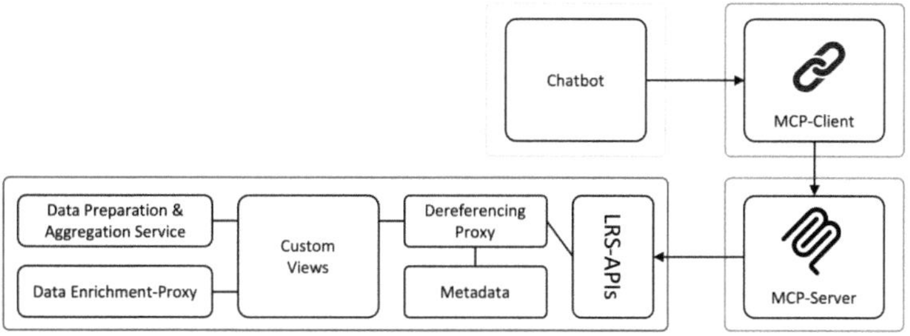

Fig. 4. MCP approach via DPAS, custom View and Dereferencing-Proxy as MCP-Tool

5 Conclusion and Future Work

In this article, we present a comprehensive concept for a LRS tailored to the needs of large-scale corporate learning environments. In discussions with stakeholders, we explored the feasibility of injecting sensitive information at runtime and processing it during requests by incorporating this information into the result set via a proxy. The implementation of the LRS as a microservice alongside other middleware demonstrated its flexibility in various contexts. Our findings underscore the importance of robust identity management, scalable data governance, and effective communication between learning systems to create a cohesive learning environment.

This concept has already been implemented as additional microservices based on open-source middleware CLM and tested in four courses as part of an operational research study for the German Armed Forces using AI services such as recommenders, learning analytics dashboards, and LLM chatbots.

Moving forward, we will continue to evaluate the LRS in user studies, to stress, optimize and evaluate the implementation. We also plan to enhance the ecosystem of xAPI producers and consumers by integrating tools like recommender systems and learning analytics dashboards, which will enrich the learning experience through personalized recommendations and actionable insights.

Acknowledgment. In this article, we would like to thank the German Armed Forces, in particular the Army Command and the Army Training Command.

References

1. Gesellschaft, F.: AI support for learning management systems (only in German) (2020). https://kilms.fraunhofer.de/
2. Dawson, S., Siemens, G.: Analytics to literacies: the development of a learning analytics framework for multiliteracies assessment. Int. Rev. Res. Open Distance Learn. **15**(4), 284–305 (2014). https://doi.org/10.19173/irrodl.v15i4.1878
3. Greller, W., Drachsler, H.: Translating learning into numbers: a generic framework for learning analytics. J. Educ. Technol. Soc. **15**(3), 42–57 (2012). https://api.semanticscholar.org/CorpusID:1152401
4. Moore, R.L.: The Role of Data Analytics in Education: Possibilities and Limitations. In: Responsible Analytics and Data Mining in Education. Routledge (2018). https://doi.org/10.4324/9780203728703-8
5. Avella, J.T., Kebritchi, M., Nunn, S.G., Kanai, T.: Learning analytics methods, benefits, and challenges in higher education: A systematic literature review. J. Asynchronous Learn. Network 20 (2016). https://doi.org/10.24059/olj.v20i2.790
6. Krauss, C., et al.: Opportunities and challenges in developing educational ai-assistants for the metaverse. In International Conference on Human-Computer Interaction, pp. 219–238. Springer, Switzerland (2024). https://doi.org/10.1007/978-3-031-60609-0_16
7. Fraunhofer FOKUS: Virtual Learning Environment of the German Armed Forces (2025). https://clm.fraunhofer.de/en/virtuelle-lernumgebung-der-bundeswehr/
8. Fraunhofer FOKUS (2024) Common Learning Middleware. https://clm.fraunhofer.de/en/clm-overview/
9. Haleem, A., Javaid, M., Qadri, M.A., Suman, R.: Understanding the role of digital technologies in education: a review. Sustainable Operat. Comput. **3**, 275–285 (2022). https://doi.org/10.1016/j.susoc.2022.05.004
10. Alam, A.: The secret sauce of student success: cracking the code by navigating the path to personalized learning with educational data mining. In: 2023 2nd International Conference on Smart Technologies and Systems for Next Generation Computing (ICSTSN), pp. 1–8 (2023). https://doi.org/10.1109/ICSTSN57873.2023.10151558
11. An, T.S., Krauss, C., Merceron, A.: Can Typical Behaviors Identified in MOOCs Be Discovered in Other Courses?. Proceedings of the 10th International Conference on Educational Data Mining (EDM 2017), Wuhan, China, June 25-28, pp. 220–225 (2017). http://educationaldatamining.org/EDM2017/proc_files/papers/paper_58.pdf
12. An, T.S., Krauss, C., Merceron, A.: On the Emergence of Typical Behaviours in LMS. Proceedings of the 16th E-Learning Fachtagung Informatik (DeLFI 2018), Frankfurt, Germany, September 10, CEUR Workshop Proceedings 2250 (2018). https://ceur-ws.org/Vol-2250/WS_LA_paper6.pdf
13. Berking, P.: Choosing a learning record store (LRS). Tech. rep., Advanced Distributed Learning Initiative (2016). https://www.adlnet.gov/assets/uploads/ChoosingAnLRS.pdf
14. Berking, P.: Choosing a Learning Record Store (LRS). Advanced Distributed Learning (ADL) Initiative White Paper (2015). https://www.adlnet.gov/assets/uploads/ChoosingAnLRS.pdf
15. Sjöblom, A., Silvola, A., Lallimo, J.: How Deployment Processes Affect the Adoption of Learning Analytics in Higher Education Institutions: Improving Potential for Impact with Better Deployment Practices. CEUR Workshop Proceedings 2985 (2021). https://ceur-ws.org/Vol-2985/paper6.pdf

16. Ferguson, R., Clow, D., Macfadyen, L., Essa, A., Dawson, S., Alexander, S.: Setting learning analytics in context: overcoming the barriers to large-scale adoption. J. Learn. Anal. **1**(3), 120–144 (2014). https://files.eric.ed.gov/fulltext/EJ1127039.pdf
17. Klein, C., Lester, J., Rangwala, H., Johri, A.: Technological barriers and incentives to learning analytics adoption in higher education: insights from users. J. Comput. High. Educ. **31**(2019), 604–625 (2019). https://doi.org/10.1007/s12528-019-09210-5
18. ADL (2016) Experience API (xAPI) Standard (Version 1.0.3). https://www.adlnet.gov/projects/xapi/
19. IEEE (2022) Experience API (xAPI) Standard (Version 2). https://opensource.ieee.org/xapi/xapi-base-standard-documentation
20. 1EdTech: Caliper Analytics Specification (2020). https://www.imsglobal.org/spec/caliper/v1p2
21. Krauss, C., Hauswirth, M.: Interoperable education infrastructures: a middleware that brings together adaptive, social and virtual learning technologies. In: ERCIM News 120 - Special Theme: Educational Technology, pp. 9–10 (2019). ISSN 0926-4981
22. Krauss, C., Streicher, A., Poxleitner, E., Altun, D., Mueller, J., An, T. S., Mueller, C.: Best-of-breed: service-oriented integration of artificial intelligence in interoperable educational ecosystems. In International workshop on learning technology for education challenges, pp. 267–283. Springer, Cham (2023). https://doi.org/10.1007/978-3-031-34754-2_22
23. ADL: xAPI Profiles Document Structure Specification (2016). https://github.com/adlnet/xapi-profiles/blob/master/xapi-profiles-structure.md#71-verbs-activity-types-and-attachment-usage-types
24. Learning Locker: The Aggregation API (HTTP Interface) in Learning Locker - Open Source - Documentation (2020). https://learninglocker.atlassian.net/wiki/spaces/DOCS/pages/106037259/Aggregation+API
25. Ifenthaler, D., Widanapathirana, C.: Development and validation of a learning analytics framework: two case studies using support vector machines. Technol. Knowl. Learn. **19**(2014), 221–240 (2014). https://doi.org/10.1007/s10758-014-9226-4
26. FWU gGmbH (2024) Schulconnex. https://github.com/Schulconnex/Schulconnex/blob/develop/docs/schnittstellen/autorisierung-dienste.md?plain=1#L126
27. Nguyen, T.A., An, T.S., Krauss, C.: A middleware for educational ecosystems–rights and access-control management by design. In International Workshop on Learning Technology for Education Challenges, pp. 166–178. Springer, Cham (2024). https://doi.org/10.1007/978-3-031-61678-5_12
28. OpenID (2023) OpenID Connect Core 1.0 incorporating errata set 2. https://openid.net/specs/openid-connect-core-1_0.html#PairwiseAlg

InsightFlow: A Generative AI Approach to Streamlining Knowledge and Learning Paths

Jiandong Cai[1], Chi Zhang[1], and Ping Ji[1,2](✉)

[1] The Graduate Center, City University of New York, New York 10016, NY, USA
{jcai,czhang2,pji}@gc.cuny.edu

[2] Hunter College, City University of New York, New York 10065, NY, USA
ping.ji@hunter.cuny.edu

Abstract. Artificial Intelligence (AI) has made significant impacts on educational technology, yet building knowledge graphs that effectively support personalized learning remains a core challenge. In this work, we introduce **InsightFlow**, a graph-aware Knowledge Tracing (KT) approach driven by large language models (LLMs) and Generative AI (GenAI). InsightFlow generates customized learning pathways that adapt to a learner's background, characteristics, and training goals. Unlike conventional KT models that focus narrowly on sequential prediction, InsightFlow integrates educator-curated knowledge graphs with Transformer-based architectures to produce high-fidelity mastery estimates over fine-grained knowledge components (KCs). These signals enable the construction of learning paths that are both highly personalized and, at the same time, aligned with specific training goals. In this paper, we also describe InsightFlow's architecture, its graph-aware extensions, and its integration with GenAI models, establishing a scalable paradigm for goal-oriented, explainable, and user-defined personalized training.

Keywords: Knowledge Tracing · Knowledge Graphs · Generative AI · Personalized Learning · Adaptive Education

1 Introduction

The accelerating pace of technological change, particularly in artificial intelligence and automation, has widened the global skill gap between traditional education and industry demands. Studies in computing education consistently report a misalignment: graduates often leave universities without the knowledge and skills employers urgently require, while enterprises struggle to fill positions in fast-evolving fields such as software engineering and data science. Large-scale analyses of software education highlight that graduates' skills "increasingly diverge from industry expectations," especially in areas such as continuous learning, creativity, and solution-oriented thinking [3, 7]. Mapping studies further

B. Fernández-Manjón et al. (Eds.): SETE 2025/ICWL 2025, LNCS 16425, pp. 240–255, 2026.
https://doi.org/10.1007/978-981-92-0042-9_18

show that this shortage of qualified professionals stems from both the rapid evolution of market demands and persistent gaps between academia and industry [5].

Traditional curricula are poorly equipped to address these challenges. University programs remain organized around large, rigid courses and lengthy degree timelines, which cannot keep pace with the short half-life of technical skills. As Jaramillo and Chiappe note, many programs continue to exhibit "substantial drawbacks" and fail to integrate adaptive, interdisciplinary learning aligned with digital transformation [9]. This rigidity leads to inefficiencies: companies face high retraining costs, while students and job seekers encounter detours in their career trajectories due to the absence of personalized, competency-driven learning pathways.

In response, researchers and educators advocate modular and personalized approaches to education. Microlearning and stackable curricula, built around small, verifiable knowledge units, have been shown to improve retention, engagement, and motivation, while allowing continual updates of content [13]. Systematic reviews further demonstrate that AI-driven personalized learning can adapt instruction in real time, tailoring pathways to individual learners' needs and improving outcomes [12]. Recent advances in knowledge tracing and recommendation also support fine-grained personalization [4,16]. Together, this evidence suggests that moving beyond static, one-size-fits-all structures toward modular, adaptive, and explainable systems is both feasible and necessary.

To address these challenges, we propose an ***A****ttainable* ***eD****ucation for* ***A****ll* - **AeDA** platform, which is organized around modular *micro-knowledge points* rather than traditional courses. Our prototype is available online [1]. Figure 1 illustrates the design of AeDA platform, which introduces three interactive portals for students, enterprises, and teachers, enabling each stakeholder to construct customized training schemes and adaptive learning paths aligned with real-world requirements. At AeDA's core lies the **InsightFlow** algorithm, which dynamically sequences micro-knowledge points into optimized, explainable learning paths. InsightFlow captures prerequisite structures among knowledge units,

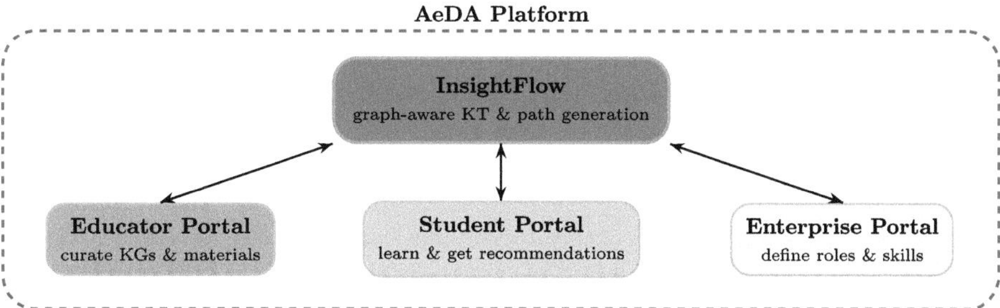

Fig. 1. AeDA platform (purple dashed boundary) with **InsightFlow** as the central engine. The **Student Portal** is emphasized at the center, with Educator and Enterprise portals on either side.

integrates learner states, and aligns outcomes with enterprise-defined competency goals [8]. We will present more details of our system design in Sect. 3.

In this paper, we present the architecture and vision of InsightFlow, outline its graph-aware extensions, and evaluate its ability to generate learning paths that are both pedagogically sound and aligned with industry needs. Guided by these objectives, we investigate the following research questions:

- **RQ1.** How well can InsightFlow capture and predict learners' evolving knowledge states in a granular manner?
- **RQ2.** How valid and efficient are the learning paths produced in terms of pedagogy and prerequisites?
- **RQ3.** What benefits do graph-aware retrieval and personalization provide for broader deployment and diverse learners?

The remainder of the paper is structured as follows. Section 2 reviews related work on knowledge tracing and curriculum graph systems. Section 3 presents the overall system design and its web-based interfaces. Section 4 introduces the InsightFlow algorithms and graph data structure with native LLM integrations. Section 5 describes the evaluation methodology, dataset, and results, including ablation studies and case analyses. Section 6 discusses limitations, implications, and opportunities for deployment, and concludes this paper with directions for future research.

2 Related Work

Knowledge Tracing (KT) is a central problem in educational data mining, aiming to infer a learner's latent mastery of knowledge components from sequential interactions. Early models such as Bayesian Knowledge Tracing (BKT) [4] used hidden Markov formulations, while Deep Knowledge Tracing (DKT) [16] employed recurrent neural networks to capture temporal dependencies, improving accuracy but limiting interpretability. Recent work leverages attention and Transformer architectures [6,15,18], and graph-based methods such as GKT [14] integrate prerequisite relations through graph neural networks. Despite these advances, most KT models focus on predicting next-response correctness rather than prescribing explainable learning trajectories [2].

Beyond KT, prerequisite and curriculum graph learning explores structural induction. Graph neural networks have been used to infer prerequisite links, and global models capture heterogeneous dependencies, for example through retrieval-augmented or graph-based reasoning approaches. Yet these approaches typically rely on static graphs without evolving learner states. A related system, K-CUBE [10], organizes curricula into course-level knowledge graphs with visualization and advising interfaces. While valuable, its scope is limited to institutional course structures. By contrast, our work focuses on *knowledge-point (KP) level* modeling, enabling finer prerequisite mappings that directly support dynamic knowledge tracing and path generation. Advances in graph-based retrieval for getting rich context based answers to questions have shown promise for educational applications. G-Retriever [8] reformulates subgraph retrieval as a Prize-Collecting Steiner Tree (PCST) optimization problem, enabling efficient extraction of relevant subgraphs from large knowledge graphs. This fits naturally in educational contexts where prerequisite relationships must be preserved while maintaining computational efficiency across large knowledge graphs. G-Retriever's optimization framework provides a foundation for scalable learning path generation, as we demonstrate in Sect. 4.3.

Learning path recommendation has also gained attention. Graph-based approaches combine cognitive diagnosis with structure for personalized sequencing [20], and reinforcement learning methods treat it as sequential decision-making [11]. However, most operate at course or skill level and lack transparent rationales, limiting adoption in practice.

Finally, explainability is increasingly recognized as essential. Reviews highlight the need for interpretable KT and transparent recommendation [19]. While some methods use attention or graphs to improve interpretability, they largely remain diagnostic. Effective path recommendation must adapt to learner states and provide traceable reasoning. This motivates approaches such as InsightFlow, which unify knowledge tracing, prerequisite reasoning, and path generation in an explainable framework.

3 System Design

As shown in Fig. 1, the AeDA system extends prior paradigms such as K-Cube through a *dynamic, cross-institutional knowledge graph.* Instead of modeling courses as atomic units, AeDA operates at the *knowledge-point (KP) level,* enabling finer representation and adaptation across institutions. This KP-centric architecture provides two key advantages:

- **Granularity.** Fine-grained KPs capture prerequisite dependencies and conceptual hierarchies beyond traditional course-level models.

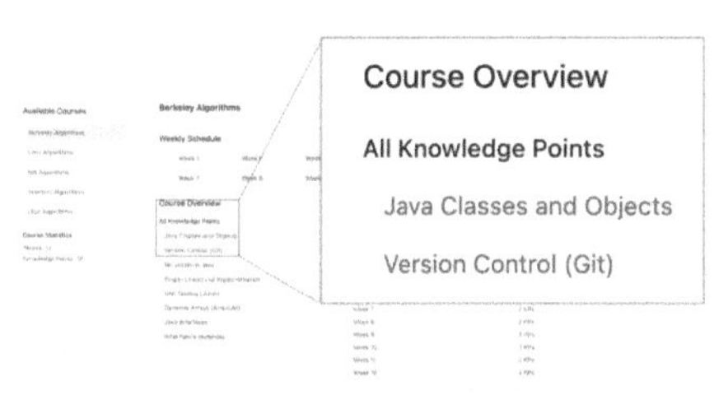

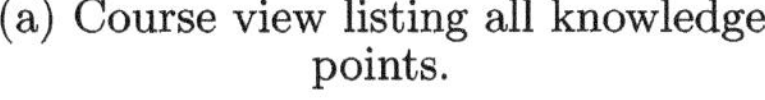
(a) Course view listing all knowledge points.

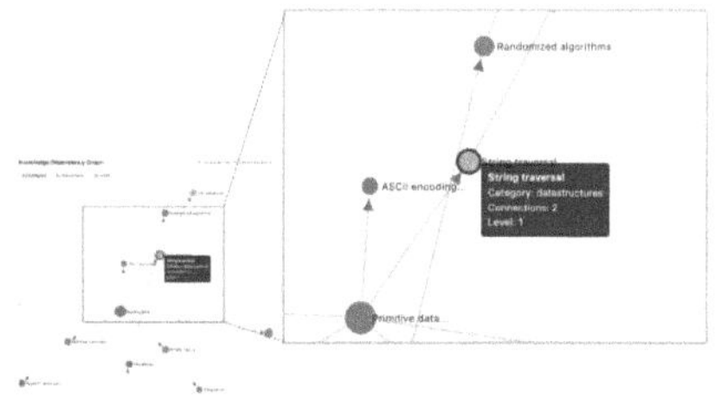

(b) Knowledge dependency graph with prerequisite links.

Fig. 2. Part of the AeDA web interface: (a) course view enumerating knowledge points; (b) interactive graph visualizing their prerequisite relations.

- **Flexibility.** Aggregating curricula from multiple universities broadens coverage and enables adaptive, cross-institution learning paths.

Together, these features allow **InsightFlow**—the core learning engine of AeDA—to support personalized, scalable education. Students receive adaptive KP-level learning paths, instructors align teaching materials with shared graphs, and institutions gain interoperable curriculum representations. Overall, this architecture bridges static visualization and dynamic knowledge tracing, laying a foundation for multi-stakeholder learning systems (Fig. 2).

4 The InsightFlow Knowledge Tracing Algorithm

In Fig. 3, we outline the design of InsightFlow - a knowledge tracing algorithm. Here, we model the curriculum as a knowledge graph:

$$\mathcal{G} = (V, E) \text{ where } V = V_0 \cup V_1, \quad E = E_{\text{prereq}} \cup E_{\text{hier}} \tag{1}$$

In the knowledge graph defined in equation (1), vertices V represent the combination of atomic knowledge components (KCs, in V_0) and courses/topics (in V_1); while edges E encode prerequisite relationships between knowledge components and hierarchical containment. Specifically, $E_{\text{prereq}} \subseteq V_0 \times V_0$, where $u \to v$ means u must be learned before v; while $E_{\text{hier}} \subseteq V_1 \times V_0$, where the topic in V_1 contains KC v. For each KC $v \in V_0$, we define its dependency structure:

- Prerequisites: $\text{prereq}(v) = \{u : (u, v) \in E_{\text{prereq}}\}$
- Descendants: $\text{desc}(v) = \{u : \exists \text{ path } v \to u \text{ in } E_{\text{prereq}}\}$
- Ancestors: $\text{anc}(v) = \{u : \exists \text{ path } u \to v \text{ in } E_{\text{prereq}}\}$
- Criticality (the fraction of curriculum depending on v): $C(v) = |\text{desc}(v)|/|V_0|$

Student state consists of mastery levels $s : V_0 \to [0, 1]$ while the learning history is denoted by $\mathcal{H} = \{(q_i, r_i, t_i)\}_{i=1}^{n}$, in which $q_i \in V_0$ is the attempted KC, $r_i \in \{0, 1\}$ is the outcome, t_i is the timestamp and $\alpha \in (0, 1)$ is the learning rate parameter. Therefore, the mastery state s follows:

$$s^{(t+1)}(v) = s^{(t)}(v) + \alpha\,(r - s^{(t)}(v)) \tag{2}$$

4.1 Learning Path Generation

To compare alternative orders of knowledge learning pathways, we introduce a pathcost model that sums the inverse *success probabilities* defined in Eq. (3), which account the weakest mastery state in prerequisites. This leads the plan to focus on building solid foundations early on in the learning pathway. For retrieval and explanation, graph-aware attention runs over a small subgraph around each step, biasing attention toward nodes that are structurally close in the prerequisite graph and relevant to the learner's learning demand. This produces the right context and provides clear rationales for why a KC is chosen. After each

InsightFlow Knowledge Tracing Algorithm

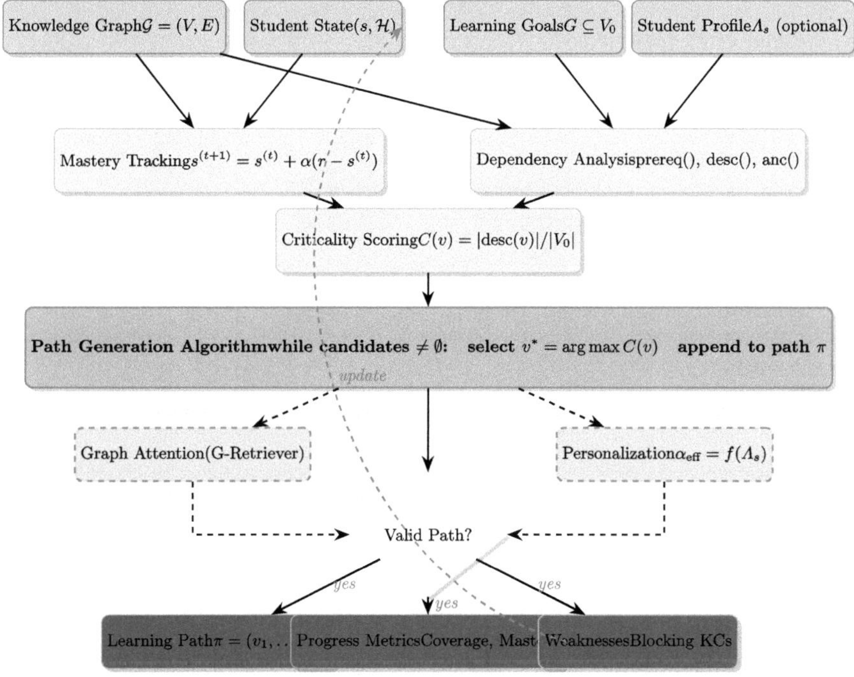

Fig. 3. InsightFlow Knowledge Tracing Algorithm. The figure illustrates how the knowledge graph, student state, and goals flow through mastery tracking, dependency analysis, and path generation, with optional graph attention and personalization.

attempt, the mastery state s is updated, the student's readiness is changed, and the plan is adapted, which closes the loop between graph constraints, prioritization, cost-aware selection, and attention-guided retrieval/explanations. We illustrate a Greedy Path Generation algorithm (GPG Algorithm), where the Success Probability P_{success} and the Path Cost π are defined in Eqs. (3) and (4) respectively.

Definition 1 (Success Probability). *For KC v given state s:*

$$P_{success}(v \mid s) = \begin{cases} p_{base} + p_{boost} \cdot avg_{u \in \text{prereq}(v)} s(u) & \text{if prereq}(v) \neq \emptyset \\ p_{base} + p_{boost} \cdot s(v) & \text{otherwise} \end{cases} \quad (3)$$

where:

- $p_{base} \in [0, 1]$*: baseline success probability without prerequisite mastery*
- $p_{boost} \in [0, 1 - p_{base}]$*: maximum increase from prerequisite mastery*

Algorithm 1. Greedy Path Generation (GPG) Algorithm

Require: Goal $G \subseteq V_0$, state s, DAG $\mathcal{G}$, threshold θ
Ensure: Learning path π

$\pi \leftarrow []$
mastered $\leftarrow \{v : s(v) \geq \theta\}$
required $\leftarrow G \cup \bigcup_{g \in G} \text{anc}(g)$
candidates $\leftarrow$ required $\setminus$ mastered
$s_{\text{current}} \leftarrow s$
while candidates $\neq \emptyset$ **do**
  ready $\leftarrow \{v \in \text{candidates} : \text{prereq}(v) \subseteq \text{mastered}\}$
  $v^* \leftarrow \arg\min_{v \in \text{ready}} \frac{1}{P_{\text{success}}(v \mid s_{\text{current}})}$
  Append v^* to π
  mastered $\leftarrow$ mastered $\cup \{v^*\}$
  candidates $\leftarrow$ candidates $\setminus \{v^*\}$
  $s_{\text{current}}(v^*) \leftarrow \theta$
end while
return π

- $p_{base} + p_{boost} \leq 1$ *ensures valid probability*

Definition 2 (Path Cost). *For path $\pi = (v_1, \ldots, v_n)$ with evolving state $s^{(i)}$:*

$$Cost(\pi) = \sum_{i=1}^{n} \frac{1}{P_{success}(v_i \mid s^{(i-1)})}, \tag{4}$$

- $\frac{1}{P_{success}(v_i \mid s^{(i-1)})}$*: is the number of expected attempts needed to master v_i.*
- $s^{(i)}$*: is the mastery state after learning nodes $v_1, \ldots, v_i$.*

State evolution: $s^{(i)} = s^{(i-1)}$ with $s^{(i)}(v_i) \leftarrow \theta$ after successfully learning v_i.

4.2 Graph-Aware Retrieval for Educational Content

Each knowledge component $v \in V_0$ contains textual attributes (course materials, explanations, exercises) stored in a content database. To enable efficient question-answering and path generation without processing the entire curriculum's content, we employ graph-aware retrieval.

Definition 3 (Graph-Aware Retrieval). *Given a user query q about the curriculum, retrieve relevant subgraph $S^* \subseteq V_0$ and associated content:*

1. ***Semantic matching:*** *Find KCs whose textual content aligns with query q*
2. ***Structure expansion:*** *Include prerequisites and descendants to maintain pedagogical completeness*
3. ***Content retrieval:*** *Fetch textual attributes only for nodes in S^* using Retrieval Augmented Generation (RAG).*

This enables conversational interaction with the knowledge graph—users can ask questions and receive responses grounded in both course content and prerequisite structure.

Definition 4 (Graph-Aware Attention for Content Integration). *To process retrieved content while respecting prerequisite relationships, attention between KCs $u, v \in S^*$ combines:*

$$\alpha_{uv} = \text{softmax}\left(\frac{\mathbf{Q}_u^\top \mathbf{K}_v}{\sqrt{d_k}} + b_{uv} \right), \quad (5)$$

- $\mathbf{Q}_u, \mathbf{K}_v$: *embeddings derived from textual content of KCs u, v*
- b_{uv}: *structural bias encoding prerequisite relationships:*
  - $(u, v) \in E_{prereq}$: $b_{uv} = \beta_1$ *(direct prerequisite)*
  - $u \in \text{anc}(v)$: $b_{uv} = \beta_2 / d(u, v)$ *(indirect prerequisite)*
  - $u \in \text{desc}(v)$: $b_{uv} = \beta_3 \cdot C(v)$ *(builds upon)*

This attention mechanism allows the model to reason about relationships between course content while respecting the curriculum's prerequisite structure.

Applications in Conversational Learning: The graph-aware retrieval enables three key capabilities: **1. Content-Grounded Q&A**: When users ask "How do neural networks relate to linear algebra?", the system retrieves relevant content from both KCs and uses attention weights to explain their relationship through actual course materials. **2. Efficient Path Generation**: Instead of loading all course content (potentially thousands of pages), GPG^2 operates on the focused subgraph S^* with pre-fetched relevant materials, reducing both computational cost and response latency. **3. Visual Highlighting**: Response generation includes node importance scores $\sum_u \alpha_{uv}$ that highlight which parts of the curriculum graph are most relevant to the user's query, creating an interactive learning experience. This approach transforms a static curriculum graph into an interactive knowledge assistant that can answer questions, explain relationships, and generate personalized paths while efficiently managing large amounts of educational content.

4.3 G-Retriever Integration for Scalable Learning Path Generation

The computational complexity of processing entire knowledge graphs becomes prohibitive as curricula grow. For a graph with $|V_0| = 1000$ KCs, processing all content for each query requires examining $O(|V_0|^2)$ potential relationships. In a recent work [8], He et al presented G-Retriever which reformulates subgraph retrieval as an optimization problem that naturally aligns with our research objectives for building knowledge learning pathways. Therefore, in this subsection, we explore the integration of G-Retriever [8] in our algorithm to enable efficient subgraph retrieval through Prize-Collecting Steiner Tree (PCST) optimization. The revised approach is described below.

Definition 5 (Educational PCST). *Given query q and knowledge graph $\mathcal{G} = (V, E)$, find subgraph $S^* = (V^*, E^*)$ that:*

$$maximize \sum_{v \in V^*} P_v(q) - \sum_{(u,v) \in E^*} C_{uv}, \tag{6}$$

- $P_v(q) = sim(q, content_v) \cdot C(v)$: *prize combining query relevance and criticality*
- $C_{uv} = \frac{1}{P_{success}(v|s)}$: *edge cost from our path cost definition*
- *Top-k relevant nodes receive descending prizes $k, k-1, \ldots, 1$*

This formulation elegantly balances three objectives: maximizing relevance to the student's query, prioritizing critical KCs with many descendants, and minimizing expected learning difficulty.

Integration with Graph-Aware Attention: G-Retriever enhances our attention mechanism by operating on optimized subgraphs rather than the full graph, as shown in Algorithm 2 below.

Algorithm 2. Greedy Path Generation with G-Retriever (GPG^2) Algorithm

---

Require: Query q, Knowledge Graph $\mathcal{G} = (V, E)$, state s, threshold θ
Ensure: Learning path π tailored to query q
Retrieval Stage: Apply G-Retriever to extract a subgraph $S^* \subseteq \mathcal{G}$ using PCST optimization:

- Score nodes by $P_v(q) = \text{sim}(q, \text{content}_v) \cdot C(v)$
- Select top-k relevant nodes and connect them with minimal-cost prerequisite bridges

Initialize $\pi \leftarrow []$, mastered $\leftarrow \{v : s(v) \geq \theta\}$, candidates $\leftarrow S^* \setminus$ mastered
$s_{\text{current}} \leftarrow s$
while candidates $\neq \emptyset$ **do**
  ready $\leftarrow \{v \in \text{candidates} : \text{prereq}(v) \subseteq \text{mastered}\}$
  Compute attention scores α_{uv} over S^* with structural and retrieval biases
  Select KC:

$$v^* \leftarrow \arg\min_{v \in \text{ready}} \frac{1}{P_{\text{success}}(v \mid s_{\text{current}})} - \lambda \sum_{u \in S^*} \alpha_{uv}$$

  Append v^* to π, update mastered and $s_{\text{current}}(v^*) \leftarrow \theta$
  candidates $\leftarrow$ candidates $\setminus \{v^*\}$
end while
return π

For example, for Machine Learning Prerequisites, consider a query "prepare for deep learning" on a graph with 500 KCs:

1. **Without G-Retriever**: Our algorithm processes all 500 nodes, examine ~2000 edges, generate paths considering all possible prerequisites

2. **With G-Retriever**: Our algorithm
   - Retrieves 18 nodes: {linear algebra, calculus, probability, optimization, neural networks, backpropagation, ...}
   - Includes critical prerequisites automatically via PCST bridge nodes
   - Generates path using only a subgraph, reducing search space by 96%

The PCST optimization ensures pedagogical completeness—if "linear algebra" is retrieved for "deep learning," its prerequisite "matrix operations" is automatically included as a bridge node, maintaining the integrity of learning dependencies.

4.4 Student Characteristics Augmentation

We augment the learning model with student-specific characteristics that affect learning dynamics. For each student s and knowledge component v, we define a learning profile $\Lambda_s(v) = [\lambda_{\text{speed}}, \lambda_{\text{motivation}}, \lambda_{\text{persistence}}]$ where:

- $\lambda_{\text{speed}} \in (0, 2]$: learning velocity multiplier ($1 =$ average pace)
- $\lambda_{\text{motivation}} \in [0, 1]$: engagement level with content v
- $\lambda_{\text{persistence}} \in [0, 1]$: resistance to forgetting (retention strength)

These characteristics modify both mastery states and path selection. The characteristic-aware mastery state s will then be captured by the following equation (7):

$$s^{(t+1)}(v) = s^{(t)}(v) + \alpha_{\text{eff}}(s, v) \cdot (r - s^{(t)}(v)), \tag{7}$$

where $\alpha_{\text{eff}}(s, v) = \alpha \cdot \lambda_{\text{speed}} \cdot g(\lambda_{\text{motivation}})$, with $s^{(t)}(v)$ being the mastery level at time t, $r \in \{0, 1\}$ the response correctness, α the base learning rate, and $g(\cdot)$ a monotonic function mapping motivation to learning efficiency.

4.5 System Input/Output Specification

In this subsection, we summarize the Inputs and Outputs of our algorithm:

The **Inputs** are: 1. Knowledge graph $\mathcal{G} = (V, E)$; 2. Student mastery s and history $\mathcal{H}$; 3. Learning goals $G \subseteq V_0$; 4. Optional: learning characteristics Λ_s.

The **Outputs** are: 1. Learning path $\pi = (v_1, \ldots, v_n)$; 2. Progress metrics (coverage, mastery, velocity); 3. Critical weaknesses W (blocking KCs); and 4. Time estimate for completion.

This multi-objective design enables InsightFlow to track knowledge, predict outcomes, and generate effective learning paths.

5 Evaluation Framework and Methodology

We assess InsightFlow through a framework designed to answer our three research questions about knowledge state tracking, path validity, and scalability benefits. Our evaluation mirrors the complexity of real-world educational environments while maintaining experimental control.

5.1 Evaluation Framework

We evaluate InsightFlow through three complementary experiments, each designed to answer a specific research question.

Knowledge Tracing (RQ1): Can InsightFlow track what students know over time? We test this by splitting each student's learning history into two parts: 70% for training the model and 30% for testing predictions. We keep these parts in chronological order the model learns from early attempts and predicts later ones. To ensure reliable results, we only include students with at least 30 total learning attempts and at least 5 attempts in the test period. We measure success using standard metrics (AUC-ROC and Accuracy) and check how many students meet our criteria to confirm the system works for different types of learners.

Path Generation (RQ2): Does InsightFlow create valid and efficient learning paths? We test this with 100 students, asking the system to create paths to 3 different learning goals for each student 300 paths total. For each path, we check four things: How long is it? Does it violate any prerequisites? Can students realistically complete it? Does it cover all necessary topics? This tells us whether InsightFlow creates paths that are both educationally sound and practical for real students.

Component Analysis (RQ3): Which parts of InsightFlow matter most? We test four versions of the system:

1. **Full Model**: The complete system with all features
2. **Without Graph**: Removes prerequisite relationships (treats all topics as independent)
3. **Without Personalization**: Treats all students the same (ignores individual differences)
4. **Without Importance Ranking**: Selects topics randomly (no strategic prioritization)

By comparing these versions, we can see exactly how much each feature contributes to the system's success and understand which components are essential for real-world use. This systematic decomposition quantifies how each component contributes to overall effectiveness and scalability.

5.2 Knowledge Tracing Evaluation

We evaluate InsightFlow's knowledge tracing capabilities on the KDD Cup 2010 Educational Data Mining Challenge dataset [17], a widely-used benchmark in intelligent tutoring systems research. The dataset contains 574 students, 28 algebra skills (knowledge components), and 295,293 step-level attempts from Carnegie Learning's Cognitive Tutor system collected during the 2005–2006 school year.

Experimental Setup: We simulate "what if InsightFlow had been observing these students?" by splitting each student's interaction history chronologically (70% training, 30% testing). We evaluate 377 students with sufficient interaction history ($\geq$30 attempts), generating 88,636 predictions. During training,

InsightFlow updates mastery estimates via exponential moving average; during testing, it predicts success probability using a weighted combination of readiness (prerequisite mastery), current mastery, student ability, KC difficulty, and temporal features (first-attempt penalties, hint usage, spacing effects).

InsightFlow Components: The model uses three core components: (1) `StudentCharacteristics` (ability, learning speed, motivation, persistence inferred from behavioral patterns), (2) `EnhancedStudentState` (tracking per-KC mastery levels $m_k \in [0, 1]$), and (3) `ModelConfig` (hyperparameters controlling prediction weights). Success probability combines these via logistic regression:

$$P(\text{success}) = \sigma(\beta_r \cdot \text{readiness} + \beta_m \cdot \text{mastery} + \beta_a \cdot \text{ability} - \beta_d \cdot \text{difficulty} - \beta_{\text{temporal}}) \tag{8}$$

Table 1 shows InsightFlow achieves 0.810 AUC with 83.7% accuracy, significantly outperforming a simplified baseline (0.715 AUC). The extremely low standard error ($\pm$0.001) and large effect size (Cohen's $d = 67.20$) indicate robust predictions across diverse students. Most importantly, ablation studies reveal that **temporal features account for 79% of performance gains**: removing first-attempt penalties, hint penalties, and spacing effects drops AUC to 0.747 (-6.3%), confirming these features capture real learning dynamics.

Table 1. Knowledge Tracing Performance on KDD Cup 2010 Dataset

Metric	Baseline	InsightFlow
Dataset Statistics		
Students Evaluated	377	377
Knowledge Components	28	28
Test Predictions	88,636	88,636
Prediction Accuracy		
AUC-ROC	0.715	**0.810** $\pm$ 0.001
Accuracy (%)	80.7	**83.7**
Statistical Validation		
Cohen's d	15.16	**67.20**
Brier Score	0.147	**0.123**
Ablation: Temporal Features		
Without Temporal Features	–	0.747 (–6.3%)
Contribution to Gain	–	**79%**

Key Insights: InsightFlow demonstrates differential effectiveness across difficulty levels, with 88% error reduction on very hard KCs versus baseline. This pattern indicates the model is *most valuable where students struggle most.*

Limitations: This evaluation tests knowledge tracing (prediction accuracy) only, not learning path generation or adaptive sequencing. Students followed the Cognitive Tutor's curriculum; we did not generate custom paths or measure impact on learning outcomes. Results are limited to algebra and require validation across other domains.

Reproducibility: All evaluation code, data adapters, and configurations are available at https://github.com/FayeZC/insightflow_icwl.

5.3 Learning Path Generation with KT Integration

We evaluate InsightFlow's path generation capabilities on the MOOCCube dataset [21], a large-scale real-world MOOC platform containing 706 courses, 700 knowledge components (KCs), 216 prerequisite relationships, and 4,723 authentic student enrollment records. The evaluation addresses two key questions: (1) Can automated approaches generate pedagogically valid learning paths? (2) Does KT integration provide added value through personalized success predictions beyond standard prerequisite planning? We evaluate 2000 students (42% of the dataset) by splitting their learning sequences (15% mastered foundations, 77% actual exploration, 8% goals), focusing on multi-goal scenarios with 5–8 learning objectives.

Comparative Approaches: We compare two path generation strategies:

1. *Baseline (Greedy)*: Topological sort selecting first available KC with satisfied prerequisites, representing standard prerequisite-aware planning without personalization
2. *KT-Aware*: Full InsightFlow combining structural criticality with KT predictions ($\text{score}_{\text{KT}}(k) = 0.5 \cdot \text{criticality} + 0.5 \cdot P(\text{success}|k) \times 10$), enabling personalized success estimation

Both approaches respect prerequisite constraints and handle circular dependencies via strongly connected components. We measure path length, prerequisite violations, goal coverage, and predicted success probability, comparing automated recommendations against actual unguided student exploration.

Table 2. Learning Path Generation Evaluation on MOOCCube (2000 Students, 8 Goals Avg.)

Metric	Baseline	KT-Aware
Path Quality		
Avg. Path Length (KCs)	11.0	**9.6**
Prerequisite Violations per Path	0.17	**0.15**
Goal Coverage (%)	99.2	99.2
Personalization (KT-Aware Advantage)		
Predicted Success Probability	–	**0.408**
Path Diversity vs Baseline (%)	–	**58.4**

Key Findings: Table 2 demonstrates that both approaches successfully generate pedagogically valid learning paths to reach 8 learning objectives, with near-perfect prerequisite adherence (<0.2 violations per path) and high goal coverage (99.2%). Baseline produces conservative paths averaging 11.0 KCs, while InsightFlow's KT-aware approach generates more efficient paths averaging 9.6 KCs (12.7% reduction) with even fewer violations (0.15 vs 0.17). Both approaches dramatically outperform self-directed exploration, which exhibited 183.0 KCs, 39.6 violations, and 0% goal achievement in our sample of 2000 students.

InsightFlow Improvements Over Baseline: *InsightFlow demonstrates measurable improvements across multiple dimensions.* First, InsightFlow generates *more efficient paths*, reducing average length from 11.0 to 9.6 KCs (12.7% reduction) by intelligently leveraging knowledge tracing to identify optimal learning sequences. Second, InsightFlow achieves *superior pedagogical correctness* with 11.8% fewer prerequisite violations (0.15 vs 0.17 per path) through KT-informed sequencing that respects student readiness while avoiding unnecessary redundancy. Third, InsightFlow provides *personalized success prediction* (40.8%) for each recommended path, enabling proactive intervention, resource allocation, and adaptive difficulty adjustments—a capability entirely absent in standard structural planning. Finally, path diversity analysis reveals InsightFlow selects different orderings than Baseline in 58.4% of cases, demonstrating that KT-based optimization yields substantively different student-centered recommendations beyond structural planning. These results from 2000 students (42% of the dataset) provide robust evidence of InsightFlow's value in large-scale learning path generation.

Limitations: Results use inferred student characteristics (ability estimated from historical success rates) rather than ground-truth calibrations. MOOCCube's sparse prerequisite graph (0.031% edge density) limits opportunities for path optimization differentiation; validation on denser structures (mathematics curricula, computer science fundamentals) would better demonstrate KT-aware selection advantages. Success predictions require longitudinal validation against actual student outcomes to confirm calibration accuracy.

This evaluation establishes that InsightFlow successfully generates educationally sound, personalized learning paths that respect curriculum structures while adapting to diverse student needs, providing a foundation for real-world deployment and iterative improvement.

6 Conclusion and Future Work

In this work, we presented **InsightFlow** - a graph-aware system that unifies prerequisite reasoning, personalization, and path generation. Our contributions lie in *(1) modeling fine-grained knowledge points with explicit prerequisite structures, (2) implementing a web platform that connects students, teachers, and institutions through a shared KP backbone, and (3) validating feasibility through simulation, showing pedagogically valid and personalized paths while identifying persistence as a challenge.*

We will enhance interpretability with advanced language models in the future, apply reinforcement learning to refine retrieval and sequencing from student feedback, and support dynamic graph updates for evolving curricula. A planned pilot deployment in 2025 will test InsightFlow against traditional advising, enabling collection of real student data for iterative refinement. In sum, InsightFlow demonstrates how transparent prerequisite reasoning and graph-aware personalization can support scalable, explainable learning paths, offering both academic and practical value in adaptive education.

References

1. AEDA: Attainable eDucation for All (2025). https://aedaversity.com/ Accessed 10 September 2025
2. Abdelrahman, G., Wang, Q., Pereira Nunes, B.: Knowledge tracing: a survey. ACM Comput. Surv. **55** (2022). https://doi.org/10.1145/3569576
3. Akdur, D.: Analysis of software engineering skills gap in the industry. ACM Trans. Comput. Educ. **23**(1) (2023). https://doi.org/10.1145/3567837
4. Corbett, A.T., Anderson, J.R.: Knowledge tracing: a model of student learning. User Model. User-Adap. Inter. **4**(4), 253–278 (1994)
5. Diniz, W., Valença, M., França, C., Santos, A., Pincovsky, M.: The skill gap in software industry: a mapping study (2024). https://doi.org/10.5753/sbes.2024.3351
6. Ghosh, A., Heffernan, N., Lan, A.S.: Context-aware attentive knowledge tracing (2020). https://arxiv.org/abs/2007.12324
7. Groeneveld, W., Vennekens, J., Aerts, K.: Identifying non-technical skill gaps in software engineering education: what experts expect but students don't learn. ACM Trans. Comput. Educ. **22**(1) (2021). https://doi.org/10.1145/3464431
8. He, X., et al.: G-retriever: retrieval-augmented generation for textual graph understanding and question answering (2024). https://arxiv.org/abs/2402.07630
9. Jaramillo, J., Chiappe, A.: The ai-driven classroom: a review of 21st century curriculum trends. PROSPECTS **54** (2024). https://doi.org/10.1007/s11125-024-09704-w
10. Li, Q., et al.: Kcube: a knowledge graph university curriculum framework for student advising and career planning. In: ICBL, pp. 358–369 (2022). https://doi.org/10.1007/978-3-031-08939-8_31
11. Ma, D., et al.: Learning path recommendation with multi-behavior user modeling and cascading deep q networks. Knowl.-Based Syst. **294**, 111743 (2024)
12. Merino-Campos, C.: The impact of artificial intelligence on personalized learning in higher education: a systematic review. Trends Higher Educ. **4**, 17 (2025). https://doi.org/10.3390/higheredu4020017
13. Monib, W.K., Qazi, A., Apong, R.A.: Microlearning beyond boundaries: a systematic review and a novel framework for improving learning outcomes. Heliyon **11**(2), e41413 (2025)
14. Nakagawa, H., Iwasawa, Y., Matsuo, Y.: Graph-based knowledge tracing: modeling student proficiency using graph neural network. In: IEEE/WIC/ACM International Conference on Web Intelligence, WI 2019, pp. 156–163. Association for Computing Machinery, New York, USA (2019). https://doi.org/10.1145/3350546.3352513
15. Pandey, S., Karypis, G.: A self-attentive model for knowledge tracing (2019). https://arxiv.org/abs/1907.06837

16. Piech, C., et al.: Deep knowledge tracing (2015). https://arxiv.org/abs/1506.05908
17. Stamper, J., Niculescu-Mizil, A., Ritter, S., Gordon, G., Koedinger, K.: Algebra i 2005-2006. https://pslcdatashop.web.cmu.edu/KDDCup/downloads.jsp (2010), challenge data set from KDD Cup 2010 Educational Data Mining Challenge. 575 students, 813,661 steps
18. Vaswani, A., et al.: Attention is all you need. In: Advances in Neural Information Processing Systems (NeurIPS), vol. 30, pp. 6000–6010 (2017)
19. Yeung, C.K., Yeung, D.Y.: Addressing two problems in deep knowledge tracing via prediction-consistent regularization (2018). https://arxiv.org/abs/1806.02180
20. Ying, S., Fu, Y.: Knowledge graph construction and personalised learning path generation mechanism for online english teaching and learning. Appli. Math. Nonlinear Sci. **9** (2024). https://doi.org/10.2478/amns-2024-3609
21. Yu, J., et al.: MOOCCube: a large-scale data repository for NLP applications in MOOCs. In: Jurafsky, D., Chai, J., Schluter, N., Tetreault, J. (eds.) Proceedings of the 58th Annual Meeting of the Association for Computational Linguistics, pp. 3135–3142. Association for Computational Linguistics, Online (2020). https://doi.org/10.18653/v1/2020.acl-main.285, https://aclanthology.org/2020.acl-main.285/

Explaining Student Performance Prediction and Generating Personalized Actionable Feedback Using Explainable Artificial Intelligence (XAI) with SHAP

Wan-Chong Choi[1,2(✉)], Iek-Chong Choi[1], Chan-Tong Lam[1], and António José Mendes[3]

[1] Faculty of Applied Sciences, Macao Polytechnic University, Macao SAR, China
wanchong.choi@mpu.edu.mo
[2] CISUC, University of Coimbra, Coimbra, Portugal
[3] Department of Informatics Engineering, CISUC, University of Coimbra, Coimbra, Portugal

Abstract. Effective student performance prediction enables timely support in Educational Data Mining (EDM). However, most predictive models lack interpretability and do not provide actionable feedback for learners. To address prediction accuracy and explanation, this study integrates an optimized XGBoost classifier with SHapley Additive exPlanations (SHAP). Using the Open University Learning Analytics Dataset (OULAD), our model employs SMOTE-based class balancing and randomized hyperparameter tuning, achieving better performance than existing research. Moreover, the model supports early predictions using demographic, assessment, and behavioral data, making it suitable for timely interventions. To address the challenge that predictive models typically function as black boxes without providing concrete guidance for instructors and students, SHAP explanations generate individualized reports that highlight the most influential features for each student's predicted outcome. These explanations are mapped to targeted, prioritized feedback aligned with students' learning needs. Case studies demonstrate how the system offers concrete and interpretable guidance for both at-risk and high-performing students. This study addresses a key EDM gap by moving beyond prediction to support personalized intervention. By linking SHAP-based explanations to personalized feedback, our method provides a scalable and interpretable framework for targeted support in education.

Keywords: Student performance prediction · Explainable Artificial Intelligence · XAI · SHapley Additive exPlanations · SHAP · Educational Data Mining · Personalized feedback · XGBoost · Early intervention · Learning analytics

B. Fernández-Manjón et al. (Eds.): SETE 2025/ICWL 2025, LNCS 16425, pp. 256–272, 2026.
https://doi.org/10.1007/978-981-92-0042-9_19

1 Introduction

Predicting student performance is a key application of Educational Data Mining (EDM), enabling the early detection of learning difficulties and the implementation of timely interventions [1, 2]. However, these models typically behave as black boxes, making it challenging to understand why a prediction was made [3].

Prior EDM research has focused on improving predictive accuracy with limited attention to model interpretability or actionable feedback [4]. Explainable Artificial Intelligence (XAI) offers solutions by interpreting model decisions and revealing key factors behind predictions [3, 5]. In education, student performance can be influenced by a wide range of factors [6]. XAI methods can highlight which behaviors or attributes contribute to success or failure, making predictions more transparent and informative to instructors or students [4].

Among XAI techniques, SHapley Additive exPlanations (SHAP) [7], grounded in Game Theory [8], has emerged as a viable approach for explaining individual predictions. SHAP attributes portions of model predictions to each feature and generates visualizations showing how predictions are formed. These insights can generate personalized recommendations, such as advising students to focus on specific activities or content areas the model identifies as influential factors.

Our study utilized the Open University Learning Analytics Dataset (OULAD) [9], providing demographic, behavioral, and assessment data from online learners, and integrated Extreme Gradient Boosting (XGBoost) [10] with SHAP-based analysis to answer the following research questions:

(1) How does the XGBoost algorithm perform in predicting student performance?
(2) How early can student performance be reliably predicted by XGBoost?
(3) How does SHAP generate individual prediction explanations?
(4) How does SHAP help generate personalized learning feedback?

The remainder of the paper is organized as follows: Sect. 2 presents the literature review, Sect. 3 describes the methodology, Sect. 4 reports the results, and Sect. 5 concludes and discusses the findings.

2 Literature Review

2.1 Student Performance Prediction in EDM

EDM techniques have been applied to predict student success or risk of failure using data from Learning Management Systems (LMS), including student interaction logs, assessment results, and demographic profiles [2]. Some studies have shown the value of mining online course data (e.g., Moodle logs) to predict course outcomes [2, 11].

The OULAD [9] is a widely used public dataset, containing anonymous records of student demographics, Virtual Learning Environment (VLE) interactions (clicks), and assessment scores for different online courses. Various studies demonstrated diverse approaches using the OULAD dataset, primarily focusing on achieving high predictive accuracy.

Several studies in the literature have utilized the OULAD dataset for predicting student performance. Heuer and Breiter [12] trained a support vector machine (SVM) [13] using demographic and behavioral predictors and reported an accuracy of 88.0% in predicting success. Rizvi et al. [14] applied a decision tree that focused on demographic attributes, such as region and socioeconomic status, and achieved an accuracy of 83.1%. Waheed et al. [15] employed an artificial neural network (ANN) that targeted behavioral features and, using an adversarial training scheme, achieved an accuracy of 89.0%. Adnan et al. [16] developed a random forest model that combined demographic, assessment, and behavioral inputs, achieving an accuracy of 91.0%. Esteban et al. [17] employed a multilayer perceptron (MLP), which was trained on demographic, assessment, and behavioral features, and reported 93.9% accuracy.

Although these models perform well, further improving predictive accuracy remains challenging. More importantly, many of them lack transparency. As noted by Romero and Ventura [18], moving beyond black-box predictions to provide actionable insights for educators is essential. Enhancing interpretability remains an important direction for future research.

2.2 XAI for Interpretability in Education

In the literature, researchers typically use interpretability and explainability interchangeably, referring to the degree to which humans can understand why AI models made specific predictions [19, 20]. XAI techniques interpret student performance prediction models, enabling educators to understand factors contributing to student success or failure [3, 5]. By improving model transparency, XAI methods support more informed educational decision-making [19, 21].

Adadi and Berrada [21] conducted a significant literature review in 2018, covering 381 papers from 2004–2018, classifying XAI methods based on applicability across machine learning algorithms, interpretability level (local or global), and timing (intrinsic or post-hoc). Intrinsic interpretability refers to implicitly explainable models due to the relatively simple structure, such as linear regression, while post-hoc interpretability involves applying additional techniques to explain complex, black-box model decisions.

Choi et al. [4] conducted another systematic review in 2024 to analyze XAI applications in predicting student performance in Computer Science and STEM education. This review found that SHAP was the most frequently used XAI post-hoc method for predicting student performance, appearing in 11 of 13 studies. However, most studies applied SHAP globally to identify important features across student populations, while relatively few studies [22, 23] used SHAP for individual-level explanations.

This limitation reduces educators' opportunities to understand why specific students might be at risk or performing well, thereby reducing the usefulness of XAI for personalized feedback. Without individual-level interpretability, providing personalized learning recommendations that address students' specific learning challenges is difficult.

2.3 Actionable Feedback and XAI

Early automated feedback systems were primarily based on expert-defined, rule-based mechanisms that mapped learner states or actions to predefined feedback schemas [24,

25]. While effective in structured environments, these systems are challenging to scale and maintain. The manual effort required to design, validate, and update rules limits their adaptability when course content or platform structure changes [26, 27].

A potential alternative is the integration of XAI into learning analytics. XAI techniques such as SHAP [7] or Local Interpretable Model-agnostic Explanations (LIME) [28] can support feedback that is both interpretable and actionable. Unlike traditional approaches, XAI leverages machine learning algorithms to first predict academic outcomes (e.g., pass or fail), then provides targeted recommendations that help identify contributing factors and suggest relevant interventions [4].

However, a recent systematic review highlights that the application of XAI to generate individualized feedback remains limited. Choi et al. [4] reported that only one study has used XAI to produce personalized recommendations in the reviewed literature. Specifically, Afzaal et al. [29] employed the Diverse Counterfactual Explanations (DiCE) library [30] to develop a feedback dashboard that integrates explainable machine learning outputs with actionable student guidance. In a university programming course, they trained predictors using LMS data, including initial assessments, quiz and assignment attributes, resource access patterns, and practical exercise attempts. Their system demonstrated how XAI can bridge predictive modeling and pedagogical support by linking explanations to specific guidance for students.

Nonetheless, further research is needed to explore how such actionable feedback can be designed to support learner decision-making and instructional adaptation. This could increase the practical value of prediction models in educational settings.

3 Methodology

3.1 Dataset

Our study utilized the OULAD dataset [9], which contains anonymized student records from online STEM courses. These records include student demographics, assessment results, and interaction logs with the VLE. We randomly selected the course CCC in OULAD as the focus of our analysis.

3.2 Tools and Environment

All analyses were conducted in Python. XGBoost model [10] development employed the scikit-learn library [31], while Pandas and NumPy were used for data preprocessing. Model interpretability was achieved using SHAP and Matplotlib, which produced web-based individual prediction reports with personalized feedback.

3.3 Optimized XGBoost Model

3.3.1 XGBoost Implementation

We employed XGBoost, a gradient boosting algorithm that iteratively constructs decision trees to correct residual errors. The choice of XGBoost was motivated by its effectiveness in capturing complex nonlinear interactions and its demonstrated performance in our prior study [3]. The problem was framed as binary classification (Pass/Fail) with an 80–20 stratified train-test split to maintain class distributions.

3.3.2 Addressing Class Imbalance with SMOTE

The dataset exhibited significant imbalance (2,756 failures vs. 1,678 passes). To prevent majority-class bias, we applied the Synthetic Minority Over-sampling Technique (SMOTE) [32] to the training set, generating synthetic minority-class samples to improve model sensitivity to underrepresented outcomes.

3.3.3 Hyperparameter Optimization

Following data balancing, we employed a randomized search [32] to enhance computational efficiency and facilitate exploration of the broader parameter space. The optimized configuration included 200 boosting rounds, a learning rate 0.05, a maximum depth of 10, a full subsample ratio, and 0.7 column sampling per tree. This combination of SMOTE and systematic hyperparameter tuning yielded improved predictive performance and better class sensitivity.

3.4 Research Design

3.4.1 Step 1. Preprocessing and Normalization

We preprocessed the OULAD dataset by removing incomplete records, resulting in 4,434 student records. Min-max normalization was applied to scale all features to a uniform range between 0 and 1.

3.4.2 Step 2. Feature Selection

Feature selection is an important step in EDM [1]. From an initial set of 22 features, we applied Chi-square testing [31, 33] to identify the most predictive variables. Features with low Chi-square scores (gender, age, total credits, disability status, attempt counts) were excluded due to minimal predictive contribution. As shown in Table 1, the final 17 features comprised: (1) Demographic data: highest education level before enrollment; (2–9) Assessment data: scores from eight assessments; (10–17) Behavioral data: click counts across eight assessments. The binary target variable classified students as Pass (1) or Fail (0).

Table 1. Overview of 17 selected features and the target variable

ID	Type	Description	Value	Description
1	Demographic Data	Educational level at course start	[0, 0.25, 0.5, 0.75, 1]	0: None 0.25: Below A-level 0.5: A-level 0.75: Higher Education 1: Postgraduate

(continued)

Table 1. (*continued*)

ID	Type	Description	Value	Description
2–9	Assessment Data	Scores across eight assessments	[0–1]	Normalized from original scores of 0–100 to [0–1]
10–17	Behavioral Data	Clicks across eight assessments	[0–1]	Normalized from original count 0 to N to [0–1]
18	Target Variable	The final grade in the course	[0, 1]	0: Fail 1: Pass

3.4.3 Step 3. Performance Prediction Using XGBoost

To address RQ1 and RQ2, we trained an optimized XGBoost classifier to predict student outcomes. We evaluated model performance at eight checkpoints aligned with the eight major assessments in the course CCC. At each checkpoint k, the model used only features available up to assessment k, enabling the progressive evaluation of prediction capability.

Model evaluation employed accuracy, precision, recall, and F1-score metrics [34]. We use the following confusion matrix: true positives (*TP*), false positives (*FP*), true negatives (*TN*), and false negatives (*FN*). Accuracy (Eq. 1) measures the overall fraction of correct predictions. Precision (Eq. 2) is the fraction of predicted positives that are correct, and recall (Eq. 3) is the fraction of actual positives that are correctly identified. The F1-score (Eq. 4) is the harmonic mean of precision and recall.

$$\text{Accuracy} = \frac{TP + TN}{TP + FP + TN + FN} \tag{1}$$

$$\text{Precision} = \frac{TP}{TP + FP} \tag{2}$$

$$\text{Recall} = \frac{TP}{TP + FN} \tag{3}$$

$$\text{F1-score} = \frac{2 \times (\text{ Precision } \times \text{ Recall })}{\text{Precision } + \text{ Recall}} \tag{4}$$

3.4.4 Step 4. Using SHAP for Generating Individual Prediction Reports

To address RQ3, we applied SHAP [7] grounded in Game Theory [8] to generate individual prediction reports for interpreting predictions from the XGBoost classifier. To generate these reports, SHAP values for the predicted class were computed to quantify the contribution of each feature to the deviation from the model's expected output.

Consistent with the SHAP definition [7], the attribution for feature i at instance x follows Eq. 5:

$$\phi_i(f, x) = \sum_{y' \subseteq x'} \frac{|y'|!(K - |y'| - 1)!}{K!}[f_x(y') - f_x(y' \backslash i)] \tag{5}$$

where y' is a binary mask over the K simplified inputs, and the sum ranges only over masks whose ones are a subset of those in x'. For any mask $y', f_x(y')$ denotes the model evaluation for x when the inputs indicated by ones in y' are treated as observed and all other inputs are treated as missing. The inner difference $f_x(y') - f_x(y' \setminus i)$ is the marginal change in the model output when feature i is added. The factorial weight $\frac{|y'|!(K-|y'|-1)!}{K!}$ carries out the Shapley averaging over all possible orders in which features can be added. Summing these weighted marginal changes yields $\phi_i(f, x)$ for each feature.

SHAP values in the reports indicate how each feature influences the prediction results: positive SHAP values push toward the predicted outcome, while negative values push against it. For students predicted to fail, features with positive SHAP values reinforce the failure prediction, while features with negative values work against it. For students predicted to pass, the interpretation reverses—positive SHAP values strengthen the passing prediction, while negative values undermine it.

These SHAP values were assembled into explanation objects, which contain base values, feature contributions, and student feature values. A bar plot enables the visualization of signed contributions, with red indicating features associated with failure and blue indicating features associated with passing. The explanation was compiled into a web-based report containing the predicted outcome, predicted probability, SHAP visualization, and personalized textual feedback.

3.4.5 Step 5. SHAP-Based Generation of Personalized Actionable Feedback

To answer RQ4, we designed a SHAP-guided method to produce personalized feedback for each student. Our method first predicts outcomes, then it uses SHAP values to identify the most influential features for that specific prediction. For students predicted to Fail, we focused on features with the most significant positive SHAP values as primary contributors to the negative prediction. For students predicted to pass, we examined the most negative SHAP values to identify areas for improvement.

Actionable feedback was generated through a mapping process where each influential feature was associated with a corresponding suggestion. For example, low assessment scores with high SHAP impact generated suggestions to revisit relevant concepts, while low interaction metrics indicated a need for stronger engagement.

The final list of suggestions was ordered according to the magnitude of the SHAP value, ensuring that the highest-impact issues were presented first in the report. This actionable feedback was positioned at the bottom of individual prediction reports.

4 Results

4.1 RQ1: Performance Results

We evaluated the performance of our optimized XGBoost model in predicting final student outcomes (Pass or Fail) across the entire dataset. The model achieved an overall accuracy of 95.22%, precision of 92.91%, recall of 97.92%, and F1-score of 95.34%, demonstrating strong classification ability.

To contextualize these results, we compared our model's performance with previous OULAD studies, as shown in Table 2. Prior research using various algorithms and different feature combinations achieved accuracies ranging from 83.1% to 93.9%. Our study, which combines demographic data, assessment scores, and behavioral features, achieved 95.22% accuracy, outperforming existing models.

This performance improvement can be attributed to comprehensive feature selection, SMOTE [32] addressing class imbalance, and randomized hyperparameter tuning [35] for the optimized XGBoost model.

These findings answer RQ1, demonstrating that our optimized XGBoost model can predict student outcomes with high accuracy and classification quality, exceeding performance reported in existing literature on the same OULAD dataset.

Table 2. Accuracy benchmarks from prior work on OULAD studies

Paper	Algorithm	Features	Accuracy
Our study	XGBoost	Demographic, Assessment, Behavioral	95.22%
[14]	Decision Tree	Demographic	83.1%
[12]	SVM	Demographic, Behavioral	88.0%
[17]	MLP	Demographic, Assessment, Behavioral	93.9%
[15]	ANN	Behavioral	89.0%
[16]	Random Forest	Demographic, Assessment, Behavioral	91.0%

4.2 RQ2: Early Prediction Across Course Checkpoints

To address RQ2, we evaluated the optimized XGBoost model's ability to predict outcomes in the course. As the course CCC includes eight assessments, we treated each assessment as a prediction checkpoint. Specifically, at checkpoint k, the model uses the first k assessment scores, associated click counts, and the student's highest education level to predict outcomes, enabling examination of how early reliable predictions can be made for timely instructor interventions.

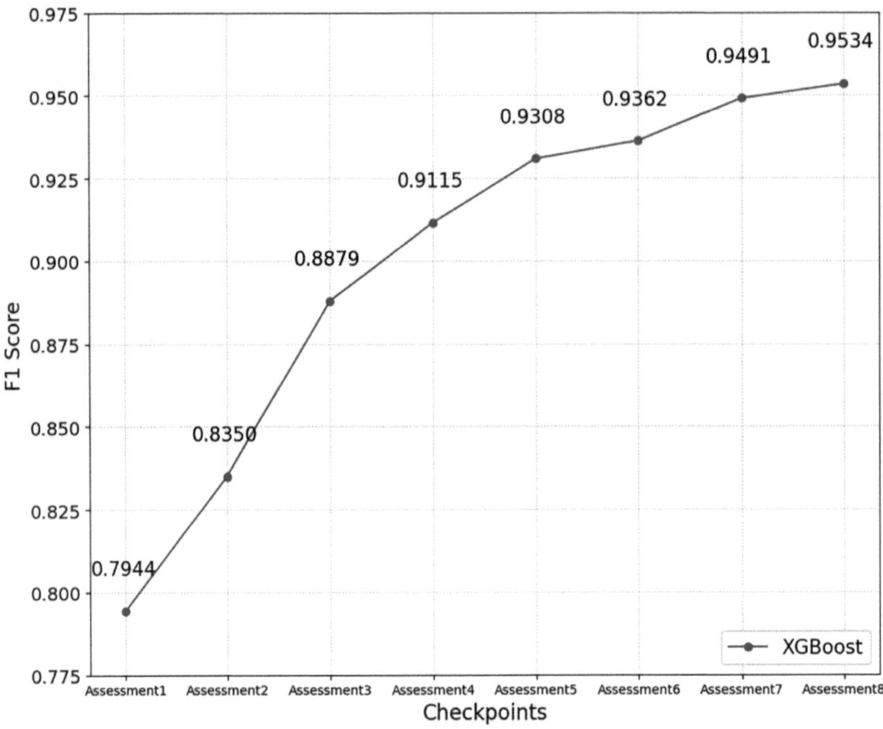

Fig. 1. Prediction results of XGBoost at different checkpoints

Figure 1 shows the progression of predictive performance across all eight checkpoints. The model accuracy improved as more assessments were included. After the first assessment, the model achieved an F1-score of 0.7944, suggesting that early signals based on initial performance and engagement already provide meaningful information about at-risk students.

Performance continued improving: F1-score reached 0.8350 after the second assessment, 0.8879 after the third, and exceeded 0.9115 after the fourth. From the fifth checkpoint onward, performance remained consistently high, ranging from 0.9308 to 0.9491. At the eighth assessment, the model achieved an F1-score of 0.9534.

These results indicated that the early checkpoint captures most predictive power, with later assessments providing only incremental improvement, enabling effective early intervention strategies.

4.3 RQ3: Individual Prediction Reports

Since the course includes eight assessments aligned with eight checkpoints, we generated individual prediction reports at each checkpoint using available data. These reports enable instructors and students to track predictions over time and identify early signs of risk, facilitating earlier and more targeted interventions.

We examined RQ3 by presenting SHAP-based explanation reports for two example students: Student A (predicted to fail) and Student B (predicted to pass). This illustrated how SHAP explains individual predictions and how explanations differ between failing and passing students.

4.3.1 Student A: SHAP Explanation for Fail Prediction

As shown in Fig. 2, Student A was predicted to fail with high probability (99.16%). The SHAP force plot indicates that strong SHAP values from the assessment scores primarily drove this prediction. In the report, red bars indicate features that increase failure probability (areas needing improvement), while blue bars show features that reduce failure risk (strengths to maintain).

The most influential negative factor was Assessment8_score (0.13, SHAP + 0.62), identified as the primary driver of failure prediction, suggesting inadequate mastery of late-course content crucial for overall success. Assessment3_score (0, SHAP + 0.52) contributed significantly with a complete lack of performance, indicating fundamental gaps in mid-course understanding. Assessment2_score (0.48, SHAP + 0.49) also had a substantial impact, showing that even moderate performance was insufficient when combined with other weak indicators. Additional assessments' scores continued this pattern: Assessment4_score (0.15, SHAP + 0.39), Assessment5_score (0.51, SHAP + 0.25), Assessment1_score (0.2, SHAP + 0.20), and Assessment6_score (0, SHAP + 0.17) all demonstrated consistent underperformance across the course timeline.

However, some course engagement data provided modest positive contributions: Assessment8_click (0.027, SHAP -0.37), Assessment7_click (0.004, SHAP -0.24), Assessment5_click (0.133, SHAP -0.09), and Assessment6_click (0.017, SHAP -0.04), indicating some degree of interaction with course materials that slightly reduced failure probability despite overall poor academic performance.

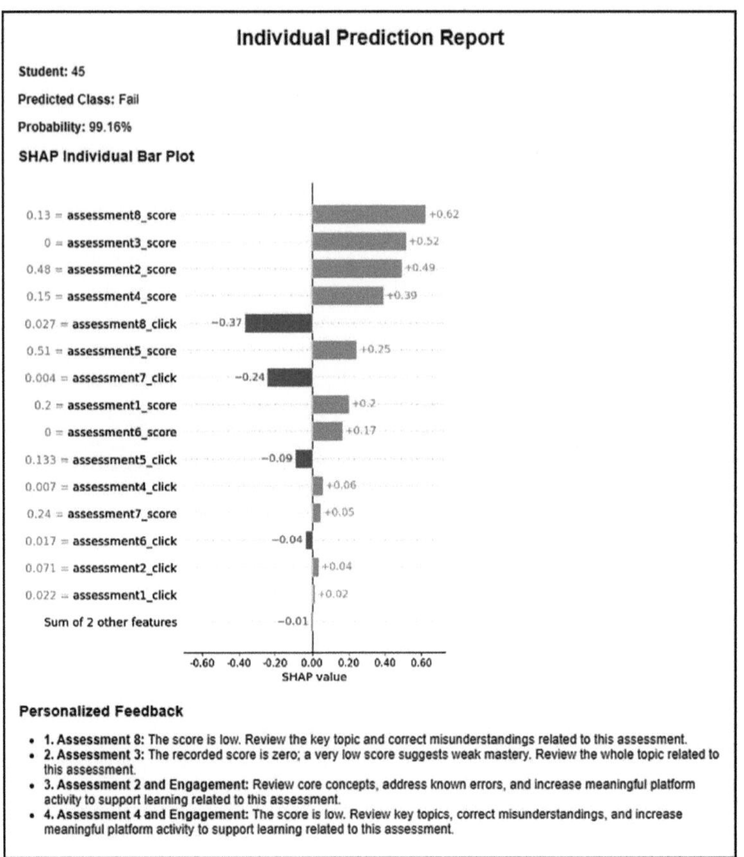

Fig. 2. Individual prediction report for fail prediction

This report enables a direct understanding of the underlying reasons for the predicted outcome, with Assessment 8 performance representing the most critical weakness and insufficient engagement patterns throughout the course.

4.3.2 Student B: SHAP Explanation for Pass Prediction

As shown in Fig. 3, Student B was predicted to pass with high confidence (99.70%). The SHAP force plot reveals strong positive contributions, primarily from high assessment scores and active engagement features.

The most influential positive factor was Assessment8_score (0.83, SHAP + 0.69), providing strong evidence of content mastery near course completion and serving as the primary driver of success prediction. High course engagement also contributed significantly: Assessment7_click (0.009, SHAP + 0.64) and Assessment8_click (0.032, SHAP + 0.56) indicated active interaction with learning materials, interpreted as strong positive behavioral signals showing sustained effort.

One notable negative contribution appeared: Assessment5_score (0.41, SHAP -0.52), representing a comparative mid-course weakness that introduced some risk into the prediction. However, this was substantially outweighed by consistent strong performance across other assessments: Assessment6_score (0.8, SHAP + 0.41), Assessment7_score (0.64, SHAP + 0.36), Assessment3_score (0.89, SHAP + 0.31), Assessment2_score (0.88, SHAP + 0.25), and Assessment1_score (0.8, SHAP + 0.20), demonstrating overall competence throughout the course.

Additional positive contributions came from various engagement metrics and assessment performance: Assessment6_click (0.023, SHAP + 0.16), Assessment5_click (0.014, SHAP + 0.13), Assessment4_click (0.012, SHAP + 0.07), Assessment2_click (0.017, SHAP + 0.06), Assessment3_click (0.019, SHAP + 0.05), and Assessment4_score (0.62, SHAP + 0.03), indicating sustained interaction with course materials and consistent academic performance that reinforced the model's confidence in pass prediction.

This case demonstrates that SHAP-based explanations provide valuable insights even for high-achieving students, identifying where further improvement efforts would be most beneficial while highlighting the factors contributing to predicted success.

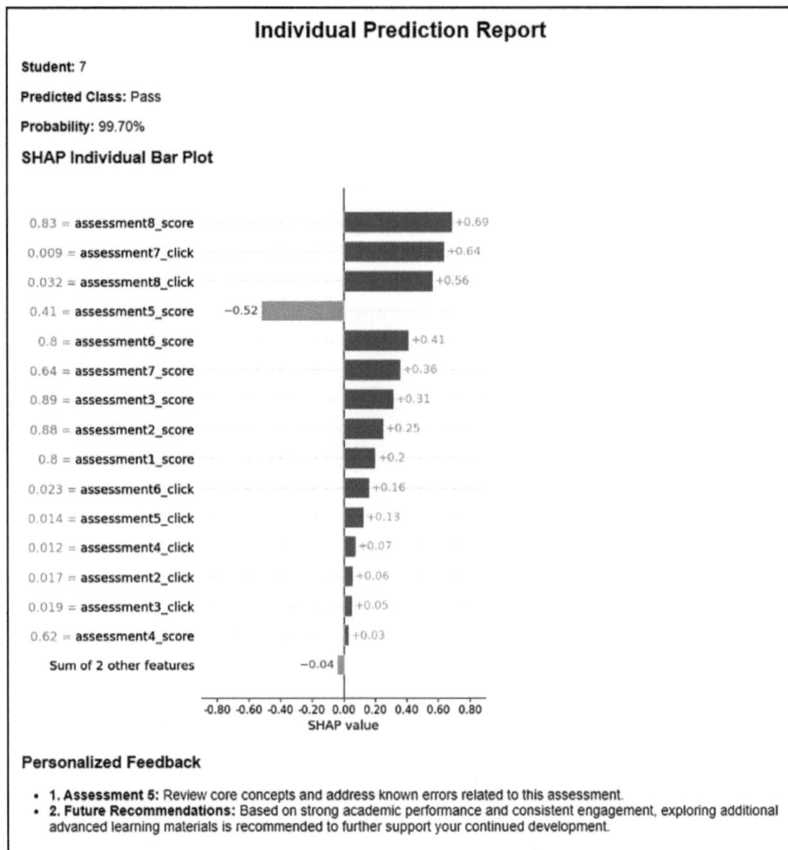

Fig. 3. Individual prediction report for pass prediction

4.4 RQ4: Personalized Actionable Feedback

The final part addressed RQ4, which examined how the SHAP explanations could be translated into personalized student recommendations. These suggestions were prioritized based on SHAP value magnitudes, where higher-ranked items reflected greater influence on the predicted outcome. As such, earlier items in the feedback list indicated areas where targeted action would have been most effective for improving student performance.

4.4.1 Student A: Actionable Feedback for At-Risk Student

For Student A, who is predicted to fail, the personalized feedback at the bottom of Fig. 2 focuses on major weaknesses identified in the individual prediction report. The suggestions directly target the most influential features driving the failure prediction, arranged by SHAP values.

The top priority addresses Assessment 8, which had the most significant positive SHAP value (+0.62) and lowest score (0.13), making it the strongest contributor to predicted failure. The first feedback recommendation is to review key topics and address misunderstandings in this assessment. The second recommendation targets Assessment 3, where the zero score contributed significantly to the SHAP value (+0.52), indicating a need for a thorough review of foundational understanding.

The third feedback item combines Assessment 2's moderate score (0.48, SHAP + 0.49) with low engagement signals from assessment2_click (0.071, SHAP + 0.04), recommending review of core concepts and increased platform interaction to address both performance and engagement deficits. Finally, Assessment 4's low score (0.15, SHAP + 0.39) and weak engagement from assessment4_click (0.007, SHAP + 0.06) receive combined suggestions for content review and increased participation to strengthen learning in this underperforming area.

This approach translates the report's top-ranked negative influences into a clear, prioritized roadmap where students can directly address their most critical learning gaps.

4.4.2 Student B: Actionable Feedback for High-Performing Student

For Student B, who was confidently predicted to pass, the feedback at the bottom of Fig. 3 focuses on maintaining strengths while addressing the single area of weakness.

The first suggestion addresses Assessment 5, with a score of 0.41 being the only feature that has a negative SHAP contribution (−0.52), recommending a review of core concepts to strengthen this comparative weakness. The second recommendation leverages the student's overall strong performance indicators by suggesting exploration of advanced materials for continued growth.

Unlike Student A's remedial feedback, Student B receives developmental guidance that aligns with their high-achievement profile. This demonstrates how the same SHAP-based methodology generates appropriately tailored feedback by mapping the most influential factors to context-appropriate recommendations. The feedback generation process ensures complete correspondence between model-derived insights and practical guidance, with suggestions directly targeting students' most impactful areas for improvement, as identified through the ranked SHAP visualization.

5 Conclusion and Discussion

This study examined how an optimized XGBoost model, enhanced with XAI techniques, can contribute to prediction and actionable support in education. We investigated four research questions using the OULAD dataset and SHAP explanations.

RQ1 focused on predictive capability. The optimized XGBoost classifier achieved 95.22% accuracy, 92.91% precision, 97.92% recall, and 95.34% F1-score, outperforming previous studies through SMOTE-based class balancing and randomized hyperparameter tuning.

To address RQ2, we examined the feasibility of early prediction. After just the first assessment, the optimized XGBoost model achieved an F1-score of 0.7944. Performance continued improving, with F1-scores reaching 0.8350 and 0.8879 by the second and third checkpoints, respectively. These results indicated that the early checkpoint captured most of the predictive power, enabling timely risk identification and intervention before learning gaps widened.

For RQ3, we explored interpretable individual predictions. SHAP-based reports visualized features influencing each student's predicted outcome. Two case studies demonstrated how SHAP force plots identified risk factors and strengths, enabling clear explanations of model decisions for instructors and students.

Turning to RQ4, we investigated the translation of SHAP explanations into personalized feedback. Suggestions were derived from the top contributing features and prioritized based on SHAP values. At-risk students received remedial feedback targeting specific assessments and engagement, while high performers received developmental recommendations.

This study addressed a critical research gap in EDM, where predictive models typically function as black boxes with limited practical application. While existing EDM research has focused primarily on predictive accuracy, few studies have provided actionable feedback that translates model insights into concrete guidance. Our SHAP-based methodology bridged this gap by directly linking explanations to individualized recommendations, providing a scalable approach for targeted interventions.

Future research should apply this framework in real classrooms to assess its practical impact. A key challenge is collecting sufficient data in such settings. Testing the approach on other datasets will also help evaluate its adaptability and generalizability.

Acknowledgments. This work is funded by national funds through FCT – Foundation for Science and Technology, I.P., within the scope of the research unit UID/00326 - Centre for Informatics and Systems of the University of Coimbra.

References

1. Choi, W.-C., Lam, C.-T., Mendes, A.J.: A systematic literature review on performance prediction in learning programming using educational data mining. In: 2023 IEEE Frontiers in Education Conference (FIE), pp. 1–9. IEEE (2023)
2. Romero, C., Ventura, S., García, E.: Data mining in course management systems: moodle case study and tutorial. Comput. Educ. **51**, 368–384 (2008)
3. Choi, W.-C., Lam, C.-T., Mendes, A.J.: Enhance learning performance predictions with explainable machine learning. In: 2024 IEEE Frontiers in Education Conference (FIE) (2024)
4. Choi, W.-C., Lam, C.-T., Pang, P.C.-I., Mendes, A.J.: A systematic literature review of explainable artificial intelligence (XAI) for interpreting student performance prediction in computer science and STEM education. In: Proceedings of the 30th ACM Conference on Innovation and Technology in Computer Science, vol. 1, pp. 221–227 (2025)
5. Choi, W.C., Lam, C.-T., Mendes, A.J.: Analyzing the interpretability of machine learning prediction on student performance using SHapley Additive exPlanations. In: 2024 IEEE International Conference on Teaching, Assessment and Learning for Engineering (TALE), pp. 1–8. IEEE (2024)
6. Choi, W.-C., Lam, C.-T., Mendes, A.J.: How various educational features influence programming performance in primary school education. In: 2024 IEEE Global Engineering Education Conference (EDUCON), pp. 1–8. IEEE (2024)
7. Lundberg, S.M., Lee, S.-I.: A unified approach to interpreting model predictions. In: Advances in Neural Information Processing Systems, vol. 30 (2017)

8. Shapley, L.S.: A Value for n-Person Games. Princeton University Press (1953)
9. Kuzilek, J., Hlosta, M., Zdrahal, Z.: Open university learning analytics dataset. Sci. Data **4**, 1–8 (2017)
10. Chen, T., Guestrin, C.: XGBoost: a scalable tree boosting system. In: Proceedings of the 22nd ACM SIGKDD International Conference on Knowledge Discovery and Data Mining, pp. 785–794 (2016)
11. Waheed, H., Hassan, S.-U., Nawaz, R., Aljohani, N.R., Chen, G., Gasevic, D.: Early prediction of learners at risk in self-paced education: a neural network approach. Expert Syst. Appl. **213** (2023)
12. Heuer, H., Breiter, A.: Student success prediction and the trade-off between big data and data minimization. In: DeLFI 2018-Die 16. E-Learning Fachtagung Informatik (2018)
13. Cortes, C., Vapnik, V.: Support-vector networks. Mach. Learn. **20**, 273–297 (1995)
14. Rizvi, S., Rienties, B., Khoja, S.A.: The role of demographics in online learning; A decision tree based approach. Comput. Educ. **137**, 32–47 (2019)
15. Waheed, H., et al.: Balancing sequential data to predict students at-risk using adversarial networks. Comput. Electr. Eng. **93**, 107274 (2021)
16. Adnan, M., et al.: Predicting at-risk students at different percentages of course length for early intervention using machine learning models. IEEE Access **9**, 7519–7539 (2021)
17. Esteban, A., Romero, C., Zafra, A.: Assignments as influential factor to improve the prediction of student performance in online courses. Appl. Sci. **11**, 10145 (2021)
18. Romero, C., Ventura, S.: Data mining in education. Wiley Interdisc. Rev. Data Min. Knowl. Discov. **3**, 12–27 (2013)
19. Gilpin, L.H., Bau, D., Yuan, B.Z., Bajwa, A., Specter, M., Kagal, L.: Explaining explanations: an overview of interpretability of machine learning. In: 2018 IEEE 5th International Conference on Data Science and Advanced Analytics (DSAA), pp. 80–89. IEEE (2018)
20. Mathrani, A., Susnjak, T., Ramaswami, G., Barczak, A.: Perspectives on the challenges of generalizability, transparency and ethics in predictive learning analytics. Comput. Educ. Open **2**, 100060 (2021)
21. Adadi, A., Berrada, M.: Peeking inside the black-box: a survey on explainable artificial intelligence (XAI). IEEE Access **6**, 52138–52160 (2018)
22. Mendez, G., Galárraga, L., Chiluiza, K.: Showing academic performance predictions during term planning: effects on students' decisions, behaviors, and preferences. In: Proceedings of the 2021 CHI Conference on Human Factors in Computing Systems. Association for Computing Machinery, New York, NY, USA (2021)
23. Adnan, M., Uddin, M.I., Khan, E., Alharithi, F.S., Amin, S., Alzahrani, A.A.: Earliest possible global and local interpretation of students' performance in virtual learning environment by leveraging explainable AI. IEEE Access **10**, 129843–129864 (2022)
24. Pardo, A., et al.: Ontask: delivering data-informed, personalized learning support actions. J. Learn. Anal. **5**, 235–249 (2018)
25. Varank, İ., et al.: Effectiveness of an online automated evaluation and feedback system in an introductory computer literacy course. Eurasia J. Math. Sci. Technol. Educ. **10** (2014)
26. Maier, U., Klotz, C.: Personalized feedback in digital learning environments: classification framework and literature review. Comput. Educ.: AI **3**, 100080 (2022)
27. Troussas, C., Papakostas, C., Krouska, A., Mylonas, P., Sgouropoulou, C.: Personalized feedback enhanced by natural language processing in intelligent tutoring systems. In: International Conference on Intelligent Tutoring Systems, pp. 667–677. Springer, Cham (2023)
28. Ribeiro, M.T., Singh, S., Guestrin, C.: "Why should I trust you?" Explaining the predictions of any classifier. In: Proceedings of the 22nd ACM SIGKDD International Conference on Knowledge Discovery and Data Mining, pp. 1135–1144 (2016)

29. Afzaal, M., et al.: Generation of automatic data-driven feedback to students using explainable machine learning. In: International Conference on AI in Education, pp. 37–42. Springer, Cham (2021)
30. Mothilal, R.K., Sharma, A., Tan, C.: Explaining machine learning classifiers through diverse counterfactual explanations. In: Proceedings of the 2020 Conference on Fairness, Accountability, and Transparency, pp. 607–617 (2020)
31. Pedregosa, F., et al.: Scikit-learn: machine learning in Python. J. Mach. Learn. Res. **12**, 2825–2830 (2011)
32. Chawla, N.V., Bowyer, K.W., Hall, L.O., Kegelmeyer, W.P.: SMOTE: synthetic minority over-sampling technique. J. Artif. Intell. Res. **16**, 321–357 (2002)
33. Chugh, A.: ML: CHI-square test for feature selection. GeeksforGeeks (2018). https://www.geeksforgeeks.org/ml-chi-square-test-for-feature-selection/
34. Powers, D.: Evaluation: from precision, recall and F-measure to ROC, informedness, markedness & correlation. J. Mach. Learn. Technol. **2**, 37–63 (2011)
35. Bergstra, J., Bengio, Y.: Random search for hyper-parameter optimization. J. Mach. Learn. Res. **13**, 281–305 (2012)

Discrimination-Free Condensation for Large-Scale Graphs

Runze Mao, Xiao Chen, Chun Hin Chan, Xiangmeng Wang, Wenqi Fan, and Qing Li(✉)

The Hong Kong Polytechnic University, Hong Kong SAR, China
runzemao2-c@my.cityu.edu.hk, shawn.chen@connect.polyu.hk,
{xiangmengpoly.wang,wenqi.fan,qing-prof.li}@polyu.edu.hk

Abstract. Graph condensation has become a prominent method for reducing the size of large-scale graphs into manageable, synthetic forms, significantly decreasing the resources needed for training graph neural networks (GNNs). While these condensed graphs allow GNNs to achieve performances comparable to those trained on original, larger graphs, the potential bias and resulting unfairness in such condensed representations have not been adequately addressed. Our research indicates that subgroup unfairness—across both binary and multi-attribute groups—intensifies significantly with existing condensation techniques, leading to ethical and societal concerns when such models are deployed in real-world settings. Considering the condensed graphs have lost original subgroup information, it is prohibitive to directly train fair GNNs on them using existing algorithms. In this paper, we introduce a novel approach, **G**raph **C**ondensation through **O**ptimal **T**ransport (GCOT), designed to ensure subgroup fairness in the graph condensation process. GCOT utilizes multi-marginal optimal transport to equalize the hidden representation distributions among different subgroups effectively, theoretically reducing unfairness in GNNs trained on condensed graphs. This method addresses both degree and attribute biases and is versatile enough to accommodate multi-group scenarios. Our extensive experiments on four real-world datasets demonstrate that GCOT not only promotes fairness but also maintains high accuracy, paving the way for more equitable GNN applications.

Keywords: Graph Condensation · Fairness · Graph Neural Networks

1 Introduction

Graphs, as a fundamental data structure in web applications [4,15,35], are capable of encapsulating intricate relationships across various domains, including recommender systems [13,14,39], molecular structures [27,37], and natural language processing [6]. Graph Neural Networks (GNNs) have been developed to exploit

R. Mao and X. Chen—Equal contribution.

B. Fernández-Manjón et al. (Eds.): SETE 2025/ICWL 2025, LNCS 16425, pp. 273–284, 2026.
https://doi.org/10.1007/978-981-92-0042-9_20

these relationships by extending deep learning to graph-structured data [12,33]. Utilizing message-passing algorithms, GNNs effectively aggregate local neighborhood data to generate meaningful node representations [3,18,26]. However, their application to large-scale graphs introduces significant scalability issues, notably increased training times and GPU demands [38]. Graph condensation [21,22] has emerged as a promising approach for efficient training on large graphs by learning a smaller synthetic graph that preserves the performance of GNNs. This process involves adjusting the synthetic graph's representations to match the GNN gradients on the original graph, thus mimicking the training dynamics of GNNs.

Despite their effectiveness, most graph condensation techniques prioritize performance, potentially overlooking fairness issues and exhibiting biases on node degrees or sensitive attributes. To explore this, we conducted preliminary studies using the DosCond method [21] on two datasets, Ogbn-arxiv [20] and Credit-defaulter [1]. We condensed these datasets using DosCond, trained a standard GCN model [26] on both the original and condensed graphs, and assessed performance disparities across designated subgroups. As illustrated in Figure 1, performance disparity between two subgroups is heavily amplified when the GCN is trained on the condensed graph, leading to unfair outcomes. This empirical investigation has suggested that certain node subgroups get underrepresented in condensed graphs, leading to significant increase in performance disparity, and raising concerns of deployment in safety-critical applications.

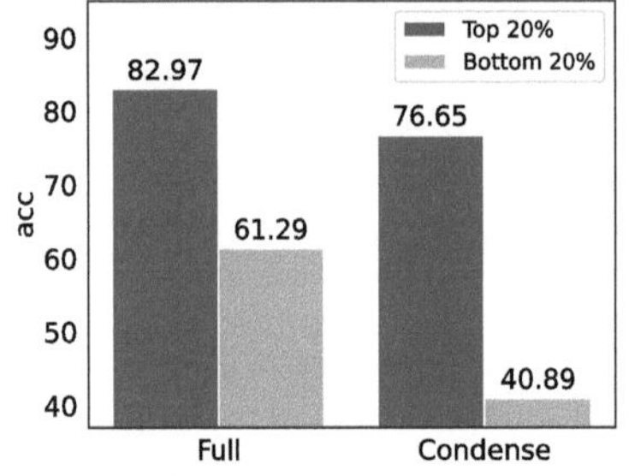

(a) Ogbn-arxiv dataset. Degree bias.

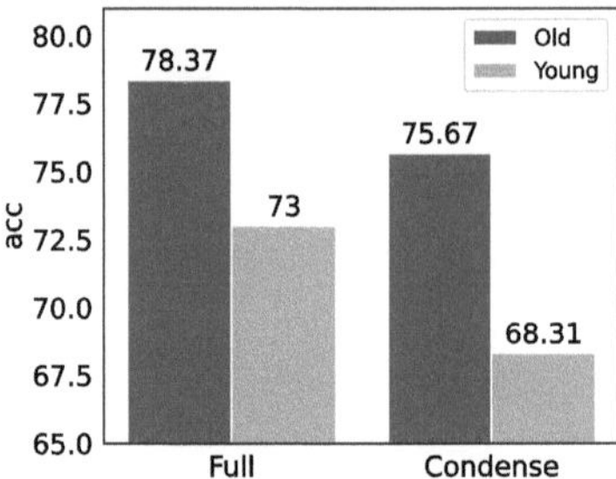

(b) Credit dataset. Attribute bias.

Fig. 1. The subgroup accuracy of GNNs trained on *full* graphs vs. *condensed* graphs. Our empirical evaluations on two datasets find that subgroup unfairness (i.e., performance disparity) is exacerbated after condensation.

In this paper, we address fairness issues in GNNs trained on condensed graphs, highlighting two main challenges. First, the condensation process reorganizes graph structure and transforms node attributes into dense features, causing the loss of original subgroup information, which makes ensuring fairness difficult. Second, the reasons for increased unfairness during graph condensation are unclear, with limited theoretical support for addressing this. Our approach begins with a theoretical analysis of existing condensation techniques, revealing that condensed node features result from aggregating original node embeddings into a weighted sum. Based on this insight, we introduce a new method called **G**raph **C**ondensation through **O**ptimal **T**ransport (GCOT). GCOT aims to ensure fairness by aligning hidden representations of different node subgroups during the condensation process, using multi-marginal optimal transport to minimize the Wasserstein distance between subgroup distributions, thus promoting more uniform treatment across groups.

Our contributions can be summarized as follows: (1) Our empirical investigations have revealed the shortcomings of existing graph condensation methods regarding fairness. (2) We introduce a novel graph condensation framework GCOT, which leverages multi-marginal optimal transport to align subgroup representations during condensation, thereby achieving fair graph condensation. (3) Our comprehensive experiments demonstrate that GCOT alleviates both degree and attribute unfairness in graph condensation. The overall performance of condensed graphs can also be enhanced.

2 Related Work

Graph Reduction. Graph size reduction [19,22] plays a crucial role in preserving the utility of large-scale graphs while making them more computationally manageable [5]. These techniques are typically performed in an unsupervised manner, ensuring that the reduced graph remains a faithful approximation of the original without relying on labeled data [19,25]. Graph condensation, a newer supervised method, reduces graph size by learning a synthetic graph with tailored node features and edges, preserving label information for effective GNN training [21,22]. Methods such as GCond and DosCond use gradient matching between the original and condensed graphs, while GC-SNTK accelerates the process by omitting bi-level optimization [30]. This approach has also been extended to compressing user-item interaction graphs in recommender systems [36].

Fairness in Graph Learning. Bias widely exists in graph-structured data [10], manifesting in two main forms: imbalanced node degrees [32], and presence of sensitive attributes such as gender and race [1]. As a result, GNNs often inherit such bias and exhibit discrimination against minority node subgroups, known as *fairness* issues. To mitigate these issues, two primary approaches have been predominantly adopted: adversarial debiasing [9] and fairness constraint [1,31]. Recently, [28] also investigated the fairness issues of graph condensation, and proposed a simple adversary-based solution. Nonetheless, adversarial methods are often unstable and may suffer from mode collapse during training [2,4]. Meanwhile, fairness constraint methods tend to target only one specific type of bias at a time. Alternatively, in this paper, we propose to leverage multi-marginal optimal transport to address the fairness issues.

3 Preliminary

Notations and Definitions. We use $\mathcal{G} = (A, X, Y)$ to represent an undirected graph with adjacency matrix $A \in \mathbb{R}^{N\times N}$, node features $X \in \mathbb{R}^{N\times D}$, and node labels $Y \in \mathbb{R}^N$. In this paper, we focus on a transductive node classification setting where $\mathcal{G}$ includes both training and testing nodes. We use cross-entropy loss, denoted by L_{cl}, for classification tasks. A GNN, represented as GNN_θ, outputs $\text{GNN}_\theta(A, X)$ at its final layer. The nodes are divided into K subgroups based on characteristics like degree or sensitive attributes (e.g., race, gender, age), and each node is assigned a subgroup ID from 0 to $K - 1$.

Graph Condensation via Gradient Matching. Graph condensation involves creating a synthetic graph $\mathcal{S} = (A_\mathcal{S}, X_\mathcal{S}, Y_\mathcal{S})$ with $N_\mathcal{S}$ nodes from a larger target graph $\mathcal{T} = (A_\mathcal{T}, X_\mathcal{T}, Y_\mathcal{T})$ with $N_\mathcal{T}$ nodes, aiming for a GNN trained on $\mathcal{S}$ to perform similarly to one trained on $\mathcal{T}$. This approach initializes the node features $X_\mathcal{S}$ of the synthetic graph as learnable parameters. It uses a fully connected network Φ to predict adjacency $A_\mathcal{S}$ and a GNN with parameters θ to condense the graph. During training, gradients computed from both the original and condensed graphs guide the updates. Specifically, at each iteration t, gradient matching loss $D(g_t^\mathcal{S}, g_t^\mathcal{T})$, calculated using cosine similarity between gradients from the two graphs, is minimized to optimize Φ and $X_\mathcal{S}$. The objective function of GCond is $L_{gc} := \min_{X_\mathcal{S},\Phi} D(g^\mathcal{S}, g^\mathcal{T}) + \min_\theta L_{cl}(\text{GNN}_\theta(\Phi(X_\mathcal{S}), X_\mathcal{S}), Y_\mathcal{S})$.

4 Fair Graph Condensation

As revealed in our preliminary studies, existing graph condensation methods are vulnerable to data bias and exacerbate unfairness for GNN training. Motivated by these findings, we propose to regularize the condensation process by aligning subgroup node representations generated by the condensation GNN, thereby alleviating data bias in the condensed graph. Concretely, we adopt multi-marginal optimal transport to minimize the distances among the distributions of different subgroup representations.

Optimal Transport (OT) provides a principled framework for measuring discrepancies between probability distributions [8,17]. A key benefit of OT is its ability to define a *metric* [24] between probability distributions, a property notably absent in methods like Kullback-Leibler (KL) divergence.

Though canonical OT primarily targets two probability distributions, our research considers a multi-group fairness problem. To adequately model the representation distributions of these subgroups, we adopt Multi-Marginal Optimal Transport (MMOT), which computes the distance among K distributions ($K \geq 2$), with the optimal value measuring their dissimilarity.

Accordingly, we propose **G**raph **C**ondensation through **O**ptimal **T**ran-sport (GCOT), which effectively utilizes MMOT to align the distributions of subgroup representations during condensation. The framework of our method is illustrated in Fig. 2. At each step of learning the condensed graph, we initially feed the original graph into the condensation GNN to obtain node representations for each

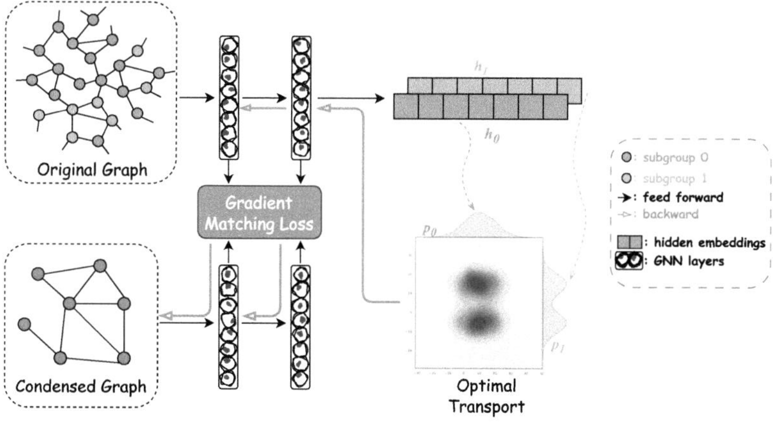

Fig. 2. The framework of GCOT.

subgroup. These representations are denoted as $Z_i \in \mathbb{R}^{N_i \times D}, \quad i = 1, \ldots, K$, where N_i is the size of the i-th subgroup. Next, we transform the representations into probability distributions using differentiable histogramming methods [29]. Specifically, we first apply a sigmoid activation function to the representations to squeeze them into the range $(0, 1)$. Subsequently, we allocate d bins in the range $(0, 1)$, each with width $1/d$. For each bin and each Z_k, we calculate the distance between the activations and the bin location. If an activation value falls within the bin range (i.e., its distance δ to the bin is smaller than $1/d$), the *size* of that bin is incremented by $\mathrm{ReLU}(1/d - \delta)$. In this way, we acquire K histograms $p_1, \ldots, p_K \in \Delta^{d-1}$ as the probability distributions of subgroup representations. To measure the dissimilarity among the subgroup representations, we compute the MMOT distance among $p_1, \ldots, p_K$ as L_{ot}:

$$\begin{aligned} L_{ot} := \min_{P \in \mathbb{R}_+^{d^K}} & \sum_{i_1, \ldots, i_K} C(i_1, \ldots, i_K) P(i_1, \ldots, i_K) \\ \text{s.t.} & \sum_{i_2, \ldots, i_K} P(i_1, \ldots, i_K) = p_1(i_1), \forall i_1 \in [d] \\ & \vdots \\ & \sum_{i_1, \ldots, i_{K-1}} P(i_1, \ldots, i_K) = p_K(i_K), \forall i_K \in [d], \end{aligned} \tag{1}$$

where $C \in \mathbb{R}_+^{d^K}$ is a tensor of Monge cost and $C(i_1, \ldots, i_K) := \max_k i_k - \min_k i_k$. The objective function (1) targets finding a joint distribution P such that the marginals of P correspond to $p_1, \ldots, p_K$ and P minimizes the total cost of moving probability masses among these distributions.

To achieve fair graph condensation, we minimize L_{ot} with respect to the condensation GNN parameters θ to align the distributions of subgroup representations. The total loss function of GCOT is defined as:

$$\min_{X_S,\Phi,\theta} L := L_{gc} + \lambda \cdot L_{ot}, \tag{2}$$

where λ is a hyperparameter that balances the utility and fairness of the condensed graph.

5 Experiments

5.1 Experiment Setup

Table 1. Main results on Cora, Ogbn-arxiv, Credit-defaulter and Recidivism datasets. Best results are marked in bold.

Dataset	Metric	GCond	Reg	Adv	Rawls	Ours	DosCond	Reg	Adv	Rawls	Ours	Whole
Cora	$acc \uparrow$	80.98	80.80	81.03	80.08	**81.18**	80.06	80.25	80.32	78.19	**80.64**	81.92
	$\Delta_{acc} \downarrow$	9.80	9.83	9.56	9.54	**8.73**	9.43	9.31	9.07	9.22	**8.98**	8.95
	$\sigma_{acc} \downarrow$	4.50	4.41	4.28	4.31	**3.90**	4.18	4.14	4.15	4.07	**3.99**	3.96
Ogbn-arxiv	$acc \uparrow$	**59.23**	58.89	59.37	58.71	58.23	58.61	58.08	57.81	**58.66**	58.60	71.21
	$\Delta_{acc} \downarrow$	31.36	30.75	30.22	31.32	**29.79**	31.79	30.53	29.85	32.43	**28.98**	22.04
	$\sigma_{acc} \downarrow$	10.98	10.75	10.71	11.01	**10.40**	11.15	10.63	10.35	11.41	**10.16**	7.57
Credit	$acc \uparrow$	74.53	74.60	74.37	75.24	**75.37**	74.30	74.66	74.96	73.60	**75.02**	75.22
	$\Delta_{SP} \downarrow$	11.21	11.20	10.98	10.97	**8.20**	13.99	10.10	10.90	11.93	**9.32**	10.23
	$\Delta_{EO} \downarrow$	8.87	8.91	8.74	8.81	**6.57**	11.39	8.15	8.82	9.54	**7.50**	8.21
Recidivism	$acc \uparrow$	80.04	82.43	81.97	81.58	**83.15**	80.08	80.88	**81.16**	81.59	80.52	81.01
	$\Delta_{SP} \downarrow$	4.47	4.46	3.98	4.24	**3.40**	4.76	4.90	4.68	6.30	**4.64**	3.59
	$\Delta_{EO} \downarrow$	3.40	2.76	2.52	2.13	**1.35**	3.45	3.61	3.43	4.21	**3.09**	1.21

Datasets. Our study uses four graph datasets for transductive node classification: Cora [26], Ogbn-arxiv [20], Credit-defaulter [1], and Recidivism [1]. For Cora, we minimize the graph to 35 nodes, achieving a 1.29% compression rate. Ogbn-arxiv is trimmed to 90 nodes, yielding a 0.053% compression rate. Credit-defaulter and Recidivism are reduced to 120 and 200 nodes with compression rates of 0.4% and 1.06%, respectively.

Bias Type. We consider both degree and attribute bias in graphs. For the Ogbn-arxiv dataset, we sort nodes by degree and select 20% to form 5 subgroups. The Cora dataset is similarly divided into 3 subgroups due to its smaller size. For the Credit-defaulter and Recidivism datasets, we use the sensitive attributes *Age* and *Race* to split nodes into 2 subgroups each, following [1].

Baselines. We choose two latest and representative graph condensation algorithms: GCond [22] and DosCond [21]. We implement GCOT and the following fairness methods on both GCond and DosCond: **i)** ***Vanilla*** is the original GCond or DosCond method; **ii)** ***Reg*** penalizes the condensation GNN with the relaxed demographic parity [7]. For K subgroups and C classes, the penalty term is $\frac{1}{K}\sum_{k=1}^{K} \max_{y_j \in [C]} |P(\hat{y} = y_j) - P(\hat{y} = y_j | s = s_k)|$ where $\hat{y}$ is the predicted label and s is the subgroup ID. **iii)** ***Adv*** utilizes adversarial learning to eliminate the subgroup information from node representations [28]. We adopt it on the output of the condensation GNN. **iv)** ***Rawls*** is a preprocessing method that debiases the input graph using Rawlsian difference principle [23].

Evaluation. In our experiments, all methods first condense the original graph into a synthetic version to train the GNN, which is then tested on the original test set. We assess the models using overall classification accuracy and fairness metrics. For Cora and Ogbn-arxiv datasets, which consider degree bias, we measure the classification accuracy of each subgroup individually and report the *max-min difference* and *standard deviation* to evaluate accuracy disparities. For Credit-defaulter and Recidivism, where subgroups are based on sensitive attributes, we use *statistical parity* and *equal opportunity* [10] as fairness metrics.

Hyperparameters. For all datasets, we utilize SGC [34] as the condensation GNN, and train GCN [26] on the condensed graph. The search spaces for λ, d and ρ are $[0.001, 0.01, 0.1, 1]$, $[10, 20, 30]$ and $[0.0001, 0.001, 0.01]$ respectively.

Table 2. Versatility of our condensed graphs to train different GNN architectures. Best results are marked in bold.

Dataset	Method	Metric	GCN	GraphSage	SGC	MLP	APPNP	Cheby	Average
Cora	DosCond	$acc \uparrow$	80.06	**79.07**	79.58	**70.50**	78.50	70.14	76.31
		$\Delta_{acc} \downarrow$	9.43	10.01	10.32	**10.21**	10.43	10.95	10.23
		$\sigma_{acc} \downarrow$	4.18	4.43	4.63	**4.43**	4.71	4.68	4.51
	Ours	$acc \uparrow$	**80.64**	78.97	**79.69**	69.95	**78.55**	**72.15**	**76.66**
		$\Delta_{acc} \downarrow$	**8.98**	**9.47**	**10.14**	10.45	**9.67**	**9.84**	**9.76**
		$\sigma_{acc} \downarrow$	**3.99**	**4.22**	**4.60**	4.63	**4.33**	**4.30**	**4.34**
Ogbn-arxiv	DosCond	$acc \uparrow$	**58.61**	**57.33**	58.55	**58.39**	**57.50**	**51.55**	**56.99**
		$\Delta_{acc} \downarrow$	31.79	32.04	30.88	31.48	31.89	30.48	31.43
		$\sigma_{acc} \downarrow$	11.15	11.27	10.84	10.91	11.21	10.77	11.02
	Ours	$acc \uparrow$	58.60	56.91	**58.91**	57.24	57.48	51.49	56.77
		$\Delta_{acc} \downarrow$	**28.98**	**31.42**	**30.35**	**29.89**	**30.57**	**29.10**	**30.05**
		$\sigma_{acc} \downarrow$	**10.16**	**11.07**	**10.64**	**10.35**	**10.72**	**10.21**	**10.52**
Credit	DosCond	$acc \uparrow$	74.30	74.73	74.63	74.64	75.11	77.77	75.20
		$\Delta_{SP} \downarrow$	13.99	10.35	14.69	11.65	15.11	11.60	12.90
		$\Delta_{EO} \downarrow$	11.39	8.34	12.00	9.61	12.65	8.51	10.42
	Ours	$acc \uparrow$	**75.02**	**77.62**	**76.22**	**75.41**	**75.40**	**78.10**	**76.29**
		$\Delta_{SP} \downarrow$	**9.32**	**7.60**	**11.69**	**8.43**	**12.34**	**7.62**	**9.50**
		$\Delta_{EO} \downarrow$	**7.50**	**5.97**	**9.19**	**6.90**	**9.92**	**5.66**	**7.52**
Recidivism	DosCond	$acc \uparrow$	80.08	83.97	**82.39**	86.10	**83.85**	76.53	82.15
		$\Delta_{SP} \downarrow$	4.76	**4.39**	5.62	**4.85**	5.53	**4.71**	**4.98**
		$\Delta_{EO} \downarrow$	3.45	3.18	**3.58**	**2.98**	3.97	5.02	3.70
	Ours	$acc \uparrow$	**80.52**	**84.99**	81.80	**86.26**	83.69	**77.70**	**82.49**
		$\Delta_{SP} \downarrow$	**4.64**	4.64	**5.31**	4.95	**5.43**	5.05	5.00
		$\Delta_{EO} \downarrow$	**3.09**	**2.84**	3.70	3.14	**3.71**	**4.45**	**3.49**

5.2 Performance Comparison and Ablation Study

Fairness and Performance Comparison. We first discuss the fairness improvements of our method. As shown in Table 1, GCOT (+Ours) outperforms GCond and DosCond on all datasets, demonstrating the effectiveness of the proposed representation alignment module. On Cora, GCond+Ours even surpasses training on the whole dataset ($\Delta_{acc} = 8.73$, $\sigma_{acc} = 3.9$ vs $\Delta_{acc} = 8.95$, $\sigma_{acc} = 3.96$), and DosCond+Ours achieves similar results on Credit-defaulter ($\Delta_{SP} = 9.32$, $\Delta_{EO} = 7.5$ vs $\Delta_{SP} = 10.23$, $\Delta_{EO} = 8.21$). GCOT also excels in most fairness metrics on Credit (Δ_{EO}) and Recidivism (Δ_{SP}). These results highlight GCOT's potential as a promising solution for fair graph condensation.

We also discuss the improvements in overall classification accuracy achieved by GCOT. GCOT further narrows the accuracy gap to that of training on the original graph, compared to GCond and DosCond. As shown in Table 1, our method outperforms GCond on all datasets but Ogbn-arxiv, and outperforms DosCond on all datasets. Notably, GCond+Ours surpasses the accuracy of training on the original graph on Credit and Recidivism (75.37 vs 75.22, 83.15 vs 81.01). Regularization techniques such as Reg and Adv also show promising improvements. Rawls' performance is less stable, e.g., GCond+Rawls drops to 78.19% on Cora. This instability is likely due to Rawls' preprocessing nature. In sum, GCOT generates better representations for condensed graphs and enhances the classification accuracy of GNNs.

Table 3. Cross-architecture evaluation of GCOT on the Credit-defaulter dataset. Left: accuracy. Right: equal opportunity.

	SGC	GCN	APPNP	GraphSage
SGC	76.22 (+2.13%)	75.02 (+0.97%)	75.40 (+0.38%)	77.62 (+3.87%)
GCN	76.97 (-0.78%)	77.23 (+0.37%)	76.94 (-0.20%)	77.34 (+0.89%)
APPNP	77.74 (+1.03%)	77.17 (+0.63%)	77.62 (+1.59%)	76.45 (+0.87%)
GraphSage	76.61 (-0.99%)	77.23 (+0.37%)	77.14 (-0.09%)	77.74 (+0.27%)

	SGC	GCN	APPNP	GraphSage
SGC	9.19 (+23.46%)	7.50 (+34.15%)	9.92 (+21.54%)	5.97 (+28.39%)
GCN	3.53 (+12.98%)	1.59 (+69.00%)	6.67 (-8.92%)	1.57 (+80.05%)
APPNP	7.28 (+8.81%)	6.00 (+20.26%)	6.79 (+10.02%)	6.55 (+33.36%)
GraphSage	2.77 (+45.37%)	1.59 (+69.00%)	5.79 (-0.77%)	1.26 (+79.82%)

Compatible with Various GNN Architectures. We also demonstrate the generalizability of our method by exploring additional GNN architectures and their combinations, with DosCond as the backbone of GCOT. First, we set the condensation GNN to SGC and vary the tested GNN among GCN [26], GraphSage [18], SGC [34], MLP[1], APPNP [16] and Cheby [11]. As results presented in Table 2, GNNs trained on the synthetic graph condensed by our method consistently perform better than the baseline in both accuracy and fairness. Second, we vary architectures of both the condensation GNN and the tested GNN on

[1] When using MLP on graphs, it discards the adjacency matrix and only uses node features for prediction.

the Credit-defaulter dataset. The results are presented in Table 3. Significantly, GCOT surpasses the baseline in both accuracy and fairness metrics across almost all combinations of GNNs. These outcomes reveal the model-agnostic nature of GCOT and its ability to integrate with various GNN architectures and its broad applicability in real-world deployments.

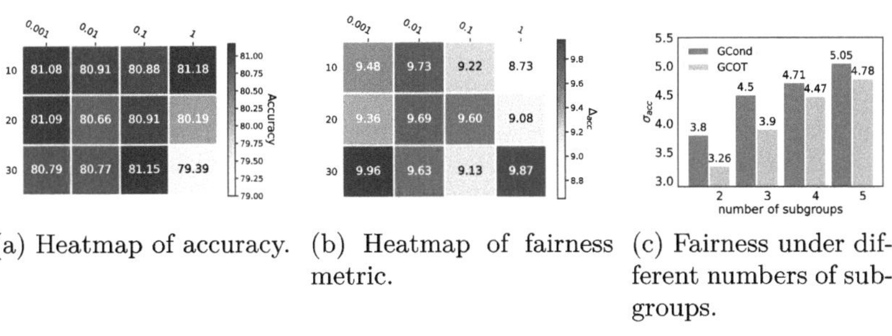

(a) Heatmap of accuracy. (b) Heatmap of fairness metric. (c) Fairness under different numbers of subgroups.

Fig. 3. Hyperparameter sensitivity of GCOT on the Cora dataset.

Hyperparameter Analysis. We evaluate the hyperparameter sensitivity analysis of GCOT using the Cora dataset with GCond as the backbone. Figures 3a and 3b show heatmaps of prediction accuracy and fairness against two hyperparameters: the weight of L_{ot} and the number of histogram bins. The results indicate minimal fluctuation, demonstrating GCOT's stability across configurations. Additionally, when partitioning the Cora dataset into 2, 3, 4, or 5 subgroups, GCOT consistently outperforms GCond, achieving lower σ_{acc}, confirming that the MMOT loss effectively handles varying subgroup numbers.

6 Conclusion

Graph condensation is key for efficient GNN training and deployment. However, existing methods worsen fairness of GNNs trained on condensed graphs, posing critical safety concerns. In this paper, we present empirical evidence that highlights the shortcomings of these methods. Besides, we theoretically analyze existing methods, and find that condensed node features are weighted sums of aggregated representations of original nodes. To mitigate the fairness issues, we propose a novel approach, GCOT, which utilizes multi-marginal optimal transport to align subgroup representations during condensation. Empirical studies show that GCOT enhances both accuracy and fairness of condensed graphs. In conclusion, GCOT marks a significant advancement in graph condensation, offering potential improvements for GNNs in real-world applications.

Acknowledgments. The research described in this paper has been partially supported by the General Research Funds from the Hong Kong Research Grants Council (project no. PolyU 15207322, 15200023, 15206024, and 15224524), internal research funds from Hong Kong Polytechnic University (project no. P0042693, P0048625, and P0051361). This work was supported by computational resources provided by The Centre for Large AI Models (CLAIM) of The Hong Kong Polytechnic University.

References

1. Agarwal, C., Lakkaraju, H., Zitnik, M.: Towards a unified framework for fair and stable graph representation learning. In: Proceedings of Conference on Uncertainty in Artificial Intelligence (2021)
2. Arjovsky, M., Chintala, S., Bottou, L.: Wasserstein generative adversarial networks. In: Proceedings of the 34th International Conference on Machine Learning (2017)
3. Chen, J., et al.: Knowledge-enhanced black-box attacks for recommendations. In: Proceedings of the 28th ACM SIGKDD Conference on Knowledge Discovery and Data Mining, pp. 108–117 (2022)
4. Chen, X., et al.: Fairly adaptive negative sampling for recommendations. In: Proceedings of the ACM Web Conference 2023, pp. 3723–3733 (2023)
5. Chen, X., Ma, C., Fan, W., Zhang, Z., Qing, L.: C2kd: cross-layer and cross-head knowledge distillation for small language model-based recommendation. In: Findings of the Association for Computational Linguistics: ACL 2025, pp. 17827–17838 (2025)
6. Chen, Z., Mao, H., Li, H., Jin, W., Wen, H., Wei, X., Wang, S., Yin, D., Fan, W., Liu, H., Tang, J.: Exploring the potential of large language models (llms) in learning on graphs (2023)
7. Chuang, C.Y., Mroueh, Y.: Fair Mixup: Fairness via Interpolation. In: International Conference on Learning Representations (2021)
8. Cuturi, M.: Sinkhorn distances: lightspeed computation of optimal transport. In: Advances in Neural Information Processing Systems (2013)
9. Dai, E., Wang, S.: Say no to the discrimination: learning fair graph neural networks with limited sensitive attribute information. In: Proceedings of the 14th ACM International Conference on Web Search and Data Mining (2021)
10. Dai, E., et al.: A comprehensive survey on trustworthy graph neural networks: privacy, robustness, fairness, and explainability (2022)
11. Defferrard, M., Bresson, X., Vandergheynst, P.: Convolutional neural networks on graphs with fast localized spectral filtering. In: Advances in Neural Information Processing Systems (2016)
12. Fan, W., et al.: Jointly attacking graph neural network and its explanations. In: 2023 IEEE 39th International Conference on Data Engineering (ICDE). IEEE (2023)
13. Fan, W., Liu, X., Jin, W., Zhao, X., Tang, J., Li, Q.: Graph trend filtering networks for recommendation. In: Proceedings of the 45th International ACM SIGIR Conference on Research and Development in Information Retrieval, pp. 112–121 (2022)
14. Fan, W., et al.: Graph neural networks for social recommendation. In: The World Wide Web Conference (2019)
15. Fan, W., et al.: A graph neural network framework for social recommendations. IEEE Trans. Knowl. Data Eng. (2020)
16. Gasteiger, J., Bojchevski, A., Günnemann, S.: Combining neural networks with personalized pagerank for classification on graphs. In: International Conference on Learning Representations (2019)

17. Gordaliza, P., Barrio, E.D., Fabrice, G., Loubes, J.M.: Obtaining fairness using optimal transport theory. In: Proceedings of the 36th International Conference on Machine Learning (2019)
18. Hamilton, W.L., Ying, R., Leskovec, J.: Inductive representation learning on large graphs. In: Advances in Neural Information Processing Systems (2017)
19. Hashemi, M., Gong, S., Ni, J., Fan, W., Prakash, B.A., Jin, W.: A comprehensive survey on graph reduction: Sparsification, coarsening, and condensation. arXiv preprint arXiv:2402.03358 (2024)
20. Hu, W., et al.: Open graph benchmark: Datasets for machine learning on graphs. In: Advances in Neural Information Processing Systems (2020)
21. Jin, W., et al.: Condensing graphs via one-step gradient matching. In: Proceedings of the 28th ACM SIGKDD Conference on Knowledge Discovery and Data Mining (2022)
22. Jin, W., Zhao, L., Zhang, S., Liu, Y., Tang, J., Shah, N.: Graph condensation for graph neural networks. In: International Conference on Learning Representations (2022)
23. Kang, J., Zhu, Y., Xia, Y., Luo, J., Tong, H.: Rawlsgcn: towards rawlsian difference principle on graph convolutional network. In: The World Wide Web Conference (2022)
24. Kantorovich, L.V.: Mathematical methods of organizing and planning production. Manage. Sci. **6**(4), 366–422 (1960)
25. Karger, D.R.: Random sampling in cut, flow, and network design problems. In: Proceedings of the Twenty-Sixth Annual ACM Symposium on Theory of Computing (1994)
26. Kipf, T.N., Welling, M.: Semi-supervised classification with graph convolutional networks. In: International Conference on Learning Representations (2017)
27. Liu, C., et al.: Generative diffusion models on graphs: methods and applications. International Joint Conference on Artificial Intelligence (IJCAI) (2023)
28. Mao, R., Fan, W., Li, Q.: GCARe: mitigating subgroup unfairness in graph condensation through adversarial regularization. Appl. Sci. **13**(16), 9166 (2023)
29. Mehta, R., Kline, J., Lokhande, V.S., Fung, G., Singh, V.: Efficient discrete multi marginal optimal transport regularization. In: International Conference on Learning Representations (2023)
30. Wang, L., Fan, W., Li, J., Ma, Y., Li, Q.: Fast graph condensation with structure-based neural tangent kernel (2023)
31. Wang, N., Lin, L., Li, J., Wang, H.: Unbiased Graph Embedding with Biased Graph Observations. In: The World Wide Web Conference (2022)
32. Wang, R., Wang, X., Shi, C., Song, L.: Uncovering the structural fairness in graph contrastive learning. In: Advances in Neural Information Processing Systems (2022)
33. Wang, Set al.: Graph machine learning in the era of large language models (llms). arXiv preprint arXiv:2404.14928 (2024)
34. Wu, F., Souza, A., Zhang, T., Fifty, C., Yu, T., Weinberger, K.: Simplifying graph convolutional networks. In: Proceedings of the 36th International Conference on Machine Learning (2019)
35. Wu, J., Fan, W., Chen, J., Liu, S., Li, Q., Tang, K.: Disentangled contrastive learning for social recommendation. In: Proceedings of the 31st ACM International Conference on Information & Knowledge Management, pp. 4570–4574 (2022)
36. Wu, J., et al.: Dataset condensation for recommendation (2023)
37. You, J., Liu, B., Ying, R., Pande, V., Leskovec, J.: Graph convolutional policy network for goal-directed molecular graph generation. In: Advances in Neural Information Processing Systems (2018)

38. Zeng, H., Zhou, H., Srivastava, A., Kannan, R., Prasanna, V.: Graphsaint: graph sampling based inductive learning method. In: International Conference on Learning Representations (2020)
39. Zhao, Z., et al.: Recommender systems in the era of large language models (llms). IEEE Trans. Knowl. Data Eng. (2024)

Contextualized Learning Assistant: A Middleware Architecture for LMS Integration

Nguyen Xuan Bach Do[1(✉)], Truong-Sinh An[1], Christopher Krauss[1], Marc Ghanime[1], Md Abdul Aziz[1], Lisa Reray[2], Almuth Mueller[3], and Daniela Altun[2]

[1] Fraunhofer FOKUS, Kaiserin-Augusta-Allee 31, Berlin 10589, Germany
{nguyenxuanbach.do,truong-sinh.an,christopher.krauss,marc.ghanime, mdabdul.aziz}@fokus.fraunhofer.de

[2] Fraunhofer FKIE, Zanderstraße 5, Bonn-Bad Godesberg 53177, Germany
{lisa.reray,daniela.altun}@fkie.fraunhofer.de

[3] Fraunhofer IOSB, Fraunhoferstraße 1, Karlsruhe 76131, Germany
almuth.mueller@iosb.fraunhofer.de

Abstract. This paper presents a novel architecture for integrating Large Language Models (LLMs) with Retrieval-Augmented Generation (RAG) into Learning Management Systems (LMS), resulting in a contextualized AI-driven Learning Assistance (AILA) that delivers personalized, real-time learning support. Leveraging a middleware approach, the system securely orchestrates relevant data, such as Learning Object Metadata (LOM) and course materials, into a modular RAG pipeline. The chatbot combines quality-assured question answering and document-grounded responses, using advanced retrieval techniques, including re-ranking and relevance filtering. A real-world evaluation in a hybrid training program demonstrated meaningful improvements in learning outcomes and strong user acceptance, validating both its pedagogical impact and technical reliability. These results highlight the potential of open-source AILA systems to enhance digital learning environments and support the development of responsive, learner-centered educational technologies.

Keywords: AI-driven Learning Assistants (AILA) · Large Language Models · Learning Management Systems · Retrieval-Augmented Generation · Chatbot for Education · Contextual Learning

1 Introduction

Learning Management Systems (LMS) have significantly shaped the landscape of digital education by providing centralized platforms for content delivery, student interaction, and assessment management. Popular LMS platforms, such as Moodle [27] and ILIAS [28], have continuously evolved, incorporating adaptive learning tools, intelligent recommendations, and automated assessment functionalities. Despite these advancements, traditional LMS platforms often fall short to

B. Fernández-Manjón et al. (Eds.): SETE 2025/ICWL 2025, LNCS 16425, pp. 285–299, 2026.
https://doi.org/10.1007/978-981-92-0042-9_21

offer real-time, context-sensitive support tailored to individual learners' needs. This gap highlights the need for contextualized, AI-driven Learning Assistance (AILA) capable of delivering relevant, subject-specific knowledge and facilitate deeper exploration of learning resources.

A fundamental prerequisite for the effectiveness of such AI-driven services is comprehensive data collection. Effective personalization and adaptive learning rely heavily on capturing and processing extensive learner interaction data, course content, metadata, and other relevant information. However, integrating diverse data sources and managing real-time data flow within traditional LMS architectures presents significant technical challenges. These platforms are primarily designed for static content delivery and lack built-in capabilities for dynamic data orchestration and advanced AI integrations.

Middleware solutions emerge as a critical enabler in overcoming these limitations. By orchestrating data flow between LMS platforms and AI-driven services, middleware ensures seamless integration and efficient management of data. Middleware not only facilitates the necessary data collection but also handles the technical complexities of interoperability, authentication, and authorization, essential for secure and context-sensitive AI support. Commonly employed standards such as Learning Tools Interoperability (LTI) and CMI5 allow middleware to register courses as external tools, streamlining integration and enabling centralized control over data flow.

To address these challenges and opportunities, this paper introduces an architecture that integrates an open-source, Large Language Model (LLM)-based chatbot enhanced by Retrieval-Augmented Generation (RAG) technology into LMS environments. Our proposed middleware-based architecture serves as the orchestrator, seamlessly collecting and managing data flow between learners, instructors, content, and AI components. The architecture is designed around open-source standards, allowing institutions to maintain control, flexibility, and data privacy, thereby avoiding vendor lock-in and proprietary dependencies.

The remainder of this paper is structured as follows: Sect. 2 reviews the relevant literature; Sect. 3 outlines our methodology, detailing the middleware-driven registration and orchestration processes, and describing the chatbot development, including its architecture and components; Sect. 4 presents a comprehensive evaluation; and Sect. 5 concludes with future research directions.

2 Related Work

The integration of AI into LMS has been a subject of extensive research, with various approaches aimed at enhancing the educational experience through personalized learning and intelligent support. This chapter reviews key contributions in the field, focusing on AI-driven solutions, particularly those utilizing LLMs and RAG techniques. By synthesizing these advancements, we identify existing gaps and outline the potential for open-source solutions that cater to the specific needs of educational institutions.

Recent studies have explored the effectiveness of AI chatbots as virtual teaching assistants. For instance, Taneja et al. (2024) introduced Jill Watson, a ChatGPT-powered assistant designed to support instructors by responding to course-related queries [1]. While this system reduced instructor workload, its limitations in content retrieval and response depth highlights the need for more sophisticated solutions capable of effectively navigating diverse educational materials. Similarly, Miladi et al. (2024) investigated the application of RAG in Massive Open Online Courses (MOOCs), demonstrating significant improvements in response accuracy [2]. Their findings suggest that RAG-enhanced models significantly improve learner's experiences by providing more relevant and precise answers. However, these approaches are often confined to specific educational contexts and do not fully address the challenges of seamless integration within traditional LMS environments.

Additionally, Neumann et al. (2025) propose a chatbot tailored for Moodle, evaluating its impact on user acceptance [3]. While their findings indicated potential benefits for the learning process, they also highlighted accuracy issues inherent to LLM-only chatbot systems, reinforcing the need for hybrid retrieval-based approaches to enhance reliability.

The emergence of **LLMs** has enabled the development of intelligent chatbots that function as **AILA within LMS**. These chatbots leverage advanced natural language processing (NLP) to provide personalized, context-aware assistance, significantly enhancing the educational experience. Interacting with students in real time, LLM-powered chatbots answer queries, offer explanations, and provide tailored feedback, simulating human-like tutoring. Research has demonstrated their effectiveness; for example, Radford et al. (2019) showed that GPT-2 could generate coherent instructional materials and respond to student inquiries [4], while BERT has been used for question answering and sentiment analysis, offering insights into student engagement. Platforms such as Moodle and Canvas [32] have explored integrating AI-driven chatbots to create interactive learning environments. These chatbots can analyze student queries and course data to provide tailored feedback, thereby improving the learning process. Additionally, Zhang et al. (2021) found that LLMs enhance personalized learning by analyzing student interactions and adapting responses accordingly [5].

One of the key benefits of LLM-based AILA is scalability, as chatbots can assist numerous students simultaneously without requiring extensive human resources. This scalability is particularly valuable in online education, where learners may require assistance at any time. Moreover, the adaptive nature of LLMs enables them to refine responses based on prior interactions, allowing for more tailored guidance. However, challenges such as data privacy, bias in training data, and interpretability must be addressed to ensure reliability and trustworthiness. The deployment of LLMs also raises concerns about accessibility, particularly since many implementations rely on proprietary models, which may lead to vendor lock-in and high operational costs. While commercial models incur token-based costs, in-house deployments require significant IT infrastructure and energy consumption, making the choice between open-source and commercial solutions highly institution-specific.

A promising avenue for mitigating these concerns is the development of open-source LLM-based AILA, which allows institutions to maintain control over their AI systems, customize solutions according to their needs, and comply with data privacy regulations. Open-source models, though currently underrepresented in research, offer significant advantages in flexibility and transparency. Furthermore, incorporating RAG into LLM-based chatbots makes these systems more effective for student support.

Retrieval-Augmented Generation combines information retrieval and natural language generation, enhancing the accuracy and relevance of responses in various applications, including education. Unlike traditional AI models that rely solely on pre-trained knowledge, RAG dynamically retrieves external information, enabling access to real-time data for more precise and reliable answers. This retrieval mechanism helps reduce the risk of *hallucinations*, a common limitation of LLMs, where the model generates confident but factually incorrect statements [7].

In education, RAG is effective for intelligent tutoring systems and chatbots. By integrating RAG with LLMs, these systems can retrieve relevant information from course materials to provide accurate answers to student queries. Research by Lewis et al. (2020) demonstrated that RAG significantly improves response accuracy compared to traditional generative models [6]. Similarly, Miladi et al. (2024) found that RAG-enhanced models improved response accuracy in MOOCs from 60% to 80%, highlighting its potential to enhance student learning experiences [2]. By retrieving real-time information, RAG helps overcome the limitations of static, pre-programmed responses, making AI assistants more adaptable to diverse educational contexts.

However, implementing RAG in education presents challenges, including selecting appropriate retrieval sources and ensuring data quality. Additionally, reliance on external databases raises data privacy and security concerns. The development of open-source RAG frameworks is gaining interest, allowing educational institutions to customize these systems for their needs. Open-source solutions facilitate the integration of retrieval-augmented technologies into LMS platforms, providing tailored experiences for educators and learners and improving educational outcomes.

The **Common Learning Middleware** [8] serves as a foundational framework for integrating AI-driven services into LMS while ensuring interoperability, secure data governance, and access control. Recent works with CLM have emphasized a Best-of-Breed approach to seamlessly connect diverse AI-powered learning tools within distributed educational ecosystems. Krauss et al. (2023) highlight the role of CLM in orchestrating AI services through a modular middleware infrastructure, enabling institutions to integrate AI-driven tutoring systems without disrupting existing LMS functionalities [9]. By leveraging standardized protocols such as LTI, xAPI, and cmi5, CLM ensures compatibility across multiple platforms while allowing adaptive AI components to access structured learning records and provide personalized recommendations.

Beyond interoperability, CLM also introduces a hierarchically structured role and authorization system that facilitates context-sensitive access control. Nguyen et al. (2024) demonstrate how CLM enables user-specific enrollment, ensuring that AI-powered learning assistants operate within defined access constraints while maintaining data sovereignty [10]. This is particularly relevant for LLM-powered RAG-based chatbots, which require fine-grained access to course data, course materials, assessments, and student interactions without compromising privacy. Additionally, CLM supports self-sovereign access models, allowing institutions to dynamically adjust permissions, ensuring compliance with regulatory standards, and mitigating risks associated with AI bias and data exposure.

3 Methodology and Architecture

This section outlines the methodology and architecture for integrating a RAG-based chatbot into an LMS. The proposed framework comprises three core components: (i) the middleware-based approach, which orchestrates data flow and enforces access control; (ii) the integration layer, which embeds the chatbot into LMS platforms via standardized interfaces; and (iii) the chatbot architecture itself, including its frontend functionalities and backend services.

3.1 The Middleware-Based Approach

Traditional LMS architectures are primarily designed for static content delivery and do not easily support the integration of external services such as AI applications or the dynamic management of diverse learning content [11]. By introducing a middleware layer utilizing the CLM, we ensure a flexible and modular system where learning content and AI-powered services can interoperate efficiently [9].

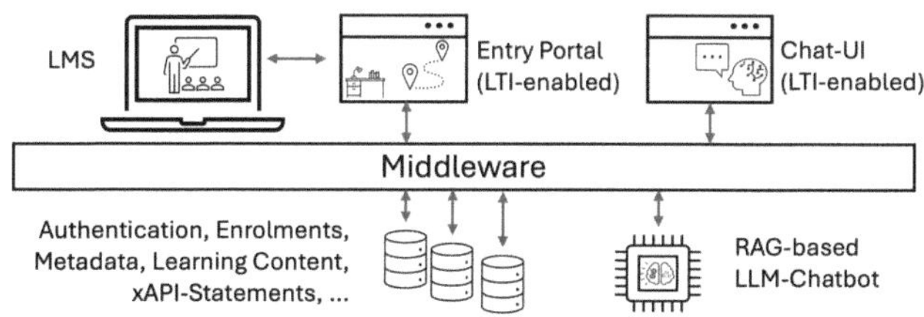

Fig. 1. Middleware-based system architecture

In this architecture, the CLM acts as a content registry, where learning materials, including IEEE Learning Object Metadata (LOM), and associated documentation, are stored and managed centrally (see Fig. 1). A CLM extension component is responsible for processing learning objects to convert them into plain text, and subsequently smaller text chunks, which are then centrally stored in a database for use by various AI applications. This allows the chatbot to retrieve structured course content dynamically, ensuring that chatbot responses remain relevant and aligned with official course materials. Through a standardized API, the chatbot queries the middleware, which facilitates content retrieval, metadata processing, and interoperability with multiple LMS platforms. To maintain controlled access, the CLM uses access rights, which comprise a list of learning object IDs associated with the user's enrollment, to filter content retrieval. This ensures that when using the chatbot, students can only access content for which they are enrolled, with any restricted material automatically excluded from the results [10]. While RAG-based retrieval techniques may further refine response accuracy, the key function of the CLM is to manage access to curated, validated learning content while enforcing authorization controls based on course enrollment. This ensures that the chatbot functions as a contextualized learning assistant, delivering relevant course materials tailored to each student's registered courses. With content orchestration and access control managed by the middleware, the next subsection focuses on the user-facing integration of the chatbot within the LMS environment.

3.2 The Integration in LMS

The chatbot's frontend, referred to as Chat-UI (see Fig. 1), was developed as a standalone web application using the *Next.js* [26] framework. To facilitate seamless authentication and interoperability, an additional application endpoint was implemented to support LTI-based authentication mechanisms. This ensures that user authentication and session management adhere to established authentication workflows, enabling secure and structured access to chatbot functionality. Additionally, the chatbot application is registered within the middleware, which extends its capabilities by wrapping the application in an LTI launch process.

Furthermore, an Entry Portal (see Fig. 1), was used in the context of this study to serve as a centralized access point for learners. Through this portal, students can directly access all registered learning content that has been activated for them. The portal itself is LTI-compliant and can be registered as an external resource within the LMS, ensuring seamless integration across different LMS platforms. To enhance usability and minimize disruption to the learning process, the chatbot is embedded within the Entry Portal. Upon activation, it triggers a PiP mode [31], enabling students to interact with the chatbot while simultaneously engaging with course materials. This design ensures that the chatbot functions as an omnipresent learning assistant, offering context-aware support without disrupting the primary learning workflow. In the following subsection, the core components of the RAG-based chatbot are described, including its frontend functionalities for learners and instructors, as well as the backend services that enable intelligent content retrieval and response generation.

3.3 The RAG-Based Chatbot

The frontend of the RAG-based chatbot comprises two main components designed to facilitate both learner interaction and instructor content management. For the learner-facing interface, users can receive two types of responses (see Fig. 2). The primary response is generated by retrieving relevant context from the learning materials via the RAG pipeline. In this mode, the AI assistant formulates answers based on the contextual information retrieved from course documents, with source details clearly displayed, either through an overlay window upon user interaction or in a separate browser tab. This approach not only enhances the transparency of the response but also helps mitigate the risk of the chatbot generating inaccurate or *hallucinated* answers by grounding its responses in verifiable sources. To further ensure response reliability and quality, the system also supports a secondary response modality that leverages pre-configured, quality-assured Q&A pairs. These curated answers are created and maintained by instructors, enabling the chatbot to provide authoritative, course-specific responses when a query matches a predefined entry.

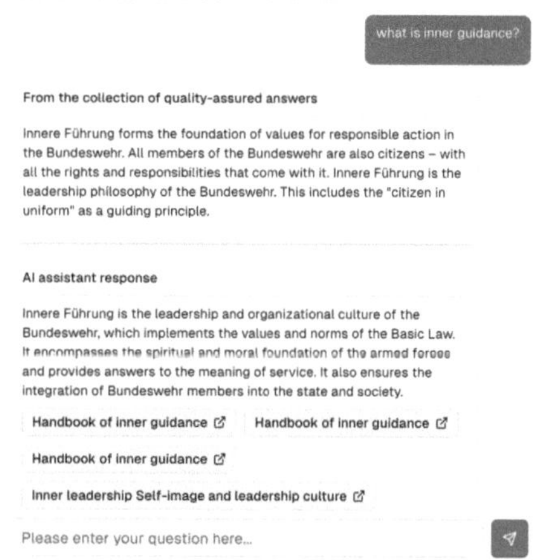

Fig. 2. Two types of responses from the chatbot: Quality-assured Answer and Generated Answer based on sources from the course content

Complementing the learner interface, a content management system (CMS) has been developed for instructors. This system enables them to manage supplementary course documents, configure and update the collection of quality-assured Q&A pairs, and adjust the cosine similarity thresholds that influence both document retrieval and quality-assured Q&A matching.

The backend consists of multiple components, each responsible for handling different aspects of data processing and AI-driven retrieval. To ensure scalability, maintainability, and efficient deployment, we employ a microservice architecture. This approach allows for independent development and scaling of individual components, improving system resilience and enabling seamless integration with various LMS platforms. Additionally, microservices facilitate modular updates, allowing specific components to be optimized without affecting the entire system.

One of the key backend components is the Embedding Service, which is responsible for converting textual data into vector-based representations. Based on the Massive Text Embedding Benchmark (MTEB) [38] [39] we opt for the *intfloat/multilingual-e5-large-instruct* model [19]. With one of the best scores for its size (560 Million Parameters), this model offers excellent performance, supports multilingual text embeddings and cross-lingual retrieval, and operates efficiently without requiring extensive computational resources. These qualities make it well-suited for handling diverse educational content. This service processes LOM metadata of the courses accessible through the CLM, ensuring that structured course information is efficiently indexed. Additionally, relevant documents uploaded by instructors via the CMS are also embedded into vector space. To enhance the quality of the RAG-pipeline, PDF documents are pre-processed by splitting them into smaller text chunks, with a chunk size of 4000 characters and an overlap of 200 characters between chunks, before vectorization, ensuring better granularity and search precision. For storing the generated vectors, we employ a Database Service that utilizes *pgvector* [20], a *PostgreSQL* [21] extension for vector storage and search. Our evaluations showed that *pgvector* outperforms alternative solutions such as *ChromaDB* [22], particularly in identifying more relevant text extracts within documents. This leads to higher-quality responses in chatbot interactions, making the system more effective in delivering accurate learning assistance. The relevance of retrieved text chunks from the Database Service can vary, particularly because cosine similarity thresholds can be adjusted by instructors through the CMS. To ensure that only highly relevant information is provided, we implement an additional filtering step before returning results. This step leverages the LLM-as-a-Judge approach [12], where the retrieved chunks and the learner's query are passed to the LLM for relevance assessment. The LLM evaluates whether each chunk appropriately addresses the query and classifies it using a Guided Generation approach [13], outputting the assessment in a pre-defined binary format ("True" or "False").

To further refine search results, a Reranking Service is incorporated into the pipeline. This component reorders retrieved passages based on semantic relevance, ensuring that the most contextually relevant information is prioritized in the chatbot's responses. We leverage the *gte-multilingual-reranker-base* model [23], which is optimized for cross-lingual ranking tasks, improving semantic alignment between queries and retrieved text segments.

For language model inference, an LLM-Server is set up to ensure on-premises deployment of the model, providing greater control over data privacy and infrastructure integration. We opt for *vLLM* [14], instead of another state-of-the-art system such as *llama.cpp* [15]. The advantage of *vLLM* lies in its efficient memory management and fast inference capabilities, particularly for serving multiple concurrent requests [14]. *vLLM*'s pipelined decoding and continuous batching significantly reduce response latency, making it well-suited for real-time chatbot applications in an LMS environment. The language model used in our system is *Teuken-7B-instruct-commercial-v0.4* [24]. It is an open-source, multilingual model designed for European languages, including German, which accounts for

8.72% of the model's training token [25], making it particularly suitable for educational applications in German-speaking institutions.

4 Evaluation

The objective of this evaluation is to assess the effectiveness of the RAG-based chatbot (AILA), integrated into a standardized training program commissioned by a public-sector partner. The evaluation focuses on two core aspects: (i) the impact of the chatbot on learner outcomes and user experience, and (ii) the technical performance of the underlying retrieval system that supports AILA's responses. This dual focus ensures a comprehensive understanding of both educational efficacy and system-level reliability.

The evaluated course was structured as a hybrid format with in-person instruction and self-study phases, spanning six weeks and involving up to 25 participants. During self-study periods, participants prepared for upcoming sessions using LMS resources.

AILA was configured to access a curated pool of quality-assured Q&A pairs aligned with the course content. In collaboration with course trainers, 70 course-specific rules and regulations were integrated into the system.

Participant feedback was collected via surveys and interviews throughout the course. This informed iterative refinements to AILA, ensuring alignment with learner needs and instructional objectives. Insights from this process also informed the development of future training modules, demonstrating AILA's potential as a sustainable educational tool.

Prior to the commencement of the course, participants were asked to self-assess their knowledge of the topics and their anticipated learning success, with the opportunity to reassess at any time during the course. Course completion was based on an external assessment by the course trainers to document the qualifications achieved.

Based on the self-assessment conducted before the start of the course, participants were divided into two groups: The **Test Group** and the **Control Group**. Both groups have equivalent access to LMS resources. The key distinction was that the Test Group had access to AILA, whereas the Control Group did not.

4.1 Learning Outcome Evaluation

To measure AILA's impact on learning performance, we conducted a quasi-experimental pilot study. Four iterations of the course were delivered, with the final iteration ($n = 20$) selected for analysis due to its comprehensive metadata and documented assessment results. Participants were randomly assigned to control ($n = 10$) and AILA ($n = 10$) groups. Prior knowledge levels were comparable (Mann-Whitney U [36], $p = 0.891$; see Table 1), enabling valid comparisons.

Learning success was measured through ten assessments that covered factual knowledge, conceptual understanding, and application skills over the course of several weeks. Participants reported interacting with AILA for 1–10 h during the course. Given the limited sample size, results should be interpreted as preliminary. Nonetheless, the observed patterns are indicative of promising effects.

Learning gains were calculated using the normalized gain formula:

$$g = \frac{\text{post\%} - \text{pre\%}}{100\% - \text{pre\%}} \quad \text{(Hake, 1998) [33]} \tag{1}$$

Due to the small sample size, Mann-Whitney U tests were used for between-group comparisons, while Wilcoxon signed-rank tests were used for within-group pre-post comparisons (Wilcoxon, 1945) [34]. Effect sizes were calculated using Hedges' g, which corrects for small sample bias (Hedges, 1981) [35].

Table 1. Learning Gains Results

Assessment Metric	Control Group	Test Group	p-value
Pre-test Mean (SD)	63.0 (3.0)	62.8 (2.8)	0.891
Post-test Mean (SD)	64.7 (2.8)	67.3 (2.5)	0.052
Absolute Gain	+1.7 points	+4.5 points	0.047*
Normalized Gain (Hake)	0.045	0.120	0.044*

*p < 0.05 (Mann–Whitney U test) [36] $n = 20$

The pooled standard deviation was calculated as:

$$SD_{\text{pooled}} = \sqrt{\frac{(n_1 - 1)SD_1^2 + (n_2 - 1)SD_2^2}{n_1 + n_2 - 2}} \approx 2.67 \tag{2}$$

Cohen's d is computed as:

$$d = \frac{M_2 - M_1}{SD_{\text{pooled}}} = \frac{67.3 - 64.7}{2.67} \approx 0.960 \tag{3}$$

Hedges' g is then:

$$g = d \times \left(1 - \frac{3}{4(n_1 + n_2) - 9}\right) = 0.960 \times \left(1 - \frac{3}{71}\right) \approx 0.919 \tag{4}$$

As shown in Table 1, the AILA group achieved significantly greater learning improvement with normalized gains of 0.120 (low-medium) versus 0.045 (low) for controls, representing **2.6 times higher normalized learning gains**. Mann-Whitney U tests confirmed statistical significance for both absolute gains ($p = 0.047$) and normalized gains using Equation (1) ($p = 0.044$), demonstrating AILA's superior learning efficiency. While post-test scores showed a strong positive trend favoring AILA (67.3 vs 64.7, $p = 0.052$), approaching the conventional significance threshold, the significant improvements in learning gains provide robust evidence of AILA's effectiveness.

Wilcoxon signed-rank tests for within-group comparisons demonstrated significant improvements from pre-test to post-test for both control ($p = 0.022$)

and AILA groups ($p = 0.003$). The lower p-value for the test group indicates stronger statistical evidence and more robust learning gains across participants.

The substantial effect size (Hedges' $g = 0.92$) from Equations (2-4) indicates large practical significance. This quantitative evaluation demonstrates that AILA integration significantly enhances learning outcomes in LMS environments, with the effect size suggesting meaningful educational impact beyond statistical significance.

Complementing the quantitative data, participant feedback offered additional insights into AILA's perceived value. Participants viewed the chatbot as a valuable enhancement to conventional LMS functionality, rating it as simple and intuitive, with no usability concerns. This positive reception highlights the importance of user experience in educational technology, as a seamless interface fosters engagement and motivation. The system excelled in theory-based learning components, where conceptual comprehension is crucial, likely due to the chatbot's ability to provide contextually relevant explanations and real-time responses to questions, reinforcing course material.

While this pilot study is limited by a small sample size ($n = 20$), it provides a strong proof of concept. Future research should replicate these findings across diverse cohorts and subject areas to evaluate the scalability and generalizability of RAG-based chatbots like AILA in enhancing digital learning experiences.

4.2 RAG Evaluation

While the learning outcome analysis evaluates the educational impact of AILA, it is also important to assess the performance of the retrieval system that powers its responses. This subsection presents the retrieval accuracy evaluation, assessing database and model impacts on performance. To ensure consistency and the use of objective performance metrics, a benchmarking framework was developed, inspired by the Hugging Face *RAG Evaluation Cookbook* [16]. The baseline used was a traditional sparse retrieval method based on the *BM25* algorithm [17]. Two vector databases, *pgvector* [20] and *ChromaDB* [22], were tested across different configurations. Embeddings were generated using the *intfloat/multilingual-e5-large-instruct* model [19], with an embedding size of 1024. When re-ranking was enabled, we employed the *gte-multilingual-reranker-base* model [23]. It is important to note that retrieval performance is influenced by both the embedding model and the design of the prompt pipeline used to integrate retrieved content into the LLM's output.

Evaluation Datasets: For this study, a synthetic dataset was created from 25 PDF documents in the training program, producing 14,088 chunk-query pairs (with minimal text-processing applied). An LLM generated one query per chunk, ensuring each chunk either directly answers the query or provides relevant information. To benchmark against real-world results, the best-performing system from the synthetic dataset was compared with the *BeIR/scifact* [37] dataset.

Accuracy: The *Accuracy@* metric evaluates the frequency of expected chunks appearing in top results, expressed as a percentage. *Accuracy@3* and *Accuracy@5* represent percentages for top 3 and top 5 results, respectively.

Table 2. Accuracy per System

System	Dataset	Re-ranking	Accuracy@3	Accuracy@5
BM25	Synthetic	No	41%	45%
ChromaDB	Synthetic	No	44%	48%
pgvector	Synthetic	No	54%	60%
pgvector – Hybrid	Synthetic	No	59%	65%
ChromaDB	Synthetic	Yes	64%	68%
pgvector	Synthetic	Yes	69%	73%
pgvector – Hybrid	Synthetic	Yes	70%	75%
pgvector – Hybrid	BeIR/scifact	Yes	71%	80%

Compared to BM25, *ChromaDB* [22] improves *Accuracy@5* by 3% (Table 2). *Pgvector* [20] achieves a 10–12% accuracy boost, while its Hybrid Search [21] adds another 5%, totaling 15–17% over *ChromaDB*. Re-ranking increases *ChromaDB*'s accuracy by 20%, but only 10% for *pgvector*'s Hybrid Search as its effect diminishes with better base performances. Based on benchmarks, we integrated *pgvector*'s Hybrid Search with re-ranking into our pipeline, achieving an accuracy of 75% with the synthetic dataset and 80% with *BeIR/scifact*.

5 Conclusion

This study presents a novel architecture for integrating LLMs with RAG into LMS, resulting in a contextualized AILA that delivers enhanced learning experiences. Through a middleware approach, the system seamlessly incorporates LOM, course materials, and related content into a dynamic, modular RAG pipeline capable of context-aware responses.

Real-world evaluation demonstrates both the educational impact and technical robustness. Learners using AILA achieved significantly greater learning gains, with a Hedges' g of 0.92 and normalized gains more than twice those of the control group. Retrieval benchmarks confirmed the system's reliability, with hybrid search and re-ranking reaching up to 80% top-5 accuracy. These results underscore AILA's potential as a scalable and effective learning assistant.

Building on these promising results, future work should explore both pedagogical and technical enhancements. On the pedagogical side, studies should broaden the participant base and investigate AILA's long-term effects on learner autonomy, motivation, and knowledge retention. Technically, AILA could evolve from a reactive assistant to a proactive agent, supported by enhanced control mechanisms that govern input and output interactions with the LLM to ensure safe, relevant, and pedagogically aligned responses. By leveraging learner analytics, particularly xAPI statements already collected, the system could support adaptive scaffolding and personalized feedback. Integrating an xAPI aggregation service would empower learners to monitor their own progress. Finally, features such as multilingual support and virtual avatars could enhance accessibility and engagement, especially in scenario-based and culturally diverse contexts. This work points to a future where scalable intelligent AILA become integral components of inclusive and adaptive educational ecosystems.

Acknowledgments. We would like to express our sincere gratitude to the German Armed Forces, in particular the Army Command and the Army Training Command, for their support of this study.

References

1. Taneja, K., Maiti, P., Kakar, S., Guruprasad, P., Rao, S., Goel, A. K.: Jill Watson: a Virtual Teaching Assistant powered by ChatGPT. arXiv (2024). https://arxiv.org/abs/2405.11070v1
2. Miladi, F., Psyché, V., Lemire, D.: Leveraging GPT-4 for accuracy in education: a comparative study on retrieval-augmented generation in MOOCs. In: Olney, A.M., Chounta, IA., Liu, Z., Santos, O.C., Bittencourt, I.I. (eds.) AIED 2024. CCIS, vol 2150, pp. 427–434 (2024). https://doi.org/10.1007/978-3-031-64315-6_40
3. Neumann, A.T., Yin, Y., Sowe, S., Decker, S., Jarke, M.: An LLM-driven chatbot in higher education for databases and information systems. IEEE Trans. Educ. **68**(1), 103–116 (2025). https://doi.org/10.1109/TE.2024.3467912
4. Radford, A., Wu, J., Child, R., Luan, D., Amodei, D., Sutskever, I.: Language Models are Unsupervised Multitask Learners. OpenAI (2019). https://cdn.openai.com/better-language-models/language_models_are_unsupervised_multitask_learners.pdf
5. Zhang, R., Guo, J., Chen, L., Fan, Y., Cheng, X.: A review on question generation from natural language text. ACM Trans. Inform. Syst. (TOIS) **40**(1), 1–43 (2021)
6. Lewis, P., et al.: Retrieval-Augmented Generation for Knowledge-Intensive NLP Tasks. Adv. Neural. Inf. Process. Syst. **33**, 9459–9474 (2020)
7. Ji, Z., et al.: Survey of Hallucination in Natural Language Generation. arXiv (2022). https://arxiv.org/abs/2202.03629
8. Common Learning Middleware — Vermittler zwischen interoperablen Bildungsinfrastrukturen. https://clm.fraunhofer.de/en/clm-start-en/, Accessed 31 Jan 2025
9. Krauss, C., Streicher, A., Poxleitner, E., Altun, D., Mueller, J., An, T., Mueller, C.: Best-of-breed: service-oriented integration of artificial intelligence in interoperable educational ecosystems. In: Uden, L., Liberona, D. (eds.) LTEC 2023. CCIS, vol. 1830, pp. 267–283. Springer, Cham (2023). https://doi.org/10.1007/978-3-031-34754-2_22
10. Nguyen, T., An, T., Krauss, C.: A middleware for educational ecosystems – rights and access-control management by design. In: Uden, L., Liberona, D. (eds) LTEC 2024. CCIS, vol. 2082. Springer, Cham, pp. 166–178 (2024).https://doi.org/10.1007/978-3-031-61678-5_12
11. Zawacki-Richter, O., Marín, V., Bond, M., Gouverneur, F.: Systematic review of research on artificial intelligence applications in higher education - where are the educators? Int. J. Educ. Technol. High. Educ. **16**, 1–27 (2019). https://doi.org/10.1186/s41239-019-0171-0
12. LLM-as-a-Judge: A Complete Guide to Using LLMs for Evaluations. https://www.evidentlyai.com/llm-guide/llm-as-a-judge, Accessed 31 Oct 2025

13. Willard, B.T., Louf, R.: Efficient Guided Generation for Large Language Models. arXiv (2023). https://arxiv.org/abs/2307.09702
14. Kwon, Wet al.: Efficient Memory Management for Large Language Model Serving with PagedAttention. arXiv (2023). https://arxiv.org/abs/2309.06180
15. Gerganov, G.: GitHub - ggml-org/llama.cpp: LLM Inference in C/C++. GitHub. https://github.com/ggml-org/llama.cpp, . Accessed 31 Oct 2025
16. Roucher, A.: RAG Evaluation - Hugging Face Open-Source AI Cookbook. https://huggingface.co/learn/cookbook/en/rag_evaluation Accessed 31 Oct 2025
17. Brown, D.: Rank-BM25: a collection of BM25 algorithms in python. Zenodo (2020). https://doi.org/10.5281/zenodo.4520057
18. Pgvector: GitHub - pgvector/pgvector: Open-Source Vector Similarity Search for Postgres. GitHub. https://github.com/pgvector/pgvector?tab=readme-ov-file#hybrid-search Accessed 31 Oct 2025
19. Intfloat: Multilingual-e5-large-instruct. Hugging Face. last accessed 2025/10/31, https://huggingface.co/intfloat/multilingual-e5-large-instruct
20. Pgvector: GitHub - pgvector/pgvector: Open-source Vector Similarity Search for Postgres. GitHub. Accessed 31 Oct 2025. https://github.com/pgvector/pgvector/
21. PostgreSQL: The World's Most Advanced Open Source Relational Database. PostgreSQL. https://www.postgresql.org/, Accessed 31 Oct 2025
22. Chroma: Try Chroma - AI Native Vector Database. https://www.trychroma.com/ Accessed 31 Oct 2025
23. Alibaba-NLP: gte-multilingual-reranker-base. Hugging Face. https://huggingface.co/Alibaba-NLP/gte-multilingual-reranker-base Accessed 31 Oct 2025
24. openGPT-X: Teuken-7B-instruct-commercial-v0.4. Hugging Face. https://huggingface.co/openGPT-X/Teuken-7B-instruct-commercial-v0.4 Accessed 31 Oct 2025
25. Ali, M., et al.: Teuken-7B-Base & Teuken-7B-Instruct: Towards European LLMs. arXiv (2024). https://arxiv.org/abs/2410.03730v2
26. Next.js: The React Framework for the Web. https://nextjs.org/ Accessed 31 Oct 2025
27. Moodle: Open-Source Learning Management System. https://moodle.com/ Accessed 31 Oct 2025
28. ILIAS: Open-Source Learning Management System. https://www.ilias.de/ Accessed 31 Oct 2025
29. Anthology Blackboard: The LMS for easier teaching and better learning. https://www.anthology.com/products/teaching-and-learning/learning-effectiveness/blackboard Accessed 31 Oct 2025
30. 1EdTech: Learning Tools Interoperability (LTI) Standard. https://www.1edtech.org/standards/lti Accessed 31 Oct 2025
31. Beaufort, F.: Picture-in-Picture. W3C Working Draft, 16 December (2024). https://www.w3.org/TR/picture-in-picture/ Accessed 31 Oct 2025
32. Instructure: Canvas Learning Management System. https://www.instructure.com/canvas Accessed 31 Oct 2025
33. Hake, R.R.: Interactive-engagement vs. traditional methods: a six-thousand-student survey of mechanics test data for introductory physics courses. Am. J. Phys. **66**, 64 (1998). https://doi.org/10.1119/1.18809
34. Wilcoxon, F.: individual comparisons by ranking methods. Biometrics Bull. **1**(6), 80–83 (1945). https://doi.org/10.2307/3001968
35. Hedges, L.V.: Distribution theory for glass's estimator of effect size and related estimators. J. Educ. Stat. **6**, 107–128 (1981). https://doi.org/10.2307/1164588

36. Mann, H.B., Whitney, D.R.: On a test of whether one of two random variables is stochastically larger than the other. Ann. Math. Stat. **18**, 50–60 (1947). https://doi.org/10.1214/aoms/1177730491
37. Thakur, N., Reimers, N., Rücklé, A., Srivastava, A., Gurevych, I.: BEIR: a heterogeneous benchmark for zero-shot evaluation of information retrieval models. In: Thirty-fifth Conference on Neural Information Processing Systems Datasets and Benchmarks Track (Round 2) (2021). https://openreview.net/forum?id=wCu6T5xFjeJ
38. Muennighoff, N., Tazi, N., Magne, L., Reimers, N.: MTEB: Massive Text Embedding Benchmark. arXiv preprint arXiv:2210.07316 (2022)
39. Enevoldsen, K., et al.: MMTEB: Massive Multilingual Text Embedding Benchmark. *arXiv preprint* arXiv:2502.13595 (2025)

Question–Explanation at the Right Level: Adaptive XAI for Introductory Programming

Boban Vesin[1,2](✉), Anders Robstad[2], Robin Lund Sadun[2], Katerina Mangaroska[1], and Michalis Giannakos[2]

[1] University of South-Eastern Norway, Vestfold, Norway
{boban.vesin,katerina.mangaroska}@usn.no
[2] Norwegian University of Science and Technology, Trondheim, Norway
anders.robstad@live.no, Robinls2000@hotmail.com, michailg@ntnu.no

Abstract. Generative AI can provide timely, individualized explanations, but it remains unclear when learners perceive them as high-quality and engaging, and how they can effectively support textbook-like practice and clarification. We investigate this in CS1 by pairing explainable-AI (XAI) feedback with adaptive questioning: an IRT-based computerized adaptive testing (CAT) engine maintains a productive difficulty range, and post-response explanations clarify concepts. In a mixed-methods, between-subjects study (N=50; one 10-item session), we compared adaptive with random sequencing. Surveys, system logs, and interviews indicated high usability in both groups (SUS $\approx$ 90) and valid alignment of difficulty with ability estimates in the adaptive condition (correlated with prior CS1 achievement). Relative to random sequencing, adaptivity increased perceived usefulness and satisfaction and showed an upward trend in feedback quality; intention to reuse did not reliably differ. Targeted difficulty was associated with longer time-on-task and more thorough reading. Learners described explanations as clear and actionable and requested adjustable depth. Overall, results suggest that an XAI-driven, adaptively sequenced question–explanation loop supports textbook-like practice and immediate clarification by aligning difficulty and delivering concise, concept-referenced explanations. Design implications include preserving difficulty alignment, offering progressive disclosure of explanation depth, and signaling coverage of learning outcomes.

Keywords: Explainable AI · Computerized adaptive testing · Generative AI feedback · Introductory programming

1 Introduction

Assessment is central to higher education as both evaluation and a driver of learning. Formative assessment improves learning by providing feedback that supports reflection, corrects misconceptions, and deepens understanding [5].

B. Fernández-Manjón et al. (Eds.): SETE 2025/ICWL 2025, LNCS 16425, pp. 300–310, 2026.
https://doi.org/10.1007/978-981-92-0042-9_22

It gives students timely, specific guidance that builds self-regulation and confidence, and offers educators actionable insights. Yet massification and digitalization intensify a quality–efficiency trade-off: large cohorts and limited resources push grading over formative feedback, leading to delays or omissions [1]. The core challenge is scalability—delivering timely, meaningful, personalized feedback at scale.

Computerized Adaptive Testing (CAT) tailors items to proficiency, improving precision, efficiency, fairness, and satisfaction [10], but it does not by itself provide formative, actionable feedback. Generative AI (GenAI) can produce concise, context-aware, personalized feedback at scale, potentially easing this bottleneck and supporting diverse trajectories [21]; its value, however, depends on learners perceiving explanations as high quality and actually using them [3].

Although CAT and GenAI each show educational benefits, their combined potential for textbook-like practice and clarification remains underexplored [17]. We investigate this integration with *DaTT-IT*, a CAT prototype augmented with explainable-AI (XAI) feedback in an introductory programming course. An IRT-based engine selects the next item after each response, and an XAI component generates brief, concept-referenced explanations grounded in the correct answer. The premise is that difficulty alignment sustains engagement, while concise explanations enable textbook-like practice and immediate clarification.

Our goal is to examine how an XAI-driven adaptive question-and-feedback system affects learners' *attitudes*, *engagement*, and *usage* in CS1:

1. **RQ1 (Attitudes).** Relative to random sequencing, do learners in the adaptive condition report more positive attitudes toward AI-generated feedback (e.g., perceived usefulness, satisfaction, perceived feedback quality, and trust)?
2. **RQ2 (Engagement).** Does adaptive selection increase engagement with the activity and the feedback (e.g., time-on-task, feedback dwell time and open rates, self-reported engagement, and intention to reuse)?
3. **RQ3 (Use).** To what extent do learners use the explanations to diagnose errors and plan next steps—and is this extent greater under adaptivity?

We conducted a between-subjects experiment in CS1 (N=50): participants completed a single 10-item session under adaptive (IRT-based) or random sequencing. We triangulated post-session surveys, system logs, and interviews to evaluate attitudes, engagement, and usage in the context of textbook-like practice and clarification.

Findings indicate that aligning item difficulty with proficiency, together with concise, concept-referenced explanations, supports textbook-like practice and immediate clarification. Relative to random sequencing, adaptivity increased perceived usefulness and satisfaction and was associated with greater engagement at appropriately challenging items. Design implications include preserving difficulty alignment, providing progressive disclosure of explanation depth, and signaling coverage of learning outcomes. Given the brief, single-session design and the absence of direct learning-outcome measures, we treat results as exploratory and focus on how the approach can practically support textbook-like practice and clarification in CS1.

2 Related Work

Recent advances in generative AI for education promise actionable, learning-enhancing feedback during classroom use, yet it remains unclear how such feedback—when paired with adaptive sequencing—can best *complement* textbook-like practice and clarification in introductory programming [6,8,13]. In educational XAI, the emphasis is on concise, concept-referenced rationales that learners can trust and act upon rather than on exposing internal mechanics [2]. However, the conditions under which such explanations are perceived as high quality, sustain engagement, and are actually used are still being established [12,18]. Building on systems that integrate item selection with post-response explanations [16], this paper tests whether an XAI-driven, adaptive question–feedback loop can function as a *lightweight, scalable complement* to textbook-like practice and immediate clarification, focusing on learners' attitudes, engagement, and concrete use of explanations.

Formative feedback is most effective when timely, specific, and actionable [13]. In intelligent tutoring systems, stepwise hints and worked examples support error diagnosis and conceptual understanding [8,20]; we follow this tradition by delivering generative explanations immediately after each response, targeting practice and clarification while preserving the immediacy and individualization of tutoring feedback. To improve reliability and perceived quality, we constrain output format and ground explanations in the item's verified correct answer [16].

In education, XAI aims to provide human-interpretable, concept-referenced explanations that clarify *why* an answer is correct or incorrect and *how* to improve, rather than exposing model internals [7,18]. Learners value concise, proficiency-sensitive rationales; accordingly, our solution offers adjustable granularity—from brief to extended detail [16,19]. We operationalize XAI at the point of use: prompts include full item context, the learner's selection, and the ground-truth answer, anchoring explanations in verified content, reducing fabrication, and retaining personalization [16].

2.1 Adaptivity and Computerized Adaptive Testing

Adaptive sequencing with item response theory (IRT) selects items informative for a learner's current proficiency, improving measurement efficiency and keeping tasks within a productive challenge band [9]. Mature CAT tooling—e.g., `catR` for selection/estimation and `mirt` for calibration/modeling—supports deployment [4,11]. We hypothesize that tighter alignment between item difficulty and estimated ability increases engagement with explanations and perceived usefulness, aligning with theories that appropriate challenge deepens processing [14,16]. Positioned at the XAI–CAT intersection, our approach differs from non-adaptive textbooks and classic ITS (which often require fine-grained step models): adaptivity and explanation operate in a lightweight loop scalable to course-level practice.

In contrast to systems offering only post-hoc hints or generic feedback, we combine an IRT engine that ensures appropriate difficulty with XAI-generated, concept-focused explanations immediately after each response. Prototype results indicate strong usability, effective alignment between task difficulty and learner ability, positive perceptions of usefulness and satisfaction, and qualitative evidence of active engagement with explanations for understanding and self-correction. These findings suggest an integrated mechanism that serves as a *lightweight, scalable complement* to textbook-like practice and conceptual reinforcement in introductory programming [16].

3 Methods

We used a mixed-methods design—a between-subjects experiment paired with qualitative interviews. Participants were randomly assigned to *adaptive* (IRT-based CAT selection) or *random* (uniform sampling from the same bank) conditions. We test whether an XAI-driven question–explanation loop supports textbook-like practice and immediate clarification in CS1.

3.1 Research Design and Questions

We address one overarching question: *To what extent can an explainable-AI–driven, adaptive question–feedback system support textbook-like practice and immediate clarification in introductory programming?* Three sub-questions operationalize this aim using post-test constructs, system logs, and interviews.

RQ1 (Attitudes). We compare conditions on Likert-scale *Usefulness*, *Satisfaction*, and *Trust*. Internal consistency is assessed via McDonald's ω; assumptions via Shapiro–Wilk and Levene. Between-group differences use independent t-tests or Mann–Whitney U as appropriate; effect sizes are Hedges' g or Cliff's δ with 95% CIs. Holm's procedure adjusts p-values across attitudinal subscales. *Trust* shows no reliable difference; interviews contextualize clarity/credibility.

RQ2 (Engagement). Behavioral outcomes include total time-on-task, mean feedback dwell, number of feedback views, and proportion of items with feedback opened; self-reports cover in-session engagement and intention to reuse. We use t-tests or Mann–Whitney U with effect sizes and 95% CIs. As robustness, count outcomes are examined with GLMs (Poisson/negative binomial if overdispersed), and per-item measures with linear mixed-effects models (random participant intercepts). Prior achievement (CS1 grade) serves as a covariate in robustness checks. GLM/LMM coefficients and CIs appear in the Appendix.

RQ3 (Use). Learning use is captured by post-test items on diagnosing errors and planning study actions, plus a behavioral proxy (proportion of items with feedback opened). Group differences use t-tests or Mann–Whitney U with effect sizes and CIs. As robustness, item-level feedback-opening is modeled with logistic mixed-effects (random participant intercept). We report group-level proportions/contrasts in the text and provide model coefficients/CIs in the Appendix.

Interviews are thematically coded to surface concrete study behaviors and mechanisms by which explanations inform next steps(Fig. 1).

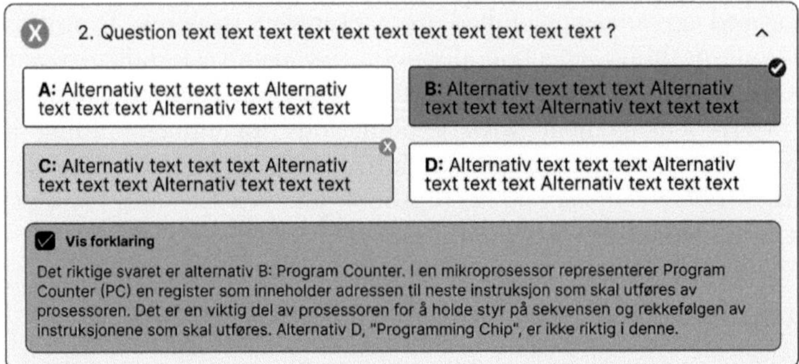

Fig. 1. User-facing explanation displayed after each response in both conditions

The working hypothesis was that the adaptive, XAI-based condition would increase the perceived value and effectiveness of feedback, thereby supporting textbook-like practice and immediate clarification in CS1 [16].

4 System and Intervention

We operationalized the "AI-as-Book" as a three-tier web system (Fig. 2) that (i) diagnoses mastery, (ii) sequences items at appropriate difficulty, and (iii) provides brief, concept-referenced explanations after each response. A uniform web front end delivered items; a middle tier orchestrated administration, logging, and LLM calls; and a dedicated service implemented IRT-based CAT to select the next item in the adaptive condition (uniform random in control). After each response, the selector returned the next item, and the XAI module generated an explanation; all prompts, outputs, item IDs, and dwell times were logged for analysis [4,11,15,16].

Item Bank and Calibration. The bank contained 248 multiple-choice CS1 items (2014–2024), deduplicated and lightly edited, mapped to the course syllabus. Items received initial difficulty tags (−3 to +3) and were refined using preparatory responses (perceived difficulty and correctness) to mitigate cold-start effects prior to CAT administration [16].

Grounded XAI Feedback. Explanations are *implemented*, not merely argued, via a grounded generation pipeline: (i) inputs include the whole item stem, options, the learner's choice, and the verified correct answer (no external retrieval); (ii) a structured prompt elicits a concise concept tag, a brief rationale, and an actionable next step under a length cap; (iii) middleware guardrails enforce low temperature, schema checks, safe fallbacks, and progressive disclosure in the UI (short preview with optional expansion). Prompts were iteratively tuned until stable, low-error runs were obtained on a held-out set [16].

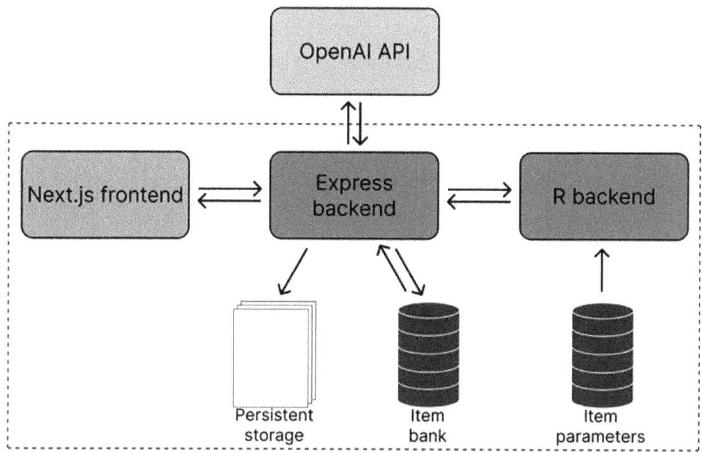

Fig. 2. System architecture of the "AI-as-Book" intervention showing calibrated item bank, adaptive (CAT) vs. random selection, response capture, and grounded XAI feedback generation.

4.1 Participants

Fifty NTNU undergraduates who had completed and passed CS1 (ITGK)—primarily in their first or second year—were recruited voluntarily via course announcements. To align with an item bank calibrated for early CS1 proficiency, students in year $\geq$3 were excluded. A subset of n=10 volunteered for semi-structured interviews [16].

4.2 Setting and Procedure

Sessions took place in a reserved room with a standardized workstation. After informed consent, participants received a unique code linking surveys and the system, enabling concealed random assignment to adaptive (IRT–CAT) or random sequencing; both participants and researchers were blind to condition. Each completed a 10-item test, reviewed results and explanations, and then a post-test questionnaire; volunteers additionally completed a short interview. Sessions ended with debriefing and a reminder of withdrawal rights [16].

4.3 Measures

Data came from post-test questionnaires, system logs, and semi-structured interviews, aligned with the three RQs. Quantitative constructs used 7-point Likert scales (item means). For descriptive comparison only, we labeled levels as low (< 4), moderate (4–5.5), and high (> 5.5); these labels were not inferential cut-offs.

Attitudes. Perceptions of AI-generated explanations were measured with adapted Likert scales for *Usefulness*, *Satisfaction*, and *Trust* [16]. Interviews probed clarity, perceived quality, and comparisons to textbook explanations.

Engagement. Logs captured time-on-task, feedback dwell time, and the number of feedback views; questionnaires measured in-session engagement and intention to reuse. For descriptive purposes, participants above the median on either behavioral or self-reported engagement were considered highly engaged.

Usage. Questionnaires asked whether explanations were used to understand mistakes, guide corrections, and plan study strategies. Interviews clarified how learners applied feedback and whether they viewed the system as complementing a textbook. The behavioral proxy was the proportion of items with feedback opened.

Taken together, these quantitative and qualitative measures assess whether the XAI system supports textbook-like practice and immediate clarification.

5 Results

System usability was uniformly high and comparable across conditions (SUS: control = 90.7, adaptive = 89.3), so downstream differences are unlikely due to interface issues. In the adaptive group (n=23), CAT ability estimates correlated with prior CS1 grade (Spearman ρ=0.588, one-tailed p=0.002; Pearson r=0.501, p=0.007), supporting the validity of the adaptive engine.

5.1 RQ1: Attitudes Toward XAI Explanations

Attitudinal constructs favored the adaptive condition on key dimensions. *Usefulness* was higher under adaptivity (M=6.14±0.51 vs. 5.82±0.59; $t(48)$=2.04, one-sided p=0.023, $d\approx$0.58) and *Feedback* quality trended higher (M=6.26 ± 0.49 vs. 5.97±0.63; $t(48)$=1.84, one-sided p=0.036, $d\approx$0.52; 95% CI included 0) (Table 1). *Satisfaction* was also higher (adaptive 6.47 ± 0.56 vs. random 6.12 ± 0.67; Mann–Whitney U=569.5, $z=-2.26$, p=0.024), whereas *Intention* did not differ (adaptive 6.00 ± 0.83 vs. random 5.72 ± 0.77; p=0.183) (Table 2). Overall means near the top of the 7-point scale ($\approx$ 6) indicate generally positive attitudes. Interviews described explanations as clear and helpful, with occasional caution about rare inaccuracies, echoing the quantitative pattern [16]. Trust showed no reliable between-condition difference and is summarized briefly.

5.2 RQ2: Engagement with the Activity and the Feedback

Behavioral and correlational evidence indicated deeper participation when item difficulty aligned with learners' proficiency. Within the adaptive group (n = 23 with complete logs), higher *Usefulness* aligned with longer time on task

Table 1. T-test results for variables Feedback quality and Usefulness

Construct	Mean (SD)		t(df)	p
	Control gr. [N = 25]	Exp. gr. [N = 25]		
Feedback quality	5.97 (0.63)	6.26 (0.49)	1.84 (48)	.036*
Usefulness	5.82 (0.59)	6.14 (0.51)	2.04 (48)	.023*

*: Indicates p<0.05 (significant result).

Table 2. Mann-Whitney U-test results of the comparison of the mean values of each factor between the experimental and control groups

Construct	U	z	p
Intention	244.500	-1.33	0.183
Satisfaction	569.500	-2.26	0.024*

*: Indicates p<0.05 (significant result).

(Pearson $r = 0.386$, $p = 0.034$), and time on task increased with estimated ability ($r = 0.371$, $p = 0.034$), consistent with appropriately challenging items prompting more sustained interaction [16]. Interviews converged on the same mechanism: "selective reading due to inappropriate difficulty" appeared only in the non-adaptive group (3 references from 1 participant) and not in adaptive (0/0); "selective reading due to not currently taking the course" occurred 2/2 (adaptive) vs. 3/3 (non-adaptive); "selective reading due to responding correctly" 4/4 vs. 3/3; and "feedback positively impacting retention" 3/3 vs. 5/2 (counts/unique participants).

5.3 RQ3: Use of Explanations for Learning

Self-reports and interviews indicated that learners used the explanations to diagnose errors and plan subsequent study steps, with the adaptive condition more frequently emphasizing that explanations matched the learner's level. A dedicated "replaceability" notion emerged qualitatively: participants compared the explanations favorably to textbook-style prose but expressed heterogeneous preferences for depth, suggesting value in offering adjustable granularity (brief *vs.* extended) to support different proficiency levels [16]. Although direct between-group differences in fine-grained "use" behaviors (e.g., per-item opening rates) were not the primary focus of the original analysis, the observed pattern of high satisfaction, perceived usefulness, and time-on-task associations under adaptivity supports substantive uptake of the explanations during practice (Table 3).

5.4 Synthesis

Taken together, (i) high and comparable usability across conditions, (ii) valid item difficulty - proficiency alignment, (iii) stronger attitudes on usefulness and

Table 3. Coding matrix for "*Perceived feedback quality*"

	Comprehension of feedback	Understanding through feedback	Quality of feedback positively impacting learning	Quality of feedback negatively impacting learning
Adaptive	10 (5*)	9 (5*)	8 (3*)	6 (2*)
Non-adaptive	5 (3*)	8 (4*)	3 (3*)	12 (2*)

Notes. Numbers indicate the count of references to each code. Asterisk (*) indicates the number of unique participants referenced.

satisfaction with supportive qualitative testimony, and (iv) engagement patterns aligned with deeper interaction under adaptivity provide converging evidence that an XAI-driven, adaptively sequenced question–explanation loop can act as a lightweight, scalable complement for textbook-like practice and conceptual clarification in CS1 [16]. Remaining design implications include the potential benefit of controllable explanation depth to accommodate heterogeneous preferences.

6 Discussion

Results indicate that an XAI-driven, adaptively sequenced question–explanation loop can support textbook-like functions—adaptive practice and immediate clarification—in an introductory CS course. Usability was uniformly high, ruling out interface confounds, and CAT ability estimates correlated with prior achievement, supporting the validity of difficulty alignment. Compared with random sequencing, the adaptive condition yielded higher usefulness and satisfaction; interviewees consistently described the explanations as clear and helpful. Engagement patterns (time-on-task and attention to explanations) align with the mechanism in which appropriately challenging items elicit deeper interaction, which in turn supports perceived value [16]. We therefore position the approach as a *lightweight, scalable complement* to existing course materials for practice and clarification.

Qualitative themes reinforce this mechanism: perceived question difficulty (including a meaningful difficulty range) shaped engagement with feedback; when items were trivial or opaque, participants reported selective reading and occasional weariness, whereas appropriately challenging items promoted thorough reading, better perceived feedback quality, and improved understanding with some reported retention benefits. Attitudes and preferences for question difficulty and feedback depth varied across learners, suggesting the need for adjustable explanations. Taken together, these themes outline a pathway from difficulty alignment → engagement with feedback → perceived quality → attitudes and reported learning use.

Three implications follow. First, *difficulty–proficiency alignment* is central: adaptivity that keeps items within a productive challenge band increases both engagement and the perceived value of explanations. Second, *adjustable explanation depth* (progressive disclosure) accommodates heterogeneous preferences—short, concept-tagged summaries with optional deeper dives. Third, *coverage signaling* via lightweight indicators of syllabus outcomes helps the system emulate textbook-style navigation and make progress transparent.

Limitations. A single-institution, post-course sample (N=50) limits generalizability and may introduce recall/motivation bias. The fixed 10-item session constrains behavioral inference. Item-bank calibration based on preparatory responses may retain noise; although adaptive ability estimates correlated with prior achievement, finer topic-level calibration is needed. *No direct learning-outcome measures were collected*, so claims are limited to attitudes, engagement, and reported/observed use.

7 Conclusion

The explainable-AI system, when combined with adaptive item selection, fostered more positive learner attitudes (e.g., perceived usefulness and satisfaction) and engagement patterns indicative of deeper interaction, while maintaining high levels of usability. In sum, our findings indicate that an XAI-driven, adaptively sequenced question–explanation loop can act as a *lightweight, scalable complement* for textbook-like practice and concept clarification in introductory programming courses. Future design refinements should emphasize alignment of item difficulty with learner proficiency, adjustable levels of explanation depth, and transparent mapping to intended learning outcomes.

Acknowledgments. The research is supported by the UTFORSK project of the Norwegian Directorate for Higher Education and Skills (HK-dir), project number: UTF-2021/10186.

References

1. Ahmad, M., Ravi, P., Karger, D., Facciotti, M.: How adding metacognitive requirements in support of ai feedback in practice exams transforms student learning behaviors. In: Proceedings of the 2025 ACM Conference on Learning at Scale, pp. 1–10. ACM (2025)
2. Baruah, B., Jahani, M., Ward, T.: Exploring ethical awareness and learning impact: a study on the use of chatgpt and generative ai in higher education. In: 2025 IEEE Global Engineering Education Conference (EDUCON). IEEE (2025)
3. Berg, J., Repstad, Ø., Serkland, T.: Student perspectives on ai-supported formative assessment in pharmacology. British J. Clin. Pharmacol. (2025)
4. Chalmers, R.P.: mirt: a multidimensional item response theory package for the R environment. J. Statist. Softw. **48**(6), 1–29 (2012). https://doi.org/10.18637/jss.v048.i06
5. Chen, Y., Ma, L., Pirzada, P., Chai, K.K.: Evaluating a guided personalised learning model in undergraduate engineering education: a data-driven approach to student-centred pedagogy. Educ. Sci. **15**(7), 925 (2025)

6. Droulers, M., Krautloher, A., Shaeri, S.: Interactive oral assessment: co-existence of formative and summative purposes. Teaching Higher Educ. (2025)
7. Ilić, M., Keković, G., Mikić, V., Mangaroska, K., Kopanja, L., Vesin, B.: Predicting student performance in a programming tutoring system using ai and filtering techniques. IEEE Trans. Learn. Technol. **17**, 1891–1905 (2024)
8. Lee, S.S., Moore, R.L.: Harnessing generative ai (genai) for automated feedback in higher education: a systematic review. Online Learning **28**(3), 82–104 (2024)
9. van der Linden, W.J., Glas, C.A.W. (eds.): Elements of Adaptive Testing. Springer, New York (2010). https://doi.org/10.1007/978-0-387-85461-8
10. Liu, Q., Zhuang, Y., Bi, H., Huang, Z., Huang, W., Li, J.: Survey of computerized adaptive testing: A machine learning perspective. arXiv preprint arXiv:2404.00712 (2024)
11. Magis, D., Raîche, G.: catr: an R package for computerized adaptive testing. J. Statist. Softw. **48**(20), 1–19 (2012). https://doi.org/10.18637/jss.v048.i20
12. Mangaroska, K., Larssen, K., Amundsen, A., Vesin, B., Giannakos, M.: Understanding engagement through game learning analytics and design elements: insights from a word game case study. In: Proceedings of the 14th Learning Analytics and Knowledge Conference, pp. 305–315 (2024)
13. Meyer, J., et al.: Using llms to bring evidence-based feedback into the classroom: Ai-generated feedback increases secondary students' text revision, motivation, and positive emotions. Comput. Educ. Artifi. Intell. **6**, 100199 (2024)
14. Mikić, V., Keković, G., Mangaroska, K., Ilić, M., Kopanja, L., Vesin, B.: Exploring learner engagement in e-learning environments: a predictive analytics perspective. Inter. J. Hum.–Comput. Interact., 1–24 (2025)
15. Possaghi, I., et al.: Integrating multi-modal learning analytics dashboard in k-12 education: insights for enhancing orchestration and teacher decision-making. Smart Learn. Environ. **12**(1), 1–34 (2025)
16. Robstad, A., Sadun, R.L.: DaTT-IT: Exploring the Effect of Combining Generative AI-Generated Feedback with Computerized Adaptive Testing. Master's thesis, Norwegian University of Science and Technology (NTNU), Trondheim, Norway (2024), master's thesis
17. Trevisan, O., Baiata, C., Gabbi, E., Luzzi, D.: From literature to patterns: a scoping review of blended learning assessment. In: EDULEARN25 Proceedings. IATED (2025)
18. Türkmen, G.: The review of studies on explainable artificial intelligence in educational research (2019–2024). J. Educ. Comput. Res. (2025)
19. Vuuren-Cassar, V.: Students' assessment experience in higher education: a trial of summative audio feedback. In: EDULEARN25 Proceedings. IATED (2025)
20. Wang, Z., Ng, J., Lo, E., Hu, X.: Advancing virtual reality creation in maker education with learning analytics and generative artificial intelligence. In: AI STEAM Conference Proceedings. CUHK (2025)
21. Zapata-Rivera, D., Torre, I., Lee, C.S., et al.: Generative ai in education. Front. Artifi. Intell. **7**, 1532896 (2024)

Workshop AIoT-MAPD

SAUNet: A Bio-inspired Spiking Attention U-Net for Energy-Efficient Semantic Segmentation with Applications to IoT-Enabled Assessment Systems

Ameer Tamoor Khan[1(✉)], Muhammad Ramzan[2], Aquil Mirza Mohammed[3], Xinwei Cao[4], and Shuai Li[5]

[1] Department of Plant and Environmental Sciences, University of Copenhagen, Copenhagen, Denmark
ameer.tamoor.khan@sund.ku.dk
[2] Department of Information Technology, University of Haripur, Haripur, Pakistan
[3] Department of Computing, The Hong Kong Polytechnic University, Hong Kong, Hong Kong
aquilmirza.mohammed@polyu.edu.hk
[4] Department of Accounting, Jiangnan University, Wuxi, China
xwcao@jiangnan.edu.cn
[5] Faculty of Information Technology and Electrical Engineering, University of Oulu, Oulu, Finland
shuai.li@oulu.fi

Abstract. The deployment of AI in IoT environments demands energy-efficient computational paradigms for resource-constrained edge devices. We present **SAUNet**, a bio-inspired Spiking Attention U-Net architecture for energy-efficient semantic segmentation. Unlike conventional ANNs using dense continuous-valued activations, SAUNet integrates Leaky Integrate-and-Fire (LIF) neurons with surrogate gradient learning, enabling event-driven temporally-aware computation. SAUNet was evaluated on the PlantDoc leaf disease segmentation dataset across temporal windows ($\boldsymbol{T = 6, 8, 10}$) against standard Attention U-Net (AUNet). Results show SAUNet$_{T=10}$ achieves Dice coefficient 0.8062 and IoU 0.6822, while reducing energy consumption by 88% versus AUNet. Temporal analysis confirms progressive prediction refinement over discrete time steps. These findings establish SAUNet as a scalable energy-aware neuromorphic architecture suitable for IoT-enabled educational assessment, medical imaging, agricultural monitoring, and edge AI systems requiring high accuracy with low energy budgets.

Keywords: Spiking Neural Networks · Bio-Inspired Computing · Neuromorphic Computing · IoT Systems · Energy-Efficient AI · Edge Computing

B. Fernández-Manjón et al. (Eds.): SETE 2025/ICWL 2025, LNCS 16425, pp. 313–324, 2026.
https://doi.org/10.1007/978-981-92-0042-9_23

1 Introduction

IoT deployments across educational technology, medical imaging, precision agriculture, and industrial monitoring demand energy-efficient AI systems for resource-constrained edge devices [1,2]. Traditional ANNs utilize dense computations with continuous-valued activations, creating substantial energy overhead limiting edge device applicability [3,4].

Spiking Neural Networks (SNNs) offer a bio-inspired alternative processing information through discrete spike events when membrane potentials exceed thresholds, enabling temporally sparse event-driven computation [5,6]. This reduces power consumption significantly, making SNNs attractive for energy-constrained IoT environments [7,8].

Bio-inspired optimization algorithms like Beetle Antennae Search [9,10] and Eagle Perching Optimizer [11] demonstrate how biological principles guide efficient computational systems for robotics [12,13] and optimization [14,15]. Similarly, SNNs leverage biological neural computation for energy-efficient IoT processing.

Despite advantages, SNN application to complex vision tasks faces challenges: non-differentiable spike functions, temporal dynamics complexity, and limited training methodologies [16]. Recent surrogate gradient advances enable deep spiking architectures competing with ANNs [17–19].

We introduce SAUNet, a comprehensive bio-inspired Spiking Attention U-Net for semantic segmentation with broad IoT applicability. SAUNet employs LIF neurons with ATan surrogate gradients throughout encoder-decoder pathways, enabling temporal feature integration while preserving energy efficiency. The key innovation integrates spiking attention mechanisms within U-Net framework, focusing computational resources on salient spatial features while maintaining temporal dynamics [20,21].

Our contributions: (1) Novel bio-inspired spiking architecture integrating attention within U-Net for energy-efficient segmentation; (2) Spiking attention modules leveraging sparse spatiotemporal encoding; (3) Comprehensive validation showing 88% energy reduction with competitive performance; (4) Detailed temporal analysis revealing progressive prediction refinement; (5) New paradigm for energy-aware IoT AI systems.

2 Methods

2.1 Dataset and Preprocessing

We employed the **PlantDoc Leaf Disease Segmentation Dataset** [22], which consists of **2,940 RGB leaf images** and their corresponding **binary segmentation masks**. The dataset is divided into **2,646 images for training** and **294 images for testing**, ensuring a balanced distribution for model development and evaluation (Fig. 2).

Representative samples from the dataset are illustrated in Fig. 1, where the *upper row* depicts RGB images exhibiting a wide range of disease symptoms across different plant species, while the *lower row* shows the associated binary masks that precisely delineate infected regions. The diversity of disease types, leaf textures, and imaging conditions demonstrates the dataset's comprehensiveness for training robust and generalizable segmentation models.

For preprocessing, all images and masks were standardized to a resolution of **640 × 640 pixels** for evaluation and subsequently **resized to 128 × 128** during training to accommodate temporal simulation constraints and reduce computational overhead. The preprocessing pipeline also incorporated extensive **data augmentation** to enhance model robustness and prevent overfitting. Augmentation techniques included:

- Random rotations within ±15°,
- Horizontal and vertical flipping,
- Scaling and cropping operations,
- Brightness and contrast adjustments within ±20%,
- Grayscale conversion (10%) to simulate illumination variation,
- Contrast Limited Adaptive Histogram Equalization (CLAHE) for improved local contrast,
- Gaussian blur and median filtering to reduce sensor noise and smooth texture variations.

This combination of standardized preprocessing and diverse augmentation strategies provided a strong foundation for effective model training and reliable evaluation.

2.2 Architecture Design

SAUNet employs discrete-time spiking neurons governed by the Leaky Integrate-and-Fire (LIF) model [23], as illustrated in Fig. 3. The LIF neuron simplifies the biological neuron dynamics by integrating the membrane potential over time and triggering a spike when the threshold is exceeded:

$$\tau_m \frac{du(t)}{dt} = -(u(t) - u_{rest}) + R \cdot I(t) \tag{1}$$

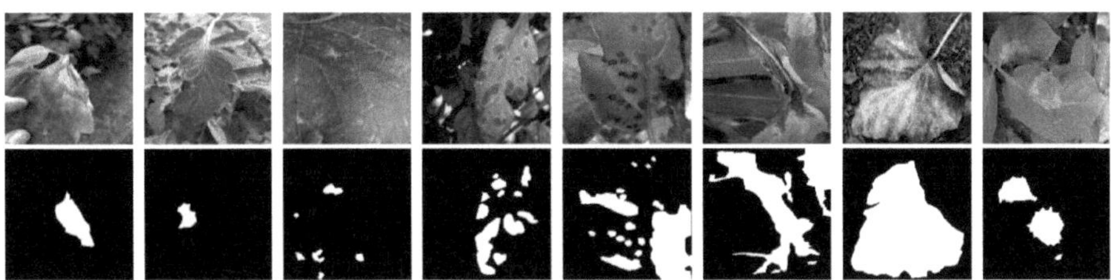

Fig. 1. Representative samples from the PlantDoc leaf disease segmentation dataset. The upper row displays RGB leaf images exhibiting various disease symptoms across different plant species, while the lower row presents the corresponding binary segmentation masks that precisely delineate infected regions. The diversity of disease manifestations and imaging conditions demonstrates the comprehensive nature of the dataset for training robust segmentation models.

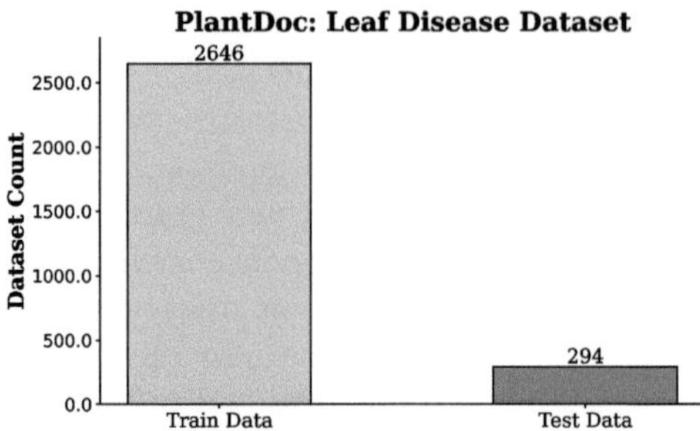

Fig. 2. Statistical distribution of the PlantDoc leaf disease segmentation dataset showing the training and testing partitions. The dataset comprises 2,646 training images and 294 testing images, providing a balanced distribution for model development and evaluation procedures.

where $u(t)$ denotes the membrane potential, τ_m is the membrane time constant, u_{rest} represents the resting potential, R is the membrane resistance, and $I(t)$ is the input current. When $u(t)$ surpasses the firing threshold u_{th}, the neuron emits a spike and resets, enabling event-based computation with temporal encoding. As shown in Fig. 3, the LIF model achieves a balance between biological realism and computational efficiency compared to the more complex Hodgkin–Huxley neuron and the simplified artificial neuron model.

The overall architecture of SAUNet follows a **symmetric encoder–decoder structure** (Fig. 5), where temporal spike dynamics are integrated within convolutional and attention modules. The network comprises three modular components, detailed in Fig. 4:

1. **SNN Convolutional Block:** Consists of two convolutional layers followed by batch normalization and LIF neuron activation using ATan surrogate gradients to maintain differentiability.
2. **SNN Up-Convolutional Block:** Performs spatial upsampling through bilinear interpolation, convolution, and spike-based activation to reconstruct higher-resolution feature maps.
3. **SNN Attention Block:** Computes attention weights using spiking neurons and sigmoid activation, modulating skip connection features via learnable scaling factors for energy-efficient selective feature enhancement.

Temporal integration operates across $T \in \{6, 8, 10\}$ discrete time steps, allowing membrane potentials to accumulate over time and refine spatial-temporal feature representations. Input pixel intensities are converted into spike trains via rate coding, ensuring compatibility with spiking neuron dynamics. Within the encoder (Fig. 5), feature maps are progressively downsampled ($640 \times 640 \rightarrow 320 \times 320 \rightarrow 160 \times 160 \rightarrow 80 \times 80 \rightarrow 40 \times 40$), while the decoder mirrors this hierarchy to reconstruct the segmentation output using skip connections and spiking attention mechanisms.

Temporal integration operates across $T \in \{6, 8, 10\}$ time steps, accumulating membrane potentials to refine representations. Spike encoding converts pixel

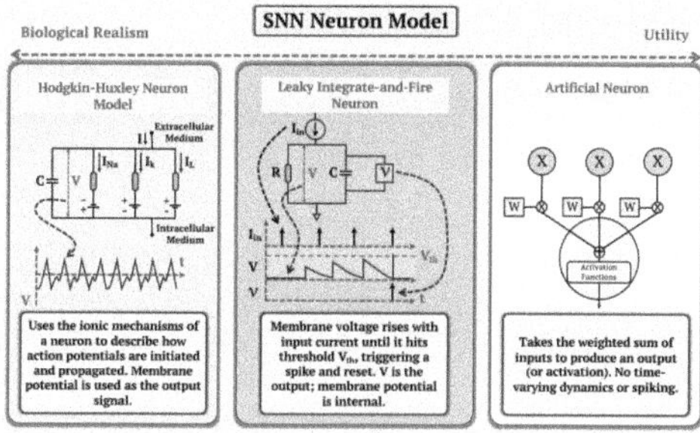

Fig. 3. Comparative analysis of neural models across the spectrum of biological realism and computational utility. The Hodgkin–Huxley model provides detailed ion-channel dynamics with high biological fidelity. The Leaky Integrate-and-Fire (LIF) model, employed in SAUNet, simplifies spiking behavior through membrane potential integration and thresholding while maintaining essential temporal dynamics. The artificial neuron model abstracts temporal considerations, relying on weighted summation and activation functions for computational efficiency.

intensities to temporal spike trains using rate coding. The encoder reduces spatial resolution ($640 \times 640 \rightarrow 320 \times 320 \rightarrow 160 \times 160 \rightarrow 80 \times 80 \rightarrow 40 \times 40$) while increasing feature channels. The decoder mirrors this using skip connections with attention mechanisms.

2.3 Training Configuration

Models trained independently per temporal configuration using Adam optimizer (learning rate 1×10^{-4}), cosine annealing schedule, batch size 8, 100 epochs with

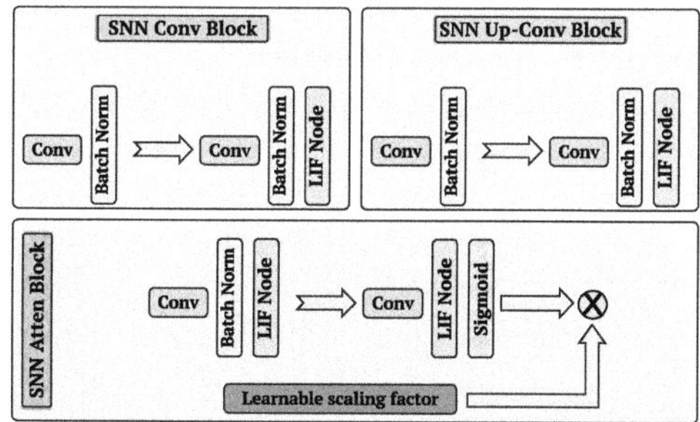

Fig. 4. Modular architectural components of SAUNet. The SNN Convolutional Block integrates sequential convolutional layers with batch normalization followed by LIF neuron activation. The SNN Up-Convolutional Block performs spatial upsampling through bilinear interpolation, convolution, and spike-based activation. The SNN Attention Block computes attention weights using spiking neurons and modulates skip connection features through learnable scaling factors, enabling selective feature enhancement within the energy-efficient spiking paradigm.

early stopping. ATan surrogate gradients enable backpropagation through non-differentiable spikes [24,25]. Network states reset per forward pass preventing temporal dependencies [26]. Training on Google Colab (NVIDIA T4 GPU, 15 GB RAM). Complete hyperparameters in Table 1.

Evaluation metrics: Dice coefficient (F1-score), IoU, precision, recall. Performance assessed across temporal configurations examining integration window effects on accuracy, computational efficiency, energy consumption, and temporal progression.

Table 1. Training specifications

Parameter	Value
GPU	NVIDIA T4
Optimizer	Adam
Learning Rate	1×10^{-4}
Batch Size	8
Epochs	100
Time Steps T	$\{6, 8, 10\}$
Training Size	128×128 px
Test Size	640×640 px
Dataset	PlantDoc (2,646/294)

3 Results

3.1 Quantitative Performance

Table 2 compares SAUNet across temporal configurations against AUNet baseline. AUNet achieves highest performance (Dice 0.8486, IoU 0.7424). SAUNet$_{T=10}$ demonstrates competitive performance (Dice 0.8062, IoU 0.6822), only 5.0% and 8.1% reduction respectively. Notably, SAUNet$_{T=10}$ surpasses AUNet in precision (0.8691 vs 0.8519), indicating superior capability for clean predictions with reduced false positives.

Temporal progression reveals clear improvements with increased integration windows. SAUNet$_{T=6}$ exhibits insufficient performance (Dice 0.6511), while SAUNet$_{T=8}$ approaches optimal configuration (Dice 0.8050). Training dynamics (Fig. 6) show stable convergence for SAUNet$_{T=10}$, closely approaching AUNet levels.

3.2 Energy Efficiency

Figure 7 demonstrates substantial efficiency advantages. SAUNet$_{T=10}$ provides 88% energy reduction versus AUNet while maintaining competitive performance.

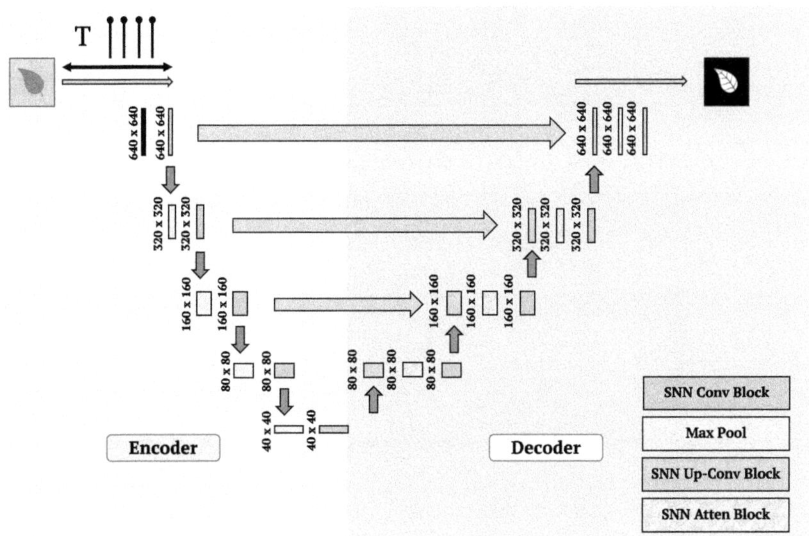

Fig. 5. SAUNet architecture: symmetric encoder–decoder with LIF neuron dynamics and ATan surrogate gradients. Input undergoes temporal spike encoding and propagates through $T \in \{6, 8, 10\}$ time steps. The encoder progressively downsamples ($640 \times 640 \rightarrow 40 \times 40$), and the decoder reconstructs the spatial resolution using skip connections and spiking attention.

Table 2. Quantitative performance comparison

Model	Loss	Dice	IoU	Precision	Recall	Accuracy
AUNet	0.164	0.849	0.742	0.852	0.853	0.948
SAUNet$_{T=6}$	0.243	0.651	0.492	0.867	0.534	0.900
SAUNet$_{T=8}$	0.204	0.805	0.677	0.839	0.782	0.929
SAUNet$_{T=10}$	0.191	0.806	0.682	0.869	0.759	0.940

This stems from sparse activation patterns where operations occur only on spike events. Activation sparsity analysis confirms SAUNet maintains <15% activation rates across layers, validating energy efficiency through spike-based computation.

Statistical testing confirms performance differences between SAUNet$_{T=10}$ and SAUNet$_{T=8}$ non-significant ($p > 0.05$), both viable depending on constraints. Gap versus SAUNet$_{T=6}$ highly significant ($p < 0.001$), emphasizing adequate temporal integration importance.

3.3 Temporal Progression

Figure 8 reveals progressive refinement across time steps. Initial steps ($t = 1, 2$) produce sparse noisy activations evolving to coherent accurate masks by final

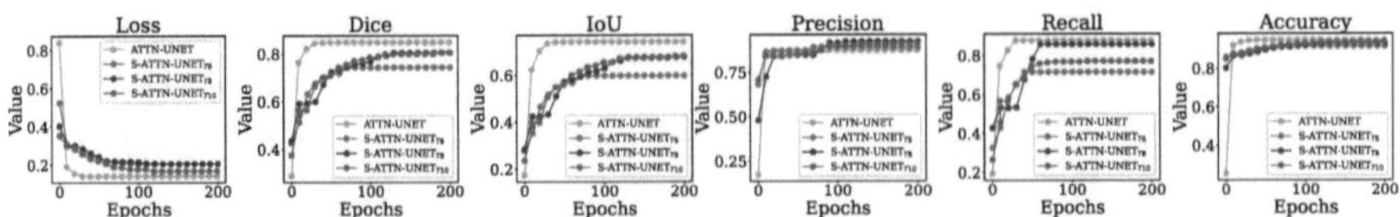

Fig. 6. Training performance over 200 epochs. SAUNet configurations show stable convergence, with $\text{SAUNet}_{T=10}$ achieving optimal balance across metrics

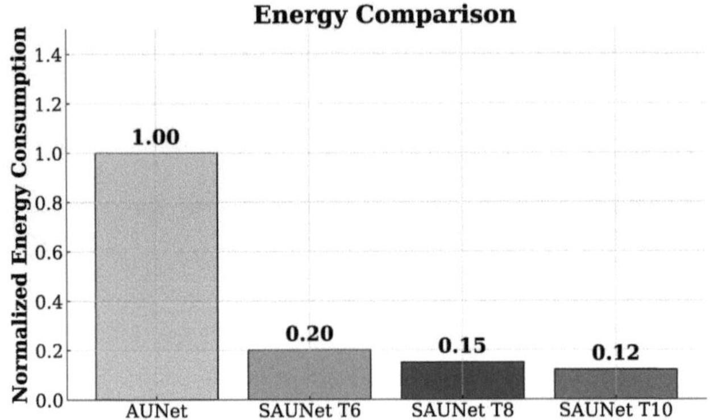

Fig. 7. Normalized energy consumption. $\text{SAUNet}_{T=10}$ achieves 88% reduction versus AUNet baseline

steps ($t = 5, 6$). This demonstrates unique SNN capability for iterative improvement through temporal integration, absent in conventional feedforward architectures. The progressive refinement illustrates effective temporal integration achieving robust detection.

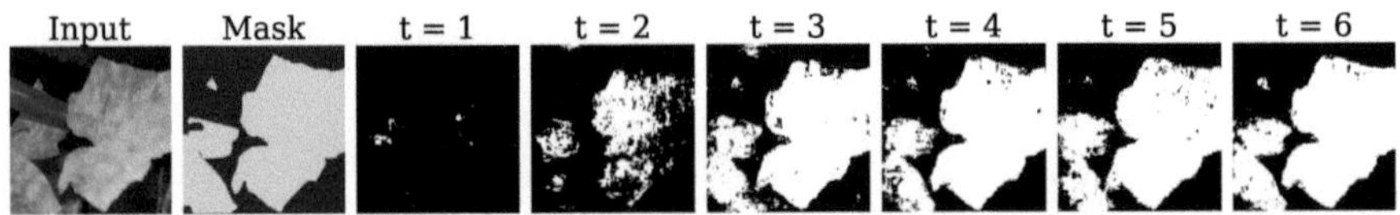

Fig. 8. Temporal progression across time steps ($t = 1$ to $t = 6$). Outputs show progressive refinement from sparse initial activations to accurate segmentations

4 Discussion

Results establish SAUNet as viable energy-efficient alternative for semantic segmentation with broad IoT applicability. Competitive metrics with only marginal reductions demonstrate temporal integration capabilities effectively compensate for sparse event-driven processing constraints. Superior precision indicates bio-inspired SNNs may exhibit inherent advantages in clean prediction generation.

Temporal progression provides insights into iterative refinement. Gradual evolution from sparse activations to coherent masks demonstrates SAUNet leverages temporal integration for robust learning—fundamental advantage over feed-forward architectures lacking iterative improvement through temporal evidence accumulation.

Drawing parallels to bio-inspired optimization algorithms (BAS [9,27], Eagle Perching [11]) demonstrating efficiency in robotics [12] and optimization [14, 15], SAUNet exemplifies how biological principles guide efficient systems. Just as nature-inspired algorithms achieve performance through selective sampling, SAUNet's selective spiking reduces overhead while maintaining accuracy.

The 88% energy reduction represents paradigm shift for deploying sophisticated vision models in resource-constrained environments. This stems from fundamental computational paradigm differences—operations only when neurons spike versus dense matrix computations. Sparse activation (<<15%) confirms biological plausibility and efficiency, demonstrating effective processing with minimal resource utilization.

Attention mechanism integration within bio-inspired spiking paradigm represents significant innovation. Successful implementation demonstrates complex computations realizable using sparse event-driven processing while maintaining efficiency advantages, opening possibilities for sophisticated architectures combining attention selectivity with spiking efficiency benefits.

Broad applicability across IoT domains: (1) Medical imaging—tumor detection, organ segmentation, anatomical identification; (2) Industrial quality control—defect detection, manufacturing monitoring; (3) Educational assessment—skill evaluation, procedural monitoring; (4) Environmental monitoring—remote sensing requiring autonomous operation.

Future directions include sophisticated temporal encoding schemes, specialized neuromorphic hardware development, multi-class segmentation extension, and IoT technology integration (sensor networks, communication protocols) for comprehensive monitoring platforms.

5 Conclusion

SAUNet successfully demonstrates SNN viability for complex semantic segmentation in resource-constrained environments. SAUNet$_{T=10}$ achieves Dice 0.8062 and IoU 0.6822, highly competitive with conventional architectures while achieving 88% energy reduction. Temporal integration enables progressive refinement absent in feedforward architectures.

Architectural innovations, particularly attention integration within bio-inspired spiking paradigm, establish new possibilities for energy-efficient systems. Sparse activation (<15%) confirms biological plausibility and efficiency. Implications extend beyond immediate applications to edge computing across educational assessment, medical diagnostics, industrial monitoring, and precision agriculture.

The work establishes new paradigm for energy-aware AI, demonstrating sophisticated vision capabilities achievable while meeting stringent IoT deployment constraints. This provides foundation for sustainable computing technologies contributing to environmentally responsible AI systems deployable across diverse domains.

Acknowledgements. This research demonstrates methodologies applicable to IoT-enabled assessment systems requiring energy-efficient AI deployment. Authors acknowledge Google Colab computational resources.

Funding. No specific funding received.

Conflict of Interest. Authors declare no conflict of interest.

Data Availability. Dataset openly available at: https://www.kaggle.com/datasets/fakhrealam9537/leaf-disease-segmentation-dataset.

Author Contributions. ATK: Conceptualization, Methodology, Software Development, Investigation, Visualization, and Writing—Original Draft Preparation. MR: Data Curation, Software Implementation, Validation, and Writing—Review & Editing. AMM: Formal Analysis, Experimental Validation, and Writing—Review & Editing. XC: Project Administration, Technical Guidance, and Writing—Review & Editing. SL: Supervision, Funding Acquisition, Conceptual Oversight, and Writing—Review & Editing.

References

1. Chen, L., Chen, P., Lin, Z.: Artificial intelligence in education: a review. IEEE Access **8**, 75264–75278 (2020)
2. Hwang, G.-J., Xie, H., Wah, B.W., Gašević, D.: Vision, challenges, roles and research issues of artificial intelligence in education. Comput. Educ. Artif. Intell. **1**, 100001 (2020)
3. Kamilaris, A., Prenafeta-Boldú, F.X.: Deep learning in agriculture: a survey. Comput. Electron. Agric. **147**, 70–90 (2018)
4. Savary, S., Willocquet, L., Pethybridge, S.J., Esker, P., McRoberts, N., Nelson, A.: The global burden of pathogens and pests on major food crops. Nature Ecol. Evol. **3**(3), 430–439 (2019)
5. Maass, W.: Networks of spiking neurons: the third generation of neural network models. Neural Netw. **10**(9), 1659–1671 (1997)
6. Ghosh-Dastidar, S., Adeli, H.: Spiking neural networks. Int. J. Neural Syst. **19**(04), 295–308 (2009)
7. Davies, M., et al.: Loihi: a neuromorphic manycore processor with on-chip learning. IEEE Micro **38**(1), 82–99 (2018)
8. Akopyan, F., et al.: TrueNorth: design and tool flow of a 65 mw 1 million neuron programmable neurosynaptic chip. IEEE Trans. Comput. Aided Des. Integr. Circuits Syst. **34**(10), 1537–1557 (2015)

9. Khan, A.T., Cao, X., Li, Z., Li, S.: Enhanced beetle antennae search with zeroing neural network for online solution of constrained optimization. Neurocomputing **447**, 294–306 (2021)
10. Khan, A.T., Li, S., Zhou, X.: Trajectory optimization of 5-link biped robot using beetle antennae search. IEEE Trans. Circuits Syst. II Express Briefs **68**(10), 3276–3280 (2021)
11. Khan, A.T., Li, S., Zhang, Y., Stanimirovic, P.S.: Eagle perching optimizer for the online solution of constrained optimization. Mem. Mater. Device Circuit Syst. **4**, 100021 (2023)
12. Khan, A.T., Li, S., Cao, X.: Control framework for cooperative robots in smart home using bio-inspired neural network. Measurement **167**, 108253 (2021)
13. Khan, A.T., Li, S., Cao, X.: Human guided cooperative robotic agents in smart home using beetle antennae search. SCIENCE CHINA Inf. Sci. **65**(2), 122204 (2022)
14. Khan, A.T., Cao, X., Li, S., Hu, B., Katsikis, V.N.: Quantum beetle antennae search: a novel technique for the constrained portfolio optimization problem. SCIENCE CHINA Inf. Sci. **64**(5), 152204 (2021)
15. Khan, A.T., Cao, X., Li, S., Katsikis, V.N., Brajevic, I., Stanimirovic, P.S.: Fraud detection in publicly traded us firms using beetle antennae search: a machine learning approach. Expert Syst. Appl. **191**, 116148 (2022)
16. Neftci, E.O., Mostafa, H., Zenke, F.: Surrogate gradient learning in spiking neural networks: bringing the power of gradient-based optimization to spiking neural networks. IEEE Signal Process. Mag. **36**(6), 51–63 (2019)
17. Zenke, F., Ganguli, S.: Superspike: supervised learning in multilayer spiking neural networks. Neural Comput. **30**(6), 1514–1541 (2018)
18. Wu, Y., Deng, L., Li, G., Zhu, J., Xie, Y., Shi, L.: Direct training for spiking neural networks: Faster, larger, better. In: Proceedings of the AAAI Conference on Artificial Intelligence, vol. 33, no. 01 pp. 1311–1318 (2019)
19. Fang, W., Yu, Z., Chen, Y., Masquelier, T., Huang, T., Tian, Y.: Incorporating learnable membrane time constant to enhance learning of spiking neural networks. In: Proceedings of the IEEE/CVF International Conference on Computer Vision, pp. 2661–2671 (2021)
20. Yao, M., et al.: Temporal-wise attention spiking neural networks for event streams classification. In: Proceedings of the IEEE/CVF International Conference on Computer Vision, pp. 10221–10230 (2021)
21. Guo, M., Huang, X., Deng, L., Li, G., Xu, B.: Recurrent spiking neural networks with memory and attention for event-based optical flow estimation. IEEE Trans. Neural Netw. Learn. Syst. (2023)
22. Singh, D., Jain, N., Jain, P., Kayal, P., Kumawat, S., Batra, N.: PlantDoc: a dataset for visual plant disease detection. In: Proceedings of the 7th ACM IKDD CoDS and 25th COMAD, pp. 249–253 (2020)
23. Izhikevich, E.M.: Simple model of spiking neurons. IEEE Trans. Neural Networks **14**(6), 1569–1572 (2003)
24. Li, Y., Guo, Y., Zhang, S., Deng, S., Hai, Y., Gu, S.: Differentiable spike: rethinking gradient-descent for training spiking neural networks. Adv. Neural. Inf. Process. Syst. **34**, 23426–23439 (2021)
25. Rathi, N., Srinivasan, G., Panda, P., Roy, K.: Enabling deep spiking neural networks with hybrid conversion and spike timing dependent backpropagation. In: Proceedings of the International Conference on Learning Representations (2020)

26. Panda, P., Aketi, S.A., Roy, K.: Toward scalable, efficient, and accurate deep spiking neural networks with backward residual connections, stochastic softmax, and hybridization. Front. Neurosci. **14**, 653 (2020)
27. Khan, A.T., Cao, X., Li, S.: Dual beetle antennae search system for optimal planning and robust control of 5-link biped robots. J. Comput. Sci. **60**, 101556 (2022)

Workshop AIPL

Efficient High Utility Itemset Mining on Massive Data

Xixian Han, Kangao Wang, and Xiaolong Wan(✉)

Harbin Institute of Technology, Harbin, China
{hanxx,wxl}@hit.edu.cn, wka@stu.hit.edu.cn

Abstract. In learning analytics and computer support for intelligent tutoring, high utility itemset mining (HUIM) is an interesting operation to find the sets of items which have high utilities. HUIM normally is considered to be more difficult than the traditional frequent itemset mining (FIM), since the utility of the itemset does not hold anti-monotone property. This paper analyzes the inefficiency of existing algorithms for HUIM on massive data. To address this, we introduce a novel algorithm named P2H, which utilizes a prefix-partitioning approach. P2H organizes the transaction table into memory-resident partitions. Each partition groups transactions that share a common initial item, enabling efficient discovery of high-utility itemsets. P2H handles the prefix-based partitions sequentially and independently. By the pre-computed data structure, P2H can skip most of the partitions and report the required high utility itemsets. For the partitions to be processed further, a set enumeration tree is proposed to compute the results quickly. Besides, a novel pruning strategy utilizing full suffix utilities is introduced to effectively reduce the exploration space. Extensive evaluation on both synthetic and real-world datasets demonstrates that P2H substantially outperforms state-of-the-art methods.

Keywords: Learning Analytics · Computer Support for Intelligent Tutoring · Massive data · HUIM · prefix-based partitioning · subtree pruning

1 Introduction

High utility itemset mining (HUIM) is a vital data mining task with significant applications in educational technologies such as learning analytics and computer support for intelligent tutoring [5], in addition to its traditional applications in cross marketing [17]. It extends frequent itemset mining (FIM) [2,6] by considering not only the frequency of itemsets but also item-specific profits and purchase quantities. While FIM identifies commonly occurring sets (e.g., $\{beer, snack\}$), it may overlook highly profitable but less frequent combinations (e.g., $\{caviar, champagne\}$). HUIM addresses this by quantifying the utility of an itemset, which combines the quantity (internal utility) in the transaction

B. Fernández-Manjón et al. (Eds.): SETE 2025/ICWL 2025, LNCS 16425, pp. 327–342, 2026.
https://doi.org/10.1007/978-981-92-0042-9_24

and the distinct profit (external utility) of the item. HUIM enables the identification of high-impact educational patterns and effective pedagogical strategies that extend beyond mere frequency analysis, particularly valuable for discovering optimal learning pathways and intervention strategies in educational contexts.

A key challenge in HUIM is the non-monotonicity of utility: unlike frequency in FIM, which exhibits an anti-monotonic property (simplifying pruning), the utility of an itemset can be higher or lower than that of its subsets or supersets. This complexity makes HUIM computationally more demanding than FIM, as traditional pruning techniques from FIM cannot be directly applied.

Current HUIM algorithms are commonly classified as either two-phase algorithms and one-phase algorithms. Two-phase algorithms [1,9,12,15,16,18] first generate candidate itemsets using an overestimated utility measure (e.g., transaction-weighted utilization) and then verify their true utility in a second pass. They often produce a large number of candidates, leading to high computational costs on massive datasets. One-phase algorithms [3,4,7,10,11,13,20] directly compute utilities without candidate generation, using structures like utility-lists or trees. However, they typically assume the entire dataset fits in memory, resulting in excessive I/O costs and performance degradation for massive data that exceeds memory capacity. In summary, current HUIM algorithms exhibit significant performance limitations on massive data.

To address this, this paper proposes a novel P2H algorithm (*P*refix-*P*artitioning-based *H*igh utility itemset mining), which utilizes the prefix-based partitioning and subtree pruning rule to find high utility itemsets on massive data efficiently. In this paper, the itemsets are arranged in lexicographic order. The transaction table is pre-split into prefix-based partitions. Each of these memory-resident partitions contains all itemsets that share the same initial item(s). P2H can process the partitions sequentially and independently. For each partition currently considered, the execution of P2H is processed in different cases according to the size of the promising item set. When high utility itemsets on the partition cannot be discovered directly, the enumeration-tree-based depth-first search is performed to find the high utility itemsets. The subtree pruning rule based on full suffix utility is devised in this paper to reduce the search space of the enumeration tree. We evaluated the P2H algorithm on both synthetic and real-world datasets. The results demonstrate that it consistently outperforms state-of-the-art methods.

The primary contributions of this work are as follows:

- This paper proposes a novel prefix-partitioning-based P2H algorithm to discover high utility itemsets on massive data efficiently.
- This paper devises the subtree pruning rule, which is based on full suffix utility, to reduce the exploration space considerably.
- Comprehensive experiments demonstrate that the P2H algorithm delivers substantially superior performance over state-of-the-art algorithms.

The structure of this paper is organized as follows. Section 2 shows the related work. Problem definition presented in Sect. 3. The key property of HUIM is analyzed in Sect. 4. Section 5 introduces the prefix-based partitioning. Section 6 proposes P2H algorithm. Section 7 evaluates the performance of P2H and Sect. 8 concludes the paper.

Table 1. Summary of symbols

Symbol	Meaning
$HUIM$	high utility itemset mining
T	the transaction table
d	the number of the distinct items
$\mathcal{I}$	the universe of the items $\{i_1, i_2, \ldots, i_d\}$
$minU$	the utility threshold
$minUP$	the utility threshold in percentage
$dbUtil$	the total utility
$G(X)$	the set of transactions containing an itemset X
P_a	the prefix-based partition of the item i_a
ps_a	the set of promising items when dealing with P_a

2 Related Work

High utility itemset mining has emerged as a prominent and actively studied area due to its high practical value [8,14,17]. Current HUIM methods are primarily categorized into two groups: two-phase algorithms [1,9,12,15,16,18] and one-phase algorithms [3,4,7,10,11,13,20].

Two-phase algorithms first generate candidate itemsets using an overestimated utility measure (like transaction-weighted utilization) and then verify their true utility in a second database scan [12]. Improvements include the isolated items discarding strategy (IIDS) [9] for candidate reduction, the IHUP tree [1] for incremental mining, and the UP-Growth algorithm [16] with a compact tree structure and pruning strategies. A fundamental limitation is that the candidate set can be excessively large for massive data, leading to high computational costs in both phases.

One-phase algorithms directly identify high utility itemsets without candidate generation. HUI-Miner [11] introduced utility-lists for this purpose. Subsequent works enhanced efficiency: HUP-Miner [7] with partitioned utility lists, FHM [4] with co-occurrence pruning (EUCP), d2HUP [10] with tighter upper bounds, and EFIM [20] with database projection and transaction merging. ULB-Miner [3] proposed a buffer structure to manage memory for utility-lists. Evaluations [19] show one-phase algorithms generally outperform two-phase ones, with EFIM excelling on dense datasets and d2HUP on sparse ones.

Discussion. While two-phase HUIM algorithms suffer from generating a prohibitively large number of candidates, leading to inefficiency on massive datasets, one-phase algorithms avoid candidate generation but are designed under the assumption that the entire dataset resides in memory. For massive datasets that exceed memory capacity, these one-phase methods incur excessive I/O costs due to repeated scans or random accesses, significantly degrading performance. Consequently, this paper aims to develop an efficient HUIM algorithm tailored for massive data that cannot be fully loaded into memory.

3 Problem Definition

Consider a transaction table T consisting of n transactions, each comprising items drawn from the set $\mathcal{I} = \{i_1, i_2, \ldots, i_d\}$. An itemset refers to any subset of $\mathcal{I}$. Every item $i \in \mathcal{I}$ is assigned a unique weight that reflects its importance or unit profit; this measure is termed its *external utility*, denoted as $eu(i)$. For every transaction $t \in T$, each item i present in t possesses an *internal utility*, expressed as $iu(i,t)$, which indicates the quantity of the item.

The utility $u(i,t)$ of an item i in transaction t is given by the product of its external and internal utilities: $u(i,t) = eu(i) \times iu(i,t)$. Then, for an itemset X that appears in transaction t, the utility $u(X,t)$ of X in t is $u(X,t) = \sum_{i \in X} u(i,t)$. Accordingly, this aggregate utility reflects the overall profit generated by the sale of itemset X in t.

Definition 1 ***(The utility of the itemset).*** *For a given itemset X, its utility $u(X)$ in transaction table T is calculated as $u(X) = \sum_{t \in G(X)} u(X,t)$, where $G(X)$ denotes the collection of all transactions in T that include X.*

The total profit attributable to the sales of itemset X is reflected in its utility.

Definition 2 ***(High utility itemset).*** *An itemset is classified as a high-utility itemset if its utility meets or exceeds the utility threshold, denoted as $minU$.*

Definition 3 ***(High utility itemset mining).*** *Given the utility threshold $minU$, high utility itemset mining (HUIM) is to discover all the high utility itemsets, denoted by HUI_T, that is: $HUI_T = \{X | X \subseteq \mathcal{I} \text{ and } u(X) \geq minU\}$.*

Definition 4 ***(Transaction utility).*** *For a transaction $t \in T$, its transaction utility $u(t,t)$ is the sum of the utilities of all items, $u(t,t) = \sum_{i \in t} u(i,t)$.*

Definition 5 ***(Total utility of the table).*** *The total utility $dbUtil$ is the sum of the transaction utility of every transaction in T, i.e. $dbUtil = \sum_{t \in T} u(t,t)$.*

Given the definition of total utility $dbUtil$, the utility threshold also can be represented as a percentage $minUP = \frac{minU}{dbUtil} \times 100\%$. The frequently used symbols are listed in Table 1.

4 Analysis of Properties of HUIM

Designing an efficient HUIM algorithm for massive data requires addressing three core challenges: (1) to produce the full collection of high utility itemsets, (2) to ensure the memory capacity is sufficient to hold the entire working data set, (3) to minimize computational overhead, including computational and I/O cost.

In practice, while the potential search space is enormous ($2^d - 1$), the actual set of high utility itemsets is typically very small. The very ideal case for HUIM is *only to retrieve the useful subset of the transactions in T, and among the useful transactions, only to read the useful items.* Given the utility threshold $minU$, an item is called promising, if it is possible to be used to generate the high utility itemsets, otherwise, it is called unpromising.

To define promising (unpromising) items, the concept of transaction-weighted utilization of an itemset is provided first, which is an over-estimation of the utility of the itemset and holds the anti-monotone property. For an itemset X, its transaction-weighted utilization (TWU) is calculated as the total sum of the utilities of all transactions in T that include X, $twu(X) = \sum_{t \in G(X)} u(t)$, where $G(X)$ denotes the set of transactions in T containing X.

Therefore, given the utility threshold $minU$, an item $i \in \mathcal{I}$ is promising, if $twu(i) \geq minU$, Otherwise, it is unpromising.

Obviously, $\forall i \in \mathcal{I}$, if i is an unpromising item, i will not appear in any high utility itemsets. Given a transaction table T, we can pre-compute the transaction-weighted utilization of the single item, and find the set of promising items. When performing HUIM, we only need to concern the promising itemsets in each transaction.

5 Prefix-Based Partitioning

This paper assumes items are ordered lexicographically ($i_1 \prec i_2 \prec \ldots \prec i_d$). The set of all high utility itemsets HUI_T is partitioned into $G_1, G_2, \ldots, G_d$, where G_a contains high utility itemsets beginning with the item i_a, $\bigcup_{1 \leq a \leq d} G_a = HUI_T$.

To handle massive data, we propose a partitioning approach based on item prefixes. The transaction table T is split to d prefix-based partitions $P_1, P_2, \ldots, P_d$, where each partition $P_a (1 \leq a \leq d)$ keeps the transactions which begins with the item i_a. This allows each group G_a to be processed independently by loading only P_a into memory, minimizing I/O overhead.

Partitioning is done via a single sequential scan of T. For each transaction $t[1] \prec t[2] \prec \ldots \prec t[k]$ (items in lexicographic order), every suffix $((t[b], t[b+1], \ldots, t[k]))$ is written to partition P_a corresponding to item $t[b]$. This process is performed once, and the resulting partitions support efficient incremental updates for new transactions. The details are shown in Algorithm 1. The P2H (***P***refix-***P***artitioning-based ***H***igh utility itemset mining) algorithm leverages this structure for scalable HUIM on massive datasets.

Discussion. We assume that each partition P_a can be held entirely in memory, which is reasonable for typical applications (e.g., supermarket products).

Some Useful Pre-constructed Data Structures. To optimize performance, the data structure UIP_a (***U***tility ***I***nformation in ***P***artition) is constructed. UIP_a is an array with d elements, each of which contains three parts $(twu, iutil, putil)$. $\forall 1 \leq b \leq d$, $UIP_a[b]$ represents the transaction-weighted utilization of the item b in P_a, the utility of the item b in P_a and the utility of the item pair (i_a, i_b) in P_a, respectively. Of course, if $a = b$, $iutil = putil$. The data structure UIP_a can be generated by a single scan on P_a.

Algorithm 1. PrefixbasedPartition(T, $\mathcal{I}$)

Input: T is the transaction table, $\mathcal{I}$ is the universe of the items.
Output: Prefix-based partitions $P_1, P_2, \ldots, P_d$

while T has more transactions **do**
    retrieve the next transaction t of T
    $t = (t[1], t[2], \ldots, t[k])$
    for $b = 1$ to k **do**
        Let $t[b]$ be the ath item in $\mathcal{I}$
        Write $(t[b], t[b+1], \ldots, t[k])$ to partition P_a.

6 P2H Algorithm

This part describes the detailed execution of P2H algorithm, which is shown in Algorithm 2.

Given the utility threshold *minU*, P2H computes HUI_T by considering the partitions individually. As described from Line 3 to Line 5 in Algorithm 2, $\forall 1 \leq a \leq d$, let P_a be the partition considered currently. By the information in UIP_a, the set ps_a of the promising items in P_a can be acquired, i.e. $ps_a = \{i_b | \forall 1 \leq b \leq d, UIP_a[b].twu \geq minU\}$. The value of $|ps_a|$, i.e. the cardinality of the set, corresponds to four cases, whose processing is introduced as follows.

Case 1 ($|ps_a| == 0$)**.** The value of $|ps_a|$ is 0. As described from Line 6 to Line 7 in Algorithm 2, in this case, there is no promising item in P_a, also there is no high utility itemset in P_a. P2H just skips P_a and considers the next partition.

Case 2 ($|ps_a| == 1$)**.** There is only one promising item in P_a. It is proved in Theorem 1 that the only promising item in P_a is i_a. As depicted from Line 8 to Line 10 in Algorithm 2, the possible high utility itemset generated in P_a in case 2 is 1-itemset $\{i_a\}$. If $UIP_a[a].iutil \geq minU$, $\{i_a\}$ is high utility.

Theorem 1. *In case 2, the only promising item in P_a is i_a.*

Proof. Suppose that the only promising item in P_a is $i_b (b \neq a)$. According to the prefix-based partitioning strategy in Sect. 5, every transaction t in P_a begins with i_a, $twu(i_a, P_a) \geq twu(i_b, P_a)$. If i_b is a promising item, t_a is a promising item also. This contradicts the case 2 that there is only one promising item. Thus, in case 2, the only promising item in P_a is i_a.

Algorithm 2. P2H Algorithm($P_1, P_2, \ldots, P_d$, UIP, $minU$)

Input: $P_1, P_2, \ldots, P_d$ are the prefix-based partitions, UIP is the utility information of the partitions, $minU$ is the specified utility threshold.
Output: The high utility itemsets.

// Process the partitions sequentially
1: **for** $a = 1$ to d **do**
2: Begin to deal with partition P_a
// The determination of promising item set
3: **for** $b = 1$ to d **do**
4: **if** $UIP_a[b].twu \geq minU$ **then**
5: Add i_b to ps_a. // ps_a: the promising item set
// Processing P_a in different cases
6: **if** $|ps_a| == 0$ (case 1) **then**
7: Continue the next iteration of the loop
8: **else if** $|ps_a| == 1$ (case 2) **then**
9: **if** $UIP_a[i_a].iutil \geq minU$ **then**
10: Output $\{i_a\}$ as a high utility itemset
11: **else if** $|ps_a| == 2$ (case 3) **then**
12: **if** $UIP_a[i_a].iutil \geq minU$ **then**
13: Output $\{i_a\}$ as a high utility itemset
// Let i_b be the another promising item in ps_a
14: **if** $UIP_a[i_b].putil \geq minU$ **then**
15: Output $\{i_a, i_b\}$ as a high utility itemset
16: **else**
17: ProcessCase4(P_a, UIP_a, $minU$, ps_a) //(case 4)

Algorithm 3. ProcessCase4(P_a, UIP_a, $minU$, ps_a)

Input: P_a is the current considered partition, UIP is the utility information of the partitions, $minU$ is the specified utility threshold, ps_a is the promising item set.
Output: The high utility itemsets in P_a.

// Unpromising item filtering
1: **while** P_a has more transactions **do**
2: Retrieve the next transaction t in P_a
3: Discard unpromising items of t not contained in ps_a
4: **if** t has at least one promising item **then**
5: Add t to P_a^r
6: Compute the transaction-weighted utilization of any item in the set $\bigcup_{t \in P_a^r} t$ by a sequential scan on P_a^r.
7: **for** *each* $i \in \bigcup_{t \in P_a^r} t$ **do**
8: **if** $twu(i, P_a^r) \geq minU$ **then**
9: Add i to ps_a^r
// The discovery of the high utility itemsets
10: **if** $|ps_a^r| \leq 2$ **then**
11: Process similarly as described from Line 6 to Line 15 in Algorithm 2
12: **else**
13: Create root node r of $\mathcal{E}$
$r.item = i_a$, $r.pat = i_a$, $r.tset = P_u^r$ by pseudo-copy
Compute $r.iutil$ and $r.fsu$ by $r.tset$
14: DepthFirstSearch(r, $minU$, ps_a^r)

Case 3 ($|ps_a| == 2$)**.** There are two promising items in P_a. Similarly with Theorem 1, i_a is one of the two promising items. Let i_b ($b > a$) be the another promising item. As described from Line 11 to Line 15 in Algorithm 2, the possible high utility itemsets generated in P_a are $\{i_a\}$ and $\{i_a, i_b\}$. If $UIP_a[a].iutil \geq minU$, $\{i_a\}$ is high utility. If $UIP_a[b].putil \geq minU$, $\{i_a, i_b\}$ is high utility. Whether $\{i_b\}$ is high utility or not is checked when P2H considers the P_b.

Case 4 ($|ps_a| \geq 3$)**.** In case 4, there are greater than or equal to 3 promising items in P_a. P2H needs to retrieve transactions in P_a to compute HUI_a. The pseudo-code of processing in case 4 is provided in Algorithm 3.

Unpromising Item Filtering. To optimize memory and computation, P2H employs unpromising item filtering during partition processing. For each transaction in partition P_a, items that cannot contribute to high utility itemsets starting with i_a are discarded, resulting in a set of revised transactions P_a^r. This reduces the memory footprint and accelerates subsequent steps. The pseudo-code of unpromising item filtering is depicted from Line 1 to Line 9 in Algorithm 3.

After filtering, the transaction-weighted utility of 1-itemsets in P_a^r is recomputed to identify the current promising items ps_a^r. If the number of promising items is less than 3, high utility itemsets are directly enumerated. Otherwise, the further processing on the revised transactions is still required.

Regarding the current set of promising items ps_a^r, the set enumeration tree $\mathcal{E}$, as depicted in Fig. 1, is expanded using a depth-first approach to derive HUI_a from the updated transactions. It should be noted that $\mathcal{E}$ relies on a predefined lexicographic order of the items. Every node contains six attributes $(item, pat, iutil, child, tset, fsu)$. Here, *item* denotes the item associated with the node. For any node e in $\mathcal{E}$, the sequence of items along the path from the root to e forms the itemset *e.pat*. *e.iutil* stores the utility of *e.pat* within ps_a^r. *e.child* points to the child nodes of e, while *e.tset* refers to the group of transactions in ps_a^r that include *e.pat*. $e.fsu$ holds the *full suffix utility* of *e.pat* across the transactions in *e.tset*, as formally specified in Definition 7. As established in Theorem 2, the depth-first search can prune the branch at node e if $e.fsu < minU$, thereby avoiding unnecessary exploration. The corresponding subtree pruning rule is formally presented in Table 2.

Table 2. Subtree pruning rule by full suffix utility

Subtree pruning rule: During the depth-first traversal of the enumeration tree $\mathcal{E}$, if $e.fsu < minU$ for the current node e,
the entire subtree originating from e can be pruned to avoid further exploration.

Algorithm 4. DepthFirstSearch(e, $minU$, ps_a^r)

Input: e is the currently considered node in $\mathcal{E}$, $minU$ is the specified utility threshold, ps_a^r is the current promising item set.
Output: The high utility itemsets in P_a.

// Subtree pruning rule
if $e.fsu < minU$ **then**
  return
// Check whether the current itemset of e is high utility
if $e.iutil \geq minU$ **then**
  Output *e.pat* as a high utility itemset
// Expand the current node e to the next level
// $idx(i, ps_a^r)$: positional index of the item i in ps_a^r
for $b = idx(e.item, ps_a^r)$ to $|ps_a^r|$ **do**
  Create child node e_b of e
  $e_b.item = ps_a^r[idx(e.item, ps_a^r) + b]$
  $e_b.pat = e.pat + ps_a^r[idx(e.item, ps_a^r) + b]$
  Add e_b to $e.child$
for *each* $t \in e.tset$ **do**
  Add t to $e_b.tset$ if t contains the item $ps_a^r[idx(e.item, ps_a^r) + b]$
for *each* $e_b \in e.child$ **do**
  Compute $e_b.iutil$ and $e_b.fsu$ by $e_b.tset$
  DepthFirstSearch(e_b, $minU$, ps_a^r)

Definition 6 ***(The full suffix utility of an itemset in a transaction).*** *The full suffix utility $fsu(X,t)$ of an itemset X in a transaction t that includes X is given by $fsu(X,t) = \sum_{i \in X} u(i,t) + \sum_{lpos(X)+1 \leq j \leq size(t)} u(t[j],t)$, where $lpos(X)$ denotes the position of the last item of X, $size(t)$ indicates the total number of items in t, and $t[j]$ refers to the jth item in t.*

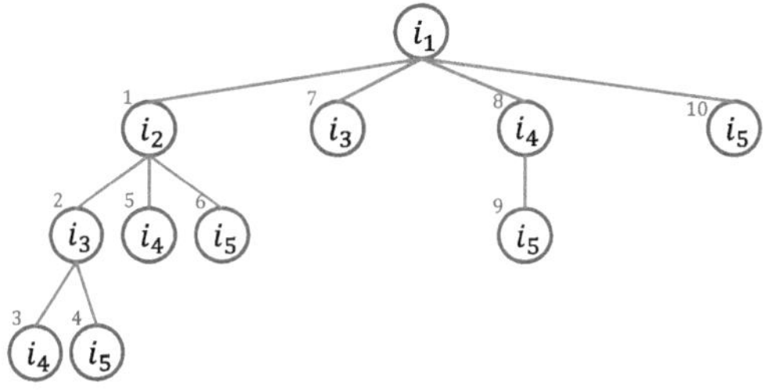

Fig. 1. The illustration of set enumeration tree in depth-first search

Definition 7 ***(The full suffix utility of an itemset in a transaction set).*** *The full suffix utility $fsu(X, tset)$ of an itemset X over a set of transactions tset, where every transaction in tset includes X, $fsu(X, tset) = \sum_{t \in tset} fsu(X, t)$.*

Theorem 2. *During the depth-first traversal of the enumeration tree $\mathcal{E}$, let e_1 be the current node, if $e_1.fsu < minU$, then for every node e_2 within the subtree rooted at e_1, $e_2.iutil < minU$.*

Proof. Since e_2 is a descendant of e_1 in $\mathcal{E}$, $e_1.pat \subset e_2.pat$, $e_1.tset \supseteq e_2.tset$. This is because every transaction that includes $e_1.pat$ must also contain $e_2.pat$. Based on the definitions of utility and full suffix utility, we have,

$$(1)\ e_2.iutil = \sum_{t \in e_2.tset} \sum_{i \in e_2.pat} u(i,t) = \sum_{t \in e_2.tset} \left[\sum_{i \in e_1.pat} u(i,t) + \sum_{j \in e_2.pat - e_1.pat} u(j,t) \right],$$

$$(2)\ e_1.fsu = fsu(e_1.pat, e_2.tset) + fsu(e_1.pat, e_2.tset - e_1.tset),$$

$$(3)\ fsu(e_1.pat, e_2.tset) = \sum_{t \in e_2.tset} \left[\sum_{i \in e_1.pat} u(i,t) + \sum_{lpos(e_1.pat)+1 \le b \le size(t)} u(t[b], t) \right].$$

Given revised t, $\sum_{j \in e_2.pat - e_1.pat} u(j,t) \le \sum_{lpos(e_1.pat)+1 \le b \le size(t)} u(t[b], t)$. Thus, $e_2.iutil \le fsu(e_1.pat, e_2.tset) \le e_1.fsu$. If $e_1.fsu < minU$, $e_2.iutil < minU$.

Pseudo-copying. The transactions in P_a^r are stored in the memory as an array, $P_a^r[1], P_a^r[2], \ldots, P_a^r[|P_a^r|]$. For any node e in $\mathcal{E}$, $e.tset$ does not physically duplicate the relevant transactions but only maintains pointers to these transactions. This approach greatly reduces memory consumption. For clarity in algorithmic description, however, we treat these transaction pointers as if they were actual copies of the transactions, a technique referred to in this paper as *pseudo-copying*.

Initially, when processing P_a^r, the root r of $\mathcal{E}$ is created with $r.item = i_a$, $r.pat = i_a$ and $r.tset = P_a^r$. The values of $r.iutil$ and $r.fsu$ are then computed accordingly.

$\forall j \in ps_a^r$, let $idx(j, ps_a^r)$ denote the positional index of j within ps_a^r. For instance, the first item in ps_a^r has an index of 1.

Table 3. Parameter Settings

Parameter	Used values
Transaction number(10^6) (syn)	5–500
Utility threshold in percentage (%) (syn)	0.1–0.9
The number of items (syn)	500–1500
The average transaction width (syn)	6–14
Utility threshold in percentage (%) (real)	0.1–0.9

Depth-First Search Procedure. Starting from the root node e of $\mathcal{E}$, the depth-first search proceeds as shown in Algorithm 4. If $e.fsu < minU$, the subtree rooted at e is pruned. Otherwise, P2H expands e to the next level, as high-utility itemsets may exist in its subtree. If $e.iutil \geq minU$, $e.pat$ is a high-utility itemset and is output. Let $e.item$ be the item labeling e. The candidate items for expanding e are those with indices greater than $idx(e.item, ps_a^r)$, specifically, $ps_a^r[idx(e.item, ps_a^r)+1], ps_a^r[idx(e.item, ps_a^r)+2], \ldots, ps_a^r[|ps_a^r|]$. For the bth child node e_b of e, we assign $e_b.item = ps_a^r[idx(e.item, ps_a^r) + b]$, $e_b.pat = e.pat + e_b.item$ where "+" is a string concatenation operator, and $e_b.tset$ is a subset of $e.tset$ which contains $e_b.item$. The values of $e_b.iutil$ and $e_b.fsu$ are computed accordingly. The depth-first search then continues recursively with the first child node, applying the same processing steps. The exploration of P_a^r concludes when no further nodes in $\mathcal{E}$ remain to be visited.

7 Performance Evaluation

We implemented P2H in Java and evaluated its performance against $d2HUP_E$ on a workstation with an Intel i7-9700 CPU and 32 GB RAM. $d2HUP_E$ was chosen for comparison as it extends $d2HUP$, which is recognized as the top-performing algorithm for sparse, large datasets with low utility thresholds [19]. We set the maximum number of transactions kept in memory to be 5M(5,000,000). In the process of execution, this consumes the memory space of up to 11.18 gigabytes.

Parameter Settings and Datasets. Table 3 shows the parameter settings. We use a synthetic dataset, generated with established methods [2] where internal utilities range from 1 to 10 and external utilities follow a log-normal distribution [11], and a real OnlineRetail dataset from the UCI repository (archive.ics.uci.edu/ml/datasets/Online+Retail), processed with similar utility assignments.

The Pre-construction of Prefix-Based Partitioning. Given $d = 1000$ and $w = 10$, this part introduces the results of the prefix-based partitioning with the varying transaction numbers. Figure 2(a) and Fig. 2(b) show the execution time and I/O cost of prefix-based partitioning, respectively.

Exp 1: The Effect of Transaction Number. Experiment 1 evaluates P2H with $minUP = 0.5\%$, $d = 1000$, and $w = 10$ across varying n. As shown in Fig. 3(a), the runtime of both P2H and $d2HUP_E$ increases with n, but P2H

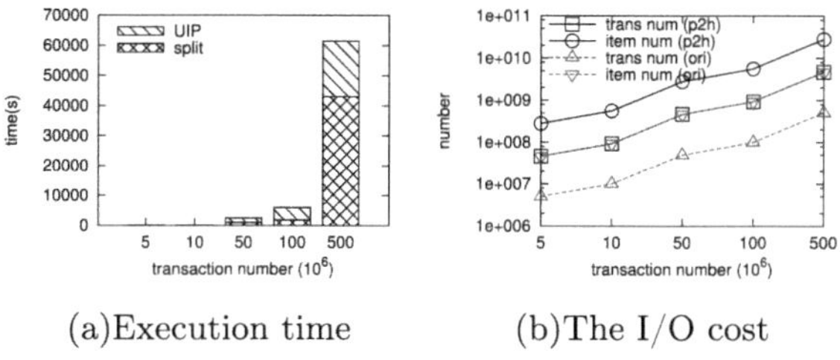

(a)Execution time (b)The I/O cost

Fig. 2. The pre-construction of prefix-based partitioning

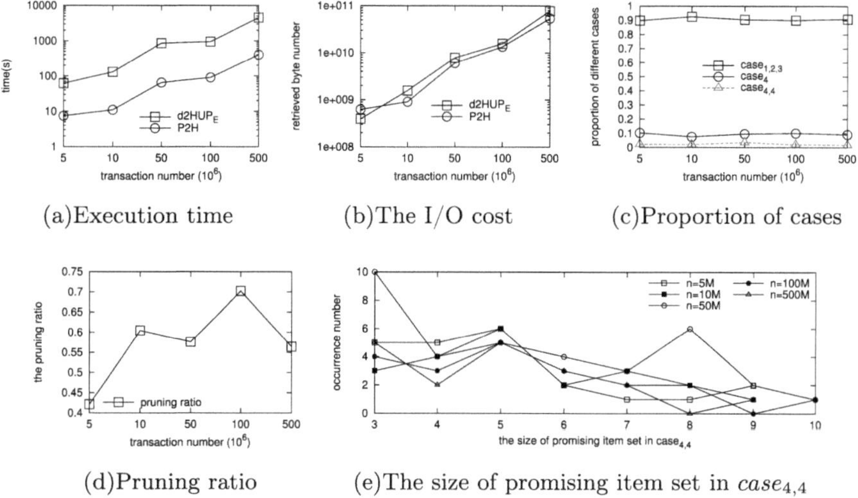

(a)Execution time (b)The I/O cost (c)Proportion of cases

(d)Pruning ratio (e)The size of promising item set in $case_{4,4}$

Fig. 3. The effect of transaction number

runs 11.03 times faster on average. Because P2H eliminates the need for a separate candidate refinement phase, and its prefix-based partitioning and subtree pruning significantly reduce computational cost. Figure 3(b) shows that P2H incurs 1.26 times less I/O than $d2HUP_E$, except at $n = 5M$. P2H's partitioning ensures consistent processing regardless of n. Figure 3(c) reveals that over 90% of partitions are skipped entirely (cases 1–3). Only about a third (3% total) require expensive tree construction (case 4), keeping computational overhead low. The subtree pruning rule (Fig. 3(d)) effectively prunes a large portion of the search space, though the ratio varies with data distribution. While the original table has over 700 promising items, the maximum per partition in P2H is only 10 (Fig. 3(e) and Table 4), confirming a massive reduction in exploration space.

Exp 2: The Effect of Utility Threshold. Experiment 2 evaluates P2H with $n = 100M$, $d = 1000$, and $w = 10$ across varying $minUP$. As $minUP$ increases from 0.1% to 0.9%, the execution times of both P2H and $d2HUP_E$ decrease. P2H demonstrates a more significant reduction, running 18.08 times faster than

Table 4. Promising item size of the transaction table in experiment 1.

$n(10^6)$	5	10	50	100	500
size	728	713	732	746	717

Table 5. Promising item size of the transaction table in experiment 2.

$minUP(\%)$	0.1	0.3	0.5	0.7	0.9
size	941	860	732	630	519

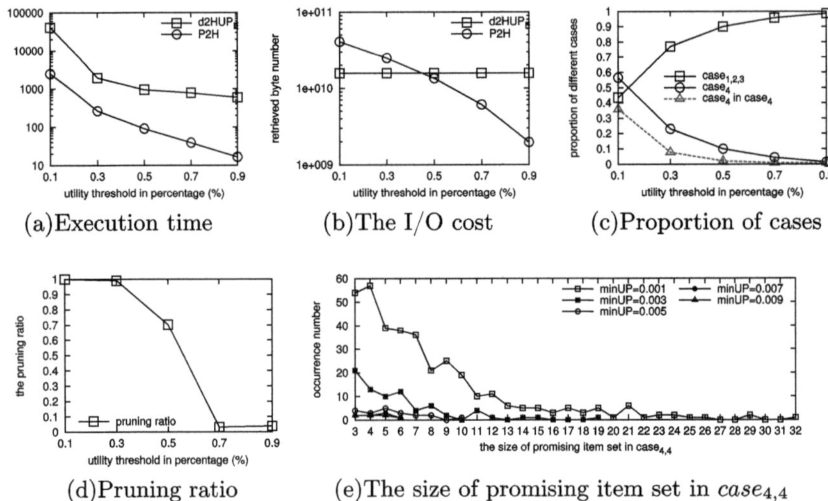

(a)Execution time (b)The I/O cost (c)Proportion of cases

(d)Pruning ratio (e)The size of promising item set in $case_{4,4}$

Fig. 4. The effect of utility threshold

$d2HUP_E$ on average. The I/O cost for $d2HUP_E$ remains constant as it requires two full table scans regardless of the threshold. In contrast, P2H's I/O cost decreases substantially with higher $minUP$ (Fig. 4(b)). Figure 4(c) shows that at a low threshold ($minUP = 0.1\%$), over half of the partitions require retrieval and processing. This proportion declines rapidly as $minUP$ increases, dropping to just 1.4% at $minUP = 0.9\%$. The subtree pruning ratio is extremely high (0.9999744) at $minUP = 0.1\%$ but decreases with higher thresholds (Fig. 4(d)). A lower threshold results in larger promising item sets, as shown in Fig. 4(e), creating larger potential search trees and thus more opportunities for pruning. The core advantage of P2H is confirmed: the number of the promising items is drastically smaller than that in the original table (Table 5), showing that prefix-based partitioning effectively reduces exploration space.

Table 6. Promising item size of the transaction table in experiment 3

d	500	750	1000	1250	1500
size	435(0.87)	587(0.78)	732(0.73)	809(0.65)	903(0.60)

Table 7. Promising item size of the transaction table in experiment 4

w	6	8	10	12	14
size	581	631	732	747	802

Table 8. Promising item size of the transaction table in experiment 5

$minUP(\%)$	0.01	0.05	0.1	0.5	1
size	1560	938	674	198	99

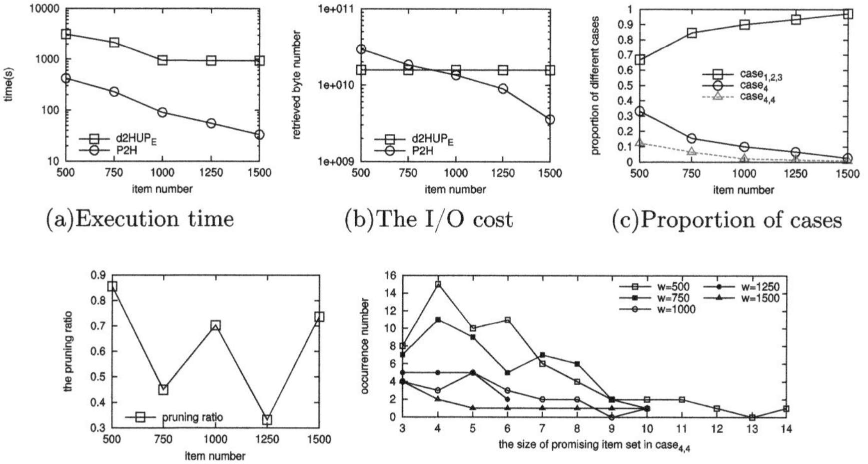

(a)Execution time

(b)The I/O cost

(c)Proportion of cases

(d)Pruning ratio

(e)The size of promising item set in $case_{4,4}$

Fig. 5. The effect of item number

Exp 3: The Effect of Number of the Items. Experiment 3 evaluates P2H with $n = 100M$, $minUP = 0.5\%$, and $w = 10$ across varying numbers of items d. As shown in Fig. 5(a), P2H runs 14.43 times faster than $d2HUP_E$ on average, with the speedup ratio improving as d increases. The I/O cost for $d2HUP_E$ remains constant, as it requires two full table scans regardless of d. In contrast, P2H's I/O cost decreases with larger d (Fig. 5(b)), because fewer partitions need to be retrieved and processed. Figure 5(c) shows that a larger d leads to a greater proportion of partitions being skipped entirely, reducing computational overhead. Figure 5(d) shows that the subtree pruning ratio varies with data distribution but remains highly effective. The size of the promising item set within each partition decreases as d increases (Fig. 5(e)), further reducing in-memory computational cost. This is consistent with the observation that the proportion of promising items in the original transaction table declines with larger d (Table 6), demonstrating the efficiency of P2H's partitioning strategy.

Exp 4: The Effect of Average Transaction Width. Experiment 4 evaluates P2H with $n = 100M$, $minUP = 0.5\%$, and $d = 1000$ across varying transac-

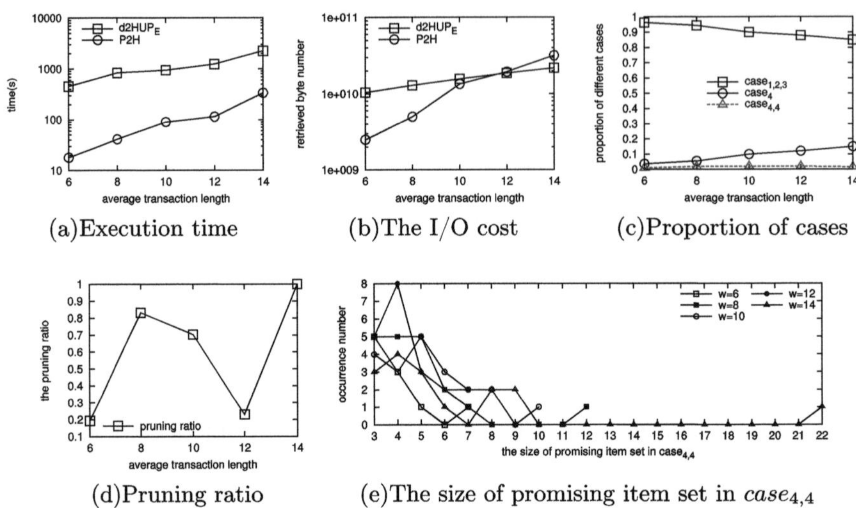

(a)Execution time (b)The I/O cost (c)Proportion of cases

(d)Pruning ratio (e)The size of promising item set in $case_{4,4}$

Fig. 6. The effect of average transaction width

tion widths (w). As shown in Fig. 6(a), the execution times of both algorithms increase with w and P2H runs 14.71 times faster than $d2HUP_E$. The I/O costs of both algorithms are illustrated in Fig. 6(b). With a greater value of w, the I/O cost of P2H increases and exceeds that of $d2HUP_E$. The proportion of different cases is depicted in Fig. 6(c), and it conforms with the explanation above. The pruning ratio of subtree pruning is affected by the actual data distribution and as shown in Fig. 6(d), but the subtree pruning operation still can reduce the exploration space effectively. Figure 6(e) shows the size of the promising items. As shown in Table 7, the number of promising items in the original transaction table increases with the average transaction width. However, the number of promising items handled in each partition remains much smaller, which confirms that prefix-based partitioning effectively reduces the exploration space.

Exp 5: Real Data - OnlineRetail Data Set. Experiment 5 evaluates P2H on a scaled OnlineRetail dataset (5.4M transactions, 2603 items) with varying utility thresholds $minUP$. P2H significantly outperforms $d2HUP_E$, running 39.35 times faster on average. As shown in Fig. 7(a), the speedup is most dramatic at very low thresholds, reaching two orders of magnitude at $minUP = 0.01\%$. The I/O cost for $d2HUP_E$ is constant as it requires two full table scans regardless of the threshold. P2H's I/O cost, however, decreases significantly as $minUP$ increases (Fig. 7(b)) because it can skip a larger proportion of partitions directly at higher thresholds (Fig. 7(c)). The subtree pruning rule is highly effective, especially at low thresholds where the potential search space is vast (Fig. 7(d)). P2H processes each partition using a drastically reduced set of "promising items" compared to the original dataset (Fig. 7(e) and Table 8). This efficient reduction of the problem space is a key factor in its superior performance, particularly on large real-world data.

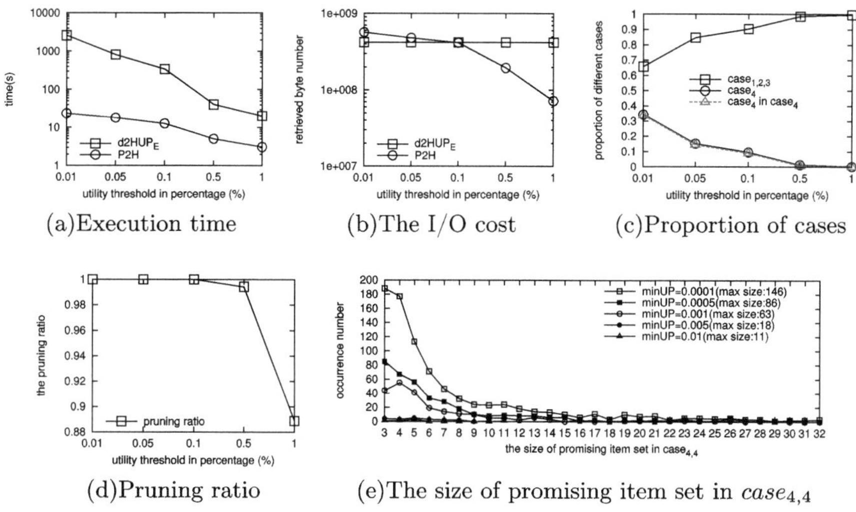

(a)Execution time (b)The I/O cost (c)Proportion of cases

(d)Pruning ratio (e)The size of promising item set in $case_{4,4}$

Fig. 7. The effect of real data set

8 Conclusion

This paper addresses the significant challenge of high utility itemset mining (HUIM) on massive datasets that exceed memory capacity. We propose P2H, a novel algorithm based on prefix-based partitioning, which divides the transaction database into manageable, lexicographically-ordered segments. Each partition is processed independently in memory, leveraging pre-computed utility information and efficient pruning strategies like subtree pruning and unpromising item filtering to drastically reduce both computational overhead and I/O costs. Experimental results demonstrate that P2H achieves substantial speedups-up to orders of magnitude-compared to existing extended methods like $d2HUP_E$.

Acknowledgment. This work was supported in part by NSFC U21A20513, NSFC 62402135, Taishan Scholars Program of Shandong Province grant tsqn202211091, and Natural Science Foundation of Shandong Province grant ZR2023QF059.

References

1. Ahmed, C.F., Tanbeer, S.K., Jeong, B., Lee, Y.: Efficient tree structures for high utility pattern mining in incremental databases. IEEE Trans. Knowl. Data Eng. **21**(12), 1708–1721 (2009)
2. Djamégni, C.T., et al.: Support estimation in frequent itemsets mining on enriched two level tree. Inf. Syst. **133**, 102559 (2025)
3. Duong, Q., Fournier-Viger, P., Ramampiaro, H., Nørvåg, K., Dam, T.: Efficient high utility itemset mining using buffered utility-lists. Appl. Intell. **48**(7), 1859–1877 (2018)

4. Fournier-Viger, P., Wu, C., Zida, S., Tseng, V.S.: FHM: faster high-utility itemset mining using estimated utility co-occurrence pruning. In: Foundations of Intelligent Systems - 21st International Symposium, ISMIS 2014, Roskilde, Denmark, 25–27 June 2014. Proceedings, pp. 83–92 (2014)
5. Han, M., He, F., Zhang, R., Li, C., Meng, F.: High utility itemset mining in data stream using elephant herding optimization. Knowl. Inf. Syst. **67**(3), 2357–2394 (2025)
6. Han, X., Liu, X., Chen, J., Lai, G., Gao, H., Li, J.: Efficiently mining frequent itemsets on massive data. IEEE Access **7**, 31409–31421 (2019)
7. Krishnamoorthy, S.: Pruning strategies for mining high utility itemsets. Expert Syst. Appl. **42**(5), 2371–2381 (2015)
8. Li, M., Han, M., Chen, Z., Wu, H., Zhang, X.: FCHM-stream: fast closed high utility itemsets mining over data streams. Knowl. Inf. Syst. **65**(6), 2509–2539 (2023)
9. Li, Y., Yeh, J., Chang, C.: Isolated items discarding strategy for discovering high utility itemsets. Data Knowl. Eng. **64**(1), 198–217 (2008)
10. Liu, J., Wang, K., Fung, B.C.M.: Mining high utility patterns in one phase without generating candidates. IEEE Trans. Knowl. Data Eng. **28**(5), 1245–1257 (2016)
11. Liu, M., Qu, J.: Mining high utility itemsets without candidate generation. In: 21st ACM International Conference on Information and Knowledge Management, CIKM 2012, Maui, HI, USA, October 29 - November 02 2012, pp. 55–64 (2012)
12. Liu, Y., Liao, W., Choudhary, A.N.: A two-phase algorithm for fast discovery of high utility itemsets. In: Advances in Knowledge Discovery and Data Mining, 9th Pacific-Asia Conference, PAKDD 2005, Hanoi, Vietnam, 18–20 May 2005, Proceedings, pp. 689–695 (2005)
13. Peng, A.Y., Koh, Y.S., Riddle, P.: mHUIMiner: a fast high utility itemset mining algorithm for sparse datasets. In: Advances in Knowledge Discovery and Data Mining - 21st Pacific-Asia Conference, PAKDD 2017, Jeju, South Korea, 23–26 May 2017, Proceedings, Part II, pp. 196–207 (2017)
14. Song, W., Ren, G., Gan, W.: Fast mining local high-utility itemsets. Eng. Appl. Artif. Intell. **145**, 109960 (2025)
15. Tseng, V.S., Shie, B., Wu, C., Yu, P.S.: Efficient algorithms for mining high utility itemsets from transactional databases. IEEE Trans. Knowl. Data Eng. **25**(8), 1772–1786 (2013)
16. Tseng, V.S., Wu, C., Shie, B., Yu, P.S.: Up-growth: an efficient algorithm for high utility itemset mining. In: Proceedings of the 16th ACM SIGKDD International Conference on Knowledge Discovery and Data Mining, Washington, DC, USA, 25–28 July 2010, pp. 253–262 (2010)
17. Tung, N.T., Nguyen, T.D.D., Nguyen, L.T.T., Vu, D., Fournier-Viger, P., Vo, B.: Mining cross-level high utility itemsets in unstable and negative profit databases. IEEE Trans. Knowl. Data Eng. **37**(9), 5420–5435 (2025)
18. Yun, U., Ryang, H., Ryu, K.H.: High utility itemset mining with techniques for reducing overestimated utilities and pruning candidates. Expert Syst. Appl. **41**(8), 3861–3878 (2014)
19. Zhang, C., Almpanidis, G., Wang, W., Liu, C.: An empirical evaluation of high utility itemset mining algorithms. Expert Syst. Appl. **101**, 91–115 (2018)
20. Zida, S., Fournier-Viger, P., Lin, J.C., Wu, C., Tseng, V.S.: EFIM: a fast and memory efficient algorithm for high-utility itemset mining. Knowl. Inf. Syst. **51**(2), 595–625 (2017)

A Brief Discussion on Improving Analog Electronics Teaching from the Perspective of Sensing and Systems

Hai Wang[1,2](✉), Yifan Wu[1,2], Zhidan Zhang[1,2], Hao Chen[1], Lei Huang[1], Xiangyan Kong[1,2], Yangong Zheng[1], and Yuejun Zhang[1]

[1] The School of Electrical Engineering and Computer Science (EECS), Ningbo University, Ningbo 315211, China
wanghai@nbu.edu.cn
[2] The Institute for Future Wireless Research (iFWR), Ningbo University, Ningbo 315211, China

Abstract. This paper focuses on the teaching and practice of *Fundamentals of Analog Electronics* under the background of "New Engineering" education and the development needs of electronic information disciplines. By integrating device principles, amplifier circuits, and high-sensitivity magnetic detection systems, the study aims to enhance students' learning interest and innovation ability. Starting from PN junctions, diodes, and optoelectronic devices, their applications in communication and magnetic field detection are introduced to bridge theory with practice. The principles of field-effect transistors and transimpedance amplifiers are then analyzed, including the effect of temperature on device performance and circuit gain. In the experimental section, an embedded control and data processing system based on LabVIEW is designed to achieve displacement control, signal acquisition, and imaging, combined with digital filtering to suppress interference. This work not only enriches classroom teaching but also provides a practical platform for nondestructive testing, weak signal extraction, and low-noise circuit design.

Keywords: Fundamentals of Analog Electronics · Low-Noise Circuit Design · High-Sensitivity Magnetic Sensor

1 Introduction

Fundamentals of Analog Electronics is an essential branch of electronic technology. At present, the educational content covers areas such as signal processing, circuit design, and integrated circuits, aligning with the development needs of the Internet of Things, artificial intelligence, and communication technologies. In 2017, the Chinese Ministry of Education launched the "New Engineering" initiative, emphasizing interdisciplinary innovation, practical skills, and industry–academia–research integration to promote talent cultivation and the transformation of achievements. Internationally, companies such as Texas Instruments [1] and ADI have made continuous breakthroughs in analog electronics, while domestically, firms like ZYNALOG have developed high-performance

B. Fernández-Manjón et al. (Eds.): SETE 2025/ICWL 2025, LNCS 16425, pp. 343–353, 2026.
https://doi.org/10.1007/978-981-92-0042-9_25

products widely applied in communications, healthcare, automotive electronics, and industrial control.

As a core course for electronic information majors, fundamentals of Analog Electronics build upon physical circuits and bridges toward high-frequency and integrated circuits. Its content covers diodes, transistors, field-effect transistors, operational amplifiers, and amplifier circuits, with applications in computation, filtering, waveform generation, and power supply design. However, due to the complexity of knowledge and the lack of frontier applications in classroom teaching, students' learning interest is often insufficient. Currently, many innovative teaching methods have been proposed internationally. For example, the Digital Spine-Enabled Hybrid Passive-Active Learning Design [2] integrates online and offline learning to enhance student engagement and learning outcomes.

This paper aims to foster students' mastery of device principles and circuit analysis methods, while leveraging high-sensitivity magnetic detection systems to enhance their understanding of basic circuits, low-noise amplification, and weak signal detection, thereby promoting their innovation capacity and overall competence.

2 Single PN Junction Device

A PN junction [3] is the fundamental structure formed when a P-type semiconductor comes into contact with an N-type semiconductor. The P-type region contains a large number of holes, while the N-type region contains a large number of electrons. At the junction, these carriers diffuse and recombine, creating a depletion layer and a space charge region. The built-in electric field within this region prevents further diffusion of carriers and gives the junction its characteristic unidirectional conductivity.

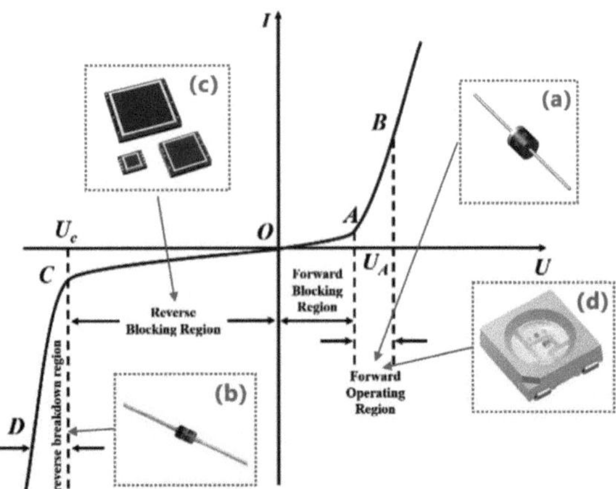

Fig. 1. The current–voltage (I–V) characteristic curve of a PN junction and different types of diodes: (a) diodes, (b) Zener diodes, (c) photodiode, (d) light-emitting diode.

The I–V characteristic curve of a PN junction (see Fig. 1) describes the relationship between the voltage across the junction and the resulting current. This curve can generally be divided into three regions: the forward conduction region on the right, the reverse cutoff region in the middle, and the reverse breakdown region on the left.

In traditional classrooms, teaching often emphasizes the transmission of theoretical knowledge while paying little attention to practice and application. As a result, students tend to passively absorb information without sufficient opportunities to apply what they have learned to real problem-solving. To spark students' interest in studying single PN junction devices, this paper begins with the three regions of the I–V characteristic curve. By introducing the distinct applications of the device in each region, theory is integrated with practice, enabling students to master the knowledge more effectively.

2.1 Diode and Zener Diode

In traditional teaching, the focus is mainly on diodes and Zener diodes [4]. The basic structure of a diode is a PN junction, once packaged with electrodes, it forms the device (see Fig. 1(a)). The primary application of a general diode lies in its unidirectional conductivity, which enables the realization of rectifier circuits [5], detector circuits, switching, and protection circuits.

The Zener diode, on the other hand, is a special type of diode (see Fig. 1(b)) that mainly operates in the reverse breakdown region. Unlike a conventional diode that may be damaged by excessive current during breakdown, a Zener diode makes use of its stable breakdown voltage characteristic. It is commonly employed in circuits as a voltage reference or voltage regulator. When a reverse voltage is applied across a Zener diode and reaches its breakdown voltage, the diode enters the breakdown conduction state, where its voltage remains nearly constant while the current varies according to the external circuit. This property allows the Zener diode to effectively stabilize voltage in electronic systems.

2.2 Light-Emitting Diode and Photodiode

A photodiode [6] (see Fig. 1(c)) is a device that operates based on the photoelectric effect of a semiconductor PN junction. It typically works in the reverse-bias region of the diode. Compared to a standard diode, the PN junction of a photodiode is designed to be sensitive to light. When light illuminates the junction, photons generate electron–hole pairs, producing a photocurrent in the external circuit. The magnitude of this photocurrent is proportional to the intensity of the incident light.

In an optical pumping magnetometer [7], when the atomic gas is excited by the pump laser, the spin state of the atoms is modulated by the external magnetic field. By using a photodiode to detect changes in the intensity of light passing through the atomic vapor and converting the optical signal into an electrical signal, magnetic field information can be electronically measured and recorded.

A light-emitting diode (LED) [8] (see Fig. 1(d)) primarily operates in the forward conduction region of I–V characteristic curve. Its working principle is based on the PN junction properties of semiconductors and the radiative transitions that occur when carriers recombine. Unlike a standard diode, an LED is made from specialized semiconductor compounds.

When the PN junction is forward biased, electrons and holes recombine in the junction region. During this process, electrons transition from a higher energy state to a lower energy state, releasing energy in the form of photons. The energy of these photons corresponds to the bandgap of the semiconductor material, so the emission color of the LED depends on the material used. Table 1 lists various materials along with their corresponding emission colors and operating voltages.

Table 1. Parameters of LEDs with Different Materials

Wavelength range (nm)	Color	Operating voltage@20mA	Material
<400	Ultraviolet	3.1–4.4	GaN
400–450	Purple	2.8–4.0	InGaN
450–500	Blue	2.5–3.7	ZnSe
500–570	Green	1.9–4.0	AlGaP
570–590	Yellow	2.1–2.2	InGaAlP
590–610	Orange	2.0–2.1	GaAsP
610–670	Red	1.6–2.0	AlGaAs
>760	Infrared	<1.9	GaP

3 Amplifiers Electronic Circuits

3.1 Key Parameters of Junction Field-Effect Transistors (JFETs)

A junction field-effect transistor (JFET) is a type of semiconductor device in which the current is controlled by an electric field [9]. It can be modeled as a voltage-controlled current source and features high input impedance and low noise. In the small-signal model, the transconductance (g_m) of a JFET is defined as:

$$g_m = \frac{\partial I_D}{\partial V_{GS}} \tag{1}$$

where I_D is the drain current and V_{GS} is the gate–source voltage. In a typical common-source amplifier, the circuit gain is given by:

$$A_v = -g_m R_D \tag{2}$$

where g_m is the transconductance of the JFET and R_D is the drain resistor. The negative sign indicates a 180° phase shift between the input and output signals. Moreover, the gate current of a JFET is extremely small, giving it an input impedance ranging from 10^7 to 10^{12} Ω, far exceeding that of bipolar junction transistors (BJTs). Its output impedance is typically on the order of several kilo-ohms. In terms of frequency response, the low-frequency cutoff is usually determined by the coupling and bypass capacitors, ranging from a few Hz to several tens of Hz, while the mid-frequency gain remains stable. The high-frequency cutoff is influenced by the gate–source capacitance (C_{gs}, a few pF) and the gate–drain capacitance (C_{gd}, around 1–5 pF) through the Miller effect, resulting in bandwidths that can reach the MHz range. Additionally, JFETs exhibit low current noise and a low flicker (1/f) noise corner frequency, making them highly suitable for low-frequency sensor applications such as optically pumped magnetometers (OPMs) [10].

3.2 Applications of Amplifiers

In practical systems, the amplitude of useful signals is often very small and buried in noise. For example, in an OLED non-destructive testing system based on magnetic sensors [11], it is necessary to detect the weak magnetic signals generated by the tiny currents of the display driver IC. During acquisition and analysis, these signals are inevitably affected by various noise sources, including thermal noise, power-line interference, and complex environmental electromagnetic interference. In such cases, amplifiers are used to build circuits for amplification, filtering, and other processing, enabling the extraction of the desired useful signals from the noise.

3.3 Effect of Temperature on Basic JFET Parameters

In magnetic detection systems based on superconducting quantum interference devices [12], the sensors typically operate at liquid helium temperatures (4.2 K) or liquid nitrogen temperatures (77 K) [13]. To investigate whether the amplifier and sensor can function properly in the same environment, it is necessary to study the effect of temperature on the basic characteristics of JFETs. In this experiment, the JFET amplifier circuit was tested at both room temperature (298 K) and liquid nitrogen temperature (77 K). It can be observed that when tested in a low-temperature environment, the circuit's gain is significantly lower than under room-temperature conditions. (see Fig. 2(a)).

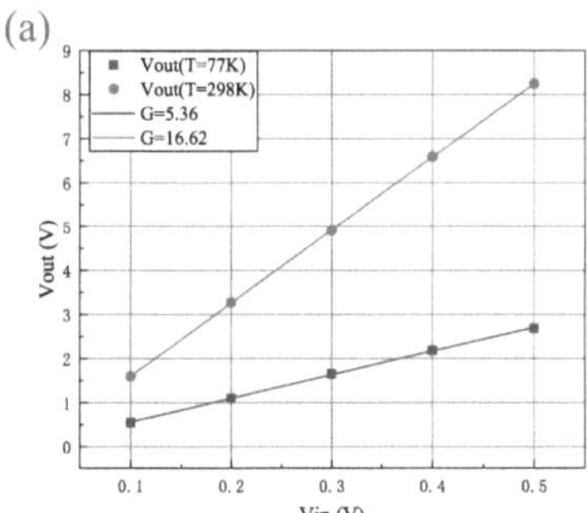

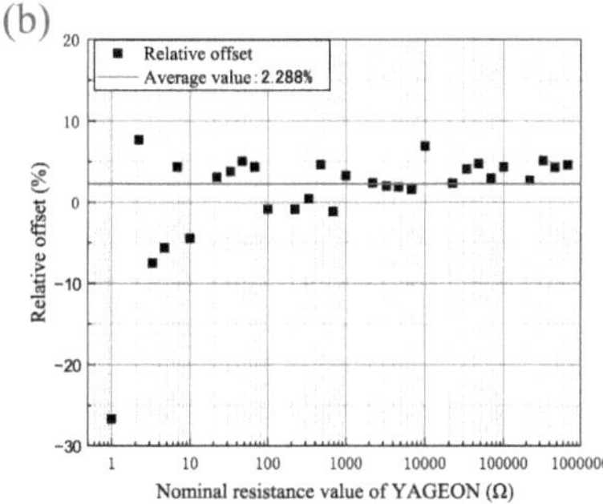

Fig. 2. Figures (a) shows comparison of JFET Amplifier Gain at Room Temperature and Low Temperature. Figures (b) shows relative deviation of YAGEO resistor values at liquid nitrogen temperature

Under low-temperature conditions, changes in the JFET's transconductance (g_m) and variations in resistance values may both affect the gain of the amplifier circuit.

Therefore, the relative deviation of YAGEO resistors at liquid nitrogen temperature was first measured (see Fig. 2(b)). For each resistance specification, 10 measurements were performed on resistors of the same value, and the results were averaged. The results show that the average relative resistance deviation is only 2.288%, indicating that it has negligible impact on the gain of the JFET common-source amplifier.

By maintaining the drain current $I_d = 2$ mA of the JFET LSK170, it was observed that when the environment changed from room temperature to a low-temperature condition, the static operating point of the JFET shifted from $U_{gs} = -298$ mA to $U_{gs} = -9.65$ mV (see Fig. 3). This change in the operating point altered the transconductance g_m thereby affecting the circuit's gain.

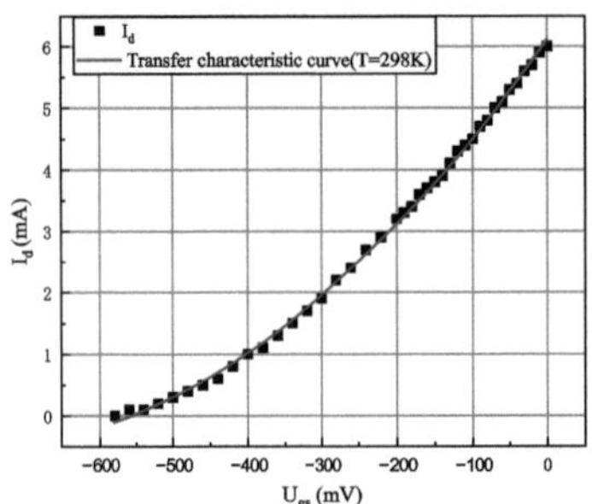

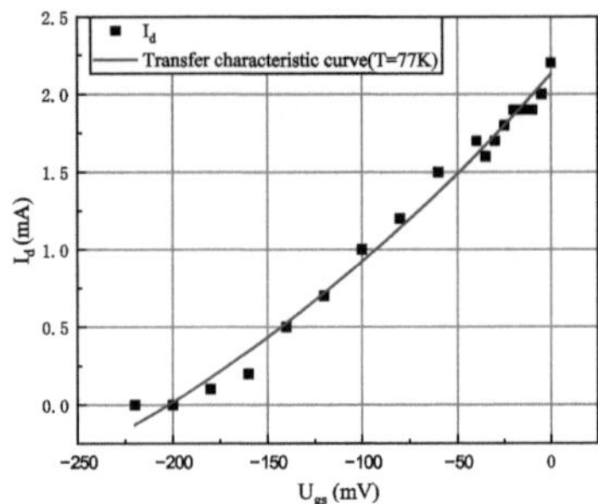

Fig. 3. Transfer characteristics of LSK170 at room temperature (298K) and low temperature (77K)

3.4 TIA Amplifier Circuit

To bridge theory with practice, a transimpedance amplifier (TIA) circuit based on the OPA657 operational amplifier was implemented in LTspice [14] (see Fig. 4). This circuit converts an input current into an output voltage and is widely employed in photodetectors, primarily to amplify weak current signals generated by photoelectric conversion devices such as photodiodes and photomultiplier tubes. The fundamental operating principle of the circuit is to use the feedback resistor Rf to transform the input current into an output voltage. The signal is then processed through an RC low-pass filter, producing both the original signal and an AC-coupled output.

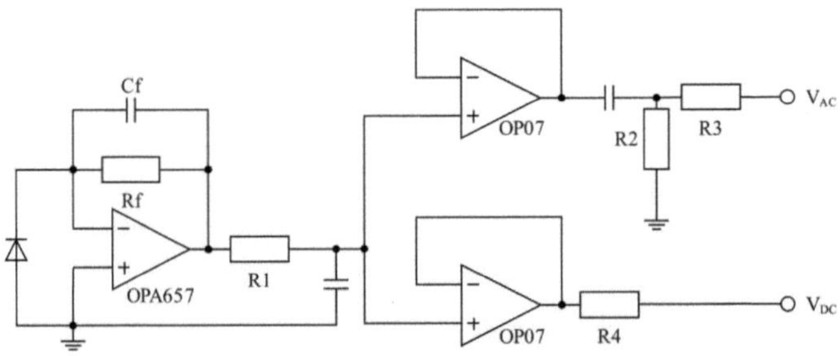

Fig. 4. OPA657-based TIA circuit

By using the simulation software LTspice, the operating state of the circuit can be essentially predicted. In the simulation circuit, the feedback resistor Rf was set to 10 kΩ, and the RC low-pass filter consisted of a 1.2 kΩ resistor and a 1nF capacitor. The LTspice simulation results show an amplification gain of 10 kV/A and a bandwidth of 133.8 kHz (see Fig. 5). The upper curve represents the amplitude–frequency response of the circuit, while the lower curve corresponds to its phase–frequency response.

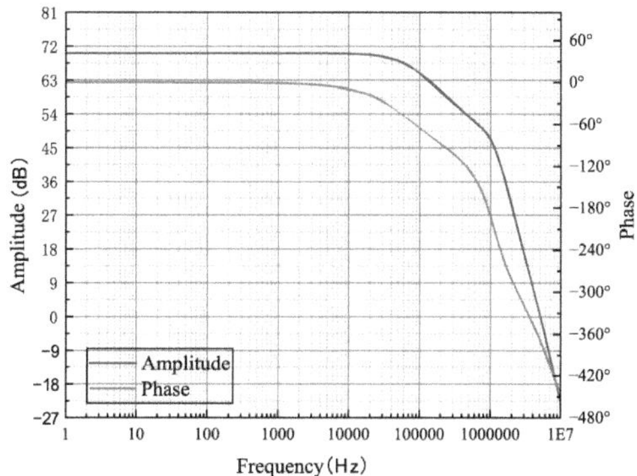

Fig. 5. LTspice circuit simulation results

4 Experimental Design

4.1 Embedded Software Design

This nondestructive testing (NDT) system based on a high-sensitivity magnetic sensor consists of four main modules: a probe composed of a TMR sensor and a coil, a power amplification and signal amplification readout circuit, a DSP, and a three-axis motion platform. The upper computer of this NDT system is developed based on LabVIEW [15], enabling three-axis displacement platform control, voltage acquisition, and image processing. During operation, the platform is first initialized and moved to the specified position. After completing voltage acquisition, the data are stored, and each point is subsequently measured in sequence. Finally, all the collected data are processed to generate a defect imaging map (see Fig. 6).

The embedded software interface (see Fig. 7) consists of two parts, with the left section dedicated to controlling the three-axis motion platform. Through serial communication with the platform's console, it enables independent control of the X, Y, and Z axes, including motion parameters such as direction, speed, distance, and acceleration. Meanwhile, the display section provides real-time information on the current position and velocity of the platform. In addition, this section integrates convenient shortcut functions, such as one-click stop and three-axis homing, to facilitate operation.

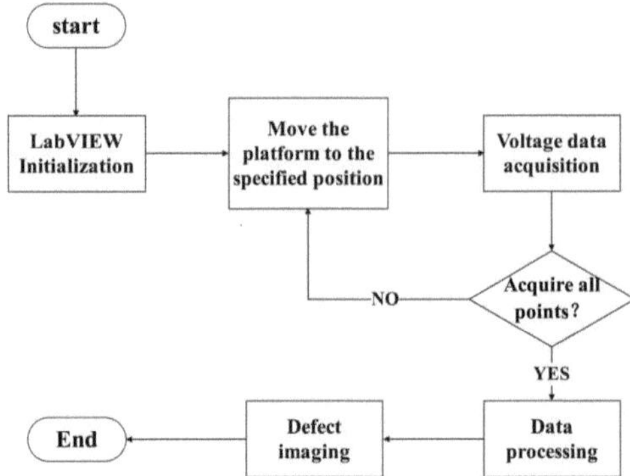

Fig. 6. Flowchart of the upper-computer control in the nondestructive testing system

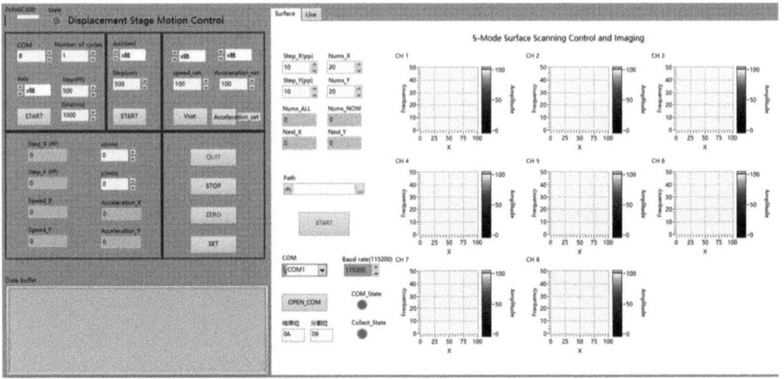

Fig. 7. Embedded system interface diagram

On the right side of the system interface is the S-shaped surface scanning and imaging module, which transmits eight-channel voltage data via serial communication. Before scanning, the range and step size must be set, and the port, baud rate, and protocol initialized. Once started, the program displays the serial communication status, scanning positions, and progress, while the left section allows real-time monitoring of the received data. After the scan is completed, the eight-channel data are plotted for imaging. The program adopts a producer/consumer architecture to achieve multi-loop data sharing and ensure acquisition integrity (see Fig. 8).

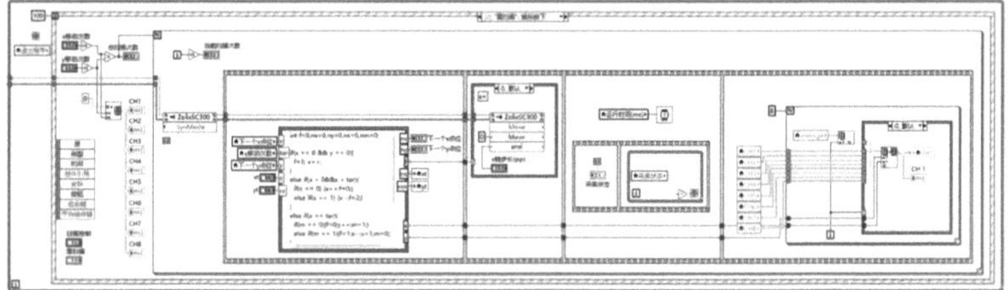

Fig. 8. Partial program block diagram of S-shaped surface scanning and imaging

4.2 Filter Algorithm Design

Under unshielded conditions, the measured signals of the system often contain strong power-frequency and high-frequency interferences. Therefore, in order to extract useful information, suppress noise, and enhance the stability and reliability of the system, filtering must be applied after voltage data acquisition.

According to the processing method, filters can be classified into analog and digital types; based on frequency characteristics, they can be categorized as low-pass, high-pass, band-pass, and band-stop filters. Moreover, different types of filters exhibit distinct passband and stopband characteristics, allowing selection based on specific requirements. Figure 10 illustrates the amplitude–frequency responses of Butterworth, Chebyshev, elliptic, and Bessel low-pass filters.

From the amplitude–frequency response curves in Fig. 9, the differences among the four filters can be observed. The Butterworth filter provides the flattest passband but with a slower stopband roll-off; the Chebyshev filter introduces ripples in the passband but achieves a faster stopband attenuation; the elliptic filter offers the steepest stopband roll-off but introduces ripples in both the passband and stopband; while the Bessel filter, although inferior in amplitude–frequency characteristics, provides the best phase response with a maximally flat group delay.

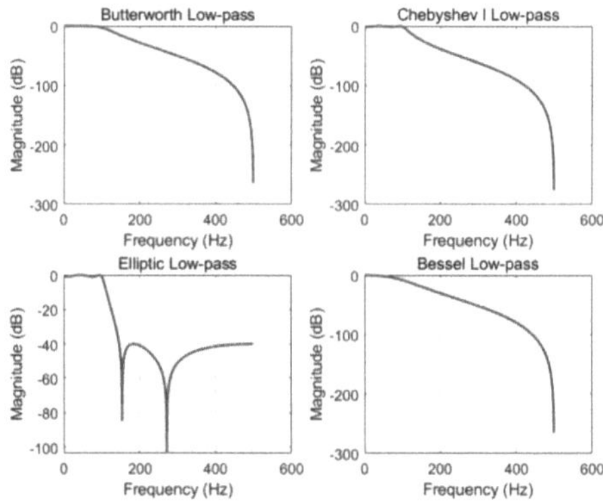

Fig. 9. Amplitude–frequency response characteristics of four different types of low-pass filters

In LabVIEW, multiple filter functions are already encapsulated (see Fig. 10). By simply invoking the appropriate filter and configuring parameters such as filter type, cutoff frequency, sampling frequency, and order, the design of the filtering algorithm can be accomplished.

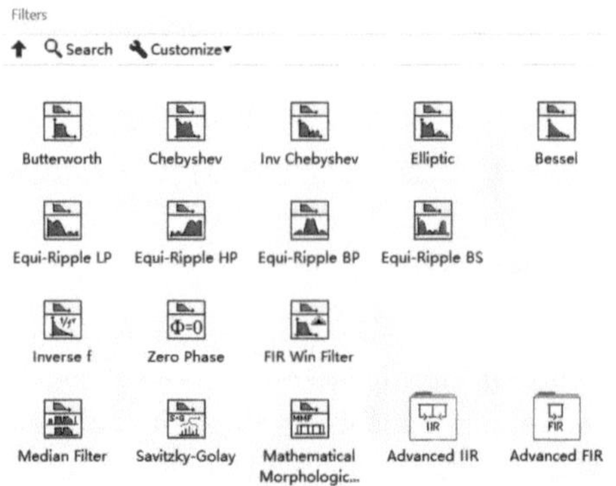

Fig. 10. Different types of filters provided in LabVIEW

5 Conclusion

This paper establishes a complete chain of "theory–simulation–experiment–application," closely integrating traditional teaching of Fundamentals of Analog Electronics with cutting-edge application scenarios. On the one hand, by introducing the applications of PN junctions, photodiodes, and JFETs in magnetic sensing and low-noise amplification, students' intuitive understanding of abstract circuit knowledge is enhanced. On the other hand, through practical modules such as the LabVIEW-based upper computer system, filter algorithm design, and transimpedance amplifier simulations, a teaching and research platform oriented toward practical nondestructive testing is constructed. This study not only improves students' comprehension of device characteristics and signal processing methods, but also plays an active role in cultivating hands-on ability, interdisciplinary thinking, and innovative awareness. Overall, the work provides valuable exploration and practical experience for the reform of analog electronics education and the application research of high-sensitivity magnetic detection systems.

Acknowledgements. This work was supported by the Teaching Reform Research Project of Analog Electronics at Ningbo University (JYXM2024097). Hai Wang and Yifan Wu contributed equally to the work.

References

1. Gass, W.: Early history of Texas instrument's digital signal processor. IEEE Micro **41**(6), 129–130 (2021)
2. Wang, K., Scott, J., Jollands, M.: Enhancing analog electronics education in undergraduate degrees through digital spine-enabled hybrid passive-active learning design. IEEE Access **13**, 104679–104691 (2025)

3. Li, D., Lin, W., Wang, Q., Lv, X., Zhang, T., Li, L.: Trenched diamond PN junction diode with enhanced conductance modulation effect designed by simulation. Microelectron. J. **139**, 105903 (2023)
4. Suetsugu, T., Kazimierczuk, M.K.: Voltage clamped class-e amplifier with zener diode. IEEE Trans. Circuits Syst. Fundam. Theory Appl. **50**(10), 1347–1349 (2003)
5. Dirgantoro, K.P., Yang, Y.-M.: Feasibility study on the rectifier diode and bridge circuit theory. J. Intell. Fuzzy Syst. **35**(1), 559–564 (2018)
6. Yu, G.: SBIR phase II: Flexible polymer photodiode arrays for image scanning and digital camera applications (1998)
7. Gilles, H., Hamel, J., Chéron, B.: Laser pumped 4He magnetometer. Rev. Sci. Instrum. **72**(5), 2253–2260 (2001)
8. Moiseyev, L.V., Odnoblyudov, M.A.: A review of modern light-emitting diode technologies in light sources for general illumination. Light Eng. **22**(3), 11–19 (2014)
9. Chen, Z.: Model for power SiC vertical JFET with unified description of linear and saturation operating regimes. IEEE Trans. Ind. Appl. **47**(4), 1853–1861 (2011)
10. Pedersen, M., Abbott, D.F., Jackson, G.D.: Wearable OPM-MEG: a changing landscape for epilepsy. Epilepsia **63**(11), 2745–2753 (2022)
11. Zhu, H., Wang, H., Li, Z., Kong, X.: OLED current detection using tunneling magnetoresistance sensor. Chin. J. Liq. Cryst. Disp. **38**(5), 595–601 (2023)
12. Jin, I.: Low-noise dc superconducting quantum interference devices for gravity wave detection (1997)
13. Takemoto, M., Akai, T., Kitamura, Y., Hatsukade, Y., Tanaka, S.: HTS rf-SQUID microscope for metallic contaminant detection. IEEE Trans. Appl. Supercond. **21**(3), 432–435 (2011)
14. Kularatna, N.: LTspice® for linear circuits. IEEE Electr. Insul. Mag. **40**(5), 44 (2024)
15. Whitley, K., Blackwell, A.: Visual programming in the wild: a survey of LabVIEW programmers. J. Vis. Lang. Comput. **12**(4), 435–472 (2001)

Submodular Merging with Superpixels for Ocean Remote Sensing Image Segmentation

Qianna Cui(✉) and Yilin Xu

School of Computer Science and Information, China Three Gorges University, Yichang 443000, Hubei, People's Republic of China
cuiqianna@ctgu.edu.cn

Abstract. In image segmentation, superpixels composed of locally adjacent similar pixels have the effect of suppressing noise sensitivity and reducing feature calculation, and further improving the performance of segmentation in terms of both accuracy and efficiency. With a number of superpixels, an image can be segmented well with a perfect merging condition. However, existing superpixel-based segmentation methods are highly dependent on the dataset, extremely time-consuming, and lack generalization and explainability. For that, we design an interpretable mathematical programming model with submodular function to merge superpixels in this paper. After we map the superpixels and their adjacency relationships into a graph structure, the image segmentation problem is transformed into a graph partition problem. Through the application of the submodular function to the constructed graph, the partition problem the partition problem is flexibly transformed into that of finding a cut set. To figure out this problem, we design an approximate algorithm within the time complexity of $O(n)$, where n is the total number of superpixels. We demonstrate that the approximation ratio of the algorithm is $(1 - \frac{1}{e})$, which is proven with an arbitrarily small constant $e > 0$. An ocean remote-sensing dataset is used to verify its high performance and efficiency. It indirectly demonstrate that our merging model is generalizable and explainable.

Keywords: Superpixel merging · Remote sensing image segmentation · Submodular function · Approximate algorithm · Graph cuts

1 Introduction

Image segmentation is one of the core tasks in the field of computer vision, and plays an important role in applications such as medical image analysis, autonomous driving, and remote sensing interpretation [1–4]. In most scientific fields, related research relies on experimental data. For researchers, the prevailing idea is to segment images by identifying similar features within a given dataset—an approach known as data-driven methods, such as deep learning methods [5,6].

B. Fernández-Manjón et al. (Eds.): SETE 2025/ICWL 2025, LNCS 16425, pp. 354–368, 2026.
https://doi.org/10.1007/978-981-92-0042-9_26

However, this approach is often based on datasets with different assumptions, making it difficult to apply the same segmentation criterion to different datasets and requiring training on a large number of datasets. In addition, even after extensive training, the ideal segmentation results are still hard to attain. This is due to the fact that the segmentation problem is a discrete partitioning problem on the pixel set, which is an NP-hard problem in the field of combinatorial optimization [7,8].

Since the collection of datasets is often affected by the environment, the images contain more noisy pixels. Traditional pixel-level segmentation methods are difficult to meet actual segmentation needs due to their high computational complexity and susceptibility to noise [9,10]. Superpixel technology significantly reduces the complexity of subsequent processing by dividing the image into perceptually consistent local areas [11]. Image segmentation based on superpixels mainly includes three steps: (1) generating superpixels; (2) extracting superpixel features; (3) dividing the superpixel set according to the features [12]. However, how to use superpixels to achieve segmentation with consistent regional features still faces challenges: the global optimization of segmentation targets lacks theoretical guarantees. Up to now, superpixel merging process is mapped to a few explainable models, such as set maximum coverage [13]. Another kind of superpixel merging method employs a pre-set given merging criterion [14,15]. However, these merging methods need to traverse all potential merging results in each iterative step, which suffer from low efficiency. When the image size increases, the merging cost rises exponentially. Based on the above analysis, the existing superpixel merging methods hardly generalize to practical datasets with large size.

In recent years, submodular function optimization has gained increasing importance in computer vision due to its theoretical advantages in combinatorial optimization problems (such as guaranteed approximation ratios and efficient solutions), including object detection [16,17] and video information extraction [18]. These studies are based on image segmentation and thus provide new approaches to global optimization in the task [19,20]. Shen et al. proposed a quadratic submodular energy approximation maximization framework with knapsack constraints, which regards computer vision problems as a generalization of the classic 0/1 knapsack problem [19]. By mapping image pixels and their related relationships into a graph structure, we transform the image segmentation task into a graph topology selection problem [20,21]. In the aforementioned studies, the image segmentation problem is explicitly transformed into a submodular function maximization problem involving selecting subsets from a base set.

However, these methods all design objective functions at the pixel level and incorporate the final pixel cluster balance constraint into the objective function in a relaxed manner, thereby obtaining pixel clusters with high homogeneity and a balanced number of clusters. At present, the research on superpixel-based image segmentation models has not deeply involved the global optimization level, and has not guaranteed the heterogeneity between different regions, resulting in low generalization of existing segmentation methods.

Inspired by the above research, this paper transforms the superpixel-based image segmentation problem into a graph topology selection problem, and divides the vertices in the graph into different clusters according to the selected graph topology structure. Superpixel-based segmentation essentially seeks to partition superpixel clusters such that the segmented regions corresponding to each superpixel cluster are highly homogeneous, while the segments themselves are highly heterogeneous. Based on the principle of maximum entropy for random walks on a graph, this paper designs an entropy rate function to select graph topology. By maximizing this entropy rate function, we achieve compact, highly homogeneous segmented regions [21,22]. In addition, we add a heterogeneity constraint by extracting the texture features to increase heterogeneity among different regions as much as possible. On the basis of the above mentioned analysis, we build a submodular merging model, and propose a lazy greedy algorithm by its diminishing marginal benefit property, reducing the complexity from the merging process from $O(n^2)$ to $O(n \log n)$. Futhermore, our proposed merging model relies on the distinguishing conditions for different segmentation regions, which have provable theoretical guarantees, and demonstrate promising performance on diverse datasets. Our designed approximation algorithm has the $(1 - \frac{1}{e})-$ ratio.

2 Related Work

2.1 Submodular Function

Assume E is a finite set. The set function $F : 2^E \to \mathbb{R}$ is a submodular function that satisfies:

$$F(A \cup \{a_1\}) - F(A) \geq F(A \cup \{a_1, a_2\}) - F(A \cup \{a_2\}) \quad (1)$$

Or equivalently, for all $A \subseteq E$ and $a_1, a_2 \in E \setminus A$, there are

$$\delta F_{a_1}(A) \geq \delta F_{a_1}(A \cup \{a_2\}) \quad (2)$$

where

$$\delta F_{a_1}(A) = F(A \cup \{a_1\}) - F(A) \quad (3)$$

represent the marginal gain from adding element a_1 to the set A. This property is also known as the property of diminishing marginal returns, meaning that the gain gained by adding elements later becomes smaller [23].

If for $\forall A \subseteq E$, the set function F satisfies $F(A) \leq F(A \cup \{a_1\})$, then F is said to be monotonically increasing. This property is referred to as monotonicity in this paper.

2.2 Random Walk

In a random walk model, the uncertainty of a random variable is measured by the entropy H [21,24]. The entropy of a discrete random variable X with probability mass function p_X is defined as:

$$H(X) = -\sum_{x\in\mathcal{X}} p_X(x)\log p_X(x) \tag{4}$$

where $\mathcal{X}$ is the support set of X. The conditional entropy $H(X|Y)$ is used to quantify the uncertainty in X given the value of the associated random variable Y. It is defined as:

$$\begin{aligned} H(X|Y) &= \sum_{y\in\mathcal{Y}} p_Y(y) H(X|Y=y) \\ &= -\sum_{y\in\mathcal{Y}} p_Y(y) \sum_{x\in\mathcal{X}} p_{X|Y}(x|y)\log p_{X|Y}(x|y) \end{aligned} \tag{5}$$

where $\mathcal{Y}$ is the support of Y and $p_{X|Y}$ is the conditional probability mass function.

The entropy rate is a measure used to quantify the uncertainty of a random process $\boldsymbol{X} = \{X_t|t \in T\}$, where T is a set of metrics. In discrete random processes, the entropy rate is defined as an asymptotic measure:

$$\mathcal{H}(\boldsymbol{X}) = \lim_{t\to\infty} H(X_t|X_{t-1}, X_{t-2}, \cdots, X_1) \tag{6}$$

It measures the uncertainty that remains in the random process after observing past trajectories. For stationary random processes, the limit in the above equation always holds. For stationary first-order Markov processes, the entropy rate has a simple form:

$$\begin{aligned} \mathcal{H}(\boldsymbol{X}) &= \lim_{t\to\infty} H(X_t|X_{t-1}) \\ &= \lim_{t\to\infty} H(X_2|X_1) = H(X_2|X_1) \end{aligned} \tag{7}$$

The first equality is due to the first-order Markov property, while the second equality is due to stationarity.

Assume that $\boldsymbol{X} = \{X_t|t \in T, X_t \in V\}$ is a random walk on the graph $G = (V, E)$, where w is a non-negative similarity measure. Based on the random walk model [25], the transition probability is defined as:

$$p_{i,j} = \Pr(X_{t+1} = v_j|X_t = v_i) = \frac{w_{i,j}}{w_i} \tag{8}$$

where $w_i = \sum_{k:v_{i,k}\in E} w_{i,k}$ is the sum of the incident weights of the vertex vi and the following formula gives the stationary distribution:

$$\boldsymbol{\mu} = (\mu_1, \mu_2, \cdots, \mu_{|V|})^T = \left(\frac{w_1}{w_T}, \frac{w_2}{w_T}, \cdots, \frac{w_{|V|}}{w_T}\right)^T \tag{9}$$

where $w_T = \sum_{i=1}^{|V|} w_i$ is a normalizing constant. Stationary distributions are not unique in disconnected graphs. However, $\boldsymbol{\mu}$ in the above equation is always a stationary distribution. We can easily verify that $\boldsymbol{\mu} = P^T \boldsymbol{\mu}$, where $P = [p_{i,j}]$ is the transition matrix. The entropy rate of a random walk can be calculated using the above equation $H(X|Y)$:

$$\begin{aligned}\mathcal{H}(\boldsymbol{X}) &= H(X_2|X_1) = \sum_i \mu_i H(X_2|X_1 = v_i) \\ &= -\sum_i \sum_j \frac{w_{i,j}}{w_T} \log \frac{w_{i,j}}{w_T} + \sum_i \frac{w_i}{w_T} \log \frac{w_i}{w_T}\end{aligned} \tag{10}$$

3 Problem Formulation

To segment an ocean remote sensing image into some homogeneous regions, generating superpixel is an effective technique to eliminate the negative effect of noise first. Thereby , the image segmentation problem is a superpixel clustering issue which merges the adjacent similar superpixel into the same region. We map the superpixel image into a graph structure, then the superpixel merging problem translates into a graph-partition problem . In other words , the problem is to find k-connected subgraphs, where each subgraph has the maximum similarity for each node cluster.

3.1 Graph Construction

After producing superpixels for an image, we map them into a graph $G = (V, E)$ with its adjacent relationships, where V is the set of nodes, and E is the set of edges. For the superpixel set $I = \{S_1, S_2, \ldots, S_n\}$, we let each node $v_i \in V$ denote the superpixel S_i, where $i \in [1, \ldots, n]$. Proper edge-construction options include the nearest-neighbor graph, the fully-connected graph, and the region-adjacent graph [21,26]. The merging significance is insignificance between two superpixels that are far apart , fully connected graph is not necessary, which is time-consuming. However , the region adjacent graph may miss opportunities to merge the closer but not adjacent superpixels. So, we construct the nearest neighbor graph for merging similar superpixels, we set the number of nearest neighbors to 8. In the graph G, each edge $e_{i,j} \in E$ connects two superpixels S_i and S_j that are among each other's 8 nearest neighbors , the locations of which are computed with the center position. For each superpixel S_i, we can extract the RGB, LAB, and HSV color features $f_c^\rho(S_i)$, by which the distance between two different superpixels can be computed directly. The distance is computed with the following equation:

$$d_{i,j}^c = \|f_c^\rho(S_i) - f_c^\rho(S_j)\|^2 \tag{11}$$

The color distance can measure the dissimilarity between two nodes in the graph, thus each edge can be weighted by the color distance, which is computed as follows:

$$w_{i,j}^c = \exp(-(d_{i,j}^c)) \tag{12}$$

The graph construction process is presented in Fig. 1 in detail .

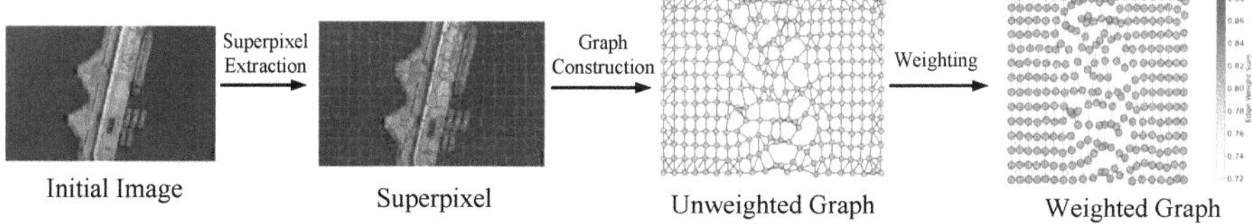

Fig. 1. Graph Construction with superpixels for an ocean remote sensing image.

Our goal in superpixel merging is to split the graph into disjoint components. It is achieved by finding a subset of edges $A \subseteq E$ such that the resulting graph, $G = (V, A)$, contains K-disjoint subgraphs. A good expectation of the graph partition is that all nodes in each subgraph are as similar as possible. It has been proven that the compact and homogeneous cluster can be achieved by the entropy rate via random walks [21,25,27]. So, the random-walk model is a effective way to generate the required set A. In the random walk model, to keep the total outgoing weight constant , we add a self-loop to each vertex to represent the edge weights that have not been selected into the set A. In other words, the edge weights are symmetric, i.e. $w_{i,j}^c = w_{j,i}^c$. Therefore, a self-loop $e_{i,i}$ is constructed for each vertex. The weight of $e_{i,i}$ is defined as: $w_{i,i}^c = \sum_{j:e_{i,j} \in E \setminus A} w_{i,j}^c$, which represents the sum of the weights of the unselected edges connected to vertex v_i in the initial graph. It should be noted that the increased self-loop has no effect on the graph partitioning.

3.2 Entropy Rate-Based Superpixel Merging

To obtain a compact set of vertices with high similarity, this paper uses the entropy of random walks based on the constructed graph model structure to calculate and obtain a set A that satisfies the segmentation objective, thereby obtaining a connected subgraph set $\{G_1 = (V_1, E_1), \ldots, G_K = (V_K, E_K)\}$.

Based on the random walk model, the transition probability $p_{i,j}$ from vertex v_i to vertex v_j is calculated as follows:

$$p_{i,j}(A) = \begin{cases} \dfrac{w_{i,j}^c}{w_i^c}, & if \quad i \neq j \quad and \quad e_{i,j} \in A \\ 0, & if \quad i \neq j \quad and \quad e_{i,j} \notin A \\ \dfrac{w_{i,i}^c}{w_i^c} = 1 - \dfrac{\sum_{j:e_{i,j} \in A} w_{i,j}^c}{w_i^c}, & if \quad i = j \end{cases} \tag{13}$$

Here, $w_i^c = \sum_{k:e_{i,k}\in E} w_{i,k}^c$ represents the sum of the weights of the edges connected to vertex v_i in the initial graph structure. The state distribution of the random walk is as follows:

$$\mu = (\mu_1, \mu_2, \ldots, \mu_{|V|})^T = (\frac{w_1^c}{w_T^c}, \frac{w_2^c}{w_T^c}, \ldots, \frac{w_{|V|}^c}{w_T^c}) \tag{14}$$

where $|V|$ represents the total number of vertices in the vertex set, and $w_T = \sum_{i=1}^{|V|} w_i$ is the sum of the weights on all vertices. The entropy rate of a random walk on a graph $G = (V, E)$ can be calculated using the following entropy rate function:

$$\mathcal{H}(A) = -\sum_i \mu_i \sum_j p_{i,j}(A) \log p_{i,j}(A) \tag{15}$$

Maximizing the formula (15) encourages to maximize $p_{i,j}(A)$, which makes the similarity of each node cluster as large as possible.

3.3 Partition Penalty-Based Superpixel Merging

Using only the entropy-rate term, the graph partition process may group nodes into an incorrect cluster when the nodes have similar color features, especially for superpixels with the same color as the background. The reason is that no constraint term is designed to separate dissimilar clusters as much as possible. To overcome it, we propose a partition penalty by combining spatial and texture dissimilarity. First, we extract the texture feature and position feature of superpixel S_i, which are $f^t(S_i)$ and $f^p(S_i)$ respectively. Then, the distance of superpixel S_i and S_j is computed using Eq. (11), which are called $d_{i,j}^t$ and $d_{i,j}^p$. Then, two additional weights $w_{i,j}^t$ and $w_{i,j}^p$ are obtained using Eq. (12). When the new weights of two subgraphs are calculated, we can utilize them to measure the dissimilarity of each subgraph, and then separate the dissimilar subgraph by the following partition penalty:

$$\mathcal{P}(A) = (\alpha_1 * \sum_{e_{i,j}\in A} w_{i,j}^t + \alpha_2 * \sum_{e_{i,j}\in A} w_{i,j}^p) = (\alpha_1 * w_{i,j}^t(A) + \alpha_2 * w_{i,j}^p(A)) \tag{16}$$

where α_1 and α_2 are the standardization factors for texture feature and position feature, respectively. Note that smaller intra-subgraph differences yield a larger penalty, and vice versa.

By the formulation of entropy rate and partition penalty, the mathematical programming model is designed to merge superpixels with following formula:

$$\max_{A\subseteq E} \mathcal{F}(A) \quad s.t. \quad N_A \geq K \tag{17}$$

where $\mathcal{F}(A) = \mathcal{H}(A) + \lambda * \mathcal{P}(A)$. The factor of λ is to control the effect of partition penalty in the whole merging function.

Theorem 1. *The superpixel merging function $\mathcal{F}(A)$ is a monotonically increasing submodular function under the proposed graph construction.*

The entropy rate function $\mathcal{H}(A)$ has been proven to be a monotonically increasing submodular function theoretically proven [19,21,25]. From Eq. (16), we can see that each component $w^t_{i,j}(A)$ or $w^p_{i,j}(A)$ is a linear additive function, which is a monotonically increasing submodular function with well-established in the literature [28–30]. Therefore, the penalty function $\mathcal{P}(A)$ is a monotonically increasing submodular function due to the two linear functions $d^t_{i,j}(A)$ and $d^p_{i,j}(A)$.

3.4 Submodular Optimization of Superpixel Merging

The maximum of a submodular function is an NP-hard problem, which cannot be solved in linear time. To solve the model, we design an approximate algorithm based on a greedy thought and the submodular property. A submodular merging algorithm is proposed as follows:

Algorithm 1. Submodular Merging Algorithm

Input: $G = (V, E)$, $w, d^t, d^p : E \rightarrow \mathbb{R}^+$, K, controlling factor γ
Output: A
$A \leftarrow \emptyset$, $U \leftarrow E$
for $|A| < K$ **do**
  $e_{i,j} \leftarrow arg \max_{e_{i,j} \in E} \mathcal{F}(A \cup \{e_{i,j}\}) - \mathcal{F}(A)$
  if $A \cup \{e_{i,j}\}$ is a cycle-free graph **then**
    $A \leftarrow A \cup \{e_{i,j}\}$
  end if
  $U \leftarrow U - \{e_{i,j}\}$
  if $U = \emptyset$ **then**
    break
  end if
end for

Through the selected edge set A, the original graph G can be split into the $|A|$ subgraphs.

The submodular merging algorithm satisfies the conditions of Theorem 2.

Theorem 2. *The submodular merging algorithm is an approximate method with the $(1 - \frac{1}{e})$−ratio.*

Proof. Suppose that the optimal solution of the model is A_{OPT}. If the greedy algorithm can obtain the result A_i at step i, then the marginal gain at that step is:

$$\delta_i = \mathcal{F}(A_i) - \mathcal{F}(A_{i-1}) \tag{18}$$

Since $\mathcal{F}(\cdot)$ is a submodular function and $A_i \subseteq A_{OPT}$, it follows that:

$$\mathcal{F}(A_{OPT}) - \mathcal{F}(A_i) \leq \sum_{e \in A_{OPT} \setminus A_i} (\mathcal{F}(A_i \cup \{e\}) - \mathcal{F}(A_i)) \tag{19}$$

From Eq. (18) and the submodular-function property (1), for $\forall e_x \in A_{OPT} \setminus A_i$, we have:

$$\delta_{i+1} \geq \mathcal{F}(A_i \cup \{e_x\}) - \mathcal{F}(A_i) \tag{20}$$

The $|A_{OPT} \setminus A_i| \leq K$, then:

$$\delta_{i+1} \geq \frac{1}{K} \sum_{e_x \in A_{OPT} \setminus A_i} \mathcal{F}(A_i \cup \{e_x\}) - \mathcal{F}(A_i)) \geq \frac{1}{K}(\mathcal{F}(A_{OPT}) - \mathcal{F}(A_i)) \tag{21}$$

Based on the above analysis, we can obtain:

$$\mathcal{F}(A_{i+1}) \geq \mathcal{F}(A_i) + \frac{\mathcal{F}(A_{OPT}) - \mathcal{F}(A_i)}{K} \geq (1 - \frac{1}{K})\mathcal{F}(A_i) + \frac{1}{K}\mathcal{F}(A_{OPT}) \tag{22}$$

From the above inequality, it follows that:

$$-\frac{1}{K}\mathcal{F}(A_{OPT}) - (1 - \frac{1}{K})\mathcal{F}(A_i) \geq -\mathcal{F}(A_{i+1}) \tag{23}$$

Adding $\mathcal{F}(A_{OPT})$ to both sides of the above formula, we obtain:

$$(1 - \frac{1}{K})\mathcal{F}(A_{OPT}) - (1 - \frac{1}{K})\mathcal{F}(A_i) \geq \mathcal{F}(A_{OPT}) - \mathcal{F}(A_{i+1}) \tag{24}$$

That is:

$$\mathcal{F}(A_{OPT}) - \mathcal{F}(A_{i+1}) \leq (1 - \frac{1}{K})(\mathcal{F}(A_{OPT} - \mathcal{F}(A_i)) \tag{25}$$

Then,

$$\begin{aligned}
&\mathcal{F}(A_{OPT}) - \mathcal{F}(A_{i+2}) \leq (1 - \frac{1}{K})(\mathcal{F}(A_{OPT}) - \mathcal{F}(A_{i+1})) \\
\leq &(1 - \frac{1}{K})[(1 - \frac{1}{K})(\mathcal{F}(A_{OPT}) - \mathcal{F}(A_i))] \leq (1 - \frac{1}{K})^2(\mathcal{F}(A_{OPT} - \mathcal{F}(A_i))
\end{aligned} \tag{26}$$

After K iterations of recursion, it can be deduced by induction:

$$\begin{aligned}
&\mathcal{F}(A_{OPT}) - \mathcal{F}(A_K) \leq (1 - \frac{1}{K})^K(\mathcal{F}(A_{OPT}) - \mathcal{F}(A_0)) \\
\leq &(1 - \frac{1}{K})^K(\mathcal{F}(A_{OPT}) - \mathcal{F}(\emptyset)) \leq (1 - \frac{1}{K})^K\mathcal{F}(A_{OPT}) \leq \frac{1}{e}\mathcal{F}(A_{OPT})
\end{aligned} \tag{27}$$

The last inequality holds because:

$$\lim_{K \to +\infty} (1 - \frac{1}{K})^K = \lim_{n \to +\infty} (1 + \frac{1}{-n})^{-n} = e^{-1} \tag{28}$$

Thus,

$$\mathcal{F}(A_K) \geq \mathcal{F}(A_{OPT}) - \frac{1}{e}\mathcal{F}(A_{OPT}) = (1 - \frac{1}{e})\mathcal{F}(A_{OPT}) \tag{29}$$

So,

$$\mathcal{F}(A_{OUT}) \geq (1 - \frac{1}{e})\mathcal{F}(A_{OPT}) \tag{30}$$

Hence, the theorem is proved.

3.5 Implementation

To find the optimal edge in E at each iterative step, the submodular algorithm examines all edges, the time complexity of which is $O(|E|)$, where $|E|$ is the number of edges. At each iteration of edge selection, it travels all edge list to identify the edge with the largest gain. Thus, the time complexity is $O(|E|^2)$, which is impractical for practical superpixel merging tasks. Due to diminishing marginal returns, we propose a lazy greedy method to speed up the algorithm.

Suppose the optimal edge is selected as the one with the largest marginal benefits at a certain step, the next edge can be found by its guidance. In the next step, due to submodularity, the marginal benefits of most elements will only be smaller than the value calculated in the previous step (or remain the same). Therefore, we do not need to recalculate the marginal benefits of all elements accurately at each step. The lazy greedy method maintains a "marginal benefit upper bound" for each element, with which we can construct a max heap ordered by the current upper bound. At each step, we only examine the element at the top of the queue. Then update the top value and a new heap can be constructed until convergence. In this way, the algorithm avoids computing the exact marginal benefits for all elements at each step, significantly speeding up execution, especially in the later stages of the problem.

Algorithm 2. Fast Submodular Merging Algorithm

Input: $G = (V, E)$, $w, d^t, d^p : E \to \mathbb{R}^+$, K, controlling factor γ
Output: A
$A \leftarrow \emptyset$, $U \leftarrow E$
Construct a max heap H_p, compute the initial marginal benefit $\delta(e) = \mathcal{F}(e) - \mathcal{F}(\emptyset)$, push the pair $(\delta(e), e)$ into the heap H_p.
for $|A| < K$ **do**
  Push out the top element $(\delta_{\max}, e)$ from the H_p.
  Compute the current marginal benefit $\delta(e)_{i,j} = \mathcal{F}(A \cup \{e_{i,j}\}) - \mathcal{F}(A)$.
  Look at the new top element of H_p and record its upper bound as δ_{next} (if the queue is empty, set it to $-\infty$).
  if $\delta(e)_{i,j} \geq \delta_{next}$ and $A \cup \{e_{i,j}\}$ is a cycle-free graph **then**
    $A \leftarrow A \cup \{e_{i,j}\}$
    Let $\delta_{next} = \delta(e)_{i,j}$
    $U \leftarrow U - \{e_{i,j}\}$
  else
    Push the pair $(\delta(e)_{i,j}, e_{i,j})$ into the heap H_p again.
  end if
  if $U = \emptyset$ **then**
    break
  end if
end for

With the heap in place, the submodular merging algorithm can reduce the running time to $O(|E|)$. That is because the improved method can find the optimal edge in $O(1)$ time at each iteration. Because the number of edges is the constant multiple of the number of node in the 8-neighbor graph, the algorithm runs in the $O(n)$-time, where n is the number of superpixels.

4 Experiment

To evaluate our proposed method in the ocean remote sensing images, we collect a small dataset from the paper [31]. The dataset has 50 ocean remote sensing images, each of which is in the scope of the inshore area. We compute the boundary recall (BR), boundary precision (BP), and the boundary F1-score (BFS) to measure the superpixel merging result [32–34]. We use the SLIC method as the superpixel segmentation method [32], by which we can obtain superpixels with $O(N)$ time, where N is the total number of image pixels. All experiments are done on Windows 11, with 16 GB RAM, the Intel Core i5-11600KF, running at 3.9 GHz.

4.1 Visual Display

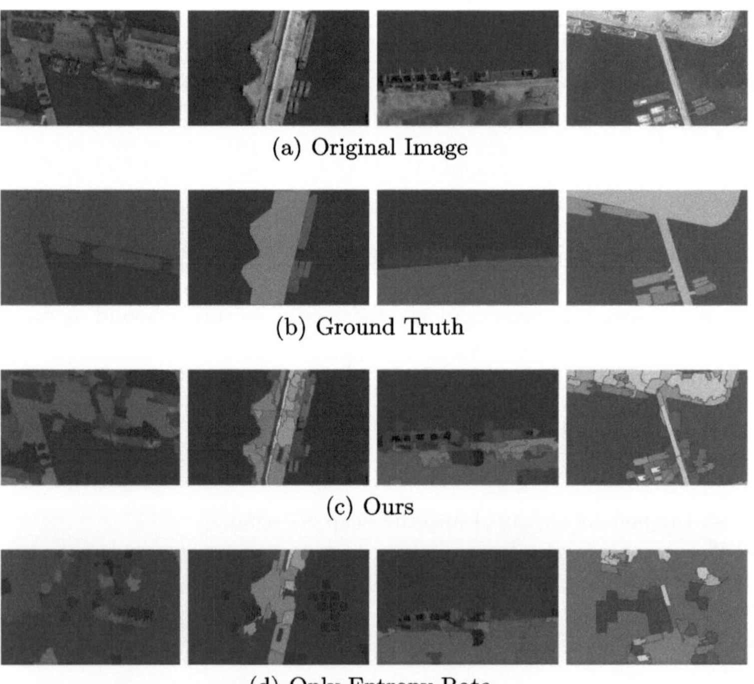

(a) Original Image

(b) Ground Truth

(c) Ours

(d) Only Entropy Rate

Fig. 2. An example shown of superpixel merging results

Setting the number of superpixels to 200, certain superpixel merging results are shown in Fig. 2. From the image, we can see that some adjacent superpixels can be clustered into the same region when we use the partition penalty. However, the merging result may contain significant errors when only the entropy rate term is used.

4.2 Quantitative Analysis

We compute the three performance values to verify the benefit of partition penalty. These values are obtained by the average level of the small datasets. We can see that, all the three performance values are far better than that of the other method. Although, the running time of our method is higher than the other method, we can ignore such a minor difference. In fact, the higher running time of our method is derived from the addition calculation of partition penalty (Table 1).

Table 1. Performance metrics of different merging methods at the small dataset.

Method	BR	BP	BFS	TIME/s
Ours	**0.6342**	**0.1229**	**0.2060**	0.14
Only Entropy	0.3687	0.09185	0.1470	**0.12**

In this paper, we address an improvement algorithm to accelerate the submodular merging process. We perform an experiment without the heap construction, and observe that the first algorithm needs to run 130.88 s. Therefore, the faster algorithm is essential for the practical superpixel merging task.

5 Conclusion

This paper constructs a graph structure based on superpixels, and proposes an optimized objective function for image segmentation based on the entropy rate expression of the random walk model on the graph. It designs an image segmentation model by joining with a novel partition penalty constraint, which is proven as a submodular function. According to the objective function of superpixel merging, an approximate algorithm with a greedy mechanism is proposed, and it is proved that the approximation ratio of the algorithm is $1 - \frac{1}{e}$. The proposed method in this paper is verified on two different types of datasets, and it can obtain segmentation results similar to the benchmark segmentation images, and has high generalization ability. Experiments also verify that our proposed method has high efficiency. However, there are other constraints in image segmentation that affect the segmentation results, such as the selection and combination of feature types. In the future, based on the research foundation of this paper, we will combine feature selection and other studies to develop segmentation models with higher performance and better generalization.

Acknowledgments. This study was funded by the Talent Startup Fund of China Three Gorges University (No. 8243325), and the Hubei Provincial Natural Science Foundation (No. 2024AFB217).

Disclosure of Interests. The authors have no competing interests to declare that are relevant to the content of this article.

References

1. Minaee, S., Boykov, Y., Porikli, F., Plaza, A., Kehtarnavaz, N., Terzopoulos, D.: Image segmentation using deep learning: a survey. IEEE Trans. Pattern Anal. Mach. Intell. **44**(7), 3523–3542 (2021)
2. Liu, S., et al.: Rotated multi-scale interaction network for referring remote sensing image segmentation. In: Proceedings of the IEEE/CVF Conference on Computer Vision and Pattern Recognition, pp. 26 658–26 668 (2024)
3. Wang, Y., Zhang, J., Chen, Y., Yuan, H., Wu, C.: An automated learning method of semantic segmentation for train autonomous driving environment understanding. IEEE Trans. Industr. Inf. **20**(4), 6913–6922 (2024)
4. Wu, Y., et al.: Diversified and personalized multi-rater medical image segmentation. In: Proceedings of the IEEE/CVF Conference on Computer Vision and Pattern Recognition, pp. 11 470–11 479 (2024)
5. Gao, C., et al.: Deep learning in pulmonary nodule detection and segmentation: a systematic review. Eur. Radiol. **35**(1), 255–266 (2025)
6. Iqbal, S., Khan, T.M., Naqvi, S.S., Naveed, A., Meijering, E.: Tbconvl-net: a hybrid deep learning architecture for robust medical image segmentation. Pattern Recogn. **158**, 111028 (2025)
7. Wu, D., Guo, Z., Yu, L., Sang, N., Gao, C.: Structural pruning via spatial-aware information redundancy for semantic segmentation. In: Proceedings of the AAAI Conference on Artificial Intelligence, vol. 39, no. 8, pp. 8368–8376 (2025)
8. Adityaja, A.M., Shigwan, S.J., Kumar, N.: Unsegmedgat: unsupervised medical image segmentation using graph attention networks clustering. In: IEEE 22nd International Symposium on Biomedical Imaging (ISBI), vol. 2025, pp. 1–4. IEEE (2025)
9. Fang, M., Wang, G., Wang, Y., et al.: Anomaly-aware superpixel segmentation for sar images via deep feature learning. Expert Syst. Appl. 128216 (2025)
10. Zeng, S., Zhu, L., Zhang, X., He, H., Lu, Y.: Supercl: superpixel guided contrastive learning for medical image segmentation pre-training, arXiv preprint arXiv:2504.14737 (2025)
11. Li, N., Xiang, D., Sun, X., Hu, C., Su, Y.: Multiscale adaptive polsar image superpixel generation based on local iterative clustering and polarimetric scattering features. ISPRS J. Photogramm. Remote. Sens. **220**, 307–322 (2025)
12. Hossain, M.D., Chen, D.: Segmentation for object-based image analysis (obia): a review of algorithms and challenges from remote sensing perspective. ISPRS J. Photogramm. Remote. Sens. **150**, 115–134 (2019)
13. Yang, X., Zhang, Z., Zhang, L., Fan, X., Ye, Q., Fu, L.: Global superpixel-merging via set maximum coverage. Eng. Appl. Artif. Intell. **127**, 107212 (2024)
14. Zeyu, X., Xiao, L., Defang, Z., Xinyu, C.: Fuzzy c-means clustering algorithm based on superpixel merging and multi-feature adaptive fusion measurement. IET Image Proc. **18**(1), 140–153 (2024)

15. Yang, X., LiShen, J., Xu, S., Ye, Q., Fu, L.: Remote sensing image segmentation via global superpixel-merging, Available at SSRN 5269354
16. Liu, D., Zhou, K.S., Bernhardt, D., Comaniciu, D.: Search strategies for multiple landmark detection by submodular maximization. In: IEEE Computer Society Conference on Computer Vision and Pattern Recognition, vol. 2010, pp. 2831–2838. IEEE (2010)
17. Zhu, F., Jiang, Z., Shao, L.: Submodular object recognition. In: Proceedings of the IEEE Conference on Computer Vision and Pattern Recognition, pp. 2457–2464 (2014)
18. Xu, J., Mukherjee, L., Li, Y., Warner, J., Singh, V.: Gaze-enabled egocentric video summarization via constrained submodular maximization. Comput. Vis. Pattern Recogn. (2015)
19. Shen, J., Dong, X., Peng, J., Jin, X., Shao, L., Porikli, F.: Submodular function optimization for motion clustering and image segmentation. IEEE Trans. Neural Netw. Learn. Syst. **30**(9), 2637–2649 (2019)
20. Tan, H., Li, Q., Peng, Z.: A novel interactive image segmentation algorithm based on maximization of submodular function. Int. J. Pattern Recognit Artif Intell. **37**(03), 2354005 (2023)
21. Liu, M.-Y., Tuzel, O., Ramalingam, S., Chellappa, R.: Entropy-rate clustering: cluster analysis via maximizing a submodular function subject to a matroid constraint. IEEE Trans. Pattern Anal. Mach. Intell. **36**(1), 99–112 (2013)
22. Jaynes, E.T.: Information theory and statistical mechanics. Phys. Rev. **106**(4), 620 (1957)
23. Nemhauser, G.L., Wolsey, L.A., Fisher, M.L.: An analysis of approximations for maximizing submodular set functions–i. Math. Program. **14**, 265–294 (1978)
24. Nau, R.: Notes on the random walk model. Fuqua School Bus. **1**, 1–19 (2014)
25. Zheng, J., Jiang, Z., Chellappa, R.: Submodular attribute selection for visual recognition. IEEE Trans. Pattern Anal. Mach. Intell. **39**(11), 2242–2255 (2016)
26. Zhang, X., Xiao, P., Feng, X., He, G.: Another look on region merging procedure from seed region shift for high-resolution remote sensing image segmentation. ISPRS J. Photogramm. Remote. Sens. **148**, 197–207 (2019)
27. Yang, F., Jiang, Z., Davis, L.S.: Submodular reranking with multiple feature modalities for image retrieval. In: Asian Conference on Computer Vision, pp. 19–34. Springer (2014)
28. Fujishige, S.: Submodular Functions and Optimization. vol. 58. Elsevier (2005)
29. Bach, F., et al.: Learning with submodular functions: a convex optimization perspective. Found. Trends® Mach. Learn. **6**(2-3), 145–373 (2013)
30. Liu, X., Li, W., Yang, J.: A primal-dual approximation algorithm for the k-prize-collecting minimum vertex cover problem with submodular penalties. Front. Comp. Sci. **17**(3), 173404 (2023)
31. Cui, Q., Pan, H., Li, X., Zhang, K., Chen, W.: Cmsug: competitive mechanism-based superpixel generation method for image segmentation. J. Intell. Fuzzy Syst. **43**(4), 4409–4430 (2022)
32. Achanta, R., Shaji, A., Smith, K., Lucchi, A., Fua, P., Süsstrunk, S.: Slic superpixels compared to state-of-the-art superpixel methods. IEEE Trans. Pattern Anal. Mach. Intell. **34**(11), 2274–2282 (2012)

33. Wu, C., Zheng, J., Feng, Z., Zhang, H., Zhang, L., Cao, J., Yan, H.: Fuzzy slic: fuzzy simple linear iterative clustering. IEEE Trans. Circuits Syst. Video Technol. **31**(6), 2114–2124 (2020)
34. Achanta, R., Susstrunk, S.: Superpixels and polygons using simple non-iterative clustering. In: Proceedings of the IEEE Conference on Computer Vision and Pattern Recognition, pp. 4651–4660 (2017)

Closing Digital Textbook's Intention-Behavior Gap in Vocational Education: a Case Study with TAM Method

Deyi Wang(✉), Qing Li, and Jianchuan Zhao

Guangdong Mechanical and Electrical Polytechnic, Guangzhou 510515, China
deyiwang@gdmec.edu.cn

Abstract. At present, digital textbooks (DTs) are a key development direction in higher vocational education in China, but research on their application remains limited. To fill this gap, this study adopts the Technology Acceptance Model(TAM), takes the course Digital Electronic Technology as the research context, and evaluates digital textbooks usage effectiveness through a combination of questionnaires, facial recognition, and backend data analysis. It reveals a contradiction in digital textbooks usage: while students show high Behavioral Intention to Use for digital textbooks and recognize their Perceived Usefulness, 34.7% of in-class usage of digital textbook carriers (mobile devices) focuses primarily on non-academic activities.

Analysis highlights two key causes. First, defects in Perceived Ease of Use, such as difficulties in task switching, and the suppression of Attitude Toward Use by distractions weaken Behavioral Intention to Use's ability to drive actual digital textbooks use. Second, insufficient digital textbook functions and classroom management fail to channel high Behavioral Intention to Use into learning-related behaviors. In response, this study proposes a framework of digital textbooks simplification & task-bound usage & time-limited access, which not only provides empirical evidence for resolving the behavioral intention-behavior conversion issue in digital textbooks promotion but also offers references for the integrated application of digital technologies in higher vocational education.

Keywords: Digital textbook · Higher vocational education · Technology Acceptance Model · Cross validation

1 Introduction

Digital transformation is a key trend in Chinese higher vocational education [1,2]. Educational digitalization enhances equity and offers efficient learning experiences [3]. However, while existing studies show vocational students have high Behavioral Intention to Use Digital Textbooks(DTs), classroom observations find their primary DT-access device (mobile phones) is mostly used for

B. Fernández-Manjón et al. (Eds.): SETE 2025/ICWL 2025, LNCS 16425, pp. 369–381, 2026.
https://doi.org/10.1007/978-981-92-0042-9_27

non-academic activities. This contradiction undermines DTs' educational value, which requires further investigation.

DTs have been gradually applied in teaching; they not only covers traditional textbook content, but also add in-class quizzes, multimedia, and AI-powered Q&A ability [4] (Fig. 1).

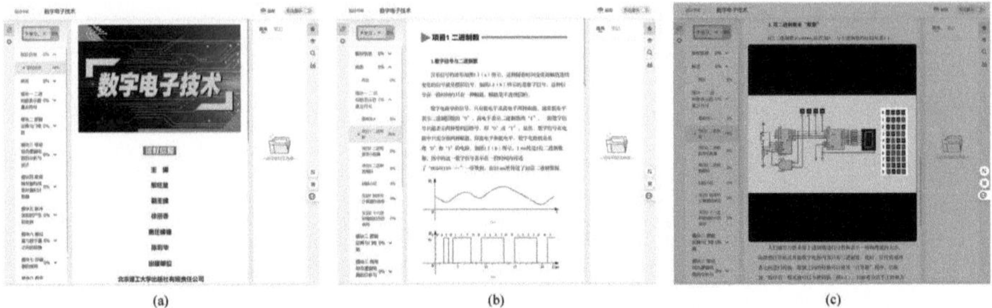

Fig. 1. Digital Electronics Technology Digital Textbook sample: (a) cover, (b) content page, (c) multimedia example.

To this end, via questionnaires and classroom video verification, this paper aims to: reveal the divergence between students' Digital Textbooks Behavioral Intention to Use and in-class non-academic Digital Textbooks device usage, analyze its causes using TAM and multi-platform data, and provide bases for DT optimization and classroom management. The main contributions of this work are:

1. Investigate DTs' role in China's higher vocational teaching, focusing on the contradiction phenomenon.
2. Analyze causes of the contradiction phenomenon via TAM and multi-platform data verification.
3. Propose the Technology Acceptance Model Feedback-Monitoring-Backend Data Cross Validation (TAM-FMBDCV) method, in order to analyze this phenomenon.

2 Related Works

This section summarizes recent findings on educational equity, teaching methods based on digital technology, teaching evaluation methods for digital technology, and computer vision applications in education evaluation.

From the perspective of digital methods and educational equity, machine learning has been used to analyze the learning gap between indigenous and non-indigenous students, revealing indigenous-driven inequality and discrimination [5]. Singaporean researchers have utilized examination pass rates to analyze the learning performance of different ethnic groups [6].

In terms of the application of digital technology in education, studies have explored the role of mobile phones in adult literacy training in India, assessing their suitability for initial, targeted literacy interventions [7]. Other works have analyzed how adolescent learners interact with mobile vocabulary apps to predict learning experiences and self-assessment outcomes [8], and explored the impact of digital device types on computerized standardized learning assessments [9]. In China, university teachers' integration of mobile phones into classrooms has been identified as a factor influencing learning performance [10], while mobile-based learning has been shown to enhance adults' knowledge acquisition [11]. Additionally, machine learning has been used to identify key factors predicting East Asian students' reading scores based on classroom [12]. Notably, while these studies confirm digital tools' potential, a critical gap persists: several works point out that learners' positive Behavioral Intention to Use digital tools often fail to translate into actual academic use, due to factors like flawed tool functionality and environmental distractions.

For the evaluation of digital teaching technology effectiveness, Cameroonian researchers have studied the relationship between speech attitude and secondary school students' academic performance [13], with similar findings corroborated in Scotland [14], while other studies have explored high school students' smartphone use during school hours and its links to digital labor in educational settings [15].

Advances in computer vision have driven its application in education too. Li et al. [16] developed the UCEC-Face dataset to address classroom facial recognition challenges and improve recognition accuracy; DeLyser et al. [17] proposed "Engineering Applications III" to enhance students' practical and theoretical skills; and a teaching model was invented to boost learning motivation and efficacy, it is shown to improve learning outcomes [3]. Gordon et al. [18] found that text length affects reading behavior, recommending concise explanations and active learning integration, while the EmotionCues system [19] adopted classroom videos to assess learning status.

These studies discussed topics related to educational inequalities and challenges, and explored the role of technology in reshaping education and student behaviors-highlighting mobile literacy potential, digital devices' assessment impact, computer vision in education, and key learning factors. They clarify education's complexity and guide policies and practices. However, there is little research on digital textbooks in higher vocational education practice. Thus, this paper explores the role of digital textbooks and analyzes their utility.

3 Research Method

3.1 Research Carrier and Research Subject

The digital textbook (DT) used in this course is *Digital Electronics Technology* by Professor Li (Fig. 1) [4], which supports multi-platform access. All students use mobile phones as their DT reading platform.

The study involves 4 classes (referred to as A, B, C, and D) from the 2024 cohort at Guangdong Mechanical & Electrical Polytechnic (GDMEP), with Class

A having 58 students, Class B 58 students, Class C 56 students, and Class D 55 students, totaling 227 participants, among whom females account for 27%. All four classes take the *Digital Electronics Technology* course and are taught by the same teacher; they were randomly divided into two groups:

DT Encouragement Group (Classes A and D): Students were allowed free mobile phone use in class, and the teacher assigned one DT-based interactive task per class.

Mobile Phone Restriction Group (Classes B and C): Students were only permitted to use mobile phones to access DTs in the last 30 min of class; non-academic mobile phone use was prohibited during all other class periods.

3.2 Technology Acceptance Model Feedback-Monitoring-Backend Data Cross Validation (TAM-FMBDCV) Method

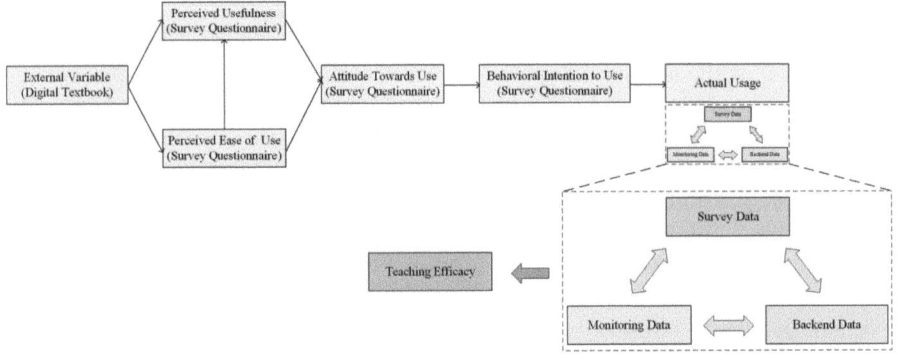

Fig. 2. Schematic diagram of TAM-FMBDCV method.

The proposed TAM-FMBDCV assesses actual use of DT. However, as most feedback relies on research subjects' subjective opinion, quantitative verification of survey authenticity is needed. Students often use mobile phones for entertainment during in-class DT application; this study proposes TAM-FMBDCV to analyze DT effectiveness. The schematic is presented in Fig. 2; it mainly uses cross-validation via questionnaires, classroom monitoring data analysis, and DT backend data. Since backend data comes from the DT platform, this subsection introduces the questionnaire and classroom behavior monitoring algorithm in TAM-FMBDCV[1].

Survey Questionnaire. In order to investigate the mobile phone usage in vocational college students, this paper developed a 94-item survey covering aspects including use frequency, influencing factors, personal perceptions, and network

[1] All data in this article were obtained with research subjects' consent.

security awareness. Created and distributed via the Questionnaire Star platform[2], the survey was promoted through vocational college students' online communities, learning management systems, and social media to reach the target group.

Post-distribution, 210 responses were collected, rigorously screened, and cleaned, resulting in 153 valid responses after data cleaning. Merged response category data is presented in Table 1.

Table 1. Merged Category Information with TAM Variables

Category	TAM Variable	Description
Personal Information and Habits	External Variables	Includes personal basic information such as grade, gender, and daily mobile phone usage duration, which may influence the initial perception of DT.
Classroom Behavior and Learning Attitude	PEU	Focuses on the frequency and attitude of students using mobile phones in class, as well as the impact on learning outcomes, reflecting technology acceptance.
Effectiveness of digital textbook	PU	Assesses the effectiveness of digital textbooks in enhancing students' awareness of learning.
Mobile Phone Usage and Educational Effectiveness	ATU	Discusses the impact of mobile phone usage on learning outcomes and the effectiveness of teachers' management policies.
Learning Outcomes and Student Satisfaction	BIU	Focuses on the impact of mobile phone usage on classroom learning and students' expectations and satisfaction with the course.
Mobile Phones and Learning Burden	PEU, ATU	Studies the impact of in-class mobile phone usage on social interaction and health, including technology application understanding and network security awareness.

Classroom Student Engagement Evaluation Method. The workflow of the classroom student engagement evaluation method is shown in Fig. 3, where (a) presents the implementation details of our previously proposed Akconv-Retinaface method [20] and (b) displays its workflow diagram. This study employs this high-precision algorithm to assess in-class student engagement. Specifically, it has been verified to reach 98% accuracy in teaching scenarios, supports real-time detection on laptop platforms, and determines whether students

[2] https://www.wjx.cn/.

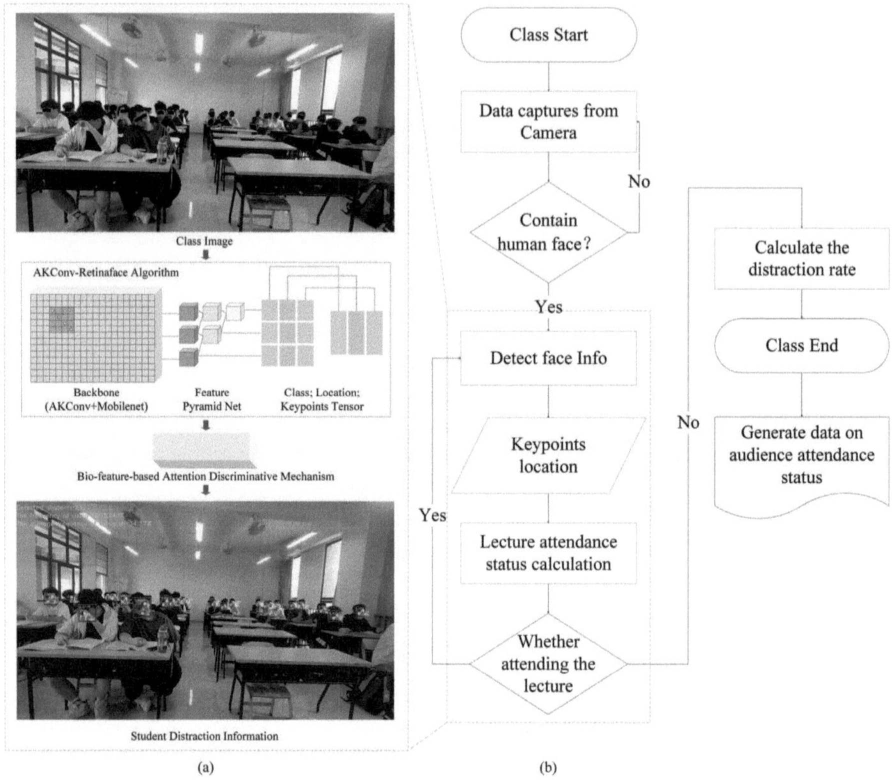

Fig. 3. Processing procedure for the method of obtaining student engagement information.

use mobile phones for entertainment by recording their distraction duration. At the start of class, the system activates the camera to capture real-time data: it first detects faces in the frame; if a face is detected, the system records the current time, extracts facial features, and obtains key facial point coordinates before analyzing students' engagement status to judge their attention. After class, data collection stops, and a classroom monitoring and engagement report is generated. This requires no classroom video recording and enables the creation of distraction reports for the course.

4 Experimental Results

4.1 Survey Questionnaire Results

(1) To ensure the rigor of the analysis, we used Spearman analysis to verify the correlation between the obtained data. The relevant data analysis results are presented in Tables 3, 4, and Fig. 4. Figure 4 shows that the questionnaire data meet Cronbach's α criteria, confirming the questionnaire's internal consistency

for measuring digital textbook (DT) perceptions. Structural Equation Modeling (SEM) (Table 2) further validated the TAM pathways: Perceived Ease of Use (PEU) positively affected Perceived Usefulness (PU) but not Attitude Toward Use (ATU); PU strongly positively affected ATU; and ATU positively affected Behavioral Intention to Use (BIU). From the above analysis results, it can be concluded that the obtained data are feasible for analyzing DT acceptance.

(2) We analyzed Table 3, and the conclusions are as follows: Question Pair 1 focuses on "Mobile Phones and Learning Burden," most responses are affirmative; Question Pair 2 is about "Effectiveness of Digital Textbooks," where

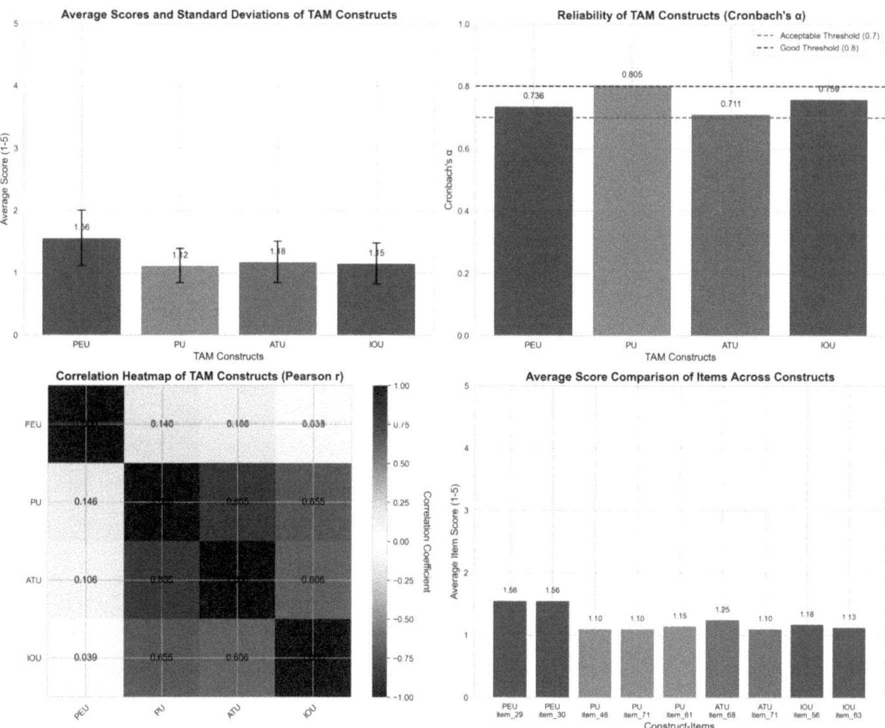

Fig. 4. TAM Reliability Analysis Result Figure.

Table 2. TAM Structural Equation Modeling (SEM) Results for Digital Textbook Acceptance

Path	Coefficient (β)	p-value	Significance	R^2
PEU → PU	0.156	0.0018	**	0.063
PEU → ATU	-0.049	0.2333	ns	0.542
PU → ATU	0.871	< 0.001	***	–
ATU → BIU	0.610	< 0.001	***	0.411

Question 69 receives mostly negative responses, it indicaties digital textbook design has not effectively reduced students' learning burden; Question Pairs 3–5, are all related to "Learning Outcomes and Student Satisfaction," show varying patterns: Question Pair 3 gets mostly neutral responses, Question Pair 4 receives mostly positive feedback while Question 64 (Pair 4) gets mixed neutral and positive responses, and Question Pair 5 has varied responses; Question Pair 6 focuses on mobile phones' impact on classroom performance, with most responses indicates that they believe mobile phone use affects in-class learning.

Table 3. Questions with High Correlation

Pair	Questions	Correlation
1	30 & 31	0.8237
2	46 & 69	0.7775
3	57 & 64	0.7559
4	61 & 64	0.7880
5	61 & 71	0.8158
6	66 & 72	0.7639

(3) We further analyzed Table 3, Table 1, and survey data. We used the Technology Acceptance Model (TAM). Our core focus was to check how common students' Behavioral Intention to Use (BIU) digital textbooks (DTs) is.

In the "Mobile Phones and Learning Burden (PEU, ATU)" category, most students answered "yes" to Questions 30 and 31. This matches TAM's premise that "usability boosts acceptance." This positive view of PEU creates a psychological foundation for students' potential BIU toward DTs. TAM says that positive feelings about usability indirectly support the willingness to use related digital tools. The "learning burden" category (ATU) needs more analysis. We need to see if frequent use causes cognitive overload. But this analysis does not take away the initial basis for BIU.

In the "Effectiveness of Digital Textbooks (PU, PEU/ATU)" category, Question 46 shows something. Students recognize that DTs help with learning and gaining knowledge. This matches TAM's hypothesis that "functional value drives acceptance." In the TAM framework, PU is a key factor that leads to BIU. So students' recognition of DTs' functional value directly confirms they have positive BIU. In contrast, Question 69 shows a problem: DTs are "useful but not user-friendly." This gap between content value and design ease affects ATU and BIU a little. But it does not remove the overall positive BIU that comes from PU.

We looked at "Learning Outcomes and Student Satisfaction (BIU, PU)." This is the TAM dimension directly linked to usage willingness. Analysis shows that BIU is common. Question 61 confirms that mobile phones help promote classroom interaction. This factor may strengthen students' ongoing BIU toward

DTs. Questions 57 and 64 show unclear attitudes in specific situations. But they do not show negative BIU. Even Question 71 shows that students do not fully notice one DT function. But this limitation does not reduce their general willingness to use DTs.

In the "The Impact of Mobile Phones on Classroom Performance (PEU, ATU)" category, most students answered "yes" to Questions 66 and 72. These responses point out factors that stop BIU from becoming actual behavior. They do not question that BIU exists. Question 66 shows that students find it hard to manage multiple tasks (low PEU). Question 72 shows that mobile phones disrupt learning. TAM logic notes that such factors stop BIU from being shown. But they do not take away BIU itself. This further shows that students' willingness to use DTs is still common.

Table 4. Details of high correlation questions with TAM Variables

Category	TAM Variable	Question Number & Content	Majority Response
Mobile Phones and Learning Burden	PEU, ATU	30. Does using mobile phones affect students' ability to collect information?	Yes
	PEU, ATU	31. Does using mobile phones enhance students' understanding of classroom information?	Yes
Effectiveness of digital textbook	PU	46. Do digital textbooks provide enough learning support to help students understand new knowledge?	Yes
	PEU, ATU	69. Is the design of digital textbooks effectively reducing the learning burden on students?	No
Learning Outcomes and Student Satisfaction	BIU	57. How is students' ability to understand complex concepts when using digital textbooks?	Neutral
	PU	61. How do mobile phones promote classroom interaction and student participation?	Good
	BIU	64. What is the overall satisfaction with the use of digital textbooks?	Neutral
	PU	71. How is students' ability to transfer knowledge with the help of digital textbooks?	Neutral
The Impact of Mobile Phones on Classroom Performance	PEU, ATU	66. How challenging is it for students to switch tasks when using mobile phones?	Challenging
	ATU	72. Does the use of mobile phones lead to the distraction of students' attention in the classroom, thereby affecting learning outcomes?	Yes

4.2 Classroom Video Analysis Results

By analyzing the monitoring data from 8 class sessions across 4 target classes (via Akconv-Retinaface method [20]), we found the average in-class mobile phone usage frequency was 34.7%, which differs by less than 1% from the 33.8% rate reported in the questionnaire. This consistency further validates the reliability of the questionnaire data. And the distraction detection function of method [20] revealed that the mobile phone usage was non-academic. This confirms the prevalence of in-class non-academic mobile phone behavior.

4.3 Backend Data and Final Grades

Table 5. Digital Textbook Cloud Platform Backend Data

Class	Average Duration (h)	Average Progress (%)	Average Audio (h)	Average Video (h)	Quiz Performance (%)
Encourage Group	0.09	1.609	0	0.001	0.1379
Restrict Group	0.061	0.8	0	0	0

Digital Textbook Backend Data. Table 5 presents the digital textbook cloud platform backend data, covering key metrics: average DT usage duration, average learning progress, average audio/video usage, and quiz performance. As can be seen, the Encourage Group outperforms the Restrict Group across all DT-related indicators, the absolute values of the Encourage Group's DT engagement remain extremely low. Specifically, the Encourage Group's average audio usage is 0h, average video usage is only 0.001h, and quiz performance is a mere 0.1379%. These figures indicate that even in the group allowed free in-class mobile use (and with confirmed high BIU for DTs), students rarely utilized DT functions for learning.

Table 6. Examination Score(AS is short for Average Score)

Class A AS	Class B AS	Class C AS	Class D AS	Grade AS
54.41	58.15	65.66	59.90	59.62
Encourage Group AS	Restrict Group AS	Encourage Group Bias	Restrict Group Bias	
57.16	61.91	0.0414	0.0383	

4.4 Final Grades

Table 6 presents the average scores of Class A-D, grade-level average score, and the Encourage/Restrict Groups' average scores with bias data.

As verified in Sect. 4.1, the Encourage Group exhibited widespread positive BIU toward DTs; however, its average score (57.16) is lower than that of the Restrict Group (61.91). Such results indicate that positive DT usage intention alone does not drive improved academic outcomes-unregulated mobile access in the Encourage Group likely diverted students to non-learning activities, undermining potential DT benefits.

Additionally, the Restrict Group's smaller bias (0.0383) compared to the Encourage Group's 0.0414 reflects more stable overall performance. This stability can be attributed to the Restrict Group's stricter mobile access rules, which reduced non-academic distractions, consistent with the group's minimal non-academic mobile use observed in video data and lower but more focused DT utilization in backend metrics.

5 Discussion

5.1 TAM Mechanisms of the "Intention-Behavior Gap" in DT Use

The core "intention-behavior gap" can be explained via the Technology Acceptance Model (TAM), with three key points:

First, Perceived Usefulness (PU) drives BIU but not actual learning behavior. Questionnaire results show students recognize DTs' PU in "providing learning support" (Question 46) and "promoting classroom interaction" (Question 61), which fosters positive BIU as per TAM. However, backend data reveals the Encourage Group (high BIU) has a lower average score (57.16) than the Restrict Group (61.91) and near-zero quiz performance (Table 5), as students divert phones to non-learning activities despite recognizing DT utility.

Second, Perceived Ease of Use (PEU) has scenario defects that block BIU translation. Students affirm PEU in mobile information collection (Question 30) and classroom comprehension (Question 31) but struggle with task switching (Question 66), creating an "ease of use trap." Combined with the 34.7% in-class mobile usage (video analysis), students prioritize low-effort non-academic activities over DT use, even with positive BIU.

Third, Attitude Toward Use (ATU) mediates to suppress BIU. Despite partial PU/PEU positivity, neutral DT satisfaction (Question 64, BIU) and knowledge transfer ratings (Question 71, PU), plus the Restrict Group's stable grades (Table 6), confirm that negative ATU inhibits action. This negative ATU stems from DT design failures (Question 69, no learning burden reduction) and mobile distractions (Question 72, attention disruption), with backend data showing these attitudes prevent function-to-behavior conversion.

5.2 Non-TAM Cause: Classroom Management's Role in the Gap

Beyond TAM variables, classroom management strategies directly influence non-academic use and the gap. The Encourage Group, without mandatory interactive tasks, leads to unconstrained mobile phone usage.

In contrast, the Restrict Group's "time-limited DT access" reduced non-academic distractions. This management lowered non-learning use and promoted focused DT engagement, leading to more stable grades. This confirms that classroom management is a key unaddressed factor in the original TAM-focused discussion.

5.3 Intervention Pathways to Narrow the Gap

Interventions must target TAM variables and management to close the gap:

First, Optimize DT Functions for PEU/ATU. Simplify interfaces, prioritize core functions, and add "one-click return to learning" to fix task-switching issues (Question 66). Integrate non-academic app blocking to reduce distraction-driven negative ATU (Question 72).

Second, Reform Classroom Management with Task-Driven DT Use. Drawing on the Restrict Group's stability, assign 1–2 DT interactive tasks per class to the Encourage Group; free mobile use is allowed only after task completion. This channels high BIU into DT learning, reducing unstructured non-academic use.

Third, Guide Students to Link BIU, Behavior, and Outcomes. For high PEU/low ATU students, provide personalized "goal-oriented" DT guidelines. For low PU/low BIU groups, use case teaching to boost value perception. Share "high BIU to high DT use to good grades" examples to build cognitive links.

6 Conclusion

In order to evaluate the performance of digital textbooks in China's higher vocational education. This study adopted the Technology Acceptance Model(TAM) and further validated the effectiveness of acquired data. We found there is an "intention-behavior gap" in digital textbook usage. Through the TAM analysis, two reasons were found: usefulness makes students want to use digital textbooks but not actually use them, ease of use has task-switching issues, bad attitudes stop use, and not good enough classroom management. Based on these reasons, this paper propose directions to improve digital textbook: more simple interfaces, and block non-study apps, use tasks to guide classroom deigital textbook use, and teachers should encourage students' interest in using digital textbooks. However, this framework lacks longitudinal validation, and the study sample was limited to students enrolled in Digital Electronics Technology.

In future research, we will expand the sample to include students across diverse disciplines and regions and conduct longitudinal validation of the framework.

Acknowledgments. This research was supported by the Foundation for Young Talents in Higher Education of Guangdong under Grant 2024KQNCX314, the Guangdong Mechanical and Electrical Polytechnic Research Project(No. Gccrcxm-202303, YJYB2023-73). Research and Innovation Team for High-Quality Development of Science, Education, and Industry Integration in Vocational Education (2024WCXTD058)

Disclosure of Interests. The authors have no competing interests to declare that are relevant to the content of this article.

References

1. Rizk, J., Hillier, C.: Digital technology and increasing engagement among students with disabilities: interaction rituals and digital capital. Comput. Educ. Open **3**, 100099 (2022)
2. Novak, E., McDaniel, K., Li, J.: Factors that impact student frustration in digital learning environments. Comput. Educ. Open **5**, 100153 (2023)
3. Lin, F.L., Lin, H.H., Chang, S.L.: Programming e-books: Culture, English, and scratch for schoolchildren of rural taiwan. IEEE Trans. Educ. **66**(1), 62–72 (2023)

4. Li, W.: Digital Electronics Technology. 1 edn. Beijing Institute of Technology Press (2024)
5. Delprato, M., Frola, A., Antequera, G.: Indigenous and non-indigenous proficiency gaps for out-of-school and in-school populations: a machine learning approach. Int. J. Educ. Dev. **93**, 102631 (2022)
6. Ali, F.: Gaps in educational outcomes: analysing national examination performance of singaporean malay and non-malay students in the past 20 years. Asia Pacific J. Educ. **36**(4), 473–487 (2016)
7. Chudgar, A.: The promise and challenges of using mobile phones for adult literacy training: data from one indian state. Int. J. Educ. Dev. **34**, 20–29 (2014)
8. Wei, W.: Understanding and supporting the use of feedback from mobile applications in the learning of vocabulary among young adolescent learners. Stud. Educ. Eval. **78**, 101264 (2023)
9. Rutkowski, L., Rutkowski, D., Valdivia, D.S., Underhill, S., Canbolat, Y.: Measurement properties as a possible cause of digital device effects on a standardized assessment of learning. Stud. Educ. Eval. **77**, 101261 (2023)
10. Sijia Xue, J.D., Yang, Y.: Institutional influences on teachers' classroom technology integration: a multi-case study of teachers' uses of mobile social media at universities in china. Asia Pacific J. Educ. **43**(4), 1306–1327 (2023)
11. Alkasirah, N.A.M., Nor, N.M.M.: Potential usage of mobile learning via short messaging system (sms) for enhancing islamic knowledge of adult learners (2019). https://api.semanticscholar.org/CorpusID:133082431
12. Shuqiong Luo, Ronnel B. King, F.W., on Leung, S.: English digital reading achievement for east asian students: identifying the key predictors using a machine learning approach. Asia Pacific J. Educ. **0**(0), 1–17 (2024)
13. Nguemkap Kouamo, R.: On and off line hate speech and academic performance in secondary education in cameroon. Int. J. Educ. Dev. **109**, 103081 (2024)
14. Sharp, A., Thomson, G.: Performance in external examinations and pupils' orientations to studying. Educ. Rev. **36**(1), 37–51 (1984)
15. Paakkari, A., Rautio, P., Valasmo, V.: Digital labour in school: smartphones and their consequences in classrooms. Learn. Cult. Soc. Interact. **21**, 161–169 (2019)
16. Li, N., et al.: Chinese face dataset for face recognition in an uncontrolled classroom environment. IEEE Access **11**, 86963–86976 (2023)
17. DeLyser, R., Quine, R., Rullkoetter, P., Armentrout, D.: A sophomore capstone course in measurement and automated data acquisition. IEEE Trans. Educ. **47**(4), 453–458 (2004)
18. Gordon, C.L., Lysecky, R., Vahid, F.: Less is more: students skim lengthy online textbooks. IEEE Trans. Educ. **66**(2), 123–129 (2023)
19. Zeng, H., et al.: Emotioncues: emotion-oriented visual summarization of classroom videos. IEEE Trans. Visual Comput. Graphics **27**(7), 3168–3181 (2021)
20. Wang, D.Y., et al.: A method for assessing student online class status based on deep neural networks (2024), patent Application No. CN202410759902.7

Workshop LAAPL

Avatar-Mediated Reflection in VR: An Agentic AI Approach to Personalized Learning

Bo Hui[1], Chen Chen[2], Xinyang Bao[3], and Yong-Hong Kuo[1(✉)]

[1] Department of Data and Systems Engineering, The University of Hong Kong, Hong Kong, China
boOoOo@hku.hk, yhkuo@hku.hk

[2] The Faculty of Education, The University of Hong Kong, Hong Kong, China
logancc@hku.hk

[3] Department of Electrical and Electronic Engineering, The University of Hong Kong, Hong Kong, China
u3595298@connect.hku.hk

Abstract. Personalized learning systems increasingly leverage large language models (LLM) to offer adaptive learning plans and real-time support. While such systems excel at content adaptation, the other critical process, self-reflection, is still under development. Traditional reflection methods and even advanced reflective dialogue systems remain limited by reliance on self-immersed, first-person perspectives. Recent work shows Virtual Reality (VR)'s capacity for embodied presence can externalize internal dialogue and promote self-distancing, which could improve emotional regulation and foster deeper insights [3,16]. Building on this foundation, we propose a novel framework that integrates an AI agent in a mobile-based interview and a virtual avatar in VR to provide second-person perspectives for embodied and personalized self-reflection. Based on a database of personal interviews, learners can converse with a virtual self in VR. By reframing reflection as an embodied dialogue with a virtual self, this approach aims to establish a new paradigm of agentic AI that transforms reflection from an isolated task into a dynamic conversation, thereby enabling deeper and more personalized self-reflection.

Keywords: Virtual Reality · Self-distancing · Self-reflection

1 Introduction

Nowadays, personalized learning can provide customized instructions according to learners' goals, abilities, and learning status with the power of LLM. LLM could significantly enhance personalized learning by serving as virtual tutors, coaches, and study partners across diverse educational settings, as the system can use users' data to provide specific feedback, adaptive learning plans, and real-time support [4,9,13,23]. LLM is being integrated into learning management systems, recommendation engines, and interactive platforms to address

B. Fernández-Manjón et al. (Eds.): SETE 2025/ICWL 2025, LNCS 16425, pp. 385–394, 2026.
https://doi.org/10.1007/978-981-92-0042-9_28

individual learner needs and enhance engagement [4,13]. Beyond content adaptation, Self-reflection should be also very important for learning, which has not been explored thoroughly. Extensive research indicates that self-reflection not only facilitates personal growth and professional development, but also enhances learning outcomes, strengthens psychological resilience, and improves self-awareness [2,11,12,17]. People also wish to go beyond the simple review but to have deeper and more challenging insights [5].

Traditional approaches to reflective practice, such as keeping written journals or seeking feedback from mentors, often have limitations in terms of interactivity and learner engagement. Furthermore, these methods present significant challenges for students to detect the transfer. There is a course named MEDD8894 Design Thinking and Education in the University of Hong Kong asked students to write a reflective design journal. The objective is to systematically cultivate design thinking awareness by documenting real-world design opportunities and people-centric practices [6]. Through continuous observation, application of design tools, and a reflective journal, the aim is to develop transferable insights in problem-solving. Attending a class promotes knowledge enrichment and cognitive transfer. Regular and periodic review will be beneficial for students to gain a better understanding of their own learning progress. However, capturing evidence of transfer remains challenging because of its abstract nature. Learners may struggle to sustain engagement or may find reflection to be a solitary and abstract exercise. Therefore, the reflective dialogue system is explored for a more interactive system. Early systems are predominantly rule-based chatbots that guide users through reflection using predefined questions and scripts [15]. With advancements in LLM, an increasing number of systems now employ LLM and generative pre-trained models to provide more natural, contextually relevant dialogues [7,22]. However, these tools only allow individuals to reflect from a first-person viewpoint, which can sometimes limit objectivity, deeper insights, and emotional regulation.

Immersive technologies and intelligent agents may open new possibilities for creating interactive, embodied, and personalized reflective experiences. VR has been widely studied as a tool for immersive and experiential learning. Research indicates that the high interactivity and physical involvement in VR effectively boost learning motivation, interest, and outcomes [14,18]. Beyond the engagement, VR, with its capacity for embodied presence and immersive simulation, presents a transformative opportunity to externalize and reframe the reflective process, which is self-distancing. Self-distancing, which uses a second-person perspective instead of a first-person perspective, could externalize internal, abstract self-dialogue into visible, concrete social simulations. The process could improve emotional regulation, promote wiser reasoning, and facilitate cognitive reappraisal from an immersed to an observer perspective [3,16]. Researchers are exploring ways to use the embodiment of virtual bodies, as well as VR avatars, as a self-reflection medium for different purposes. The self-conversation method, grounded in self-distancing principles, was shown to elicit a stronger perception of behavioral change compared to text-based reflection [21]. Similarly, the

ConVRSelf platform demonstrated high user acceptability by employing body-swapping to enable autobiographical narrative review and lifestyle reflection [1]. Osimo et al. [20] illustrated that embodying a Sigmund Freud avatar in VR improved self-counselling through deepened self-distancing and reflective engagement. Researches show that virtual body swapping promotes therapeutic self-distancing via third-person perspective-taking, leading to enhanced emotional regulation and self-reflective capacity [8]. We would like to explore how the way could be designed for the self-reflection process in personalized learning. We propose a VR-based intervention where users engage in dialogue with an LLM-driven avatar representation of their past self, serving as a conversational partner that embodies participants' prior thoughts and experiences (Table 1).

Table 1. Comparative Analysis of VR Self-Reflection Systems

Core Aspect	ConVRSelf [1]	Freud Avatar [20]	Our System
Interaction Mode	Observational Review	Self-Dialogue	Conversation
Enabling Technology	Body-Swapping Scene Re-build	Body Ownership Pre-defined Roles	Data-based LLM Agentic AI
Primary Advantage	Objective Behavioral Review	Guided Role-Playing	Conversation with past-self

This work makes a primary contribution by introducing the concept of a 'Past-Self Avatar' and establishing a framework for embodied dialogue with it. Our system leverages an agentic AI to transform self-distancing into a simulated social interaction with a data-driven representation of one's past self. This paradigm shift reframes reflection from an isolated cognitive task into a dynamic, interpersonal conversation, thereby opening new pathways for facilitating deep and highly personalized self-reflection.

2 System Architecture and Workflow

The proposed framework is designed to facilitate self-reflection by integrating three core components: a mobile application for semi-structured interviews, a central database for storing participant data, and an immersive VR environment featuring a conversational avatar, as shown in Fig. 1.

2.1 Technical Implementation of the Interview Module

The process is initiated by the mobile conversational agent, which conducts semi-structured interviews with learners. Learners first need to select their own representative avatar in the application before starting the interview. The interview process itself constitutes the first stage of self-reflection. The agent, powered

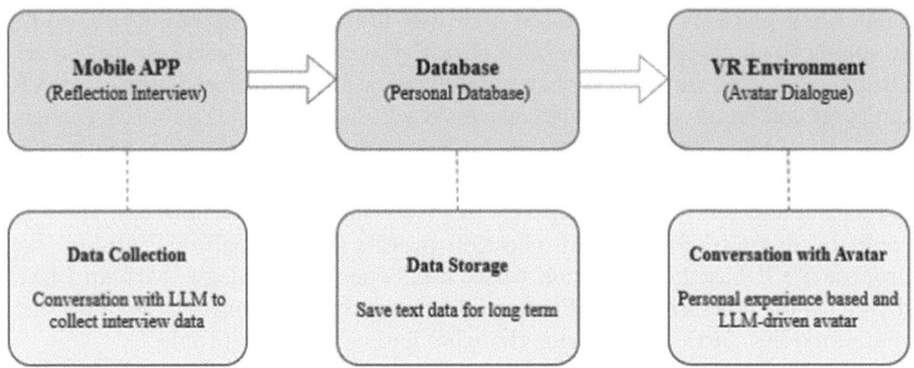

Fig. 1. Flowchart of VR Avatar Reflection System

by LLM, begins with a set of predefined questions before engaging in dynamic, adaptive questioning to elicit rich and detailed narratives from the learners. The interview module on the mobile app is architected around an integrated pipeline to enable seamless voice and text interaction. The specific models implemented are SenseVoice for Speech-to-Text (STT), GPT-4 as the LLM, and EdgeTTS for Text-to-Speech (TTS). To accurately detect the endpoints of user speech and initiate processing, a Voice Activity Detection (VAD) model, Silero, is integrated. The workflow operates as follows: the learner's spoken responses are first transcribed into text by the STT model (with an option for typed responses also provided). This text is then passed as input to the LLM, which generates a contextually relevant subsequent question or feedback. The LLM's textual response is subsequently synthesized into speech by the TTS model, completing the interactive cycle (Fig. 2).

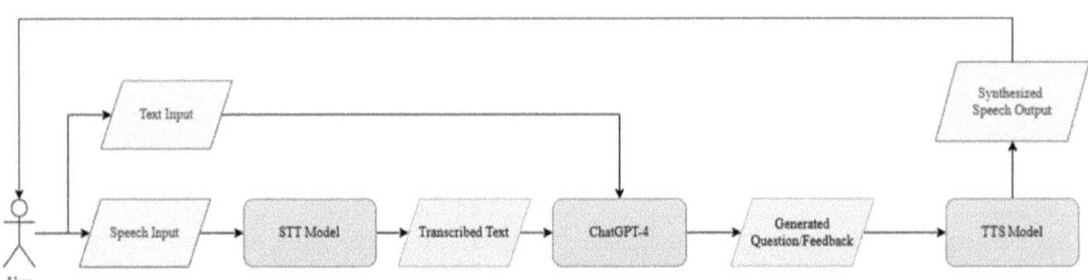

Fig. 2. Workflow of the conversational AI interview system

2.2 Data Persistence and Future Personalization

All conversational data from these interviews, along with learner information, is persistently stored in a centralized MySQL database. This systematically organized personal database forms a knowledge base of the learner's experiences and reflections. To further enhance the personalization and context-awareness of the system, a Retrieval-Augmented Generation (RAG) framework is planned for future implementation. This framework will connect the LLM to the personal database, enabling the generation of responses that are deeply grounded in the learner's entire historical narrative.

2.3 Immersive Reflection in Virtual Reality

The personal database will enable a deeply personalized reflective experience in the final component. A VR environment developed by Unity will allow learners to engage in real-time dialogue with a representative avatar embodying a past version of themselves. This avatar is driven by LLM, potentially augmented by a retrieval-augmented generation (RAG) system, enabling it to dynamically draw upon the learner's stored autobiographical experiences. Through this setup, learners can externalize and reflect on their past thoughts and experiences.

3 Evaluation Plan

We will aim for those courses with around 30 students enrolled. At the commencement of the academic term, students will select a digital avatar to serve as their virtual representative throughout the course. This avatar will be prominently featured within a dedicated mobile application designed to facilitate the design thinking journaling process. Rather than maintaining traditional handwritten journals, students will engage in semi-structured digital interviews via the mobile platform throughout the semester, allowing for systematic documentation of their reflections, insights, and experiential findings. All recorded data will be securely stored within individualized personal databases. At the conclusion of the semester, students will utilize VR headsets to engage in an immersive, reflective dialogue with their representative avatar, facilitating a review of their learning journey and developmental trajectory.

To rigorously assess the effectiveness of the proposed framework, a mixed-methods evaluation strategy will be employed, combining quantitative, qualitative, and comparative measures. This multi-faceted approach is designed to capture changes in awareness, the depth of reflective engagement, the relative efficacy of the intervention compared to established practice, and participants' engagement and motivation.

3.1 Quantitative Analysis of Reflection Awareness

To directly measure the construct of self-reflection, this study plans to use the Self-Reflection and Insight Scale (SRIS) [10]. The SRIS consists of two subscales: the Self-Reflection Scale, which assesses the tendency to engage in self-reflective thinking, and the Insight Scale, which measures the clarity and understanding gained from such reflection. An increase in scores on the Self-Reflection Scale indicates that learners are engaging in more frequent reflective thinking, while a significant rise in Insight Scale scores suggests that their reflection has not only increased in frequency but also enhanced in quality, resulting in clearer self-understanding. A pre-test/post-test design will be adopted to evaluate the intervention's effect. Participants will complete the SRIS prior to the intervention and again after engaging with the framework, which includes mobile data collection and VR avatar-mediated dialogue. Quantitative analysis will focus on both the total score and the two subscale scores. Statistical significance of pre-post differences will be assessed using paired-sample t-tests, with non-parametric alternatives (e.g., Wilcoxon signed-rank test) employed if assumptions are violated. This analysis aims to determine whether the intervention leads to significant improvements in self-reflective tendencies and insightful self-understanding.

3.2 Qualitative Analysis of Reflective Depth

To gain a richer, nuanced understanding of the reflective experience, qualitative data will be collected and analyzed. This will include: 1) Thematic analysis of the dialogue transcripts generated during the VR session, coded for indicators of reflective depth (e.g., presence of causal reasoning, critique of assumptions, evidence of perspective-taking); and 2) Semi-structured interviews conducted post-intervention to explore participants' subjective experiences, perceived insights, engagement, motivation, and the perceived impact of the embodied avatar interaction on their self-awareness.

3.3 Comparative Experimental Design

A quasi-experimental study will be conducted to contrast the novel framework against a traditional reflective method. Over two separate semesters of the same course, students will engage in different reflective exercises. One cohort will participate in the mobile application reflection interview throughout the semester. The subsequent cohort will experience extra VR avatar-mediated conversation. Both cohorts will complete identical end-of-semester evaluations, including the SRIS and qualitative interviews. This design will enable a direct comparison of the influence of avatar conversation on reflection awareness and the quality of reflection, controlling for course content and learning objectives.

4 Discussion

The proposed framework, situated at the intersection of personalized AI, immersive technology, and deep introspection, invites a discussion that transcends its immediate pedagogical outcomes. This section aims to situate the work within a wider context by confronting the critical questions of responsibility and realism. We first undertake a thorough examination of the ethical imperatives, given the handling of sensitive autobiographical data. Subsequently, we assess the practical feasibility of the system, addressing the infrastructural and accessibility barriers that must be overcome for successful adoption.

4.1 Ethical Considerations

The deployment of an AI-driven avatar that leverages deeply personal autobiographical data necessitates a rigorous examination of its ethical implications. Among the most pressing concerns are data privacy and security, given the sensitivity of the information collected, and potential psychological impacts, which arise from users' immersive interactions with a digital representation of their past selves. Informed by the seminal ethical framework for VR proposed by Madary and Metzinger [19], our study design incorporates several key safeguards to address the unique risks associated with avatar-mediated introspection. First, we adhere to the principle of a dynamic, multi-stage informed consent, ensuring participants are fully apprised not only of technical procedures but also of the potential psychological impacts, such as emotional distress when confronting past selves. Second, upholding the crucial right to withdraw, users are able to terminate the VR experience at any moment without penalty. Furthermore, participant data will be pseudonymized and encrypted to protect the profound privacy of their autobiographical disclosures and behavioral data. Finally, we will exercise heightened caution regarding participant eligibility, particularly screening out vulnerable populations who may be disproportionately affected by the immersive and self-referential nature of the intervention.

4.2 Practical Feasibility and Scalability

The scalability and broader deployment of the proposed framework are potentially constrained by practical challenges related to hardware requirements and accessibility. Operating an immersive VR environment in real-time requires substantial computational resources. While this requirement can be managed in our initial pilot study by providing qualified laptops and VR headsets for in-class use, it becomes a major barrier for broader adoption in less controlled, real-world settings. The limited availability of high-performance computing devices and VR equipment could hinder widespread implementation. To maintain access to the core reflective functionality under resource-limited conditions, one viable pathway is to develop a desktop or mobile version of the system. Nevertheless, it should be acknowledged that this alternative platform would inherently lack the immersive presence and embodied interaction that are central to the VR-based reflective experience.

5 Conclusion

This paper has introduced a novel framework for avatar-mediated self-reflection that integrates LLM, VR, and personal databases. Our primary contribution lies in extending the role of LLMs beyond content adaptation to the dynamic personalization of the self-reflection process itself. By situating learners within an immersive VR environment and using their own personal narratives as the foundational context, the framework facilitates a uniquely personalized and embodied reflective experience. A key innovation is the strategic use of a self-distanced, second-person perspective through the avatar, a design grounded in psychological theory to enhance the efficacy of introspection.

We anticipate that this approach will yield significant outcomes for users. Specifically, we expect it to cultivate a more disciplined capacity for introspection, develop a finer-grained ability to articulate complex emotional states, and ultimately foster integrative insight. This entails the ability to construct coherent narratives that connect feelings, thoughts, and actions, thereby transforming self-reflection from a passive awareness into an active tool for personal growth and adaptive functioning.

The potential significance of this work is multifaceted. It represents a step toward a new paradigm of AI-driven systems focused on fostering reflection skills rather than merely delivering information. For the fields of educational technology and psychology, it offers a testable model for how immersive technologies can be leveraged to support profound psychological processes like self-reflection. Future work will focus on the implementation of this framework, including the refinement of the avatar-led dialogue and rigorous empirical validation to measure its impact on reflective depth and personal insight.

Acknowledgments. The authors wish to express sincere gratitude to the programme committee and reviewers for their valuable feedback and suggestions. We are grateful to the Innovation and Technology Commission and the Government of the Hong Kong Special Administrative Region of the People's Republic of China for supporting our research on virtual reality (e.g., through the Innovation and Technology Fund Tier 1 Platform project ITP/006/24LP). We would also like to acknowledge the support from the Tam Wing Fan Innovation Fund and Philomathia Foundation Innovation Fund. Moreover, we thank Dr. Tobey H. Ko and Votanic Company for technical guidance and support, as well as Professor Henry Lau for his great efforts in establishing the daseCAVE. Finally, we appreciate all Visioneers members of the Human-System Interaction and Simulation lab's support and participation during the project development.

References

1. Anastasiadou, D., et al.: Virtual self-conversation using motivational interviewing techniques to promote healthy eating and physical activity: a usability study. Front. Psychiatry **14**, 999656 (2023)
2. Ardelt, M., Grunwald, S.: The importance of self-reflection and awareness for human development in hard times. Res. Hum. Dev. **15**(3–4), 187–199 (2018)
3. Ayduk, Ö., Kross, E.: Analyzing negative experiences without ruminating: the role of self-distancing in enabling adaptive self-reflection. Soc. Pers. Psychol. Compass **4**(10), 841–854 (2010)

4. Bany Abdelnabi, A.A., Soykan, B., Bhatti, D., Rabadi, G.: Usefulness of large language models (llms) for student feedback on h&p during clerkship: artificial intelligence for personalized learning. ACM Trans. Comput. Healthcare (2025). https://doi.org/10.1145/3712298, just Accepted
5. Brownhill, S.: Asking additional key questions of self-reflection. Reflective Pract. **24**(3), 400–412 (2023). https://doi.org/10.1080/14623943.2023.2190578
6. Chen, C., Lo, C., Hui, B.: Design journal instruction. MEDD8894 Design Thinking and Education, The University of Hong Kong (2024), course assignment specification
7. Deng, Y., Liao, L., Lei, W., Yang, G.H., Lam, W., Chua, T.S.: Proactive conversational ai: a comprehensive survey of advancements and opportunities. ACM Trans. Inf. Syst. **43**(3), 1–45 (2025)
8. Döllinger, N., et al.: Virtual body swapping: a vr-based approach to embodied third-person self-processing in mind-body therapy. In: Proceedings of the 2024 CHI Conference on Human Factors in Computing Systems, CHI 2024, ACM, New York, NY, USA (2024). https://doi.org/10.1145/3613904.3642328
9. Gan, W., Qi, Z., Wu, J., Lin, J.C.W.: Large language models in education: Vision and opportunities. In: 2023 IEEE International Conference on Big Data (BigData), pp. 4776–4785 (2023). https://doi.org/10.1109/BigData59044.2023.10386291
10. Grant, A.M., Franklin, J., Langford, P.: The self-reflection and insight scale: a new measure of private self-consciousness. Soc. Behav. Personal. Int. J. **30**(8), 821–835 (2002)
11. Grossmann, I., Dorfman, A., Oakes, H., Santos, H.C., Vohs, K.D., Scholer, A.A.: Training for wisdom: the distanced-self-reflection diary method. Psychol. Sci. **32**(3), 381–394 (2021)
12. Gün, B.: Quality self-reflection through reflection training. ELT J. **65**(2), 126–135 (2011)
13. Huang, M., Ma, J., Bo, S.: Design and implementation of a multi-level personalized teaching framework based on llm. In: 2025 14th International Conference on Educational and Information Technology (ICEIT), pp. 8–14 (2025). https://doi.org/10.1109/ICEIT64364.2025.10975909
14. Johnson-Glenberg, M.: Immersive vr and education: embodied design principles that include gesture and hand controls. Front. Robot. AI **5** (2018). https://doi.org/10.3389/frobt.2018.00081
15. Kocielnik, R., Xiao, L., Avrahami, D., Hsieh, G.: Reflection companion: a conversational system for engaging users in reflection on physical activity. Proc. ACM Interact. Mob. Wearable Ubiquitous Technol. **2**(2), 1–26 (2018)
16. Kross, E., Grossmann, I.: Boosting wisdom: distance from the self enhances wise reasoning, attitudes, and behavior. J. Exp. Psychol. Gen. **141**(1), 43 (2012)
17. Kross, E., Ong, M., Ayduk, O.: Self-reflection at work: why it matters and how to harness its potential and avoid its pitfalls. Annu. Rev. Organ. Psych. Organ. Behav. **10**(1), 441–464 (2023)
18. Liu, Z., Wang, L.: Study on the style construction of embodied cognitive learning supported by vr technology. Educ. Inf. Technol. **30**, 403–419 (2024). https://doi.org/10.1007/s10639-024-13049-4
19. Madary, M., Metzinger, T.K.: Real virtuality: a code of ethical conduct. recommendations for good scientific practice and the consumers of vr-technology. Front. Robot. AI **3**, 180932 (2016)
20. Osimo, S.A., Pizarro, R., Spanlang, B., Slater, M.: Conversations between self and self as sigmund freud–a virtual body ownership paradigm for self counselling. Sci. Rep. **5**(1), 13899 (2015)

21. Slater, M., et al.: An experimental study of a virtual reality counselling paradigm using embodied self-dialogue. Sci. Rep. **9**(1), 10903 (2019)
22. Tan, Z., et al.: In prospect and retrospect: reflective memory management for long-term personalized dialogue agents. arXiv preprint arXiv:2503.08026 (2025)
23. Wang, X.J., Lee, C.P., Mutlu, B.: Learnmate: enhancing online education with llm-powered personalized learning plans and support. In: Proceedings of the Extended Abstracts of the CHI Conference on Human Factors in Computing Systems. CHI EA 2025, ACM, New York, NY, USA (2025). https://doi.org/10.1145/3706599.3719857

LLM-Driven Adaptive Pictography: A Novel Framework for Personalized Chinese Character Learning

Yuetong Guo, Yantong He, and Kanoksak Wattanachote(✉)

Faculty of Information and Communication Technology (ICT), Mahidol University, Salaya 73170, Nakhon Pathom, Thailand
kanoksak.wat@mahidol.ac.th

Abstract. The acquisition of Chinese characters (Hanzi) presents a significant challenge for learners worldwide, from young native speakers to second language (L2) adults, primarily because rote memorization is ineffective. This paper introduces the LLM-Driven Adaptive Pictography (LLMDAP) framework, a novel AI-powered system that transforms Hanzi learning into an active, creative, and highly personalized process. LLMDAP leverages a three-stage pipeline. The first stage, Visual Capture, allows learners to sketch concepts using pictorial cues. The second stage, Multimodal Mapping, uses a heuristic/AI-based recognizer to map sketches to characters and trigger learning content. The last stage is the Personalized Reinforcement, where the system dynamically generates a multimodal poster showcasing the character's etymological chain and provides text-to-speech feedback. We present the complete system architecture and a fully implemented proof-of-concept that demonstrates the technical feasibility of this approach for a core set of pictographic characters. Our work contributes a novel framework grounded in cognitive theory, a functional prototype, and a detailed technical walkthrough. The LLMDAP framework marks a significant step towards highly personalized, AI-powered language education for a global audience, and we provide a clear roadmap for its future expansion and empirical validation.

Keywords: Personalized Learning · Large Language Models · Multimodal AI · Chinese Character Acquisition · Pictography · Educational Technology

1 Introduction

The acquisition of Chinese characters (汉字, hànzì) represents a significant cognitive and pedagogical challenge not only for second language (L2) learners [1] but also for native Chinese children (识字, shízì) [2]. Unlike alphabetic writing systems that rely on phonetic correspondence, Hanzi are logographic, requiring learners to memorize the visual form, pronunciation, and semantic meaning of thousands of distinct characters. For Chinese children, literacy development demands years of repetitive practice and exposure, as each character must be learned as a unique visual pattern with subtle distinctions in stroke order and radicals. Studies in cognitive psychology [3] have shown

B. Fernández-Manjón et al. (Eds.): SETE 2025/ICWL 2025, LNCS 16425, pp. 395–410, 2026.
https://doi.org/10.1007/978-981-92-0042-9_29

that the working memory load involved in recognizing and recalling characters is substantially higher than in alphabetic systems, as learners must simultaneously integrate orthographic, phonological, and semantic information [4]. This complexity makes early literacy acquisition in Chinese a gradual and often effort-intensive process, even for native speakers immersed in the language environment.

For L2 learners, the difficulty of mastering Hanzi is compounded by the lack of phoneme-grapheme transparency and the absence of familiar linguistic anchors. Learners must overcome a steep learning curve [5] to connect visual forms with both pronunciation (pinyin) and meaning, often without the aid of cognates or consistent spelling rules. The cognitive load is particularly high because learning to read and write Chinese involves building parallel systems of recognition and recall, enabling both the identification and reproduction of characters from memory. Despite these challenges, interest in Mandarin Chinese has surged globally, with millions of learners studying it as a foreign language due to China's growing cultural and economic influence [6]. This worldwide trend [7] underscores the universal nature of the challenge: whether in Beijing or Boston, mastering Hanzi requires sustained cognitive effort, visual memory, and contextual understanding that go far beyond phonetic decoding [8].

Traditional methods like 抄写 (repetitive copying) strengthen motor memory and visual familiarity but rarely foster deep semantic or cultural understanding of Hanzi. Learners focus on surface form rather than internalizing structural logic or etymology, leading to shallow encoding, short-term recall without meaningful retention.

Digital tools such as flashcards and mobile apps (e.g., Anki, Pleco, Skritter [9, 10]) modernize this process with spaced repetition and multimedia cues but largely digitize passive learning, replicating rote recall in a digital format.

Both traditional and digital approaches lack personalization and semantic grounding. They do not adapt to learners' cognitive styles or emotional engagement, leaving characters as arbitrary symbols rather than meaningful constructs, particularly for L2 learners, where motivation and retention often stagnate despite increased exposure. To operationalize this vision, we propose the LLMDAP framework, a unified, three-stage pipeline designed to support personalized Hanzi learning for both L1 and L2 learners:

Sketch Recognition and Semantic Mapping: The learner submits a hand-drawn sketch representing their interpretation of a character's meaning. A heuristic or AI-based recognizer then interprets the sketch using both Geometric Heuristics (low-level strokes/shapes) and Semantic Heuristics (high-level pictorial cues), mapping these visual features onto candidate Hanzi or radicals.

Dynamic Poster Generation: Once the system identifies the relevant character(s), it generates a multimodal "learning poster," a dynamic visual layout combining the character's etymology, phonetic cues, radicals, and example usages, all customized to reflect the learner's sketch and level.

Personalized Reinforcement: Set up practice modules, including character recognition (listening, viewing, and understanding meanings) and writing exercises. Based on the learners' practice feedback, use LLMDAP to provide corresponding personalized guidance. For example, strengthen feedback on the correct stroke order of characters and review pronunciation.

Personalized Multimodal Feedback. A Text-to-Speech (TTS) and multimodal generation module produces personalized audio narration and interactive cues, allowing learners to see, hear, and feel the meaning simultaneously. This feedback loop closes the gap between creative expression and structured linguistic knowledge.

Together, these stages form a closed-loop learning system: user creativity feeds system adaptation, and system feedback refines user understanding. LLMDAP, therefore, bridges the gap between rote reproduction and meaningful creation.

2 Literature Review and Theoretical Foundation

2.1 Cognitive Theories of Learning

According to Dual Coding Theory [11], learning is most effective when information is encoded through both verbal and non-verbal (visual) systems. The LLMDAP framework operationalizes this principle by integrating two complementary modes: the learner's sketch as a visual code and the character's etymological and linguistic narrative as a verbal code. When learners create a sketch representing the meaning or structure of a Hanzi, they engage the visual channel to encode imagery and spatial relationships. The subsequent system-generated narrative, linking the sketch to the character's pronunciation, meaning, and cultural context, activates the verbal channel.

This dual activation strengthens associative memory, as learners can retrieve the character through both its visual imagery and linguistic description. Unlike rote memorization or flashcards, which rely primarily on verbal repetition, LLMDAP ensures that visual and verbal representations reinforce one another, leading to richer, more durable learning outcomes.

Cognitive Load Theory [12] distinguishes between intrinsic, extraneous, and germane load in learning. Traditional rote copying and uncontextualized digital drills impose a high extraneous load, forcing learners to process disconnected visual and semantic elements without an organizing schema.

LLMDAP reduces this burden by providing meaningful integration: the sketch, narrative, and etymological visualization are all tied together in a coherent multimodal story. This structure minimizes unnecessary cognitive effort and channels mental resources toward schema formation, the linking of visual form, phonetic sound, and semantic meaning into a unified mental model. As a result, learners experience reduced frustration and improved retention, since the content is presented in cognitively aligned formats that support comprehension rather than overload it.

2.2 Memory Retention and Reinforcement Technologies

The effectiveness of long-term language acquisition depends critically on reinforcement strategies that combat the natural decay of memory. Hermann Ebbinghaus's forgetting curve [13] demonstrates that memory retention declines exponentially without reinforcement, with most information lost within days of initial learning. This phenomenon is particularly relevant for Chinese character acquisition, where learners must retain thousands of distinct visual-symbol associations.

Spaced Repetition Systems (SRS) directly address this challenge by scheduling review sessions at optimal intervals to strengthen memory traces before they fade. Algorithms such as the Leitner system or SM-2 (used in Anki) calculate these intervals based on recall performance, ensuring that difficult items receive more frequent review while well-mastered content appears less often [14]. LLMDAP incorporates these principles in its Personalized Reinforcement stage, using performance metrics to dynamically adjust review schedules and maximize retention efficiency.

Adaptive Learning Algorithms extend beyond simple spaced repetition by personalizing the entire learning pathway based on individual progress, error patterns, and cognitive preferences. These systems employ knowledge tracing models [15] that estimate the probability of mastery for each learning component, allowing for real-time adjustment of content difficulty and presentation style. In LLMDAP, this adaptivity manifests through customized practice modules that focus on each learner's specific challenges, whether in stroke order, tonal pronunciation, or radical recognition.

Multimodal Feedback Systems in language learning leverage multiple sensory channels to reinforce memory formation. Text-to-Speech (TTS) technology, when accurately implemented with proper tonal representation for Mandarin, provides crucial phonological reinforcement that complements visual learning [16]. Research in computer-assisted language learning (CALL) [17–19] has demonstrated that bimodal presentation, combining visual characters with auditory pronunciation, significantly improves character recognition and recall compared to unimodal approaches [20]. LLMDAP's integration of TTS with visual etymological narratives creates a rich multisensory experience that aligns with how the brain naturally processes and stores linguistic information.

2.3 The Pictographic Opportunity and AI's Role

The very feature that makes Hanzi appear daunting—their visual complexity—is also the source of their mnemonic potential [21, 22]. A significant portion of the Chinese writing system's foundational characters originated as pictographs (象形, xiàngxíng) or ideographs (表意, biǎo yì) [23], representing concrete objects or abstract concepts through stylized drawings. For instance, the modern character for "mountain" (山, shān) evolved from a drawing of three peaks in Oracle Bone Script, while "water" (水, shuǐ) derived from a flowing river. This etymological heritage provides a natural, intuitive roadmap for understanding and memorizing character forms.

However, in traditional pedagogy, this etymology is often presented as static, passive information in textbooks or apps, a historical footnote rather than an active learning tool. The cognitive leap from a 3,000-year-old pictograph to a modern, abstracted character can be difficult for a learner to make independently. The connection remains impersonal and external.

This is where the transformative potential of Artificial Intelligence, specifically Multimodal Large Language Models (MLLMs) [24], emerges. MLLMs like GPT-4V [25] and Gemini possess the unprecedented capability to understand, interpret, and generate content across different modalities, most critically, for our purposes, both images (a hand-drawn sketch representing their interpretation of a character and a character's handwriting) and text. This allows them to act as intelligent, dynamic mediators between a learner's personal expression and formal linguistic knowledge.

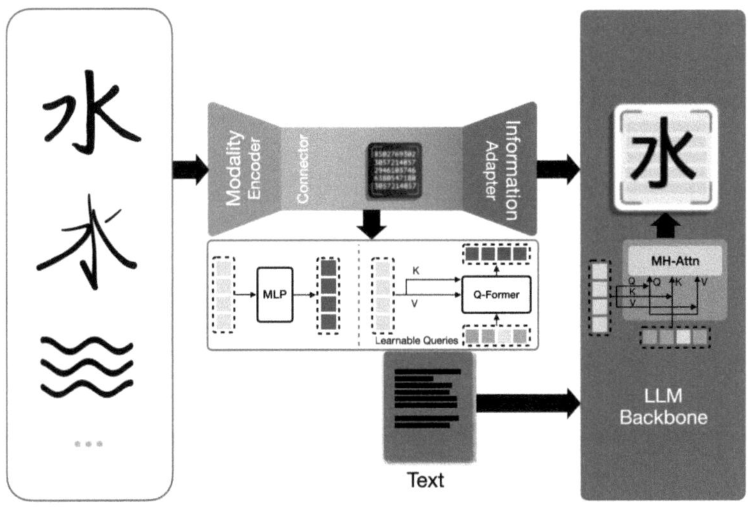

Fig. 1. Multimodal understanding of LLMDAP: the components of the stage of multimodality.

The core innovation of the LLMDAP framework, as in Fig. 1, is the repurposing of this advanced AI capability to ground the learning process in personal creative output. Instead of passively observing ancient pictographs, the learner actively creates their own visual representation of a concept. The MLLM's role is to analyze this personal sketch, recognize its semantic intent, and dynamically construct a coherent narrative that bridges the learner's unique drawing with the character's historical evolution and modern usage. This process transforms the AI from a simple information retrieval system into a personalized etymological tutor, making the ancient pictographic principle a living, interactive, and deeply personal experience. The mnemonic connection is no longer between the learner and a generic image, but between the learner and a story generated from their own creation.

3 The LLMDAP Framework: System Architecture

3.1 High-Level Overview

The LLMDAP framework is designed as a modular three-layer system integrating user interaction, AI-based processing, and structured linguistic data (Fig. 1). Each component corresponds to a stage in the pipeline, from learner input to personalized multimodal output, ensuring seamless flow and interoperability.

The LLMDAP's Input Layer enables learners to sketch, view generated posters, and receive auditory feedback. The AI Processing Layer performs sketch recognition, semantic mapping, and multimodal poster synthesis. The database in the Retrieval Layer stores linguistic, etymological, and phonetic knowledge in a relational structure for efficient retrieval.

System Data Flow (see Fig. 2):

Input: The learner draws a conceptual sketch in the browser interface.

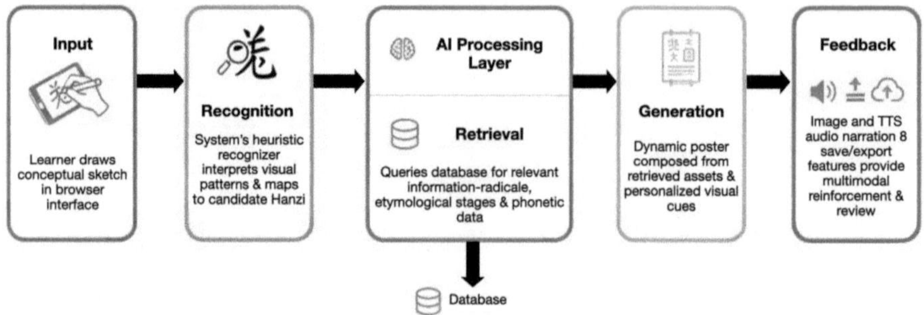

Fig. 2. The diagram illustrating our LLMDAP system's conceptual data flow.

Recognition: The system's heuristic recognizer interprets visual patterns and maps them to candidate Hanzi.

Retrieval: The AI Processing Layer queries the database to fetch relevant information—radicals, etymological stages, and phonetic data.

Generation: A dynamic poster is composed of retrieved assets and personalized visual cues.

Feedback: Image and TTS audio narration and save/export features provide multimodal reinforcement and review functionality.

This layered structure emphasizes interoperability: each module can be improved independently (e.g., replacing the heuristic recognizer with an MLLM) without disrupting the overall flow of the system.

3.2 Stage 1: Visual Capture and Heuristic Sketch Recognition

The first stage enables the learner to externalize their understanding of a character through a hand-drawn sketch, creating a personal mnemonic anchor that transforms abstract linguistic data into a concrete visual artifact.

For the proof-of-concept system, LLMDAP employs a deterministic, heuristic recognizer rather than a deep-learning model. This decision was guided by three practical factors:

Speed: Lightweight heuristic analysis provides immediate feedback suitable for classroom or demo settings.

Cost: It requires no GPU inference or external API calls, ensuring accessibility.

Clarity: Deterministic rules are transparent and interpretable, allowing easy debugging and reproducibility.

This recognizer establishes a baseline architecture for the system's pipeline, while leaving the module plug-and-play, readily replaceable by an advanced MLLM for future research.

Technical Details

The recognizer analyzes geometric primitives extracted from the learner's sketch (using the ipycanvas API in Colab or a web canvas). Each writing stroke (Table 1) is converted

Table 1. Low-Level Stroke Recognition using Geometric Heuristics.

Feature	Description	Target Hanzi	Heuristic Logic
number_of_peaks	Count of distinct pointed regions	山 (mountain)	≥3 vertical peaks
is_closed_circle	Presence of enclosed loops	日 (sun), 目 (eye)	Closed shape ratio > 0.8
has_curved_lines	Presence of smooth, sinusoidal curvature	水 (water)	≥2 curved segments
stroke_divergence	Outward, branching stroke pattern	火 (fire)	≥2 diverging lines
vertical_axis_symmetry	Degree of mirror symmetry	树 (tree)	Symmetry > 0.7

into a feature vector based on basic geometric descriptors such as stroke count, curvature, symmetry, and enclosure (see Fig. 3).

Each feature is normalized and evaluated via simple rule-based thresholds to infer the most probable Hanzi candidate. When multiple candidates fit a pattern, the recognizer ranks them by geometric confidence and sends the top match to the next stage.

Moreover, our LLMDAP framework proposed another concept-level approach (Table 2) that complements the geometric stroke logic by mapping semantic or pictorial cues, patterns that the learner might naturally draw when visualizing meaning. Together, the two tables demonstrate how LLMDAP's heuristic recognizer bridges form-based analysis (strokes, shapes) and meaning-based interpretation (conceptual sketches), as demonstrated in Fig. 3.

3.3 Stage 2: Multimodal Mapping and Dynamic Poster Generation

The second stage of the LLMDAP framework, multimodal mapping, is responsible for translating a learner's visual sketch into a semantically and visually aligned Chinese character while dynamically generating a personalized multimodal poster. The central objective is to create a learning artifact that merges linguistic knowledge, etymological evolution, and personalized visual memory cues, transforming static memorization into an active, creative process.

Once the learner's sketch is captured in the first stage, it is processed through a hybrid recognition approach that compares the input with a curated visual database of Hanzi radicals and pictographic primitives. For the current prototype, this employs the deterministic heuristic recognizer described in Stage 1, while the architecture is designed for future integration with Multimodal LLMs. The goal is to map conceptual similarity rather than exact shape matching, encouraging learners to associate ideas and visual metaphors rather than perfect form reproduction. This semantic-flexible recognition allows the system to identify a corresponding Hanzi candidate and initiate poster generation, thereby grounding abstract characters in the learner's own creative imagery (see Fig. 4).

Table 2. High-Level Concept Recognition using Semantic Heuristics.

Feature	Description	Target Hanzi	Heuristic Logic
wave_pattern	Sketch contains 2–4 flowing, curved horizontal or diagonal lines resembling waves	水 (water)	Detect repetitive sinusoidal curves; interpret as fluid motion symbol
stick_figure	Simple human shape with circular head and 4–5 limb strokes	人 (person)	Presence of central vertical body line with symmetric branch strokes
enclosed_circle_with_lines	Circle enclosing rays or short outward lines	日 (sun)	Central closed contour + radial extensions → solar imagery
vertical_line_with_branch	Trunk-like vertical stroke with side branches	树 (tree)	Main vertical stroke with two lateral extensions; high symmetry
triangular_peak_pattern	Sketch with pointed mountain-like outline	山 (mountain)	≥3 ascending peaks in y-axis profile; stable base width
radiating_spark_lines	Multiple short diverging strokes from a central node	火 (fire)	Stroke divergence > threshold; radial symmetry ratio ~0.6
box_with_dot	Square or rectangular shape containing one centered mark	田 (field)	Detect enclosure and interior mark ratio; suggests cultivated grid

Database Schema and Knowledge Graph

At the core of this process lies a MySQL-based knowledge graph, which stores interconnected data describing each character's structural, historical, and phonetic attributes. The schema includes three principal tables:

characters: Contains the main attributes of each Hanzi, including *id*, *unicode*, *modern_form*, *pinyin*, *meaning*, and *etymology_summary*.

etymology_stages: Stores a timeline of glyph evolution (Oracle bone script, Bronze script, Seal script, Clerical, and Modern), each linked to the corresponding character id, image URLs or font references, and brief semantic annotations.

glyphs: Contains vectorized or bitmap representations of both modern and ancient forms, tagged with their Unicode range and metadata about the script origin.

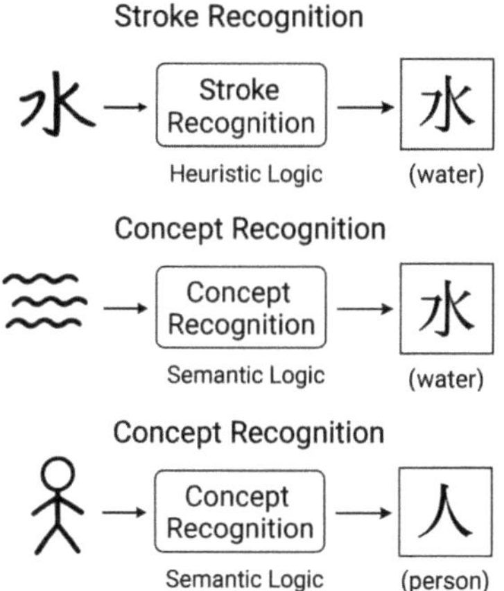

Fig. 3. LLMDAP: Integrated geometric and semantic concept recognition.

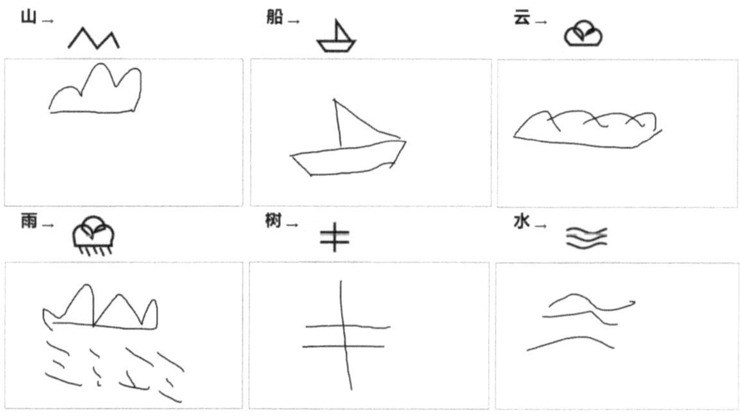

Fig. 4. LLMDAP: Our multimodal mapping outputs of pictorial cues (from top left to bottom right they are 山(shān)-mountain, 船(chuán)-boat, 云(yún)-cloud, 雨(yǔ)-rain, 树(shù)-tree, and 水(shuǐ)-water.

This structure allows dynamic querying and hierarchical traversal from semantic concept to character evolution, forming the knowledge backbone for multimodal visualization. The system can retrieve a character's full historical chain within milliseconds, feeding it into the rendering engine for contextualized display.

Technical Implementation Challenges

Font Integration Challenge and Solution: One of the major technical challenges encountered in Stage 2 is rendering ancient scripts, such as Oracle Bone (甲骨文) and Bronze Script (金文), which are often unavailable in standard Unicode fonts. To address this, LLMDAP integrates a hybrid font management solution combining specialized Unicode-compliant fonts (e.g., Hanazono Mincho, Noto Sans CJK SC, and AllText Ancient Chinese) and custom raster glyph assets manually curated from open-source etymological datasets. When a requested script form is missing from the local font set, the system gracefully falls back to pre-rendered PNG glyphs stored in the glyphs table. This ensures visual continuity and scholarly accuracy while maintaining lightweight rendering performance in both web and Colab environments.

Poster Generation Algorithm: Poster generation is handled through a combination of ipycanvas and Pillow (PIL) libraries, ensuring compatibility across Jupyter/Colab interfaces. The layout process follows a modular pipeline:

Canvas Initialization: Define poster dimensions (e.g., 1080 × 720 px) with a neutral background.

Modern Character Placement: Center the contemporary Hanzi in large type, using a high-resolution CJK font.

Icon Overlay: Superimpose the learner's original sketch as a semi-transparent overlay to visually connect personal input and canonical form.

Evolution Timeline Rendering: Sequentially render historical glyphs from oldest to newest, spaced horizontally or vertically, forming a clear visual chain of etymological transformation.

Text Wrapping and Annotation: Using Pillow's ImageDraw.textbbox() and textwrap modules, add brief annotations, pinyin, meaning, and etymology, aligned with each glyph.

Final Composition and Export: Merge layers into a unified PNG or PDF output, ready for display or reinforcement in the next stage.

This dynamic poster functions as a cognitively enriched artifact that merges semantic, phonetic, and visual information into a single, memorable representation, transforming abstract knowledge into a tangible multimodal experience.

3.4 Stage 3: Personalized Reinforcement Modules

The third and final stage, Personalized Reinforcement, focuses on retention and long-term memory formation through interactive, multimodal feedback. Once a poster has been generated, the system transitions from production to reinforcement, engaging both auditory and visual channels to consolidate learning in accordance with Dual Coding Theory and the Cognitive Load Theory.

Text-to-Speech Integration: A key feature of Stage 3 is the bimodal reinforcement loop enabled by text-to-speech (TTS) synthesis. LLMDAP leverages the Web Speech API (for browser implementations) or gTTS/pyttsx3 (for offline and Colab environments) to provide naturalistic pronunciation and semantic description. When a learner interacts with a generated poster, by hovering over a glyph or clicking the modern character, the system plays the Mandarin pronunciation, tonal contour, and English or L1 translation. This auditory reinforcement enhances phonological encoding and strengthens orthographic-phonological mapping, which is particularly beneficial for L2 learners struggling with tone discrimination and phoneme recall.

Adaptive Review and Save Functionality: To promote spaced repetition and personalized learning continuity, LLMDAP enables learners to save each generated poster into a local or cloud-based gallery. Each artifact is tagged with metadata (character ID, timestamp, user ID, and difficulty level) and reintroduced at intervals based on learner performance. The database logs user interactions (e.g., number of correct identifications, playback requests) to compute adaptive review schedules using a simple exponential decay function. This ensures that characters with weaker recall are presented more frequently in subsequent sessions, aligning the system's pedagogy with well-established memory models such as Ebbinghaus's forgetting curve. In combination, the TTS and adaptive save mechanisms transform static learning artifacts into living, interactive memory anchors. Learners can revisit, listen, and visually trace their prior creations, reinforcing cognitive links across form, sound, and meaning in a personalized feedback loop. Stage 3 thus completes the LLMDAP cycle, transforming passive rote learning into an adaptive, creative, and multimodal language experience.

4 Implementation and Demonstrative Walkthrough

4.1 Development Environment and Tech Stack

The LLMDAP prototype was developed as a fully functional, end-to-end system using an accessible, open-source technology stack. The primary goal was to ensure technical feasibility, reproducibility, and cross-platform operability, particularly within Google Colab and standard web environments. Our software environment consists of the programming language: Python 3.9. The interface and visualization: Jupyter Notebook and Google Colab environment. Graphics Libraries, we applied ipycanvas (v8.0.0) for interactive sketch capture, and Pillow (v10.0.0) for layout rendering and image composition.

Backend database, we implemented on MySQL 8.0, providing structured storage for the *characters*, *etymology_stages*, and *glyphs* tables (the system's internal Knowledge Graph).

Web Backend (for our future task), we planned to utilize Flask 2.3 for serving the system as a browser-based prototype with API endpoints for recognition and poster generation.

For AI and Recognition, we applied a lightweight heuristic recognizer (OpenCV + LLM-assisted semantic disambiguation) for the second stage of mapping.

Text-to-Speech (for our future task), we planned to apply Web Speech API (browser) or gTTS (offline mode) for audio synthesis and bimodal learning reinforcement.

All components were designed for modular extensibility, allowing future integration with vision-language models (e.g., GPT-4V or LLaVA) without major architectural changes.

4.2 A Demonstrative Case Study: Learning the Character "水" (Water)

To illustrate LLMDAP's workflow and pedagogical affordances, we present a step-by-step demonstration using the pictographic character "水" (shuǐ, water), one of the most ancient and visually representative Hanzi, see Fig. 5. The initial clean user interface consists of a drawing canvas, a prompt box, and a "Recognize" button. The learner begins by sketching freely within the canvas area, expressing the concept of water through intuitive visual metaphors. The learner inputs a series of wavy lines, loosely resembling flowing streams. This spontaneous drawing acts as a visual hypothesis rather than a test of accuracy; the system is designed to capture semantic intent, not artistic precision. Once submitted, the Multimodal Mapping engine compares the drawn pattern with stored radical shapes and semantic embeddings. As shown in Fig. 5, the system successfully matches the input to the character "水", displaying a recognition message and confidence score. This demonstrates the heuristic recognizer's ability to generalize across stylized or imperfect input, mirroring how human learners interpret form and meaning flexibly.

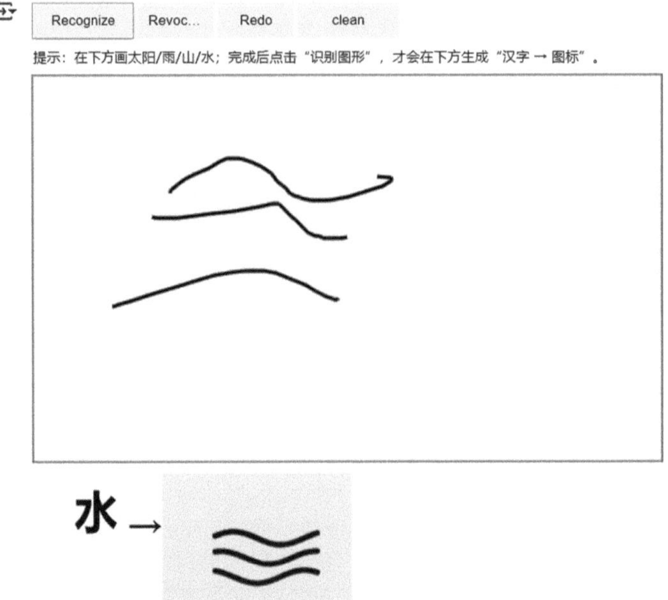

Fig. 5. An illustration of LLMDAP's workflow and pedagogical affordances, a step-by-step demonstration using the pictographic character "水" (shuǐ, water).

4.3 Discussion of System Capabilities and Preliminary Insight

The walkthrough demonstrates that LLMDAP's three-stage pipeline, sketch capture, multimodal mapping, and reinforcement, is both technically implementable and pedagogically coherent. The modular Python-based implementation successfully integrates multimodal I/O (visual, textual, and auditory) in a single interactive loop. This confirms the framework's engineering feasibility as a foundation for AI-powered Hanzi education.

Table 3. Internal Recognition Accuracy on Canonical Test Sketches.

Character	Test Samples	Correctly Recognized	Accuracy
水 (water)	50	50	100%
树 (tree)	50	40	80%
日 (sun)	50	50	100%
人 (person)	50	50	100%
Overall	**200**	**190**	**95%**

Internal validation was conducted using 200 test sketches covering four basic pictographs (水, 树, 日, and 人), with five stylized variants per character. Each sketch was drawn by different users simulating diverse input styles. The recognizer's results are summarized in Table 3.

These results indicate that even the heuristic recognizer is sufficient for early-stage pictographic characters, validating the technical soundness of the pipeline before introducing a vision-language model.

5 Discussion and Limitations

5.1 The LLMDAP Framework as a New Paradigm

LLMDAP introduces a paradigm shift in Hanzi learning, from passive memorization to co-creative exploration. Learners become active participants who construct meaning through multimodal interaction, while the AI acts as a personalized curator rather than a static tutor. In this sense, LLMDAP operationalizes the emerging educational paradigm of LLM-based Personalized Learning, in which language models dynamically scaffold learning experiences. Furthermore, LLMDAP aligns with the vision of Agentic AI: systems that empower learners to act, create, and reflect rather than merely consume predefined content. By turning each character into a story co-authored by the learner and the system, LLMDAP demonstrates how AI can mediate culturally grounded, individualized learning journeys.

5.2 Limitations with Candor

While promising, LLMDAP remains a prototype with several limitations that warrant transparency.

Scope: The current implementation supports a small corpus of basic pictographs (e.g., 水, 树, 日, and 人), primarily due to the manual curation required for etymological glyph data.

Recognition Engine: The heuristic visual recognizer, though effective for canonical forms, cannot generalize to highly abstract or complex sketches. Replacing it with a multimodal LLM (e.g., GPT-4V) would provide more robust interpretation and contextual mapping.

Lack of Formal User Study: As a system demonstration paper, LLMDAP has not yet undergone empirical validation. A formal, comparative user study is a critical next step to evaluate its actual impact on learning outcomes, engagement, and retention.

6 Conclusions and Future Work

This work has addressed a universal challenge in language education, the difficulty of mastering Chinese characters, and proposed a novel, AI-driven solution grounded in cognitive theory and user creativity. Through the LLMDAP framework, we demonstrated how sketch-based interaction, multimodal mapping, and personalized reinforcement can transform rote memorization into an engaging, learner-centered process. A functional prototype, built with modern open-source tools, validates the technical feasibility and conceptual promise of the approach.

Beyond Hanzi learning, LLMDAP illustrates how agentic, multimodal AI systems can redefine the learner's role, from a passive recipient of information to an active co-creator of knowledge. By combining cognitive science, AI, and design thinking, LLMDAP charts a concrete path toward personalized, creative, and evidence-based AI education. Future work will focus on empirical validation, large-scale MLLM integration, and pedagogical scaling, positioning LLMDAP as a key step toward the next generation of intelligent learning environments.

The next development milestone involves replacing the heuristic recognizer with a Multimodal Large Language Model (MLLM) such as GPT-4V or LLaVA. Through prompt engineering, the model will be guided to interpret sketch intent, generate candidate characters, and explain radical composition, thereby improving recognition accuracy and interpretive richness.

LLMDAP will be extended to compound and ideographic characters, enabling conceptual instruction beyond pictographs. For instance, learners might be prompted to sketch "a person next to a tree," allowing the system to introduce 休 (xiū, rest). The MLLM will then explain how the radical composition reflects semantic relationships, offering a deeper insight into Chinese morphology and cognitive linguistics. To empirically validate LLMDAP, we plan to conduct a mixed-methods study with approximately 60 participants, comprising both Chinese children and adult L2 learners. Participants will be randomly assigned to one of two groups: 1) LLMDAP Group: Using the adaptive pictography interface. 2) Control Group: Using traditional flashcard-based learning.

The study will follow a pre-test/intervention/immediate post-test/delayed post-test design. Quantitative measures will assess retention and pronunciation recall, while qualitative instruments, such as the Intrinsic Motivation Inventory (IMI), will capture engagement and learner perceptions. This research will provide the first empirical evidence of LLMDAP's pedagogical effectiveness and inform iterative refinements of the framework.

References

1. Bigelow, M., Ennser-Kananen, J.: The Routledge Handbook of Educational Linguistics, 1st edn. Routledge, New York (2014)

2. Shu, H., Anderson, R.C.: Role of Radical Awareness in the Character and Word Acquisition of Chinese Children: Center for the Study of Reading. Production Note. University of Illinois at Urbana-Champaign Library, Illinois (2007)
3. Perfetti, C.A., Liu, Y., Tan, L.H.: The lexical constituency model: some implications of research on Chinese for general theories of reading. Psychol. Rev. **112**(1), 43–59 (2005)
4. Perfetti, C.A., Tan, L.H.: The time course of graphic, phonological, and semantic activation in Chinese character identification. J. Exp. Psychol. Learn. Mem. Cogn. **24**(1), 101–118 (1998)
5. Shen, H.H., Ke, C.: Radical awareness and word acquisition among nonnative learners of Chinese. Mod. Lang. J. **91**(1), 97–111 (2007)
6. Pitutacha, W.: An Exploration of the Increasing Popularity of Chinese Language Education relative to English Language Education. Language Institute, Thammasat University (2024)
7. Ministry of Education of the People's Republic of China. International promotion of the Chinese language continues to grow. https://en.moe.gov.cn. Accessed 13 Aug 2025
8. Khaohongshu Blog: Learning Chinese with Google Gemini – Can it beat ChatGPT? https://kaohongshu.blog/2024/11/03/learning-chinese-with-google-gemini-can-it-beat-chatgpt/. Accessed 20 Sept 2025
9. AD7GD. Flashcards: Anki vs Pleco vs Skritter in detail. https://www.reddit.com/r/ChineseLanguage/comments/ad0gvn/flashcards_anki_vs_pleco_vs_skritter_in_detail/. Accessed 01 Oct 2025
10. Hooshmand, D. Skritter Review. How I Learned 2,500 Chinese Characters. https://discoverdiscomfort.com/skritter-review-learn-chinese-characters/. Accessed 01 Oct 2025
11. Clark, J.M., Paivio, A.: Dual coding theory and education. Educ. Psychol. Rev. **3**(3), 149–170 (1991)
12. Sweller, J., Mestre, J.P., Ross, B.H.: Chapter Two - Cognitive Load Theory. Psychology of Learning and Motivation, vol. 55, pp. 37–76. Academic Press (2011)
13. Ebbinghaus, H.: Memory: a contribution to experimental psychology. Ann. Neurosci. **20**(4), 155–156 (2013). https://doi.org/10.5214/ans.0972.7531.200408
14. Settles, B., Meeder, B.: A trainable spaced repetition model for language learning. In: Proceedings of the 54th Annual Meeting of the Association for Computational Linguistics, vol. 1 (2016)
15. Corbett, A.T., Anderson, J.R.: Knowledge tracing: modeling the acquisition of procedural knowledge. User Model. User-Adap. Inter. **4**, 253–278 (1994)
16. Zhao, L.: Production and Perception of Lexical Tone Variation in Mandarin Dialects. Language and Linguistic Science, University of York (2023)
17. Kaburise, P.: Practicalities of a computer-assisted language learning project. Int. J. Educ. Sci. **7**(3), 747–754 (2014)
18. Pirasteh, P.: The effectiveness of computer-assisted language learning (CALL) on learning grammar by Iranian EFL learners. Procedia Soc. Behav. Sci. **98**, 1422–1427 (2014)
19. Chen, C.M., Li, M.C., Lin, M.F.: The effects of video-annotated learning and reviewing system with vocabulary learning mechanism on English listening comprehension and technology acceptance. Comput. Assist. Lang. Learn. **35**(7), 1557–1593 (2022)
20. Mayer, R.E.: Multimedia Learning, 3rd edn. Cambridge University Press, Cambridge (2020)
21. Chang, L.Y., Tang, Y.Y., Lee, C.Y., Chen, H.C.: The effect of visual mnemonics and the presentation of character pairs on learning visually similar characters for Chinese-as-second-language learners. Front. Psychol. **13**, 783898 (2022)
22. Leminen, F., Bai, S.: Applying visual mnemonics enhances Chinese characters learning for Chinese as second language learners: a mixed-method study. In: Proceedings of the 7th International Conference on Digital Technology in Education (ICDTE), pp. 150–154. Association for Computing Machinery, New York, NY, USA (2023)
23. Yong, H., Jing, P. Chinese Lexicography: A History from 1046 BC to AD 1911. Oxford University Press (2008)

24. Zhang, J., Khayatkhoei, M., Chhikara, P., Ilievski, F.: MLLMs Know Where to Look: Training-free Perception of Small Visual Details with Multimodal LLMs. arXiv (2025)
25. Yao, Y., et al.: Efficient GPT-4V level multimodal large language model for deployment on edge devices. Nat. Commun. **16**, 5509 (2025)

EMGen: Human-AI Collaboration to Generate Educational Material

Raymond Morland[1], Fuhua Lin[1(✉)], and Qun Jin[2]

[1] Athabasca University, Athabasca, AB T9S 3A3, Canada
rmorland1@learn.athabascau.ca, oscarl@athabascau.ca
[2] Waseda University, Tokorozawa 359-1192, Japan
jin@waseda.jp

Abstract. This paper investigates the use of large language models for automatically generating educational content, with a focus on specifying precise, pedagogy-aligned requirements for AI-assisted authoring. We introduce EMGen, a web-based system that combines prompt design patterns with an iterative generate-review-revise process, grounded in a structured curriculum model and specialized educator-AI interfaces. These interfaces translate instructor intent into actionable constraints (e.g., content type, learning methodology, and question validation criteria) and, when paired with instructor-provided resources via retrieval-augmented generation, help align outputs with curricular goals. Through initial testing, we illustrate how EMGen supports the creation and refinement of materials; formal instructor evaluations of UI/UX and content quality are forthcoming. Our contribution is a practical workflow and toolchain that reduces ad hoc prompt engineering, keeps educators in control of pedagogical decisions, and shows promise for improving the quality and relevance of AI-generated educational materials.

Keywords: Large Language Models · Content Generation · Educational Material · Human-AI Interaction · Adaptive Learning

1 Introduction

In the dynamic realm of educational technology, the transformative potential of large language models (LLMs) such as OpenAI's GPT, Anthropic's Claude, and Meta's Llama is becoming increasingly evident [7]. These advanced AI systems typically operate through chat-based interfaces, simulating one-on-one conversations. However, such conversational user interfaces often prove inadequate for generating complex, context-specific educational materials, particularly for instructors who lack prior experience with AI tools or prompt engineering, thereby creating a significant barrier to effective use in educational contexts [15].

Research has found that eliciting and articulating precise requirements for AI-powered educational content generation presents a significant challenge for

B. Fernández-Manjón et al. (Eds.): SETE 2025/ICWL 2025, LNCS 16425, pp. 411–424, 2026.
https://doi.org/10.1007/978-981-92-0042-9_30

educators [13]. The complexity of translating educational objectives into clear and actionable prompts is multifaceted and nuanced. Achieving optimal alignment between human intent and AI-generated output often requires extensive and iterative interaction between the user and the model [3]. Consequently, the refinement of AI-generated content (AIGC) should be viewed not as a linear process, but as a dynamic, cyclical, and collaborative dialogue between human and machine. In this process, educators must engage in continuous clarification, communicating contextual nuances, pedagogical constraints, and clearly defined learning objectives (LOs) to effectively guide the model's output. Through this extended, iterative interaction, the AI system progressively refines its understanding, adapting to the intricate requirements of educational material design. Yet, because educational content creation inherently involves ambiguity and contextual variability, such refinement cannot rely on simple or concise instructions alone.

Effective human-AI collaboration (HAIC) therefore demands a sophisticated approach, one that embraces complexity, encourages detailed explanation, and supports iterative feedback mechanisms [5]. By acknowledging the limitations of brief prompt engineering, educators can adopt more robust strategies for leveraging generative AI (GenAI) in instructional design. Consequently, the success of GenAI-assisted educational-material generation depends on the depth and quality of the human-AI interaction (HAII), turning what might appear as a challenge into an opportunity for intentional, precise, and tailored content creation.

In this research, we developed a web-based LLM-powered AI system called EMGen, designed for HAIC. Specifically, the system was developed as an automated AI assistant capable of executing actions via a user interface (UI), targeting the generation of educational material for adaptive personalized learning. The UI of this innovative system is designed to reflect a collaborative real-life approach between teachers and AI, going beyond traditional chat-based models. Furthermore, the system has been designed to generate educational material based on learning science. For example, the system is capable of generating multiple-choice questions (MCQs) for formative assessment using question validation criteria (QVC) grounded in instructional design principles to ensure their effectiveness and usability.

Our approach is grounded in domain and curriculum models, which provide a structured framework to organize and represent educational concepts [10]. By leveraging these models, we aim to bridge the gap between AI capabilities and educators' needs, ensuring that generated content aligns with pedagogical goals and learning theories. In addition, the proposed HAIC model is designed to support an iterative and incremental optimization process, allowing educators to refine and improve AI-generated materials over time. This approach not only addresses the current limitations of AIGC tools, but also empowers educators to maintain control over the content creation process while benefiting from AI assistance. Our work contributes to HAII in education by detailing an educator-AI collaboration workflow and an evaluation design for the development of educational material.

The remainder of this paper is organized as follows. Section 2 reviews the related work in HAIC for AI-generated educational content; Sect. 3 describes the EMGen methodology; Sect. 4 details the implementation; Sect. 5 presents a discussion of initial and future testing; and Sect. 6 concludes and outlines directions for future work.

2 Related Works

Recent research in the field of HAIC in education supports the significance and timeliness of this study and the implementation of EMGen. For example, Atchley et al. [1] explore the integration of AI in higher education, positioning it as both a transformative opportunity and a challenge. The authors highlight how AI tools, such as ChatGPT, can facilitate learning when thoughtfully incorporated while addressing risks such as cognitive offloading and misinformation. They emphasize the importance of developing meta-cognitive skills and collaborative approaches to prepare students for effective HAIC in the evolving workforce.

Several researchers have implemented frameworks and systems for using AI tools to generate content. Dickey and Bejarano [4] introduced GAIDE, a framework designed to assist educators in the efficient development of course content using GenAI. GAIDE integrates practical steps for leveraging AI tools to generate, refine, and adapt educational materials, reducing instructional workload while maintaining quality and diversity of content. By emphasizing iterative refinement and contextual integrity, GAIDE empowers educators to harness AI for scalable, engaging, and inclusive curriculum design.

To determine how collaboration between AI systems, students, and instructors can be facilitated, crowd-sourcing and learnersourcing have been investigated. Khosravi et al. [8] explore the concept of learnersourcing, where students and educators collaborate with AI to create educational content, addressing challenges such as content quality and engagement. Moreover, Mohammadreza Tavakoli et al. [18] proposed a system that combines AI and crowd-sourcing to develop personalized curricula, detailing an iterative process involving human contributors and AI recommendations. Although these methods may enable collaborative development of educational content, we seek methods that are more immediate and do not require the work of many people.

In the field of automated question generation (AQG), validation is a critical component [6,16]. Maity et al. [11] conducted an investigation of the capabilities of GPT-4 Turbo to generate educational questions aligned with Bloom's Revised Taxonomy. The integration of QVC into LLM prompts represents a potential avenue to enhance the quality and effectiveness of AQG utilizing LLM. By providing LLMs with this additional contextual information, it is hypothesized that the generated questions will demonstrate improved alignment with specific LOs, maintain appropriate difficulty levels, and mitigate redundancy, thus increasing their relevance and educational value. In addition, the incorporation of QVC into the generation process can facilitate the production of questions by LLMs that exhibit greater clarity, reduced bias, and improved consistency with educational standards, ultimately contributing to more accurate and reliable assessments in educational contexts.

Several recent reviews have covered the recent impact of AI on education. Brusilovsky [2] reviewed the current state of AI in education, focusing on user control and collaboration between learners and AI, and suggested future research directions to enhance these interactions. In general, the impact AI will have on the creation of educational material is undeniable. We seek to further the progress made so far by implementing a system that brings together several fundamental principles of educational content creation and HAII.

3 Methodology

Our method of effectively generating educational material incorporates three fundamental components: curriculum modeling, an iterative design process, and established learning methodologies. We discuss these components in this section and their implementation in the EMGen system in Sect. 4.

3.1 Supporting Models

To enable effective HAIC for the generation of educational material using GenAI, we use a hybrid curriculum model as shown in Fig. 1 [10]. The model starts with a curriculum and its learning outcomes. A curriculum consists of a set of courses. Each individual course within the curriculum has its own set of outcomes. These are specific and tailored to the subject matter of the course. Course-level outcomes act as bridges between curriculum goals and the fundamentals of daily teaching or learning.

Below the course-level are unit-level learning outcomes. These outcomes break down the course material into manageable chunks, often corresponding to the main themes or concepts within the subject. They provide a road map for both instructors and students, highlighting key competencies to be mastered within a given time frame. Units are further broken down into sections, and at the most granular level, we find section-level LOs. These are the day-to-day, lesson-by-lesson objectives that guide individual class sessions or learning activities. They are highly specific, often using revised Bloom taxonomy action verbs to describe observable behaviors or demonstrable skills [9].

This layered approach to curriculum modeling ensures that every learning activity, assessment, and resource are purposefully aligned with the broader educational goals. This not only facilitates clear communication of expectations to students, but also aids in curriculum mapping, assessment design, and continuous improvement efforts. By meticulously crafting and aligning LOs at each layer, educators can create a cohesive, goal-oriented learning experience that guides students from the big picture to the smallest details of their educational journey. This curriculum model enables logical sequencing of learning materials, guided by learning experiences.

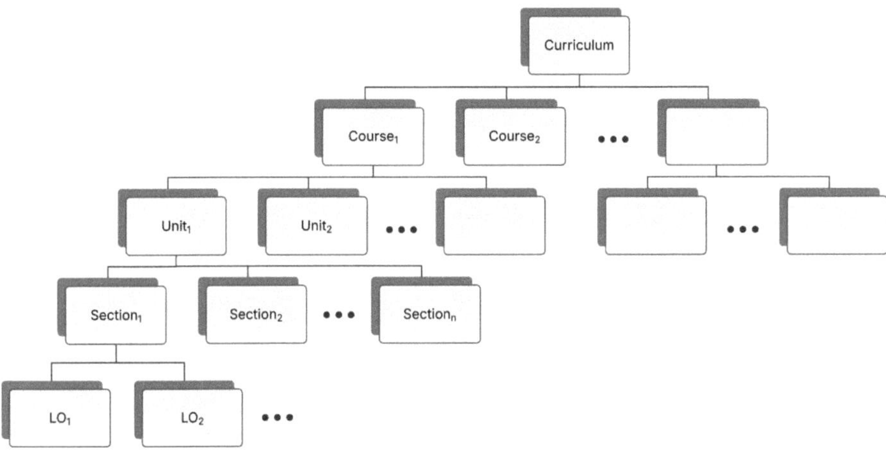

Fig. 1. The curriculum model supporting EMGen.

3.2 Iterative Design Workflow

The iterative design process for creating AIGC in EMGen is illustrated in Fig. 2. The process begins with Phase 1 Initial Requirement Gathering, in which the course author specifies subject matter and topic details, LOs, type of material to generate (e.g., tutorial, assessment items). Phase 2 consists of the AIGC phase, in which an AI tool, powered by LLMs, generates and displays initial content based on the teacher's input. Next, in Phase 3, the educator reviews the generated content and provides feedback, which can include accuracy of information, alignment with the LO, appropriateness for the target audience, areas needing improvement or expansion. In Phase 4, the AI tool refines the content based on the teacher's feedback; this may include adjusting difficulty levels, expanding on specific concepts, generating additional examples or questions. The process repeats phases 3 and 4 until the author of the course is satisfied with the output. The last phase, Phase 5, is finalization and integration, in which the author of the course finalizes the content and integrates it into their course materials.

This iterative process allows for continuous improvement of the content generated, leveraging both AI capabilities and the course author's expertise. The interface design focuses on ease of use, clear feedback mechanisms, and seamless integration of AIGC into the course author's workflow.

3.3 Guiding the LLM

To ensure that the specific type of content generated by the LLM aligns not only with the desired LO of the course but also with the instructor's pedagogical strategies, additional guidance is provided to the LLM in the prompt. Depending on the type of content an instructor wishes to produce, they can supply additional information in the form of learning methodologies, for tutorial-type content, or QVC, for MCQ-type content.

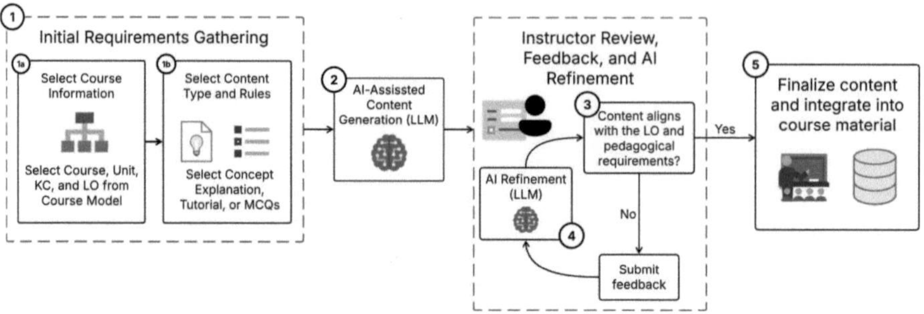

Fig. 2. The iterative design process for generating educational material with EMGen.

Learning Methodologies. As part of the initial requirement gathering to generate tutorials, the instructor has the option to select the specific type of learning methodology that they would like the educational material to follow. For each learning methodology, a unique string of context is injected into the prompt to guide the alignment of the LLM. This context is added in conjunction with the LO metadata, content type, and other information in the prompt. In the current implementation, we explore two learning methodologies: the Feynman Learning Techniques and the GROW model.

The Feynman Technique. This is a method to allow students to develop a deep understanding of a subject and has been shown to be especially effective in e-learning environments [17]. The technique was developed by the Nobel Prize winning physicist Richard Feynman, a master of demystifying complex topics. His key insight into learning was that complexity and jargon often mask a lack of understanding. By following his technique, students can break through this complexity to understand the underlying principles. Feynman's learning technique comprises four key steps:

1. Select a concept to learn.
2. Teach it to a child.
3. Review and refine your understanding.
4. Organize your notes and revise them regularly.

The GROW Model. This is a widely recognized coaching framework that is used to set goals and solve problems [14]. This framework serves as a guide for developing a structured learning plan, customized to an individual's present circumstances and the specific knowledge or skills they aim to acquire. There are several variations of the GROW model. In the version of the GROW model by Panchal and Riddell [14], the "O" can signify Obstacles or Options. Obstacles represent barriers that prevent people from reaching their goals. Identifying these obstacles is crucial, as addressing them is necessary to make progress. The GROW model comprises four stages:

1. Goal (G): Define the desired outcome.
2. Reality (R): Assess the current situation.
3. Options (O): Explore potential strategies to achieve the goal.
4. Will (W): Determine the actions to be taken.

Depending on which learning methodology the instructor selects, the Feynman technique steps or the GROW model stages are injected into the LLM prompt.

Question Validation Criteria. To guide and align automatically generated MCQs, we adopt a literature-derived QVC framework synthesized from established item writing guidelines [12]. The QVC included are: (1) Alignment with the stated LO and cognitive level; (2) Fairness/Bias minimization; (3) Clarity/Completeness of the stem; (4) Plausible, homogeneous distractors; (5) Readable option ordering (logical/alphabetical/chronological/numerical as appropriate); (6) Avoidance of test-wise/logic cues (length, grammar, style inconsistencies); (7) Independence of options (no overlap or extremes); and (8) Instructive feedback at the option level. Instructors select from this predefined list when generating MCQs and may add custom QVC as needed. The selected QVC are injected into the LLM prompt as explicit acceptance criteria.

4 EMGen Architecture and Implementation

EMGen is implemented as a client-server web application, consisting of a server application, a teaching application, and a database. The server application is implemented in NodeJS[1] and is responsible for managing database transactions, data modeling, and content generation. To access LLMs, the LangChain[2] JavaScript library was used and integrated into the NodeJS web server. LangChain provides wrapper classes to many popular LLMs APIs and makes integrating LLMs into an application easy. All content is generated using the OpenAI gpt-4o-mini model for its cost effectiveness. To store all course models, content type, content data, and vector embeddings, the MongoDB[3] document database is used. The front-end instructor application is built using the Next.js[4] React framework. The EMGen architecture is shown in Fig. 3.

EMGen's instructor application separates source assets from generated content. In the *Learning Resources* module, instructors upload slides, lecture notes, and other materials; these are processed into vector embeddings and indexed for retrieval-augmented generation (RAG). In the *Educational Content* module, instructors browse, filter, and search previously generated items or start new ones by selecting Generate Material. When generation begins, a draft document is created in the database, and progress is automatically saved at each step,

[1] https://nodejs.org.
[2] https://js.langchain.com.
[3] https://www.mongodb.com/.
[4] https://nextjs.org/.

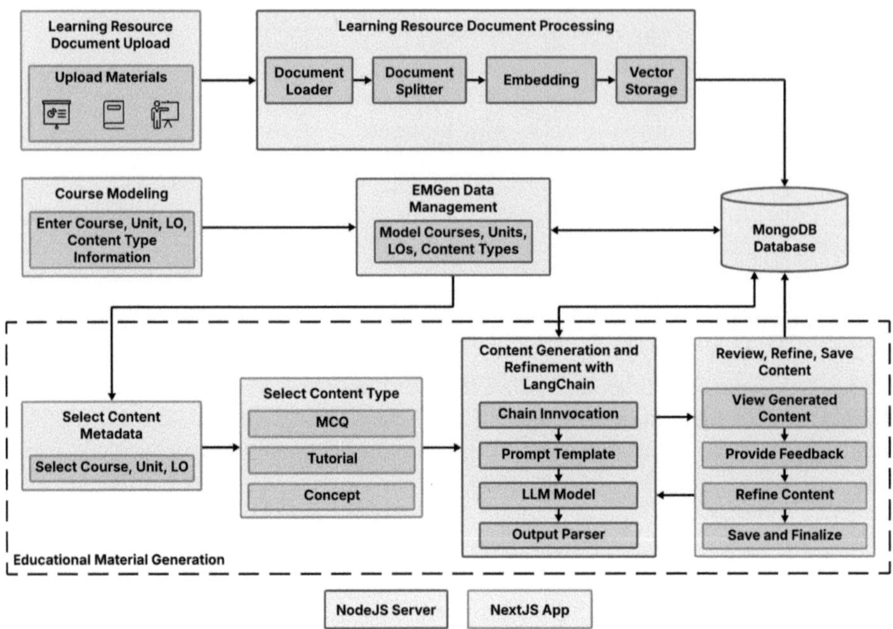

Fig. 3. The EMGen system architecture.

allowing instructors to exit and resume later without loss. The content generation form then guides users through the iterative design workflow shown in Fig. 2.

First, in the "Info" step, the instructor selects the course, unit, section, and LO for which to generate content (see Fig. 4). The course information displayed in this interface is authored in the *Courses* module using the course modeling tools.

Second, in the "Type" step, the instructor selects the type of content to generate for the LO (see Fig. 5). The types of content are organized into two categories: *Assessment Items*, used in automated assessments, and *Instructional Material*, used for remediation and student learning. The currently available options are tutorials (instructional material) and MCQs (assessment items). Each type of content includes a description and an output format that is injected into the prompt template so the LLM generates the appropriate item.

Third, after selecting the type of content, the instructor configures the pedagogical options in the "Pedagogy" step. For MCQs, the instructor selects a set of QVC (see Fig. 6), choosing from predefined items or adding custom ones. The selected QVC are injected into the LLM prompt to align the questions with the instructor's pedagogical preferences. For tutorials, the instructor chooses a learning methodology from those described in Sect. 3.3 (see Fig. 7). After completing this step, the instructor clicks "Refine Content" to generate the material. The selected LO and content type, together with the chosen QVC or methodology,

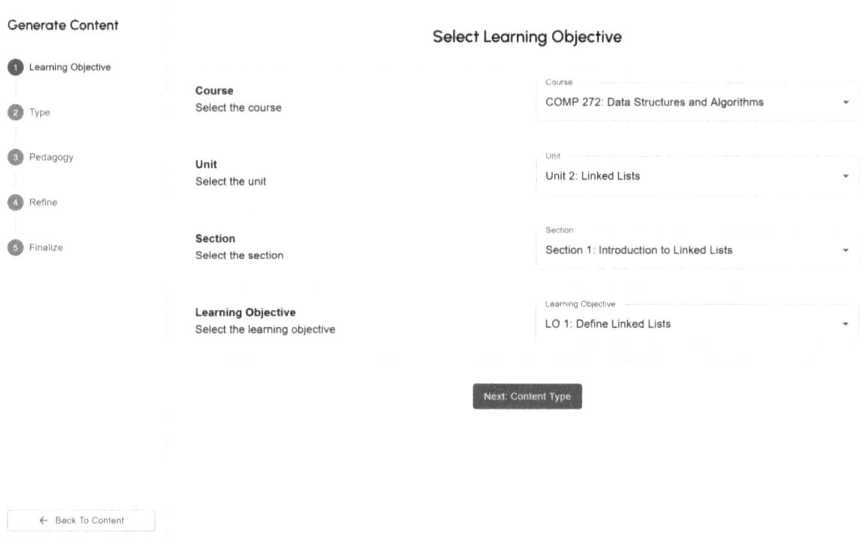

Fig. 4. Selecting learning objectives for educational content in EMGen.

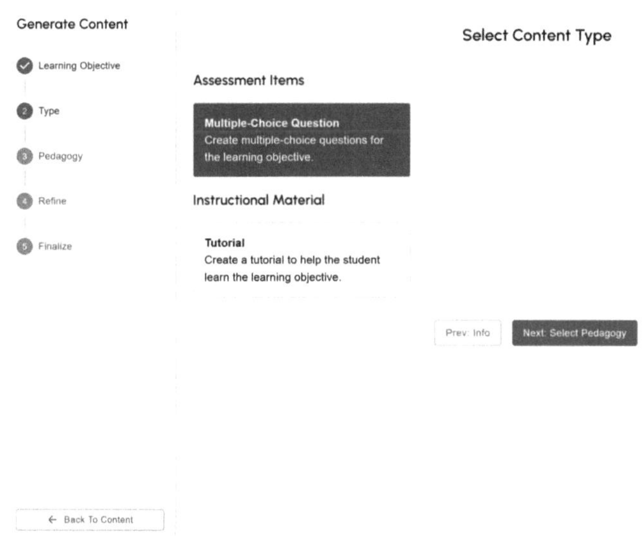

Fig. 5. Selecting content types for educational content in EMGen.

are injected into the prompt template; the LLM generates the content, and the server returns it to the application.

Finally, when satisfied with the content, the instructor clicks "Finalize,", which completes the creation and removes the item from the draft status. The

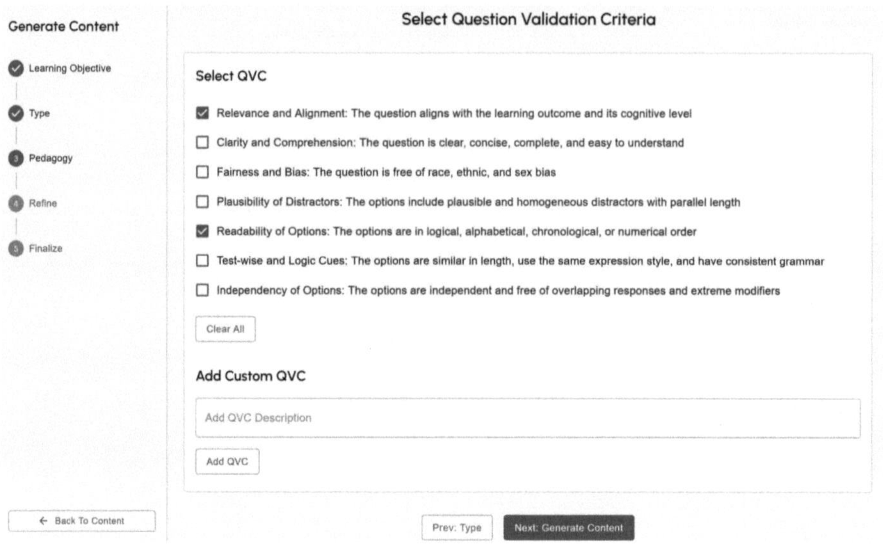

Fig. 6. Selecting the QVC for a MCQ in the EMGen educational material generation process.

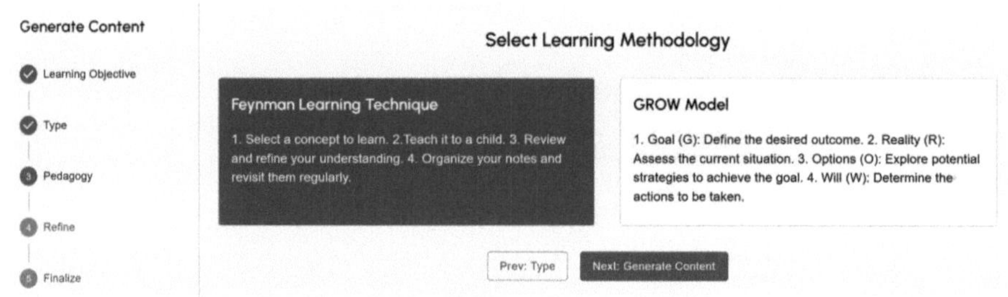

Fig. 7. Selecting the learning methodology for a tutorial in the EMGen educational material generation process.

final screen then offers options to export as PDF, create additional materials, or view all generated content (see Fig. 9).

Fourth, in the "Refine" step, once the generated content is loaded into the application, the instructor reviews and improves it (see Fig. 8). They may provide structured feedback to guide revisions or edit the text directly. All fields in the form are fully editable through text input and the Quill.js[5] rich text editor (WYSIWYG). After entering feedback and selecting options, the instructor clicks the submit button which sends the feedback together with the current content to the server. The LLM then revises the material based on this input, and the updated version is returned to the application. This enables iterative refinement

[5] https://quilljs.com/.

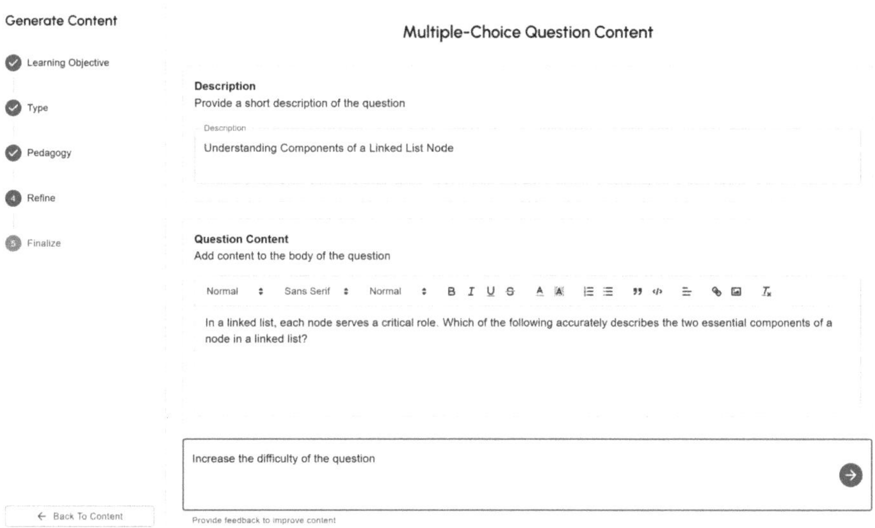

Fig. 8. Instructors iteratively refine generated content in the EMGen interface by providing feedback.

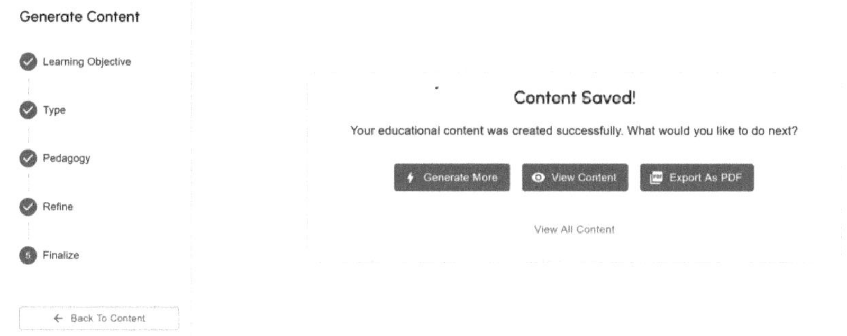

Fig. 9. Instructors have the option to export generated content to a PDF, generate more content, or view all content on the finalize screen.

across multiple cycles. Each version is saved and instructors can revert to any prior version as needed.

5 Discussion

MCQs produced with our system have undergone initial testing; previous work evaluated the quality of the questions and found the approach capable of generating usable items [12]. We have since conducted internal checks on other content types, and formal instructor evaluations across all content types are forthcoming. In these studies, instructors will create courses in EMGen, upload learning resources to seed the RAG corpus, and generate instructional materials. The evaluation will address (1) UI / user experience (UX), usability, workflow efficiency, and satisfaction; and (2) quality of content, curricular alignment, topical relevance, clarity, and correctness. We will also assess the effect of iterative refinement by comparing first-pass outputs with versions revised through one or two feedback cycles.

Integrating our iterative content generation methodology into EMGen offers clear advantages over the ad hoc, chat-based use of LLMs. The output can be structured according to the instructor's learning management system's schema and open standards such as LTI[6], allowing automatic validation, reuse, and interoperability. EMGen also provides end-to-end integration, automating ingestion, storage, versioning, and publishing, so materials flow directly into the instructor's system and can be deployed immediately in learning objects (e.g. adaptive assessments, course modules), eliminating copy-and-paste from external chat interfaces (e.g. ChatGPT, Perplexity). In addition, the system auto-injects QVC, content type, learning methodology, and course-model metadata into prompt templates and applies predefined prompting strategies, reducing cognitive load and obviating ad hoc prompt engineering, so instructors can focus on course modeling and content refinement. Collectively, these capabilities shorten the pipeline from instructor intent to student-facing resources.

6 Conclusion and Future Work

This paper presents a novel human-AI interface for iterative educational material authoring, addressing persistent challenges in leveraging AIGC within education. Grounded in domain knowledge models and learning theory, our approach provides a structured workflow for organizing and generating content that remains aligned with pedagogical goals.

EMGen shows early promise for improving the quality and relevance of AI-generated materials. By combining user-centered design with pedagogical constraints and built-in mechanisms for iterative refinement, the system keeps educators in control while harnessing the capabilities of modern LLMs. Our key contributions are as follows.

1. An HAIC model that supports iterative, incremental optimization of course materials and transparent instructor control,
2. Integration of domain knowledge models (and RAG) to improve the relevance and accuracy of generated content,
3. A UI tailored to educator workflows for course modeling, generation, review, and revision, with versioning and rollback, and
4. Initial evidence from pilot use in computer science courses and a clear plan for forthcoming UI/UX and content-quality evaluations.

Although this work establishes the foundation of our HAIC model for AIGC, several directions remain. We will assess generalizability across disciplines by

[6] https://www.1edtech.org/standards/lti.

adapting domain models and interfaces, conduct longitudinal studies to quantify effects on learning outcomes and engagement, evaluate integration with adaptive learning to personalize content, and expand authoring to richer modalities, interactive simulations, video, and auto-generated figures, to address the current lack of visual aids. We also plan to support multi-instructor collaboration for shared authoring and best-practice exchange, and to embed ethical safeguards, including bias and fairness auditing, privacy protection, and transparency. Advancing these areas will produce more robust, equitable, and widely applicable HAIC tools.

Acknowledgments. We acknowledge the support of the Natural Sciences and Engineering Research Council of Canada (NSERC), Alberta Innovates, and Athabasca University, Canada.

Disclosure of Interests. The authors have no competing interests to declare that they are relevant to the content of this article.

References

1. Atchley, P., Pannell, H., Wofford, K., Hopkins, M., Atchley, R.A.: Human and ai collaboration in the higher education environment: opportunities and concerns. Cogn. Res. Principles Implications **9**(1), 20 (2024). https://doi.org/10.1186/s41235-024-00547-9
2. Brusilovsky, P.: AI in education, learner control, and human-AI collaboration. Int. J. Artif. Intell. Educ. **34**(1), 122–135 (2024). https://doi.org/10.1007/s40593-023-00356-z
3. Cain, W.: Prompting change: exploring prompt engineering in large language model ai and its potential to transform education. TechTrends **68**(1), 47–57 (2024). https://doi.org/10.1007/s11528-023-00896-0
4. Dickey, E., Bejarano, A.: GAIDE: a framework for using generative ai to assist in course content development. In: 2024 IEEE Frontiers in Education Conference (FIE), p. 1–9. IEEE (2024). https://doi.org/10.1109/fie61694.2024.10893132
5. Gomez, C., Cho, S.M., Ke, S., Huang, C.M., Unberath, M.: Human-AI collaboration is not very collaborative yet: a taxonomy of interaction patterns in AI-assisted decision making from a systematic review. Front. Comput. Sci. **6** (2025). https://doi.org/10.3389/fcomp.2024.1521066
6. Gorgun, G., Bulut, O.: Exploring quality criteria and evaluation methods in automated question generation: a comprehensive survey. Educ. Inf. Technol. **29**(18), 24111–24142 (2024). https://doi.org/10.1007/s10639-024-12771-3
7. Kasneci, E., et al.: Chatgpt for good? On opportunities and challenges of large language models for education. Learn. Individ. Differ. **103**, 102274 (2023). https://doi.org/10.1016/j.lindif.2023.102274
8. Khosravi, H., Denny, P., Moore, S., Stamper, J.: Learnersourcing in the age of AI: student, educator and machine partnerships for content creation. Comput. Educ. Artif. Intell. **5**, 100151 (2023). https://doi.org/10.1016/j.caeai.2023.100151
9. Krathwohl, D.R.: A revision of Bloom's taxonomy: an overview. Theory Into Pract. **41**(4), 212–218 (2002). https://doi.org/10.1207/s15430421tip4104_2

10. Lin, F., Morland, R.: Curriculum modeling for adaptive learning. In: Sottilare, R.A., Schwarz, J. (eds.) Adaptive Instructional Systems, vol. 15813, pp. 57–72. Springer Nature Switzerland, Cham (2025). https://doi.org/10.1007/978-3-031-92970-0_5
11. Maity, S., Deroy, A., Sarkar, S.: How effective is GPT-4 turbo in generating school-level questions from textbooks based on bloom's revised taxonomy? (2024), https://arxiv.org/abs/2406.15211
12. Morland, R.D., et al.: Can question validation criteria improve the quality of LLM-generated multiple-choice questions? In: Proceedings of the 1st International Workshop on Smart Education in the Age of Generative AI (SEGA) (2025, in press). Accepted for presentation
13. Office of Educational Technology: Artificial intelligence (AI) and the future of teaching and learning: insights and recommendations. Report ED631097, U.S. Department of Education, Washington, DC (2023). https://eric.ed.gov/?id=ED631097. eRIC Number: ED631097
14. Panchal, S., Riddell, P.: The grows model: extending the grow coaching model to support behavioural change. Coaching Psychol. **16**(2), 12–24 (2020). https://doi.org/10.53841/bpstcp.2020.16.2.12
15. Pozdniakov, S., et al.: Large language models meet user interfaces: the case of provisioning feedback. Comput. Educ. Artif. Intell. **7**, 100289 (2024). https://doi.org/10.1016/j.caeai.2024.100289
16. Raina, V., Gales, M.: Multiple-choice question generation: towards an automated assessment framework (2022). https://arxiv.org/abs/2209.11830
17. Reyes, E.P., Blanco, R.M.F.L., Doroon, D.R.L., Limana, J.L.B., Torcende, A.M.A.: Feynman technique as a heutagogical learning strategy for independent and remote learning. Recoletos Multidisc. Res. J. **9**(2), 1–13 (2021). https://doi.org/10.32871/rmrj2109.02.06
18. Tavakoli, M., Faraji, A., Molavi, M.T., Mol, S., Kismihók, G.: Hybrid human-AI curriculum development for personalised informal learning environments. In: LAK22: 12th International Learning Analytics and Knowledge Conference, LAK22, pp. 563–569. Association for Computing Machinery, New York, NY, USA (2022). https://doi.org/10.1145/3506860.3506917

Active Learning with Generative AI to Enhance Learning Experience: Experiment Design and Verification

Miyuki Ri[1], Ruichen Cong[2], and Qun Jin[2(✉)]

[1] School of Human Sciences, Waseda University, Tokorozawa, Japan
[2] Faculty of Human Sciences, Waseda University, Tokorozawa, Japan
jin@waseda.jp

Abstract. The COVID-19 pandemic has accelerated changes in educational methods, while rapid technological advancements underscore the need for adaptable talent in an evolving society. In this study, we design an experiment and verify the effectiveness of utilizing generative AI tools as a partner based on active learning. In our experiment, we compare the learning experiences and outcomes between participants provided with generative AI tools and those without, within active learning environment. After experiment, participants are asked to conduct a questionnaire to assess motivation and perceived engagement. The results indicated that overall active engagement was higher for those participants who did not use generative AI. However, learning effects were significantly observed when participants engaged deeply with generative AI, such as providing detailed materials, pointing out AI's mistakes, and sharing prior knowledge. Furthermore, participants utilized generative AI tools as a discussion assistant in the group learning condition, which had a higher rating. In contrast, participants in the individual learning condition had a lower rating, who reported that the interaction with generative AI may disrupt their thinking.

Keywords: Active Learning · Generative AI · Learning Effect · Learning Design

1 Introduction

The COVID-19 pandemic significantly transformed various aspects of daily life, particularly in the field of education. During the pandemic, the decline in in-person learning opportunities led to a rapid increase in the adoption of e-learning. In 2020, 83.8% of universities in Japan were conducting distance learning classes in various forms [1]. However, while overall satisfaction was reported, many students faced challenges such as decreased motivation, feelings of isolation, and difficulties in understanding the material. Syahputri et al. [2] confirmed that many students experienced isolation during the online classes and have uncertainty about whether they have mastered the learning content.

While in the post-pandemic period, Japanese universities have largely reverted to in-person classes. For example, 75.2% of large-scale lecture-style classes in 2024 were conducted either fully or mostly in-person [3]. In contrast, in the United States and

B. Fernández-Manjón et al. (Eds.): SETE 2025/ICWL 2025, LNCS 16425, pp. 425–436, 2026.
https://doi.org/10.1007/978-981-92-0042-9_31

Australia, there has been little change since 2022, with online classes continuing to comprise more than half of all courses. Furthermore, about half of Japanese faculty members indicated a preference for face-to-face teaching methods, while only a small fraction (less than 5%) favored fully online instruction [4]. It can be considered that factors such as ineffective with the effect of online classes and insufficient infrastructure are likely contributors.

At the same time, the widespread experience with online learning during the pandemic also led many students to recognize its advantages. According to a 2022 survey by the Japan Association of Private Universities and Colleges [5], some students favored face-to-face classes, others favored online, and many preferred hybrid approaches. This highlights a need not to simply revert to traditional in-person instruction, but rather to improve the quality of online learning and explore more effective, flexible learning methods.

On the other hand, the arrival of the Society 5.0 era has transformed the educational landscape. Society 5.0, as proposed in Japan's fifth Science and Technology Basic Plan, envisions a "super-smart society" that integrates cyberspace and the physical world through advanced technologies such as AI, big data, and IoT [6]. The plan emphasizes the importance of fostering talent capable of both discovering breakthrough knowledge and applying it to societal challenges [7]. Such individuals, who can maximize the potential of AI and data while engaging across diverse fields, are expected to play a central role in the new era.

To address the challenges of online learning, such as student isolation and decreased motivation, a shift from passive information transmission to more engaging methods is required. One promising educational approach is active learning. Bonwell and Eison [8] defined active learning as instructional activities involving students in doing things and thinking about what they are doing. Similarly, Matsumoto and Akiyama [9] described it as a method that deepens foundational learning through application, enabling learners to actively construct and reconstruct knowledge through engagement and collaboration. Therefore, active learning can be expected to address the passivity often associated with conventional online lectures. This shift toward proactive and collaborative learning is not only an approach to the challenges of online learning but also aligns with the future direction of society 5.0.

Recent advancements in conversational generative AI present a new opportunity to facilitate active learning. However, its effectiveness in addressing the specific challenges remains to be explored. In this study, we aim to investigate how conversational generative AI, was utilized as an AI partner based on the active learning method, can overcome challenges such as improving learning motivation in online learning environments. We design an experiment that uses Generative AI tools during active learning to enhance the learning experience and verify the learning effects. It can be expected to explore the potential for active learning and generative AI in increasingly diverse educational contexts.

The remainder of this paper is organized as follows. In Sect. 2, related work on learning effectiveness in active learning and the use of generative AI is reviewed. Section 3 describes the experiment design. Section 4 presents the results of the analysis, including the students' deliverables, questionnaires, and dialogue logs with generative AI Finally, Sect. 5 concludes the paper and highlights future directions.

2 Related Work

2.1 Learning Effectiveness in Active Learning

Related studies have highlighted the effectiveness of active learning in enhancing student engagement. For instance, a study on the effectiveness of active learning classes for the same subject found that learners in the active learning format were more motivated to engage in self-study, and actually did so, compared to those in the regular format [10]. Furthermore, in an attempt to employ active learning in university online courses, a post-evaluation showed that students rated the classes highly in terms of interest, willingness to participate, and other factors. In particular, it was confirmed that organizing small groups fostered caring and encouraging behaviors among students, which may help reduce the stress of attending online classes [11]. These findings suggest that the major distinction between active learning and regular classes lies in the enhancement of students' motivation and interest, often facilitated through communication with others.

In addition to its effects on motivation and interest, the impact of active learning on student comprehension has also been investigated. Active learning is classified into two forms, which are weakly participatory and strongly participatory. The weakly participatory is defined as students were able to communicate their opinions to the instructor through some channel without verbal expression, and the instructor was able to gauge feedback from students. The strong participatory included these features, and all students directly provided their opinions and discussed with others. Matsumoto and Akiyama [9] examined the differences in student grades between these two forms. They conducted the same class in both participatory and compared the student grades. The results indicated that while grades in the weakly participatory class were varied considerably, the distribution of grades in the strongly participatory class shifted toward higher performance.

While active learning has been shown to enhance student engagement and deepen understanding, it also presents several challenges. Previous studies on Student Active Learning (SAL) have identified multiple barriers, including physical and institutional constraints, as well as student-related barriers [12]. These include issues in self-regulation, insufficient effort, a lack of individual accountability, and difficulties with collaborative skills [12]. Therefore, the use of generative AI as a partner in active learning holds potential for addressing these challenges. By functioning as a consistently available conversation partner, generative AI may support students who lack confidence in their collaborative abilities or who are working individually, thereby providing consistent opportunities for dialogue and reflection.

Furthermore, a challenge in active learning is the documented discrepancy between actual learning gains and students' feelings of learning. Students often perceive traditional lectures as more effective, even when active learning yields superior results [13].

2.2 Learning Effectiveness in Using of Generative AI

Previous studies have begun to examine the effectiveness of generative AI as an educational tool. For instance, an examination of students' use of ChatGPT in flipped programming classes confirmed that ChatGPT could replace a portion of Internet searches and serve as a useful learning assistant [14]. Similarly, Giannakos et al. [15] highlighted that large language models (LLMs) can function as personal tutors or study partners, offering continuous, 24-h support for learners, thereby expanding the possibilities for personalized and active learning.

Hiramoto et al. [16] investigated autonomous learning effects using ChatGPT among university students. The results showed that while students' awareness of ChatGPT's usefulness improved after instruction, usage pattern differed depending on the learning setting. In group work, students actively incorporated ChatGPT, whereas in individual tasks, only about half used it proactively. Furthermore, an evaluation of proposals created during group work revealed that in the nine total groups, those utilizing ChatGPT accounted for both the top-three and the bottom-three submissions. These findings indicate that integrating ChatGPT into learning does not guarantee positive outcomes. It can lead to polarized results, either enhancing or decreasing the quality of the learning outcomes.

Matsushima and Ozaki [17] incorporated Generative AI into debates to analyze how students collected information, constructed arguments, and assigned roles with AI support. The results revealed that AI promoted learning by reducing anxiety and expanding knowledge, but also hindered it by causing information overload and encouraging overreliance, which reduced students' initiative. In addition, Zhang et al. [18] found that students with higher learning motivation tended to evaluate online courses more negatively than face-to-face ones. They also emphasized that online learners often feel uncertain about their progress due to limited feedback and a lack of visibility regarding peer reactions, underscoring the need for more opportunities for exchange and confidence-building.

2.3 Position of This Study

While existing studies on the learning effects of generative AI have primarily compared learning outcomes between individuals and groups, they have often overlooked how the AI was specifically utilized. Therefore, this study aims to clarify not only whether learning effectiveness differs, but also what kinds of approaches and purposes in using generative AI led to higher learning effectiveness. The conversational generative AI can be positioned as a promising solution to address motivational and learning effectiveness challenges in online learning by facilitating an active learning framework.

3 Experiment Design

3.1 Basic Concept

This study conducted an experimental survey with university students to examine the learning effects of active learning supported by generative AI in an online learning environment. Specifically, to investigate differences between individual learning and face-to-face group work, and to evaluate the impact of generative AI in both contexts, two experimental conditions were compared: (1) AI-assisted active learning in small groups, and (2) one-on-one active learning between an individual student and generative AI. The individual learning condition was designed to simulate an online learning environment without the presence of other learners.

The participants included students from various majors and academic years, ensuring a diverse background. Crucially, all participants were novices to the specific theme of the discussion task, which focused on "eliminating or reducing disparities in children's experiences using digital technology".

Regarding the learning environment, the group learning condition (1) was conducted with three participants gathering face-to-face around a single table in an empty classroom. The individual learning condition (2) took place remotely, with participants participating from their usual online learning settings.

In total, the participants included (1) five groups of three participants in the group learning condition, and (2) 12 participants in the individual learning condition. All participants first watched a common online instructional video to acquire basic knowledge. They then spent 20 min working under their assigned condition to produce a deliverable. The deliverables were created on worksheets where participants expressed their ideas using both text and diagrams. The use of generative AI was optional, meaning that learners had full discretion over whether and how to use it. Only GPT o4-mini and GPT-4o, available in the free version of ChatGPT, were permitted. The use of other generative AI tools or internet searches, including accessing external websites through ChatGPT, was prohibited.

In this study, generative AI was conceptualized as a conversational partner, analogous to peers in face-to-face group discussions. Through dialogue with the AI, participants gained opportunities to share their own thoughts, encounter different perspectives, and critically evaluate and modify the AI's responses as needed. This design reflects the assumption that dialogic interaction with AI can simulate key elements of collaborative learning, such as exchange of perspectives and critical feedback.

The learning task was to "propose a way to eliminate or reduce disparities in children's experiences using digital technology." Participants were free to use the document's open-response section in any way they wished, but they were required to indicate a single final proposal and specify who would be responsible for its implementation.

3.2 Data Collection and Analysis

After the active learning session, all participants completed a questionnaire survey. The quantitative indicators included: frequency of AI use, learning motivation, evaluation of the active learning experience, and evaluation of the effectiveness of the generated AI (5-point). In addition, qualitative data were collected through open-ended questions, which asked about the purpose of using the AI, difficulties in AI interaction, new insights, and perceives learning gains. For the active learning experience, reference was made to the active learning (externalization) scale developed by Mizokami et al. [19]. Six items were then established, each using the five-point scale method, to correspond to the six general characteristics of active learning identified by Bonwell and Eison [8].

Furthermore, participants who used AI were asked to submit all interactions with ChatGPT during the creation of deliverable. These interaction logs were analyzed in relation to their questionnaire responses. The analysis focused on how participants with higher self-evaluations use the generative AI, with the aim of identifying more effective strategies for AI-supported learning.

4 Experiment Results and Discussion

4.1 Results of Questionnaire Survey

First, the actual status of daily use of the generated AI was ascertained from the questionnaire we administered to the subjects, and the results are shown in Table 1. Overall, the largest number of respondents, 9, answered that they used the AI several times a month, followed by 4–5 days a week and 2–3 days a week. The largest number of respondents in the group learning condition (1) answered that they used the AI 4–5 days a week, and in the individual learning condition (2) answered that they used the AI 2–3 days a week. However, overall, the distribution of the respondents was found to be broad, ranging from every day to a few times a month.

Next, Table 2 shows whether the participants used ChatGPT in this experiment. Overall, the number of subjects who used the generative AI was twice that of those who did not use it. In the group learning condition (1), three out of five groups used the generative AI, while two groups did not use it, and in the individuals learning condition (2), 9 respondents used the generative AI. In both conditions, the number of respondents who used the generative AI was larger than the number of those who did not.

Table 1. Actual condition of daily use of the generated AI

Frequency of Use	(1) Group	(2) Individuals	Overall
Every day	2	2	4
4–5 days a week	6	1	7
2–3 days a week	2	5	7
Several times a month	5	4	9
Several times a year	0	0	0
Never used	0	0	0

Willingness to Learn. The questionnaire results were used to examine how willingness to learn changed after experiencing the learning method that allowed participants to freely use generative AI to complete the task. Respondents were categorized into the group learning condition (1) and the individual learning condition (2), and then further divided according to whether they used generative AI. The mean values of the three questionnaire items are shown in Table 3. However, for the second item, only those who

Table 2. The use of generative AI during experiment

Whether Used or Not	(1) Group	(2) Individuals	Overall
Used	9	9	18
Did not use	6	3	9

Table 3. Mean ratings of the learning motivation

Use of Generative AI	(1) Group		(2) Individuals	
	Used	Did not use	Used	Did not use
I was more motivated to learn compared to regular lectures	3.44	3.50	3.78	3.67
I was more motivated to learn compared to flipped classroom	3.44	5.00	3.25	3.00
I would like to continue studying in this way	3.33	3.67	3.56	3.33

had previously taken flipped classrooms were asked to answer, resulting in a smaller number of valid responses compared to the other items.

From Table 3, it can be observed that the learning method that allowed the free use of the generative AI conducted in this study had an overall positive impact on the willingness to learn. In particular, evaluations of increased willingness to learn were high across all categories when compared to regular lectures. Interestingly, even among participants in the group learning condition who did not use the generative AI, many respondents answered that their motivation to learn had increased, and mean scores were high.

Active Learning Experience. Next, the six items related to the active learning experience were analyzed. As with the evaluation of learning motivation, participants were divided into the group learning condition (1) and individual learning condition (2) and then categorized by whether they used generative AI. The distribution of ratings for each item, including the median, quartiles, and range, is summarized in the box plot shown in Fig. 1.

The box plot reveals that the median ratings for participants who did not use generative AI tended to be higher across most items compared to those who used generative AI. However, since the number of participants who did not use generative AI was less than half of those who did, the results may be highly dependent on everyone's evaluation, which could explain the relatively high average scores. Meanwhile, the plot also clearly shows the presence of outliers (indicated by dots) and high maximum scores in the AI-using conditions, suggesting that some individuals who used AI reported an exceptionally high active learning experience.

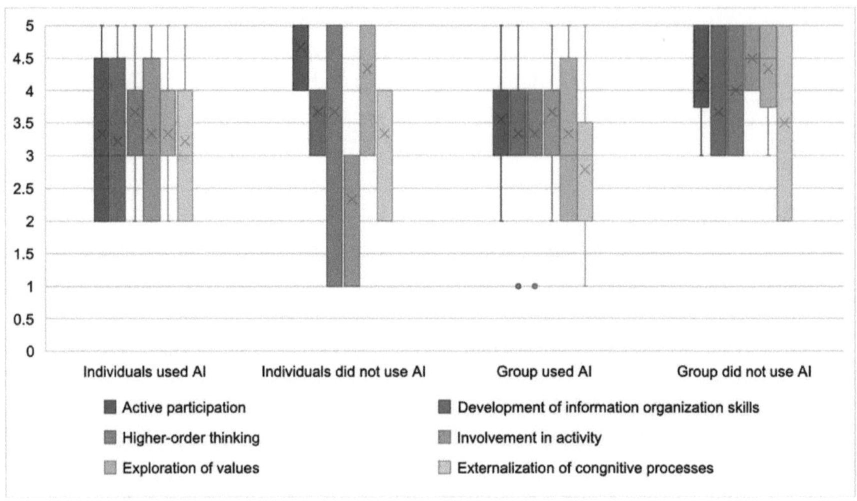

Fig. 1. Distribution of ratings for active learning experience across conditions

In addition, the items "development of information organization skills" and "externalization of cognitive processes" showed lower median ratings among individuals who used generative AI. Notably, the distribution also indicates that some participants who used generative AI still provided high evaluations (ratings of 4 or 5) for these items, suggesting a diversity in the learning experience.

Effects of Using Generative AI. Only participants who used generative AI in this study were asked to rate how their activities changed because of its use. The mean scores are summarized in Table 4.

Table 4. Mean ratings of effectiveness of using generative AI

Effectiveness of Use	(1) Group	(2) Individuals	Overall
Increased activity of discussion and thinking	4.00	3.67	3.83
Deepening of understanding of the theme	3.78	3.78	3.78
Improvement in quality of deliverables	4.22	4.00	4.11

Overall, participants who used the generative AI gave a high evaluation of the effects of using the generative AI. For the three items of "Increased activity of discussion and thinking", "Deepening of understanding of the theme", and "Improvement in quality of deliverables", the mean ratings of the two learning conditions were compared using Welch's t-tests. The results indicated that there were no statistically significant differences between the two conditions on any of the items.

Thus, within the limitation of the sample size and study design, no clear difference was identified between group and individual use with respect to the effectiveness of generative AI. However, the mean scores tended to be slightly higher for group use in “Increased activity of discussion and thinking”, and “Improvement in quality of deliverables”, suggesting that further investigation with larger samples is warranted.

Results of the Use of Generative AI and Conversation Logs. Next, the conversation logs with ChatGPT were analyzed to find out what questions participants paid attention to and the frequency of their interactions with the AI. First, Table 5 summarizes the number of interactions with generative AI. The results show that individual learning condition had higher overall number of interactions compared to the group condition.

Next, participants' purpose for using generative AI were identified from selected and open-ended questions. The results, summarized in Table 6, indicate that all users employed generative AI primarily for idea generation.

Table 5. Number of interactions with generative AI

Statistical Result	(1) Group	(2) Individuals
Average	4.00	5.67
Maximum value	8.00	13.00
Minimum value	1.00	2.00

Table 6. Reported purposes of using generative AI

Purpose of Use	(1) Group	(2) Individuals	Overall
Sentence elaboration	0	2	2
Idea generation	9	9	18
Organizing ideas	2	2	4
Rationale for opinions	2	4	6

According to participants' answer, the participants' efforts in using the generative AI can be broadly divided into three strategies: (1) articulating their own opinions, (2) providing detailed contextual information and prior knowledge, and (3) identifying inconsistencies. Conversely, participants reported difficulties arising from the imprecision and ambiguity of AI-generated information and its reliance on existing ideas, which limited their ability to produce deliverables with confidence. Furthermore, some also noted that the need to define a clear purpose before engaging with the AI forced them to adapt their usual thought processes.

In terms of perceived learning outcomes compared with regular classes, participants reported that use of generative AI: (1) Provided new perspectives and ideas that they could not have come up with on their own, (2) Functioned as a trigger for idea generation and discussion, facilitating the exchange of opinions and brainstorming, (3) Reduced the time required for ideation phase, thereby improving the quality of discussions and completeness of deliverables while maintaining concentration, (4) Offered a sense of security through its complementary support, lowering psychological barriers for starting the learning process, and (5) Altered their approaches to thinking, as they acquired more structured thinking and engaged in more proactive questioning.

4.2 Discussion

The findings of this study indicate that allowing participants to use generative AI tools can lower their psychological barrier to engaging in the task and enhance their motivation. However, participants who did not use generative AI tools reported a higher overall sense of engagement. In contrast, some individuals who did use generative AI tools provided high ratings for specific aspects of active learning. Most participants reported using generative AI tools primarily for idea generation, brainstorming, and asking for open-ended responses. This indicates that participants recognize generative AI as a tool for expanding thinking.

However, for deeper learning, participants under the individual learning condition reported significant learning benefits when they actively engaged with the generative AI. They mentioned strategies such as providing detailed materials, pointing out AI's mistakes, and sharing prior knowledge obtained from class materials. One participant noted that AI reduced the time spent generating initial ideas, enabling greater focus on refining solutions, which helped sustain concentration and foster more structured thinking. These findings suggest that participants who benefited most did not passively accept generative AI outputs. They engaged in active involvement, including refining prompts, evaluating responses, and integrating contextual knowledge.

Additionally, participants under the group learning condition rated more highly than those in the individual learning condition regarding the increased activity of discussion and thinking. It can be considered that the interaction required for prompting AI, such as formulating questions and evaluating responses, can disrupt the cognitive workflow of an individual learner. This interpretation is supported by qualitative feedback from individual learners, who expressed difficulty in sustaining focus due to the time required for typing and confusion over how to maintain the discussion's primary focus while interacting with the AI. In contrast, in a group context, the generative AI may function as an intelligent assistant for discussion. While one member queries the AI, the cognitive and social processes of the group continue, as other members can discuss the output or prepare the next inquiry.

Furthermore, the findings of this study can offer insights relevant to emerging research directions. Recent research explored student-AI interaction with multiple agents to provide personalized learning support [20]. Similarly, Zhang et al. [21] proposed the SimClass framework, utilizing multiple LLM-empowered agents to simulate dynamic classroom interactions, focusing on collaborative learning environments. Our preliminary results provide evidence that points to the most beneficial interaction pattern between AI and individuals for personalized learning and verify that a single AI can act as a discussion assistant in group settings for collaborative learning. Therefore, these findings can be expected to contribute to the development of Agentic AI by informing the design principles for both personalized learning and collaborative learning.

A limitation of this study is that it did not assess the impact of potentially biased or inaccurate information produced by generative AI on participants' learning outcomes.

5 Conclusion

In this study, we designed an experiment and verified the use of conversational generative AI as a partner in online environments based on an active learning method. The results indicated that while the use of generative AI enhanced initial motivation, overall active engagement was higher for those participants who did not use generative AI. However, learning effects were significantly observed when participants engaged deeply with generative AI, such as providing detailed materials, pointing out AI's mistakes, and sharing prior knowledge. Furthermore, participants utilized generative AI tools as a discussion assistant in the group learning condition, which had a higher rating. In contrast, participants in the individual learning condition had a lower rating, with qualitative feedback suggesting that the interaction with generative AI may disrupt their thinking.

For future work, we plan to evaluate the impact of AI-generated misinformation on learning effects and to explore optimal approaches for integrating AI into real classroom settings, thereby informing the development of agentic AI for personalized and collaborative learning. In addition, it will be important to incorporate objective measures of learning effectiveness, such as external expert evaluations or standardized scoring of deliverables, to complement the self-reported data. Furthermore, we plan to conduct an in-depth analysis of AI conversation logs (e.g., through text mining) to identify specific usage strategies that contribute to higher learning effects, particularly among participants who provided high self-evaluations.

References

1. Ministry of Education, Culture, Sports, Science and Technology: Education in Japan beyond the crisis of COVID-19—Leave No One Behind (2020). https://www.mext.go.jp/en/content/20200904_mxt_kouhou01-000008961_1.pdf (Last accessed on 13 May 2026)
2. Syahputri, V.N., Rahma, E.A., Setiyana, R., Diana, S., Parlindungan, F.: Online learning drawbacks during the Covid-19 pandemic: a psychological perspective. EnJourMe (English Journal of Merdeka): Cult. Lang. Teach. Engl. **5**(2), 108–116 (2020)
3. Yamada, R.: Japan Shift Back to In-Person University Classes —Leveraging COVID-Era Online Experience for Future Applications. Nikkei (2025). (in Japanese)
4. Yamada, R.: Post-Corona University Education and future improvements: concerning a survey of faculty members and a case study survey. J. Jpn. Assoc. Coll. Univ. Educ. **46**(1), 53–58 (2024). (in Japanese)
5. The Japan Association of Private Universities and College. Report on Student Survey Regarding the Impact of the COVID-19 Pandemic. The Japan Association of Private Universities and College (2022). (in Japanese)
6. Council for Science, Technology and Innovation Cabinet Office, Government of Japan: Report onthe 5th Science and Technology Basic Plan. Cabinet Office (2015)
7. Ministry of Education, Culture, Sports, Science and Technology: Human Resource Development for Society 5.0: Changes to Society, Changes to Learning (Summary) (2018). https://www.mext.go.jp/b_menu/activity/detail/pdf2018/20180605_001.pdf (Last accessed on 13 May 2026)

8. Bonwell, C.C., Eison, J.A.: Active learning: creating excitement in the classroom. 1991 ASHE-ERIC Higher Education Reports. ERIC Clearinghouse on Higher Education, The George Washington University, Washington, DC (1991)
9. Matsumoto, K., Akiyama, T.: A Study on the Development and Educational Effects of Active Learning in Large-Scale Classes—Focusing on Differences Arising from Adopting Various Active Learning Formats. Nagoya Gakuin University Annual Research Report, vol. 25, pp. 1–39 (2012). (in Japanese)
10. Tsuji, Y., Sugiyama, S.: Effect verification of active learning classes for the same subject. Jpn. J. Educ. Technol. **40**(Suppl.), 45–48 (2017). (in Japanese)
11. Matsushita, K.: A trial of active learning activities in distance learning classes at university. Bull. Educ. Res. Teach. Dev. Kagawa Univ. **41**, 89–98 (2020). (in Japanese)
12. Børte, K., Nesje, K., Lillejord, S.: Barriers to student active learning in higher education. Teach. High. Educ. **28**(3), 597–615 (2023)
13. Lombardi, D., Shipley, T.F., et al.: The curious construct of active learning. Psychol. Sci. Publ. Interest **22** 1), 8–43 (2021)
14. Ozeki, M., Ochi, M.: Utilization of ChatGPT by students in the flipped classroom of programming. In: Research Report of JSET Conferences, vol. 4, pp. 149–156 (2023). (in Japanese)
15. Giannakos, M., et al.: The promise and challenges of generative AI in education. Behav. Inf. Technol. **44**(11), 2518–2544 (2025)
16. Hiramoto, T., Kameda, T., Shimada, T.: Basic research on proactive learning methods using ChatGPT for university students in SDGs education and ESD. Beyond SDGs Innov. Res. **4**(6), 1–14 (2023). (in Japanese)
17. Matsushima, R., Ozaki, H.: Relationship between university students' evaluation of online classes, self-regulated learning strategies, and learner characteristics. Jpn. J. Educ. Technol. **45**(Suppl.), 5–8 (2021). (in Japanese)
18. Zhang, Z., Sun, B., An, P.: Breaking barriers or building dependency? Exploring team-LLM collaboration in AI-infused classroom debate. In: Proceedings of the 2025 CHI Conference on Human Factors in Computing Systems, pp. 1–19 (2025)
19. Mizokami, S., et al.: Developing the active learning (externalization) scale by bifactor model. Kyoto Univ. Res. High. Educ. **22**, 151–162 (2016). (in Japanese)
20. Hao, Z., Cao, J., Li, R., Yu, J., Liu, Z., Zhang, Y.: Mapping student-AI interaction dynamics in multi-agent learning environments: supporting personalized learning and reducing performance gaps. Comput. Educ.. Educ. **241**, 105472 (2026)
21. Zhang, Z., et al.: Simulating classroom education with LLM-empowered agents. In: Proceedings of the 2025 Conference of the Nations of the Americas Chapter of the Association for Computational Linguistics: Human Language Technologies (NAACL 2025), vol. 1, pp. 10364–10379 (2025)

Workshop LLMNE

Privacy-Preserving Pronunciation Assessment: Implementation and Validation of a GOPT-Based English Pronunciation Assessment System

Mingchun Liang[1(✉)], Enpin Ren[1], Cheukhang Lee[1], Cheongyin Choy[1], and Rouchen Liu[2]

[1] Department of Computing, The Hong Kong Polytechnic University, Hong Kong, China
{gordon.liang,enpin.ren,cheuk-hang-regular.lee, cheong-yin.choy}@connect.polyu.hk

[2] Department of Computing, Central South University, Changsha, China
ruochen@csu.edu.cn

Abstract. Cloud-based pronunciation assessment in education introduces material risks to student voice-data privacy and compliance under FERPA, COPPA, and GDPR, motivating an on-premises alternative that eliminates external transfer of recordings [6,7]. This paper presents a fully containerized English pronunciation assessment system that executes end-to-end locally while delivering actionable feedback for instruction [5]. The pipeline standardizes audio to 16 kHz mono WAV, extracts 40-dimensional MFCCs with CMVN and LDA+MLLT, performs phoneme-level forced alignment, and computes 84-dimensional GOP features composed of 42 LPP and 42 LPR components [5]. A compact GOPT-based Transformer consumes GOP sequences to produce phoneme-, word-, and utterance-level scores across accuracy, completeness, fluency, and prosody [1]. The implementation integrates Kaldi, PyTorch, and FastAPI on a Windows 10 CPU host and is packaged for reproducible on-premises deployment [5]. Validation on representative utterances shows robust discrimination across pronunciation quality conditions, supporting the feasibility of privacy-preserving institutional deployment without sacrificing reliability or operability [1].

Keywords: Pronunciation assessment · Privacy preservation · Educational technology · On-premises deployment · GOPT · System validation

1 Introduction

Pronunciation assessment is critical for communicative competence, yet classroom settings rarely provide timely, individualized feedback at scale, creating a persistent gap between instruction and actionable guidance for learners [2].

M. Liang and E. Ren—These authors contributed equally to this work.

B. Fernández-Manjón et al. (Eds.): SETE 2025/ICWL 2025, LNCS 16425, pp. 439–453, 2026.
https://doi.org/10.1007/978-981-92-0042-9_32

Recent advances in automatic pronunciation assessment (APA) combine forced alignment–based Goodness of Pronunciation (GOP) features with compact neural scorers to deliver multi-granularity judgments that correlate well with expert ratings, enabling practical deployment in education [1,3].

However, cloud-first delivery models introduce material privacy and compliance risks for student voice data under FERPA, COPPA, and GDPR, and many institutional stakeholders increasingly require solutions that avoid external transmission and maintain full data sovereignty [6,7].

This work addresses these tensions by implementing a fully on-premises, containerized English pronunciation assessment system that processes audio end-to-end locally while returning interpretable, multi-dimensional feedback suitable for instruction [1,5].

Background and Problem. Traditional GOP-based methods quantify phoneme realizations via Log Phone Posterior (LPP) and Log Posterior Ratio (LPR), but earlier statistical pipelines struggled to capture context and provide robust sentence-level scoring [2]. The GOPT architecture remedies this by feeding 84-dimensional GOP sequences into a lightweight Transformer to predict scores at phoneme, word, and utterance levels across accuracy, completeness, fluency, and prosody, achieving utterance-level PCC up to 0.743 on SpeechOcean762 [1,3].

Motivation and Challenges. Educational deployments require: (1) strict privacy guarantees that preclude any external transfer of voice data, (2) reproducible, open-source implementations that institutions can audit and operate, and (3) low-latency inference on modest CPU hardware without sacrificing diagnostic value for instruction [5–7]. From a systems perspective, realizing GOP at scale demands careful reconciliation between alignment recipes and downstream feature needs, robust data standardization, and a compact scorer that remains accurate under constrained resources [1,5].

Intuition and Method. The core idea is to preserve the proven GOP→ Transformer scoring paradigm while relocating the entire pipeline on-prem within a Dockerized stack that standardizes audio, extracts MFCCs with CMVN and LDA+MLLT, computes 84-D GOP features via phoneme-level forced alignment, and feeds fixed-length sequences into a 26,577-parameter GOPT model for multi-aspect scoring [1,5]. A minimal FastAPI service exposes local REST endpoints and an optional web UI, enabling secure classroom or lab deployment without data egress; Fig. 1 summarizes the end-to-end flow [5].

Experiments and Findings. The implemented system achieves complete on-prem execution on a Windows 10 host with CPU-only processing, delivering end-to-end latency of roughly 6 s per utterance and robust discrimination across pronunciation quality conditions on representative utterances [1,5]. Using pretrained LibriSpeech/PAII acoustic and GOPT variants, validation shows utterance-level correlations consistent with prior reports (e.g., PCC $\approx$ 0.743 for the LibriSpeech model) while maintaining interpretable sub-scores for pedagogy [1,3,4].

Contributions.

- A privacy-preserving, fully containerized APA system that performs audio standardization, GOP extraction with Kaldi, and GOPT inference entirely on institution-owned hardware, eliminating external data transfer [1,5].
- A practical deployment blueprint with FastAPI services and optional web UI, supporting secure local operation, configurable retention, and 6 s utterance-level latency suitable for interactive feedback [5].
- A compact GOPT implementation (26,577 parameters) that yields phoneme-, word-, and utterance-level scores across accuracy, completeness, fluency, and prosody for actionable instruction [1].
- Empirical validation with pretrained models demonstrating reliable discrimination of pronunciation quality conditions and correlation consistent with SpeechOcean762 benchmarks, supporting feasibility for institutional deployment [1,3].

Together, these results indicate that institutions can retain data sovereignty while deploying accurate, interpretable APA, thereby aligning pedagogical value with privacy and compliance requirements [1,6,7].

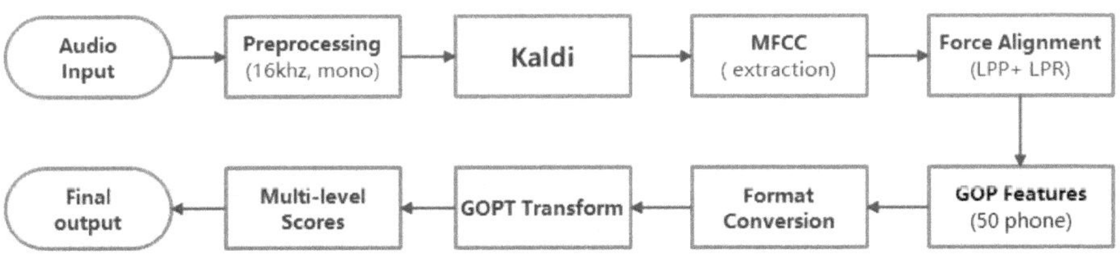

Fig. 1. System Architecture Flowchart

2 Related Work

2.1 Pronunciation Assessment Technologies

Early pronunciation assessment systems relied on Goodness of Pronunciation metrics introduced by Witt and Young [2], quantifying quality as log posterior probability of canonical phoneme sequences. The GOPT model by Gong et al. [1] represents current state-of-the-art, extracting GOP features through forced alignment then processing these through transformer encoders with task-specific prediction heads. However, the GOPT did not explore practical considerations such as privacy preservation or reproducible implementation within fully open-source environments.

Commercial pronunciation [8] assessment services provide cloud-based access but require data transmission creating privacy concerns. Service level agreements typically include provisions allowing vendors to analyze usage patterns and improve services using customer data, which may conflict with educational privacy requirements.

2.2 Privacy in Educational Technology

Growing awareness of privacy risks in educational AI has motivated research into privacy-preserving techniques. Differential privacy adds calibrated noise but may degrade performance [9]. Federated learning enables collaborative improvement without centralizing data but requires coordination infrastructure. For institutional deployment, on-premises processing provides privacy benefits with computational resources exceeding personal devices.

3 Preliminary

3.1 Model Overview

The Goodness of Pronunciation Transformer (GOPT) [1] is a compact Transformer-based encoder architecture designed to process GOP (Goodness of Pronunciation) features and generate multi-granularity, multi-aspect pronunciation assessment scores. With only 26,577 trainable parameters, GOPT is specifically engineered for deployment in resource-constrained educational environments while maintaining sufficient capacity to capture complex pronunciation patterns.

3.2 Architecture Design

Input Representation. GOPT processes two input feature types: 84-dimensional GOP vectors and one-hot encoded canonical phonemes. Both feature types are projected to a shared hidden dimension of $d_{\text{model}} = 24$ through separate fully connected layers, then combined via element-wise addition:

$$\mathbf{h}_i^{(0)} = \mathbf{W}_{\text{gop}}\mathbf{g}_i + \mathbf{W}_{\text{phn}}\mathbf{e}_{\text{phn}_i} \tag{1}$$

where $\mathbf{g}_i \in \mathbb{R}^{84}$ is the GOP feature, $\mathbf{e}_{\text{phn}_i} \in \mathbb{R}^{40}$ is the one-hot encoded phoneme, and $\mathbf{W}_{\text{gop}} \in \mathbb{R}^{24\times 84}$, $\mathbf{W}_{\text{phn}} \in \mathbb{R}^{24\times 40}$ are learnable projection matrices.

Sequence Construction. Following BERT conventions, GOPT prepends five learnable classification tokens (CLS tokens) before the phoneme sequence, each corresponding to a sentence-level assessment task: accuracy, fluency, completeness, prosody, and total score. The input sequence is constructed as:

$$\mathbf{X}^{(0)} = [\mathbf{cls}_1; \ldots; \mathbf{cls}_5; \mathbf{h}_1^{(0)}; \ldots; \mathbf{h}_N^{(0)}] + \mathbf{P} \tag{2}$$

where N is the sequence length and $\mathbf{P} \in \mathbb{R}^{(N+5)\times 24}$ is a learnable positional encoding matrix.

Encoder Stack. The encoder comprises $L = 3$ stacked Transformer blocks. Each block contains multi-head self-attention and feed-forward components with residual connections and layer normalization:

$$\begin{aligned} \mathbf{Z}^{(\ell)} &= \text{LayerNorm}(\mathbf{X}^{(\ell-1)} + \text{MultiHeadAttn}(\mathbf{X}^{(\ell-1)})) \\ \mathbf{X}^{(\ell)} &= \text{LayerNorm}(\mathbf{Z}^{(\ell)} + \text{FFN}(\mathbf{Z}^{(\ell)})) \end{aligned} \tag{3}$$

Due to dataset scale constraints, GOPT employs single-head attention ($H = 1$) with a feed-forward hidden dimension of 96.

Prediction Heads. GOPT uses eight independent regression heads at different granularities:

- **Phoneme-level**: One head for phoneme accuracy scores
- **Word-level**: Three heads for word accuracy, stress, and total scores (obtained by averaging phoneme predictions)
- **Utterance-level**: Five heads for utterance accuracy, fluency, completeness, prosody, and total scores (applied to CLS tokens)

Each prediction head applies layer normalization followed by linear projection: $\hat{y} = \mathbf{w}^T \cdot \text{LayerNorm}(\mathbf{X}^{(L)}) + b$

4 Methodology

4.1 Pronunciation Assessment Task

Automatic pronunciation assessment takes an audio recording as input and outputs pronunciation scores at multiple granularities. Specifically, the system produces four sets of scores: phoneme-level accuracy s^{phone}, word-level accuracy s^{word}, stress s^{stress}, and total s^{total}, while also providing additional metrics including fluency s^{fluency}, completeness s^{complete}, and prosodic ratings.

To extract robust pronunciation features, we employ the Goodness Of Pronunciation (GOP) features computed from acoustic model posteriors. For each phoneme p, the Log Phone Posterior (LPP) is calculated as:

$$\text{LPP}(p) \approx \frac{1}{t_e - t_s + 1} \sum_{t=t_s}^{t_e} \log p(p|o_t) \tag{4}$$

where t_s and t_e denote the start and end frame indices of the phoneme, and o_t represents the input acoustic observations at frame t. The posterior probability is computed by aggregating HMM state posteriors:

$$p(p|o_t) = \sum_{s \in p} p(s|o_t) \tag{5}$$

Additionally, we compute the Log Posterior Ratio (LPR) as a confidence measure:

$$\text{LPR}(p_j|p_i) = \log p(p_j|o; t_s, t_e) - \log p(p_i|o; t_s, t_e) \tag{6}$$

The GOP feature vector **g** for each phoneme combines both LPP and LPR components into a comprehensive representation that captures pronunciation quality across multiple aspects.

4.2 Privacy Requirements

To ensure compliance with FERPA [6], COPPA, and GDPR [7] regulations while implementing the GOPT-based pronunciation assessment system, we quantify privacy safeguards through the following metrics. Audio data is processed locally on institution-owned infrastructure without transmission to external servers, with only essential information transmitted for immediate user feedback.

The encryption security index measures the proportion of audio data protected through end-to-end encryption:

$$\text{ESI} = \frac{E_{\text{encrypted}}}{E_{\text{total}}} \times 100\% \tag{7}$$

where $E_{\text{encrypted}}$ denotes the volume of encrypted audio data and E_{total} represents the total volume of all processed audio data. This metric ensures data confidentiality throughout the assessment pipeline.

The privacy compliance score provides a comprehensive assessment of regulatory adherence across multiple requirements:

$$\text{PCS} = \frac{1}{n}\sum_{i=1}^{n} C_i \tag{8}$$

where C_i is a binary variable indicating compliance status (1 = compliant, 0 = non-compliant) for each privacy requirement i, and n is the total number of privacy requirements. A score of 1.0 indicates full compliance with all privacy regulations.

Data retention is optimized to support immediate user feedback while minimizing information exposure:

$$T_{\text{retention}} = T_{\text{feedback}} + T_{\text{buffer}} \tag{9}$$

where T_{feedback} is the duration required for real-time pronunciation correction and T_{buffer} represents an optional buffering period. This framework ensures that personally identifiable information is retained only as long as necessary.

4.3 GOP Feature Extraction

GOP features quantify alignment quality between observed speech and expected patterns [2]. We computed two complementary representations following established practice.

Log Phone Posterior (LPP) represents the primary GOP metric. For each frame t aligned to canonical phoneme p, we compute posterior probability $P(p|\mathbf{o}_t)$ where $\mathbf{o}_t$ denotes acoustic observation. Phone-level LPP aggregates frame-level log posteriors:

$$\text{LPP}(p) = \frac{1}{N_p} \sum_{t \in T_p} \log P(p|\mathbf{o}_t)$$

where T_p denotes frames aligned to p. High LPP values indicate accurate pronunciation.

Log Posterior Ratio (LPR) accounts for phoneme confusability:

$$\text{LPR}(p,t) = \log P(p|\mathbf{o}_t) - \log \max_{q \in \mathcal{Q} \setminus \{p\}} P(q|\mathbf{o}_t)$$

High LPR indicates canonical phoneme strongly preferred over alternatives.

For each utterance, we extracted both LPP and LPR values for all 42 English phonemes, yielding an 84-dimensional feature vector. Processing time averaged approximately 6 s per utterance for the complete pipeline.

4.4 GOPT Transformer Architecture

The GOPT model [1] processes GOP feature sequences to predict pronunciation scores. An embedding layer projects 84-dimensional GOP features to 24-dimensional hidden representation. A transformer encoder processes embedded sequences through three layers of single-head self-attention. Five special classification tokens enable task-specific aggregation. Task-specific prediction heads implement linear projections to scalar scores for phoneme, word, and utterance level predictions. The complete model contains 26,577 trainable parameters.

5 Results

5.1 System Architecture Overview

Our pronunciation assessment system implements an integrated four-stage pipeline within a Docker-containerized environment. Initially, audio inputs undergo preprocessing conversion to 16 kHz mono WAV format using standard tools. Subsequently, the system performs MFCC feature extraction with CMVN normalization and LDA+MLLT transformation, yielding 40-dimensional acoustic features. Forced alignment is then executed using LibriSpeech Chain Models with phoneme-level accuracy, computing 84-dimensional GOP features comprising 42-dimensional Log Phone Posterior (LPP) and 42-dimensional Log Posterior Ratio (LPR) [2]. Finally, the extracted GOP features are padded or truncated to 50 phonemes and fed into a GOPT Transformer model [1] featuring 26,577 parameters with embedding dimension 24, single attention head, and 3 stacked layers. The model predicts multi-granular quality scores at phoneme, word, and sentence levels. All pipeline stages have been completed and comprehensively validated on the SpeechOcean762 dataset, achieving 0.743 Pearson Correlation Coefficient on utterance-level assessments.

5.2 Experimental Setup

Our experimental environment comprises a Docker-containerized system running on a Windows 10 host with CPU-based processing (GPU acceleration available as an optional enhancement). The core framework integrates three major components: (1) **Kaldi ASR Toolkit** for Goodness of Pronunciation (GOP) feature extraction [4], (2) **GOPT (Goodness of Pronunciation Transformer)** models for multi-level pronunciation assessment [1], and (3) REST API and Web interface for inference and visualization.

For GOP feature extraction, we employ LibriSpeech ASR [4] Chain Models pre-trained on LibriSpeech and PAII datasets. Audio inputs are preprocessed to 16 kHz, mono-channel WAV format. The extraction pipeline performs Mel-Frequency Cepstral Coefficient (MFCC) analysis with CMVN normalization and LDA+MLLT transformation, followed by forced alignment at the phoneme level. The resulting GOP features comprise 84 dimensions: 42-dimensional Log Phone Posterior (LPP) and 42-dimensional Log Posterior Ratio (LPR).

We evaluate three GOPT models: LibriSpeech [4], PAIIA, and PAIIB variants, each with 26,577 parameters. The Transformer-based architecture features an embedding dimension of 24, single attention head, and 3 stacked layers. Extracted GOP features are padded or truncated to 50 phonemes before model inference. Model predictions generate multi-granular scores at phoneme, word, and sentence levels. Our validation employs SpeechOcean762 test set, using Pearson Correlation Coefficient (PCC) as the primary evaluation metric.

5.3 Experimental Validation

To validate the complete pronunciation assessment system, we conducted experiments using three test utterances representing different pronunciation quality levels. All test utterances use the same content text: *"I WOULD LIKE TO HAVE A CHEESE CAKE"*, ensuring consistent baseline pronunciation patterns. The assessment results are presented in Table 1, providing comprehensive multi-dimensional pronunciation scores across three pronunciation quality scenarios.

Test Utterance 1: Normal Pronunciation. Normal, native-like pronunciation with clear articulation; Accuracy 1.16, Completeness 1.93, Fluency 1.41, Prosody 1.25, and Total 1.29, indicating high completeness and smooth, natural delivery (Fig. 2).

Test Utterance 2: Speech with Pronunciation Errors. The second test utterance contains intentional pronunciation errors including incorrect phoneme substitutions and articulation defects. Under GOPT assessment, this utterance achieved an accuracy score of 0.97, representing a 16.4% reduction compared to normal pronunciation. The reduced accuracy reflects the presence of articulation quality defects and phoneme substitutions. Notably, the completeness score remained relatively high at 1.90, indicating that while errors occurred,

Fig. 2. Normal Pronunciation Result

all phonemes were still present in the utterance. The fluency score decreased to 1.21 compared to normal speech, showing approximately 14.2% reduction, which reflects the disruption introduced by pronunciation errors affecting speech smoothness. The prosodic rating of 1.08 shows 13.6% reduction from normal pronunciation, indicating that intonation and stress patterns were also affected by the articulation difficulties. The overall total score of 1.12 represents a 13.2% decline from normal pronunciation. This pattern demonstrates the system's nuanced sensitivity to different quality degradation mechanisms, distinguishing between phonetic accuracy issues, continuity of speech delivery, and prosodic aspects (Fig. 3).

Fig. 3. Speech with Pronunciation Errors Result

Test Utterance 3: Non-fluent Speech. The third test utterance represents non-fluent, hesitant speech with reduced confidence and multiple delivery issues.

The GOPT assessment revealed severe pronunciation degradation across multiple dimensions. The accuracy score dropped to 0.75, representing a substantial 35.3% reduction compared to normal pronunciation, indicating significant articulation quality deterioration characteristic of non-fluent or non-native speakers lacking confidence. The completeness score remained high at 1.91, suggesting that despite fluency and accuracy challenges, all phonemes were still attempted and present. The fluency score decreased substantially to 0.97, showing a 31.2% reduction from normal pronunciation, reflecting hesitations, unnatural pauses, and disconnected speech delivery. The prosodic rating of 0.87 demonstrates a 30.4% reduction from normal speech, indicating disrupted intonation patterns and inappropriate stress placements. The overall total score of 0.94 represents a 27.1% overall decline from normal pronunciation. This test case effectively demonstrates the system's ability to detect and quantify severe pronunciation and delivery quality degradation across multiple independent dimensions while maintaining the completeness dimension relatively stable, providing educators with detailed diagnostic information about whether students are attempting correct phonemes but lacking delivery confidence versus attempting different phonemes altogether (Fig. 4).

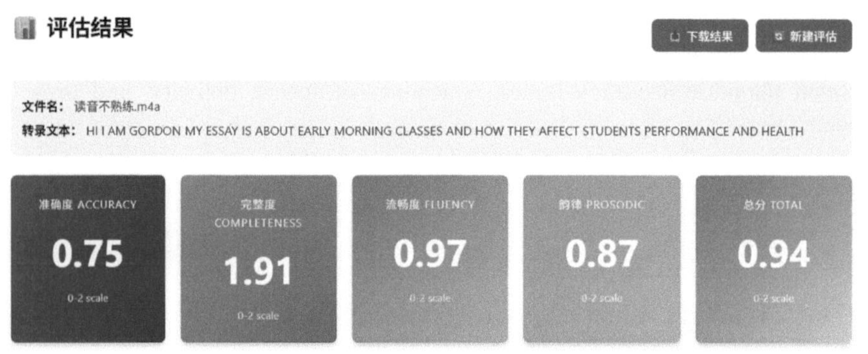

Fig. 4. Non-Fluent Speech Result

5.4 Comparative Analysis of Assessment Results

Table 1 presents the complete assessment results and comparative analysis. The GOPT model demonstrates consistent discrimination capability across pronunciation quality levels. Accuracy represents the dimension most sensitive to pronunciation quality variations, showing 16.4% reduction between normal and error-containing speech, and 35.3% reduction between normal and non-fluent speech. Completeness remains relatively stable across all three test cases (1.90–1.93 range), suggesting that all test utterances maintained phonetic completeness

Table 1. GOPT Assessment Results Across Three Test Utterances (0–2 Scale)

Test Case	Accuracy	Completeness	Fluency	Prosody	Total
Normal	1.16	1.93	1.41	1.25	1.29
With Errors	0.97	1.90	1.21	1.08	1.12
Non-Fluent	0.75	1.91	0.97	0.87	0.94
Normal vs. Errors	−16.4%	−1.6%	−14.2%	−13.6%	−13.2%
Normal vs. Non-Fluent	−35.3%	−1.0%	−31.2%	−30.4%	−27.1%

Table 2. Processing Time for Complete Pipeline

Pipeline Stage	Time (sec)	Status
Audio preprocessing	0.8	Validated
MFCC extraction	1.2	Validated
GMM-HMM alignment	2.5	Validated
GOP computation	0.9	Validated
GOPT inference	0.6	Validated
Total	**6.0**	-

despite quality variations. Fluency and prosody demonstrate intermediate sensitivity, with score reductions of 14–31% across quality levels. The overall total score reflects weighted combinations of individual dimensions, ranging from 0.94 for non-fluent speech to 1.29 for normal pronunciation.

5.5 Performance Metrics

Table 3 presents acoustic model performance. We validated alignment quality on test utterances by examining phoneme boundary predictions using the methodology described by Witt and Young [2]. Forced alignment successfully identified phoneme boundaries with reasonable durations (40–150 ms). GOP feature vectors exhibited expected characteristics with LPP values ranging from −8 to −2 and LPR values from −4 to 2.

Table 2 breaks down processing time for completed pipeline stages. The complete pipeline processes approximately 6 s per utterance. Forced alignment represents the computational bottleneck at approximately 2.5 s. GOPT inference [1] requires approximately 0.6 s, yielding total latency around 6 s, acceptable for interactive educational applications.

The tri3b acoustic model contains 4,116 tied triphone states modeled by 19,963 Gaussian mixture components, achieving alignment probability 94.42% with failure rate of only 3.31%. The complete training pipeline executed in approximately 35–40 min on our CPU system.

Table 3. GMM-HMM Acoustic Model Performance on mini LibriSpeech

Metric	Value	Interpretation
Alignment Probability	94.42%	Successfully aligned frames
Retry Rate	2.27%	Required adjustment
Failure Rate	3.31%	Could not align
HMM States	4,116	Tied triphone states
Gaussian Components	19,963	Mixture components
Training Time (total)	35–40 min	All stages on CPU

6 Discussion

6.1 System Validation and Pronunciation Quality Discrimination

The experimental validation demonstrates that the GOPT model effectively discriminates across different pronunciation quality levels within the on-premises deployment environment. The three test cases systematically showed appropriate score degradation corresponding to pronunciation quality reduction. The accuracy metric showed the highest sensitivity to pronunciation variations, with maximum change of 35.3% between normal and non-fluent speech. This pattern aligns with the primary assessment objective of evaluating phoneme articulation quality. Notably, completeness remained stable across all test cases, suggesting that the assessment correctly recognized all phonemes were present despite delivery quality variations. This feature is pedagogically valuable as it can provide independent feedback on whether students are attempting all required phonemes versus incorrectly articulating them.

The distinction between accuracy, fluency, and prosody scores enables multidimensional feedback. A learner with low accuracy but high fluency would receive different guidance than one with high accuracy but low prosody. Such granularity facilitates more targeted pronunciation instruction. The system's ability to assess multiple dimensions independently while computing an overall score provides both comprehensive and integrated feedback.

6.2 Privacy Benefits and Regulatory Compliance

Our on-premises approach offers educational institutions concrete privacy benefits. Processing all audio data locally eliminates data transmission to external services, inherently satisfying FERPA [6] and COPPA requirements. GDPR [7] compliance is simplified because institutions maintain complete control over retention policies. Cross-border data transfers are eliminated. Beyond regulatory compliance, on-premises deployment supports transparency by providing straightforward assurances that voice recordings never leave institutional control. Cost predictability represents an additional benefit, as on-premises systems incur primarily one-time hardware costs rather than recurring usage-based fees.

Table 4. Comparison of On-Premises and Commercial Cloud Solutions

Feature	On-Premises	Cloud Services
Data transmission	None (local only)	Required upload
Privacy model	Complete sovereignty	Trust vendor
Cost model	One-time hardware	Recurring fees
Languages	English (expandable)	Multiple languages
Setup complexity	High	Low (API calls)

The processing latency of approximately 6 s per utterance is acceptable for educational feedback scenarios where students typically allow several seconds for system response.

6.3 Comparison with Commercial Services

Table 4 compares our on-premises approach with commercial cloud services. Commercial services offer advantages including production-ready implementations, no hardware investment, and support for multiple languages. However, these advantages come at the cost of requiring data transmission creating privacy concerns. Our system accepts tradeoffs of higher initial setup effort in exchange for complete privacy protection and institutional control.

6.4 Implementation Insights

The incompatibility between chain acoustic models and GOP computation [2] represented our most significant technical challenge. Chain models are prominently featured in Kaldi recipes [5] but do not produce frame-level phoneme posteriors required for GOP. This experience taught us the importance of considering downstream task requirements when selecting algorithms. Feature dimensionality alignment between acoustic and neural models also required careful attention to ensure output dimensions matched requirements. The successful demonstration across three test utterances with varying pronunciation quality validates that the complete pipeline architecture functions correctly for practical pronunciation assessment scenarios.

6.5 Limitations and Future Work

Our work has several limitations. Most fundamentally, our validation consists of three curated test utterances rather than evaluation on standard benchmark datasets such as SpeechOcean762 [3]. The acoustic model training data consists of adult native speakers from LibriSpeech [4], introducing potential domain mismatch with child learners or non-native speakers. Our test utterances, while systematically varying pronunciation quality, do not represent comprehensive evaluation across diverse speaker populations and speech variation patterns.

End-to-end application integration with user-friendly interface remains future work. Comprehensive evaluation on SpeechOcean762 [3] with diverse speaker populations represents our immediate next step, along with extended deployment in realistic classroom environments.

7 Conclusion

This work demonstrates that on-premises pronunciation assessment systems can provide viable alternatives to cloud-based solutions while maintaining robust pedagogical effectiveness. By implementing the GOPT architecture on cost-effective, CPU-only hardware and validating system functionality through empirical assessment experiments, we establish the technical feasibility and practical applicability of deploying advanced speech processing models within institutional environments.

The experimental validation demonstrates that the GOPT model produces reliable multidimensional pronunciation assessment across diverse speech samples. The system successfully discriminates pronunciation quality variations, with quantified assessment differentials indicating 35.3% score reduction between fluent and non-fluent utterances, thereby confirming the reliability of the system for providing meaningful educational feedback.

This research contributes to the broader landscape of privacy-preserving language education technologies. We establish a framework for deploying acoustic models using accessible open-source tools, identify salient technical challenges inherent in implementing on-premises speech processing pipelines, and articulate the privacy and regulatory advantages associated with institution-based deployment models. Furthermore, our empirical validation confirms that sophisticated pronunciation assessment models remain functionally reliable within constrained computational environments.

The findings suggest that educational institutions need not compromise student data protection or institutional autonomy when implementing advanced AI-based assessment systems. This work provides a foundation for developing privacy-conscious educational applications that maintain pedagogical sophistication while respecting fundamental principles of data security and institutional independence.

Acknowledgments. This work was conducted at the Research Institute for Artificial Intelligence of Things (RIAIoT) and supported by PolyU Internal Research Fund BDZ3 and TDLEG25-28/IICA/P/05. We acknowledge the open-source communities behind Kaldi [5], PyTorch, LibriSpeech [4], and SpeechOcean762 [3] whose tools and datasets made this work possible.

References

1. Gong, Y., Chen, Z., Chu, I.H., Chang, P., Glass, J.: Transformer-based multi-aspect multi-granularity non-native English speaker pronunciation assessment. In: Proceedings IEEE ICASSP, pp. 7262–7266 (2022)
2. Witt, S.M., Young, S.J.: Phone-level pronunciation scoring and assessment for interactive language learning. Speech Commun. **30**(2–3), 95–108 (2000)
3. Zhang, J., Huang, Z., Huang, Y., Wang, H.: Speechocean762: an open-source non-native English speech corpus for pronunciation assessment. In: Proceedings Interspeech, pp. 2116–2120 (2021)
4. Panayotov, V., Chen, G., Povey, D., Khudanpur, S.: LibriSpeech: an ASR corpus based on public domain audio books. In: Proceedings IEEE ICASSP, pp. 5206–5210 (2015)
5. Povey, D., Ghoshal, A., Boulianne, G., et al.: The Kaldi speech recognition toolkit. In: Proceedings IEEE ASRU (2011)
6. U.S. Department of Education: Family Educational Rights and Privacy Act (FERPA). 20 U.S.C. §1232g (1974)
7. European Parliament and Council: General Data Protection Regulation. Official J. Eur. Union **L119** (2016)
8. Microsoft Azure AI Services: Pronunciation assessment - Azure AI services. Microsoft Learn Documentation (2025). https://learn.microsoft.com/en-us/azure/architecture/
9. Liu, Q., Shakya, R., Khalil, M., Jovanovic, J.: Advancing privacy in learning analytics using differential privacy. arXiv:2501.01786 [cs.CR], January 2025. https://arxiv.org/abs/2501.01786

An Approach for Effective Remote Assistance in Practical STEM Courses

Bruno Silva, Raphael E. Nkrow, Dutliff Boshoff, and Gerhard P. Hancke(✉)

Department of Computer Science, City University of Hong Kong, Hong Kong SAR, China
{bdecarva,gp.hancke}@cityu.edu.hk, {renkrow2-c, dboshoff2-c}@my.cityu.edu.hk

Abstract. As part of their curriculum, several STEM courses include practical sessions where students have to complete a number of tasks under the supervision of several teaching assistants (TAs). For online classes, or lectures that take place across several venues concurrently, it is challenging to provide assistance since it is not always possible to have physically present TAs. In this paper, we investigate the use of web technologies to address the problem of remote assistance in practical STEM courses. We combine existing tools to implement a system where TAs can remotely assist students present in different locations in real-time. We have tested our implementation, and the results show that this is an effective approach, particularly for online lectures.

Keywords: Computer science education · remote assistance · web-based learning

1 Introduction

STEM (Science, Technology, Engineering, and Mathematics) education emphasizes not only the acquisition of theoretical knowledge but also its application in experimental and practical problem-solving contexts. Practical sessions—ranging from programming, computer, and networking security labs to physics simulations and engineering design projects—are essential to prepare students for professional practice [1]. In traditional face-to-face settings, these sessions are supported by immediate instructor feedback, peer collaboration, and access to laboratory infrastructure. However, in some cases, it is impossible for all entities (Professors, teaching assistants, lab assistants and students) to be physically present in one venue due to several factors such as the capacity of classroom sizes, large student numbers, etc.

The growth of online and hybrid learning models, accelerated by the COVID-19 pandemic, has challenged educators to replicate such experiences in virtual environments [2]. While learning management systems (LMSs) and video conferencing platforms support lecture delivery, they fall short in enabling real-time troubleshooting, experimentation, and collaborative problem-solving in practical lab sessions. The result is a pedagogical gap in remote STEM education.

B. Fernández-Manjón et al. (Eds.): SETE 2025/ICWL 2025, LNCS 16425, pp. 454–459, 2026.
https://doi.org/10.1007/978-981-92-0042-9_33

This paper presents a tested Online LMSs (OLMSs) suited for collaborative hands-on practical lab sessions with a strong focus on allowing students, or groups of students, to be offered instant help when needed. The proposed model was tested on a hands-on information security course in a university in Hong Kong with over 350 students. The integrated approach uses existing tools such as Virtual Network Computing (VNC) viewer, Virtual Machines (VMs), Capture the Flag (CTF), and Zoom.

2 Background and Motivation

Laboratory and practical sessions are fundamental to STEM pedagogy because they help students to 1) develop problem-solving and critical thinking skills, 2) provide experiential learning opportunities [3], 3) cultivate teamwork and professional collaboration, and 4) enhance retention of theoretical knowledge through application. In disciplines such as computer science, cybersecurity, and engineering, hands-on skills are not supplementary—they are core competencies required in professional practice [4]. While digital platforms have enabled continuity of learning, several limitations exist:

- **Technical barriers:** students face difficulties installing or configuring specialized software without direct instructor assistance.
- **Monitoring challenges:** instructors struggle to observe student workflows, detect errors, or intervene in real time.
- **Loss of engagement:** remote students often experience reduced motivation and interaction, especially in practical tasks [5]
- **Equity concerns:** Disparities in hardware, internet access, and digital literacy create uneven learning outcomes.

These challenges highlight the need for solutions that replicate the immediacy, safety, and interactivity of practical lab sessions.

3 Methodology

We use existing tools to implement our proposed model. In this section, we describe the function of each tool.

3.1 Virtual Machines as Practical Learning Environments

We create VMs that contain the necessary configuration to complete all tasks. This approach solves the following problems that we have encountered in the past: the VM is pre-configured, which avoids spending time configuring each individual machine; the students do not have to install any comprehensive (large) software, apart from a VNC client program to access the VM. Additionally, running a local VM would require students to download a large image (>10 GB) that contains the VM.

In addition, remotely hosted VMs offer the following benefits:

1) **Flexibility:** we can dynamically create/delete the required number of VMs depending on the class size since all the VMs are cloned from a single image and managed at one central point.

2) **Concurrent usage:** students and TAs can access the same VM concurrently. For assistance, the TAs can remotely log into the same VM and provide assistance in real-time and students can see the TA's actions.
3) **Privacy**: if a TA needs to remotely log into a student's machine, there are privacy issues. By hosting the VM remotely, the privacy issues are eliminated.
4) **Simplicity:** the configuration difficulty is reduced so that students start to immediately work on the exercises rather than getting stuck on trying to set up their own VM.

The other two important aspects that we need to address are communication and progress tracking. A more detailed discussion of our implementation follows.

3.2 VNC as a Remote Assistance Tool

VNC allows one system to remotely control another by transmitting keyboard, mouse, and display signals across a network [6]. Within STEM education, this enables instructors to 1) observe student progress in real time, 2) provide immediate feedback by taking control of the student's environment, and 3) demonstrate troubleshooting procedures directly on student systems. The main benefits of a VNC viewer in our model include:

- **Enhanced instructor presence:** students feel supported when instructors can intervene directly when needed
- **Cross-platform compatibility:** works across operating systems and devices.
- **Low hardware requirements:** minimal computational overhead.

3.3 Capture-the-Flag as a Gamified Learning Strategy

CTF challenges are competition-style tasks commonly used in cybersecurity. They present students with puzzles or vulnerabilities to exploit in order to retrieve "flags" [7]. The same model can be extended across STEM disciplines, embedding problem-solving tasks within gamified frameworks. CTFs offer an innovative way to sustain engagement in remote online hands-on lab sessions and other benefits such as:

1. **Motivation:** gamification increases engagement and persistence [8].
2. **Teamwork:** challenges often require collaboration, mirroring workplace practices.
3. **Feedback:** scoring systems provide immediate indicators of progress.

4 Implementation

Our implementation consists of three core components: a set of VMs, a platform to enable students to interact/communicate with the TAs, and a platform to effectively track the students' progress so that TAs can offer assistance if students fall behind while completing the exercises.

For the VM set, we opted for Azure as a Cloud provider, mainly because we need to run concurrent lectures with CityU Dongguan, therefore we need a Cloud provider that is accessible in Mainland China. Each VM is accessible via the VNC viewer software that is installed on the TAs' and students' computers. The VMs run Linux and have all the required tools for the activities pre-installed.

For communication between students and TAs, we selected Zoom. It is a platform that is already familiar to the TAs and students, and it offers the functionality that we require. Breakout rooms can be used for each discussion with the TA. Secondly, there is no need to share screens since TAs and students can access the same VM at the same time, therefore any actions taken by the TA while assisting are visible on the students' VNC viewer in real-time.

To track the students' progress, we implemented a CTF server, which is often used in cybersecurity competitions. CTF servers offer a standardized way to pose questions (support for multiple choice plug-ins, etc.), and assign points to each question, which allows the TAs to track the progress of every student through a live scoreboard, and proactively provide assistance to any student that falls behind. Figure 1 illustrates our system. It is noted that although only two students and one TA are shown, the system is scalable.

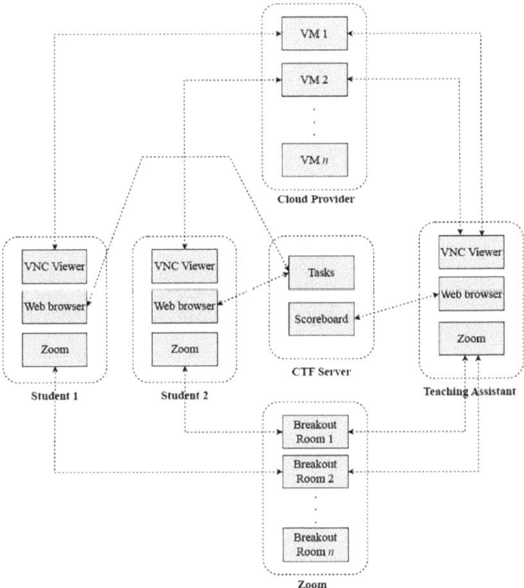

Fig. 1. System implementation.

5 Results

At the end of every online practical session, the students completed a survey sharing their opinions of the proposed approach. The survey included several questions related to how the students perceived the practical sessions: if they enjoyed the sessions, if they found them engaging, and whether they would recommend them. Figure 2.a) and Fig. 2.b) show how engaging and how effective, respectively, the students found the lectures. Figure 3 shows how likely students are to recommend this approach for future online classes.

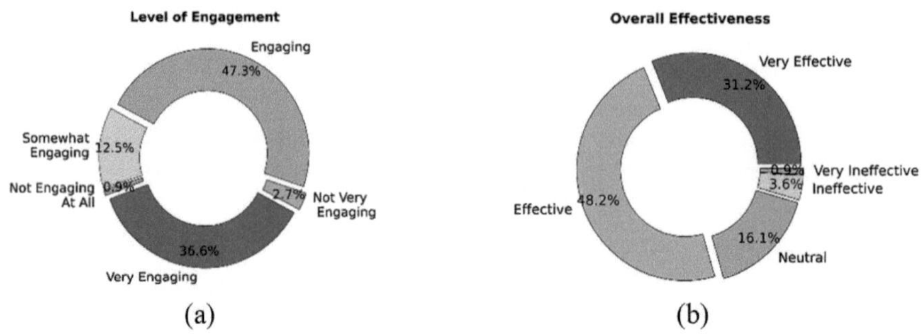

Fig. 2. a) Engagement level, b) overall effectiveness.

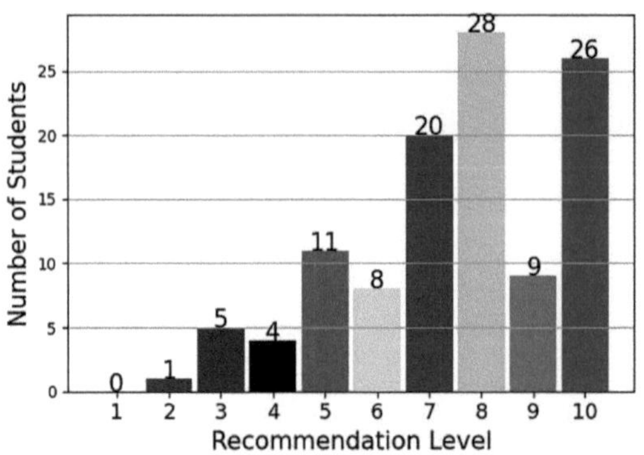

Fig. 3. Recommendation level.

6 Discussion

Based on the survey results, the charts in Figs. 1, 2 and 3 show what the students thought about the effectiveness of the remote assistance approach and how engaging they thought the online lectures were. The majority (83.9%) of students found the course engaging/very engaging. The results also show that the majority of students (79.4%) are of the opinion that it is effective, including 31.2% who found the approach to be very effective.

We also asked the students, on a scale of 0 to 10, how likely they are to recommend this approach for online lectures. The results in Fig. 3 show that over 70% of the students responded with a recommendation level >7. In summary, it is evident that the feedback from the students is positive: they find our proposed method effective, engaging and they highly recommend it to future online lectures.

7 Conclusion

STEM education must extend beyond lectures and discussion forums to include interactive, practice-based experiences. In this paper, we proposed an integrated framework combining existing technologies to deliver an OLM suited for collaborative hands-on lab sessions and online lectures with strong focus on enabling students to obtain instant help or guidance when needed. The proposed model can replicate many of the benefits of in-person laboratories. By addressing logistical, pedagogical, and motivational challenges, this framework ensures that remote students remain engaged, supported, and prepared for professional STEM careers.

Acknowledgments. This paper was significantly supported by City University of Hong Kong (Project 6953003).

References

1. Zhang, T., Zhang, Y., Huang, S.: Exploration and innovation in practical teaching for computer science majors. J. Soc. Sci. Cult. Dev. **1**(1), 1–13 (2024)
2. Cheung, S.K.S., Wang, F.L., Kwok, L.F.: Online learning and blended learning: new practices derived from the pandemic-driven disruption. J. Comput. High. Educ. **35**, 1–5 (2023)
3. Remington, T.F., Chou, P., Topa, B.: Experiential learning through STEM: recent initiatives in the United States. Int. J. Train. Dev. **27**, 327–359 (2023)
4. Text="CE: Unable to parse this reference. Kindly do manual structure" ABET: Criteria for Accrediting Engineering Programs. ABET, Baltimore, MD (2019)
5. Hodges, C., Moore, S., Lockee, B., Trust, T., Bond, A.: The difference between emergency remote teaching and online learning. Educause Rev. **27** (2020)
6. Eljak, H., et al.: E-learning-based cloud computing environment: a systematic review, challenges, and opportunities. IEEE Access **12**, 7329–7355 (2024)
7. Zhang, L., Grossman, D., Anderson, R.: Capture the Flag as a pedagogical tool for cybersecurity education. ACM Trans. Comput. Educ. (TOCE) **21**(4), 1–26 (2021)
8. Li, C., et al.: Enhance learner engagement through experiential learning in a gamified simulation: a longitudinal study. In: Ma, W.W.K., Cheung, S.S.K., Li, C., Prayadsab, P., Mungwattana, A. (eds.) ICBL 2025. LNCS, vol. 15721, pp. 191–202. Springer, Singapore (2025). https://doi.org/10.1007/978-981-96-8430-4_15

Workshop UMLL

Virtual Reality Metaverse with Personalised AI Tutor for English Presentation Training

Venus W. M. Chan and Billy T. M. Wong(✉)

Hong Kong Metropolitan University, Hong Kong, China
{vwmchan,tamiwong}@hkmu.edu.hk

Abstract. This paper presents AI-powered Metaverse for Speaking (AIMS)—a platform integrating AI and virtual reality (VR) metaverse for English presentation training. AIMS features an immersive environment for accessing learning materials with an AI tutor to provide personalised assistance in preparing for presentations. A preliminary study on learner experience and perceptions of the platform was conducted. Interview results indicate that the immersive nature of the platform was effective in engaging learners in training activities. The AI tutor was viewed as advantageous for its immediate recommendations, though participants noted its limitations in providing nuanced, context-specific advice compared to human feedback. Usability challenges, including technical glitches and headset discomfort, were identified as barriers to adoption. The findings suggest the platform's potential to enhance presentation training by addressing limitations of traditional approaches, while facilitating conditions such as hardware infrastructure and user support also play a key role in ensuring success.

Keywords: AI tutor · personalised recommendation · presentation training · virtual reality · VR · Metaverse

1 Introduction

The rapid development of generative artificial intelligence (AI) in recent years has revolutionised various aspects of education. Its ability to analyse vast amounts of data and provide tailored outputs has enabled the personalisation of learning processes, addressing individual learner needs and preferences. AI-powered systems are increasingly adopted to deliver personalised recommendations to learners, which is critical for skill acquisition and improvement [1, 2]. This shift toward personalised learning aligns with the broader trend of leveraging technology to create adaptive and learner-centred environments [3].

This study focuses on the development of presentation skills for which personalised recommendations are particularly valuable. Effective presentations require mastery of multiple components, such as language proficiency, delivery techniques, audience engagement, and confidence. Traditional methods of training often rely on human instructors or peer feedback, which can be inconsistent, limited in scope, and subject to time and effort constraints. AI-powered systems offer the potential to provide

B. Fernández-Manjón et al. (Eds.): SETE 2025/ICWL 2025, LNCS 16425, pp. 463–471, 2026.
https://doi.org/10.1007/978-981-92-0042-9_34

detailed and consistent recommendations, enabling learners to identify specific areas for improvement and track their progress over time [4].

Furthermore, the integration of AI into virtual reality (VR) metaverse environments has opened new possibilities for immersive and interactive learning experiences. VR metaverse provides a dynamic and controlled space for language learners to engage in learning activities in an immersive environment, and receive immediate AI-generated recommendations to address their needs [5]. This combination of AI within the VR metaverse is particularly helpful for English presentation training, as it allows learners to access learning materials as well as personalised tutoring for their context-specific enquiries [6, 7].

This paper introduces our work on developing an AI-powered VR metaverse platform—AI-powered Metaverse for Speaking (AIMS)—for English presentation training, focusing on its personalised recommendation feature and learner experience. AIMS leverages generative AI to provide tailored advice on preparing for a presentation and corrective feedback by analysing the context and situation of a learner's specific presentation task. As a preliminary study, we examined learners' experience with the platform and perceptions of the AI tutor in relation to its effectiveness in supporting presentation skill development. The findings provide insights into the role of AI in offering personalised recommendations to enhance learning experiences within immersive environments.

2 Related Work

2.1 Presentation Skills Development

Public speaking anxiety is a common social phobia, affecting approximately 20% of the population [8]. Factors such as stage fright, audience-related anxiety, personality traits, and lack of confidence in speaking skills contribute to this issue [9]. In English-speaking contexts, foreign language anxiety further exacerbates the problem, particularly among students from non-English-speaking backgrounds, such as Chinese learners [10].

Traditional classroom settings often fail to adequately address these challenges. Teachers face constraints such as limited class time, large class sizes, and diverse student proficiency levels, which hinder their ability to provide detailed, individualised feedback on presentation skills [11]. These skills require extensive practice and mastery of multiple components, including content organisation, verbal and non-verbal communication, fluency, pronunciation, and audience engagement. The lack of personalised attention in traditional settings underscores the need for innovative solutions to support learners in developing these competencies.

2.2 VR and Metaverse in Education

The educational metaverse represents a novel approach to teaching and learning, combining digital identities and 3D virtual worlds to create immersive and interactive environments [12]. This technology offers significant advantages, such as overcoming time and location constraints, enabling ubiquitous learning, and fostering independent, active, and sustainable learning [13].

In language education, the metaverse has shown promise but remains underexplored. For instance, Park [14] demonstrated that metaverse-based task-oriented teaching enhanced learner interaction in Korean language education. Similarly, Christoforou [15] proposed a metaverse platform for English for specific purposes, highlighting benefits like immersion and contextualised practice, though lacking empirical evidence. While these studies suggest the potential of the metaverse in language learning, most existing research is descriptive, with limited experimental studies comparing metaverse-based learning to traditional classroom methods.

The integration of AI into the metaverse has further expanded its educational possibilities. AI-powered chatbots in metaverse environments have been shown to enhance learning experiences. For example, Lee et al. [16] found that interacting with AI chatbots in the metaverse positively impacted learners' awareness of global Englishes. Similarly, Hwang et al. [17] demonstrated that pre-service English teachers using chatbot-metaverse platforms developed more interactive and authentic learning activities compared to those using chatbot-only systems. Despite these promising findings, more empirical research is needed to fully understand the pedagogical potential of AI-powered metaverse platforms, particularly for developing presentation skills.

2.3 AI-Powered Personalised Learning

AI has become a transformative force in language education, offering personalised learning experiences and automating repetitive tasks. Intelligent Computer-Assisted Language Learning systems, which integrate AI with language practice, have garnered significant attention for their ability to customise learning and provide immediate feedback. AI applications have been explored across various language skills, including writing, speaking, and pronunciation. For instance, AI tools have been used for automated writing assessment [18], natural language processing for speech scoring [19], and corrective feedback on speaking skills [20]. These studies highlight the potential of AI to enhance learners' proficiency and confidence while reducing anxiety.

In the context of speaking skills, AI-powered systems such as AI Tutor [21] and Language Student [22] have demonstrated their ability to improve learners' language proficiency through automated error correction and navigational support. Zou et al. [20] found that AI speech evaluation programs significantly improved the speaking skills of English as a Foreign Language (EFL) learners, though the specific contexts and program details were not elaborated.

Despite these advancements, much of the existing research focuses on commercial applications, often neglecting pedagogical considerations and theoretical grounding. Furthermore, there is a lack of empirical evidence on the integration of AI in metaverse environments for developing English presentation skills. While AI has shown potential in providing personalised feedback, its application in immersive, interactive settings like the metaverse remains underexplored. This gap highlights the need for studies that combine AI and metaverse technologies to address the unique challenges of teaching and learning presentation skills.

3 Features of AIMS

AIMS was developed to address the challenges associated with presentation training. This AI-powered platform leverages the immersive capabilities of VR metaverse and the adaptive intelligence of AI to enhance learners' presentation skills for prepared speeches. Its design is grounded in Herbein et al.'s [23] conceptual framework for public speaking competence that integrates three core components: knowledge, skills, and motivation. By combining these elements, AIMS aims to foster holistic development in learners, enabling them to overcome presentation anxiety and improve their overall performance.

AIMS supports diverse learning modalities, including ubiquitous learning, blended learning, and personalised learning, making it adaptable to various educational contexts. The platform is designed to enhance learners' attitudes—such as motivation, engagement, and satisfaction—while simultaneously improving learning outcomes, particularly the acquisition of presentation skills.

In the VR metaverse environment, learners can access a wide array of learning materials, such as instructional videos, textual guides, and interactive exercises (Fig. 1).

Fig. 1. [Left] The VR metaverse of AIMS, where learners access diverse learning materials; and [Right] an example of instructional video on academic public speaking.

AIMS also features an AI tutor which serves as a personalised learning companion, offering tailored guidance to help students prepare for presentations (Fig. 2). By analysing the context and specific requirements of each presentation task, the AI tutor provides feedback and suggestions for improvement. These recommendations span critical areas such as content organisation, clarity, delivery techniques, and audience engagement. Additionally, the AI tutor assists learners in analysing the presentation's nature, formality, and audience characteristics, offering context-specific advice to refine their delivery and maximise impact.

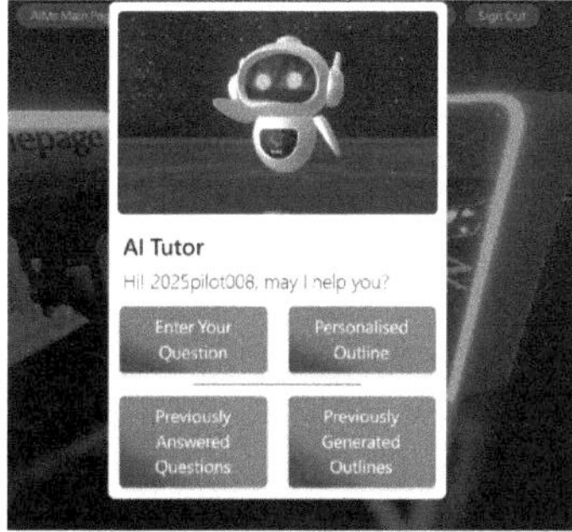

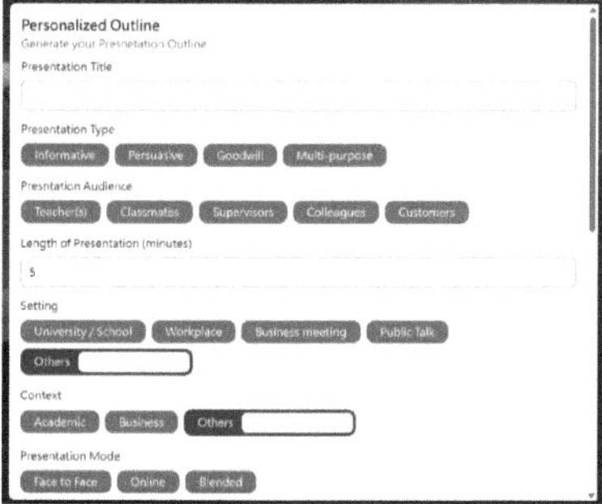

Fig. 2. [Left] The AI tutor which provides personalised assistance; and [Right] the personalised outline feature for presentation preparation.

4 Preliminary Study

To evaluate the effectiveness of AIMS, including its VR metaverse and AI tutor features, a preliminary study was conducted. This study aimed to gather initial insights into students' experiences with the platform.

4.1 Research Methodology

Participants. Six undergraduate students majoring in language and communication were recruited through convenience sampling. Given this small sample size, the study was exploratory in nature, aiming to collect insights into the students' experiences with AIMS.

Data Collection. Data were collected through semi-structured interviews after participants tried the features of AIMS. Each participant used a VR headset (Meta Quest 3) to interact with the platform and experience its features, including the AI tutor. The interview was designed based on a framework adapted from the Mobile Augmented Reality Acceptance Model [24]. The adapted framework encompasses seven dimensions: perceived relative advantage, VR self-efficacy, perceived enjoyment, perceived ease of use, perceived usefulness, attitude, facilitating conditions, and intention to use. Thematic analysis was employed to identify patterns and themes in participants' perceptions of AIMS.

4.2 Results

The interview results reveal the participants' experiences with AIMS for VR presentation learning activities and the AI-powered personalised recommendation feature. The results are organised according to the framework categories: perceived relative advantage, VR self-efficacy, perceived enjoyment, perceived ease of use, perceived usefulness, attitude, facilitating conditions, and intention to use.

Perceived Relative Advantage. Students generally perceived the VR metaverse as advantageous for presentation training due to its immersive learning activities. Particularly, the AI tutor was praised for its detailed and tailored advice on presentation design for a customised topic and context, including structure, flow, and content. However, compared to teacher feedback, students noted that teachers allow for follow-up questions, which AI does not.

Some students noted limitations, such as difficulty seeing text clearly when wearing the VR headset and the "uncanny valley effect"—"a phenomenon where humanoid, almost lifelike virtual agents evoke feelings of discomfort in the observers" [25] —which made virtual characters seem less realistic. While VR was seen as more effective than traditional methods like classroom lecturing, some participants felt it was not essential for presentation training, as alternatives like practising with friends or accessing materials with smartphones were available.

VR Self-efficacy. Students' confidence in using the VR platform varied. Those with prior experience using smartphones or VR gaming reported higher self-efficacy, as familiarity with immersive technologies facilitated an easier transition. However, technical issues, such as occasionally unresponsive buttons and difficulties with loading learning materials, negatively impacted confidence.

Perceived Enjoyment. The immersive experience of VR was appreciated for its novelty and realism. Students found the AI tutor feedback engaging and timely. However, technical problems, such as distance adjustments and chaotic zoom angles in the metaverse environment, detracted from the overall experience. Additionally, some students expressed that presentation training itself is not inherently enjoyable, and the complexity of using the equipment reduced motivation.

Perceived Ease of Use. Ease of use was a mixed experience for students. While some found the controls intuitive and easy to learn with repeated use, others viewed the bulkiness of the VR headset and the need for a location suitable for using the headset as limiting factors. Suggestions for improvement included providing a user guide and addressing focal length adjustments to enhance usability.

Perceived Usefulness. The VR platform was widely regarded as useful for improving presentation skills. The AI tutor feature was particularly valued for its actionable insights, such as identifying content and structural weaknesses in presentations. However, some students felt that the platform had minimal impact on their skills, particularly if they were already confident in their abilities.

Attitude. Overall, students expressed positive attitudes toward the VR platform, recognising its potential to boost confidence and improve communication skills. Many felt the immersive environment and AI recommendations were helpful and feasible for students, particularly those with limited experience in public speaking. However, drawbacks such as eye strain and dizziness tempered enthusiasm for extended use.

Facilitating Conditions. The need for facilitating conditions, such as reliable Wi-Fi, quiet environments, and sufficient power supply, was emphasised by students. Many felt that schools providing VR resources, such as booking facilities and lighter, more comfortable equipment, would encourage adoption. The importance of overcoming feelings of awkwardness when using VR in public spaces was also noted.

Intention to Use. Students expressed varying levels of intention to use the VR platform for presentation training. While some were enthusiastic about incorporating VR into their learning and recommended it to classmates, others preferred traditional methods but were open to using VR occasionally, particularly if resources were provided. VR was seen as suitable for shorter learning sessions but less appealing for extended use due to physical discomfort. The AI tutor feature was highlighted as a motivating factor for improving performance and self-discipline through practising presentation design and preparation.

5 Discussion and Conclusion

The findings of this preliminary study provide insights into the potential of integrating AI-powered personalised recommendations within a VR metaverse platform for English presentation training. The results offer implications for the future development and broader applications of these technologies in education.

The immersive and interactive nature of the VR metaverse was widely appreciated by participants. This aligns with prior research suggesting that VR can reduce public speaking anxiety and enhance learner confidence by providing controlled, low-pressure learning settings [5, 12]. However, the "uncanny valley effect" [25] and technical limitations—such as blurry text and occasional glitches caused by challenges in customising VR headset settings to accommodate individual participants' vision needs, as well as network issues—detracted from the overall realism and usability of the platform. These findings suggest that while VR offers advantages for presentation training, refinements in hardware and software are necessary to enhance user experience and engagement.

The AI tutor's personalised recommendation feature was a standout aspect of AIMS, with participants praising its detailed insights into various aspects of presentation design. This supports existing literature on the effectiveness of AI in providing immediate, actionable feedback for skill development [1, 4, 20]. However, participants noted that AI recommendation lacks the interactive and adaptive qualities of human feedback, such as the ability to address follow-up questions. This limitation underscores the need for developing new approaches to maximise learning outcomes, such as allowing learners to interact with AI to receive further feedback.

The study also revealed mixed perceptions of the platform's effectiveness. While some participants found the controls intuitive and appreciated the novelty of the VR experience, others were deterred by the bulkiness of the headset, technical issues, and physical discomfort. These findings are consistent with prior research highlighting the ergonomic and usability challenges of VR technologies [5, 26]. Furthermore, learners' individual proficiency in presentation skills was shown to affect their perceptions of the usefulness of the VR platform. Addressing these issues through improved hardware design, user-friendly interfaces, and more customisation of personalised features could enhance the accessibility and appeal of VR learning platforms.

Given the exploratory nature of this study and its small sample size, the findings should be interpreted with caution. Further research with larger, more diverse participant groups is needed to validate these results and explore the long-term impact of AIMS on presentation skill development. Comparative studies examining the effectiveness of AIMS against traditional and other technology-enhanced presentation training methods would also provide valuable insights into its relative advantages and limitations.

Acknowledgments. The work described in this paper was supported by grants from Hong Kong Metropolitan University (CP/2022/04 and TLRF2024(04)).

Disclosure of Interests. The authors have no competing interests to declare that are relevant to the content of this article.

References

1. Li, K.C., Wong, B.T.M.: Artificial intelligence in personalised learning: a bibliometric analysis. Interact. Technol. Smart Educ. **30**(3), 422–445 (2023)
2. Li, K.C., Chong, G.H.L., Wong, B.T.M., Wu, M.M.F.: A TAM-based analysis of Hong Kong undergraduate students' attitudes toward generative AI in higher education and employment. Educ. Sci. **15**(7), 798 (2025)
3. Li, K.C., Wong, B.T.M.: Features and trends of personalised learning: a review of journal publications from 2001 to 2018. In: Cheung et al. (eds.), Personalized Learning: Approaches, Methods and Practices, pp. 4–17. Routledge (2024)
4. Chan, V.: A qualitative study of an XR-enhanced and AI-powered mobile app for public speaking training: student perceptions and experiences. SN Comput. Sci. **6**, 796 (2025)
5. Li, K.C., Wong, B.T.M.: A literature review of augmented reality, virtual reality, and mixed reality in language learning. Int. J. Mob. Learn. Organ. **15**(2), 164–178 (2021)
6. Chan, V.: Investigating the effects of extended reality (XR) on interpreter competencies: an experimental study of a pioneering XR mobile-assisted language learning application for interpreting training. J. Comput. Assisted Learn. **41**(3), e70055 (2025)
7. Chan, V.: Impact of an extended reality-powered mobile application: an experimental study in interpreting classes. Interact. Learn. Environ. https://doi.org/10.1080/10494820.2025.2519702(2025)
8. Poeschl, S.: Virtual reality training for public speaking—a QUEST-VR framework validation. Front. ICT **4**, 1–13 (2017)
9. Chan, V.: Investigating the impact of a virtual reality mobile application on learners' interpreting competence. J. Comput. Assist. Learn. **39**(4), 1242–1258 (2023)
10. Liu, M., Jackson, J.: An exploration of Chinese EFL learners' unwillingness to communicate and foreign language anxiety. Mod. Lang. J. **92**(1), 71–86 (2008)
11. Chan, V.: Using a virtual reality mobile application for interpreting learning: listening to the student's voice. Interact. Learn. Environ. **32**(6), 2438–2451 (2024)
12. Chen, Z.: Exploring the application scenarios and issues facing Metaverse technology in education. Interact. Learn. Environ. **32**(5), 1975–1987 (2024)
13. Inceoglu, M.M., Ciloglugil, B.: Use of Metaverse in education. In: Gervasi, O., Murgante, B., Misra, S., Rocha, A.M.A.C., Garau, C. (eds.) Computational Science and Its Applications – ICCSA 2022 Workshops. LNCS, vol. 13377, pp. 171–184. Springer, Cham (2022). https://doi.org/10.1007/978-3-031-10536-4_12

14. Park, J.: Exploring the possibility of using Metaverse in Korean language education. J. Int. Netw. Korean Lang. Cult. **18**(3), 117–146 (2021)
15. Christoforou, M.: Enhancing the ESP lesson with IMMERSE: a pedagogical example of a Metaverse language learning platform. In: Proceedings of 14th International Conference Innovation in Language Learning (2022). https://hdl.handle.net/20.500.14279/27320
16. Lee, S., Jeon, J., Choe, H.: Enhancing pre-service teachers' global Englishes awareness with technology: a focus on AI chatbots in 3D Metaverse environments. TESOL Q. **59**(1), 49–74 (2025)
17. Hwang, Y., Lee, S., Jeon, J.: Integrating AI Chatbots into the Metaverse: pre-service English teachers' design works and perceptions. Educ. Inf. Technol. **30**, 4099–4130 (2025)
18. Uzun, C.: The role of artificial intelligence in teaching Turkish to foreigners and Chat GPT assessment for writing skills. In: Zaremohzzabieh, Z., Abdullah, R., Ahrari, S. (eds.) Exploring Youth Studies in the Age of AI, pp. 231–248. IGI Global (2024)
19. Toprak-Yıldız, T.E.: Natural language processing applications in language assessment: The use of automated speech scoring. In: Köroğlu, Z.Ç, Çakır, A. (eds.) Fostering Foreign Language Teaching and Learning Environments with Contemporary Technologies, pp. 216–234. IGI Global (2024)
20. Zou, B., Du, Y., Wang, Z., Chen, J., Zhang, W.: An investigation into artificial intelligence speech evaluation programs with automatic feedback for developing EFL learners' speaking skills. Sage Open **13**(3) https://doi.org/10.1177/21582440231193818 (2023)
21. Kim, W.H., Kim, J.H.: Individualised AI tutor based on developmental learning networks. IEEE Access **8**, 27927–27937 (2020)
22. McClain, D.M.: Artificially intelligent computer-assisted language learning system with AI student component. Capstone Res. Projects **188** (2016). https://knowledge.e.southern.edu/senior_research/188
23. Herbein, E., Golle, J., Tibus, M., Schiefer, J., Trautwein, U., Zettler, I.: Fostering elementary school children's public speaking skills: a randomized controlled trial. Learn. Instr. **55**, 158–168 (2018)
24. Koutromanos, G., Mikropoulos, A.T., Mavridis, D., Christogiannis, C.: The mobile augmented reality acceptance model for teachers and future teachers. Educ. Inf. Technol. **29**, 7855–7893 (2024)
25. Diekhof, E.K., Kastner, S., Deinert, D., Foerster, M., Steinicke, F.: The uncanny valley effect and immune activation in virtual reality. Sci. Rep. **15**, 30473 (2025)
26. Souchet, A.D., Lourdeaux, D., Pagani, A., Rebenitsch, L.: A narrative review of immersive virtual reality's ergonomics and risks at the workplace: cybersickness, visual fatigue, muscular fatigue, acute stress, and mental overload. Virtual Reality **27**, 19–50 (2023)

AI Education Developer Community: A Study on the Evolution of DAOs

Caiyan Tang[1], Chengzu Dong[2], Qin Wang[3], Qi Cai[4], Shiping Chen[3](✉), and Yuhui Huo[5]

[1] The University of Sydney, Sydney, Australia
[2] School of Data Science, Lingnan University, Hong Kong, China
chengzudong@ln.edu.hk
[3] CSIRO, Data61, Sydney, Australia
shiping.chen@data61.csiro.au
[4] Chongqing Electric Power College, Chongqing, China
[5] Eagle Plus Technology Pty Ltd., Dongguan, China
yuavision@sina.com

Abstract. We study how decentralized autonomous organizations (DAOs) evolve in an AI education developer community. We propose a four-stage evolution path, a "5D + O" governance principle set, and a 70-20-10 resource structure. We combine case evidence, qualitative interviews, and social network analysis. We show that decentralized screening, transparent voting, and contribution based allocation help early incubation, risk dispersion, and fast coordination. We also highlight the role of community education onboarding, capability building, and norm internalization in sustaining governance at each stage. We discuss limits and future research.

Keywords: DAO · Decentralised Governance · AI Education · Privacy Protection · Cross-Community Interoperability

1 Introduction

Decentralized Autonomous Organizations (DAOs) represent a novel governance paradigm enabled by blockchain technology, characterized by decentralized decision-making and enhanced management transparency [6]. Unlike traditional hierarchical structures, DAOs leverage smart contracts and consensus mechanisms to replace managerial layers, thereby mitigating single points of failure and surpassing the limitations of flattened organizational models like the amoeba management system. Furthermore, compared to publicly listed companies that consolidate power through equity distribution, such as the "Huawei model," DAOs' self contained governance frameworks and education system are notably more flexible and adaptable [7, 8, 22].

This study proposes an evolutionary framework for DAOs, which unfolds in four distinct stages. The process begins with an initial enthusiast phase, focused on community formation and project proposal. This is followed by the selection of a core team, facilitated by decentralized mechanisms such as communication and election. The third

B. Fernández-Manjón et al. (Eds.): SETE 2025/ICWL 2025, LNCS 16425, pp. 472–481, 2026.
https://doi.org/10.1007/978-981-92-0042-9_35

stage involves the establishment of a "quasi-corporate" structure, which is driven by a contribution value model. This model integrates key production elements, including talent, capital, and technical expertise. Within the AI context, this stage demonstrates the aggregation of 20 angel investors, 70 technical professionals, and 10 successful entrepreneurs. The final stage is characterized by business expansion and operational optimization.

Our research specifically examines the AI developer community, an exceptionally dynamic and innovative sector in the current AI landscape. This community serves as an ideal experimental platform for observing DAO evolution. Amidst the rapid growth of AI entrepreneurship and angel investments, DAOs' "end-to-start" resource allocation model significantly enhances project success rates while decentralizing the high failure risks inherent in early-stage ventures [9, 10].

This study seeks to answer the following key research questions:

1. How can DAOs rapidly aggregate resources and talent during their nascent stages?
2. Can decentralized screening and voting mechanisms effectively substitute traditional team selection processes?
3. Is the contribution value model a viable foundation for supporting business model incubation and organizational expansion within the AI domain?

This article ultimately aims to demonstrate how DAO governance principles can enable rapid project incubation, efficient resource aggregation, risk dispersion, high transparency, and an overall increase in project success rates.

2 Preliminary Concepts

2.1 Defining Decentralized Autonomous Organizations (DAOs)

A Decentralized Autonomous Organization (DAO) represents an internetnative form of governance and coordination, operating without a central authority and governed by rules encoded in smart contracts on a blockchain. At its core, a DAO is a transparent, distributed, and self-organizing entity that empowers its members to collectively make decisions and manage resources through a secure, verifiable, and intermediary-free system. This model fundamentally challenges traditional corporate hierarchies by replacing centralized control with a decentralized, token- or contribution-based consensus mechanism, thereby fostering greater transparency and member participation.

2.2 Typologies and Participant Roles in DAOs

DAO members typically fulfill diverse roles, ranging from core contributors and developers who build and maintain the project, to token holders who participate in governance voting, and general community members who contribute through discussions and feedback. These participants collectively shape the organization's trajectory. DAOs are not monolithic; they can be categorized into various types based on their function, such as protocol DAOs (governing blockchain protocols), grant DAOs (managing funding for projects), and social DAOs (focused on community building). Understanding these different roles and structures is crucial for analyzing a DAO's operational dynamics and governance effectiveness.

2.3 The AI Developer Community: Rationale for a Case Study

This study specifically focuses on the AI developer community as a case study for DAO evolution. This choice is predicated on several key factors. First, the AI field is highly dynamic and innovation-driven, characterized by rapid technological cycles and a high degree of collaboration among a globally distributed network of experts. This environment is particularly conducive to the decentralized and agile nature of DAOs. Second, AI-related ventures often involve high initial risk and a need for flexible resource allocation, areas where traditional corporate models struggle. By examining an AI developer community, this research can effectively illustrate how DAOs mitigate these risks, accelerate project incubation, and efficiently aggregate talent and resources in a high-stakes, innovation-intensive domain.

3 Related Work

Since 2015, Decentralized Autonomous Organizations (DAOs) have emerged as a significant area of blockchain research, representing a key advancement in decentralized governance mechanisms. Existing literature primarily investigates three main dimensions: (1) technical governance structures [11, 12]; (2) consensus mechanisms and incentive designs [13, 14]; and (3) community-driven evolutionary paths [15, 16]. However, the foundational social layer and the role of social capital within these decentralized structures remain largely underexplored [4].

Recent studies by Tang et al. have expanded this foundation in more concrete ways. In their survey work, Tang et al. [23] systematically analyze DAO typologies, governance mechanisms, and the interplay between structural rules and participant behavior, positioning DAOs as socio-technical systems rather than solely technical artifacts. In their empirical case study, Tang et al. [24] investigate Meta-IP Chain DAO, a pioneering tokenless DAO, by examining its proposal-to-vote workflows, resource allocation logic, and how contributions (rather than tokens) mediate governance power in practice.

These concrete findings bridge the gap between abstract models and real-world DAO operations, and provide a more grounded baseline for our own re-source allocation framework.

However, there is a notable gap in current DAO research concerning effective resource allocation strategies. Specifically, within the high-risk and rapidly evolving AI industry, a clear model for the efficient aggregation and distribution of resources remains underdeveloped.

The *70-20-10 resource allocation model* proposed in this study draws inspiration from the well-established 70-20-10 rule in corporate innovation [17, 18]. This model aims to provide DAOs with a logical framework for resource distribution that effectively balances organizational stability with innovative flexibility. While still in its experimental phase, this model has evolved through the continuous optimization of team structures and investment efficiency in AI projects, offering a viable pathway for the construction of robust resource governance models within decentralized organizations.

4 Research Methodology

This study employs a mixed-methods research design, integrating case studies, qualitative interviews, and Social Network Analysis (SNA) to provide a comprehensive analysis of DAO evolution.

4.1 Data Sources

The data for this research was collected from several primary sources:

- Community governance documents, including "5D" documents and internal proposal records.
- Off-chain governance records from Snapshot and community communication channels.
- Qualitative feedback from in-depth interviews with 12 community members.
- Quantitative data, such as voting metrics, participation behavior, and communication logs.

4.2 Analytical Methods

We utilized the NetworkX tool to perform a social graph analysis. Our focus was on key network metrics such as Degree Centrality, Betweenness Centrality, and propagation paths. This approach allowed us to move beyond simple interaction counts to quantitatively assess the structural roles and influence of individual members [2]. These metrics were combined with other indicators, including voting rates, proposal completion rates, and participation frequency, to quantitatively assess the real-world effectiveness of the governance mechanisms.

4.3 Methodological Foundation

The core methodological framework of this study is *case-based theory building*. This approach, initially proposed by Eisenhardt and later refined and widely applied by Yin, is particularly well-suited for research on nascent organizational forms and governance mechanisms. Eisenhardt's approach emphasizes the inductive construction of theoretical models from multiple real-world cases and diverse data sources. In contrast, Yin's methodology stresses the importance of rigorous case design, clear logical chains, and data triangulation.

In this study, the AIer Link community serves as a representative and evolving case of DAO governance, providing a real-world context for the development of a grounded theory.

Building upon this foundation, the study incorporates *Social Network Analysis (SNA)* using tools like NetworkX to model member interactions and information diffusion. By employing key metrics such as degree centrality, closeness centrality, and betweenness centrality, we identified influential bridge nodes and core connectors, thereby revealing the structural characteristics of internal governance behaviors within the community.

Furthermore, we adopted a *Participatory Observation* approach. The researcher actively engaged in the daily governance practices of the AIer Link community, including proposal submissions, topic discussions, team collaborations, and resource allocation. This immersive involvement provided firsthand behavioral insights, enabling the study to capture informal rules, consensus formation, and trust-building mechanisms that are often inaccessible to external observers.

In summary, the integration of case study analysis, social network modeling, and participatory observation provides a comprehensive and multi-dimensional understanding of DAO evolution. This multi-faceted approach also establishes a robust methodological foundation for future theoretical modeling and cross-case comparative analysis in decentralized governance research.

5 DAO Evolution Model

5.1 Evolutionary Structure

The DAO evolutionary process, as observed in this study, progresses through four distinct stages: (1) enthusiast gathering, (2) core member selection, (3) a contribution-driven organizational structure, and (4) community governance leadership. This progression is not determined by time but by the successful acquisition and availability of resources necessary to initiate each subsequent stage.

5.2 The "5D + O" Governance Principles

This study introduces the "5D+O" principles, a set of core tenets designed to guide DAO governance. These principles are:

- **Debug**: Focused on bug removal and system integrity.
- **Decentralized**: Emphasizing decentralized control and decision-making.
- **De-confrontation**: Aimed at reducing conflict and fostering collaboration.
- **De-risking**: Involving proactive risk management strategies.
- **Distributed**: Highlighting the distribution of responsibilities and resources.
- **Open-source**: Promoting transparency and collaborative development.

This system provides a foundational framework for building trust, mitigating risks, and effectively attracting productive contributors during the community's early development phases.

Table 1. Key SNA Metrics of the AIer Link Community

Metric	Meaning	Median Value	Maximum Value
Degree Centrality	Frequency of node recommendation or interaction	8	27
Betweenness Centrality	The ability of a node to connect others and be connected	0.014	0.371

(continued)

Table 1. (*continued*)

Metric	Meaning	Median Value	Maximum Value
Propagation Depth (Average Path Length)	The average path length from seed nodes outward	2.3	4.1
Clustering Coefficient	Degree of interconnection among adjacent nodes	0.42	0.81

5.3 The 70–20-10 Resource Structure Model

The proposed **70-20-10 resource allocation model** divides community resources into three distinct categories based on their strategic purpose:

- **70%**: Allocated to core technology and tool development, which forms the primary foundation of the project.
- **20%**: Dedicated to incubation and exploratory projects, fostering innovation and new ventures.
- **10%**: Reserved for strategic research and governance upgrades, ensuring the long-term health and adaptability of the organization.

The allocation of these resources is governed by publicly submitted proposals and consensus mechanisms. Furthermore, team equity, salaries, and funds are managed in accordance with these established governance rules, which also in-corporate flexible adjustment mechanisms.

5.4 Limitations and Future Modeling

At this stage of the research, complex mathematical modeling is considered inappropriate due to the limited sample size and propagation mechanisms. The current study is focused on a phase where the data is readily comparable, and the underlying mechanisms are clear and transparent. Future research, however, will introduce more sophisticated methods, including the quantification of behavioral indicators and the development of a scalable resource weight function system.

6 Research Findings

6.1 Core Member Identification and Propagation Path Analysis

Through a Social Network Analysis (SNA) of community members' propagation behavior and interaction structures using NetworkX, we identified key nodes with significant influence and propagation power. The main quantitative findings are summarized in Table 1.

graphicx

The structural analysis revealed that the early community formed two to three "core propagation groups," each with recommendation paths traceable to 3-5 early evangelists. These individuals were responsible for key functions such as team building, operational coordination, and development guidance. The bridge nodes identified through the SNA diagram demonstrate significant information integration and coordination capabilities, effectively serving as "informal central hubs" in the community's nascent governance structure.

Furthermore, the chain-like propagation structure, where information spreads through multiple levels, in some cases exceeded five levels. This indicates that even without formal on-chain governance mechanisms, the "distributed recommendation system" built on social networks had already developed robust "influence diffusion" and "decentralized mobilization" capabilities.

Our social network analysis of member relationships confirmed that a few core early enthusiasts held pivotal positions within the network. These members exhibited significantly higher Degree Centrality and Betweenness Centrality than others, highlighting their crucial role in connecting community nodes and disseminating information [19, 20]. For instance, within the community's early social graph, the top 5% of members by Degree Centrality attracted and connected over 50% of newly joined members, reflecting a "strong center-weak periphery" network structure. This concentration of centrality implies that resources (including information and opportunities) are primarily disseminated and aggregated through a limited number of highcentrality nodes.

6.2 DAO Governance Voting Mechanism

Although the AIer Link community has not yet implemented an on-chain voting system, all proposal activities have been comprehensively documented through community communication chains, WeChat public account comments, webpage declarations, and group chat screenshots. Data from 32 valid proposals submitted throughout 2023 is summarized in Table 2.

Table 2. Summary of 2023 Proposal Activity

Metric	Value
Number of Valid Proposals	32
Average Participation per Person	5.4 times
Proposal Approval Rate	78% (25 proposals approved)
Average Response Time	Initial consensus within 23 h
Proposal Implementation Rate	64% (20 implemented)

6.3 Contribution Structure and Initial Resource Allocation Results

Guided by the 70-20-10 resource structure model, the AIer Link community achieved the following results during the incubation of two key projects, as detailed in Table 3.

Table 3. Resource Allocation and Project Outcomes

Project Code	Pool	Est. I/O Ratio	Progress
AIL-2023-NLP	70% Core Pool	1:2.5	POC completed; investment interest
AIL-2023-VQA	20% Exploration Pool	1:1.1	Qualified for incubation; resources allocated
AIL-2023-GOV	10% Strategic Pool	Zero output (long-term)	In preparation as a governance research project

6.4 Preliminary Conclusions and Insights

The findings from this research demonstrate that even with a small data sample and an incomplete on-chain mechanism, the DAO governance model exhibits a powerful combination of high transparency, rapid response, and structural consensus in the early organizational stages.

- Social network analysis tools are highly effective for member screening and for identifying paths of trust flow.
- Although the voting mechanism is not fully formalized, the community's communication channels have successfully established a "behavior-driven consensus proxy mechanism."
- The contribution structure and resource allocation mechanism have proven to be effective, confirming the practical applicability and potential for organizational efficiency of the DAO governance framework in the AI field.

In summary, the research findings presented in this chapter show that social network analysis can be leveraged to identify and accelerate the aggregation of resources and talent during the early stages of DAO development. While the decentralized voting mechanism has shown promise in terms of fairness and effectiveness in team selection, it still requires improvements to increase participation and prevent the concentration of power. The contribution value-driven 70-20-10 resource allocation model has effectively promoted project incubation and organizational expansion within the AI developer community DAO, providing valuable insights for DAO governance practice. These findings will be further discussed in Chapter 6 regarding their theoretical and practical implications.

7 Discussion

The DAO evolution model proposed in this study shows clear advantages in resource integration, risk management, and allocation efficiency: its decentralized structure aggregates diverse resources across geographic and organizational boundaries, enabling transparent, intermediary-free decisions that speed innovation and project progress; its open, distributed decision-making mitigates waste and single-point failures common in centralized firms, dispersing entrepreneurial risk and improving flexibility under uncertainty; and its smart contract–based processes streamline proposals and real-time voting, cutting approval layers, delays, and costs while boosting responsiveness. This shift marks a move from traditional hierarchies toward networked, collaborative production [1].

8 Limitations and Future Research Directions

While this study provides an effective analysis of the DAO governance model, its limitations should be acknowledged. First, the research is based on a single-case study of the AIer Link community, which may limit the generalizability of the findings. Although AIer Link serves as a representative case demonstrating the potential of DAO governance in the AI field, DAOs in different industries and of varying scales may encounter distinct challenges and opportunities. Future research should expand the sample size to include a broader range of industries and DAO communities to validate the universality of these findings. Second, the data collected in this study is somewhat limited and does not provide a comprehensive examination of all aspects of DAO governance implementation. For instance, in large-scale communities, complex issues such as balancing decision-making efficiency with democratic participation and addressing potential power concentration from token holdings have not been fully explored. Future studies should focus on the performance of DAO governance models in different contexts, analyzing the effects of varying governance structures and organizational sizes. Furthermore, as DAO technology and models continue to evolve, future research should also focus on optimizing member selection algorithms, enhancing the transparency and security of voting mechanisms, and addressing more complex governance challenges.

9 Conclusion

This study demonstrates the considerable potential of DAO governance models within modern, internet-native communities, particularly for resource aggregation, decentralized governance, and the dispersion of entrepreneurial risk, by analyzing the real-world case of AIer Link to confirm their effectiveness in improving resource allocation efficiency, promoting innovation, and mitigating risks; specifically, the DAO model facilitates information flow and the sharing of innovation resources while helping entrepreneurs navigate risks and adapt quickly to volatile markets. Theoretically, the research proposes a novel framework for DAO governance that highlights how decentralized structures foster collaboration, enhance transparency, and improve decision-making efficiency, and it introduces a 70-20-10 resource allocation model that guides distribution in early-stage DAO communities so they can remain flexible and innovative while scaling rapidly. Practically, the study offers experience-backed guidance and theoretical support for adopting DAOs, anticipating that as AI entrepreneurial projects and DAO practices mature, the DAO model will be applied across more industries, contributing to a more equitable, efficient, and transparent global governance system.

Acknowledgment. This work is supported by the project titled 'AI and Digital Technology in International Education: Enhancing Teaching Methods and Student Engagement through Online Platforms, Virtual Reality (VR), and Augmented Reality (AR).' The funding code is 102738.

References

1. Benkler, Y.: The Wealth of Networks: How Social Production Transforms Markets and Freedom. Yale University Press (2006)
2. Borgatti, S.P., Everett, M.G.: A graph-theoretic perspective on centrality. Soc. Netw. **28**(4), 466–484 (2006)
3. O'Brien, K.A., Lim, E.D.T.: Distributed agile teams: a systematic review. J. Inf. Technol. (2020)
4. Wasserman, S., Faust, K.: Social Network Analysis: Methods and Applications. Cambridge University Press (1994)
5. Barabasi, A.L., Albert, R.: Emergence of scaling in random networks. Science **286**(5439), 509–512 (1999)
6. Buterin, V.: DAOs, DACs, DAs and more: an incomplete terminology guide. Ethereum Blog (2014)
7. Inamori, K.: Amoeba Management. Oriental Press (2010)
8. Ren, Z.: How Long Can Huawei's Red Flag Last?. CITIC Press (2020)
9. CB Insights: State of AI startups 2023 (2023)
10. Horowitz, A.: The future of DAOs. A16Z Crypto Research (2022)
11. Wright, A., De Filippi, P.: Decentralized blockchain technology and the rise of LEX cryptographia. SSRN Electron. J. (2015)
12. Xu, X., et al.: A systematic review of blockchain. ACM Comput. Surv. (2019)
13. Beck, R., Mu¨ller-Bloch, C., King, J.: Governance in blockchain networks. MIS Quart. Executive **17**(3), 165–179 (2018)
14. Atzori, M.: Blockchain technology and decentralized governance. Ledger **2**, 45–62 (2017)
15. Reijers, W., O'Brolchain, F., Haynes, P.: Governance in Blockchain Technologies & Social Contract Theories. Ledger, vol. 3 (2018)
16. Zhang, J., Xie, K., Wang, H.: Towards autonomous governance: a case study of DAO in DeFi ecosystem (Preprint) (2021)
17. Lombardo, M.M., Eichinger, R.W.: The Career Architect Development Planner. Lominger (1996)
18. Viima: The 70-20-10 rule for Innovation (2021). https://www.viima.com/blog/70-20-10-rule-of-innovation
19. Freeman, L.C.: Centrality in social networks: conceptual clarification. Soc. Netw. **1**(3), 215–239 (1979)
20. Scott, J.: Social Network Analysis, 4th edn. SAGE Publications (2017)
21. Reijers, W., O'Brolchain, F., Haynes, P.: Governance in blockchain technologies & social contract theories. Ledger **1**, 134–151 (2016)
22. Jiang, X., Wang, R., Hoang, T., Ranaweera, C., Dong, C., Myers, T.: AI-powered gamified scaffolding: transforming learning in virtual learning environment. Electronics **14**(13), 2732 (2025)
23. Tang, C., Cai, Q., Dong, C., Wang, Q., Chen, S.: Decentralised Autonomous Organizations (DAOs): an exploratory survey. Distributed Ledger Technologies (Research & Practice) (2025). https://doi.org/10.1145/3716321
24. Tang, C., Cai, Q., Dong, C. Wang, Q., Chen, S., Jiang, M.: An empirical case study of meta-IP chain DAO: the pioneer tokenless DAO. In: Proceedings of the 2024 IEEE 9th International Conference on Data Science in Cyberspace (DSC), pp. 24–31 (2024). https://doi.org/10.1109/DSC63484.2024.00011

Workshop OPEA

A Conceptual Integrated AI Framework and Research Agenda for Personalized Adaptive Assessment Using NLP, Reinforcement Learning, and Adversarial Response Modeling

Tahmina Akter Anondi(✉) and Ezekiel Nwokolo

Louisiana State University Shreveport, Shreveport, USA
tahmina.akter.anondi@gmail.com

Abstract. Personalized adaptive assessment has emerged as a cornerstone of modern educational technology, aiming to provide learners with tailored evaluation pathways that evolve in response to their performance, behaviors, and contextual cues. While existing research has made progress using isolated techniques—such as automatic question generation, reinforcement learning–based item selection, or NLP-driven scoring—current systems remain fragmented, limited in transparency, and insufficiently sensitive to human factors. This paper presents a unified conceptual framework that integrates five complementary paradigms: (1) Natural Language Processing for open-response understanding, (2) Reinforcement Learning for dynamic item sequencing, (3) Adversarial Response Modeling for robustness against guessing and generative-AI misuse, (4) Emotion-Aware Modeling to adapt assessments based on affective states, and (5) Knowledge Graph–Driven Concept Routing to ensure pedagogical coherence. We additionally introduce a multi-agent architecture in which specialized agents coordinate to deliver adaptive question selection, emotion monitoring, explanation generation, and bias-aware scoring. Drawing from established findings in adaptive testing, cognitive diagnostics, fairness in automated assessment, and intelligent tutoring systems, this work articulates a research agenda focused on transparency, explainability, fairness, and real-time adaptation. The proposed framework is conceptual yet technically grounded, supported with formal equations for RL-based item selection, formal architectural schematics, and illustrative examples that mirror real classroom use cases. By unifying emotion-aware analytics, multi-agent coordination, and adversarial robustness, the paper aims to lay the foundation for a next-generation assessment paradigm that is human-centric, pedagogically aligned, and resilient to emerging forms of misuse.

Keywords: Personalized Adaptive Assessment · Computerized Adaptive Testing (CAT) · Reinforcement Learning · Generative AI · Fairness in Educational AI

1 Introduction

Traditional examinations often treat students as static data points—unchanging, context-free, and emotionally neutral. This assumption stands in sharp contrast to real learning, where students hesitate, reason aloud, get confused, recover, and occasionally guess

B. Fernández-Manjón et al. (Eds.): SETE 2025/ICWL 2025, LNCS 16425, pp. 485–499, 2026.
https://doi.org/10.1007/978-981-92-0042-9_36

strategically. Yet most assessment systems measure only the final answer, offering limited insight into the cognitive or emotional processes underlying a learner's performance. As adaptive digital platforms proliferate, the demand for assessments that recognize learners as dynamic, evolving participants has become increasingly urgent. Recent advances in educational AI highlight what is possible. NLP techniques now support automatic question generation [1, 3], refinement of examination items [4], and sensitive evaluation of written explanations. Reinforcement learning (RL) systems can shape question paths based on performance trajectories [10–13]. Meanwhile, a growing body of research on fairness, bias, and explainability [15–18] exposes the limitations of opaque scoring mechanisms, particularly for students whose linguistic styles diverge from dominant norms. Despite this progress, these components typically function in isolation. A system may personalize difficulty but remain blind to frustration; another may analyze free-text explanations but cannot prevent AI-generated answers; others may map conceptual relationships but lack mechanisms for real-time adaptation.

This siloing leaves several critical gaps unaddressed.

- First, adaptive models rarely incorporate affective cues, even though emotional states such as frustration or confusion are strong predictors of disengagement.
- Second, current platforms remain vulnerable to adversarial behavior—ranging from intentional guessing to the use of large language models to fabricate responses.
- Third, many systems rely on linear item sequences rather than structured representations of knowledge, limiting their ability to make pedagogically coherent decisions about what a learner should encounter next.

To address these challenges, this paper introduces an integrated framework that combines NLP-based response interpretation, RL-driven sequencing, adversarial response modeling, emotion-aware analytics, and knowledge-graph-guided concept routing. The core innovation lies in a multi-agent architecture where specialized agents interact through a lightweight message-passing protocol. Rather than centralizing authority in a single "oversight" module, the architecture supports distributed coordination:

- the Emotion Agent signals affective states,
- the Knowledge Graph Agent constrains allowable concept transitions,
- the Item Selection Agent proposes candidate items via RL, and
- the Scoring Agent evaluates semantic correctness.

These agents follow a negotiated consensus model: each produces action proposals with confidence scores, and the system selects the next step according to predefined arbitration rules (e.g., prioritizing conceptual prerequisites over difficulty optimization when conflicts arise). This interaction mechanism transforms assessment from a monolithic decision process into a transparent, distributed reasoning workflow.

This paper articulates a mechanically grounded architectural design for such an assessment system. The framework includes the logic by which agents exchange information, the constraints that govern item sequencing, and the integration of adversarial signals and affective cues into real-time decision-making. By embedding these components within a coherent design, the work offers a structured research agenda for building next-generation assessment systems that are adaptive, emotionally aware, and resilient to emerging forms of misuse.

2 Background

AI-driven assessment research spans multiple domains—NLP-based question generation, psychometric adaptive testing, reinforcement learning, knowledge-graph modeling, affective computing, and multi-agent systems. Despite strong progress in each area, these technologies largely evolve in isolation, preventing the emergence of assessment systems that are simultaneously adaptive, emotionally aware, pedagogically coherent, and robust against misuse. This section synthesizes the relevant literature and identifies the conceptual and technical gaps motivating the proposed framework. Natural Language Processing (NLP) has significantly advanced question generation and automated response interpretation. Early AQG systems rely on rule-based linguistic templates and shallow learning to construct short-answer and multiple-choice items from text corpora, typically targeting lower-level cognitive skills such as recall and comprehension [1, 2]. More recent approaches integrate Bloom's taxonomy into question templates, giving models explicit control over cognitive level and linguistic complexity [1]. With the rise of large language models (LLMs), question generation has become one of the most adopted educational applications of generative AI. LLM-based agents can generate, refine, and quality-check exam items aligned with curricular outcomes [4], while small generative models show promise for lightweight educational question generation in resource-constrained settings [3]. Generative AI has also been deployed for interactive discourse, feedback, and scaffolded learning tasks in intelligent learning environments [5, 6]. However, these systems remain linguistic silos: they generate or evaluate text but do not exchange structured information with adaptive testing engines. None of the existing frameworks integrate NLP-derived signals—such as semantic uncertainty, partial correctness, conceptual drift, or reasoning depth—into the dynamic control logic of adaptive assessment. As a result, rich linguistic insights are lost before influencing item selection or learner modeling.

2.1 Reinforcement Learning in Adaptive Testing

Reinforcement Learning (RL) has emerged as a promising mechanism for adaptive pedagogical decision-making. RL-based tutors have been shown to support lower-performing learners in mathematics [10], orchestrate metacognitive interventions across multiple ITS platforms [12], and optimize content sequencing and hint selection [13]. Meanwhile, psychometric adaptive testing frameworks such as CAT and CD-CAT rely on information-based heuristics to select items that maximize measurement precision [7, 11]. Despite these advancements, RL in education remains contextually isolated. Standard RL policies optimize difficulty based only on performance trajectories and are not designed to ingest multimodal cues such as emotional state, linguistic uncertainty, or knowledge-graph constraints. Furthermore, IRT-based CAT systems generally require numeric response vectors, making them incompatible with semantic or behavioral embeddings produced by NLP and affective models [7, 8]. Consequently, RL currently functions as a standalone optimization engine rather than a holistic decision-maker within a multi-agent pedagogical ecosystem. Growing reliance on AI-driven scoring has intensified concerns about fairness and interpretability. Deep learning models for short-answer scoring exhibit systematic item-level and demographic biases [15], and similar inequities appear in automated writing assessment [16]. FairAIED and related frameworks emphasize that fairness risks may emerge from data collection, model design, or deployment workflows, requiring iterative, context-aware auditing and mitigation strategies [17]. Ethical analyses of AI-assisted educational assessment further highlight transparency, accountability, and privacy concerns across all stages of the assessment pipeline [18]. Empirical studies show that academic staff expect robust governance and clear institutional guidelines before adopting AI-based assessment [19]. Despite this broad literature, operational fairness—fairness embedded directly into the assessment logic—remains missing. Existing adaptive assessment systems do not incorporate adversarial detection, bias monitoring, or integrity modeling within the decision engine itself. These processes are typically performed as post-hoc analyses rather than real-time constraints. Knowledge graphs (KGs) have become increasingly important for organizing conceptual dependencies, from materials science domains [14] to intelligent tutoring systems. KGs enforce prerequisite relationships, support concept-level diagnosis, and structure problem-solving pathways. Recent research demonstrates that emotion-aware KG-driven agents can represent learner experiences more holistically by linking conceptual mastery with affective cues [20]. Empirical studies also show that AI-based emotion detection can meaningfully inform teaching and assessment strategies [21]. However, within adaptive testing, KGs are still underutilized. Many systems treat concept relationships as static labels or metadata rather than dynamic constraints on item routing. Furthermore, existing models do not integrate KG constraints with emotional signals or adversarial indicators, resulting in item transitions that may be pedagogically incorrect, emotionally inappropriate, or vulnerable to misuse. Even state-of-the-art graph-based multi-agent architectures, such as GraphMASAL, do not incorporate real-time affective states or adversarial risk into their routing algorithms, limiting their suitability for high-stakes assessment [22].

Multi-agent systems have been deployed in collaborative learning, intelligent tutoring, and classroom orchestration. However, dominant designs rely on hierarchical control structures—commonly known as Pedagogical Managers or Orchestrators—that make centralized decisions while subordinate agents perform specialized tasks. This model creates a single point of failure and prevents agents from negotiating conflicting objectives such as difficulty optimization (RL), emotional stabilization (Affective Computing), and integrity protection (Adversarial Modeling). No existing educational architecture employs distributed, constraint-driven negotiation among autonomous agents. The absence of such a mechanism limits system flexibility, transparency, and resilience. This gap directly motivates the decentralized, multi-agent design introduced in this paper.

3 Conceptual Framework and Methodology

This section defines the architectural specification for the integrated adaptive assessment framework, as shown in Fig. 1. While later sections introduce algorithms and internal component logic, the objective here is to clarify the structural interactions that enable a dynamic, emotionally aware, and pedagogically coherent assessment process.

The framework operates as a distributed multi-agent system rather than a hierarchical controller-based design. Five autonomous agents cooperate through a shared state representation—the Assessment Knowledge Base—which functions as a message and constraint exchange layer. Instead of a central controller dictating the flow, the system applies Constraint-Driven Arbitration: each agent contributes constraints that define the feasible region of the decision space, while the optimization agent (RL Item Selection Agent) operates strictly within these boundaries.

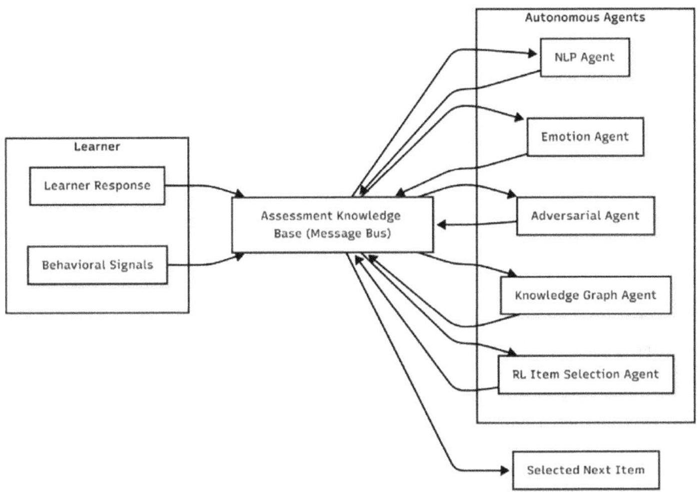

Fig. 1. High-Level Architecture (Schematic)

3.1 Architecture: The Five-Agent Consensus Model

The assessment process is decomposed into five specialized agent roles. Each operates independently, contributes its own view of the learner state, and communicates through the shared knowledge base.

1. **NLP Agent (Response Interpreter)**

Role: Analyzes open-ended student responses.
Outputs: Semantic embeddings, Partial-credit likelihood, Linguistic uncertainty indicators (e.g., hedging, incomplete reasoning)

2. **Emotion Agent (Safety Barrier)**

Role: Monitors affective patterns using behavioral features such as: Response latency, Number of revisions, Input hesitations, Abrupt answer submission
Outputs: Affective constraints (e.g., limit difficulty escalation under frustration), Stability indicators for pacing decisions.
Example constraint:

$$\text{MaxDifficulty} \leq 0.5$$

3. **Adversarial Agent (Integrity Monitor)**

Role: Detects signs of gaming or misuse, including: Rapid guessing patterns, AI-generated text signatures, Inconsistent reasoning across attempts

Outputs: Integrity constraints (e.g., exclude items vulnerable to exploitation)

Example constraint:

$$\text{Exclude}(Item_{\text{ambiguous}})$$

4. **Knowledge Graph Agent (Structure Enforcer)**

Role: Maintains the learner's conceptual position within the domain's knowledge topology (prerequisites, dependencies, concept clusters).

Outputs: Set of conceptually valid next steps, Pedagogical constraints based on prerequisite mastery

5. **RL Item Selection Agent (Optimizer)**

Role: Maximizes expected learning reward given the learner's current state.

Evaluates only the candidates allowed by all other agents.

Outputs: The optimal next item under the active constraint set

5.1. **The Constraint-Driven Arbitration Protocol**

As shown in Fig. 2, A core contribution of this work is the replacement of implicit "controller logic" with a **formal, set-theoretic arbitration mechanism**.

Let:

- $\mathcal{X}$= the full item universe
- $S_{\text{KG}} \subseteq \mathcal{X}$= conceptually valid items from the Knowledge Graph Agent
- $S_{\text{Emo}} \subseteq \mathcal{X}$= items satisfying emotion-derived pacing/difficulty constraints
- $S_{\text{Adv}} \subseteq \mathcal{X}$= items deemed safe under adversarial status

The **Valid Candidate Set** is:

$$C_{\text{valid}} = S_{\text{KG}} \cap S_{\text{Emo}} \cap S_{\text{Adv}}$$

The RL agent then optimizes its Q-function only over this constrained set:

$$x_{t+1} = \text{argmaxx} \in \text{Cvalid}\ Q(s_t, x)$$

This decision architecture ensures:

- **Pedagogical validity:** No concept jump violates prerequisite structure.
- **Emotional safety:** Difficulty adaptation respects cognitive load.
- **Integrity:** Vulnerable items are filtered before optimization.
- **Auditability:** Every discarded item has a documented constraint-based reason.

5.2. **Illustrative Scenario: Constraint Interaction in Practice**

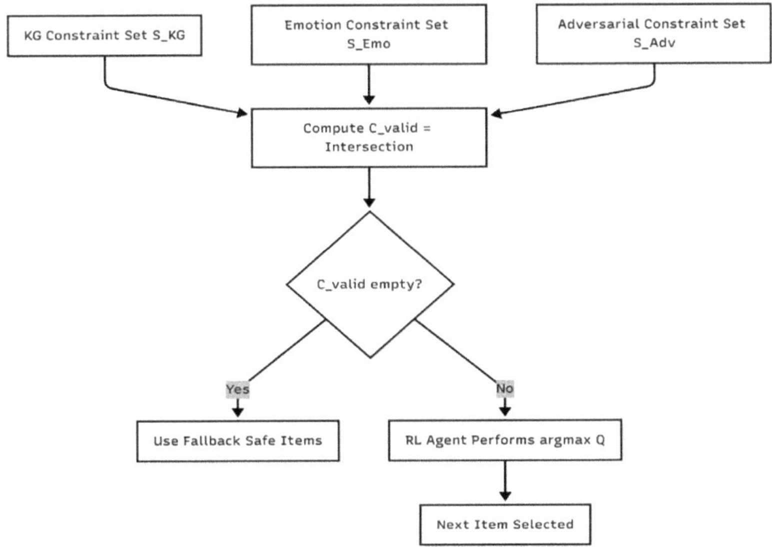

Fig. 2. The Constraint-Driven Arbitration Pipeline

Consider a learner navigating a unit on **Rational Numbers**.

They complete a question on *Fractions* and get it correct, but their interaction pattern suggests high cognitive strain (long pauses, multiple deletions, tentative phrasing).

Agent Analyses:

- **NLP Agent:** Identifies semantically correct reasoning with minor conceptual drift.
- **Emotion Agent:** Detects "High Frustration / High Uncertainty" → imposes stability constraints.
- **Knowledge Graph Agent:** Permits two concept transitions:
  - *Advanced Fractions* (A)
  - *Intro to Decimals* (B)
- **Adversarial Agent:** No anomalies detected → no items excluded.

Constraint Sets:

- $S_{\mathrm{KG}} = \{\mathrm{Items}(A) \cup \mathrm{Items}(B)\}$
- $S_{\mathrm{Emo}} = \{i \in \mathcal{X} \mid \mathit{Diff}(i) < 0.6\}$
- $S_{\mathrm{Adv}} = \mathcal{X}$

Arbitration Result: The intersection filters out high-difficulty items from *Advanced Fractions*.

Remaining candidates:

- Low-difficulty Fraction reviews
- Intro to Decimals (moderate complexity, conceptually permissible)

RL Optimization:
Among the allowed set, the RL agent evaluates expected learning gain and selects an item from *Intro to Decimals*—a forward progression that respects both cognitive load and pedagogical structure.

4 Algorithmic Specification and System Logic

The methodology defines the complete operational logic of the proposed adaptive assessment system. Unlike hierarchical designs that rely on a single master controller, this framework distributes computation across five autonomous agents. Each agent produces constraints or proposals, and the final assessment decision emerges through **Constraint-Driven Arbitration**. This section formalizes the underlying algorithms, state transitions, and message-passing mechanisms.

4.1 System State Representation

1. Let the overall learner state at time t be:

$$s_t = \{r_t, e_t, k_t, a_t\}$$

2. where:

   - r_t: semantic response features from NLP
   - e_t: affective state from Emotion Agent
   - k_t: conceptual position from Knowledge Graph Agent
   - a_t: adversarial risk indicators

The **Assessment Knowledge Base (AKB)** stores s_t and all agent outputs at each timestep.

4.2 Agent Output Formalization

3. Each agent produces its own function, mapping s_t to constraints.

(1) **NLP Agent**

$$\text{NLP}(s_t) = \{emb_t, score_t, drift_t\}$$

4. Where:

   - emb_t: semantic embedding
   - $score_t$: partial credit estimate
   - $drift_t$: conceptual drift score

(2) **Emotion Agent**

$$\mathrm{Emo}(s_t) = \{E_t, \mathrm{DifficultyCap}(t)\}$$

5. where $E_t \in$ {stable, overloaded, frustrated}.
6. Example difficulty cap:

$$\mathrm{DifficultyCap}(t) = 1 - E_t$$

As illustrated in Fig. 3, this mechanism transforms behavioral signals (latency, pauses) into tangible pacing constraints.

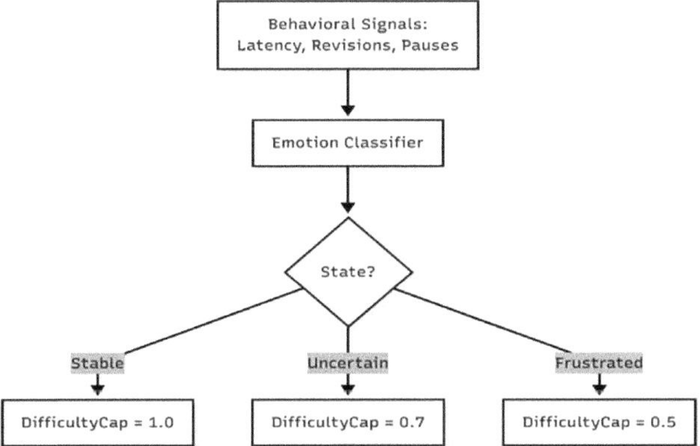

Fig. 3. Emotion-State Interpretation Diagram

7. (Emotion Agent reduces permissible difficulty when overloaded.)

(3) **Adversarial Agent**

$$\mathrm{Adv}(s_t) = \{A_t, \mathrm{ExcludeSet}(t)\}$$

where A_t is a binary anomaly flag.

The workflow for detecting these anomalies and generating the exclusion set is shown in Fig. 4.

(4) **Knowledge Graph Agent**

$$\mathrm{KG}(s_t) = S_{\mathrm{KG}} = \{x \in \mathcal{X} \mid \mathit{prereq}(x) \subseteq \mathit{mastered}(t)\}$$

(5) **RL** Item Selection Agent

8. Produces Q-values:

$$Q(s_t, x)\forall x \in \mathcal{X}$$

But can only optimize over constraints, not the entire domain.

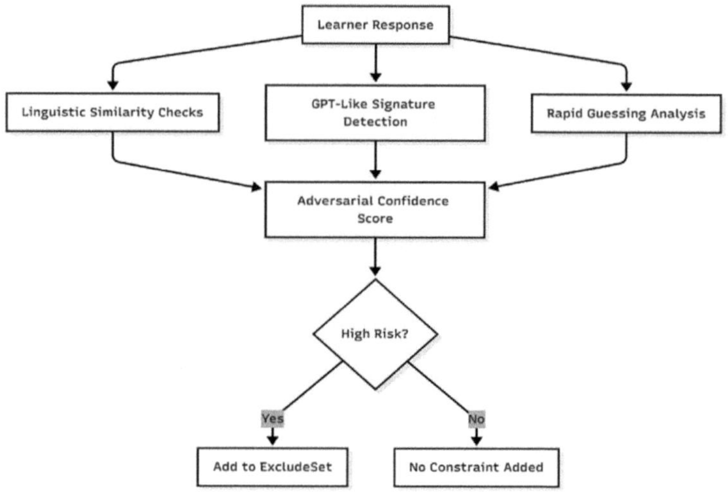

Fig. 4. Adversarial Detection Pipeline Diagram

4.3 Constraint Generation Logic

9. Each agent produces a filtered candidate set.

$$S_{\mathrm{KG}} = \text{Items satisfying conceptual prerequisites}$$
$$S_{\mathrm{Emo}} = \{x \in \mathcal{X} \mid \mathit{Diff}\,(x) \leq \mathrm{DifficultyCap}(t)\}$$
$$S_{\mathrm{Adv}} = \mathcal{X} \setminus \mathrm{ExcludeSet}(t)$$

10. The **Valid Candidate Set** is:

$$C_{\mathrm{valid}} = S_{\mathrm{KG}} \cap S_{\mathrm{Emo}} \cap S_{\mathrm{Adv}}$$

11. (If $C_{\mathrm{valid}} = \varnothing$, , the system falls back to teacher-defined safe items.)

4.4 RL Optimization Under Constraints

12. The RL agent selects the next item:

$$x_{t+1} = \mathrm{argmaxx} \in \mathrm{Cvalid}\; Q(s_t, x)$$

13. Reward function:

$$R_t = \alpha \cdot \mathrm{Correctness} + \beta \cdot \mathrm{LearningGain} - \gamma \cdot \mathrm{AffectiveCost}$$

14. This integrates both cognitive and emotional objectives.

4.5 Multi-agent Message Passing Protocol

15. Agents communicate through the AKB using a **broadcast-and-filter** strategy.

Broadcast Phase

16. Each agent posts:

$$m_t^{(i)} = \{constraints_i, metadata_i\}$$

Filter Phase

17. The Arbitration Engine computes: C_valid = S_KG ∩ S_Emo ∩ S_Adv

Decision Phase

18. RL selects from C_{valid}.

4.6 Pseudocode: End-To-End Operation

```
Algorithm AdaptiveAssessmentStep
Input: learner_response, AKB_state
r_t ← NLP_Agent.process(learner_response)
e_t ← Emotion_Agent.infer_state(learner_response)
a_t ← Adversarial_Agent.check(learner_response)
k_t ← KG_Agent.update_position(r_t)
S_KG  ← KG_Agent.generate_constraints(k_t)
S_Emo ← Emotion_Agent.generate_constraints(e_t)
S_Adv ← Adversarial_Agent.generate_constraints(a_t)
C_valid ← S_KG ∩ S_Emo ∩ S_Adv
if C_valid = Ø then
      C_valid ← fallback_safe_items
end if
x_next ← RL_Agent.select_argmax_Q(AKB_state, C_valid)
AKB_state ← update(AKB_state, r_t, e_t, a_t, k_t, x_next)
return x_next
```

4.7 Operational Interpretation

The system achieves:

- **Pedagogical coherence** → enforced by KG constraints
- **Emotional stability** → via Difficulty Cap
- **Integrity and robustness** → via adversarial filtering
- **Learning optimization** → via RL
- **Auditability** → every constraint is explainable

5 Proposed Evaluation Methodology

Because this work introduces a novel multi-agent architectural framework, immediate empirical testing with real students is not feasible until a full engineering implementation is available. To bridge this gap, we adopt a Simulation-Based Validation Strategy. This approach allows the architectural logic—especially the Constraint-Driven Arbitration protocol—to be tested under controlled, repeatable conditions. By simulating a wide range of learner behaviors, we can examine how effectively the agents negotiate constraints and maintain system stability without involving human participants. This ensures that preliminary validation is both ethically sound and technically meaningful.

To evaluate the coordinated behavior of the agents, we propose a simulated environment built using Gymnasium (formerly OpenAI Gym). The simulation environment contains "Synthetic Learners," autonomous agents designed to replicate real educational behavior profiles. These profiles allow us to examine how the system responds to cognitive difficulty, emotional volatility, and adversarial misuse. We define three core synthetic profiles. The first is **Profile A (The Struggling Learner)**. This learner begins with low domain mastery ($\theta < -1.0$) and exhibits high sensitivity to frustration. The key expectation is that the Emotion Agent will intervene frequently, applying difficulty caps that override the RL agent's natural tendency to escalate challenge. This profile tests whether the system effectively prioritizes emotional stability over rapid measurement. The second is **Profile B (The Adversarial User)**. This learner is programmed to attempt gaming strategies such as rapid guessing (responses under 3 s) and patterned input behaviors. The Adversarial Agent is expected to detect these anomalies early—ideally within the first few interactions—and modify the Valid Candidate Set (C_{valid}) accordingly. The anticipated result is that the system restricts the learner to items that cannot be easily gamed, particularly open-ended or reasoning-heavy items. The third is **Profile C (The Standard Learner)**, representing an average student with moderate mastery and a typical learning curve. This profile serves as the control condition. We expect the proposed architecture to behave similarly to standard Computerized Adaptive Testing (CAT) systems, allowing efficient ability estimation while adding minimal latency. This ensures that the additional safety layers do not hinder the assessment experience for typical learners. To evaluate system performance, we define three Key Performance Indicators. The first is the **Arbitration Conflict Rate (ACR)**, which measures how often the intersection of constraint sets results in an empty candidate set ($C_{valid} = \varnothing$). A low ACR indicates that the various agents' constraints are compatible and rarely conflict in ways that halt progress. The second KPI is **Affective Stability Variance**, which measures fluctuations in the synthetic learner's frustration score across an episode. Lower variance suggests that the Emotion Agent successfully prevents emotional spikes by regulating difficulty and pacing. This metric is essential for demonstrating the value of emotion-driven constraints. The third KPI is **Measurement Efficiency**, calculated as the reduction in the standard error of the ability estimate per item administered. This ensures that the introduction of safety filters, adversarial checks, and emotional constraints does not diminish the statistical efficiency of adaptive testing.

5.1 Evaluation Workflow

The validation plan involves running 1,000 Monte Carlo simulations for each learner profile. Each simulation consists of $T = 50$ timesteps, imitating the length of a typical adaptive assessment. At each timestep, a synthetic learner generates a response, the five agents evaluate it, the constraint sets are updated, and the arbitration logic determines the next item. As detailed in Fig. 3, this loop captures how the Valid Candidate Set expands or contracts dynamically over the course of an assessment.

After collecting the simulation logs, we will generate trajectory maps that visualize how decisions are shaped by the interaction of the agents. Additionally, we will conduct **Ablation Studies**, running simulations with specific agents disabled—such as removing the Emotion Agent or the Adversarial Agent—to measure the marginal contribution of each component. This analysis allows us to quantify how each agent affects fairness, stability, and measurement precision, supporting the claim that the full multi-agent configuration is superior to simplified alternatives. As illustrated in Fig. 5, the interaction loop repeats for $T = 50$ timesteps per episode. The resulting interaction logs will be analyzed to generate trajectory maps, visualizing how the "Valid Set" expands and contracts dynamically based on constraints. Furthermore, we plan to conduct Ablation Studies by running the simulation with specific agents disabled (e.g., "No Emotion Agent") to quantify the marginal contribution of each component to fairness and learning outcomes.

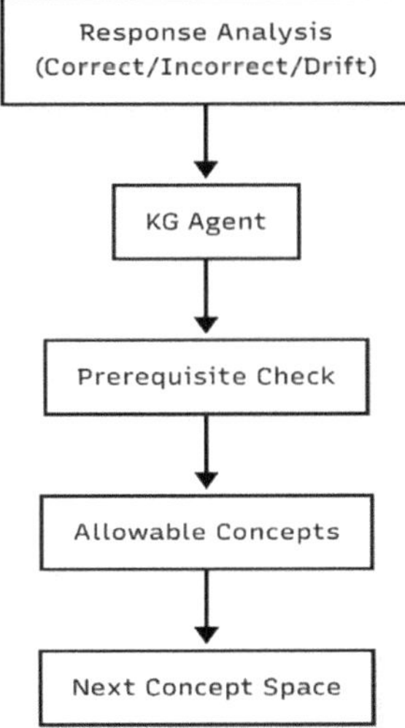

Fig. 5. Simulation Workflow Diagram

6 Conclusion

This paper introduced a unified multi-agent framework for personalized adaptive assessment, addressing long-standing limitations in current educational AI systems. Whereas existing approaches often treat NLP processing, reinforcement learning, emotion detection, and adversarial modeling as isolated components, the proposed architecture weaves these capabilities into a single coherent decision structure. The core contribution lies in the mechanism of Constraint-Driven Arbitration, through which conceptual prerequisites, emotional stability conditions, and integrity safeguards jointly shape the space of possible assessment actions. This design replaces hierarchical "controller" logic with a distributed, interpretable negotiation process that aligns technical optimization with pedagogical and ethical considerations. By integrating NLP-based semantic understanding, affective modeling, knowledge graph–driven concept routing, adversarial detection, and RL-driven sequencing, the framework advances a vision of assessment that treats learners as dynamic participants rather than static datapoints. The system's emphasis on transparency and auditability ensures that each decision—whether selecting a next item, moderating difficulty, or filtering adversarial risks—can be traced to clear and intelligible constraints. This represents a meaningful step toward assessment systems that are both technologically sophisticated and educationally trustworthy. The evaluation strategy outlined through simulation-based "Synthetic Classrooms" offers a practical and rigorous pathway for validating architectural soundness before real-world deployment. The proposed KPIs—Arbitration Conflict Rate, Affective Stability Variance, and Measurement Efficiency—provide measurable and interpretable indicators of system performance. Moreover, the ablation experiments establish a foundation for understanding the unique contribution of each agent to overall system behavior. While this work is primarily architectural, the methods, algorithms, and evaluation protocol presented here open multiple avenues for future experimentation. Implementing the full system within real learning environments, extending the agent negotiation mechanism with meta-learning, and exploring psychometric alignment across diverse populations remain promising directions. Ultimately, the proposed framework offers a foundation for next-generation assessment systems that are adaptive, fair, explainable, and robust—capable of meeting the evolving demands of modern education.

Acknowledgements. Parts of the manuscript were refined with the help of a language-model–based writing assistant, while all methodological decisions and interpretations were made by the authors.

References

1. Ghuge, A.R., et al.: Automatic question generation system using natural language processing. Int. J. Res. Appl. Sci. Eng. Technol. (2025)
2. Hidalgo-Mayorga, M., de los Á., Puente-Riofrio, M.I., Pérez-Salas, F.P., Guerrero-Arrieta, K.G., López-Naranjo, A.L.: Financial literacy as a tool for social inclusion and reduction of inequalities: a systematic review. Soc. Sci. **14**(11), 658 (2025). https://doi.org/10.3390/socsci14110658
3. Selvam, P., et al.: Small generative language models for educational question generation. In: Proceedings of the NeurIPS Workshop on Generative AI for Education (GAIED) (2023)
4. Nikolovski, V., Trajanov, D., Chorbev, I.: Advancing AI in higher education: a comparative study of large language model-based agents for exam question generation, improvement, and evaluation. Algorithms **18**(3), 144 (2025). https://doi.org/10.3390/a18030144
5. Melzer, S., Asselborn, T., Möller, R.: Generative AI for interactive learning in education. Datenbank-Spektrum **25**, 87–93 (2025). https://doi.org/10.1007/s13222-025-00507-7

6. Lee, A.V.Y., et al.: Designs and practices using generative AI for sustainable student discourse and knowledge creation. Smart Learn. Environ. **10**, 59 (2023)
7. Barrada, J.R., Olea, J., Ponsoda, V., Abad, F.J.: Item selection rules in computerized adaptive testing: accuracy and security. Methodology **5**(1), 7–17 (2009). https://doi.org/10.1027/1614-2241.5.1.7
8. Han, K.T.: Components of the item selection algorithm in computerized adaptive testing. J. Educ. Eval. Health Professions **15** (2018)
9. Zheng, C., Chang, H.-H.: High-efficiency response distribution–based item selection algorithms for short-length cognitive diagnostic computerized adaptive testing. Appl. Psychol. Meas. **40**(8), 608–624 (2016). https://doi.org/10.1177/0146621616665196
10. van de Sande, S., et al.: Reinforcement learning tutor better supported lower performers in a math task. Mach. Learn. **113**, 3023–3048 (2024)
11. G. Jatobá, V.M., Farias, J.S., Freire, V., Ruela, A.S., Delgado, K.V.: ALICAT: a customized approach to item selection process in computerized adaptive testing. J. Braz. Comput. Soc. **26**(1), 1–13 (2020). https://doi.org/10.1186/s13173-020-00098-z
12. Abdelshiheed, M., et al.: Leveraging deep reinforcement learning for metacognitive interventions across intelligent tutoring systems. In: Proceedings of the 24th International Conference on Artificial Intelligence in Education (AIED) (2023)
13. Schmitt, C., et al.: Reinforcement learning in education: a systematic literature review. Int. J. Artif. Intell. Educ. (2025)
14. Xu, K., Xiao, X., Wang, L., Lou, M., Wang, F., et al.: Data-driven materials research and development for functional coatings. Adv. Sci. **11**(42), 202405262 (2024). https://doi.org/10.1002/advs.202405262
15. Heine, C., et al.: Algorithmic fairness in automatic short answer scoring. Int. J. Artif. Intell. Educ. (2025
16. Matta, M., et al.: Implications of bias in automated writing quality scores for fair and equitable assessment decisions. School Psychol. **38**(3), 173–181 (2023)
17. Chinta, S.V., et al.: FairAIED: navigating fairness, bias, and ethics in educational AI applications. arXiv:2407.18745 (2024)
18. Lim, T., et al.: What students really think: unpacking AI ethics in educational assessments through a triadic framework. Int. J. Educ. Technol. High. Educa. **22**, 56 (2025)
19. Qouzah, L., et al.: AI in education: enhancing learning potential and addressing ethical considerations among academic staff—a cross-sectional study at the University of Jordan. Int. J. Educ. Integrity **21**, 16 (2025)
20. Zall, A., Kangavari, M.: Towards emotion-aware intelligent agents by utilizing knowledge graphs of experiences (2024). https://www.researchgate.net/publication/384021242_Towards_emotion-aware_intelligent_agents_by_utilizing_knowledge_graphs_of_experiences
21. Vistorte, A.O.M., Silva, A.G.T., Sbicigo, J.B.: Integrating artificial intelligence to assess emotions in educational settings. Front. Psychol. **15** (2024). https://pmc.ncbi.nlm.nih.gov/articles/PMC11223560/
22. Zeng, L., Li, Y., Huang, J.: GraphMASAL: A graph-based multi-agent system for adaptive learning. arXiv preprint. https://arxiv.org/abs/2511.11035 (2025)

Author Index

B. Fernández-Manjón et al. (Eds.): SETE 2025/ICWL 2025, LNCS 16425, pp. 501–502, 2026.
https://doi.org/10.1007/978-981-92-0042-9

MIX
Papier aus verantwortungsvollen Quellen
Paper from responsible sources
FSC® C105338

If you have any concerns about our products,
you can contact us on
ProductSafety@springernature.com

In case Publisher is established outside the EU,
the EU authorized representative is:
Springer Nature Customer Service Center GmbH
Europaplatz 3, 69115 Heidelberg, Germany

Printed by Libri Plureos GmbH
in Hamburg, Germany